Autobiographies 2

Each book in the evocative and richly entertaining autobiography of Sean O'Casey is essential reading for a proper appreciation of this major Irish dramatist whose plays were among the most exciting developments in modern drama.

Born in the back streets of Dublin, suffering from weak and diseased eyes, he lived in poverty and physical hardship for many years. In his late teens he became a manual labourer, and after working on the roads or in the docks from five in the morning to six at night he would spend his evenings helping the cause of the Gaelic League and Sinn Fein. He became Secretary of the Irish Citizen Army and a founder member of the Irish Labour Party. Although his first published work was in 1907, not until the success of *Juno and the Paycock* in 1925 did he give up manual work and become a full-time writer.

Independence and the Civil War heralded O'Casey's early triumphs at the Abbey Theatre, Dublin. In his autobiography of those years he vividly recreates the period and its personalities, and sets out the reasons for his departure from Dublin for London in 1926. In the final books O'Casey writes of the crowded years of his life in England, his marriage to the actress Eileen Carey, America, the war and his friendship with G. B. Shaw, but at the back of it all there remains his fundamental concern for the people of Ireland.

Sean O'Casey
Autobiographies 2

Inishfallen, Fare Thee Well
Rose and Crown
Sunset and Evening Star

PAPERMAC

Inishfallen, Fare Thee Well first published 1949
Rose and Crown first published 1952
Sunset and Evening Star first published 1954

First combined edition published by Macmillan and Company Ltd 1963
This edition published 1992 by
P A P E R M A C
a division of Pan Macmillan Publishers Limited
Cavaye Place London SW10 9PG
and Basingstoke

Associated companies in Auckland, Budapest, Dublin,
Gaborone, Harare, Hong Kong, Kampala, Kuala Lumpur, Lagos,
Madras, Manzini, Melbourne, Mexico City, Nairobi, New York,
Singapore, Sydney, Tokyo and Windhoek

1 3 5 7 9 8 6 4 2

ISBN 0-333-58251-9

A CIP catalogue record for this book is available from the British Library

Printed in Hong Kong

CONTENTS

INISHFALLEN, FARE THEE WELL

ROSE AND CROWN

INISHFALLEN, FARE THEE WELL

The wheel of th' wagon's broken,
It ain't goin' to turn no more;
The wheel of th' wagon's broken,
An' there's weeds round th' ranch-house door.

To Walter McDonald, D.D.,
Professor of Theology in St. Patrick's
Roman Catholic College, Maynooth,
for forty years; a great man
gone, and almost forgotten;
but not quite forgotten

HIGH ROAD AND LOW ROAD

THINGS had changed, but not utterly; and no terrible beauty was to be born. Short Mass was still the favourite service, and Brian Boru's harp still bloomed on the bottles of beer. But the boys were home again from prison camp and prison cell. First the venial sinners from Frongoch; then the mortal sinners from Wakefield, Reading, Dartmoor, and other jails. They've had their lesson, thought the sophisticated British Authorities, and from this out they will be pure and prim. The convicts, warned by the spitting and hissing of their departure to their prisons, hoped they'd steal quietly through the city to fireside and bed; but the people had changed utterly, and thronged their streets to cheer them. The wail of the Irish ochone had changed into the roar of the Irish hurrah. Again, the felon's cap had become the noblest crown an Irish head could wear. Nothing could be too good for the boys. When one spoke, all had to remain silent. They led at all meetings, dominated committees, won at cards, got everything anyone had to give, and were everywhere forced to lay down the law on all philosophy, patriotism, foresight, prophecy, and good manners. Was he out in Easter Week? became the touchstone of Irish life. And it was those who hadn't been out themselves who roared silence at anyone venturing to send a remark into a conversation led by a lad home from a prison or a concentration camp; for the lads, themselves, were exceedingly modest about it all, and were often embarrassed by their hangers-on, who forgot that most of Dublin, willy-nilly, was out in Easter Week; that there weren't many Dublin houses without bullet-holes in them; and that casualties were heavier among those who weren't out than among those who were. So for a long time, Easter Week became the Year of One in Irish history and Irish life.

Now the manœuvring began: the young leaders, still alive, circled round each other, wary and watchful, eager to snap up a well-considered trifle of position that would give them the power to govern. Spirals of political movement began to appear, with Michael Collins dancing a jig in one; Arthur Griffith doing a new Irish-Hungarian dance in another; and Eamonn De Valera, a fresh young fellow, a bit of a dancer himself, side-stepped from one group to the other, hands on hips, advising them to join hands, and foot it featly here and there, pointing a pliant toe himself to show others the way — now glide! De Valera was very supple.

At the big Sinn Fein Ard Fheis, stout with unity, the choice for President lay between a young man, a middle-aged one, and an old veteran; between De Valera, a soldier and a man; Arthur Griffith, the politician; and Plunkett, Count of the Holy Roman Empire — wherever that was. There was the freshman, in a prominent place, waiting to blot out the figure of the old stager, Griffith, from the view of the people; just, too, when he was about to have a life-size picture taken. The modest young man was about to turn into the daring young man on the flying tripeace. Griffith was threatened with the job of sitting behind De Valera for the rest of his life, and he looked glum. Plunkett had only his prayers to help him; and Griffith had no chance, for the fires of Easter Week were still a halo round De Valera's head; he had been the last to surrender, and had shown such ability in minor military manœuvres, that had he had a fuller direction of the whole contest, the British would have been given a far tougher job to do. Griffith heard all bassi, tenori, soprani, and baritoni in the country singing, top-voiced, *We'll Crown De Valera King of Ireland*. So Griffith stood out to say, I withdraw in favour of Mr. De Valera, a soldier and a man. The white-bearded Vatican Count Plunkett stood forth to say, I withdraw in favour of Mr. De Valera, a man and a soldier, and the thing was done; so with a mighty cheerio, Ireland elected an heroic homily to be her leader.

It was a curious choice to Sean, for to him De Valera seemed to be no Gael either in substance or in face, though he was probably one in theory. Though, it is recorded, he played hurley when he was a kid, Sean couldn't see an excited De Valera rushing round a hurling field; and, certainly, he had never known him in the team attached to the Central Branch of the Gaelic League; he couldn't see De Valera abandoning himself to sweat and laughter in the dancing of a jig, nor could he see him swanking about in sober green kilt and gaudy saffron shawl; or slanting an approving eye on any pretty girl that passed him; or standing, elbow on counter in a Dublin pub, about to lower a drink, with a Where it goes, lads. No, such as he would be always in a dignified posture at Dail or Council, or helping to spray prayers at a church gathering. He knew, like Griffith, next to nothing about the common people. He was of the house with the bow-window, lace curtains, and the brass knocker — planetoids to the planet of the Big House. He was outside of everything except himself. Sean had listened often to him pouring out phrases by the ten thousand, not one of which had on it even the glisten of a tinsel dew-drop. There seemed to be no sound of Irish wind, water, folkchant, or birdsong in the dry, dull voice; not that of lark, linnet, blackbird, or thrush; not even the homely caw of an Irish crow: the entire man was invested with a mantle, made whole with half from the cloak of Dan O'Connell and half from that of Thomas Davis, pinned wide in front by an inscription of the Sacred Heart. Griffith's voice, at least, was cold; De Valera's was neither cold nor hot — it was simply lukewarm, and very dreary. But it inspired his followers, now almost the whole of Catholic Ireland, who looked upon him as a Bonnie Prince Charlie in sober suiting, and bruited his fame about the land with many banners. De Valera had chained together all ambitious and disagreeing Irishmen in the bond of peace and unenduring fellowship, so that England got nervous at this unforeseen sight, and began to order men in Connacht to go into Ulster, and men in Leinster to go into Munster, putting those in jail who waited to pack up a pair of pyjamas, because delays were dangerous.

Sean, to help on the good work, wrote a stirring ballad called *The Call of the Tribe*, and hurried to Liberty Hall to get Seumas Hughes, who was then secretary, or something there, to the Transport Union, to put music on it. Seumas thrilled over the verses, saying he'd do all a man could to compose an air worthy of the song's sentiments. So in a week's time, off Sean hurried again to get the song adorned with the promised music, but it was handed back to him without a mark; Hughes telling him that he had had orders from above not to have anything to do with that fellow Casside. Dejected and oppressed, Sean tore the song into little pieces, and threw them from him into the silent square so that they might be lost with the valour, the enter-prise, and the bold endeavour that had graced and lighted up the place when the indomitable Larkin spoke his flaming words from the window above, now sealed up and dumb with the gloom of a fell and angry caution. Orders! From whom? Not, surely, from Bill O'Brien, for he was a democrat of democrats, blandly tolerant of all men, and eager, as few other men were, to love his neighbour as himself?

Still, an odd man, this Bill O'Brien who now guided the workers of Ireland with the more cautious marching command of Right, right, right, right, right, instead of the old fiery one of Left, left, left, left, left, when the hearts of men stirred to the shout of the militant workers. Liberty Hall had been shoved back into order after the battering it had got from the guns of the Helga, but there was a woebegone look on its face, for its great men had gone, and Ichabod was its name now. It was but a hatchway now for the payment of dues by its members. Odd the building looked, disarmed of its temper and temerity, and it seemed to be ashamed of still standing there with one of its champions dead, and the other in a far-away prison. The Union's Executive had gone far from the madding crowd of workers, and had taken over a Georgian house in Rutland Square whose dignified doorway, tiled hall, plate glass, pinewood counters, and stately desks gave it a presence that made it ashamed of its parent, Liberty Hall, with its raucous voice, turbulent manner, and defiance of all power inimical to the workers' cause. Here, behind a formidable desk, sat William O'Brien, known among the workers as Old Bill, thinking deeply, and manœuvring cleverly, to gather all Ireland's workers into what was called The One Big Union.

Bill had no look of a Labour leader about him, but rather that of a most respectable clerk at home in a sure job; though Sean had met him at a Socialist gathering where little Walter Carpenter, the Wicklow Englishman, had auctioned tiny red flags — the first, he said, seen in the streets of Dublin — a man named Lee buying one for a fiver, and Bill taking one of a few left for ten shillings; the joyful event ending by a Mrs. Cogley singing *The Marseillaise*, and all singing, in unison, *The Red Flag*. O'Brien had a cold, keen mind, masked by a set, pale face, beaded by two small eyes darting out a point of light in any quick and sudden glance taken at another; a short brown beard covered the chin, its line carried along by two dark brows sprouting harshly across a bony-looking forehead. His body was usually bent forward at the waist from the habit of constantly stooping forward to balance away an imperfection in a foot. Sean had often listened to his cold voice speaking; and, at times, when angry, the face waxed deadly white, and the cold voice took on a bitter tone, without a spark of warmth in it, so that its intensity made a sensitive listener shiver.

He seemed to be a self-centred man, finding in himself all that was needed to live a cool and concentrated life; hardly ever seeming to take notice of things left or right of him. Riding his bicycle, he invariably looked straight ahead, as if he were passing through deserted streets; and at a meeting, the rather sour, but certainly sharp, face never wavered a hair's breadth from a straight-out stare to the centre of him. A frozen sense of self-importance animated the man; and the clever, sharp, shrewd mind at white heat behind the cold, pale mask, was ever boring a silent way through all opposition to the regulation and control of the Irish Labour Movement. So this curious, silent shape, always neatly dressed, wearing in the lapel of his coat an invisible last shred of the tattered red flag, once held high by Larkin and Connolly, could be seen only at meetings, or on a bicycle on his way to one; or in his newly-furnished office, if one had a passport for admission; but never, as far as Sean knew, at a picture gallery, at a play, at a music-hall; or in a pub with a pint before him, or a half a malt waiting at his elbow; never even to be seen rambling a country lane with a lassie on his arm; too high-minded, too busy, too full of all sweet, good things in himself to be troubled with these things of the earth, earthy. With De Valera, he would share the eternal glory of sacrificing himself for the common good; a bud that was to open into the tripartite government of all Irish life, the one to be supreme in politics, the other in labour, with a churchman to see that all went well with the faith, so that a new trinity, one and indivisible, should live in peace, unity, joy, and quadragesimal jubilation under the siestal shadow of the mighty mitre of Armagh.

As Sean couldn't be busy one way or another, he forged a third method, and joined the few who formed the little Socialist Party of Ireland, a Lett named Sidney Arnold (who since the Red Revolution in Russia, said his name was Semyon Aronson), Hector Hughes, a young barrister, and others. So Sean went about campaigning for Meals for Necessitous Schoolchildren; delivering handbills in the streets to the few who wanted them, hastily organising meetings, and doing most of the work while the others did most of the talk. To keep himself from the sin of idleness, he got together a concert, including a one-act play, in which he himself took one of the principal characters, and persuaded Arthur Armstrong to give them the Olympia free for the great occasion. On the night of the event, Armstrong met Sean, who had come early to prepare, and told him, angrily, that the thing hadn't been advertised, and no-one would be there, the bleak result of which would hurt the good name of his theatre; and he exploded into wrath when Sean told him his one trouble was that the Olympia wouldn't be able to hold all who came. Some time later, the stage carpenter came in, and the anxious Armstrong asked him if there was any sign of an audience collecting outside. Audience? echoed the carpenter; Jasus, th' street's jammed, an' they're holdin' up th' traffic! Then there came upon Armstrong fear that his theatre would be wrecked, and he rushed round, madly, looking for stewards. With tremendous difficulty, the doors were opened, and the stewards were swept off their feet by the incoming tide of people; so swift and sweeping that many with tickets for the boxes were carried up to the gallery, and some of those with tickets for the gallery were borne, almost shoulder-high, into the boxes. When the theatre was full, the doors bolted and barred, Sean, dressed for his part in plus-fours and gorgeous pullover, stood on a window-sill high up in the building, and appealed to a great crowd below in the street to go home quietly, and forgive the theatre for not being a bigger one. And, when all was done, Sister Helena, of the St. Laurence O'Toole Sisters of Charity, received a goodly sum to furnish out penny dinners for the poor.

Prime dinners, wholesome dinners here — only a penny each! and Sean smiled ironically to himself, as he cautiously passed out over the polished floor of the convent, when he thought that no-one needed a penny dinner more than his mother and himself; but pride kept the two of them miles away from one. Oh, pride, oh, foolish pride! Oh, sweet and generous God, who bringest the harvest in due season and fillest the heart of man with good things, here are two of Thy children who need a dinner of some sort, but who haven't a ha'penny to buy a penny one. Let us say a silent prayer of thanks for what we've got, and what we are to receive in the sour bye and bye: Oh, God the Father, God the Son, and God the Holy Ghost, we whisper hearty thanks well up to Thee for the fruits of the earth which Thou hast not bestowed upon us, though Thy intention was good; though Thou hast failed to fill our hearts with food and glad-ness, we praise Thee, at least, for the fine display of all Thy good gifts in the wide shop windows; for the bread that strengthens the hearts of a few men; and for the wine that maketh glad the hearts of others: moselle, hock, those of the Rhine, Sauterne, Burgundy, and the heady joy coming from Champagne. Though our hearts and those of our neighbours be thin with meagre joys, and fading towards dry-ness, we magnify Thee for the feverish dreams we have had some-times, during fasts and the higher festivals, of all good things; of cheeses, camembert, stilton, cheddar, and roquefort; of the dark-gold sherries of Spain and the rich, red vintage of Portugal. We rejoice in our foiled dreams of the luscious plums, pears, and peaches of Europe, the delicious citrus fruits of Africa, the dates and figs of Barbary, making our poor mouths water, and our hearts widen out in free-will acknowledgement of Thy goodness and fair play; not forgetting the coffee of Mocha, pineapples of the Indies, and the gold-crusted bread born of the grain from Canada and Illinois, which, with well-brewed tea, gathered from the aromatic plant of

Assam, enables us to live on, and enjoy, in dreams, the goodly things Thou hast bestowed upon the children of men. We bless Thy name, too, for the kind hearts, that are more than coronets, who have got together the valuable penny dinners for the poor, invoking St. Anthony, himself, that he may induce Thee to provide the miracle that will put a cigar in every grimy hand when each gorgeous feast has ended.

Two fierce fights were going on for liberty: one on the little green dot in the world's waters, called Ireland; and the other over a wide brown, grey, blue, and scarlet expanse of land, later to overflow into the many-coloured, gigantic bloom of the Soviet Union. The first for a liberty of the soul that was to leave the body and mind still in prison; the other for the liberty of the body that was to send the soul and mind as well out into the seething waters of a troubled world on a new and noble adventure. Dublin was astir, for many were busy in its secret places hammering out in thought the iron nature of an ironic people into a shape of an Irish Republic. Young men, in slum and shady avenue, were concerning themselves with the idea of giving up any comfort they had, and risking their lives, that they might be numbered among those who would be remembered, if not forever, for awhile anyhow. Some had died already, and Thomas Ashe was dead now. Killed through the rigours of forcible feeding. In Mountjoy Jail, one of Eire's golden boys was changing into dust.

Sean had written two laments for Thomas Ashe, for he had been an old friend of his when both had been pipers; and now, with a Fergus O'Connor, who had published the two laments, he was on his way to the prison to get news as to when the body of the dead man would be allowed out for burial. This most handsome man, Ashe, six foot tall, straight as a standard, with a leonine head, bannered by a mass of hair that was almost golden, this most handsome man was dead. Turning into the long avenue leading to the prison, with a few birds still twittering on the languid trees, the entrance gate looked like a toy door in a toy fort in the distance, with a few tiny black figures before it, waiting permission to go in to a toy dead brother, a toy dead son. But the gate grew rapidly larger as they came closer, and beside it, then, the thing towered high over them all, fitting and frowning the figures now into the look of sad humanity, waiting to go forward and endure the last act of reluctant charity of burying their beloved dead.

In silence, there they stood. Sean in his old clothes, his broken cap pulled sullenly down over his eyes; O'Connor in well-cut Irish tweeds and costly cap; and the relatives in solemn black, stood before the heavy, dull-brown gateway, with its subsidiary wicket to one side for admission of privileged persons on business bent; silently praying, the lips of the black figures moved slightly in an unheard murmur of *Eternal rest grant to him, O Lord, and let perpetual light shine upon his brave soul*; acting as a chorus to O'Connor chanting in a low whisper Sean's lament for the dead man, the pity in it forcing the tears to trickle down his cheeks before the high and heavy oaken gateway, braced with many a thick and unbreakable iron clamp.

And here, now, was another sad moment, the tale of the death of another young man for another cause, though both fought and died for freedom. The young man who died holding a Rhine bridge at Arnhem has been awarded the Victoria Cross. Defending a bridge and a blazing house for three days, he fell at last and went away forever. Sean tried to picture this young man, Lieutenant John Grayburn, wounded twice, leading his little group of gallant paratroops to safety before he died, with the questioning, kindly-truculent face of the Scot, tall and determined in his battledress; but no figure like unto the picture he tried to think of came before his eyes. Instead, he saw a little fellow, well made and promising, in a nicely-ordered sailor suit, the gold insignia of a petty officer promoting to prominence the little sleeve; his baby eyes aglow, a face flushed with resolution to hold his own, a tiny human storm of sturdy stands and gallant rushes to keep what he called his goal safe. A bud appearing to flaunt forward to a flower so soon; a red flower to fade quicker than it formed; so soon to fall, to die, and disappear forever. Nothing now to Sean, but the misty sight of a young man, dim, and a little boy, clear, wending slow along the low road to the bonnie banks of Loch Lomond, or sailing over the sea to Skye. Ah, Johnny Grayburn, Johnny Grayburn, Sean will often see these two — the little fellow countering him in childish football; this one clearly; and a dim, tall fellow, wounded shoulder and back, fighting, till he falls forward to be lost in the tangle of the earth's sad fruitfulness. And what have you left of yourself behind for coming life to see, to honour, and admire? A blink o' scarlet ribbon holding up a copper cross, with a golden centre. Not enough, not enough, Johnny Grayburn; not enough to pay for your sturdy body, your handsome face, the promise of the future man. I was very fond of you, Johnny Grayburn, for you were all that every youngster ought to be; the makings of a fine, intelligent, colourful human being. Fresh as an angel over a new inn door. So strong, so sure of life, so sure of fame, maybe; so sure of his own boyish pride, so sure that God was with him. The day of his youth was the day of his glory; and that day passed off into everlasting darkness. His life a short and gallant story with a swift ending. Both of them: Ashe and Grayburn. They had an intimation of immortality, and then they died. They had not time to grow old. *They shall not grow old as we that are left grow old* — Oh, whining heresy of sentimental age, condoning the crime that young life has to die, turning life to a whimper. That youth's sweet, scented manuscript should close is never sad, for age is no weariness after a well-fought fight; and the years welcome the young mind journeying on to the elder thought, a life where hope is merged into a fuller conquest. The grey is never far beneath the golden locks, and when it shows itself, it but tells that life has ripened.

So there these two lie, but a few moments or so apart from each other; the one who died for Ireland's humanity, the other who died for the world's; the one in the grey-green of an Irish Volunteer, the other in the muddy-yellow of England's battledress; both now lost, swallowed up in the greed of eternity. There they lie together — but a moment apart in time, inert, motionless forever. Maybe their end is soft and simple to those who have been furnished with the means of handing over the early and the little later years of youth to mannerly nurses, to be nurtured in the midst of polished nursery, resplendent toys, neat skirts, and spotless caps with saucy streamers stretching out like flimsy wings behind them. But the bereft mother, who has suffered all of her boy's turbulent rising into a steadier life, will always find a sorrow in another's son, a ghost in an empty chair; she will have a cold heart when she hears a youthful laugh, or the free step of one outside on the pavement; her lips will be as cold as ice when she feels again the warm kiss from the soft lips of the past of one who is forgotten by all, though she remembers. Let mitred souls who think they can outlive Time, stealing men's sense with sign of stole and chasuble, say what they will away from these dead forms; insomuch as Christ is risen, and become the first-fruits of them who sleep; that these dead shall go through the endless endlessness of eternity, knowing all, and known of all within their grade of sanctity; shall sojourn actively where is neither sun nor moon to shine in it; for the light thereof is the glory of God; where all the ageing ages shall be but as the time wasted in the blinking of an eye; and the life of the longest-lived universe shall be to them less than the life of a bubble afloat in the swift air.

No, thought Sean; this is but a serious fancy, hiding human foolishness and frailty; no more possible for the sad dead to achieve than for a fair lady to stretch a white arm, seize the moon, and hang it round her neck. It would be a dream to say amen to the hope of Christians. All that man can do is to make what man's life may be; to make what man's life must be; to ensure that life coming on to the stage when the curtain rises shall play its part out till the curtain falls. That is as much as we know; that is as far as we can go. Then —

> *Then star nor sun shall waken,*
> *Nor any change of light:*
> *Nor sound of waters shaken,*
> *Nor any sound or sight:*
> *Nor wintry leaves nor vernal,*
> *Nor days nor things diurnal;*
> *Only the sleep eternal*
> *In an eternal night.*

The rest, if there be a God, must be left in His cool, accommodating hands.

MRS. CASSIDE TAKES A HOLIDAY

SEAN had at last written something for money. It was a tiny booklet called *The Story of the Irish Citizen Army*, and the Dublin publishers, Maunsel & Son, had promised to print it, provided it passed the British Censor. He was to get fifteen pounds on its day of publication, and all the energy left to him became a curse as day after day, week after week, passed without showing any sign of the censored manuscript. Beyond an occasional day of scrappy work they were living on Mrs. Casside's old-age pension, which, when four shillings rent was paid, left six to provide them with all the bad things of life. When the manuscript did come back, it was a creased and tangled mass, with Sean's small, cramped longhand heavily underscored on every page with red, green, and blue pencil lines. With his eyes the way they were, it took him a week to get the sheets into orderly rotation. They were curious-looking documents now: the first Censor had encircled with red anything he thought to be dangerous to the British Government, peace, and God's truth; the second Censor, mind superior, went over what had been marked in red, and confirmed whatever he thought damaging by adding a green circle to the red one; and the third, mind *superiorum*, decided, finally, what was indeed dangerous, by encircling the red and green attempts with a lofty blue one of his own. After what seemed to be ages of labour, Sean filled the gaps in, the Censors, with a few more alterations, passed it, and Sean found himself waiting for fifteen pounds.

Fifteen pounds! Enough, with the pension, to keep them for seven months; for five, if they bought lavishly to give themselves the clothes they needed so badly. The sun became by day a golden sovereign, the stars by night turned into glittering silver shillings. Though the walk was a long one, every second day, or so, Sean tramped up to Baggot Street to stare at the humble façade of the publishers who were to give to the world his book. One day he went in to ask for the cheque, or a portion of it, but was told it wasn't due yet. Next week, he returned, to be told the Manager was away. The golden sovereign in the sky began to dim, and the shimmer of the stars at night began to tarnish. At last he was told, if he came in a week's time, the cheque would be waiting for him.

A few days before he was to call, he heard his mother coughing, and asking what was wrong, received the usual reply that it was but a bit of a cold. He persuaded her into bed, and gave her a hot cup of tea; all that he had to give; all that remained in the house to give its head. If he only had enough of the promised fee to buy a little brandy. He heard her coughing through the night, and grew frightened, for he dreaded her death. He had lived so long beside her, from the day she had brushed his brown childish hair from his forehead to the one that found grey hairs tingeing his temple. She had been his comforter, his rod and his staff, his ever-present help in time of trouble. She had been so understanding, too; never crossing him. Ever silent when she saw him thinking out things in a reverie; breaking into the quiet crooning of some favourite song when she saw the reverie was over. Night after night, when he had been stretched on the old sofa, dreading the onset of paralysis, to screw up his courage he had sung, full-voiced, almost every song he knew, and hymns when the songs gave out; and she had joined in discreetly, adding her sincere and quavering tone to the more militant sound of his voice. Tired of singing, he had read to her from Scott and Dickens, stopping often to listen to her young, fresh, and gleaming laughter, so strange from one who had gone through so hard, bitter, and thankless a life for nearly eighty years; fifty of them little less than terrible; years that had withheld joy, raiment, food, and even hope; for she never had a hope that she could ever be better than she was. But she was always a proud woman, hating charity as an enemy, and never welcoming it, so that all these bitter years had never mastered her, never diminished the sturdiness of her fine nature. Tom's death had silenced her for awhile; Ella's pitiable end had been a battering blow, but she recovered enough to sing a swan-song: a confident, patient, lovely folk-version of the Nunc Dimittis. She went jauntily to her death; whether to another life or no, death scored no victory over her; she never felt its sting. God or Nature had, at least, given her that reward.

On the day he was to go for the fifteen pounds he bent over the sofa, a little fearful of leaving her alone.

—I'm off now, he said, trying to speak cheerily as he put his hand on her hot forehead, and I won't be long.

—You never watered the poor flowers last night, she complained, for I had to get up in the night to do it myself. I don't know what they'd do without me.

—You're not to get up, he said earnestly; and as she stayed silent, d'ye hear me? You're not to stir from where y'are.

—I'm really a lot bether, Jack, she smiled up at him, and wouldn't hurt if I got up for a little. There's a few things to be washed, and hung out to dhry.

—I'll wash them when I come back, he said irritably, and put them out to dhry. I've already left them soaking.

—You're not to get up. Promise me, mother, he added appealingly, that you'll stay comfortably where you are; for he knew the quick urge in all women like his mother to be forever useful in illness or in health. He was afraid, too, of the epidemic of influenza raging everywhere, killing hundreds of the young and vigorous weekly, so that street after street had dark convoys of funerals passing through them daily. If she got that in her low state she was done. Mother, he repeated, you're not to get up.

—If you go on pamperin' me this way, she said, her deep eyes a bonny twinkle, you'll spoil me forever from doin' anything again.

Pampering her! There she was, feverish, cough-ridden, lying on a hard, flea-infested sofa, a few scraps of blanket covering her — and she thought she was being pampered! She who hadn't had for years a sound boot on her foot, a solid meal in her belly, or a warm stitch on her back. The Christian iron of resignation had entered her soul!

—An' don't worry, she called out as he reached the door, if you don't manage to get th' money today — we'll manage somehow.

He went out thinking of her. She had had a quiverful of children — some said thirteen; and but five of them had reached an adult age.

Two went in their infancy from croup, and a third — a lively little girl, by all accounts, called Susan, after her mother — from the same complaint at the age of six. She had never mentioned the little lass; but Michael and Ella had spoken of her to him. Of the two Johnnies she had spoken, because he, the third, had managed to live. Ella had told him her mother had spoken about Susan several times. When Susan died, she seemed to have crept into her mother's heart, for, Ella said, tears had always decked her eyes whenever the little one's name had been mentioned.

All who had survived were clever, each in his own way: Archie, clever-handed, could do almost anything with wood and a few tools, and could model astonishing things from papier mâché; Tom, with method and order in his slower cleverness, would have made a grand soldier; Michael had been a superb hand with pencil and crayon, and would, if chances had been good, have made a fine artist; while Ella, graceful and retentive, with her white hands at home on the keys of a piano, reading music easily at first sight, full of Scott's poetry, familiar with Shakespeare and Milton, might have become a gleam from the beauty of Beethoven and Bach. But they were all four failures: no-one was there to point a way further on from where they found themselves when they entered into personal and responsible life. Social surroundings and the Idylls of Religion persuaded, or shoved, them back to where they had started from; the colours of life gradually faded, and they groped boastfully and defiantly about in the gloom again. Social privilege and Christian conduct took their talents away from them, and buried them in a wasteland.

It lay in his pocket at last with his good right hand surrounding it — the cheque for fifteen pounds. Pay to Sean O'Casside, on Order, the sum of fifteen pounds sterling; so he started homewards, face flushed, heart panting, lips murmuring thanks to God. He'd buy a hot-water bottle to keep his mother's feet cosy; oranges to cool her hot tongue; some meat to make beef-tea to renew her strength, and some sugar, tea, and a few eggs — for a start. Oh, yes, and he'd call in on his way, and get Dr. Delany to see her; a five-shilling fee, and she was worth it. But first, he'd have to get this cheque turned into money.

Here was the Bank named on the cheque. Here was the Bank. A heavy door against which he had to push his full weight to open it. A place rich in polished mahogany and the shining of brass grilles. A solemn, subdued air, like what you'd feel in a church. A glass-panelled door, well behind the mahogany barricades, with the title of *Manager* written across it in letters of purest gold. Wise-looking heads, some old, some young, bent down, battling over big books. Sean felt awed, and a feverish feeling swept over him so that his hand trembled when he held out the cheque. Cash for that, please, he had asked with a dry tongue that made his voice husky. He got it back again. Couldn't cash it, oh, no. It was crossed or something. Find one with an account, and, maybe, he'd do it. Sorry; no, couldn't oblige him. He hastened out, and hurried into another. Sorry; they couldn't possibly do it for him either. Where did he get it? What did he get it for? Where did he live? No; they couldn't cash it for him: rules were rules. He hurried out frightened, and ran back to Maunsel's. Mr. the Manager was out. Oh, no; they never paid in money. Rules were rules; but anyone would cash it for him.

He hurried homewards again, excited and afraid. Now his way was blocked by a crowd staring towards Trinity College; blocked his way, and held him there, fuming, and cursing silently. A hell-blast blight them all! His mother might well be in her last moments, might be calling for him, and he stuck there among these gapers! A stream of coloured pennons fluttered over the College entrance. He could hear his mother calling faintly, Jack, Jack; where's Jack? He tried to push into the crowd to get by, but he was stopped by a policeman. Can't I pass? I have important business to do. No; have to wait now till he goes in. Wait till who goes in? The Lord Lieutenant. Why, what's on? Cricket match, or something. Jasus! hold up a finger, and you'll get a Dublin crowd. How often had his mother said that to him! Here they were hard at it. Supposing she wanted anything, and he wasn't there to get it! Here comes the gent now; Life Guards round the carriage drawn by snow-white animals flecked with golden-brown patches, and a squadron of arrogant hussars to follow. Trit-trot, trit-trot goes Dublin's dearest toy into trit-trot Trinity College. Six hundred pounds a week for going about all plumes and pleasures. Wonder what would happen if I went in and asked him to cash the cheque for me? In duty done in a state of life, God sorted men out in a comical way; here am I with fifteen pounds in my pocket that are no good to me; there he goes trit-trotting into a temple of learning with more money than he can inconveniently spend. If his mother was ill, there'd be nurses sitting on every chair in the house, doctors coming in by every door and trying to climb in by every window, with chemists in every store compounding medicines. There'd be silk sheets under and over her on a bed as cosy as a well-built bird's nest in the heart of a sunny tree; while silky white magnolias and crimson rhododendrons nodded anxiety outside a window discreetly curtained with brocade. And if she died, no less a protestant than an archbishop, no less a catholic than a cardinal, would be robing themselves in chasuble and stole, afire with embroidery, to go trit-trot to where the coffin lay, and there waft her upward with a first-class testimonial to the reception saints and angels waiting to set her down among heaven's best people.

—Wait a minute, he thought as he went on when the crowd had scattered — a skirt and a warm petticoat for the mother — say a pound; trousers, boots, and a cap for himself — say another one; five weeks' rent owed — a third; and near two more for tea, sugar, coal, bread, and milk. They go quick, one after another — five of them vanished already at one swoop!

He went into McCartan's hardware and crockery shop; asked to see some hot-water jars; chose one, and presented the cheque. The girl assistant took it into an inner part of the shop and came back with the boss, who stared at Sean as he returned the cheque.

—We don't do business this way here, he said. We'd soon be out on the street if we done that. Put that hot-wather jar back in its place, Sarah; and he watched her till she did it, then came to the door to stare after Sean as he hurried down the street. A curse seemed to doom the coloured bit of paper in his pocket. Where was he to get the beef, the jar, the fruit, and other things he needed for the sick woman? He made towards home, the sweat running down him with the dint of hurrying from place to place, the cheque getting crumpled from the nervous fingering of his hand: a moment ago, a treasure; now a drop of poisoned anxiety in the core of his mind.

Taking a last gamble, he burst into Murphy's, to whom he was indebted for goods, easing up to stroll jauntily into the store that was but two ordinary houses knocked into one, but which was stacked with everything from milk and coal to oil, bacon, tobacco, sweets, and fruit. He stretched the cheque over the counter to Murphy, who stared at it wonderingly, wiping hands, smeared with the grease of bacon, before taking it gingerly between his fingers with a murmured Wha's this?

—Just come to pay what I owe, Sean said, carelessly; that's a cheque, Mr. Murphy — just want you to cash it for me.

—Ah, said Murphy, I daren't do that, now, for how do I know it's genuine?

—Oh, it's genuine all right, said Sean gaily; you can tell by the weight of it.

—We have to be on our guard. I'll let th' bank see it, an' if they say it's a good one, I'll get you th' money.

—I want the damned money now! said Sean tersely.

—Well, you can't have it; even was I willin', I haven't got such a quantity o' money in th' house.

—Well, let's have half of it then.

—I couldn't, so I couldn't — it mightn't be passed.

—How it mightn't be passed?

—The payer mightn't have a thing in the bank to meet it; I got caught wanst that way before.

Here was another anxiety for Sean! Something new he had never heard of before. Thieves and tricksters — the world was crawling with them! The whole thing mightn't be worth the half of an honest-to-god ten-shilling note! May the flaming weirdness of hell envelop them all!

—How long will it take to get passed? asked Sean.

—Aw, not more'n a week or so.

—I want some money now, said Sean fiercely; the mother's ill, and there isn't a thing in the house!

—Well, I tell you wha', said Murphy sympathetically, I'll let you have credit to another five shillings — that's as fair as I can do.

—That's no use! said Sean furiously, I want to get a hot-water jar for her feet.

—Oh, that? Wait now; th' missus's got one she'll lend you. He ran off to come back with an old white jar in his hand. There y'are, and he handed it over to Sean. A half a crown for it, if it doesn't come back. If th' cheque's passed, you can have what's comin' when I take what's owed.

—Give me five shillings, damn you, said Sean, or hand back the cheque and you can whistle for what's owed to you.

—I make it a rule never to lend money, grumbled Murphy, as he slowly counted five shillings into Sean's eager, outstretched hand.

He hurriedly bought a pound of beef, a few eggs, some corn-flour, and several oranges, fancying all the time he heard her calling him, though very faintly the shrivelled lips moved in the crinkled, pallid face in the midst of the fuchsia, the geranium, and the musk. He ran back, softly mounted the stairs, and crept into the room. She appeared to be sleeping quiet. Good! He got a small sack, went to Murphy's, and carried back two stone of coal, bread, sugar, tea, and a small jug of milk. Soon he had a good fire going, and when the kettle boiled, he filled the jar, wrapped it in an old torn shift, and carefully shoved it under the old bedclothes to her feet which to his touch felt icily cold. He sensed her feet stretching towards the jar, and heard her lips giving a purring murmur of pleasure. He put the beef into a saucepan to stew; peeled the oranges; squeezed with the pressure of his hands as much juice as he could from them into a tumbler, adding some sugar and hot water. He brought it to her, and she swallowed it in a few quick gulps, though her forehead, when he felt it, seemed now to be as cold as her feet. He noticed that she never asked him about the cheque, and seemed to have forgotten all about it. Too sleepy, maybe, he thought, pushing away the dread that cheques even of the highest value wouldn't interest her any longer now. A tap at the door. Christ! he'd forgotten the doctor, and here he was now without the money to pay his fee! With steady and gentle hands the doctor examined her while she stared at him with a vacancy Sean didn't like.

—A great old woman, said Sean, trying to be bright after the examination was over. Had a hard life, but can stand anything. She'll be all right in a few days; and as the doctor remained silent, added, think so, sir?

—She's a very old woman, the doctor remarked, very old; and tired, too. The pulse is weak; very weak; and he stood, staring at the still figure on the sofa — waiting for the fee, Sean thought bitterly.

—I can't give you the five shillings just now, he said aloud, flushing crimson, for a cheque I got hasn't been cashed yet.

—Cheque? The doctor was startled. What cheque would you have? and he set his soft hat firmly on his head, looking searingly into Sean's face.

—One I got for writing a book, said Sean; it's to be published soon.

—A book? Indeed? Well, the next time you haven't a fee handy, get the Dispensary doctor, please; that's what he's for — to attend to you people. And without another word he left the room, leaving the house without telling Sean what was to be done for his mother.

He went to the fire, stirred the beef-tea, and tasted it. It was good, better than any medicine for her, he thought. When it had cooled a little, and hearing her stir, he touched her gently into noticing it. Sitting on the old red-covered box, he fed her from a spoon till half of it was gone. Then with a murmured, Grand; that was grand, Jack, she sank back on to the hard horsehair pillow that Sean had covered with an old towel to try to keep the bristles from annoying her neck and shoulders.

—Everything's grand to her, he thought; she has accepted anything given to her without a murmur of complaint. A cup of tea; a glass of beer; a sip of orange juice; and now a few drops of beef-tea — all grand, and welcome gifts from the giver of all.

Going down to the yard to fill a kettle to make himself some tea, he was greeted by a neighbour hanging out some ragged clothes on to a rope line.

—Your mother was in great fettle this morning, she said thickly, for she held a clothes-peg crossways in her mouth; she'll live to be a hundhred.

—Why! Were you up to see her?

—Up? No; but wasn't she down here early on puttin' out her few old things to dhry, after washin' them out, an' she laughin' an' jokin' with any that happened to come into th' yard. You could hear her a mile off!

Now he knew why her heart had gone weak and her pulse slow. She had risen while he was away, had washed the clothes, and had hung them out to dry. There they were, hanging limp on the line, a last testimony to a brave and resolute woman. In his mind's flurry over the cheque, he hadn't noticed them before. She had used up her last spark of energy keeping useful in life. It was done now. He might have known that she couldn't keep a promise to lie still and stay in bed.

He went back to the room, and looked steadfastly down at the dear, wrinkled face; and his heart sank to see how worn it was, how pale it seemed to be growing. There were the humorously-curving mouth, now tightly, almost grimly, closed; the strongly-made nose, and the firm, resolute chin; the sleek hair, still with many dark hairs threading a pattern through the grey locks, that he had combed and brushed every morning for a week now. Life would be chill for him when that warm heart had ceased to beat.

He shook himself violently. It was neither honest nor manly of him to wish her to live longer. If ever a woman in this world had earned a rest from her labours, this was the one. He didn't wish her to live because of any pleasure death might take away from her. He wished it simply because she seemed to make life easier for him. Nay, not seemed; she did. To wish her to live was a great weakness that he couldn't shake aside. He was the one of her children who had been with her all the time. Thirty-five years or so she had cared for, and defended, him. Her works would follow her. What works? Attending to him! That wouldn't fetch her even a good-conduct medal from a local G.H.Q. of heaven! This woman's spiritual hardihood, her unshakable energy, her fine intelligence had all been burned to unusable ashes in the tedious smokiness of a hapless life. Life had wasted all her fine possessions. None, save he, could recognise her for what she was; and he was powerless to yield her any words of praise, for if he spoke them, there were none to hear. She would die alone — unhonoured and unsung. Unwept, too? Almost, indeed; for who was there to weep for her going? The poor had precious little time or chance to weep. She seemed to expect these things from no-one. She was far above any praise that could be given for anything she had done. Silence was the highest praise that could be given her. And the resolve that he, too, would become as she had been — indifferent to the phases of fortune; indifferent, if possible, to what the world regarded as praise, peace, and prosperity; to bear all things — while fighting them fiercely — pain, poverty, and wretchedness, with dignity and silence; and, finally, to meet death with a careless nod of greeting, to suffer his cold clasp with a calm closing of the eyes, and a silent hail and farewell to a world left living.

His beginning of bravery wasn't too good. Grief was tightening his breast, and his breath came too quick at the thought of losing her. Self-pity had ambushed his hardy designs, and before he knew it, tears had welled from his eyes, and had splashed down on to the pale face so full of settled peace. The black eyes of her suddenly opened and, startled, stared up at his anxious face. His tears had roused her from a graceful quietness, just as she was about to round off life with a little sleep.

—Ah! Jack, she murmured pitifully, her lips quivering, her worn and gnarled old hand stroking his, resting on the edge of the old sofa; ah! Jack, Jack, Jack!

He bent down and kissed her warmly, and the black eyes, still agleam with pity, closed slowly, and her head sank back on to the hard old pillow, as she murmured, I'll be up and about again soon. With another shake of his body, he calmed his emotion, rearranged the old clothes over her as comfortably as he could, glad to see her sliding into her quiet sleep again.

He felt a little more hopeful now. She hadn't coughed for quite a time. He listened; she seemed to be breathing more easily. She might get over it. She had, so far, escaped the plague that had darkened every Dublin street with mourning, hanging crêpe from the knocker of every door, white ribbons for the young, black for the old; the heavenly slogan of R.I.P. on every one of them. He'd disturb her no more: he'd let her come out of it her own way, or quietly go her own way out of the world.

He went over to the fire, and set the kettle on it for a cup of tea. He pulled over the little table, set pen, ink, and paper on it, stiffening himself to go on writing his *Three Shouts on a Hill* — a shout at the Gaelic League, a shout at Sinn Fein, and a shout at Labour. Most of it had already been written, and he was now working at the epilogic chapter called Descending the Hill. When it was done, maybe, he'd send it to Shaw, and ask him to write a preface praising it. He wouldn't part with this new work for less than twenty-five pounds. With cunning, that would keep him going for a year, and give him time to think of something else to do.

He went to the window, and looked out at the sky. It was stridently lovely in green and purple and crimson. Like a fat, fully-robed cardinal giving a blessing to the world. Curious that Oscar Wilde hurried to pull down the blind whenever a sunset reddened his room, calling it old-fashioned, belonging to the time when Turner was the last note in art. A lily-like, drooping sky murmured to him in delicate phrases, but this red-faced, impudent lass, arrayed in crimson taffeta, was too much for him. It was too familiar, and came too close. And yet the pearly chasteness of the evening star swung in its folds, soothing the rowdy showiness of the vaunting heavens. Sean gave welcome to its manly warmth; bawdy it might be, and rough-toned, too; but it had life, and shared it lavishly with the earth beneath. When the sky was thoughtful in its pale and dreamy colours, let the lute be vocal; when the sun flared red and purple, let the trumpet sound.

How quiet the house had grown. Not a mouse stirring. He had never sensed the house so still before, as if life had gone, and left it breathless. Quieter than a nun, breathless with adoration; as still as death itself. He shivered as if a creepy silent wind had entered the room; cold, as cold could be. As cold as heaven would be if God cast a cold look on a well-loved saint.

He went back to the little table to resume his work, but strive as he might, no thought allowed itself to enter his mind. The curious silence remained, as if some virtue, some warmth had gone from the little room forever. He glanced over at his mother, and saw her face calmly lying still in a deep sleep. She was just asleep. This curious feeling was but imagination, gone fretful and cold; yet a great dread crept over every beat of his quickening heart. He got up slowly, and walked over firmly to the sofa. He bent down low over her, listening,

listening; and then he knew that she was dead. He felt her forehead
— it was turning into the coldness of marble. She had gone from him
when the silent wind had crept into the room. She had died without
one murmur for attention; unbreakable, tireless, and quite confident.
Indomitable woman. She had stretched out only when all usefulness
had left her body, possessing nothing but the sweet peace that gave
courage to her fine, gay heart. She had taken a holiday from life at
last. She had come very close to her Michael now; he had won her
away from the world at last. She had died divested of decoration,
even of one glittering word of praise. No matter. No earthly diadem
would be brilliant enough to wear well on that seamed and fearless
brow. All the perfumes of Arabia could add no further beauty to
those worn and gnarled hands. Only such a gem as the evening star
on that forehead could safely set off that hardy, gentle, patient face.
He bent down and kissed her. Her lips were very cold now. Careless,
he let the tears fall on the wrinkled cheeks, but no lids fluttered open
to let the bright, dark eyes stare hope and courage into his own now;
nor did the cracked lips give as much as a quiver. Ah! Jack, Jack, she
is dead indeed!

Through a gay, warm, golden haze, curtained with a magenta sky,
Sean moved to the business of his mother's burial. But no summer
sun could gild the streets with hope, or make them genial for him.
Each street was a paved courtyard to a tomb. Although he hurried
about, getting three pounds advance fom the Agent on his mother's
five pounds life insurance, registering her death, seeking a coffin, he
scarcely seemed to move. Under the magenta sky, through the
shimmering golden haze, everything seemed to come towards him,
passing by ere he could see the shapes plain, or mind comment on
what he saw, as they flowed by him under the magenta sky, through
the quivering golden haze. Streams of funerals came moving towards
him; black plumes for the old, now and again, nodded a timely
farewell from the horses' heads; but white plumes for the young
never seemed to cease nodding a sad greeting from the golden haze
enlivening their last hour among the living; the bold, black hearses
moving with glossy impudence, the brown coffins aglitter with brass,
their lids bearing up a burden of blossoms trying to smile away the
silent grief that lay beneath them.

Throughout the golden haze he saw neither bird nor bee; yes, a
butterfly; just one, a tiny white one, lost, knowing not whether to
come or go, seeking, maybe, a sad sip of nectar from flowers decking
the top of a coffin. Out of the enveloping haze a girl's hands wrapped

up for him in tissue paper, tying it with black tape, a snowy shroud and soft pillow; the finest shift his mother had ever worn, the softest pillow her head had ever touched; while dimly he realised that a pound of his had gone into the sunny hilarity around him. Then the hand of another girl, in some faintly sketched-in shop, gave him half a dozen crimson gladioluses, that they might shine a torch of defiance beside the grey head of the brave, dead woman.

Out of the dancing shimmer came the thin voice of a drowsy clerk in the cemetery office droning out the order for the opening of the grave, purchased in perpetuity by the deceased years and years ago for the family, the one piece of property she ever had possessed, and proving to be a sound investment now; and again he felt that another pound had vanished into the bright-blue and gorgeous haze from his store of three.

Then from the satisfied splendour of the sun crept the rectory garden with the sensitive face of Mr. Griffin, white and worn from a recent illness, quietly looking at Sean, his shoulders heavily shawled, murmuring comfortable words towards Sean's dull ear, words that were coloured soberly with sympathy, that one of God's dear children had come closer to Him to be calmly received into a quiet order of sainthood, with all heaven watching her stepping shyly into the joy of her Lord; for her heavy afflictions had been but for a moment, and had worked for her an exceeding weight of eternal glory; who, having had nothing, now possesses all things; bringing no thrill to Sean's heart, for he welcomed words like these no longer; and through all the sunnied harmony of the day a dark path led him everywhere, and crêpe bordered the zenith and nadir of all he saw.

Hard he found it to get a coffin — the last gift he was to give her; for, in the shimmer, piles of coffins shone outside the doors of them who made them, and within were towering barricades of them, already sold, yet many more were needed for those who had died in the epidemic. Busy and sweating hands, raised above the coffins, impatiently motioned him away; and hammers thudded ceaselessly, day and night, down on elm and oak and pine to meet the needs of those eager to bury their dead.

At last, when he found a merciful dealer, he was satisfied and tired, his legs so numb that no feeling came to them when he moved. He was glad when he passed out from under the magenta canopy, out of the golden haze, into the house, into the cooler room, where Mrs. Casside, dressed in her spotless wedding-garment, lay still, something of a smile on her face, maybe because she had quietly prevented any further discouraging interference with the beginning of her long journey from where she had secretly crept silently away from life.

Over the white shroud, over the coffin, he draped the red cloth that had covered the box on which she had so often sat. It would be her red flag, ignorant as she was of all things political, and seemingly indifferent to the truth that the great only appear great because the workers are on their knees; but she was, in her bravery, her irreducible and quiet endurance, her fearless and cheery battle with a hard, and often brutal, life, the soul of Socialism; and the red symbol, draping her coffin, honoured itself in warming the dead-cold breast of an indomitable woman.

He was glad, after waiting five days, when the morning of the funeral came. Strive as he might, he couldn't force himself to realise that all life had left the frail body lying so safe and still in its faintly-polished box. He would have been shocked, but not surprised, if he had heard her voice crooning quietly some old, sweet song, or seen her suddenly lean out of the window to send a greeting down to a passing neighbour. Perhaps, a young, black-haired miss once more, she was with her Michael again; he with his white brow and bronze beard, looking down at her, stroking her hand, and murmuring, You took a long time to come to me, Sue; a long, long time. And she would say, I came quick as I could, Michael; and when I found the way, I hurried.

Sean broke off a sprig of fuchsia, another of musk, and a crimson disk from the geranium, and carefully arranged them under a fold of the shroud, near her right hand. They would be her gold, her frankincense, and myrrh; her credentials to show to the first guardian saint she'd meet. I cared for these, she'd say, and honoured them, for they were of the gifts that the good God gave me. Then, maybe, with a dim smile, he'd ask her what favours she expected to get in return for these trivial things; she'd answer, permission to sing a few old songs, some useful work to do in the daytime, and a chance to walk with Michael under the evening stars.

He knew well that what he saw in his mind's eye was but a fantastic remembrance of one, now gone; one whom he thought he loved because she had been very useful to him. He knew that this hurly-burly of thought and confused vision would gradually resolve itself into a newly-ordered life; a life broken sharply from the more immediate past; and that his new life would go on striding ever further away from the geranium, the fuchsia, and the musk. She had come the way all had come, and had gone the way all had gone; as he would go. The rest was silence. Death wasn't a lonely thing. Here, before him, with all outside lively and quick, death looked sad and separated; but great multitudes had died as she had, in the same way, at the same moment. Never morning wore to evening but some heart did break. Leaves of grass, all, which today is, and tomorrow is cast into the oven. *In memoriam ad gloriam sed asthoriam non nomoreum*, amen. Leaves of grass, all; that the dews spangled, the frosts bit, the sun burned. It was passing strange — set beside the supercilious contempt some had for mass production; or the passionate, almost idolatrous, honour paid by so many to the individual — that the biggest mass production known to man came from the mind of God! Or, if no god lived, then, from the indifferent energy of nature. God imitated His creations, not in two or thousands, but in millions; they were poured out in crowds, from dread and useful viruses, through the leaves of grass up to the innumerable flaming suns. Mass production, mass order, and mass community life seemed to be the fullest and happiest manifestation of heaven's many laws. It wouldn't do to say that each differed from each in some trivial, imperceptible way, blade of grass from blade of grass; leaf of tree from leaf of tree; human face from human face. Who is he who having examined each blade of grass, every leaf of every tree, would say no one of them was like its like? And though human faces might differ, and did, the darkness of hatred, the light of love, the glint of fear, the lightning flash of courage shone the same from every human eye, and the thoughts surrounding them were, in essence, the same in every human heart.

He went to the window and looked out. A few cabs had gathered to carry a few neighbours to help in the carrying of Mrs. Casside to the grave. Carry me back to old Virginny; back to where she came from, back to ashes and back to dust. All for the forbidden bite of an apple. A benevolent sentence from a benevolent god. Nonsense. Death is but change, and change has been with us, in us, through us, since the world began. We are frightened at the thought of ceasing to be, because the thought implies that consciousness of annihilation persists. But we shall never know that we are dead.

Here came the hearse, crawling along like a polished black beetle under the vivid blue sky, through the golden haze. He felt for coins in his pocket, and slid them through his fingers, counting; just enough to pay his cab fare, tip the hearsemen and the grave-diggers. She'd soon be buried now out of the world's way. Heavy steps came up the stairs, and when he said, Come in, to a knock on the door, two hearsemen entered, clad in the blue-black suits of their kind, their heads furnished with high top-hats, their faces firmly set in seriousness. They were followed by some neighbours who came to help carry the coffin down.

—We'll miss her, Sean, said one of them; and the kids will too — badly. A great oul' woman gone west — th' light o' heaven to her!

—There y'are, said the leading hearseman, handing an envelope to Sean; that's for you — th' bill.

—The bill? Oh, righto, said Sean carelessly, thrusting the envelope into his pocket. You can start to screw her down now.

—There'll be no screwin' down, nor no effin' funeral here till th' money's paid, said the hearseman harshly. Right, Bill? he added, turning to his mate.

—The bill'll be paid, said Sean, as soon as a cheque I have is cashed — your manager knows about it.

—I'm tellin' you no funeral'll leave here till th' money's paid, repeated the hearseman fiercely; we want no thricks with cheques.

—Aw, murmured one of the neighbours, you couldn't leave th' poor woman sthranded like that; th' money'll be paid.

—Sthranded or no, said the hearseman, if th' money owed, four pound nineteen shillings an' sixpence, isn't in them two hands — stretching them out — in ten minutes' time, we sail off, an' you can do what you like with th' stiff; an' them's th' last words!

Sean jumped down the stairs, rushed along the road, darted into a side street, and burst into Murphy's to splutter out the way things were, pleading for God's sake to let him have enough to pay the bill for coffin and hearse.

—Wait, now, said Murphy slowly; for it never does to rush money matthers. Cheque passed awright, couple o' days ago; so we're all serene. Had I known you were in a hurry, I'd 'a had things ready. I don't know there's as much as you want in the till — th' day's young yet. He stuck a hand into the till, raking forward some coins, and fingering gently a few pound notes. Wait till I see. One, two, three, four — there's four o' them, anyway, for a start; an' five, ten, fifteen shillins in half-crowns — for a funeral you should ha' warned me beforehand — sixteen, seventeen, eighteen — if I hadda known, I'd ha' had everything ready — nineteen; now which'll you have — two thrupenny bits or six coppers?

—When'll I get the rest due to me? asked Sean, swiftly gathering up the notes and coin as they were handed out to him.

—Aw, sometime at th' end o' th' week, when I've taken what's mine, an' when th' till's flush. If I hadda known you were in a hurry, I'd ha' had things ready; but Sean heard only the beginning of the sentence, for he was racing back, breathless, to where his mother patiently lay, waiting to be laid to rest. He handed the money to the hearseman, who signed the receipt, the lid of the coffin was screwed down, and then the hearseman gestured to the neighbours to bear the box below.

—The burial docket? he asked of Sean, and carefully put it into a breast pocket. We'll have t'hurry, Bill, he said to his mate, if we're to get to th' cemetery in time to settle th' old lady properly.

Sean heard them hurrying down the stairs, heard the coffin bumping against the corners, and with a bitter heart stood watching at the top, tense with shame at the scene about the money that had been played before the neighbours. He'd wait till the coffin had been rolled into the hearse, till the neighbours had climbed into their cabs, then he'd run down and jump quietly into his own. Hearing a half-threatening, half-coaxing mutter of gee-up gee-up, there, he glanced from a window, and saw the funeral moving off at a quick trot without him, while the driver of his own cab, standing on the footboard, was trying to flick the window with his whip to draw Sean's attention to the departure. He rushed hither and thither looking for his cap, and finally tore down bareheaded, opened the door of the cab, and sprang headlong into it.

—Where'r all the others? came from the head of the driver which had suddenly thrust itself in at the window.

—T'others? What others?

—What others! testily — why, them's acomin' with you.

—There's no others coming with me, and Sean saw a look of dazed dismay spreading over the driver's face.

—Wha' — ne'er a one?

—No, ne'er a one. It doesn't matter.

—It matthers a helluva lot to me! he half shouted. A cab at a funeral with only a single one in it was never known before in th' world's histhory! If the cab carried you there on your own, I'd never be able to lift me head again in th' light o' day!

—Please go on, said Sean plaintively, or I'll not be in time to take a part in the burial. I'll let you have five shillings for your pains.

—Five shillins, an' a funeral a gala occasion? With a load o' four, now, I'd look complete, an' be in ten shillins; with a full cab o' six, I'd look complete, an' feel complete, an' be fifteen shillins to th' good. Is there ne'er a one o' yous, he shouted to a sniggering group near by, ne'er a one o' yous man enough to lep into a cab beside a neighbour, near suicide with loneliness an' sorra, an' cheer him up with a glowin' pipe an' a warm word from t'other seat opposite? Ara, this is a poor place for a poor soul to set out on its last journey to meet its God.

Sean was about to jump from the cab and overwhelm the driver with a burst of curses, but thinking better of it he sank back on the seat and sighed. History was repeating itself; something like this had happened at his sister's funeral. What did it matter in the end? He had seen the last of her long ago. It was an empty world, an empty world for him.

—I tell you wha', said the driver, sticking his head in again at the window; I'll take you fifty foot from th' gate, where I won't be seen, an' dhrop you there, if you pay me six shillins, an' say no more about it, for fair's fair.

—Yes, yes; agreed, said Sean, after he had slid the coins in his pocket through his fingers to make sure he had enough to meet the demand.

Sean heard the driver flinging curses at his mare, heard the swish of a whip, and felt the animal surging forward at a clumsy gallop; so maybe he'd be in time to see the coffin lowered, when Mrs. Casside, baptized Susan, would be committed to the ground amid the trumpet obbligato of the Christian faith, sending its notes, boastful and satisfying, into every present ear save that of the dead woman, and his own. Fearful consciences would believe the proclamation that, at the last day, at the sound of the trump, the dead would rise, and each individual body would be reunited to its individual soul; when the natural would be changed for the spiritual, the corrupt for the incorruptible; that which was mortal for amazing immortality. A tall order. A mystery. That is Paul's only explanation. But what is the soul? Where is it when the body is present, and where does it go when the body is but dust? A substantial form of the body? But how can that be? If I cease to be myself, how can I persist as myself? If, when I die, I become a disembodied spirit, then I am no longer what I once knew myself to be, and so how can it be said that I am what I once was and now am not? The being which is I gets all my joy and exhilaration, feels all my pain, sees things lovely and things evil, hears all soft and harsh sounds through the senses, through the nerves, all in delicate and delightful union with the coarser parts of the body; but when I die, all these die, too, and I that was am then no more: nothing left but a fading memory among a few. No; say what they like, there's nothing above but the blue air, or the soft, grey cloud taking the gay sun's gilding; or the black one hoarding a storm for our heads. No; the banner waving over every grave is silence.

But let them say out their jewelled words over Susan's body, to the last word; unto this last; for they were part of her strange and happy dream, and dear to all her secret thoughts; though Sean knew that, unattended, though the mind was lovely and the body pure, the clay of the grave would bring forth coarse grass that would soon hide it from the sight of man forever.

HAIL AND FAREWELL

SEAN was leaving forever the room where his mother had lived so long, and in which she had, at last, died. His brother, Michael, wasn't a congenial man to live with. Never had been, and but for the foolish, peace-loving anxiety of his mother, Sean would have come into violent collision with him long ago. Michael had gone his own sour way, and had dwindled into a wreck before he had come to the end of it. He had treated his mother as a bully would treat an amiable fag in a second-hand public school. She had always dreaded his appearance in the house; and felt fully alert and all at ease whenever he happened to be far away. His glittering gate had always been the door of a public-house, and drunkenness was to him an inward sign of outward majesty and strength. When he had money, he was popular with those who had none; a merry fellow, heart of the roll. Spending the little he had on others, who had less, so that he could enjoy the telling, before a rough and reverent gang, of the brief chronicles of half-imagined escapades, seen in the tawdry visions of a drunken bout. Paint him as he was twenty golden years ago, and paint him as he is now, and one would have a horrifying picture of a worker Dorian Gray. Now there is no trace whatever of his young and sturdy grace, fine, intelligent face, well-made manhood, or delicately-moulded hands; no trace whatever. His lovely masculine manhood hadn't lived to grow old; first it had been marred, then utterly destroyed by the life he led, ere a grey rib appeared in his raven-hued hair. Coarseness, vulgarity, and a vicious meanness glowered from his features now, though at times one caught a sudden flash of dark pride, lighting a gleam of grandeur for a second in the penury of the lined and battered face of the man.

Time and again, Sean had lain awake through the night, cursing deep, while he listened to the drunkard keeping their mother from a tardy sleep, lying patient and coaxingly amiable on her hard and bitter sofa-bed; Michael singing sloppily to himself; cursing his hard lot, falling heavily off his chair when he feared she had dozed off, leaving him alone; for he knew she would arise in her old shift to gently help him on to the chair again; or put her own rough pillow under his head if he was too drunk to move. How often had Sean's blood raged into angry heat, longing to run out and encircle the rough, withering throat with his still sinewy hands, to choke and choke the life out of him; always failing in his desire because Sean knew his mother would cling to him and pull at him, begging them both to remember that they were brothers. The end of it would have been his mother in tears, afflicted with dire trembling, and full of a bitter, taunting fear of the future. So Sean had stayed still, and lay on, listening.

Now it was very different: no mother to wail, to plead, to sigh her heart half away from herself. He had a few pounds just received for an article which would keep him going quietly for more than a month of Sundays. He had thought that the mother's death would work a change in Michael. Surely, he would remember, and remembering, regret all the vicious anxiety he had poured into so many hours of her gentle and resistant life? Remember, and be sorry for it, and repent; become a soberer and a wiser man? Sorra a bit of it!

Sean was trying to think out the words of a song in the dead of night when he heard the heavy, lurching steps stumbling up the stairs and the raucous, beery voice forcing itself to shape a song, masquerading a spurious delight in the heart of the braggart, hating himself. From the corner of an eye he saw the tousled figure staggering into the room, knocking clumsily and intentionally against the table at which Sean was sitting, while an envious, dirty hand, sliding along it, sent the little ink-bottle flying to the floor. Sean said nothing, but sat quietly where he was.

—Writin', be God, again! murmured the blurred voice of his brother; some fellas are able to give themselves airs! Scholar, is it? Scholar, me arse! Well, th' ink's gone, so wha'll we do now? Here's one who's forgotten moren' some'll ever learn. There's a man here. Takes a few dhrinks, but a man, all th' same; a man with two good mitts. Writin'! If I was someone, I'd thry to be a man first! But Sean sat still, quiet, where he was.

The malice-wreathed face, blasted away from all humanity, had suddenly thrust itself close to his own, half sickening him with the steam of a reeking savour spurting from the slobbering, panting mouth.

—Who d'ye think y'are, eh? were sodden words borne to his ear by a gust of rotting breath, and Sean, standing up from the chair, stepped back to avoid the stare of the bloodshot eyes; but the luridly drunken face, staring viciously, followed his own closely, while the wobbling mouth slobbered out a black rosary of curses, many of the soiled words slimy with self-pity for the drunkard himself, who felt he could never get back one jot or tittle óf the fair things gone from him forever. Sean, half retching, and savage, conjuring up some of the old vigour still lingering in his muscles, shot his shoulder against the chest of the calibanic splutterer, lifting him clean off his staggering legs, and sent him, with the table, crashing heavily to the floor, to lie there, a hand twisted under him, snoring heavily in a drunken and concussive stupor.

Sean got an old sack, filled it with as many of his books as it would hold, and set out on his first trip to fresh woods and pastures new, carrying his knowledge with him, estimating that he would have to make three trips at least before he put the last book into the old bag. When he came into the open, Sean shivered, for there was as yet no sign of the dawn, and it was bitter cold. No rosy auroran fingers would be opening the dawn of this morning; but a chill, bony hand, with the cold moisture of death gemming the fingers, would pull apart, surlily, the opening gates of the day. Half of a wan moon hung hesitating in the sky, as if she had lost her way in the heavens, and waited for some influence to come and guide her again on to a right road. The street as far as an eye could carry was silent and still as a sick animal crouched in some forgotten corner. The poor blinds and curtains in every window were closely united in hiding everything behind them, as far as unsteady and timorous hands could conceal things behind tatters. The little shops were tightly shuttered so that no sign of loaf, tray of tea, root or leaf of vegetable, newspaper, or sweet, showed itself, seeming to say that here older life no longer ate, drank, or read; and that younger life had gone fasting from the lure of caramel and rock. Indeed, it looked as if life had gone, and left the lonely street behind it.

—Hello, Sean! a voice sounded in a steady way in his ear, and then he noticed two young fellows walking softly beside him. Are you doin' a moonlight flit, or wha'?

—Where are you two off to? asked Sean, ignoring their question; a little innocent ramble, eh?

—Ay, replied the one who had greeted Sean, that's it — with a little sup in a bottle for th' Tans, he added, tapping his side.

—Come on, Ned, said the other, we can't keep th' Tans waitin'; and getting into their silent stride again, a loping trot, they vanished into the gloom ahead.

—The Curfew! He had clean forgotten that till these two who had dissolved into the shadow had whispered their mission. A second two would linger at a corner, and a third two at another so that the Tans would face fire from several directions; cross-fire that would send bullets soaring through the windows of houses where the sleeping people were depending on their guardian angels. Soon, somewhere, he would hear the bursting of a grenade, orchestrated by the odd emphatic report of rifle and automatic revolver, in another tussle between Saxon and Gael. A most dangerous thing to be out at Curfew hour without a pass, with the excuse that he was on his way to find a doss-down for a few nights; with a sack on his back; nothing would convince the Tans that his business was no concern of theirs. Everybody's business was a concern of theirs. In the absence of an ambush, there might be a chance of a few minutes' chat with them; but immediately after one, they wouldn't waste time on talk. Would he go back to wait till the daybreak, and the shadows fled away? He'd have to go back and forward three times at least to bring all his books away; but an interview with the Tans wouldn't be much worse than several more long hours spent with a drunken, sprawling brother. There he stood, thinking, his fingers numb with the cold, gripping the mouth of the sack; stood thinking whether to go on or go back, under a sky that was a wide canopy of squalid, haggard grey, muddied by the sleety humours of the night that had gone, weighed down with bellied swathes of clouds, black and lowering; while over where he guessed the sun to be, shone a cold, steely light, like the slim blade of a rapier that the dew had rusted.

Whisht! The whine of a motor. He listened. Away over to the left, he saw the light of a searchlight flickering over the roofs. The Tans! He hurried from the broader street into a narrow lane, to crouch in the recess of a back doorway, his bag of books resting beside him. He heard the motor swinging along the street he had just left, saw the beam of light sweeping down the lane, covering him with a dreadful glory; but it darkened again in a second, and Sean, near a faint, felt his heart panting fiercely.

The ambush! There it was; he heard the sullen bursting of grenades, the solid, piercing reports of rifle-fire, shouts that must come from the Tans, for he knew the Republicans remained sullenly silent, firing impassively, firing steadily at the head, the chest, or the belly of a Tan; and may God make their eyes keen and their hands steady! added Sean piously. But it was very annoying, thought Sean as he shivered in his corner, listening to the not very distant gunfire. The people were getting a little tired of the fighting. Gun-peals and slogan-cries were things happy enough in a song; but they made misery in a busy street, or along the quiet, unassuming walks of a village. If it went on much longer, most of the cosy Irish homes would become but handfuls of ashes to be poured reverently into jars, and put safely away on a shelf for sweet remembrance. The sovereign people were having a tough time of it from enemies on the left and friends on the right. Going out for a stroll, or to purchase a necessary, no-one knew when he'd have to fall flat on his belly, to wait for death to go by, in the midst of smoke and fire and horrifying noises. Armoured cars clattered through the city; lorries, caged in with wire and crowded with Tans pointing guns at everyone's breast, cruised through the streets; and patrols, with every rifle cocked to the last hair, crept along every kerb. Every narrow lane seemed to be the dark dazzling barrel of a rifle. Christian Protestant England and Christian Catholic Ireland were banging away at each other for God, for King, and Country. All forgot, for the time being, the deeds alleged to have been done in Russia, so that they could show, in a ripe example, what Christ's faith, hope, and charity could do in a private and confidential war of their own. Christ's faithful soldiers and servants were busy bestowing the chrism of death upon each other.

Sean had gone on safely when the firing had died away, had found a room in which to live, fortunately; for his few friends were afraid to guard his books during an interval because of the many Irish works that were among them. They might damn the holder if the Tans made a raid. So here he was back in the old room again, filling his sack with books for the last time. There still lay the woe-spattered figure of Michael, mingled with pieces of the broken table, still snoring riotously in the stupor of drink. Sean glanced round the old room for the last time. Farewell, now, forever, to Nelson on his way through a fishing-village street, bound for Trafalgar's Bay; to Victoria in her deep-purple bodice, divided by the pale-blue sash, the golden crown, sprinkled with red and blue jewels, set firm on her

arrogant head; the mantelpiece clock, veneered to parade as mahogany, with its glass panel of painted flowers below its innocent face,
centred by a plain circular piece of glass that showed the pendulum
going to and fro, ceaselessly — a wedding present to his mother
from her husband. A great old clock. Sean had never known it to
need repairing. His mother had loved it, never forgetting to wind it
the last thing at night, reminding others of its need whenever she
lay ill, as if the thing had life that grew tired; the winding of it providing the energy for another day's work. Anything that moved had
life to her — the ticking clock no less than the growing flowers. Two
old wooden chairs, the squat little cupboard that he had used to hold
his books, a broken fender; a few battered things barely capable of
boiling an egg or frying a rasher; the old box by the fire, still covered
by the red cloth, where she had sat out many hours of a lonely life;
and the clay-grimed tins that once held so proudly the geranium,
the fuchsia, and the musk. They had withered when their good
guardian went away. Farewell to them all. Little connected with the
civility of life remaining here. Everything here to Sean was dead and
gone; he would never set eye on them again, and he never wanted to;
without the honour of his mother moving among them, they had
fallen from whatever grace they once had, and were damned forever.

Ah! He had near forgotten the old horse-hair sofa where she had
slept so uneasily for so long; where she had flung off many an illness,
with him attending on her as best he could. No, not quite as best he
could; not near it. How often had he neglected to attend to her, to
even think of her when she lay ill! No, not too often, maybe, for she
was seldom ill; and most times put an ailment over on her feet; but
he had neglected her often enough, content to do what he could the
last thing at night when he was about to go to bed. She had borne
everything without a murmur, laughing even, at times, when a
quiver of pain went through her; like a stoic, calm as a Buddha. And
death, himself, recognising her courage, had kissed her hand before
he led her away quietly. Sean laid a hand reverently on the old sofa
for a moment; had he had one, he'd have dropped a red rose on its
tattered cover.

Yet with all his feeling, he had never put as much as one green
sprig on her grave; never paid it a visit after having helped to lay her
there; and never would. The dead, worthy of remembrance, are
worth more than a decorated grave yielding profit to the selfish and
the vicious. Out of hell comes the thought and deed of making profit

from grief and sorrow. God's acre let out to the dead for so much per square foot. Holy roods of soil! The growing bush, however green, the climbing rose, however lovely, the sculptured stone, however grand, are neither seen nor wanted by the dead. If we wish to remember loved ones gone, then let us place the sculptured stone, the green bush, the climbing rose, apple-bloom, and cherry-blossom in public places where the sun shines, children play, and the living pass to and fro. Only the thoughts of the living can give the mortal immortality.

Sean looked down for the last time at the form of the sprawling castaway. Not a sign, not a shadow, of the earlier elegance; the clever, sinuous movement of the finely-fixed hand holding a pencil, weaving vibrant and charming lines over the bare whiteness of paper. No; not even a withered sign of a long-lost artist. And yet in that dreary and distorted face there must be some of the youthful glory hidden away; something, like a palimpsest, under the blear and dreadful misery of the countenance. No, not a mark of anything other than what all men see today. And yet, not so long ago, Sean had seen that perished face lit up with a courage that he could never summon to himself. Standing aimlessly idle on a slip down by the mouth of the river Liffey, Sean and Michael were smoking and watching the bathers swimming about in the deep and murky waters. Suddenly, one of them began to splash and cry out, unable to control himself in the swift flow, frightening the other swimmers who moved away from him, shouting out for the lifebuoy which a man frantically tried to disentangle from its nest in the wet stone wall. Sean saw Michael's scattered face tense into a fine, firm eagerness, saw him bend swift, stiff-jointed and all as he was, whip off his boots, sling aside his coat, and take a short run to plunge into the brown, swift-rippling waters, saw him shoot over to the struggling, drowning man. He swam like an otter, tumbling and forcing himself through the water with a strange, brave movement of glee. Standing ashiver and dripping on the slip again, Sean heard the policeman asking Michael for his name and address, and Michael's reply that a shilling for a glass of malt would serve him better.

To Sean's own knowledge, he had saved more than ten lives in this way, though no mention of any appeared on the face of the earth or the brow of heaven. In the sea, in a river, or in the calm, deep pool of a quarry, Michael would plunge forward to pull a drowning soul to safety. Never, either, would he don the dark motley of blackleg or scab. Ay, there was that much to be said for him. Had he had his due, a streak of red ribbon would be glaring from his faded coat now.

Sean stared down at the gaping mouth, the once well-formed face, now miscast with many evil markings, the frizzly moustache caked into horrid lumps with stale, dried droppings of beer, the seamed forehead, and the twisted cheeks: how could anyone who saw, say that that repellent figure bore on its breast the red badge of courage! Perhaps the sign of the sword was equal to the sign of the cross, for here lay stretched a fellow who risked laying down his life many times, not for friends, but for those whom he did not know, and, having saved them, would never see again. Those shapely hands of his were never made for the cankered pastime of handling pints. Clever and cunning, they did many things in their time, from holding a hawser, carrying new-baked, creosoted railway sleepers, hot and stinging, to guiding the delicate movements of pencil and pen. God's curse on today's way of the world! It was not that this prone man in younger days had digged in the earth to bury his talents there: no; he had been quietly robbed of them by the careless and criminal indifference of teachers, spiritual pastors, and masters, who had thoroughly buried them for him.

Curse of God on the way of the world today!

Sean hoisted the bag of books on to his shoulder, gave a last glance round the broken room, and then turned to leave it forever.

THE RAID

THE cold beauty of frost glittered everywhere outside, unseen, unfelt, for the slum was asleep. An uneasy silence echoed over the house, for awake or asleep, everyone knew that death with his comrade, the inflicter of wounds, roamed the darkened streets. Stretched out in a truckle bed in a tenement room, its murky window facing on to the street, Sean thought of the tapestry of the day. He could see the street stretching along outside, its roughly cobbled roadway beset with empty match-boxes, tattered straws, tattered papers, scattered mounds of horse-dung, and sprinkled deep with slumbering dust waiting for an idle wind to come and raise it to irritating life again. Lean-looking gas-lamps stood at regular intervals on the footpaths, many of them deformed from the play of swinging children, bending over like old men standing to gasp, and wait for a pain in the back to go. The melancholy pathway meandered along by the side of the tall houses, leading everywhere to tarnishing labour, to consumption's cough, to the writhings of fever, to bitter mutterings against life, and frantic calls on St. Anthony, The Little Flower, and Bernadette of Missabielle to be absent helps in time of trouble. Upon these stones I will build my church.

There were the houses, too — a long, lurching row of discontented incurables, smirched with the age-long marks of ague, fevers, cancer, and consumption, the soured tears of little children, and the sighs of disappointed newly-married girls. The doors were scarred with time's spit and anger's hasty knocking; the pillars by their sides were shaky, their stuccoed bloom long since peeled away, and they looked like crutches keeping the trembling doors standing on their palsied feet. The gummy-eyed windows blinked dimly out, lacquered by a year's tired dust from the troubled street below. Dirt and disease were the big sacraments here — outward and visible signs of an inward and spiritual disgrace. The people bought the cheapest things in food they could find in order to live, to work, to worship: the cheapest spuds, the cheapest tea, the cheapest meat, the cheapest fat; and waited for unsold bread to grow stale that they might buy that cheaper, too. Here they gathered up the fragments so that nothing would be lost. The streets were long haggard corridors of rottenness and ruin. What wonderful mind of memory could link this shrinking wretchedness with the flaunting gorgeousness of silk and satin; with bloom of rose and scent of lavender? A thousand years must have passed since the last lavender lady was carried out feet first from the last surviving one of them. Even the sun shudders now when she touches a roof, for she feels some evil has chilled the glow of her garment. The flower that here once bloomed is dead forever. No wall-flower here has crept into a favoured cranny; sight and sign of the primrose are far away; no room here for a dance of daffodils; no swallow twittering under a shady eave; and it was sad to see an odd sparrow seeking a yellow grain from the mocking dust; not even a spiky-headed thistle, purple-mitred, could find a corner here for a sturdy life. No Wordsworth here wandered about as lonely as a cloud.

> The decent dead provoke no blood-congealing fear,
> Like the dread death that lives to fester here.
> Here children, lost to every sense but life,
> Indulge in play that mimics social strife;

And learn from strenuous practice that they may
Act well their part at home some future day:
The girl trains her lungs to scream and shout,
The boy his arms to knock a wife about.

And yet this riddled horridness had given root to the passion
flower. What had been lost was found; what had been dead came to
life again. The spirit beneath the coat brocaded, with slender sword
quivering, had come into being again, not in brocade, but in rags;
not with sword or dainty phrases, elegant in comedy and satire, but
with bitter curses, blows as hard as an arm can give, and a rank,
savage spit into a master's face. Fought, these frantic fools did,
led by Larkin and by Connolly; fought till the day-star arose in their
shivering hearts, the new and glorious light, the red evangel, the
light of the knowledge of the glory of God, manifested in the active
mind and vital bodies of men and women and little children. And
now something stronger than bare hands was in the battle. Many a
spear-point flame from a gun frightened a dark corner or a shadowy
street, making armed men in khaki or black crouch low in their
rushing lorries, firing rapidly back at the street grown shadowy
again, or the corner now darker than ever before.

Now the old house was still. Comely Bessie Ballynoy, on her way
up, had knocked; but finding Sean in bed, had bid goodnight, and
gone. Lazy sleep had crawled in by the dark hallway to soothe restlessness and to hush the clamour from the attic above to the basement below. A lousy sleep, dreary-eyed, in loosely slippered feet,
torn and muddy, calling in a shoddy whisper for quietness; creeping
in yawning, leaving no-one on watch, though every night now was
a perilous night for Dublin. In all the rooms, all the cheap crockery
stood quiet on the shelves; the chairs leaned against the shaky walls;
rosy-faced fires had all gone pale; the patter of children's feet had
long since ceased; only dreams crept slyly in to fill the ugly rooms with
sparkling peace for a few dark moments, clothing the sleepers with
a cautious splendour; setting them, maybe, to sip rare wines from
bulging bottles, or leading them to yellow sands bordering a playful
sea. A younger lass, perhaps, dreamed of scanty night attire between
snowy sheets, with a colour-robed prince by the bedroom door in
haste to come in, and bid her a choice goodnight; while the younger
men saw themselves, sword in hand, driving the khaki cut-throats
out of Eire's five beautiful fields.

Every guardian angel relaxed now, and nodded sleepily by tattered
counterpane and ragged sheet, for sin usually curled up like a dog

to sleep at their feet, waiting for the tenement life to go on again in the morning. So after Curfew the silent tenement slept, unconscious even that every whining wail of every passing motor sang a song of death to someone; for in sleep the slimy roof above them had slid aside, and left the stars but a hand's breadth out of reach.

When will the day break in Eirinn; when will her day-star arise? How often had he heard these words sung in a languishing voice after an eight-hand reel or a high-cauled cap at *ceilidh* or *sguorid-heacht*! Well, no day would ever break here, nor would the shadows ever flee away. Sean's eyes were closing, and dimming thoughts swooned faintly from his mind into the humming whine of motor-engines coming quick along the road outside. Up on his elbow he shot as he heard the sound of braking, telling him that the lorries were outside of his house, or of those on either side. Then he shot down again to hide as a blinding beam from a searchlight poured through the window, skimming the cream of the darkness out of the room. It silvered the old walls for a few moments, then withdrew like a receding tide to send its beam on another part of the house. Then there was a volley of battering blows on the obstinate wooden door, mingled with the crash of falling glass that told Sean the panels on each side of it had been shattered by hammer or rifle-butt.

A raid! All the winsome dreams of the house had vanished; sleep had gone; and children dug arms and legs into the tensing bodies of their mothers.

Which were they — the Tommies or the Tans? Tans, thought Sean, for the Tommies would not shout so soullessly, nor smash the glass panels so suddenly; they would hammer on the door with a rifle-butt, and wait for it to be opened. No; these were the Tans.

He heard the quick pit-put, pit-put of stockinged feet, faint as it was, coming down the stairs, turning left at the bottom of them, and hurrying along the hall towards the back-yard. His ears were so cocked that he heard the soft, silky pad of the hurrying feet plainly through the storm of blows falling on the street door; then he thought he heard the back door open softly and gently close again.

—Who could that be? he thought. Might be any one of the men. Those who didn't take part in ambushes often carried ammunition to those who did; and the dockers and seamen gave a ready hand to the smuggling in of arms. If it wasn't for his own poor sight, he'd probably be doing it himself. All were friendly, save the thin and delicate husband of Mrs. Ballynoy, who cared for no manner of politics. Someone, anyway, slipping into the back to dodge over the wall into the dark lanes, with fear but without fuss. The Dublin slums at war with the British Empire; all the power of an army, flanked by gangs of ruthless ruffians; all the ordered honour of a regal cabinet and the mighty-moneyed banks fighting the ragged tits of the tenements. An unequal fight, by God, but the slums would win! There goes the door!

A great crash shook the old house and shook the heart of Sean, for well he knew the ordeal that might be in front of him once the light from a Tan's torch smote the darkness of the room. A mad rush of heavy feet went past his door, to spread over the stilly house; for no-one had come from a room to risk sudden death in the dark and draughty hallway. He remembered the two boys brought bound from Dublin Castle to a dump-field on the edge of the city by two Auxie-Tan officers, who set them sitting against an old stone wall, extinguishing each young head under an old bucket picked from a rubbish heap. Then going away forty paces or so, they fired away at the buckets till they were full of holes, leaving what they had done behind them to put the fear of the Tans into the hearts of the surviving I.R.A. men. He thought, too, of Clancy, Clune, and McKee, caught and brought to the Castle, where the Tans interviewed them with the stimulant of bayonets, prodding them gamely till none of the three could sigh any longer, for each at last was dead. Now he could hear neither sound nor murmur — all had gone quiet after the crashing fall of the door. No sound even of a child's protest, though that wasn't surprising, for all of them would be too frightened to squeal till a gun exploded somewhere: all was quiet — the sad silence of a sleeping slum. Yet Sean knew that the house must be alive with crawling men, slinking up and down the stairs, hovering outside this door or that one, each with a gun tensed to the last hair, with a ready finger touching the trigger. He guessed that a part of them were the Auxies, the classic members of sibilant and sinister raiders. The Tans alone would make more noise, slamming themselves into a room, shouting to shake off the fear that slashed many of their faces. The Auxies were too proud to show a sign of it. The Tommies would be warm, always hesitant at knocking a woman's room about; they would even be jocular in their funny English way, encouraging the women and even the children to grumble at being taken away from their proper sleep.

All Sean could do was to try to lie dead still, digging down deeper without a sound into the hard mattress of his truckle bed, stifling any desire to steal to the door to listen; to try to modify his breathing till it became unnoticed by himself, for a profound silence might make the Tans disinclined to probe a way in to find out the cause of it; though the Auxies cared nothing for silence, but would lift a corpse from a coffin to search for a gun. He always left his door unlocked now, for past experience had shown him that the slightest obstacle to a swift entrance to a room always irritated them.

From the corner of an eye he could see through the window the searchlight gliding, now up, now down the street, and once for a few moments it blinded him by flooding the room. Then he heard sullen, but loud, thuds of heavy iron falling on heavy wood, coming from the back, and he guessed they were breaking in the entrance to the large shed that was said to be used as a carpenter's shop, and in which Mrs. Ballynoy's husband sometimes worked. Now he heard soft, sly steps going down the hallway to the back. After whomsoever had crept away while the door was being broken down. He had climbèd the wall, thought Sean, and somewhere — maybe just behind it — crouched silently in the darkest corner of the narrow lane, a revolver tight in his hand, his shoes slung round his neck, so that, if he had to run, no sound of running feet would give an enemy a cue of a direction through which to send a hail of bullets: a bitter night for a pair of bare feet.

Sean could sense the women, and, maybe, the men, praying while the hammering lasted, to cease at once when silence came again, for it wouldn't serve them to let the Auxies hear them trying to talk to God. These silences were the worst: during the hammering one knew where they were; throughout the silences one didn't. Then they might be anywhere; might be opening his very own door snakily, softly, now; some of them might be even in the room, for their black uniforms fitted the darkness they loved, and black juices, smeared over their cheeks and brows, mixed them cosily with the dárker shadows of the night. Any moment a brilliant torch might blind his slatted eyes, and a string of shouted questions blast his ear; a pressed-in, cold pistol-barrel make a tiny livid rim on his naked chest. He tried to forget thought, making his mind one with the darkness, losing his fear in the vastness of space; but it was no use, for thought never got farther than that the Tans were there, and his mind came back to think of how it would feel to have a bullet burning a swift channel through the middle of his belly.

Azrael, Azrael, gentle, dignified being of spirit, graceful spirit of death, come, and minister unto us, and save us merry gentlemen!

Come lovely and soothing death,
Undulate round the world, serenely arriving,
Arriving
In the day, in the night, to all, to each,
Sooner or later, delicate death.

Ah! Whitman, Walt Whitman, you never knew the Tans! Death doesn't arrive serenely here, his hands are desperate, and neither is he delicately formed. Here the angel of death is a biting bitch!

The silence was startled by the sound of a motor-engine warming up, getting ready to go. He heard steps now in the hall, and the sound of *bravura* jests from a few voices. They were going. They mightn't be, though: they pretended that at times, driving the lorries away a bit, but leaving the men behind, to come with a rush into the house again among foolish people hurrying in their night-clothes out of their rooms to ask questions of each other. Stay still; don't move; not a stir: some of them still might be just beyond the door.

He lay there for what seemed a long time, the sweat of fear damping his body, and making him shiver. Stay still; don't move — someone was beside the door. He heard the handle giving a faint, brassy murmur. Soon, a black-clothed arm would thrust itself within, and a shot might go off that he would never hear. He silently squirmed deeper into the bed, and left the rest to God.

—Eh! he heard the voice of Mrs. Ballynoy whisper from the darkness. Are you there, or did they take you? Are you gone, or are you asleep, or wha'?

—That woman again! he thought resentfully — what a fright she gave me! Awake, Mrs. Ballynoy, he whispered back.

—Well, she said softly, you can take your ayse now, an' sleep tranquil, or get up, an' talk about th' queer things done in a Christian age.

—Wait till I light a candle, he said, making a great creak as he heaved himself out of the bed's hollow.

—You'll light no candle while I'm here, young man, said her voice, dressed in a titter, for a slip of an overall's th' only shelter between me and a piercin' look from a young man's eyes; an' it wouldn't be good to go from one exthreme to another on an identical night.

—Did they discover anything? asked Sean.

—Not a thing, though they took two o' th' men away with them. A sudden end to them all, an' a short fall to th' hottest hob that hell can heat! Don't light that candle yet, she added, for minds that have safely passed a danger near them are often reckless in their dealin' with an innocent female; though you're not that kind of a man, I know.

He heard the door softly closing and her hand fumbling with the lock. He hoped she wasn't going to stay. Ah! here's the key, for it's safer to put a locked door between eyes that pry into other people's affairs day an' night, tintin' everything with the colour of their own minds.

—Hadn't you better go back to your room, Mrs. Ballynoy? he warned. You need all the sleep you can get these days. We all do; and someone might be prowlin' round an' see an' think th' worst.

—Ay, she said; bad minds, th' lot o' them — that's why I've locked th' door. An' call me Nellie, for you know me well enough be now. Light th' candle now you can, but leave it on th' far side of where I'll be, for it's only a flimsy apron-overall I have between me an' all harm; and she tittered gaily as Sean very slowly lighted a candle on a box beside his bed.

She was a fine-looking heifer, right enough: long reddish hair coiled up into a bunch that rested neatly on the nape of a white neck; a well-chiselled, pale face, with large grey innocent eyes that seemed to be shrouded in a mist from the valley of the Missabielle; a fine figure set these charms off, and when she slyly waved this sweet figure in front of a man, he no longer saw, or wanted to see, the mist of Missabielle. A rose of Tralee, without the flower's serenity, maybe; but certainly a lovely rose of the tenements. But Sean was in no mood now to enjoy the charm of her fine figure and face. Once let a soul see she had been in his room and the whole house would be declaring that he was carrying on with Mrs. Ballynoy. He should have had the courage to get up and push her out. He almost wished now that the Auxies had stayed a little longer.

In the sober light of the candle he saw that she had just decorated her delightful body in a pair of brown slippers and a flowered overall reaching only half-way down her thighs, and showing a wide part of her white swelling bosom; a show that was very charming, but damned uncomfortable to one who was determined to take no notice of it.

—Oh! There y'are, she said, when the candle-light got steady, nice an' snug an' all alone. She came over and sat down on the edge of the bed beside him. I'm askin' meself why a land, overflowin' with prayer an' devotion, should be so often plunged into dhread in the dead o' night for nothin'? An' they tellin' me it's for Ireland's sake. Them politics'll be the death of us some day. I feel terrible shy in this

get-up, she said suddenly. Afther washin' the one good nightgown
I have, I was sleepin' in me skin, an' this overall was th' first thing I
laid hands on when the Tans came thundherin' at the door. Pansies
on it, she said, giggling, pulling it a little from her thigh, pansies for
thought! and she poked Sean in the breast, playfully, with a hand
reddened by the soda she used in the washing of clothes.

—Isn't Mr. Ballynoy at home? said Sean, trying to get her mind
away from the overall, while he thought of a way to get rid of her.

—Didn't I tell you this mornin', on the stairs, that he was on a
counthry job! He would be when the Tans come; though it's little
good he'd be in any emergency, bein' born timid, with a daisy in his
mouth. So I'm a poor lone lassie now, and she gave him another
poke — this time in the thigh.

—Don't you think you ought to get back? he warned; the Tans
might come again.

—Ay, indeed, they might; a body can never know what them
fellas'll do. An' it only a little way from Christmas, too. Ah! she said
suddenly, looking away into a dream distance; it's good to be near
one of your own: th' only two protestants in th' house, not countin'
me husband. Of the crowd, not countin' him, only two who have th'
proper way o' worshippin', an' are able to foresee th' genuine
meanin' of th' holy text.

—There's me for you, said Sean, thinking neither you nor your
husband bothered about religion, one way or another.

—Then you're sadly mistaken. I can't remember a year we missed
feelin' the curious chantin' glow in th' air of a Christmas mornin',
an' us on our way to church. In a proper mood, an' that was often,
I could see what you'd think's th' star, ashine on the tip of the spire's
top; an' me ears can hear th' dull plod of the three camels' feet in th'
deep sand, bearin' th' three kings with th' three rich gifts from
Persia, or some other place in th' wilds of a far-away world; an' all
th' time an anxious man seekin' shelter for his good woman, with
the valleys levelled an' th' hills hidden be th' fallin' snow, dyein' her
rich dark hair grey with its fallin' flakes, a sly soft carpet for her
sandalled feet, an' sore they were from th' sting in its frosty tendher-
ness; while th' tired Joseph thrudged demented behind, wondherin'
if they'd find their lodgin's only on the cowld, cowld ground. But
God was good, an' found the shelther of a stable for the bewildhered,
half-perished man, with his thin gown sodden, his toil-marked hands
a hot ache, an' his poor feet blue with the bitther penetration of th'
clingin' snow; an' afther Joseph had shooed th' puzzled animals to a

safe an' ordherly distance, th' little fella was soon snug in a manger
on top o' warm heaps of sainfoin, thyme, rosemary, an' lavender.

—You're wrong there, said Sean; for how in such a bitther season
could anyone come on spring and summer plants like those?

—I dunno, she murmured, unless God turned th' hay an' th'
sthraw into th' sweet-savourin' herbs. But it's far betther not to
thry to go into them things. Are you afraid to look at me, or what?
she ejaculated, turning away from her dream; for Sean had turned
his head away to escape the charm of the white bosom and soft
thighs. As long as you don't make too free, I don't mind, though I
feel a little shy in this scarce get-up.

A shoulder-band of the overall had slipped down, and she had
saucily drawn an arm out of it altogether so that near half of her
body to the waist was bare, and he saw a breast, rather lovely in the
light of the candle, looking like a golden cup with a misty ruby in its
centre. If he only had her in a shady corner of the Phoenix Park, or
in a room of his own in a house where she wasn't known, the world
would be well lost for a period of ecstasy. But not here.

—Your husband's a good fellow, he said, trying to keep his mind
off her, and would rejoice to see you as you are now. He thinks a lot
of you.

—He oughtn't, she said sarcastically; where'd he get another like
me? He means well, poor man; but honest, it's pathetic when we're
alone, an' he thries to get goin'. Askin' me to tell him when he's
hurtin' me! She went into a soft, gay, gurgling laugh, putting a hand
over her mouth to quench the merry sound of it. It's funny to talk
of it here, but maddenin' when I'm with him. I'm often near worn
out thryin', thryin' to coax a little flash of endeavour outa him. He
does his best, but the little sting he once had's gone with the wind —
joy go with it! She now laughed venomously and loud, making Sean
fearful of someone hearing her. Wait till I tell you, she went on —
you'll die laughin'! You should see Charlie when he's at the he-man
business — Are you sure you won't get faint, Nellie? Don't forget to
say if I'm hurtin' you, dearie! One night, when he was — you know
— I jerked him clean outa th' bed on to th' floor — th' bump shook
th' house! D'ye know, honest t'God, he just lay stunned there. Put
th' heart across me. Ever afther, d'ye know, I've had to handle him
like a delicate piece of china! No; poor Charlie's style's too shy for
me. Not like Jim Achree's. J'ever hear o' his?

She slid down till she was half lying over him, and sang sedulously
beside his ear:

Jim Achree's style has a wondherful way with it,
All th' girls' minds are in sad disarray with it;
Whenever they venture to have a short play with it,
Good girls want to stay with it, ever an' aye.
Oh! Jimmy Achree, shure your style is your own,
Amazin' th' way it has flourished an' grown,
With lovely threats shakin', tense with mischief-makin',
Knockin' poor women flat like a gorgeous cyclone!

—Looka, she said breathlessly, th' least bit o' fondlin' now an
I'd swoon away, helpless an' benighted.

—In the midst of death we are in life, thought Sean. He tried to
turn his head away so that he wouldn't be prompted by the white
breast that was like a golden cup with a misty ruby in its centre; but
his head refused to stir. Instead, he found his hand was sliding over
her fair bosom. He felt her arm pushing a way under his head till it
was firmly round his neck, while the other pushed the clothes from
covering him. He was lost, unless he yelled for help, and that he
couldn't do.

—You're a good young man, he heard her whispering, an' would
never take advantage of a woman alone in your room in th' dead o'
night, with but a loose slip between you an' a swift lie-down on a
bed o' meadow-sweet. Don't sthruggle, man, or you'll upset things!
Why'r you thryin' to keep me from gettin' th' clothes down? You've
far too many on you; a little cool air'll do you good. Take th' good
things while they're goin'. She whipped the clothes down with a
fierce jerk, and lying beside him, pressed her mouth to his. Her big
innocent eyes looked frantic now.

—G'won, she muttered, panting, be as rough as you like with
me — it's what I'm longin' for for weeks! And half mad himself now,
he gripped her like a vice, and sank his fingers into her flesh.

Then they suddenly went still as death, listening; listening to the
whine of a motor-engine cruising down the road outside. Then
another whine followed that, and another, the last, till they mingled
into one shrill, threatening whine that went echoing round the walls
of the old house.

—Out in strength tonight, thought Sean; more'n three of them;
each of them crooning a song of death to someone. Ireland's modern,
senseless Tanshee!

Suddenly the shrill whine lifted into a shrill, quavering scream,
the scream fading into the throb-throb of active engines as the
lorries stopped outside, or very near, the house.

—They've stopped at this house, or th' next one! said Nellie, loosening her arm from around his neck, and sliding swift from the bed to the door. Who'd ha' thought th' bastards would bother to come twice th' same night? Christ! It's this house they're makin' for! And swiftly came a great hammering on the door again. Nellie frantically twisted and turned at the key, but she couldn't get the door of the room open.

—In they'll come, she squealed softly, an' I'll be exposed to th' world as a fast woman. She tugged and writhed till the slip fell from her shoulders, leaving her naked, fuming, at the door. You it was, she half shouted, turning a red and bitter face towards Sean, that lured me into this predicument, never able to let any decent woman pass without thryin' to meddle her!

Sean, as eager as she was herself that she should go unseen, leaped out of bed, hurried over, and with a hard twist turned the key. Snatching up her flowered overall, she whipped the door open, rushed out, and up the stairs, without another word. Shutting the door again, he fled back to bed, digging himself down deep into it once again, listening to hear if it was Tan or Tommy who had entered the house.

The door spun open, and a torchlight shot terror into his eyes. Silently he waited for a blow or a shot, but neither came. He opened his eyes, and saw a young khaki-clad officer just inside the door, a torch in one hand, a revolver in the other. Behind him were two soldiers with rifles at the ready. The officer stared at Sean, then slowly returned the gun to a holster, and the soldiers, at this sign, stood at ease, and rested the butts of the rifles on the dirty floor.

—Get up; dress; go out to the street, said the officer tersely; this house has to be searched room by room. Don't try to go farther than the wire cordon ringing the district: orders are to fire on any who do. He watched Sean dressing, and when he saw him clap a cap on his head, asked, Haven't you an overcoat?

—A sort of a one, said Sean.

—Better than nothing; you'd better put it on — it's damned cold outside.

—Decent man, thought Sean, putting on his old coat; has an occasional thought for others. Thank God, the Tans are absent!

He went out into the dark hall, and near bumped into a Tan standing there, fingering a heavy revolver. A cold shiver trickled down his spine.

—Where are you going? he was asked.

—Outside to street — officer's orders, said Sean.

—What officer? asked the Tan.

—Military officer, sir.

—Oh! Military officer, eh? Well, we give the orders here — understand?

—Yessir, said Sean promptly.

—Are you a Sinn Feiner? he questioned, twisting the gun in his hand.

—A Sinn Feiner? Me? No fear.

—You were one, then.

—No; never, said Sean emphatically. Thank God, thought Sean, he didn't ask if I had ever been a Republican. The ignorant English bastard doesn't know the difference.

—Well, you're an Irishman, anyway — you can't deny that!

—No, sir, I can't deny that: I'm an Irishman, right enough.

—Well, shout To Hell with Ireland, and you can go — no mutter, but a shout the house can hear. Now!

But Sean fell silent. God damn him if he'd do that! He knew his face was white; he felt his legs tremble; but he fell silent, with a stubborn look on his face.

—Go on, you Sinn Fein rat, shout it!

A streak of light fell on them, and Sean saw the young officer coming to them. He stopped, looked at Sean, then looked at the Tan.

—What's wrong here? he asked. Let that man go into the street.

—You mind your own damned business, snarled the Tan.

—I am minding it, said the young officer. I happen to be an Irishman, too. Have you any objection to it?

—I don't take orders from you! said the Tan roughly.

—I'm not sorry for that, the officer said; but this man does — didn't I give you an order to go into the street? he asked, turning to Sean.

—Yessir.

—Carry it out, then, he said sharply; and Sean, turning swiftly, made a quick march through the hall, out by the door, into the street.

It was very cold, and by the timid gleams from a waning moon Sean saw that path and road were white with a covering of rich rime frost. Groups of people were standing, huddled up against the railings of the houses, while more were oozing sleepily out of the remaining ones, shepherded into bunches by armed soldiers. The women were trying to coax warmth into their tearful and shivering children by wrapping flimsy rags round their shoulders, and tucking the little ones under them into their arms.

Several searchlights wandered through the street, flashing over the groups of people, or tinselling along the walls of the houses. At one end stood an armoured car, the lids raised, showing the heads of several Tommies who were quietly chanting an advice to the shivering people to pack up their troubles in their old kit-bags. Along the road, over the calm, quiet chastity of the white frost, slid a diamond-shaped tank, looking like a dirty, dangerous, crawling slug, machine-guns sticking out from slits, like ugly protruding eyes staring at the cowering people.

He saw a commotion round the door of the house he lived in. He mooched over till he was beside the steps to look over the shoulders of a rank of soldiers. A prisoner! Who could it be? He whisperingly asked the soldier in front of him what had happened.

—An awrsenal! whispered the soldier hoarsely. Rear of th' 'ouse, an awrsenal discovered! 'Nough gelignite to blow up 'ole neighbour-hood. A blighter there drew a gun, but was shot through hand afore 'ee could pull trigger. 'Ere's the bawstard coming

Amid a group of soldiers with rifles at the ready marched a thin forlorn figure, but the lips in the pale face were tight together, and the small head was held high. Peering closer, Sean saw that handcuffs kept the two small hands locked together, and that from one of them red blobs were dripping on to the white frost on the path, leaving little spots behind like crimson berries that had fallen on to snow. In the hall he heard the voice of Nellie shouting.

—That's me husband! he heard her shout; a good man an' a brave one! Yous'll never shoot the life outa Ireland, yous gang o' armed ruffians! Here, take me, too, if yous aren't afraid. Keep your pecker up, Charlie — Ireland's with you!

Sean peered closer. Good God — the prisoner was the timid, insignificant Charlie Ballynoy who took no interest in politics! A lorry, full of soldiers, swirled into the kerb. The handcuffed prisoner was pushed and lifted into it. Standing there in the middle of the soldiers, with the searchlight covering him with glory, he held up his iron-locked hands from which clouts of blood still dripped.

—Up th' Republic! he shouted with the full force of his voice.

The lorry drove off, and the red specks in the rime turned brown and lonely. Heads that had lifted bent again, and all was quiet once more. A bleak dawn at last began to peel the deeper darkness from the sky, and the scene crept into a ghostly glamour, brightened by the pale faces of the waiting people; the pale moon sinking deeper into a surly sky, and the rimy frost on pathway, road, and roof grew whiter. Dirty-yellow-clad figures moved into the whiteness from one dark doorway, to move out of it again into another blacker still; while the brown, slug-like tank crept up and down the road, charring the dainty rime with its grinding treads — the new leviathan that God could ne'er control.

PAX

A LORDLY, laughing sun covered the city with a hazy veil of strident heat; and all that moved through it seemed to lazily dance along, slow, quivering, as if lost to their earthy origin, and were tremulous, but trying to be brave in another world.

Sean was walking slow down the elegant part of Dublin's North Circular Road, where the daintier houses stood, each aloof from the dust of the street; each flounced with a trimly-kept garden; all looking like nicely-reared children, tidied up to go to Sunday school, or to receive their first communion. Along this way George Moore could have safely extended his particular nose to take in the fragrant scent from bush and blossom giving a cooler charm to the molten air.

Passing by Phibsboro Church, its Vincentian spire thrusting into the deep blue of the sky, looking like a huge spear left behind on the field of one of heaven's battles with Lucifer and his lost angels, he crossed Blaquiere Bridge to enter into the lower part of the thoroughfare. On his right now was the great high stone wall surrounding the outspread and dour-bodied Mother of Mercy Hospital, while on his left rose the grimly-grey walls of Mountjoy Jail, where a contingent of Black and Tans smoked the pipe of war, waiting for orders to go forth again and give the Irish another lesson in light and leading. No fragrance from the further flowers came stealing down here; a black van went swiftly up the drive to the jail bringing prisoners to their quiet and scanty quarters, while vans as black brought the dead away from the silent and senseless hospital.

Then Sean saw them — an army patrol, dressed in dirty-white drill, filing along towards him, on each side of the road, each man with a rifle at the ready, an officer walking on the pathway, midway between the head and tail of the patrol. As Sean went nervously on, he saw the officer glance at his wrist-watch, turn, and say something to his men, and then he saw the soldiers suddenly squat down on the kerb, leaving their rifles carelessly by their sides; he saw them lighting cigarettes, and stretching their legs gorgeously out in front of them. The Truce had come. Rifle and revolver wore a friendly look now. Passing people stopped to speak to the soldiers and some shook happy hands with them; some hurried out of the houses near by, and doled out cups of tea to them; a few did a few violent steps of a dance in the centre of the street; but, now and again, men and women passed without looking right or left, going on with a fixed stare forward.

> The fight was over, and the Truce was here;
> The busy quietness seemed lone and queer;
> For ev'ry twisty lane became a golden street,
> Where generals and commandants each other greet,
> Festoon'd with glowing deeds from head to feet;
> Talking the tir'd night away ere they arrang'd to meet
> When morning came to tell to exil'd fear,
> How each, 'gainst odds, with but a questing gun,
> And two grenades, made slick from cast-out cans,
> Destroy'd three lorry-loads of Black and Tans!

Golden boys in golden streets: there they stood, midstream, in a torrent of talk, rambling, delicious and delirious talk, the dust of death still in their eyes, — all that remained of Ireland's tattered, nerve-worn, gallant army; or they leaned against a fence in a country lane, canopied by the sly innocence of woodbine's dangling stems; farmer's son and farmer's lad, girls listening; shy, white fingers sometimes stroking the faded, maybe blood-stained, cloth of a coat; there they stood, their faces turned from danger — the nerve-racked, exhilarant Fianna Fail.

Free for the time, anyhow, from the danger of a dreadful night in a barracks, or in a silent room, fitted up for a tomb, in Dublin's Castle, if any of them happened to be taken alive. Free from the searing thoughts of having the toes hammered flat with rifle-butts, cloaking the bones of the feet with a bloody squash; the tender belly punctured with merry bayonet-jabs; the face unbalanced with blows; the finger-nails pulled out with pincers, forcing yells from the man who was losing them; free from cords twisting tight on a neck till all the breath was gone. Good to be merry, for tomorrow we don't die. Warriors all, for warriors they were to fight with the bare chance of a restless rest now and again, and the certain chance of an agonising end; to fight against a force outnumbering them a hundred to one, so well armed that each could lose a gun to save his life; while an Irishman would risk his life to save his gun; so well armed that the Black and Tans wearied with the weight of what they had to carry, while the Irish lad often had to beg his quartermaster for another bullet.

Pax. Peace was here. *Pax vobiscum* to all in this fair land, first flower of the earth and first gem of the See. The people dwelt now in peaceable habitations. Bread could again be eaten in quietness; people could lounge at their doors to gossip, or lean from a window to throw down a greeting to a passing neighbour. Peace was dropping now from the veils of the morning to where the cricket sang. The wild-rose in the hedge could push her face and fragrance forward without being troubled by the rude and careless hands of hidden gunmen. The busy wren could build a delicate dome over her cosy nest without the uncertainty of having it desecrated by a grim grenade exploding. The last grave had been dug; the last lád buried. The tear at this moment shed is the last one too. Now we can see the sun shine, feel the rain falling, and watch the jaunty corn grow. Three shouts on two hills for peace: on Croagh Patrick, in Mayo, where Irish Christianity was confirmed, and on Cave Hill, in Antrim, where Republicanism was brought to life: three shouts on these two hills for peace in Eire's green, unpleasant land.

The whole country became a rhapsody of bands, banners, and bonfires. Bonfires blazed in the meanest streets, even when door and stairway had to provide the fuel. And God wasn't forgotten — don't go away thinking that, now. Thanksgiving ascended from every altar; the floor of heaven was lifted with the storm of te deums that swept up under it; and prayers were offered up that the peace might last forever and a day after. In places paraded honour was shown to God. Down in Sandymount, a suburb of Dublin, a parade was held in honour of Christ the King, and trams could hardly hold, without bulging, the crazy-joy crowds hurrying out to line the streets near the church, and watch the guard of honour, specially uniformed, groomed, and belted to pay military homage to the Blessed Sacrament. Every honest head was bowed as the Host went by, the silver-and-gold encasement standing on a velvet-floored, silk-canopied carrier, borne by Irish officers, surrounded by a thick and glittering fringe of fixed bayonets. Oh, gentle Jesus, alanna, once they came out with swords and staves to take Thee; now they come forth with bayonet and gun to keep Thee safe. What a change for the better!

—A sight worth livin' to see, said Roary O'Bawlochone to Sean.

—It would be, if Ulsther was here to see it, said the tram-conductor.

In and out of the smoky jabber, the generals astroll in their uniforms, the flame of the bonfires, the exuberant prayers of the people on their quiet way to God, and the just hopes of the country, went the long and lone chain-letter of dearsirsiamfaithfullyoursismishelemeasmor between Lloyd George at-home in London and Ayamonn De Valera half-at-home in Dublin, asking how where when why which what when Ireland could and in what way accommodate herself when she sat down or stood up in or out of the Empire, insulated from the association which would hamper and help by being beside or well away from what was canonistically known as the British Family of Nations, with a fine formula in hand to enable Ireland to be the one and a different thing at the same time, to stand on a republican rock while swimming in the sea of imperialism, the juxtapositional problem solved by alternative proposals, one in the hand of De Valera which he read to Lloyd George when he wasn't listening, and the other held by Lloyd George which he read when Dev was busy lilting I'm in my Sleeping, and don't Waken Me; each of which and both together was were to tighten things that had been loose, and loosen things that had been tight between Ireland and England for the last seven hundred years *anno domine dirige nos.*

—Looksee, said De Valera, hooking an arm in one of George's, you're a Kelt and I'm another; so we'd better have a stroll, and talk of the first four things first, before we decide everything in the discourse of time.

Away the two of them wandered, not noticing the passage of time, chatting away furiously, but in a real friendly spirit, for both of them were Kelts, thoroughly conscious that God was guiding them, and that He had given them an important place in the cosmopolitan cosmos.

—Over there, and De Valera's finger pointed to the nor'-nor'-west, is Tara, and somewhat further to the west's where Patrick kindled the turf fire that has never gone out.

—Dear me, murmured Lloyd George; a great man, your Sarsfield, Earl of Lucan.

—No, no; I'm talking of Patrick the saint, not Patrick the soldier.

—Of course — St. Patrick, said Lloyd George penitently; pity, though, he was an alien.

—He was more Irish than the Irish themselves, said De Valera emphatically; and I won't hear one word against him. Kelt or no Kelt, you must leave our saints alone.

—All are more than Irish, murmured the British Prime Minister; Anthony of Aghadoe; Ignatius, the Gael from the County Clare; the Little Flower of Lissodell; and Bernadette of Ballyvourney; I crave your worship's pardon.

De Valera, without the slightest fuss, hurried Lloyd George down the draughty Irish corridors of time; up Croagh Patrick, down Slieve Mish, around the Macgillicuddy's Reeks, till George was breathless; all the time pouring into his widened ear tales from the saga of Cuchullain, the Ranns round Rosnaree, the Dreams of Angus, the story of the bee in the bonnet of St. Finnbar; taking great care to assure Lloyd George that he personally believed, or accepted, only those records, historic, prehistoric, and preterhistoric of Eire's ruins and regulations which were substantially marked and sealed with the *nihil obstat* and *imprimatur* from the downright impression got from the signet of a bishop's ring.

—A knowledge of each of these and all together, George, went on De Valera, may suffice to form, or postulate, the possibility of a condition which might allow us to enter into some preliminary idea as to whether we should consider the status of how we feel, and what we are, in connection with your own consideration of the status as to how you feel, and what you are, in regard to whatever may be now, and subsequently, discussed between the two nations; and to endeavour to attain that desirable end, sir, you must get to know a few of the facts from all the sources I have enumerated, and will enumerate, before we can sensibly begin our talk.

—I don't know that we'll have enough time, murmured Lloyd George.

—We'll have to find enough time, said De Valera shortly; a man's never too young to learn. Another hour's trotting and we'll be in another Irish epoch — near to Avvin Macha, home of the Red Branch Knights; the great city that Macha planned on the plain with the pin of a brooch she took from the neck of her gown; so to this day it is called Avvin Macha, Armagh, Neck Pin of Macha, from *eo*, a pin; and *muin*, the neck — see?

—I see, in a kind of a way, murmured the Prime Minister, a little out of breath.

—Here's The Fews, the passage-way to Ulster, said De Valera in a half-whisper; so slow down a bit, for the people yonder aren't too hospitable, as you will soon see; for each householder has three trained cranes perched on the roof-top, the first calling out Do Not Come, Do Not Come; the second calling Get Away, Get Away; and the third Pass this House, Pass this House; so now you know the kind of fare you're facing.

—What's that I'm seeing and hearing? said Lloyd George, startled, and suddenly stopping in his tracks.

On a fence at the mouth of the Pass they saw a short, sturdy man. He was soberly dressed in neat black cloth, a trim bowler hat on his head, with a blue-and-orange feather stuck pertly in the band of it. A thumb to keep the place was inserted into a bible he had on his knees. Time and again the man would open the book, look at it, then shout up to the Mountains of Mourne coming down to the sea, saying Be ye studfast, immovable, always abounding in th' wurrk of th' lord! Then, standin' up to attention, he sang,

> Th' Pope's gut his curdinals all in a row,
> Th' lame, th' blind, the daff, en' th' dumb;
> They're comin' tae Ulsther with saint So-and-so,
> Tae silence th' boast of th' prutestunt dhrum.

> Lero, lero, all so quaro,
> Lut th' domned papists with sucrements come;
> With our guns all akimbo, we'll send them to limbo —
> Says Wullie-boy Scutt an' Dickie McCrum!

> King Bully's high up on his lully-white steed —
> Shet up th' bible, an' run for th' gun!
> We'll give th' proud Pope an' th' devil their need,
> An' show how th' Chrustian endeavour is done!

> Lero lero, do an' daro,
> Tae hull with th' Pope's devalerian chum!
> Call all the kind neighbours an' arrm them with sabers,
> Says Wullie-boy Scutt an' Dickie McCrum!

—Let's get out of here, said Lloyd George; this fellow is better left to himself.

So the two of them hastened back to safer fields, De Valera stimulating his companion with lurid and entrancing information about Ireland's right and Ireland's wrong; picturing it all so vividly that poor George, as he was stepping across the little river Nanny in County Meath, was nearly run down by a troop of Cromwell's galloping Ironsides, the windy swish of their swords taking the puff out of him before he reached the farther bank in safety. Along at a loping gallop went the two of them to the safer south, though when

they had got as far as Wexford, De Valera's revival in burning words
of things past was so glamorous that Lloyd George found himself
flying for his life from the pike men of Ninety-Eight, losing a lock
of his bushy hair, while he was swimming the Slaney, from a bullet
fired by a hasty Shelmalier, from his long-barrelled gun of the sea,
who mistook him for a Yeoman.

—Call it a day, cried the panting statesman; I'm done in entirely!

—We must suffer on, said De Valera. Surely your brain isn't
going to conk out that quick? All that we do is but the precursor to
peace, and we all want peace.

—Quite, murmured Lloyd George, quite; we've quarrelled often
enough; we must have peace now, at any price, almost.

—Well, then, don't be calling a light historical chat for twenty-four
hours a day, man. What has been said is but the point of the beginning: we haven't even got within sight of the Normans landing in
Cork and Wexford.

—And what about when I was near cleft in two by a Cromwellian
trooper up on the plains of County Meath? queried Lloyd George,
halting in his stride; and the tuft of hair whipped from my head by a
Shelmalier bullet, and I walking peaceful round the slopes of
Vinegar Hill? Didn't those things happen after the Normans came
to Ireland?

—We're going backwards, said De Valera.

—Looksee, d'ye think I'm going to permit myself to be lost in
Ireland's ranns and ruins? said Lloyd George, with the edge of
anger on his voice. D'ye not realise that a whole nation's waiting for
me over in Downing Street? How far do you want me to follow you
back? Do you imagine, sir, that an enlightened man of my dimen-
sions is ready to believe that, in his voyage to an undiscovered
America, your St. Brendan celebrated Mass on a whale's back?

—You could believe a worse thing, sir.

—I couldn't believe a thing more nonsensical, sir. A fairy-tale, a
myth!

—A myth, sir, remember, is a thing that may, or may not, be true.

—True, did you say? You make me laugh! Brendan discovered
America when no-one knew it existed! Look, he went on in tense
tones, listen, young man, listen: if you want to know the truth, and
accept a fact, it was Madoc, son of Owen Ap Gwynedd, who first
set foot on America; and you can prove this by going to the back
parts of Virginia, for there you will find communities and groups
speaking the most fluent Welsh to this very day!

—I think if we kept to the point, sir, it would be very much better murmured De Valera.

—The point? Well, to the point then. He banged his stick on a rock. Everything that has happened in the world hasn't happened in Ireland. Keep to the point And what about you, De Valera?, Haven't you ranged from a point of the present away to an imperceptible point of the past?

—That's different; that's very different.

—How is it very different?

—To get to know Ireland through her history, you must begin at the end and end at the beginning.

—I won't listen any more, cried Lloyd George; I'm tired with words; I'm perplexed; I'm fairly moidered! He walked rapidly away to a great distance, then turned to shout back, Send a man whom you can trust to me, there are too many voices speaking at the same time here. I'm off. Send me a man who's something less of an historical kaleidoscope, and we'll chat over things quietly. And remember — if you can't come to an agreement, look out for war; immediate and terrible war! I'm going home to Dixie — there now, you see how my poor mind's getting mixed here. He hurried up the slopes of Lugnaquilla. When he got to the summit, he turned, and looked down on the tiny figure of De Valera standing still in the valley below; then he shook his stick in the air, and shouted, Immediate and terrible war! Then he disappeared over the brow of the hill, making for the rocky road to Dublin.

Lonely and disturbed, the other wandered about, for he could see nothing but the mists rolling down the bog, and the mists again and they rolling up the bog, and hearing nothing but the wind crying out in the bits of broken trees were left from the great storm, and the streams roaring with the rain. Then he cocked an ear, for the crying wind seemed to be whistling, Thou art not conquered yet, dear land, thou art not conquered yet. He, too, whistled with the wind, and Mick Collins came up, and they both whistled the same thing together.

—He wants someone to go over, said De Valera; and you're the man to go, Mick.

—Aw no, no, Dev, said Mick; you'd be better. You know your own mind well, and everyone else's better; you're the man to go.

—You're the natural choice, Mick. Isn't it all prophesied in the Book of Kills?

—No, you, Dev; you as head of the State should go.

—The place for the head of the State is here in the heart of home, entrenched among the soldiers and the saints.

—But supposin' we fail, Dev?

—Fail? How fail? How could Fianna Fail fail?

These two men, after risking terrible deaths for a long time, heavy prices upon both their heads, worn and very worried with doing more than mortal men should ever be called upon to do, shook hands for the last time; shook hands, and parted; De Valera to his anxious lonely thoughts, the other to England to talk a lot of his life away.

So Mick Collins, this homely, exuberant knight of the green guerdon, fortified himself with many prayers and a splendid communion, before he went on to the boat with his companion, Arthur Griffith, to do battle for Ireland, though both of them were unsuited, either in knowledge or experience, for the fight; went forward for as much as Ireland was prepared to receive; went forward to get as much as they could out of the cunning of Lloyd George and Winston Churchill; to get as much as any man, or group of men, could have got out of things as they were then. And going up the gangway of the boat, Mick Collins wiped the sweat of anxiety from his brow, never knowing that it was the first drops from the dew of death.

And De Valera sat down in the dark valley of the shadow of anxiety, too, and waited; and so did Sean, and all the people with him; wondering when they got their freedom what would happen to the whole of them.

DRIFTING

THE bands were silent, the banners stored away, the ashes of the bonfires had gone in the wind; but Collins and his comrades were still talking under London skies. Summer had gone; autumn twilights had faded into the darkness of winter, and still De Valera pondered in Dublin, while Collins, Lloyd George, and Churchill talked and talked on in London. The people waited in the gloom, while all sorts of rumours flurried them into spreading rumours of their own. They were drifting, even as the leaves still falling from the trees drifted, idly, damp and desolate, from one place to another, the wind disallowing them to continue in their stay for long in any nook or corner where they might whirling seek for shelter and repose. The people, too, went drifting from square to square; uneasy, anxious, and suspicious, they believed this and said that, drifting from corner to square, wondering what the will of God would be. Sean began to sense that the unity of the politicians was cracking. Another split in Irish life would show itself, and then would come again the curse, the blow; and those who had so loved one another, like good Christians, would soon be in the midst of clenching teeth, the spitting on beards, and the hauling down of reputation's flag. He went his own way, thinking and writing, through a gathering murmur of bubble and squeak, listening, watching, and wondering how it would all begin.

For quite a time now, he had been working in a job, earning thirty shillings a week. Jim Larkin's sister, with a few others, had risked taking a hall that had been a school, a methodist church, and a parish dispensary. Here they had organised concerts and performed plays, building a stage themselves, while cunning hands had painted some scenery, and stitched together a few fancy and suitable costumes. Countess Markievicz had decorated the walls with a number of bad pictures. A home-made pantomime was presented, and Sean himself had acted the part of the cockney burglar in O'Duffy's play, *Special Pleading*. After more than a year's tiring effort, it was clear that these things wouldn't even pay the rent, so with the clamorous approval of many workers, who didn't care a damn about pantomime or play, a club for the playing of the game called House was started.

It was a curious game: each player bought for a penny an oblong strip of leather on which three rows of various numbers were stamped. A player could buy as many cards as his mind could manage. A caller-out at the head of the hall dipped a hand into a large tin box from which he drew out a small disk of leather, calling out the number that happened to be stamped on it. When a number was called, each player scanned the strips of leather in front of him to see if the number called was stamped on any of them; if it were, he crossed it out with a stick of chalk. As soon as any player had all the numbers on his strip of leather crossed on the top, bottom, or middle line, he shouted out House, and then received the major part of what had been gathered as payment for the cards; the rest going to pay the collectors and those responsible for the club. The men were remarkably quick in marking their cards. He had seen men with as many as ten cards. Each card had, if he remembered right, fifteen numbers, so that these players had to run over one hundred and fifty numbers every other second, marking with their chalk any number called that happened to be on any of the cards. Sean marvelled at the quickness of the eye, the swift movement of the hand holding the chalk, and the look of embattled anxiety concentrated in the rough faces of the men. A great achievement, which, in worthier circumstances of life, with mightier means of education, would have made some of these untidy, turbulent dockers and carters, unerring in their calculations, into mathematicians of the first order.

Sean's job was to come in at nine in the morning, clean up the medley of chalk, cigarette-butts, cartons, and other rubbish scattered over the hall, wash down all the benches, trim the lamps, and leave everything ready for the night's session when he left at five in the evening. For the first time for years he was able to feed himself regularly, though simply, for he devoted most of what he got to buying a complete set of Balzac, and a new set of Shakespeare's Works — all second-hand — a volume of Goya's pictures, and another of Van Gogh's paintings and drawings, as well as giving ten shillings a week for a second-hand typewriter which Michael Foley of Middle Abbey Street was keeping for him till the full amount, twenty guineas, was paid. A great machine! He had had it now for twenty-five years, and he was using it still. Well, God's help, as an Irish proverb says, is as near as the door; and so it proved to be, though it required the help from some hundreds of dockers, carters, and labourers to open the door and let Him in; and it was often a queer thought to Sean that he owed a new lease of life to the folly and thoughtlessness of these uncultured, uncouth, brave men. From the hard toil of these rough men, dishevelled in body and mind, out of what they earned so hard, he lived, ate of bread and meat, and nourished his sensuous being in art and literature. And, worst of all, in his thoughts, he never thought of thanking them.

A Committee had been formed to help get Jim Larkin released from an American jail, where he had been shoved for pronouncing publicly ethics as common as those in the Pope's *Rerum Novarum*. This Committee worked in union with one in New York, and Sean acted as Secretary. The members as well tried to parry the campaign carried on by some of the official Labour leaders to undermine, for their own ends, the value of Jim with the industrial workers of Ireland. These officials were eager to organise a state of things that would allow them to live in peace, after gaining an increase of a penny or tuppence to wages at odd and irregular times for Union members, so as to keep the workers from breaking in on their peace, and permit them to draw their salaries in a quiet and orderly way. And, of course, the church clericals gave a quiet but definite clapping of hands to their course of conduct. It was an odd attitude for the Labour leaders towards a man whose organising genius had placed most of these Labour leaders where they were.

Some thoughtful soul suggested that a greeting should be sent to Jim, sent to jail for professing the commonest ideas of Christian charity, and it was decided to send him a card holding a simple greeting to show that thousands still remembered him and wished him back in Ireland. Hearing that some of the Union officials were doing all they could to prevent the men from sending a message of affection to their much-prized champion, Sean was selected to go to see Mr. William O'Brien, the Union's new General Secretary. Sean felt that such an open-minded, fine-hearted man as O'Brien would immediately stop any interference with this effort on the part of the workers of Ireland to spiritually visit a comrade in prison. So, having first written an explanatory letter to Mr. O'Brien, Sean set out to visit him.

As he trod the way there, Sean felt angry and contemptuous that the Head office had transferred itself from the old fighting quarters of Liberty Hall to an electable house in the gardenian surroundings of Rutland Square; to a house that never had a history for the workers, and never would; where Labour would — as Sean thought — luxuriously allow itself to lie down and doze itself away to death. Official Labour had left the miry murkiness, full of the memorised shapes of battles, the shadow of which some day would take on the tougher glory of bronze remembrance, for grander quarters, where polished peace would have an easy-chair; golden-brown sherry would take the place of sombre, purplish beer; corduroy and mole-skin be replaced by the natty dinner-jacket and the black bow.

Strange influence buildings had on the memory and the heart! Thousands of buildings were passed, maybe entered, in a lifetime, but only a few were remembered in the soul and mind. Of all the buildings in Dublin, but four of them remained forever and vividly in the heart and mind of Sean: his home, the Church of St. Burnupus, the Abbey Theatre, and Liberty Hall; and, indeed, they were four symbols of his life. Each was woven deftly and deep into flesh and spirit.

Ah! Here it is! Headquarters of the Irish unskilled labourer. The silence here isn't broken by the sound of a hobnailed boot; no sharp smell from stony dust of cement, black grime from coal, or yellow dust from cattle-feed, disturbs the scents of lilac or rosebud coming from the sequestered square across the road. The evening-dress suit and the plus-four front of the Irish Labour movement. And the clergy's coy approval.

William O'Brien, General Secretary of the Irish Transport Union, would help all right in the sending of a greeting to Jim, because of his own generous heart, first; and, then, for the sake of old times in the Socialist Party of Ireland; and, lastly, Mr. O'Brien would be the last to hesitate in doing anything to hearten an old comrade now in jail for reminding Christians of the greatest of the three Christian virtues.

A vision of Mr. O'Brien, as Sean had known him, came before his eyes. The set face, like a tense white mask, crossed straight with thin red lips, fringed with a clipped moustache and short-trimmed, pointed beard; brightened by the small, shrewd eyes, like dark diamonds whose fuller light could never be coaxed into gleaming. Now a Director of the National Bank, he had then the younger vision of a great Union for all the workers of Ireland. Everywhere Sean went he saw the gigantic letters of O.B.U., One Big Union, each taller than the tallest man, forcing themselves in front of all eyes, so that he who ran could read them. Many nasty-minded workers said that the big letters really meant Old Bill's Union; and so this little fairy, that came out winged from the brain of O'Brien, danced its way through the land for a season; but died at last, like Tinkerbell, and stayed dead, for the voice of Labour was neither strong enough nor advanced enough to bring this brilliant mite to life again.

A strange man who has left his mark on the Irish Labour movement; a nature that sat at a meeting, still as death, listening; all the little thoughts expressed there, which didn't tinkle with his own, rejected, but not forgotten; for his own were great, born big, and ripe for use. He wasn't a man one would expect children to run to meet, dodge round him, laughing; swing from his hooked arm, or prattle pompous achievements into his listening ear. Too serious a man for that sort of thing. Rather might one say that youngsters would sink into silence when he came near, and reverently let him pass them by, for there seemed to be no echo of a child's voice in his own, as if he had been born ready-made, and ripe for planning. He had put childish things away from him, and was a man's man. Quiet in the crowd, William O'Brien was waiting to see what the Irish Delegates would carry back from Downing Street.

Sean went into the Irish Transport Union's Headquarters. All was business; all working steadily to create the order of the O.B.U.

Here was no talk; no glitter of a sudden laugh; no hum of a murmured song; no evidence of hurry or excitement; all bent on building
the One Big Union, the clerks bent sedately over what they had to
do. Sean heard no beating of a heart there; not even the ticking of a
clock. As the door closed behind him, he went towards the counter
where a clerk was busy emptying figures into a ledger. His footsteps
seemed to make a startling noise, and all the heads were raised to
have a look at him. He knew some of them; and the one behind the
counter, an insignificant-looking little fellow, with a heart of gold,
who had a gorgeous opinion of himself as an actor, exiled among
ordinary people through no fault of his own, stared at Sean in
astonishment, for he knew Seán had no card of entry into Transport
Union Premises since Jim Larkin had sailed away from Erin's shore.
This eminent insignificance now came out to challenge Sean. Sliding
from behind the counter like a performing flea, he stood in front of
Sean, head bent, hands outstretched as if to catch him if he tried
to dodge.

—What is the nature of your business, please? he asked in a most
efficient voice.

—No business, really, answered Sean; I'm on an errand of goodwill, and I dropped in to see Mr. O'Brien for a moment.

—We have no record of any appointment; Mr. O'Brien sees
visitors only by special appointment.

—Just you tell Bill, O'Casside's here, and he'll be glad to see me,
stretching a friendly hand out to pat the opposer's shoulder, but the
flea jumped back in alarm.

—We received no notice of your visit. Mr. O'Brien sees visitors
only by special appointment.

—He'll see me, if you'll only tell him. I wrote to him, and he
knows about the matter enticing me here.

—Mr. O'Brien sees persons only by special appointment.

—You said that before. And don't be humiliating the man by
calling him Mister; he wouldn't be pleased. Up to now, he has always
been Bill.

Two more clerks slid courageously from where they had been
working to reinforce the importantly insignificant. They arranged
themselves, one on either side of the performer, a little behind him,
so that he shouldn't waver in the discharge of his duty, and that they
would be close to help, if the need arose.

—I've come, said Sean, just to ask Mr. O'Brien to help us to send
a greeting to an old comrade, lonely in a far-off jail——

—Mr. O'Brien sees no-one, except persons who have a special——
—Appointment, added Sean. Well, my purpose is special, even
though it isn't armed with an appointment. Mr. O'Brien is a good
catholic; a man strict in his observance of the canonical orders of the
church; a Christian in spirit as well as in practice; so he will never
refuse, if you will let him know, and would easily agree to help us in
this simple act of charity of showing a thought of remembrance to
a lonely comrade; especially to the man who had lighted the flame
of Labour's revolt in the City of Dublin and Belfast, a flame that
showed the workers what they were and what they might become!

—What Larkin himself got himself into, let Larkin himself get
himself out of; and the clerks, moving forward, began to edge Sean
towards the door. He found himself out on the cold steps, the door
closed, the clerks gone; so the little clerks below, by refusing to
carry a message, prevented the greater clerk above from carrying out
a simple act of Christian charity.

And so from bad to worse.

The Round Room of Dublin's Mansion House was packed tight
with people; hushed and reverent as befitted the solemn and misereal
occasion. It was a centenary of Dante, and all who could had hurried
to enjoy the charm and refreshment of hearing Count Plunkett,
Minister of Fine Arts in the Dail, lecture about all the circles of hell,
and the many amazing things that commonly happened there. The
people, mostly the middle class, came, too, to show how they loved
fine literature, and, also, to show England they were so easy in their
minds that they could afford to think of things a long way from
Downing Street. Not knowing that the Treaty was burning a hole in
De Valera's pocket, they sat firm and quiet.

Calm as granite to their foes.
Bravely hope, and wisely waited,
Toil, join, and educate,
Man is master of his fate;
They will have their own again!

They had waited a long time; they were gloomy and doubtful;
and all were in a ready mood to furnish themselves with the fear of
what Dante had to tell them. The lecture and discussion lasted for
many hours, for all were anxious to reveal their controlled delight
in Plunkett's knowledge of Dante's hell; and soon in every ear
resounded the thunderous twisting melody of plaints innumerable
and torment and loud lament and furious rage. If the fiery speakers
had been heard by all the Irish people at the same time, the Dies

Irae would have become the national anthem of the land. The entire audience was gasping before the entertainment was over, and most of them, when they had escaped to the outer air, vowed to God and Virgin Mary that never again would they go to hear a lecture on anything higher than the poems of Thomas Davis or Barney McCoy; even though it were to be given by St. Michael himself, accompanied on a trumpet by St. Gabriel, with a young Virgil from Cork or Galway tapping out time on a solar plexus. And from that day to this, no-one has ventured to offer to give a lecture on Dante to the patient and long-suffering Irish. Ireland had hurried away from *mons tria millia* of Cassino to climb the homelier haunts of the Sugar Loaf Mountain.

Curious, thought Sean, how they couldn't see the hells out of which there was no redemption, in their own home town. During school holidays, so that children wouldn't go without a nourishing meal, spurred by a mood of dismal charity, a brother of S. T. O'Kelly, and his wife, had got a loan of the hall in which Sean worked, so that corporal charity could put another feather in its cap. Give the little lambs a meal. And such a meal! A sack of cocoa, another of split peas, some slabs of margarine, a few bags of sugar, a huge metal boiler, similar to those for boiling cattle food, and a multitude of chipped enamel mugs, were delivered to the hall. No white linen, no plates or spoons, no flowers came. Mr. O'Kelly, his wife, and a paid helper, the wife's sister, a Mrs. Murphy, came to superintend and help. The huge boiler was hitched to a little gas-ring which wouldn't heat the water in a week. Sean and a friend, at the risk of burning the hall to the ground, built a temporary furnace with loose bricks under the stage, so that the cocoa or the pea-soup could be ready before the pampered kids filed in to take their meal. They sat down in batches, for the hall wasn't big enough to take them all at one sitting. The second batch had to drink from the unwashed mugs used by the first one served, for there was no way of cleaning them; and no-one seemed to think it mattered. One day the hall reeked with the smell of cocoa, the next with the more pungent and sickening smell of pea-soup. A mug of soup, thick and stifling, and a slab of dry bread, or a mug of cocoa, with a slab of bread thinly smeared with margarine, were the feasts set forth for the young Fianna. Sean's whole being was filled with loathing when he stared from the well-dressed, well-fed, dapper figures of the server and his wife to the hunched-up, scarè-clad kids, every one of whom, as far as he could see, showed some sign of underfeeding. There they were:

of the one fold, the well-kept servers and the ill-kept kids, of the one hope, the one faith, the one baptism; the few amply supplied with corn and wine, the many gulping down as best they could the husks shaken from the finer corn. Every day Sean tidied the hall as well as he could before the hour for the kids to come, but, after two days of help in the serving, he refused to have any hand in this villainous way of showing God's love to the young, the innocent, and the helpless. A mug of heavy cocoa today for the main meal, and a mug of pea-soup tomorrow. Even to these hungry souls these things were too bitter to taste sweet. Beside the blazing fire, near sick from the smell of the soup, which Mrs. Murphy stirred with a broom-handle — a new one, thank God — Sean watched the children file listlessly in, into the soiled hall where the windows were so high that no-one, not on a ladder, could get a glimpse of the saving sun or cleansing rain outside; moving through the benches, one two one two, sitting down with neither sign nor smile on the hard seats, staring at the metallically-grinning mugs set firmly before them on the rough planks stretched on trestles to form tables, dusty with the chalk used the night before in the game of House; Mrs. Murphy patrolling along the benches, filling each mug with the strongly-smelling soup from a big enamel ewer, Mrs. O'Kelly following with a tray of bread from which each youngster took a slab as she passed them by: Pippa passes, and she does the job nicely, though no song ripples from her lips. Bring out the rich and savoury viands for those who have often been faint with hunger at the top or bottom of their street! Watching this through the steam rising from the soup and the smell that filled the hall, Sean felt that this would make as good a circle as any seen by Dante in the inferno of his imagination. Ring the bell, Watchman — ring, ring, ring! Here is something rotten, desolate, and to be destroyed by the sense of decent men and by the workers' red resentment!

Sean closed his eyes, and saw a better sight: The convents of the teaching sisters of Loretto and Ursula; the Catholic Colleges, and the higher schools of the better-off followers of episcopus and presbyter. Green grass, gravelled paths, flowers in the centre and at the sides; playgrounds made for play; clean food, and wholesome on the whole, served decently over white cloths; snowy sheets and healthy beds in rooms where the air flows freely; and, over all, the crucified Christ, in spirit, on the one hand; in actual image on the other: in one place, the hanging Saviour among the lavender; in the other, the hanging Saviour among the lice.

And so from worse to worse.

The morning dawned with a bright sun shining; then the clouds came, and the storm broke. First thing, after breakfast, the Countess Markievicz ran round telling people to be merry, for great was the Treaty brought back by the Irish Delegates. Harry Boland, Ireland's Ambassador to America, hailed it in a speech as the freedom that came from God's right hand; and Coocoo Ulla, Gaelic League President, auctioneer and valuator, put up a blackboard on the railings outside his office, which ordered every passer-by to murmur *Buidheacheas le Dia ar son saoirse*, thanks with God for the sake of freedom, finding out a short time after that he had made a mistake, and had written bad Irish; so he hurried out to take it in again. Many who ran out to cheer, ran in again to curse, when De Valera, with swift indecision, sent a letter to the Press, emphasising that this Treaty, or Articles of Association, with England partner on the one hand, and Ireland partner on the other, was in violent conflict with the wishes of the majority of the people, including the animals in brushwood and covert, and the birdies in the trees; that he couldn't recommend it; and that the Minister of Defence and Home Affairs agreed with him; making everyone more bewildered than he himself happened to be, so that thousands were for the Treaty in the freshness of morning, against it in the heat of the day, and neither for nor against it in the cool of the evening. A good chance, when it met to discuss things, thought the Larkin Release Committee, to get the Dail to pass a vote demanding the release of the workers' champion.

It was a cold bleak day in the penitential season of Advent; a grey grumbling sky overhead, with a damp, chill wind erasing the feeling of life from the flesh of the citizens crowding round, when the Delegates of the nation pushed their way through them into the puritan-faced building of the National University. A great cheer went up to God when De Valera stepped from his car, and others rang out and in when Griffith and Collins glided in after their Leader. The people gathered together to wait a decision, pushed closer together, to guard against the nipping air blowing in from the east.

The people were swaying about before the building, murmuring among themselves, murmuring words round what they thought would happen. Sean pushed through to the gate where one of his old club, the O'Tooles, was Captain of the Guard. A handsome young man, with raven-black, curly hair, eyes only a little less dark, a pale, ascetic, but humorous face, and a very slim buoyant figure. Yes, he told Sean, come along with the resolution for Jim's release; I'll slip you all into the hall, and send in any message you like; but I'm afraid it's little they'll think of Jim, and they the way they are.

Sean slid back into the crowd again, and stood for a time, watching and listening there, for it would be a while before the rest of the Committee joined him.

—It's the loppin' off of Ulsther from the rest of us's th' rough spot, said a voice beside him; yield on that, an' we yield on everything. Th' thing should never ha' been signed without first havin' submitted it to Dev: that goes without sayin'.

—How does it go without sayin'? asked a querulous voice behind the first one. De Valera can teach Mick Collins nothin'.

A venerable old man, a plaid muffler hiding chin and lower part of the nose, was being pushed, now a step forward, now a step backward, by the arguing people. He raised his nose and mouth above the muffler to say — Don't push, please. Isn't there any respect left in the land for the aged? Can't we take pattern by the members of our Dail who are quietly deciding, without any bitterness or blame, the choice the country is prepared to make? Don't push, please. Let us all preserve a decent reticence of opinion, till we learn how things go. We won't have long to wait. The questions before the Dail are simple, and reasonable men can settle them in an hour.

—D'ye call th' takin' of an oath to a foreign king a simple question?

—I refuse to reply to such an irrelevant question, said the old man coldly, hiding his nose and mouth in his muffler, immediately taking them out again, to ejaculate, Oh, don't push, please!

But they continued to argue and to push, and ugly terms of traitor, renegade, and hypocrite were hissed about among the crowd, forcing the old gentleman to prise his nose and mouth up from the deeps of his muffler to exclaim — This Treaty you are trying to condemn is giving us more than we had any right to expect.

A tall girl, standing beside Sean, gave a bitter moan when she heard the old man's vigorous remark. He had noticed her before, and had thought how good she would be to have beside him, under a hiding hedge away in the country where no-one thought of trespassing. She had a great mass of dark-brown hair rippling over her neck, big grey eyes, a tempting mouth, ripe and red as a finely born cherry; her coat was open, and underneath the blouse Sean saw that her breasts were lovely enough to make a nest for a hero's head. She had been biting her lips for some time, and he could see that she had been repressing a desire to shout out something to the people around her. She was biting them harder than ever now. Suddenly, tensing her arms and clenching her little hands, this lovely edition of sweet-and-twenty wheeled around to face the larger section of the crowd, gathering their strict attention with a screaming yell, causing the old gentleman to dive deeper into his muffler as he tried to force himself away; but she had a grip of his arm, and held him close to her.

—Look at him! she yelled; one of Griffith's toadies, mumbling his treachery here when he ought to be down among the dead men! Hear what he said? The Treaty gives Ireland more than she has any right to expect! That's what this old, dried-up palaverer tells us. The Treaty! Here's some of its good points for you, people:

> It takes away Irish Sovereignty forever.
> It gives Ulster away for ever.
> It gives Four Ports away forever.
> It makes a Guest of an English Governor-General forever.
> It makes Irishmen British Citizens forever.
> It asks an Oath of Allegiance to the English King forever.
> It Divides Ireland forever and ever and ever!

—That's what it does, and what it does it does for ever; the young girl paused to pacify the sobs that were shaking her young bosom, that was fit to comfort the head of an anxious and sorrowful hero.

Evening had fallen when Seán and his few companions stood in the shadowy hall of the great University building, waiting a chance to send in their appeal that the Dail should call collectively for Jim Larkin's release; a hallway cold, severe, and silencing. They had given in notes for Countess Markievicz, Austin Stack, and Tom Hunter to a Republican officer who had promised to see they reached the persons named on the envelopes. They stood there, cold and silent, watching young men-clerks and young women-clerks and officials, bundles of documents under their arms, coming and going on tiptoe. When any one of the clerks had something to say to another, he whispered cautiously, as if they were in the presence of some great being about to die; and so they were, for Irish Unity was at its last gasp.

After a long, long wait, two strong young men came in staggering under the weight of a gigantic roll of foolscap, which was borne on a pole, and was covered with writing of divers kinds, old Irish, middle Irish, and modern Irish, with a special translation into ogham.

—What are yous carryin' up, misther? asked the tram-conductor, tiptoeing over to the leading bearer.

—What is it, is it? queried the foremost finn maccoolie; what d'ye think it is, now?

—I dunno, but it looks important.

—So it is; it's no less than the original copy of Document No. 2.

—D'ye tell me that? An' what may that be now?

—A counther-blow at the Treathy; an amazin' thing. A document that'll be historical as long as destiny lives and time lasts. And with a final shake to get it even on their shoulders, the two carriers went off, and disappeared under the archways.

It was deeply dark now, and Sean could but guess when officials were passing by the sound of their furtive whispering. He and the tram-conductor crept over to where they heard whispering, and touched down on two of the officials.

—Any chance of having a brief talk with the Countess, or Mr. Stack, or Tom Hunter? Sean whispered cautiously in the ear of one of them.

—Don't yous know damn well yous can't, and things the way they are? Yous can't see any deputy for any talk, brief or breathless, for they're struggling in the middle of Document No. 2. That's the thing'll put the English in a quare dilemma; for they can't accept it and they can't reject it.

—Why can't they reject it, man, if they want to? asked the tram-conductor with a note of contempt in his voice.

—Because, man, if they did, they'd commit themselves to rejecting their own offer, see?

—How reject their own offer?

—Because while preserving Ireland's sovereign status, Document No. 2 provides for external association only in the Empire, with the king as head over the separated conjunction.

—What, head over Ireland's sovereign status, is it?

—No, no, man; for how could Ireland be sovereign herself if there was another sovereign authority over her?

—Isn't that what I'm askin'? insisted the tram-conductor. How can you let go of th' hand if you still hold on to it?

—What hand are you talking about?

—The King of England's hand, of course.

—Dtch dtch dtch! the whisper from the dark clicked its tongue impatiently. Look; the king's hand doesn't come into it at all. Listen: though sovereign status puts Ireland outside of the British Empire, external association keeps her inside of it — see?

Silence encircled them again, as they listened to their own

disturbing thoughts; standing in the depths of the lofty hall; thinking in the darkness, silently anxious, feeling forward in a lonely way with whispers; forming a shallow pool of defence between the quarrel of the people outside and the quarrel of the deputies in their secret chamber of open discussion.

—D'ye mean, asked the puzzled tram-conductor, at last, that Document No. 2 shifts the British Empire outside of Ireland's allegiance, while Ireland's sovereign status and external association brings the British Empire inside Ireland's external recognition?

—You see, it's this way: if Document No. 2 gets accepted, Ireland'll be what you could call a sequestered country that is still within the outlines of the British Empire.

—I don't much like the sayin' of within the outlines of the British Empire, and I don't altogether like the word sequesthered either.

—If we don't take the chance offered in Document No. 2, said the whisper, louder now than it had been before, the land'll become an improvised inferno.

All the time, the foolish fight was waging in the secret chamber of open discussion; a foolish fight, for there was as much difference between the document flourished in the upper air by De Valera and the folio of the Treaty spread out on the ground at the feet of the people by Griffith and Collins as there would be between two eggs laid by the same hen at the same time. But every meagre mind, hoodwinked by its own thoughts, praised its own devotion to Ireland, resting from its labour to spit out the charge of treachery against an opposing brother. Vainly De Valera cursed the bitter, maiming bite of politics, holding out a hand to Collins in one impulsive moment of remembrance, to have it knocked down by Mary MacSweeney; while at another moment, Collins held out a hand to De Valera, to have it set aside by the venomous speech of a supporting follower. There could be no reunion. Ireland was there in the midst of the revelling quarrellers, her chaplet of crêpe, worn for the dead who died for Ireland, going askew; there she stood distracted, or ran from Billy to Jack, shouting order order, unity unity, discipline discipline, unheard in the storm of each side shouting at the other, stamping her little foot on the floor for a silence that never came, till she sank, tired and wordless, on to the floor, anointed with the spits dribbling from the angry, twisted mouths of her own devoted children. The Kellys, the Burkes, and the Sheas were at one another's throats.

The terrible beauty was beginning to lose her good looks.

INTO CIVIL WAR

AFTER ages of talking that threatened to defy Time, and last forever, each delegate denouncing another as a traitor, recreant, or
slave, the Treaty was accepted by a majority of a few votes; many,
including De Valera, breaking out into tears when the result was
finally and forensically known.

Then those who were to become the rulers of Ireland separated
into two parties. Most of the coming middle class followed Griffith,
and the rest hallooed for freedom round the disappointed De Valera.
The clergy stood quiet on the right; the labour officials watched as
quiet on the left; both waiting to see which would prove the stronger,
hoping that some good things could be gathered from the fragments.
Not a leader left had the power or personality to check the drift,
now flowing swift to an armed fight for dominance. The laundered
people of the Big Houses shut-to the gates of their demesnes, locked
the heavy doors of the houses, pulled down the blinds, drew cosy
chairs to the marble-mannered fireplaces, sat down in them, opened
a bottle of wine, drank a health to His Majesty, and assured themselves that they were well out of it all.

The provisional government of the Free State began to cajole and
coax the people to the grandeur of their state by sending telegrams
in green envelopes, painting the postal pillar-boxes a richer green
than the green on the envelopes, crossing out the GR, and printing
in the mystic symbol of SE, while tailors worked night and day
making green uniforms for the new Free State Army. Erin was
becoming the green isle in fact as in figment. Clap hands, clap hands,
till daddy comes home, for daddy's got money, but mother has
none.

Here and now, the slick slogan of the clergy that civil war and all
deforming crimes were in the mind and way only of those who
forgot God was to be mocked at by catholic murder, catholic gun-
fire, and catholic torch setting flames to the homes of catholic people.
Here were those, now on the threshold of battle, who had not forgotten God; who went to Mass as regular as clock-work; who had
deep-cut circles in the flesh of their fingers with the never-ending
twisting of rosary beads. What atheism, the clergy said, had brought
to Russia, catholic Christianity had brought to Ireland. Catholics
who had been steeped in the Faith from the very cradle; who had
listened to every papal encyclical and episcopal pastoral; who could

find their way to confession blindfolded; who acknowledged with a bumper of bows the divine headship of the See of Rome; holy men who had the excuse of neither atheism nor paganism; yet here they were, feverishly getting ready to shoot one another in forehead and back; to torture opponents when they got a chance; to hurry a different opinion from a hasty court-martial to a quick end by a firing-squad. Righteous catholic Irishmen were about to get busy making their land a nation once again; showing, if it ever needed to be shown, that good practising catholics are very much as other men are, and sometimes a damned sight worse; that all the countless supernatural and spiritual advantages they boastfully possess do not give them any lead in grace over others, and do not fix on catholic natures any other spiritual or natural bridle than those which check the desperate anger that may try to assert itself in the heart of any common atheist or communist. The Papal yellow and white rage is worse than the rage of the red, for it is tireless in its enmity, and its revenge is swift as lightning, or as slow as the crawl of a snail through a thicket of tough grass — according to the chances conditions may put before it.

Judging by what the two parties were saying of each other, there wasn't an honest, truthful, or semi-Christian left alive in the land. Ireland's magenta sky was dark with the cloud of venomous words, hot and steaming, that came from the mouths of the delegates reviling each other. Most of them kept awake at night pondering on the bad things they could say of the others when the sun rose in the morning. Each day it grew worse, till half the hands fingered the triggers of rifles; the other half of the hands tightened on the butts of revolvers; and those who had neither nursed a hand-grenade in every pocket. To God and Ireland true; for they still went to Mass, to confession, and recited their rosaries *ad lib*.

In the midst of this seething, senseless conflict between the Treaty and Document No. 2, the Black and Tans were withdrawn in sealed vans, and crowds looked curiously on while British cavalry cautiously cantered out of the Curragh Camp; and Sean stood to watch the infantry marching stolidly down to the docks, a band playing *Come Back to Erin* to keep their hearts from failing; watching the cannon, too, as it lumbered through the streets, seeming to look, that as they had lived so long in Ireland, they didn't want to go. Well, thought Sean, as he watched them pass, at least, the Irish now will have the expansive liberty of biting each other without let or hindrance from low law of Dublin Castle or high law of heaven.

So right through this tear-up of catholic composure, the British kept quietly dribbling out of the country, puzzled as much now as they were when they first landed in Cork and Wexford near a thousand years ago. Captain Heslip, of the Free State Army, spoke a few encouraging words to a major of the Worcestershire Regiment, a plump man with a look of heavily-controlled bewilderment on his furtively-staring face, as he handed over the sacred Bank of Ireland to the wild Irishman in an officer's uniform. It was all beyond the major. It had been all so sudden. The British Government had lost its nerve. The Bank of Ireland gone, and all that therein is. Is it a dream, or are there visions about? This was more than God had fitted the major to understand. Beside the major, like a free and uneasy guardian angel, stood a Director of the Bank, in tall hat and top-of-the-morning coat, to see that everything was done according to the statutes made and provided.

And, a few steps away, in another street, Sean stood among a quiet crowd, a grin on his gob, watching the Earl of Fitzalan step from his car in a half-dazed way, not even noticing the grand salute given by a nearby police inspector; Sean watched the catholic Earl step out and trot over the pathway to hand over the place known to all as Dublin Castle, in a circumspect and affable way. Fitzalan, the Earl, seemed to be doing it all in a dream; things were turning tipsey-turvey; the dragon had conquered the knight; the lion was roaring like any sucking dove. Fitzalan happening to be a catholic in full bloom, the astute British Government naturally thought the Earl would be able to endow the Irish with a sense of order, and that the catholic Irish would yield him the respect due to his quality; but the poor man found that it was even hard to get Mass quietly, and that his catholic Irish brethren penned him up in his Vice-regal Lodge as they had penned up his protestant predecaesars. So here was the belted Earl, plundered of power, bowler-hatted now, bent at the knees, head down, slipping into the Castle quick as he could, a wistfully-reluctant look on his face, such as the face of St. Peter might show if compelled to give up the keys of the kingdom; slipped in to hand over the keys of the Citadel to the ungrateful Irish, so long the waifs and strays of history. Gone forever the knights of St. Patrick, with their orders dangling from light-blue ribbons: *Quiz seperrabit* had lost its meaning: Skibereen and Tuberneering were at home in Dublin Castle. Come all ye in. Sit down, boys, an' I'll fill your can.

—Here's the key of the Throne Room, and this one's the key of St. Patrick's Hall, my good man. A long, long trail from Fitzhenry

to Fitzalan, Alpha and Omega. Goodbye, all. Farewell, but whenever I welcome the hour of the flight of the Earl, I feel kind of sad.
The last glimpse of Erin with sorrow I see, regretting the time I've
lost in wooing; 'tis gone, and forever the time when first I met thee,
warm and young, a bright May moon was shining, love; but the
dream of those days when first I sung thee is o'er; 'tis gone, and
forever, the light we saw breaking, and no longer can you come to
rest in this bosom, my own stricken dear; so, farewell, and go where
glory waits thee, where the harp that once can function again, and
the minstrel boy will be your well-known warrior. From henceforth
you will have your own disorders, surrendering the order of Macha's
Brooch for that of Armagh's Red Hat; order of the Black Peeler and
the Green Goat; order of the Old Turf Fire; Order of Knights
Hospitallers of the Clean Sweep; Order of the Little Greyhound in
the West; the Sublime Order of Excommunication for Catholics i
Collegio Trinitatis; Order of the Banned Books; and many such,
and many more. There's nothing to stop ye now!

In spite of the cool meetings held under the care of Dublin's
catholic Archbishop; the dear pleading of Dan Breen, Eire's No. 1
Guerilla; in spite of pact and promise, broken ere they were understood, the day came when General Tom Ennis, a fawn trench-coat
mock-modestly covering a neat green uniform, with brilliant yellow
tabs on the lapels, goads his unwilling men to swing a heavy gun
swiftly, so that its angry snout may point towards the Republican
enemy barricaded deep in the Four Courts; hurries them into pulling
the lanyard that opens the cannon's mouth to send a British shell
over the walls, send it screaming over, to spread a shattering shower
of sharp steel against her greying dignity, darting hither and thither
in its effort to bring maiming death to angry comrades behind the
walls on the far side of the river Liffey; while a great crowd of excited
civilians crouches behind corners near Richmond Bridge to listen to
the crack of the cannon, and watch the smoke and flame of the
bursting shells. Rory O'Connor, chief of the Republicans, steadied
with a few doses of phospherine, taken to tighten his nerves loosened
from lack of sleep, tightens his belt, and waits; waits for a closer
attack, for he has no bullying guns to answer the dinning onslaught
of shells sent over, minute by minute, by his one-time comrade, Tom
Ennis, hidden behind the houses on the other bank of Anna Livia
Plurabelle. Thick dust hides the body of the building, and dark
smoke encircles the huge dome, making it look like the great globe
itself trekking the sky through a way of stormy clouds.

The Free Staters, having expended their shells, advanced to the building in a sharp trot, murmuring holy acts of contrition, finger on trigger and bayonet fixed; advanced, till a land-mine exploded under their passing feet, and brought the charge to a stop for a while, so that they could watch all the foolish wigs and gowns of Dublin sailing up into the sky; with all the records of the country, processes, cases, testimonies, bills of exchange, and sales of properties to church and private person, and all hereditaments chronicled since Strongbow came to Ireland, flying up after the wigs and gowns, to come fluttering down, scorched and tattered, into every Dublin back-yard and front garden.

Defeated in the Four Courts, the Republicans fortified themselves within a long portion of O'Connell Street; and Business and Banking hurried everything valuable into their safes, before retiring to the country to wait till things settled down. Once more, machine-gun and rifle-fire, rising and falling and rising again, shivered the air into a sharp and bitter moaning, pierced now and then by the strident bark of a ten-pounder sending snarling protests into buildings housing the deadliest marksmen among the Republicans. Occasionally, the shrill squealing of the gun-fire was relieved by the gentle and more musical tinkle of falling glass, splitting away from trembling windows that now began to send out flickering tongues of flame growing swiftly into steady streams of burning destruction, till the smoky skyline was changed into a rosy and tumultuous lake of fire.

At night, when the sky was nowhere, and the stars were being suffocated by an acrid smoke-pall, and all beneath them was a bewildering furnace, out from the sparks ascending, as roofs crashed in and walls tumbled down; out from the spouting flame and the grey veil of powdered rubbish, came Cathal Brugha, running; shooting at the dim, green-uniformed men bobbing about in the curly clouds of smoke; shooting at what he thought to be enemies of Ireland; shooting, till he himself was shot, to become a ghost among the ghosts of those who had fallen before him. Well, here you lie, Cathal Brugha, dying under the battle-banner of smoke-fringed flame, your couch a street of crumbling, blackened buildings; a big torch, too, lighting your last few tired steps into that unsearchable darkness reserved for life when life has ended. However strict you may have been in the holding high of an abstraction, you were a Republican; a very brave man; generous in a large way; and too honest to find comfortable companionship in the lesser men around you. Many will be carried out of life, feet first, covered with an Irish tricolour that will be too big for them; but you the flag fits well, exchanging honour for honour with the gallant dead beneath it.

Stretching himself on the old stretcher-bed by the wall that separated his room from the hall outside, Sean halted his mind from thinking out the new play he intended to write. The Abbey Theatre had accepted one, after long consideration, and he had reason to feel elated. Idly he looked around the room, while he half listened to gun-fire in the distance, or the whine of rapidly-moving lorries on the street outside. Free Staters out for a raid on the home of some old comrade-in-arms. Lift your heart up, mother Erin! Well, for the time being, he was fairly nice and snug here, if it weren't for the never-ending commotion of the families who lived in the house. He glanced round to see how he was placed: the fireplace was big and clumsy, but when a fire blazed there, it was cosy and alluring. A fine settee, to hold two comfortably, stared at its dying embers now. A large mahogany table, on which he could spread out his work, undisturbed by scattered books, a yellow-varnished desk, with a few nests of file-cabinets, gave the room a look of a shy office not knowing what to do with itself. Beside the bed was an open two-shelved locker, one of thousands cast away by the Government when the war ended, and bought by Sean for half a crown; on the shelves were his soap, shaving-kit, face-flannel, and washbasin, all discreetly hidden by a coloured print curtain. On each side of the huge windows shelving held his many books, and the windows themselves were draped with long, creamy-coloured curtains of good twill. On the table stood the lamp that gave light to him when darkness came, and, in the centre, stood a mimosa plant, faded and dry now; never likely to show its delicate yellow blossoms again. He hadn't the gift of his mother in keeping flowers friendly and responsive. No picture hung on the wall yet, for he didn't care for the cheap ones on sale in the art shops, and he couldn't afford a good one yet. On the mantel-shelf was a framed photograph of Thorwaldsen's *Venus*. On one side of the fireplace was a press in which he kept his crockery, coal, sticks for kindling, and a few saucepans. Beside this stood the small table holding his typewriter, and beside it, a suitable dignified chair to sit him straight up at his work. Not a lot to brag about, but enough for his present needs. A good nest, if it were not for the noise. The room to his right held a father, mother, and five children; the room over his head, the same with one more child: seven in the room beside him, eight in the one overhead — his was a haven of peace, a place of dignity, compared with either of them.

—There's that damned shooting again! as a volley rang out, followed by a sharp, scattered firing somewhere near the house, on the street outside. Kelt was killing Kelt as expertly and as often as he could; catholic Kelts, too. Not a freethinker among them. As diligent as the Black and Tans themselves. And just as clever. Men were shot down while at business, on pleasure, even when they whispered to a girl. A young man was swung up to a beam; as much castor oil as he could hold was poured through a funnel into him, and he was left hanging there to mutter rosaries as best he could without being able to tell his beads. And that was a merciful method.

For when Griffith and Collins had escaped into the grave, the rest of a frightened government, left breathing, ensconced itself behind the thick wall of a building near Kildare Street, protected by a generous border of barbed wire, itself defended by a running mound of sand-bags; safe nowhere, for all militant Ireland was crawling round, creeping to country hedge or street corner; prowling about to get a chance for a sure and pure shot at anything they didn't like. From their hide-in, the Government in embryo sent out warrant after warrant for the orderly execution of those caught with arms in their hands; and even those from whom the arms had been taken long before. When General Hales and Patrick O'Maille, descending from a jaunting-car to enter a hotel for dinner, fell by Republican bullets, the Provisional Government, fanged by fear, shook from sleep three prominent Republicans who had been in jail for months; led them out to a quiet corner, and, after providing them with a few moments for a private prayer, separated them by rifle-fire forever from everything they knew and loved and hated in this world. As a reprisal. Rory O'Connor, the Republican, sleeps long now, like Michael Collins, the Free Stater. Collins, fooling about in the south, just jumped to death when a random bullet fixed itself firmly in his brain. Here the Free State and all Ireland suffered a loss. Collins wasn't a great man, but he was the makings of one. He was human in a way that Griffith couldn't even try to be; he had a laugh Griffith couldn't reach, stretch he never so high. He was tolerant, and ready, even at a moment's notice, to forgive a blow, and, more difficult still, to forget about it too. Collins could never have hated militant Labour as Griffith did; nor could anyone think of him as jealous of high things in others, as Griffith was of the higher things in Yeats. One could never conceive of Griffith dancing a reel, even in the privacy of his own home; but one could easily imagine Collins doing a wild dance in the courtyard of the Castle, or of him singing a song out 'loud in the porch of Parliament House.

After the capture of Dublin by the Free Staters, ambushes began to blossom red from many a street corner; and the joyful killing spread over the whole country. Houses went up in flames, exploding often with a wild hurrah, and bridges sank sullenly down into the rivers they spanned. Republicans put land-mines under road barriers, so that when the Free Staters tried to remove them, they ascended into heaven; and when Free Staters captured Republicans, they fixed up barricades of their own, laden with land-mines, compelling the Republicans to remove the road-block, so that they too were blown to pieces. As a reprisal. The splitting of the atom. And for what? For Document No. 2! Not to abolish poverty. No; just for a spate of words that Alice in Wonderland wouldn't understand. While poor Yeats, having climbed up the winding stair of his Thoor Ballylee, looked out of a high window over the land, and wondered what it all meant. And to explain some of it, the Republicans blew up Thoor Ballylee's ancient bridge as they were leaving, shouting quite politely up to Yeats, Goodnight, sir, and thank you, as though he had given them the bridge.

Well, such good deeds were common to Christians. Ever since catholics were catholics, fire and sword became their common courtesies. The Hundred Years' War that made of Europe a great grave; the Inquisition that made torture and death holy orisons to God; the Conquistadores slaughtering tens of thousands to make the holy Faith a living thing in the hearts of men; the Crusades which so often showed the noblest killed, the meanest killing; and, now, the protestants of the north driving the catholics out of the province by bolt, bullet, and bar; while the good catholics in the south were at one another's throats, spraying death and disillusion in the minds of men. And yet these glib, imperturbable prelates, from the oldest Pope to the youngest bishop, were sloganising the lie that communistic atheism alone brought these evils upon the life of man. And has it not been recently said by one of the Pope's famed champions, a mighty man in apologetics for the Catholic Faith, that the really important thing happening was not the conquest of France by the Nazis, but the downfall of the Freemasons brought about by the fall of France? even though this Papal champion had to admit the great stand these very Freemasons had made for education, freedom of the Press, and freedom of thought in their own land. However rapidly and decidedly these prelates and apologists might pull mitre, biretta, or cap down, well over their foreheads, the mark of Cain showed through — the black cross of pure indifference to the plight of a brother. Politics has slain its thousands, but religion has slain its tens of thousands; and the Church must coax a change into her own heart before a call or a claim can be made for a change in the hearts of others.

—There isn't a room in this very house, thought Sean, as he lay awake, alert to every sound in the street outside, that hasn't a picture of the Sacred Heart hanging around somehwere; that hasn't a votive light, however tiny, burning to St. Anthony of Padua, but the house shakes with fear just as it did when the Black and Tans were howling. Look at poor Mrs. Moore, living above in the two-pair back, with her gentle, even handsome, face, that hovered unsteadily over the rushing, unreasonable agitation of the times like a trembling star in a turbulent sky. Her finely-made hands, their grace peering out even through the deep seams of age and toil, had lighted candle after candle to St. Anthony, the flickering flames mutely begging, throughout the day, throughout the night, for the safety of her little household. But St. Anthony, busy with higher things, hadn't bothered his head about her; for her two sons, who were Republicans, had been thrown into jail; their sister had quickly followed them; then this girl's sweetheart, a Republican, too, had been found on a lonely country road, more than just dead, for his belly had been kicked in, his right eye was a purple pulp, an ear had been partly shot off, and now, jagged and red-edged, stood out like a tiny fin from the side of his head, his mouth a cavity of bloody fluid, floating bits of broken teeth, while to make sure that there would be no chance of escape back into the everyday world, his body had been systematically punched full of gaping bullet-holes, so that the boy gave a lively insight and outsight of what can be done when the twitching hands of the killed twist a rosary in harmony with the twisting of companion rosaries in the hands of the killer.

So worn out, in the end, with a life daily tested to the full, the kindly soul of the old woman found rest only in restlessness. One night, while her old husband slept, she had wandered out into a windy, sleety night, to be found the morning after, stretched calmly out, indifferent to the stinging rain and the bustling wind, on the streaming pavement of a windy turning, in a last, long sleep.

Everything was embedded in a damp, dark-grey mist, spitting out a contemptuous shower of pointed sleet now and again, when Sean and a few neighbours walked beside the old man, behind the closed-in hearse, carrying the body of what had been his wife from the mortuary to the church. Sons and daughter were refused a parole from prison by the Free State Government, so they couldn't come to mingle their excited sorrow with the old man's bewildered grief; and, unable to do more, Sean and four or five neighbours had turned out to act as guards and hedge the old man's sorrow in between them. The driving, sleety rain polished the hearse into a more gleaming blackness; and Sean and his neighbours thrust themselves bending forward so that some of the showers might slide over them, slant-wise, and so fail to give them a fuller drenching. They pulled their caps well down over their brows, and thrust up their topcoat collars as high as they could make them go. Glancing up, Sean saw that the hearse-drivers were crouching forward, too, rain pouring from the rims of their top-hats, and falling with a splash on the horses' haunches.

The old man walked by himself, shaking his head with annoyance when the neighbours had surrounded him to try to shield him from some of the worst weather. He wore no overcoat, not even putting up the collar of the light jacket that held out against the rain but for a few bare minutes. He carried a newly-bought bowler hat under his arm, and with head held up, seemed to be gladly taking any dis-comfort the rain and wind could give him. Sean saw that the rain had seeped through his thin clothing, and must by now be trickling down his skin. The few white tufts left on his head were saturated, and Sean watched the globules of water gathering at the ends, their stems slowly lengthening till they parted suddenly from the edge of the tufts, now one, then two, two again, then one more, to go swiftly coursing down the nape of the old neck to disappear down inside the collar of the old man's shirt.

—You should ha' brought an old overcoat of some kind with you, Mr. Moore, said Sean.

—I wouldn't ha' felt easy if I hadda, Sean, said the old man; not after what happened the other night when who you know lay so soaked an' dead chilly the livelong night on the hard road, an' no-one mindin'. If I only hadda known.

—Well, put on your hat at least, advised Sean. It isn't good for a man of your age to go uncovered this weather.

—No, not yet. It's the one way I can show her I'm sorry I slep' while she was dyin'; the one token of respect I can offer her now.

—But, insisted Sean, if she knew, she'd be the first to tell you to do it.

—She does know, the old man said, knows well. An' by standin' up to what I'm standin' up to now, she knows I'd ha' willingly laid down with her on the cold ground in all the sleet fallin' an' all the wind blowin', the time she was dyin' alone, if only I'd known; if only I hadda known.

The whole of Ireland's following a hearse these days, thought Sean, and Ireland herself's driving the horses.

A lorry carrying two Republican prisoners, surrounded by Free State soldiers, went swiftly by them, and Sean saw it wheeling into the drive that led to Mountjoy Jail. The governors had changed, but the prison stayed there still, as brazen, as bitter as ever. As the hearse passed the gateway of the drive, Sean saw the heavy gates of the prison swing open, and the lorry pass in; saw the gate swing shut again, so that soon those two prisoners would be with the two sons of this old man whose gaze never sought the jail, but stayed fixed on the hearse moving ahead in front of him.

Why this sudden fever for killing each other on the part of the catholic Irish, so deep in the Faith, so close to God? Some there were who fought and fell, like Brugha, in the dazzling white light of their nationalistic immaculate conception. And Brugha fought openly and fair. But the others? It wasn't for want of religion — they were soaked in it from the cradle up to now. Even Ferguson, the poet, wrote that God having made the Irish brothers, and joined them in holier rites than wedlock, would never suffer them to draw opposing brands; for if He did —

> Oh, many a tuneful tongue that Thou mad'st vocal
> Would be cold and silent then;
> And songless long once more, should often-widowed Erin
> Mourn the loss of her brave young men.

What God had joined together, let no man put asunder. Poor, unhappy, futile words! Erin hadn't time even to mourn them, now, for too many were falling at the one time in different places. A gala day of death. The terrible beauty that was, is not. Like the grass, yesterday Ireland's terrible beauty had the green freshness of spring, the bright dew of the morning; today it is withered, and well in the fire. Bring out the prisoners and the firing-squad: ready! one, two, three! Fire that house! Blow up that bridge! Tighten the noose round the bugger's neck! Oh, Mary, the very thought of thee with sweetness fills me breast! Sure 'twas for this that Emmet fought, and Wolfe Tone sunk serene! Oh, young lads of Eireann, who know so little, but are so warmly wrapped up in the songs of Thomas Davis, join the Irish Republican Army, and take the chance of a death-time! Bring your own rosary beads.

But a sensible, hardy plant was rising in the place once held in Ireland's cabbage-patch by the terrible beauty's sweet pea. Sturdy stalks of petty power were springing up, and blossoms of privilege would soon be bright on them, petalled with scarlet thorns to keep envious, pulling hands away.

They stopped at Berkeley Street Chapel, took the coffin from the hearse, carried it into the church porch. A priest in cassock, surplice, and stole came dashing out, carrying a bucket and brush, muttered a few Latin invocations with bored celerity, scattered a few swift drops of water over the coffin, and ran swiftly back into church again. If the pathetic, careworn body in the coffin had been a countess, hell's bells wouldn't have kept an archbishop from sprinkling the holy water sweetly, saying the prayers slow, giving the reception an elegant and ornate look — God giving the lady value for her money and rank. Hurry up, hurry up; they carried the coffin into the church; sacristan pointed hurriedly where to put it; ran off, then; for the look of the mourners promised no tip. Hurry up. Then they went out, the old man staying behind to pray, and keep her company for a little longer. Hurry up. Sean and the rest climbed to the top of the hearse, and sat around it, their legs dangling, looking like a freak-frieze of grotesques, set in black marble, broken away from a main design.

—That old man'll catch his death in those wet clothes, said Sean.

—What's the odds, if he does aself? asked a neighbour. His children are so busy with themselves that they have time only to notice now and again that he's still there. If he catches it bad, the wind an' the rain'll be after doin' him a good turn.

A tiny vignette of the Civil War: the big church, with the light on the altar; the chalky statues of glum saints, green, blue, and brown, gawking down at the figure of an old man kneeling beside the coffin that held what remained of one who had been his lifelong comrade.

COMRADES

AH! The bould Sean! A hand clapped down on Sean's shoulder, while on his way to a sit-down in Stephen's Green, where he could dreamily deny the tale of a God existent, and test the woe of the world with thought. Sean turned, to see a wide, comradely grin on the broad, innocent face of Mick Clonervy, a rancher's son from the County of Kiltoran, whom Sean got to know when he came with cattle to Dublin, prodding hundreds of the frightened animals on to the boats for the English markets.

—Ah! me bould Sean, an' how is every bit o' yeh? asked Mick Clonervy again, his two little grey eyes agleam under the wide-peaked cap.

But Mick was Michael now. A colonel in a fine new army, one of Ireland's Own. The superfine green cloth of his uniform, the gay, dignified strip on his shoulder-strap, denoting his rank, the highly polished brown leggings guarding his sturdy limbs, or the splendid, saucily peaked cap took away no sign of the man's clumsily patterned nature. No matter how smartly he might be saluted, or how often, Colonel Michael Clonervy was Mick Clonervy still. His wide, fleshy face now beamed with joyous embarrassment as he noticed Sean scanning the prim richness of his uniform. There wasn't a button astray on it. Even the ugly-looking holster, where a gun was nesting, was neatly latched by a tongue of leather linked to a button of gleaming brass. But the wearer of this glory was ill at ease. The smart, elegant uniform fitted the body, but it failed to fit the spirit of the man. He would have felt himself happier in the old clothes spattered with cow-dung to give them taste and character. Even in the Free State Army a sergeant's job would have been a little difficult for the kindly, heavy-limbed fellow. His eyes, grey, cunning, and bright, peered at Sean from under the officer's cap. The soft, swelling, childish cheeks, red as ripe apples, the unsteady mouth, circled by thick, leechy lips, told Sean that here was a young man without a chance of ever being other than he had been years and years ago. No garment, however rich, no dignity or brightness of uniform, could make this fellow be other than Mick Clonervy who so efficiently manœuvred his father's cattle on to the boats, heedless of the sickening steam from their distended nostrils, or the slippery patches of their dung through which his hobnailed boots had one time so safely and so merrily splashed.

—This new corps of officers, thought Sean, will never do. Utterly unaware of the elements of a military life, and has no desire to learn them. How are things, Mick? he asked, hardly knowing what to say.

—Merry enough, ould son, responded Mick. Don't fret — the Republicans are finished forever. But wait till you hear: Standin' with two C.I.D. boys, guardin' a big house in Donnybrook, an' questionin' one o' them about his goin's-on with a maid in a house down further, gettin' her in the family way while he was on duty — a big breach o' discipline; an' th' damned liar thryin' to make out it was all an accident; when who d'ye think comes sailin' up th' steps on a visit but the long-haired poet, Yeats himself. You should have heard th' click o' me heels as I gave him a firm salute!

—Did he take any notice?

—Why wouldn't he take notice? 'Course he took notice; Yeats is no fool. An' he noticed that th' other two go-boys didn't budge from their loungin' against th' door-pillars, one o' them with a cigarette stuck in his ugly mouth, puffin' away. No manners! Goodmornin', General, says he — general, mind you! Only a common colonel, Misther Yeats, I says, Colonel Clonervy; just plain colonel, I says, sir.

—Yez are heirs to a great thradition, says he, while he waited for th' door t'open; th' Fianna Fail.

Sean's glance followed the Colonel's, eyeing casually a young man cycling smoothly past them, his face turned towards the Green, away from them, humming *Home to Our Mountains* from *Il Trovatore*, the cyclist's head moving emotionally to the gentle swing of the tune.

—A great thradition, says Yeats, went on the Colonel, his eyes following the quietly-moving cyclist; th' famous Fenians, says he — McCool, Oisin, Oscar; thruth on their lips, sthrength in their arms, an' purity in their hearts, says he. You're tellin' me! I says to him. Them was th' days, sir. An' listen, Misther Yeats, I says, we have as much to do today; for we have to demonsthrate a good example now to th' whole o' th' livin' world! Then th' door opened, an' th' house swallied him up.

Silently, their glances followed the lilting cyclist going along the side of the Green. When he came opposite to a tall house where Free State troops were quartered, he glided gracefully to the path's edge, guiding his machine between other cycles resting against the kerb. Still mounted, but resting his left foot on the pavement to balance himself, they saw him glance swiftly round, whip with his right hand something hanging from his waist, swing the object fast, let it go, and send it flying through the air, smashing a pane of glass, and lobbing into the room beyond.

Half deafened by a swift explosion, tempered by screams of agony from the room where the bomb had burst, shrinking from a flying shower of glass, a spear of it slicing in two the ear of a passer-by,

Sean saw Clonervy snatch the leather latch loose from the holster, pull out the gun, level it, and pull a trigger that responded only with sharp derisive clicks.

—Th' ignorant, lazy lowser of a skip's forgot to load it! he shouted, red rage masking his wide, innocent face; th' bastard sent me out helpless as a kid! Then the Colonel rushed off towards the tumult as the thrower of the bomb launched himself forward on his bicycle with a swift push of his left foot, and went tearing down the street as fast as his feet could turn the pedals.

Sean saw two plain-clothes men come running down the steps, through smoke that curled from the broken windows, to join the Colonel; saw him load his empty gun with what he got from one of the plain-clothes men; saw them spring on to bicycles resting by the kerb, to launch forward, each with an angry push from the left foot, and go careering away in the direction taken by him who had thrown the bomb.

An ambulance came tinkling up to sort out things; while Sean hurried into the Green to sit in serenity beside the lake to try to sort out things, too, among the indifferent ducks and drakes.

The bomb-thrower had dodged and twisted down, through, in and out of the lowliest streets in the district, meeting no-one showing a sign of suspicion. He could go easy now. He entered a long street, cycled slow to the end, and, as he was turning out of it, glanced back to see, in the distance, three men on bicycles coming along, one in the Free State uniform and two in civvies. He pedalled furiously up the street into which he had turned, and, at the end, glanced back again, and saw that they were still coming steadily behind, a long way off. Then he knew they were after him.

He raced along the Waterloo Road, down the Appian Way, down, and out of Belgrave Road, and whirled into Rathmines. The lady-nurses out with their lady-children, when they saw the speed of the cyclist and the speed of those who followed him, pushed their pompous perambulators into a canter away from where they were, for they knew not when shooting might burst out upon them. Passers-by hesitated, halted, then slid to a house's shelter till the panting danger had gone from view. Out of Rathgar, into Dartry, went the riders; on and on through devious ways along the river Dodder, into Rathfarnham, heading on fast, fast, faster for the Dublin hills; the lonely leader glancing back, with sweat trickling down into his eyes, murmuring, murmuring as life rolled off behind him like thread unwinding from a turning spool:

—They'll get me yet; they'll get me yet! He pedalled hard, he pedalled harder, children playing near stopping to cheer him as he shot madly by them; cheering again, after some time, when the three following, body-bent, went headlong past them, too.

—Wondher who th', who th' bugger is? jerked out one of the plain-clothes pursuers.

—Lanehin, panted the uniformed officer, Clonervy, leading; seen his gob, an' he turning' th' corner. Lanehin. Captain of the crush I was in when we were fightin' th' Tans. Lanehin — a bastard!

—Seems as if he's not got a gun on him, either, panted the plain-clothes one.

On the top of the pensive lake a modest brown duck came swimming shorewords from a pursuing drake, his brown coat, dabbed with velvety black, ashine; his glittering green head and neck stretched designedly. She climbed the shelving bank in a hurry, shook a shower of moisture off her, and made a waddling run for the grass beyond the path. He climbed calmly out, shook himself free of the clinging drops, his curly twist of a tail quivering, then waddled, slow and determined, after her.

—George Moore's Anatidean lover and his lass, thought Sean, envying the drake's comfort in having to solve but one problem at a time.

Rougher and rocky the road grew. Upupuphill now, all the time. The man who had thrown the grenade had to stand on the pedals to force them round. Sweat from thigh, chest, and back was seeping out through his clothes. No; he hadn't made a good get-away. He should never have come to the frown of these lonely hills. Better to have stayed in the busy streets. Jesus, Mary, and Joseph, he was in a bad way. And he only twenty-two. Not even that, for there was a month and more to go yet. Christ, me heart'll burst if I have to keep this up!

He slid from the bicycle sideways, letting it fall to the ground, leaving it there, while he dashed into, and pushed through, a hedge on to the rising slope of a hill, tangled with the spiny gorse, and roughly pompous with patches of purple heather. The cycle-clips had been dragged from his ankles, and the bottoms of his trousers streamed about like sombre ribbons worn by visitants to a mournful fair. Blood trickled down his legs where thorn and spine of gorse had torn the flesh. He ran on, crouching, trying to shelter his flight behind every bush, every clump of heather; he climbed in a tearing way over rocky mounds, never minding the bruising and breaking of his skin. He splashed through noisy, gurgling brooks, the gentle flow of the water cooling his aching feet and weakened ankles, now twisting under him from the stress of the fierce and long run from the terror and death following behind.

—Good God! he murmured as he raced unsteadily over the tough grass, through the thorns in bush and brake, look at the state of me trousers!

He could go no further. He was stumbling about now like a drunken fool. His legs were getting numb. He could go no further, Not another step. His whole mind encouraged his panting body to take a rest. How often he was angry when his mother used to say. You look dead tired, Kevin; you really ought to go to bed. Oh, God! If he was only at home now with the old woman urging him to go up and lie down and rest and have a good sleep!

A few more staggering steps brought him to an old stone wall, standing somewhat higher than his waist. Get behind this; lie down; sleep. He leaned his hands on the top of it, and tried to spring over; tried hard, but no spring was left in him. He leaned heavily on it, and tried to drag himself to the top and over, but no strength remained in him to do it. He spread his arms out along the top of the wall, rested his breast against it, closed his eyes, and stayed still. He'd wait here. Here in the hills. Just as he was, he'd stay. He had no gun, no gun. He had thought that after the grenade had been thrown, if any cordon was flung round where he might be, he'd have a fine chance of getting through without a gun. A mistake; a big mistake. Well, it should soon come now. Unarmed, he'd just have to take it quietly. Pity he couldn't take a chip or two out of one of them before he passed out. Couldn't though; he had no gun. Not a ghost of a chance now. Damned fool, that O.C. of his who advised him to go on the mission without a gun. *He's* all right — curse o' God on him! He shivered at the thought of sudden death. Soon now. Creeping up to him, maybe, to take him unawares. Slowly and steadily, he turned his throbbing head to see whether they were near or far or absent altogether. They were there. Only thirty feet away. The three of them; sitting ten yards apart, in a semicircle, on a grassy mound, watching him; each with a cocked gun in his right hand; the uniformed man in the centre. Jasus! sitting down, resting, and staring at him! Mick Clonervy, sergeant of his company when they had both fought the Tans; a colonel now in the Free State Army; promotion, sure! Sell his own mother for a yellow tab.

There were the two of them again! The brown duck, like a maid hid in a Franciscan habit, spurting forward when she felt the pursuer coming too close; waddling swift from the temptation following her obstinately and unerringly in the desire of the drake, brilliant as a courtier in a gay king's garden. Sean's glance followed them till both were hidden behind a curtain of flowering currant.

—Turn right round, Lanehin, shouted the Colonel; right round till we all get a full look at you! Sthretch your arms out each side of you, along the top of the wall, and rest like that till we're ready for you. Stir an inch, and we'll plug you full of holes, you creeping, cowardly, murdhering bastard!

Lanehin did as he was told, stretching his arms along the top of the wall, and leaning his back where his breast had leaned before. He watched them through half-closed weary eyes. Watched them resting there, calmly; eating something from a paper bag and drinking from a flask. Good thing they didn't come for him at once. They'd feel better after having eaten; and they'd have time to think better of what they may have thought of doing in the heat of the chase. Give them time to cool. He saw the Colonel throw away the paper bag, and one of the others putting the flask away in a breast-pocket. Now he'd see. No, not yet; they had taken cigarettes from a packet, and each was now quietly smoking, while they chatted together. The Colonel broke off a sprig of blossoming heather and slowly and carefully fixed it in the side of his cap. Suddenly he sprang to his feet, saying sharply, Come on, boys, let's get going; we can't stop here all night.

He advanced with his two men towards Lanehin; advanced without a word, till they were so close Lanehin fancied he felt their breaths tickling his cheeks. They stood as they had sat — in a closer semicircle, staring curiously at him. He stared back at them for a little; dropped his gaze; lifted his head again, knowing not what to do, for his mind overflowed with prayer, and he felt his bowels turning to water. They were quietly gazing at him, saying nothing, not lifting a hand.

—I surrendher, he said plaintively at last; what are you going to do with me? I surrendher.

—A wise thing to do, said one of the civilian-clad men.

—After all, went on the frightened man, there wasn't a lot of damage done.

—Oh, not a lot, said the Colonel; you're right there; only one of us had an eye knocked into a jelly, and another got his chest rieved asundher.

—What are you going to do with me? Make me a prisoner o' war; I surrendher.

—What are we going to do with you? echoed Colonel Clonervy. Bring you home, sit you on our knees, and nurse you? Would you like us to do that for you, eh?

—And let him sleep late in the morning, added one of the civilian-clad men.

—Make me a prisoner, murmured the unhappy lad, the hoarseness of fear darkening his voice; a prisoner of war — I surrendher.

—You asked us that before, said the Colonel; but it's easier said than done. The house at home's too crowded to take another soul. What are you sweating for, man? Are you afraid of what's coming to you, or what? I thought all Republicans were above that sort of thing.

—I'm an old comrade of yours, Mick, the young man pleaded.

—Sure I know that well, said the Colonel heartily, and I'll say this much — for the sake of oul' times, we won't let you suffer long.

—Jesus! whimpered the half-dead lad, yous wouldn't shoot an old comrade, Mick!

The Colonel's arm holding the gun shot forward suddenly, the muzzle of the gun, tilted slightly upwards, splitting the lad's lips and crashing through his chattering teeth.

—Be Jasus! We would, he said, and then he pulled the trigger.

—*Looka, Ma! shrilled a childish voice behind Sean; looka what th' ducks is doin'!*

Sean turned swift to see a fair young mother, her sweet face reddening, grasp a little boy's arm, wheel him right round, saying as she pointed out over the innocent lake: Look at all the other ducks, dear, over there on the water!

The drake had reached his goal, and he was quivering in the violent effort to fulfil God's commandment to multiply and replenish the earth.

THE CLERGY TAKE A HAND

The clergy take a hand, the clergy make a stand,
With bell, book, and candle O,
All over Spireland!

THE bishops now decided to bless one side by cursing the other from the Maynooth valley of squinting windows. For a long time they had been cautious, dubious, wondering which party had the bigger power behind it, and which of them would be the more amenable. They now realised that a good many of the people wanted anything that might bring peace; that Britain's power was behind the Free State; and that in this Free State a free people would have a dog's chance of saying a word, or a byword, against the clergy. So one fine morning, as Sean roved out, an episcopal declarion appeared in all the morning papers, fresh with dieu, condemning Unauthorised Murder on the part of the Republicans, implying to many minds that the same kind of progressive activity, on the part of the Free State followers, came within, according to the clergy, the shadow of canonical condonation. They seemed to be investing it with a kind of legal validity. But the outcry against it was so loud and clear that the clergy withdrew the manifesto the next day, shoving out a more slyly-written one in its place. So from the bishops the minor clergy got their cue: the priest followed the bishop, the deacon the priest. The holy catholic church was against the Republicans, and the Republican cause was lost. The odour of piety was mixed in with the fight where bayonets were plunged into bosoms, and brains scattered with blows from rifle-butts, so that Eire was kept busy writing down the deeds of her sons, in fair, legible characters, in the big book of death. The number of executions mounted higher; but everything was done in a rather nice way. One of the Free State ministers told us all that — 'the men who were executed this morning were, perhaps, uneducated, illiterate men, never meaning, perhaps, to get into a situation like this; men, perhaps, of no political convictions. We provided for these men all the spiritual assistance we could muster to help them in their passage to eternity. We are people who realise that man is made in the image and likeness of God, and we treat man as such. When a man is going to his death he always gets a priest.'

Now could anything be more Christian, more catholic, more decent? What nicer combination could there be than rope and cross — a natural blend. Religion, religion, what crimes are done under thy cloak of light! The jails were full, and the executions, before done to a minuet, now advanced to the quicker steps of a jig tune.

The venerable Bishop of Blarney became so hostile and bitter to Republicans that the following letter, signed by the Officer Commanding for and on behalf of Republican prisoners in Cork jails, appeared in the Republican Journal, *Eire*, on Saturday, the 23rd of June 1923:

This Bishop of Blarney, who, when the Black and Tan terror was at its worst, excommunicated the Irish Republican soldiers, and thereby nerved the British to carry out the Executions in Cork County, has now so far forgotten the principles of the religion he professes as to incite the Free State troops to murder prisoners. This incitement he uttered when addressing little children at the sacrament of Confirmation. The Catholic Faith has stood many assaults in Ireland. Its latest trial is to withstand the action of a Prelate of the Church who incites bloody-minded soldiery to further atrocities in the hearing of little Irish children at a religious ceremony. The following letter (the paper goes on) was sent to this man by the prisoners in Corca Dorcha jails: To the Most Reverend Dr. Cockadoo, Lord Bishop of Blarney; My Lord, we have read your infamous and vindictive outburst in Wednesday's *Cork Examiner* at an address given by you at the Confirmation Service in St. Peter's and St. Paul's Church. It would be a misrepresentation of fact to say that we were surprised, for we all know too well the source to be surprised at anything that emanated therefrom. We have, on previous occasions, endured outbursts in the same vein, but they were treated with the contempt they deserved. But your latest invective, however, considering the implication that runs through it, and considering the occasion on which it was spoken, calls for a response.

We wish you to understand that your opinion does not weigh with us in the slightest; the principles for which we stand are immune from such petty outbursts as yours, actuated as they are by deep-rooted imperialistic and slavish tendencies. Your incitement to murder, however, calls for strong comment, and we intend to make it. It is nothing short of scandalous that you should have chosen Confirmation day to annunciate a doctrine of pure and unadulterated murder, and endeavour to inculcate the children's receptive minds with that venomous antagonism to freedom and all it stands for, which animates your own speech and action. It is appalling to think that the Altar of God is turned by you into a political and partizan platform, from which you give free run to your own personal opinions, leaving them open to be interpreted by the uneducated as the word of God. That you would go further, and imply that the Imperial Free State troops were very lenient for not shooting all that stood for Irish independence, and that we should have been very grateful for being flung into evil-smelling, foul jails, instead of being summarily executed, is outrageous. Moreover, that you should have chosen for audience little children, many of whose relatives were doubtless imprisoned, is unprecedented.

We have too long had foisted upon us, without protest, as the teaching of our Divine Saviour, the political opinions of one who was always thoroughly unnational, and who always endeavoured to impede progress towards freedom, even to the extent of denouncing and excommunicating those who had the slightest leaning towards that holy cause. On Tuesday you surpassed yourself, and definitely implied that, had the Free State soldiers chosen to fill the graves with the bodies of Republicans, their methods would have received your commendation. You instilled into the minds of your juvenile hearers, at one of the more solemn moments of their lives, that to fight for National freedom is a crime which fully merits to be punished by death, and that such punishment would have the full sanction of the Church. That such a murderous doctrine should be preached in the house of God to innocent children, would give grounds for doubting the sanity of the preacher, were he other than your lordship's self; but we quite realise that your venomous mind is perfectly capable of it. You are now what you always were.

You are *now* an expressed exponent of the will of the people. When the people elected an overwhelming Republican majority, it did not enter into your slavish mind to recognise it, although the Republican Government was then, *de jure* and *de facto*, the government of Ireland. Now, however, that the settlement, dictated by England's Government, has been accepted by some of your countrymen, behold, you are a stout champion of the will of the people! We will not accept our politics from you, nor do we intend to allow you, unchallenged, to allocate to yourself the power of deciding our fate, even though you may have chosen to become the champion of a much bigger opinion, which leads us to believe what we have for some time suspected — that the campaign of executions received the tacit approval, if not the official sanction, of the Bishops of Ireland. O/C Prisoners. Signed for and on behalf of the prisoners in Free State jails.

The bishops again! The Men of Ninety-Eight; the Fenians; Parnell; and now the unfortunate Republicans in the Irish jails recommended to the hangman, or to a firing-squad. A way of thought that seems to be nothing new to the Vatican bishops. No episcopal voice raised, nor word spoken, asking the executioners to go slow. Republicanism had in it the seed of anti-clericalism, so let it be banished by rifle-fire, or dangle dead at the end of a rope. St. Patrick'll see they get their strict due wherever they may have to go. Let their denouncing voices be smothered in the coldness of inanimate clay. Maybe shamrocks will grow over them. Recite the Office for the Dead; pray for the sweet repose of their souls: they can do no harm to us now. Don't be stingy or mean to the poor dead chaps. *Requiem aeternam dona eis, Domine* to all the dead of the Lost Legion of the Republican Rear-Guard. They can do no more harm to us; no more harm to us now. Another one? Two more? Ah, well, we'll soon be used to it. *Requiem aeternam dona eis, Domine.* What? The very ones who had thrown them into jail, or who had sent them to the firing-squad, were often the very fellows who had encouraged them, had persuaded, had even put them under oath to uphold the precious ideals for which they were now perishing? No! D'ye tell me that! Poor boys! Well, that's not really our business. Good will come out of it, never fear. Authority comes from God, and we must approve it, even though it makes Eire's eyelids dark with the shadow of death. No sigh for mercy from a single bishop for these misguided young men and women, though they were, with these clericals, of one faith, one hope, one baptism; yet, many years after, the bishop of bishops was to send a finely-polished plea of mercy for a saurian-souled ruffian who had slain thousands and had tortured tens of thousands, with satisfaction, and in great glee.

And Sean, alone on a Dublin pathway, thought that since they could pass by so sedately on the other side while young members of their own flock were going through the agonies of execution, how rancorous, how cool and bitter they would be in handing over to death the Socialist, the Communist who might deny their importance and ignore their power in those lands where the bishop and the priest had in their white, jewel-circled hands the keys of the kingdom of life as well as those of the kingdom of heaven. Well, he had done his best to get a word in edgeways. He had written a one-act play, satirising the contesting parties and putting official Labour against the wall for its stupid and selfish pursuit of jobs, instead of flinging themselves between the opposing guns, calling out the question of which of you will fire first! Sean could never hear a word about his little play, though he had sent it to *The Plain People*, and though he asked many who were connected with the distribution of the Journal. It was ten years after, when he was living in London, that a priest from Kerry visited him and reminded him of his play, *The Robe of Rosheen*, which had appeared so long ago in the Republican paper, though ne'er another soul, apparently, had ever noticed it.

He had shifted away from the active Ireland, and was growing contentedly active in himself. Instead of trying to form Ireland's life, he would shape his own. He would splash his thoughts over what he had seen and heard; keep eyes and ears open to see and hear what life did, what life had to say, and how life said it; life drunk or sober; life sickly or sturdy; life sensible or half demented; life well-off or poor; life on its knees in prayer, or shouting up a wild curse to heaven's centre. His first play, *The Frost in the Flower*, which he had sent to the Abbey Theatre, had been returned, with a note saying how interested they were in the play, which was promising, but one of the main characters had been too critical, reminding them of various characters in Abbey plays, a characteristic that tended to become tiresome and irritating.

Sean guessed that this comment was wrong, and a little ridiculous, since he had been in the theatre but twice, and had seen only *Blight*, by Gogarty, *Androcles and the Lion*, by Shaw, *The Jackdaw*, by Lady Gregory, and another one-act play built up on a short story by James Stephens. He had seen nothing that he could try to imitate. The play dealt with a young man, a lay teacher in a Christian Brothers' school, who, though full of confidence on gigantic questions he was never called upon to touch, was timid as a new-born mouse over simple questions concerning himself. He got a very small salary from the Brothers, paid to him quarterly, mostly in sixpenny pieces and threepenny bits. A teacher-ship in elementary mathematics and elementary English fell vacant in a Technical School, the gift of a Dublin Council Committee, and Sean's timid friend, certain he hadn't a chance of getting it, applied for the job. To his frightened dismay, he was elected by a fine vote, and everyone in the parish brought him all kinds of books to help in preparing him for the work he would have to do. Though he had the ability, he hadn't the will-power; and the play ended in the midst of a party given in his honour, at which it became known that he had resigned from the job, to become the scorn of his family and the joke of the parish. The second one, called *The Harvest Festival*, dealt with the efforts of militant members of the unskilled unions to put more of the fibre of resistance to evil conditions of pay and life into the hearts and minds of the members of the craft unions whose gospel was that what was good enough for the fathers was good enough for the sons. The action took place in the busy preparations made by a church for holding the annual harvest festival, which the Anglo-catholics sneeringly called the Feast of Saint Pumpkin and all Vegetables. The play brought back to Sean a letter saying that the work was well conceived, but badly executed; with an added note from Mr. Lennox Robinson, then the Manager of the Abbey Theatre, saying that he liked very much the character of the clergy-man in the play,—which was something, though not enough for Sean.

A shadow showing a familiar figure passed by the window, and formed a memory in his mind: of Father Michael O'Flanagan. An unselfish man, with more than a little courage to make him a marked man; a brilliant speaker, with a dangerous need of more respect for bishops dressed in a little brief authority; a priest spoiled by too many good qualities. He had been priest of the poverty-stricken parish of Cliffoney in Sligo, and when, one cold, ice-proud winter, he saw his people shivering for the lack of fuel, he said to them — Go ye even unto the boglands where there is turf and to spare, and gather all ye need; and they said to him — How can we venture to do this thing, seeing that the bogland is owned by one who got the place from God? And he answered them, saying — Let him, of his plenty, give unto you of your need. They answered, saying — We have gone to him, and, behold, he turned us away, using us despite-fully, setting the dogs on us, and saying — Begone, for none but those who can buy are welcome here. And Father O'Flanagan, raising his hand to heaven, saith unto them — Go, and take what ye need, for it is written, The earth is the Lord's, and the fullness thereof; so go again, for the Lord will not refuse ye in your extremity; and take what ye need, and the Lord will bless the doing of it. And they went, and took of the turf every man, according to his need; and the owner thereof was afraid, for he was but one, and they were many.

But it came to the ears of the righteous bishops whose deep affection and profound respect for the common people, the children of God, could not be denied by any fair-minded person. The bishops knew that this sort of thing would not be good for the people; that the finest way of keeping them close to God was to disencourage any attempt to cock them up with any kind of comfort. Their flock came first with them. So they laid hold of the foolish Father Flanagan and drove him from his parish. Time to do it, too, for in a few places held by the Republicans, red flags were fluttering over the roofs. God Almighty, what was catholic Ireland coming to! Another priest was sent to replace Father Flanagan; but the poor people locked the chapel door, and so the poor man had to climb in through a window to celebrate Mass; but lacking any support of thought or action, the poor people of Cliffoney soon had to submit, and resume their old pilgrimage along the way of hunger and cold. If they were cold for want of fuel and had no money to pay for it, then they must remain cold; if they were hungry for want of food, and had no money to pay for it, then they must remain hungry; and all these light afflic-tions would work for them an exceeding weight of glory in the world to come. So Father Flanagan wandered here and there, subdued, beaten, making odd speeches that became calmer and more reticent as the days passed, till he died in a quiet corner, forgotten by almost all, save the kindly bishops, who shook their mitred heads and mur-mured — Poor misguided man whom we could not help to a higher honour than a quiet death.

With a shake of his shoulders, Sean banished the memory of Father Flanagan's decline from a hawk to a hernshaw, and thought again of the plays he had written, and of those he would write. He had a fight of his own to make. There had been a good chance of his third play, *The Crimson in the Tri-Colour*, being produced, for Lady Gregory had written that she was very interested in it; that it was evident that the author had something in him; that Mrs. Rosebud was a delightful character and Mr. Rosebud a fine foil to her. A play that was somewhat confused, but one of ideas might be made from it. But it could not be put on till the Revolution was over; and it must be typed by the theatre, for no-one could possibly attempt the reading of such written manuscript a second time. And then came a letter from Mr. Robinson saying — that in moving from Clare Street to Foxrock, he had mislaid the play, and would Sean please furnish them with a copy. And Sean had clenched his teeth, for there was no copy; not even notes from which a copy might be built. So his last state was as bad as his first. A double jolt — one to mind and body, for a sick stomach followed a disturbed mind. So much hard work had gone for nothing.

There was nothing to do but forget, and go on; forget, and go on. He had made up his mind years ago that the Abbey Theatre curtain would go up on a play of his; and up it would go, sooner or later. First decide slowly and deeply whether it is in you to do a thing; if you decide that you can, then do it, even though it kept you busy till the very last hour of life. Maybe, too, the play would be found again; and, so, in the meantime, he would go on writing another play. A year after, or more, when he was just finishing the play he was working on, news came that the play was found; that it had been typed; that each of the Directors had read it, and that rejection was their final decision. Well, refusal wasn't so bitter now, for the new play was all but done. Now that he had another to offer, he felt no grievance; his heart was calm and steady. It was years after, when he had left Ireland forever, that bitterness, mingled with scorn, overtook him, for he began to realise that the plays refused by the Abbey Theatre were a lot better than many they had welcomed, and had played on to their stage with drums and colours

The young girl below was coughing again. He could see in his mind's eye the bed in which she lay, a heap of clothing, confused with the restless tossing and turning of one in an advanced state of consumption. A basement dweller, she lived with an old mother, a brother who was a plumber, and a little girl, child of a sister, who, too, had lived with consumption for years before she had died. They lived in a basement set of two rooms, one a bedroom, the other a kitchen. Two days before, the young brother had shown Sean the floor of the bedroom that had rotted under the oilcloth till the boards were of the texture of rain-soaked wallpaper. Sean and the young man had pointed this terrible condition of the room out to the sanitary inspector, and the family were living together in the kitchen while the landlord took his time to put in a new floor. Sean had advised Peter, the sick girl's brother, to get her into the Hospice for the Dying, since there was no hope of recovery, and grave danger that the rest of them should be infected with the repulsive complaint. The cringing girl had screamed an outcry against going, saying she was not as bad as that; she would rise out of it; she already felt her strength returning day by day; so they let her lie on, mixing their poor life with a poorer one still. Answering an appeal by the mother, Sean had gone down to try to persuade the sick girl; but she had turned her face to the wall, had cried the whole time, and screamed occasionally while he was there, so he had returned to his room without a word spoken. He had left her there in the glory of dying diseased, for, it is written, whom the Lord loveth, He chasteneth.

Anyway, it surely was the priest's job to get the dying girl to dimly realise the inevitable end of this illness in a tenement. But the priests, as far as Sean could see, were chary of crossing the border into the hidden horridness of a slum — the hidden Ireland! Usually, they'd hurry in to fortify the dying with the last rites of the church, and then hurry out again. No priest, as far as Sean knew, had ever visited this dying lass to say even the Lord be with thee. There wasn't much to be got out of these places. So the lass lay there, all that had been she, diminished now almost to the bones; animated now only with the large rich eyes, luminous with the glare of feverish fear, and the long, silky black hair coiling from the ridged skull down to the withered shoulders, and flowing mockingly over the bony breast. How often in the stilly night had he listened to the sad symphony of her coughing on her lonely bed in the miserable room below, unheard by mother or brother enveloped in the thickness of a tired sleep.

A knock sounded quick on the door, the door opened — as it usually did — before the last rap was given, and young Peter came into the room, fervour in his eyes, and a curious defiance shown in the stiffened contour of his shoulders.

—Look Sean, he said, rough and ready; look, I'm fed up! If she isn't taken out of this, we'll be all goin' to the grave together. The sisthers have a snug place for her in the Hospice for the Dying, an' I can't see why she's not willin' to go.

—No-one's willin' to go there, said Sean; we all take the last few steps to the grave as slow as possible. But, Peter, she'll be far more comfortable there than she can be where she is, and she won't die a second sooner.

—Amn't I tired tellin' her that! She's so damned selfish, she won't listen. She can't walk, an' she wouldn't be able to sit in a cab, so the only way is to get hold of the Fire Brigade Ambulance; but where the hell's th' fee to come from?

—From me, thought Sean; that's why he came here. He's asking for it round the corner. Aloud, he said, I'll lend the money, Peter. You can pay it back when things improve; though Sean well knew they would never improve enough to pour back the money jingling into his pocket. Six or seven new books gone west, he sighed. Look, he said aloud, don't tell her anything. Let the ambulance men come suddenly down on her, so that she won't have time to know what's happening when she's being whisked from the festered dusk of her bed to be brought away from the world forever.

—I'll go ring up the Hospice from the pub outside, said Peter, after Sean had handed him thirty pieces of silver, to say she's comin', an' then the ambulance to come an' take her off at once. I won't whisper a word till she's on the way. Thanks, Sean.

Another knock at the door, and before the two could look towards it, the tram-conductor, quick and excited, hurried into the room.

—He's found! he said breathless; found at last! Young Captain Wogan: away in a lone counthry lane, beyond Finglas, half hidden in hemlock. Taken out an' murdhered! Near unrecognisable; his belly kicked in, ears frayed, an eye gouged out, and the nose broken, with a bullet through his brain as an amen. The bastards only left a batthered memory of him! He sank down on the sofa, and wiped warm sweat from his brow. There's Irish freedom for you!

—But Wogan shot a man before he himself was shot, said Sean.

—Ay, in fair fight, though; and it was a clean shot; not like what made the thing I saw. Sweet Jesus, have mercy on th' poor lad's soul.

—I'm goin', Sean, said Peter at the door, to settle things finally, and he closed the door softly behind him.

The conductor pulled a chair to the fire, and sat down to brood.

Sean saw that the years were weighing heavy on his crouching shoulders; that the mane of hair was very grey now; and that the seamed hands shook slightly while he lighted his pipe: the model of an ageing *semper fidelis*.

They're lavishin' contracts on each other, said the conductor suddenly, a Senathor gettin' more for eggs, with cheaper tendhers for eggs, as good, refused, making as much as fifty quid a week clear; an' th' same with butther; an' I know a lamp-lighter who's a Free State Quarther-masther now, gettin' a lift for givin' th' contract to a friend for the fittin-out of his battalion. Holy God! what's catholic Ireland comin' to!

Sean heard the engine-whinge of the ambulance stopping beside the door; heard the heavy tread of the men carrying the stretcher through the sullied hall, heard the heavier, more carefully-planted steps going down, one two three, the basement steps, seeping with rottenness, on their errand of mercy — the love of God among the mildews. Then came silence, to be broken soon, Sean knew well. There it goes — a frightened, weary wail; frenzied too, like a soul descending, vanishing, before it ended, in a hurried, hacking fit of coughing.

Sean went to a window, and looked out on the street. The bright green leaves of the sycamore sapling were weaving patches of scarlet and gold into their quiet loveliness. A fine, fair evening, with a touch of a chill in the shining of the sun. Boys were playing at Free Staters and Republicans, their voices imitating the sound of bomb-burst and rifle-shot; shouting the slogans of each party at each other that were to bring peace and goodwill to Ireland. These had halted now from their mimic work of death and wounding to stare at the dull, dread ambulance, waiting with expansive bosom to receive a dying body. Sean heard the thud of the heavy feet again, walking this time slow and in unison through the hall, carrying what was now but the life of a lung-cough. He saw the red-shirted men go down the stone steps, on to the pathway, out to the wide-open door of the ambulance, carrying on the stretcher a flicker of life away from where a ruddier life had at last refused to live along with it. All Sean could see was a thin, frail hand, white as snow, clawing timidly at a brown blanket tumbled over the stretcher; a thin, white hand paying its last respects to the life it was losing.

—What's up, what's wrong? asked the tram-conductor, trying to stiffen the shoulders that had crouched too deep to straighten, and half turning towards where Sean stood.

—A citizeness being brought to the Hospice for the Dying to hand over a life that has lived too long.

—What's amiss with her?

—Consumption.

—That's not much to get excited about. We have more stringent things to think of today than a case of simple consumption.

—She was very young — just on the verge of womanhood; and, one time, she was handsome and gay.

—Aw, what signifies that, Sean? That sort o' thing's a daily occurrence in these places. You ought to be well used to them things be now. She's a lucky lady compared with poor Jack Wogan. Looka, he went on, tapping Sean's knee when Sean had sat down again by the fire, I'll betcha anything you like, the clergy'll never raise a hand or say a word to stop this quiet, cool killin' of our poor best boys. As men — I say nothin' again' them as priests, mind you, Sean, — as men, it's poor Saint Pathrick himself must be woebegone lookin' down to see the clergy dumb while th' counthry's becomin' a murdherin' fiasco!

Saint Patrick, thought Sean; holy Saint Patrick, pray for us! Dear saint of our Isle; the isle of bullets, beads, and bombs.

Beads round every rifle sending a bullet to kill a man; beads twined round every rope, prepared to hang another.

Upon thy dear children bestow a sweet smile. The tear and the smile. The tear was there, all right; so what we want, now,

Saint Patrick, is a smile, a sweet smile. So Saint Patrick, jewel of the Gaels, pack all your troubles in your oul' kitbag, and smile, smile, smile.

BLESSED BRIDGET O' COOLE

THERE she was before him. The lean, wand-like arm of Lennox Robinson had waved her out of her chair in a dark corner of the Abbey Theatre office; waved her out to meet Sean, whose play, at last, had been accepted for production. There she was, a sturdy, stout little figure soberly clad in solemn black, made gay with a touch of something white under a long, soft, black silk veil that covered her grey hair and flowed gracefully behind half-way down her back. A simple brooch shyly glistened under her throat, like a bejewelled lady making her first retreat, feeling a little ashamed of it. Her face was a rugged one, hardy as that of a peasant, curiously lit with an odd dignity, and softened with a careless touch of humour in the bright eyes and the curving wrinkles crowding around the corners of the firm little mouth. She looked like an old, elegant nun of a new order, a blend of the Lord Jesus Christ and of Puck, an order that Ireland had never known before, and wasn't likely to know again for a long time to come.

The first night was very disappointing, for few came, and only thirteen pounds' worth of tickets were bought; the second night was much better, for it was more than half full; and the third capped the previous two, for the house was packed. Going to the theatre early, Sean enjoyed a look of ecstasy on the Old Lady's face as she stood to watch the people gathering round her little theatre. She ran to him when she saw him, caught his hand in hers, and led him out to see the queues forming a long, long trail right round the famous building. Well, he had done what he had set himself to do seven or more years ago: he had mounted a play of his on the Abbey stage. Odd, he felt no great elation; no more than he would have felt in the middle, or at the end, of a speech in Irish delivered before a crowd of Gaels. He felt, though, as he stood quiet in the vestibule, that he had crossed the border of a little, but a great, new kingdom of life, and so another illusion was born in his poor susceptible soul. He didn't know enough then that it was no great thing to be an Abbey playwright; and, afterwards, when he knew a lot more, he was glad he had suffered himself to feel no jubilation to mar his future by thinking too much of a tiny success: life remained a mystery to him. He thought, not of what he had done, but of what he had to do in the form and substance of his second play; realising, though unaware of it at the time, that to be a great playwright was a very different thing from merely being one who had had one, two, or even three, plays produced by the Abbey Theatre. Coming out of the theatre, however, he shook himself, thinking in himself that sufficient for the day is the good thing thereof. Some time after, he sent in two one-act plays, *Cathleen Listens In* and *The Cooing of Doves*; the first a skit on the Irish politics of the day, the second full of wild discussions and rows in a public-house. The first play was taken by the Abbey, the other returned, and later was used to form the second act of another play. This was the first shock given to Sean by the selective committee of the theatre, for the second work was definitely better as a play than the first. This was the first jolt he got, but he was to get many more before he was much older, and from the same source, too.

The third play was the biggest success of all, for the theatre was booked out in a few days for the whole week. Lady Gregory began to get young again, for all the weight of her seventy years and more. Hands everywhere were shaking Sean's. After his first play, during the recess, the Abbey Company had engaged the theatre to produce a play of their own selection, to keep themselves from the sin of idleness. The play they choose was Ervine's *Mary, Mary, Quite Contrary*; and Sean went to it as a token of his thanks for what they had done for him in the performance of his two works. He was damned glad he did. There he saw, for the first time, an actor, Barry Fitzgerald, glorifying comedy on the Abbey stage. He had never met the man, and no-one had ever mentioned his name to him. Seething with excitement, when the play ended, Sean ran behind the stage to pour out his enthusiasm into the unwilling ears of the other actors. Fitzgerald's not bad, he was told, when he gets a part that exactly suits him. Not bad? echoed Sean; why, he's a born clown! And, when he went with his third play, he had a suggestion for the cast: Fitzgerald was to play the chief comedy part in it. Mr. Robinson demurred, and mentioned the name of another fine actor, F. J. McCormick, for the part; but Sean held firm for Fitzgerald, knowing in his heart that he, and he alone, could get the arrogant, boozy humour from the character. Fitzgerald himself was very hesitant about taking it on, and Sean, with another member of the Company, Gaby Fallon, who had a very fine understanding of acting, stage and production, spent a long time arguing, demonstrating, and cursing, before Fitzgerald finally could be convinced he would do well in the part. The first night showed Dublin that Fitzgerald stood in the front rank of comedy actors, and Sean and Lady Gregory were delighted.

Letters came asking him for his autograph; he was stopped in the street by levelled fountain-pens and pencils held firm by persons demanding his signature on scraps of paper; notes, bearing dignified addresses on their summits, came from others, announcing that They would be At Home on a certain day, at a precise hour, with a hope, in letters of purest gold, that he would be found among the number knocking nicely at Their big hall doors; and, lastly, a letter from Mr. Robinson inviting him to a monthly dinner furnished by a Thirteen Club (or some name of that kind), with a gilded addendum that W. B. Yeats would be there. The ritual was held in a well-known Dublin restaurant bearing a sturdy poetical name. This invitation couldn't be set aside, for it was one conferring real honour; so, trimly dressed and neat as he could make himself, Sean hurried

off to mingle with the elect people of Ireland in a ceremonial meal.
Hiding his nervousness, Sean quietly greeted Mr. Robinson and
Arthur Shields, brother to Barry Fitzgerald, who gently led him, the
first before, the second behind, to a table for three, hedged safely in
a corner of the room. Away in the dim distance, a far larger table
served a number of persons whom Sean did not know yet, though,
through a murmur of submissive conversation, he heard the booming voice of Yeats chatting in a lordly lilt about Utumara, Brahmin
Mohini, birds born out of the fire, the two inflows to man's nature
— the one common to him and all animals, which is natural; and
the second, which is intellectual, coming from the fire. Yeats murmured about coming through the fire as if it were but coming
through the rye; going on from that to chatter about *anima hominis*
and *anima mundi* and spirits that walked only once on a Sunday,
while his listeners cocked their ears and bowed their heads, murmuring, *Lord, Lord, thou hast the words of infernal life.*

It was all very mysterious to Sean, and he realised that he had not
yet entered within the veil of the temple, and still was allowed to but
stand reverent on the doorstep. So he did what he could to ingratiate
himself with his hosts, eating what he thought was a badly-cooked
meal as delightfully as he could; answering the questions put to
him as wisely as possible; but discovering that he knew nothing
about writers that were common names in the mouths of those who
sat beside him. No, he had never seen or read *The Life of Man*, by
Andreiev, or *Falling Leaves*, by Giacosa, or *Monna Vanna* and
Joyzelle, by Maeterlinck; no, nor Benavente's *Passion Flower*, or
Pirandello's *Right You Are (If You Think So)*; while Sean whispered
the names of Shaw and Strindberg, which they didn't seem to catch,
though he instinctively kept firm silence about Dion Boucicault,
whose works he knew as well as Shakespeare's; afterwards provoking an agonised My Gawd! from Mr. Robinson, when he stam-
mered the names of Webster, Ford, and Massinger. So Sean
hunched his shoulders, and sat silent, while the other two went in
and came out with arguments about them and about the works of
playwrights whose names Sean had never heard of, much less
read. He shut an ear to the talk nearby, and cocked the other to the
voice of Yeats blossoming into a fuller booming about Megarithma,
who had told him he must live by bread and water and avoid woods,
because the woods concentrated the solar rays; afterwards asking
himself why woods concentrated the solar rays, and deciding to
reject that part of the counsel as an error (Petrushka deciding to

fight rather than to run away); though Sean wondered if he didn't know why the solar rays did, or did not, concentrate in woods, how he could decide that what Megarithma said must be an error; but the voice went on booming about the divine spirit of the path Samekh, the golden heart that was the central point of the cabbalistic Tree of Life, corresponding to the Sephiroth Tippereth. The rest round the table bowed their minor heads, murmuring *This same is a voice that is more than the wind among the reeds.*

Sean was awakened out of the booming by the voice of Mr. Robinson asking him if he had enjoyed the dinner, Sean dazedly and innocently replying with The Rhubarb and Custard were Fine, thanks, but the rest of the things were badly cooked; to be startled by Mr. Robinson ejaculating What a Terrible man you are to bring to Dinner! Another shock for Sean, and he felt his face go red. What was there terrible in saying food was badly cooked? He based his remark on his mother's skill. Whenever she and he had had anything worthwhile, steak, mutton, liver, or fish, garnished with vegetables, they were always sure to be handed up in a simple but first-class style of cooking. And all done on a plain open coal fire. Seldom it happened, but when it did, there was always the next thing to perfection. To this day, he remembers the soiled, sloppy look of the greens and the tattered, dry look of the meat served in the poetically-named restaurant. A ceremonial meal to Megarithma, or any other deity, wasn't going to make him say what he felt to be badly-cooked food was good and appetising. There was make-believe there, he thought, in spite of the solid aura of Keltic twilight that envelops the group.

Well, he'd take things easy; but he wouldn't be let take things easy. Some in Dublin hated Yeats, official catholics feared him, and a group of younger writers disliked his booming opinions on literature and insubstantial things without any local habitation or name. A number of these last, headed by F R. Higgins, the poet, Liam O'Flaherty and Brinsley Macnamara, the novelists, and Cecil Salkeld, the young painter, had started a Radical Club to nourish the thoughts and ambitions of the young writers, in opposition to the elderly and wild speculation of Yeats and the adulatory group that trailed longingly after him. Some of these wanted to hook in Sean so that his newer influence might be useful in putting Yeats in his improper place. As a preliminary, O'Flaherty brought Edward Garnett to the tenement where he lived, and coaxed Sean to tell Garnett a good deal about the play he was then trying to write, for foolish, innocent Sean had told O'Flaherty something about it. Garnett said he was delighted with the description given, and O'Flaherty bravely simulated the happiness of his companion. On the strength of this praise, O'Flaherty built a hope that Sean would do anything he wished; and so for long, and continuously, he argued against the influence of Yeats on literary thought in Ireland and elsewhere, saying Yeats was too damned arrogant, too assured of the superiority of his own work over that of all the others. Sean, however, had no bubbling desire to be O'Flaherty's gillie, so he countered the arguments used, for he saw clear enough that O'Flaherty, in the way of arrogance and sense of being a superior being, was worse than Yeats, without the elder man's grace and goodwill; while the cloak worn by the story-teller wasn't near so fine or colourful as the fine, silken mantle of poetry draping the shoulders of the poet.

Afterwards, when the play he had been writing then appeared on the Abbey stage to merge into conflict, the gnashing of teeth, and fearful outcries, Sean found he had to pay for his refusal to join in the campaign to make Yeats a little humbler. F. R. Higgins sent a letter to *The Irish Statesman* that emptied reproaches over the head of the defiant poet for his daring advocacy of Sean's play. Higgins referred to the play as *a technique largely based upon the revue structure, in the quintessence of an all-Abbey burlesque, intensified by diversions, and Handy Andy incidents with the more original settings offered by O'Casey. That aspect of comedy so gushly over-portrayed from Dublin artisan life, as seen only by this playwright, merely affords laborious bowing on a one-string fiddle. O'Casey in his new play entirely lacks the sincerity of an artist.* Austin Clarke, the poet, joined in the fight, gently, but none the less bitterly, indicative of what he thought about the play, saying, *The playwright seemed to be trying to exploit the poor*; and O'Flaherty, full of zeal and national righteousness, in a letter to the Press, said emphatically that the play was a bad one, protesting loudly, as he strutted about in his crying, that Yeats was a pompous fool; while an Englishman from a pleasant residence in Kingston-on-Thames, out to defend the workers and proletarian art, shouted out as far as his lungs could lean that this O'Casey was nothing but a dramatic Pontius Pilate; though poor Sean, almost at that very moment, had parcelled up the books of the plays published by Macmillan's, and had posted them off to the Soviet Union, filling the first leaf of the book with fervent good wishes for the future of the great Socialist Federation of States.

It all bewildered Sean for awhile; but, afterwards, he became certain that the attack was born of no sudden impulse, but was thought of long before the cry came. In it there was no tint of fear for Ireland's honour, the integrity of art, or the dignity of the Irishman. It was aimed at Yeats, and if it obliquely hurt and bothered Sean, all the better. It revealed to Sean for the first time the divisions in Ireland's family of literature. But these things were still in the womb of the future, and, for the moment, Sean knew peace. He had entered places unfamiliar; he had done things he did not yet fully understand; and he was quietly excited about it all. Anyway, he was quite at ease with the Old Lady. They got on grand together. They had many things in common besides the theatre. He loved pictures, and she was brimful of what her nephew, Hugh Lane, had done to diamond-clothe the walls of precious buildings with fair paintings of the men of the day, and with those done by their fathers in the old time before. She loved good books, and Sean felt that he was a little ahead of her there. She saw humour sparkle from things thought to be dead, or dull, and so did he; and they often talked and laughed together over tea in a hotel that overlooked the fair form of Stephen's Green; Sean trying to look at home in the posh place, and succeeding in a way; she eating bun after bun, murmuring that she was very, very hungry; and saying that their talk was lovely; though, best of all, she rejoiced that his plays were forcing queues to stand outside her little theatre, ringing a chime of cheeriness into all their chat. So here was Sean, sober and thoughtful, reading a warm invitation to come and spend a week or two in Coole Park, in Galway; eager to go, but a little nervous at the thought of setting out to visit foreign parts.

The Galway Express left Dublin at 8 A.M. He was to get out at Athenry, the King's Ford, where she would be there to meet him so that they could go together to Gort, and on to Coole Park on her own side-car — she had carefully planned it all out in a previous letter to him. He booked a Dublin jarvey to call for him at seven-twenty so that he could have plenty of time to get his ticket and take a seat in peace. He rose at six, made and ate his breakfast, and was well ready for the car when it came. Off they went, helter-skelter, for though they had lashings of time, the jarvey drove furiously — makin' th' animal earn her keep, he said. Sean planked himself in front of the tiny arched window of the booking-office, and waited impatiently for the shutter to be removed, his money for the ticket ready in a closed fist, his suitcase at his feet — the first his life had known. Keeping an eye on the clock, he faced the window when the hands were twelve minutes before the hour, for in two more the shutter would fly open. It didn't. Thirty or forty people had gathered when the clock showed it was five minutes to eight, with the little window as tightly shut as ever. He grew anxious, and a number of tongues behind him were clicking viciously with impatience.

—Thry a rap on th' shutther, there, said a voice in the background; aw, a sharper one than that, man! for Sean had knocked gently.

—There'll be a holy rush, now, when it does open, complained a second voice.

—Ay; that's if it ever opens! said a third voice with the sound of anger hopping off it.

There, in the centre of the wide door leading to the platform, stood the guard, glaring at them, green flag in hand in readiness to wave the train away.

—Is it out again he is? queries the guard maliciously; yez are wastin' your time waitin' for that fella. He glanced at the grinning clock, and then looked at his watch. Yez have got four minutes left, so make th' most o' them, an' get your tickets, an' hurry up an' take your seats; and he hurried off to his van.

Several fists now battered an angry tattoo on the shutter of the booking-office window, but no answer came to the knocking, though the hands of the jeering clock crept close to the unhallowed hour. Nice experience for Sean, and he a respectable traveller for the first time in his life. And getting up so early in the morning to be in time!

—Is it there yez are still like a lot o' frightened crows! blared in the voice of the guard on them again. Don't yez know that the ticket-givin' boyo's undisturbed be the thought of a given thrain havin' to leave a given station at a given hour? D'yez know th' time it is? Isn't there one among yez with bráins enough to guess that the boyo's curled up in a warm sleep in a warmer bed, regardless of thrain or tickets?

—Can we take our seats without possessing tickets? asked Sean politely.

—What a gaum y'are! answered the guard sarcastically. What are yez waitin' there for, if yez haven't to have tickets? Yez are not goin' to get me to advise yez to do what yez shouldn't do. An' don't batther down th' place, either — yez are to demand your tickets in an orderly, sensible way.

—Then what are we to do? plaintively asked a voice from the crowd.

—Now how do I know what yez are to do! retorted the guard angrily. All I know, an' all that I need to know, is that th' thrain starts in a minute or two. D'ye hear that now? Th' thrain's got to set off in another minute, so make up your minds. Are yez goin' to thravel to Galway, or are yez goin' to stay where yez are? I'm warnin' yez, mind, that th' thrain'll go empty, if yez don't get your tickets an' take your seats. A shrill blast from the engine told the guard that it was time to go. There y'are — hear that now? Have yez decided to settle down where yez are, an' die there, or what? He clicked his tongue viciously; dtch dtch! An' we're supposed to be an educated people! Half a minute more's all yez have, an' if yez aren't where yez ought to be, I'll leave yez where I found yez to make your minds up in your own sweet way be tomorrow mornin'; and he walked away in scorn.

Sean seized his suitcase, hurried on to the platform, and jumped into the train. Ticket or no ticket, he'd be in Athenry to meet the Old Lady. He was astonished to see the whole crowd follow his example. Sheep, he thought, sheep. In his seat, he thought it odd the way fear took people. He had noticed two priests in the crowd who had been just as fearful and agitated as he was himself, or the old agricultural labourer on his way to Galway who hadn't, maybe, more than his bare fare to bring him there. These would surely have defied the Black and Tans, and yet they shook at the thought of venturing a journey without a ticket, through no fault of their own. When the money was collected, Sean found he had to pay seven and six more than the ticket would have cost; and the labourer found the fare he had only enough to bring him to Athenry. There he would have to get out, and walk the rest of the way to Galway. Sean started help by offering two shillings, and the rest of the kindly passengers added enough to permit the old man to travel on in peace.

There she was waiting for him — a trim, stout, sturdy figure, standing upright and still on the platform, ready to guide him safely down to Gort, grimly patient in the midst of the talkative, quickly-moving crowd. A strange, lone figure she looked in a third-class carriage, stuck tight in a mass of peasants and small farmers, and they with baskets on their laps, or live fowl clutched in their hands; while one woman, young and lively, had a big goose, its legs and wings tied with cord, at her feet, so that it could only gabble, mixing its comic cries with the eager, animated chatter of the crowd.

—Der, said Lady Gregory, suddenly pointing out of a window, der's Craughwell where the police were always half afraid to stir, eating, drinking, and sleeping behind iron doors, thick walls, and steel-shuttered windows. We'll pass Ardrahan later on, remembering what Davis sang,

> And fleet as deer, deh Normans ran
> Tro' Curlew's Pass and Ardrahan.

—An' will again, please God, murmured a quiet voice from a corner.

She has a bit of lisp, thought Sean, and I only after noticing it now. Look at her there, with all her elegance, well at ease among the chattering crowd of common people; so why shouldn't I be steady in my mind at coming to a Big House, among rare silver and the best of china, sleeping in a bounteous bed, and handling divers tools at food never seen before. And he took heart, and felt strong, looking at the calm, handsome old face, smiling at the chatter of the people and the frightened cackling of the fowl. In the main, silent they had to sit, for she was at one end of the carriage and he at the other; so he had time to sort out his tumbling thoughts, watching her, and wondering by what devious ways she of the grandees had managed to come so close to the common people. It's little she's said herself of her younger days, dropping a bare hint, here and there, of what she thought and what she did between residence in Roxborough House, where she was born and lived her youth; and Coole Park, where she lived when she married; and Tullyra Castle, where Edward Martyn, spouse of terror, lived, told his beads, and spent most of his life like a colourless moth, fluttering between the finger and thumb of a friar.

Lady Gregory was the younger child of a large family and held a small corner in the activities surrounding her sisters, the clever Elizabeth, the musical Gertrude, and the beautiful Adelaide, afterwards the mother of Sir Hugh Lane. To the pulsing piston-beat of the hurrying train, Sean pictured her dissolving her own life into the file around her — as we all do —, but religiously preserving to herself a secret seed of thought that was to grow into a fine and sturdy understanding of literature; into a shrewd and germinant companionship with Yeats; into a wise and firm Dame Halbardier of the Irish Renaissance; into a lively prop that kept the shaky Irish Theatre standing; into the humorous dramatic writer whose plays will do their devoirs freshly on many a stage, here and elsewhere, for many a year to come.

It is most likely that she played games, went to church twice on Sundays — dwindling into a visit once, if the day happened to be very wet; committed to memory innumerable woeful and winning texts of the Bible; looked over photos of trimly-dressed relatives and friends, set down safe in the thick and gilded pages of an album; some sitting on marble or brocaded chairs, others standing beside Doric pillars, with the whole world behind them; the women floating upward out of balloon-like dresses, beset with a forest of flounces, the men denoting manliness by husky beard or oratorical moustaches. He could see her, at the end of the day, saying her prayers, before she climbed up a ladder on to a heavily-curtained bed, to try to conjure sleep out of stuffy and most respectable air. Perhaps, some night or other, she slid aside the tremendous curtains to get a glimpse of the moon whose golden disk was telling a story of loveliness to the lass of the tenement as well as to the lass of the Big House.

No Peter Pansy came flying in at her window — the curtains were a little too thick for that young mab man — to whisk her off to a never, never, forever land, turning things that were into things that were not; no Winnie the Pooh gambolled in her garden; instead, her fancies were formed from the brown wind of Connacht, in summer soft and sensitive; in winter sending the foam flying frightened from the waves, beating the Galway coast, carrying the spindrift over the land to cover her window with its healthy, bitter brine. And in the midst of the breeze or blast, she learned of the deeds of Cullen's Hound; listening with a wide-open ear to her nurse, Mary Sheridan, telling tremendous tales of him who swore by the oath of his people that *He would make his doings be spoken of among the great doings of heroes in their strength.* So he did, so did she. Has it not been all written down by her in the fine, gay book called *Cuchulain of Murhevna*? It's well Sean could see her, she sitting up in her big bed, her hair chained up for the night, her firm lips half open, her eyes intent on fancied glories that Mary Sheridan's seeding words set out before her: warriors, sages, stately queens, trancing the young girl into seeing Maeve herself, great queen of Cruachen. fixed, fine, and haughty, in the great red-repp chair of Roxborough, and she listening to the rich-bronze chariots of the Red Branch Knights thundering by in the woods outside.

She lived her young life, and rose out of the red-repp and yellow-plush life of the time: plush-covered photo-frames, plush-covered bodies and furniture, plush-covered souls full of plush-covered faith in God. That she questioned these things is certain; and that she felt another life, wider, harder, and mightier than her own, around her, is certain, too; for of all those who were with her when her busy literary and dramatic life began, she alone sat among the plain people, safe at ease, while they sat safe at ease with her. With all his scented, elegant Tony Lumpkin life, George Moore rarely had the heart to stray far beyond the border of his Aubusson carpet; and when he did so, got lost, and hurried back to its soft terra firma, giving thanks for a happy deliverance before his holy Manet icon hanging on the wall. Poor, old, clumsy-minded Edward Martyn, lurching round in the shadows of his ta ra ra Gothic house, pumping *Palestrina* out of a harmonium, trying to clap a friar's cowl on the head of life, tried to hide himself in the dim light from a holy candle clamped to his damp and pudgy hand; Yeats, who went through life with ears cocked to hear what no-one else could, heard something strange at times, shown by his letters defending the locked-out workers; didn't like what he heard, shuddered, and turning aside, chanted,

All things uncomely and broken, all things worn out and old,
The cry of a child by the roadway, the creak of a lumbering cart,
The heavy steps of the ploughman, splashing the wintry mould,
Are wronging your image that blossoms a rose in the deeps of my heart.

Shocked he was by this creak and cry, so he started to run, chanting,

Come away, O human child!
To the waters and the wild,
With a faery, hand in hand,
For the world's more full of weeping than you can understand.

But Lady Gregory wasn't afraid of the child's cry or the creak of the lumbering cart; and she stayed to speak warm words to the ploughman splashing the wintry mould. She trotted fearlessly beside all these things, sad or merry; listened to their tales, sang songs with them when they were merry; and mourned with them when a silver cord was sundered or a golden bowl was broken. The taste of rare wine mingled with that of home-made bread on the tip of her tongue; her finely-shod feet felt the true warmth of the turf fire, and beside its glow she often emptied the sorrows of her own heart into the sorrow of others. Out of her plush and plum, she came to serve the people, body and mind, with whatever faculties God had given her.

WHERE WILD SWANS NEST

A LONG, sweeping drive, left and right, gave a ceremonial pathway to Coole House, which shone out, here and there, in hand-broad patches from between majestic trees, ripe in age, and kingly in their branchiness. The House was a long, yellowish-white Georgian building, simply made, with many windows, while a manly-looking entrance — tightly shut now for a long time — faced what was once a curving expanse of lawn, smooth as green enamel in a rajah's brooch; but was now a rougher, but gayer, gathering of primrose and violet, making themselves at home where once prime minister, statesman, and governor, with their silk-gowned and parasoled women, strolled over the velvety green, their grace, charm, and power manœuvring the poor world about to their own sweet liking.

Lady Gregory was a Connachtwoman, knowing every foot of the province; every story told by every bush and stone in the counties of Galway and Clare; and she showed her Connacht rearing by compelling her seventy-odd years to climb down, like a stiff gazelle, from the high seat of the side-car, running to the threshold of the house, turning, and stretching out her two hands to say, with a beaming smile, One and twenty welcomes, Sean, to the House of Coole!

Mistress of a grand house, dying reluctantly, filled a little too full with things brought from all quarters of the known world; some of them bringing into his fancy the ghosts of a Victorian age, and others, more modern, that would send these ghosts away again, moaning; a huge gleaming marble figure of Andromeda in the drawing-room, brought in from the terrace when it had shocked the finer feelings of the people with its clean, cold nakedness; the really glorious library, walled with precious books in calf and vellum, forgotten, the most of them; unheeded, too, though they still murmured in Sanskrit, Greek, and Latin against the changing tempo of the reading world. Here was a house that for a century and more had entertained great people as well as tinkers and tailors, for every old or young fiddler, passing through south Galway, came to patronise Coole, receiving praise and largesse after playing, maybe, *Blue Butterfly Dancin'*, *The Soft Deal Board*, or *Pulse of the Bards*, *Awaken*: and as he went up the stairs (the walls covered with engraving and mezzotint so that you passed by, without knowing it, half of England's history), he fancied he heard the dancing notes of *The Red-capped Connachtman* flowing from an old fiddle, mingling with the sonorous voice of Yeats chanting out of him about the wild swans of Coole.

In the library o' nights, heavy curtains pulled taut, a blazing log fire in a huge open grate, Sean stretched out cosy in a deep settee, while she, from the gentle aura of soft candle-light, read him Hardy's Epic-Drama of the war with Napoleon, in three parts, nineteen acts, and one hundred and thirty scenes; read and read till he found himself battling sleepily for dear life to keep himself awake, and be polite to the Spirit of the Years, the Spirit of Pity, the Spirit of Rumour, the Spirits Ironic and Sinister. The poem seemed to have been begun in the dark ages, and he felt that it would roll on till the light of the sun gave out; though he murmured it was all lovely when she paused for breath, cutely conjuring her not to tire herself too much with the dint of the direful reading. But, night after night, she pegged away at it, till the very last word was spoken, and she could murmur, half exhausted, Dat's de end! Two great achievements: one for her — that she survived the reading; the other for him — that he kept awake, though feeling old and grey and full of sleep when she was finished. But, later on, Hardy came to him a far, far greater man than Sean had thought him then.

However, the gentle lady made up for the strain by reading him *Moby Dick* and Hudson's fine *The Purple Land*. Once only did he burst out into protesting: when she, full of enthusiasm, and certain of pleasing him, read a Labour play called *Singing Jail Birds*; to Sean then, to Sean now, the worst play ever written signifying its sympathy with the workers.

Oh, stop, woman, for God's sake! he had bawled, forgetful of where he was, rising, and pacing to the far end of the room: the Labour Movement isn't a mourning march to a jail-house! We are climbing a high hill, a desperately steep, high hill through fire and venomous opposition. All of those who were highest up have dropped to death; lower down, most of the climbers have dropped to death; lower still, many will drop to death; but just beneath these is the invincible vast crowd that will climb to the top by the ways made out by their dear dead comrades!

Perhaps you're right, Sean, she had said, hurriedly putting the book away, something ashamed at having so delightedly praised such an insignificant work.

One evening she came in, aglow with a surprise for Sean — a new petrol lamp into which air was pumped so that, she said, we'll have a light that makes the night even as the day of a sunny summer morning. She stood the lamp on a stand on a high table; and a lovely thing it looked with its silver-like stem and opalescent shade. Lady Gregory's maid, Bridget, hovered round while her ladyship pumped air into the petrol bowl, anxiously watching, and murmuring, Let me handle that, leave it to me, now, me lady, to be answered with the angry and impatient retort of Doh away, doh away, woman; it's twite simple, and I tan handle it myself. Turning to Sean, she added, And now you'll soon see a light dat never was on sea or land.

She was right, too, for as soon as she put a light to it, the thing gave out a mighty hiss that was half a scream, a bluish-white flame shot up high as the ceiling, the old lady's face, panic in her eyes, became as opalescent as the lamp-shade, and her wildly-puckered little mouth began to send frantic and harmless puffs of air towards the soaring, hissing flame, the agitated mouth suddenly opening wide, between the puffs, to shout at Bridget, Bring a blanket, bring a blanket, Bridget, before de house does up in fire! Sean whipped up a rug from the settee, and placed it between their faces and the flame for fear it might explode; and behind this safety-curtain the three of them juggled, blew, and smothered the thing till the fire died down; standing round it on guard till it cooled, and Bridget could safely carry the silver bowl and cracked opalescent bowl out of our sight into the kitchen.

—Oh! murmured her ladyship, sinking down to the softness of the settee, a bunishment for my banity; tinking I could do it alone; tinking I knew too much. Back to de tandles dat bring peace and surety to men of doodwill.

It was strange to see that white, frightened look flash across the face of a brave soul; that fine firm face shrinking from physical fire, though she walked calm through the ordeal of spiritual and mental fire when she fought the good fight for the freedom of the theatre against priest, peasant, and politician, howling loud and long for the putting down of Synge. Against them all she stood, fighting it all out victoriously in Ireland's heart, and dipping deep into the battle again throughout the mighty cities of America, choosing strife that was good rather than the loneliness of a false peace. Again, later on, she defended *The Shewing-up of Blanco Posnet* against Dublin Castle, its robed Lord Lieutenant, its pursuivant, its equerries, men-at-arms, scrolls, parchments, laws and crests, archer Shaw beside her, shooting many a broadcloth stinging arrow of wit into the squirming enemy, making them fall back, and yelp, and lower their banners, and seek shelter in the hollows of the hills of silence.

Again her banner of courage (a gay one, too) had gone up on a day that brought Yeats, Florence Farr, Arthur Symons, and others, to take dinner with her in London. Seeing a letter from home on the table, she took it to another room to read it quiet, finding that every line told of a new disaster, caused by the Big Wind of that year — great lime trees laid flat, oaks, elms, pine, and larch, the calm growth of near a century, had come tumbling down, shattering demesne walls, impeding the public roads; and a tremendous and lovely ilex, the pride of the place, had fallen, given up the ghost, and was no more. But not a word did she say of all this to her guests, but sedately read the play, *Riders to the Sea*, that they had come to hear.

When she got home again, she didn't sit down to wail, but set out on a journey seeking a sawmill, and picked up a second-hand one somewhere; found suitable and unsuitable men to get it going, making all sorts of things for the comfort and convenience of the local people; selling them at cost prices, so cleverly turning an evil into a good thing; the good stretching far, for when Sean came to Coole, the sawmill was still working hoarsely and jerkily, turning out things from the remnants of the fallen timber. And so this brave old Commissar of Galway turned the *Keening of Kilcash* into a busy, surging song of work, though still retaining some of its sadness for the loss of so much upright elegance.

He hadn't been ten minutes at the table before he felt he had often been there, to eat soberly, and talk merrily of books and theatre, and of the being of Ireland; she in simple and most gracious ways showing how things were handled; pointing out that dese things were done, not because of any desire for ceremony, but because dey made one more comfortable, and made things easier to eat. So he was soon at rest, she, when she wanted something from the kitchen, snapping a finger against a tiny Burmese gong that gave a soft, pensive, penetrating note, holding in its quivering sound the muted song and sadness of Burma. Once, after such a meal, they passed through a room where the blue mountains of the Barony of Loughrea nodded in at the great bow-windows; and halting his steps, Sean paused in front of a young, broad-shouldered man with an open and courageous face.

—My dear son, she murmured softly, my dear, dear son, lost leading his air-squadron over de Italian battlefield. For months and months I had dreaded it, for I knew de German planes were well ahead of ours in design and swiftness.

He wished he hadn't paused before the picture. What the hell could he say to her? He gave a quick glance, and saw that holy tears were racing down the wrinkled channels of her cheeks. He touched her old arm softly.

—Dear lady, dear friend, he said, a little savagely, the falling into death of a young, hearty man is a common thing, and may be a more common thing in days to come. The death of youth has been glorified in the damnable beauty of the belief that They will not grow old as we grow old. That is the heresy of age comforting its conscience in its own comfort and continued security. I am, and always will be, against the death of the young. It is for us who are still standing to fight for the deliverance of the young from a youthful death; from the cruel and wasteful banishment of our younger life, with all its lovely and daring visions barely outlined, becoming, when they go, a tinted breath of memory. To the old, death comes as a fair visitor; to the young, death is a savage intruder.

—We must be brave, she said, forcing her head higher; we must fence our sorrow away so that no shadow falls on those left singing and dancing around us. Come, let us doh for a walk in de woods.

The Seven Woods of Coole with their many winding paths, so many that it behoved a rambler to go warily that he be not lost in the mazes among the trees. These were among the beloved walks of Yeats, though Sean never cottoned to them, disliking their gloom, with the weight of gorgeous foliage drooping down, sombre, full of sighs and uneasy rustling, as if God had made them plaintive. Sometimes what Lady Gregory called a badger cut across their path, and red squirrels shot up the trees at their coming, moving on to the ones nearer the orchard so that they might be close to the fruit when the workers went home by the evening star. In her working overalls, which were an old black dress, an older, wide-brimmed, black straw hat, leather gauntlets over her able, wrinkled hands, one of which clutched a keen, chisel-edged stick, the Old Lady walked beside him, or a little before when the going got bad. Here, in the Wood of the Nuts, right in their way, callous and impudent, rose a mighty thistle, fully eight feet high, thrusting out its savage barbs towards their breasts, daring them to come on. Then, with the fire of defiance in her eyes, her ladyship charged down on the foe, hissing angrily, one gauntleted hand seizing a spiked branch, while the other stabbed the main butt of the thistle with the chisel-end of the stick, till the branchy spikes tottered, bent back, and fell to the ground, the victory celebrated by an uplifted stick and a fierce muttering of So perish all de king's enemies!

Occasionally, through the lusty leafage of hazel and ash, they caught a silver glimpse of Coole river flowing by, a river that bubbled up suddenly from the earth in a glade, a lonely corner, alive and gay and luminous with a host of pinkish-blue and deeply-blue and proud forget-me-nots; a secret corner that Lady Gregory had challenged Sean to find, and which had suddenly surrounded him on his third day of searching; a place so lovely in its blossoming loneliness that he felt he should not be there. Not a note from a bird disturbed its quietness; no lover and his lass, even, had passed through this glade; no breeze brought the faint lowing of far-off cattle to his ears; the blue of a serene sky overhead mantling the blue of the flowers at his feet; no sound save the musical gurgling whisper of the water calmly gushing out of the earth; so still, so quiet, so breathless, that Sean thought God Himself might well ponder here in perfect peace; and the merry Mab, in her mimic wagon, might journey home here through the tangled forest of forget-me-nots, without disturbing thoughts of things remembered in tranquillity. This was the river which, after leaving the quietness of God, ran swiftly to widen out into a lovely lake on whose soft bosom wild swans settled and wild swans rose, lifting up the noble head of Yeats to watch them,

> Scatter wheeling in great broken rings
> Upon their clamorous wings,

possibly a little envious of them, and wishing, faintly, he was one because

> Their hearts have not grown old;
> Passion or conquest, wander where they will,
> Attend upon them still.

But Yeats grew old, and cursed the dread handicap of age; yet passion lingered with him to the last, and conquest went before him till he laid himself down in rest to leave us.

Books and trees were Lady Gregory's chief charmers: the one nearest her mind, the other nearest her heart. She laboured long and lovingly in the woods of Coole. She hated rabbits and squirrels only when they nibbled the bark from her young saplings. It was she who first taught Sean to distinguish between the oak — the first dree dat Dod made, — beech, elm, hazel, larch, and pine. She marched along telling their names, the way an eager young nun would tell her beads. Away in a sacred spot of the garden, a magnificent copper beech swept the ground with its ruddy branches, forming within them a tiny dingle of its own. This was the sacred tree of Coole. On its trunk were carved the initials of famous men who had come to

visit Coole, so that they might be remembered forever. The initials
of Augustus John were there, and those of Bernard Shaw and Yeats
were cut deep into the bark that looked like hardened dark-red
velvet.

With all her bowing-down before the mystery of poetry and
painting, she never left the sober paths trod into roughness by the
feet of the common people. One very wet day, she was busy helping
to make what was called a Gort cake. When she and Sean returned
in a day or so to Dublin, the cake was to be the centre of a tea given
in the Green Room of the Abbey Theatre. She usually brought one
up for the actors when she visited Dublin. A lot of the actors and
actresses elected to regard the cake with contempt; but they ate it
all right, and when the tea was done, though the cake would feed a
regiment, he had noticed that there was little left behind. The cake
was a rich thing of spice, raisins, and currants, but the rarest thing in
its make-up was a noggin of brandy to help to damp the dough.

Sean was standing before one of the great bow-windows, watching
the rain slashing down in silvery sheets over the saturated lawn, and
listening to the sighs of the big lime tree bending discontentedly
before the sharp and bitter wind blowing its branches to and fro.
Suddenly, through the mist of the rain, he saw a dark figure, crouching to fight the wind and the rain, battling his way up the circling
drive to reach the Big House.

—Derrible day, Sean, said Lady Gregory, coming in to have a
look out of the window; derrible day!

—Whoever's coming up the drive, Lady Gregory, must feel what
you say to be true.

—Oh! It's Sammy Mogan toming to det pension papers signed,
she said, staring gloomily at the figure struggling onwards. De
foolish man to tome on a day like dis; de foolish man!

She was gone in a second. He heard the bell of the side door ring;
heard someone entering the hall, and then a long silence came.
Tired of watching the rain, he strolled about staring at the pictures
hanging on the stairway wall. Out comes an old man to the hall,
muffled up in a big coat, eyes and ears only apparent, a bundle of
soppy clothes under an arm, and he bidding her ladyship goodbye
at every step.

—You must never tome out on a day like dis aden, Sam, murmured her ladyship.

—What signifies it, me Lady? What's in it for a day but a harmless
sup o' rain? Goodbye, now, me Lady. Penethratin' though th' rain

is, it treats th' skin quietly, like th' tendher touch of a mother bird's wing reachin' over th' nest of her young ones. Well, me lady, goodbye now. An' isn't th' cordial you've just given me afther liftin' me into thinkin' th' heaviest rain on the cowldest day to be no more than the tired leaves fallin' from the high-born branchy threes. Goodbye, me Lady, for with the form signed safe in me pocket, it's whistlin' I'll be all th' way home, intherspersed with prayers for seven blessin's seven times a day on you and all your house. Goodbye, me Lady.

—Whisper, Sean, said Lady Gregory, as they went back to the fire in the library, de Gort cake will lack its warm life dis time. Sam Mogan was so perished wid. de wet and cold dat I poured de naggin of brandy into him to ,bring him back to life.

Sitting in the long and handsome garden, he saw the sun going down behind the grey garden wall and beyond the Hills of Burren, giving Coole a crimson and gold salute before it went. He realised that Lady Gregory, in the midst of her merriment and mourning, was ever running round, a sturdy little figure in her suit of solemn black, enlivened by gleaming eyes and dancing smile; ever running in and out of Yeat's Keltic Twilight, which she could never fully understand; turning his Rose Alchemica into a homely herb; and turning the wildness of his Red O'Hanrahan into the serious, steady dancing of a hornpipe on the Abbey stage. In her humorous and critical moods, swinging a critical lantern, she trespassed into A. E.'s amethystine no-man's-land where A. E. became delirious with quivering, peacock-tinted visions, seeing things innumerable and unmentionable, beings plumed, from pituitary gland to backside, with red, white, green, blue, and orange flames. There he sat, with notebook in hand, taking down divine orders of the day from brotherselfs, master-souls, ancient-beauties, elfs and faeries, madly dancing a rigadoon a dad a derry o. Here she'd trot forward impudently, pulling aside A. E.'s twilight curtains, half hiding the Pleroma, gone today and here tomorrow; disturbing the dusky grandeur of the Great Breath's breathing, and frightening away the dim moths of twilight trees, twilight hills, twilight men, and twilight women, by crying out in her quiet, determined way, through all the mumbo-jamboree of twilight thought, that there were things to cook, sheets to sew, pans and kettles to mend.

It was hard for Sean to single out the best work done by this old woman, flitting through life like a robin with the eye of a hawk; for she had as much to do with what she did not do as she had with what she did; whether it was the writing of plays, or the lofty encouragement (not forgetting the blue curtains for the windows of his little flat) given to Yeats, making the poet at home in the dignity, comfort, and quiet of a fine house; soothing him with a sunny seat under a spreading catalpa tree in a flower-lit garden, where a summer evening was full of the linnet's wings; whether it was the warm determined will that gave her little theatre a local habitation and a world-wide name; for not Yeats, nor Martyn, nor Miss Horniman gave the Abbey Theatre its enduring life, but this woman only, with the rugged cheeks, high upper lip, twinkling eyes, pricked with a dot of steel in their centres; this woman only, who, in the midst of venomous opposition, served as a general run-about in sensible pride and lofty humility, crushing time out of odd moments to write play after play that kept life passing to and fro on the Abbey stage.

On a stone wall surrounding what was once, maybe, a meadow, Sean sat one day simmering in the sun. All over the heath, the crowds of wild waste plants were covered with wide mantles of brilliant-blue butterflies. Never had he imagined such a host of blue evanescent divinity. In the formal garden, here and there, one, or maybe a pair, flew about from this flower to that one, but here they were in tens of thousands. As they settled and rose, they looked like a multitude of tiny blue banners carried by an invisible army. Or the bright blue mantle of St. Brighid down from the sky, fluttering near the half-remembered things of earth. How delightful the sturdy black figure of her ladyship would look doing a slow, graceful, if a little stiff, minuet among the brilliant-blue fluttering things. Sean wondered if Yeats had ever set eyes on these. Hardly, for they were off the beaten, formal track of his strolling: garden, lake, woods were as far as he got; and so the gurgling rise of the river and these brilliant-blue angels of an hour were denied the lyric their loveliness commended.

She loosened the tautness of her own work by taking too much time helping others, Sean thought as he sat on the wall, encircled with the cloud of blue butterflies. She became foster-mother to some plays of Yeats, weaving in dialogue for *Cathleen ni Houlihan* and his *Pot of Broth*; helping in the construction of *The King's Threshold* and *Where there is Nothing*, throwing in, for good measure, scenarios from which Douglas Hyde made *The Poorhouse* and *The Marriage*. In the theatre, among the poets and playwrights, herself a better playwright than most of them, she acted the part of a charwoman, but one with a star on her breast. Ay, indeed, this serving eagerness of hers was a weakness in her nature. She thought too much of the work of others, foaming with their own importance, leaving her but little time to think of her own. So signs on it, a good deal of what she did shows hurry, hinting in its haste that no matter if mine be not good so long as that of others be better.

Once troubled with the pushful realism of the younger writers, she started to write a romantic play around Brian Boru, called *Kincora*. She made many false starts, but kept hammering away, in spite of Yeats's advice to give it up; and, though the play got its share of applause, it wasn't in itself, she says, the success it might have been, and so hindered a welcome from critic and audience. Give it up! No wonder it wasn't the success it might have been. Why didn't Yeats mind his own business! A pity the woman was so near to Yeats while she was writing the play: he had a bad effect on her confidence in her own creation. She was concerned with him and her play; he concerned only with himself. He had no right to tell her to give up writing the play; but she served so frequently in so many common ways that Yeats easily dismissed from his mind her natural vigour in the creation of imaginative drama. It was a shame that the modelling of the play should have been chilled by a scornful wave of a delicate hand from a poetical mind that so often dismissed everything save what was dissolving in the wonder of his own thought.

Lady Gregory had her own Three Sorrows of Storytelling; three sorrows that were rifling her heart when Sean first came across her, and founded a friendship with Coole. The tumbling, burning death of her son, Major Robert Gregory, on the battlefield of Italy, was but being softened slowly by her transferred devotion to his three young children. His death, too, was a loss to Ireland, for to his many qualities he added that of a fine and sensitive designer for the theatre. In the play, *Kincora*, the king's Great Hall was shown by the hanging of vivid green curtains; there were shields, embossed with designs of gold, upon the walls, and heavy mouldings over the doors. For Brian's tent at Clontarf, a great orange curtain filled the background, with figures standing out against it in green, red, and grey. In *The Shadowy Waters*, he made the whole stage the sloping deck of a galley, blue and dim, the sails and dresses were green, and the ornaments all of copper. When Robert Gregory fell on the hilly soil of Italy, Ireland may have lost an Irish, and more colourful, Gordon Craig.

The Second Sorrow was the Atlantic weaving with her waves a winding-sheet for Sir Hugh Lane, her nephew, when he went down in the *Lusitania*, almost within view of his birthplace in the county of Cork. He it was who, through heavy opposition, gave many gems of painting to many galleries, scattering these lovely things all over Dublin, as another would scatter rose-petals about in the heat of a carnival. A loss he was, a great loss to his people, though only a very few felt it, besides the lonely woman in her home at Coole. To Sean, then, he was none; he felt it not; knew it not; but he knew it well now.

The Third Sorrow was the taking away of the Lane pictures from Dublin by the then British Authorities. A scurvy trick, one of the many done by British authority on Ireland. The lousiest and meanest of robberies ever perpetrated by one country on another. To her last breath, she followed after them, seeking them, seeking them, and often Sean had gone with her. They are still exiled from their native land; but they will be brought back. Though many in Ireland were blind to their beauty, so were others, better placed than the Irish to recognise their loveliness; for one of them, Renoir's *Umbrellas*, lay for a long time deep in the cellar of the National Gallery, too trivial, as the big shots thought, for a hanging on a respectable wall. A scurvy trick, England!

What shall we bring to the place where she now lies asleep forever? Easy enough to answer; easy enough: A promise not to forget the Lane pictures; some of the shining forget-me-nots from the glade where the fresh river rises; a branch from the copper beech that bore the initials of those who had sat at her table and walked in her garden; an old fiddler to play *The Blackberry Blossom*; a butterfly from the gorgeous blue swarm that clouded the heath, like the blue mantle of Brighid, behind the House of Coole; a vine leaf, or two, in token of her gay heart; since she elected to live and die a Christian, a cross; and the voice of her poet-friend chanting:

> Here, traveller, scholar, poet, take your stand
> When all those rooms and passages are gone,
> When nettles wave upon a shapeless mound
> And saplings root among the broken stone;
> And dedicate — eyes bent upon the ground,
> Back turned upon the brightness of the sun
> And all the sensuality of the shade —
> A moment's memory to that laurelled head.

All the rooms and passages are gone, and saplings root among the broken stone, for an elevated Irish Government has broken down the House and levelled it smooth for nettles to grow upon a shapeless mound. Oh! a scurvy act for an Irish Government to do on the memory of one who was greater than the whole bunch of them put together and tied with string. The god-damned Philistines!

A TERRIBLE BEAUTY IS BORNEO

HERE it was at last — The Irish Free State; or, as it was written down officially, Saorstat na hEireann. A discordant symphony in green. After as many as possible of good men and excellent girls had been laid in the grave, the warring sections thought enough had been done to show the Irish catholic's love for his neighbour; and so De Valera got the Republican bugles to blow the Cease Fire. The I.R.A. dumped their arms, and streeled back to their homes, though many of them never got that far, for the Free State seized thousands, including De Valera, and clapped them into jail. With the exception of a half-sad, lingering shot or two, the Civil War died out, leaving many homes unhappy, many heaps of cold, grey ashes, dwindling ghosts of once fine houses; and a heart in Eire's bosom that had now neither pride nor hope; her courage broken like an old tree in a black wind; the proud step gone that was once the walk of a queen; bent now like the old Hag of Beara, old

> with wandering
> Through hollow lands and hilly lands.

Turn your back on it all, Sean, a vic o! Turn your back on the green and the gold, on the old hag that once had the walk of a queen! What's Ni Houlihan to you, or you to Ni Houlihan? Nothing now. The little brown-backed cow was in the weeds before, and she's in the weeds again.

> But when the Dark Cow leaves the moor,
> And pastures poor with greedy weeds,
> Perhaps we'll hear her low at morn,
> Lifting her horn in pleasant meads.

Never! We'll never hear her low at morn in satisfaction, nor see her lift her head in pleasant meads. The weeds, the weeds for her forever!

Ireland held no mystery now for Sean, and what he had learned, joined to all he had experienced, plundered Dublin of its privileges. The city's dignity had strengthened into a bitter and a blasting laugh. Sean no longer wondered what went on behind the imposing portico of the Bank of Ireland. It was no longer royal. Just like any huckster's shop, tossing pounds instead of pennies into a till. He no longer looked with reverence at the blue-faced clock of Trinity College, with its golden hands forever touching up its face. He had been within, and knew that a lot of it was a slum trying to be stately. Late at night, he had helped to cook kidneys and rashers in a cubby-hole of a kitchen, by the light of matches, for the light had been cut off, even from the room of a Lecturer. Professor Rudmose Brown had brought him round the place, expecting Sean to fall down and worship it. The façade of this and of that looked well, but within it was all sourness and gloom. The Engineering School was looked at, entered, and Sean was told it was after Ruskin's own heart; but, to Sean, Ruskin here had fenced away his finer vision, for it showed, in its marble and embellishment, but a tinselled grandeur. It was here, if he remembered right, that the universe was displayed on circling wires, the planets, in due proportion, strung out around a gilded sun perched in the centre — a dead child's dying toy. Sean's own imaginative creation of the universe was a far mightier thing than these poor paupered ghosts of planet and sun.

All the mystery that had illumined his fear had gone, for he had now met many who had curtains on their windows, had a new clock on the stairs, carpets even on the floor, and a frillied maid to hasten to open when a knock came to the door of a house having special rooms in which to eat, to sleep, or rest with a book in one hand, while the other showed the glow of wine in a crystal glass.

Few of the owners of these grand things had shocked him into respect and hesitation. Sean was himself now, serene and careless; as one having nothing, yet possessing most things. They knew no more — a lot of them less — than he did himself. He knew as much as they did about literature, enjoying its fantasy, plunging into its deeps, revelling in its luxuriance; while they wasted a lot of time discussing the articulation of its bones; on which side of its body the heart lay; never putting out a hand to feel the softness of a breast, the gay beat, or the woeful throb of a dear heart. They spent most of the time measuring beauty's body and limb, while he spent all the time he could in her arms. He knew, through feeling and sensibility, more about painting than they did, rejecting their choice, and meeting the praise of the commonplace with critical condemnation. He wanted to know more about these things, and felt that Dublin had told him all she knew.

The Free State was making itself felt in all possible ways. Tim

Healy, a catholic and a life-long Nationalist, had been chosen by the British Government to be the first Governor-General, set down, mighty and grand, in the palatial Vice-Regal Lodge.

> There's statues gracing this noble place in
> All heathen goddesses and nymphs so fair;
> Bold Neptune, Plutarch, and Nicodemus,
> All mother naked in the open air.

It wasn't long before the Dubliners were calling the Vice-Regal Lodge Uncle Tim's Cabin, for Healy was held in small respect by them. Ireland's figure-head; Governor-General of the Irish Free State — Cosgrave's great conjuring trick to astonish Ireland. A tried and true patriot; a good catholic; the hound that brought down the noble stag, Parnell.

> The old foul mouth had set
> The pack upon him.

Honoured now by all the tricksters, all the holy romans, all who caught the far-away scent of a job; all these, and a few more, were soon to be bobbing down before the man who had betrayed Parnell. One whom even the Irish Party had to drive forth as a poisoned bullet. A man who would hardly have been elected for Louth, after that departure, if the ecclesiastical hands of Armagh and Dublin hadn't caressed the hoary head. Just as they had done at the great betrayal, holding Healy out to the people instead of Parnell. The clergy got their way, and all the ruin, the bitterness, the savage hatred of brother against brother, along with their way. The stag dead, the hounds hunted the hounds. But blithely the purple biretta bears the burden, telling all that the woe of the world comes from abandoning God, forgetting the fierce woe, the frightful confusion they themselves brought to Ireland by abandoning Parnell. Now this Tim Healy had become an Excellency, and the red-robed and purple-robed were all around him, meeting him in the doorway of their churches, providing him with a special *prieu-dieu*, tucking him up in his car when he murmured Say *au revoir* but not goodbye. Now Yeats's murmur about the dead Parnell shrilled along the streets:

> Go, unquiet wanderer,
> And gather the Glasnevin coverlet
> About your head till the dust stops your ear.
> You had enough of sorrow before death —
> Away, away! You are safer in the tomb.

No, stay where you are, Parnell! Stay where you are, and touch us with your hand! The name of Healy's caught in no man's heart;

Parnell's is deep in many and many a one. Your flaming name is woven in and out of Ireland's mind. Where your dust lies will be an honoured and living place forever. But who will turn aside from his way to seek the place where Healy lies; or weave a wreath of laurel for its honour; or cast a sprig of ivy on the grave?

In the midst of it all, the first turf was cut for the Shannon Scheme; and Fitz Braze, one-time Master of Music in the Kaiser's household, was teaching the proper tempo of trumpet and trombone to Irish lads; some of the Free State officials, refusing to let bad alone, paraded in blue shirts, stretched out their arms, and shouted Hail St. Patrick, Hope of the jobless! The Free State Party began to think there was nothing more wonderful in the world than themselves. And in their world there wasn't, though poor Dr. Douglas Hyde has failed to get sufficient votes to lift him even into the Senate; and when Lady Gregory told Sean this, there were tears in her soft eyes as she murmured against The indratitude of de Irish people. Poorer De Valera and many of his comrades now had their lodgings on the cowld, cowld ground in jails; and those who were still walking the free world were outcast and downcast, trying to buoy themselves up with the hope that their immaculate conception of Irish nationalism was, and ever would be, the eternal truth. They were in the desert, meditating, till the tears came, on the Treaty that accepted the King as the head of the State, and De Valera's Document No. 2 that accepted him as the head of the family. They meditated, too, on the ruinous Civil War engendered by the difference between a few words in the two oaths — the British oath and the De Valerian one: the one was to be taken in a deep bass; the other to be meekly pronounced in a whispered falsetto.

Only the Countess Markievicz preserved her *sang freud*, dashing round the country as a sound and a fury, pouring the British Empire, the Free State, De Valera's wistful Document No. 2, and her own mighty misapprehension of things Irish into her little mould of an Irish co-operative commonwealth.

Then, while a host of Irish harps were sounding *Let Erin Remember the Days of Old* at a mass meeting, the new politicians and people decided that they must become genteel, with really nice manners, to show how fit for self-government they were. So all who could, and many who couldn't, spare the money, got themselves fitted adequately for the short black jacket and the black tie, and the tailed coat with the white tie for more formal functions. The cruiskeen lawn was rejected for the cocktail glass, and long, anxious questions of precedence troubled many simple souls. The women employed experts making out blue-prints to see how far their bodices could be lowered and still be consonant with diocesan doctrine and Dublin's desperate need of attraction. The teachers of up-to-date and old-world dancing were working night and day educating the vulgar hilarity of jig and reel from the joints of the adventists to the new Irish aristocracy, so that grace and a sweet easiness might take their place. Now it became a question of dignity and poise rather than one of enjoyment bred out of gaelic prancing in the dances of the wilder Irish. The ways of the dook snooks were the better ways, so all of Dublin's grander folks were feverishly fitting themselves into the cast-off manners and minor deportment of the English. Every house with curtains on the windows and an old clock on the stairs was a frenzied hubbub of endeavour to find the right way to refined demeanour.

But these good people weren't certain of themselves. They couldn't learn everything in a hurry. These things took time. There was an air of uneasiness on most of them at every public or private gathering. They hadn't yet taken root. So a gilt-edged invitation from His Excellency Timothy Healy, Governor-General, to a Levee, caused a flutter of ecstasy, mingling with dismay, to many who graciously got them. What were they to do? How were they to go? They would be facing the unknowable. They were tormented with the thought of what they would be expected to say, and the wherewithal with which to clothe themselves. Too early for evening-dress. Pity, for most of them had, or could borrow, that much. They couldn't go in what they usually wore. That wouldn't be respectful. One had to be suitably dressed to pay one's respects to the Governor-General. But how? Morning-dress? There was no way out of it. But that would cost money; and, besides, one would have to get suitable head-gear to go with it. You couldn't go wearing a cap over it, for instance. Good God, no! That would be a revolting thing to do. Well, what then? A taller! That'll cost money, too. Especially with such a sudden demand for them. Black, I suppose? One could hardly go in a green, white, and gold topper. Why not? Why not? Ah, for God's sake, man! It's not right to make a laugh of a serious occasion. Well, a white one then? No; for, as far as I know, them sort is worn only at race meetings or cricket matches. It's a worrying problem. Why not go in me nightshirt? Aw, try to be serious, for once.

As Sean was coming down Sackville Street, a little black car suddenly stopped, a thin little man sprang out, ran on to the path, caught Sean by the arm, and held him while he was recovering breath.

—Looka, Sean, he said, I've got an invitation to the Levee, and I dunno what to do. You're a friend of Lady Gregory's, and should know what a man is to do to comport himself proper.

—A man who owns a doctorate in a university should always know what to do, said Sean. But what's the gigantic problem?

—Why, what to do at the beginning and the end of a Levee. I've got the tall-hat all right; but where do you put it, and what do you do with it when you get there?

—Well, doctor, if you're any kind of a juggler, you can enthertain the guests when you get there.

—Aw, now, be serious, Sean. Listen: I can't wear the tall-hat when I'm driving the car, can I?

—Why not?

—Why not? Whoever saw a tall-hat driving a car? It would be a laugh for all Dublin. Now what am I to do with it while I'm driving?

—Put it on the seat beside you, or behind your legs.

—I thought of that; but then I'll have to be wearing it when I step from the car, and it wouldn't look decent or sensible to be fishing it from under the seat, with everyone waiting. And then you can't suddenly slap on a tall-hat the way you would a soft one. So what's a fellow to do?

—Why not ask some of the seventy-seven dead men?

—The seventy-seven — what dead men?

—The men executed by your Free State Government.

—Oh, them! I had nothing to do with their executions, anyhow. The dead are dead, and are neither here nor there now.

—They are certainly not here, said Sean with some bitterness. But it seems to me that these men were put to death to afford you the privilege of donning a tall-hat. It won't be long till the gold harp's taken out of the green flag, and a bright, black tall-hat put in its place. The terrible beauty of a tall-hat is born to Ireland.

—Look, Sean, Yeats himself wore a tall-hat at the Horse Show, and this is far more important. I've got to wear one whether I like it or no; so tell me, like a good man, what you'd don under the circumstances?

—Me? Oh, if I was going, I'd go as I am.

—They wouldn't let y' in, man!

—That wouldn't trouble me much.

—You see, you're free of the problem, Sean, so you can well

laugh. Listen, though: am I to drive to the back of the house, or right up to the front entrance?

—Looka, said Sean, laying a friendly hand on the doctorate shoulder, I can't advise you on these deep problems. They'll probably have a man in another tall-hat to show you where to go, and how to get there. So good luck to you all!

—Hold on, just a second — listen. How're we to display ourselves when we get in? I daresay there'll be someone there to take the hat and mind it?

—Sure.

—Well, then, when I go in, I suppose His Excellency'll be waiting. Do I just bow; and, if I do, how far down do I go; or do I simply shake hands, saying, Best respects, I'm honoured, or what?

—You simply put a sweet smile on your kisser, bow as low as your head will go, and then ask His Excellency who he was with last night.

—Now, Sean, no coddin'; no double-meaning talk. We're up against it. None of us never did this before. Listen; the whole population's learning how to approach him, and how to get away again. Listen, an' you'll laugh. Paddy Miskell's missus's sprained her ankle doing curtseys at home. An' if you only heard them doing the approach, you'd have a fit. The doctorate lifted his voice into a shrill falsetto: 'Your Excellency's servant, most obedient so I am. I hope I see your Excellency in good condition. For an oul' fella of your age, you're wonderful, so y'are.' Rathmines is like a fairyland with the number of candles lighted to St. Anthony asking his help in the emergency.

Every mauler of finer things who had his name in a bank-ledger, or hoped to have it there soon, now that Cathleen ni Houlihan had won back three out of her four beautiful green fields, was busy in a quiet, curtained room, the blinds well down, discussing and practising the arts of refinement when making contacts with eminent people, more eminent people, and most eminent people; of walking with genteel steps, of bowing with dignity and caution, of curtseying with confidence, and of addressing the great with decorum and respect; just a few happy sentences to please His Excellency's ear. They were active fitting on trouser and skirt; morning-coat and evening-jacket; getting used to the sit of them; a wife here acting the governor-general to her husband; a husband there acting the governor-general to his wife.

—You go too quick, Jack. You're runnin' like a news-boy. Go

back, an' come in again. Walk something like the way a judg'd do it, in his robes.

—These blasted boots are cuttin' th' feet o' me!

—You'll have to put up with them. Now thry again, an' thry to take that hump off your shoulders, an' that look of heart-sthrain off your face. I'll count the steps slow — one, two, three; go on — say something.

—Grand evening, Mr. Healy, so 'tis.

—Oh, not Mr. Healy, man! Your Excellency, your Excellency!

—Oh, yes; your Excellency, an' how d'ye do? Grand gatherin' of Excellency — excellent persons here; very, your Excellency.

—Don't stick your mug so close to mine, Jack, when you're speakin'. Keep back a little, man. An' you must leave your tall-hat outside somewhere; you can't bring it in with you.

—An' when I come out, supposin' it's gone?

—We'll just have to take that risk, Jack.

The search for beauty had begun. In the midst of the flurry and fury over the proper alignment of clothes, over the tormenting effort to rise sublime in manner and deportment, De Valera, pinched and worn and threadbare, studied the question of the oath. He seemed to turn the spiritual side of the question into a mathematical one. His Party determined, after tremendous argument, that the taking of the oath could be done without taking the oath, provided they made it plain they didn't recognise the oath when they were taking the oath; that an oath taken under duress wasn't really an oath at all, but just the appearance of one; a deceptive thing, an illusion, a shadow, a ghost-oath. If you believed it was there, it would be there; if you didn't believe it was there, it couldn't be there. Just shut your eyes, close your ears, dispel your thoughts, and speak away, and the thing was done, yet not done.

So, after it was all over, the Republicans said they had heard nothing; no-one had said a word to them indicating that they had been taking an oath; they hadn't seen such a thing in writing or in print; the officials who were present never explained a thing to them; they stayed dumb. The Republicans saw a booklet on a bench that might have been, or might not have been, a testament. No-one said it was one. So there was no reason for them to assume that it must have been one. It was there; lying alone; but no-one picked it up, or said, Gents, this here is a testament; gents, I warn you, this is a testament — anything spoken beside this book, or in the vicinity of this book, must be the truth, the whole truth, and nothing but the truth. In fact, the silence was really oppressive. So though it was recorded that an oath had been taken, no Republican of De Valera's Party could honestly swear to the taking of any oath whatsoever.

They entered the Dail, upright men, their consciences clear, their hearts aglow, for they could now take their salaries without pain of spirit, and they could fight more effectively for the dollars, left over from the American Victory Loan, which the Free State Party was impudently claiming for its own.

> A terrible beauty is borneo,
> Republicans once so forlorneo,
> Subjected to all kinds of scorneo,
> Top-hatted, frock-coated, with manifest skill,
> Are well away now on St. Patrick's steep hill,
> Directing the labour of Jack and of Jill,
> In the dawn of a wonderful morneo.

And this was the beginning of the end of Cosgrave's power and his Free State Party. Cronus was to swallow Zeus before long. De Valera was destined to reign over Irish Israel for many years, becoming the *in hoc signo vincit* of the New Gael. In fancy again Sean recalled the vision of Pearse coming from the General Post Office into the now silent street, and standing in the midst of the fair sunshine to read to a few distant listeners, one here, two there, and three away yonder, the Proclamation of the Irish Republic, while a tiny tricolour fluttered high away over his head; but the building had changed, and seemed now to be half a bank and half a church, and the words read were different:

Irishmen and Irishwomen, in the name of God, and of the dead generations from which she receives her old tradition of nationhood, Ireland, through us, summons her people to her flag, and strikes for freedom. She strikes in the full confidence of victory for —

The white tie and the tailed coat.

The right to wear a top-hat, grey or black, according to circumstance or taste, when the occasion demands it.

The banning of all books mentioning the word Love, except when the word is used in a purely, highly spiritually, insignificant way.

The banning of any mention whatsoever of the name of James Joyce.

The right to examine and to settle eternally the question of procedure as to whether Paddy or Mick, Julia or Bridget, shall be the first to shake hands with, or bow to, Tim Healy or Sean T. O'Kelly; first to ceremonially enter a room, or first to sit down to a table.

The right to excommunicate a catholic student who enters Trinity College.

The right to make it known that western rivers are swift and deep to any person, called a communist, who may be thinking of spending a holiday in Connemara.

The right of the wrong to banish even a whisper of the name of Dr. Walter McDonald, D.D., Maynooth's Professor of Theology for forty years in the wilderness.

The right to give the catholic clergy the first word, the last word, and all the words in between, whatsoever they may be, on any and every question, whatsoever, without any reservation whatsoever either.

The right to consider such men (once referred to as Irishmen) as Tone, Emmet, Mitchel, Parnell, Synge, Yeats, and Joyce; and all such women (once referred to as Irishwomen) as Betsy Gray, Sarah Curran, Fanny Parnell, Lady Gregory, Eva of the Nation, and Speranza as non-gaels, non-Irish, and so *non est perpetua*.

The fascination De Valera had, and has, over the Irish people is astonishing. There seems to be no streak of joviality, good humour, or of erring humanity in him as there is in the warmer-natured Cosgrave. His speeches are dull, his voice unattractive, and to an independent observer there is little magnetism in the man. Yet he seems to hold an unbreakable grip on the people, and is loved by very many of them. St. John Ervine once referred to him as the Pinchbeck Parnell. But it was Arthur Griffith who was a Pinchbeck Parnell, for, posing as the great silent man, who hated speechmaking, he modelled his clay to look like the steely nature of the mighty Parnell. Whatever De Valera may be, he is De Valera and no-one else. He certainly has indomitable confidence in himself and in his policy — whatever that may be. During the Easter Rising, he proved his courage and his military skill, far above that of any other of the Leaders. He is an unassuming fellow, there is no doubt about that. Sean could see any old man or woman, and any young fellow or girl, however humble their circumstances might be, going up to him, and hear them addressing him affectionately as Dev. He would encourage them, or comfort them, and give them a delusive satisfaction. Everyone to whom Sean spoke, Irish acquaintance or English journalist, said that De Valera was a most courteous man. The man seems to have in him no malice of any kind, against man or an institution. He is as if he were one who forever remembered that he must forgive the trespasses of another, if he was to get forgiveness for his own. De

Valera couldn't hate. He could deny; he could reproach; he could argue, like a duller Gladstone, against a point of view other than his own; but he could neither hate the man nor the man's point of view. There was nothing whatever of the agnostic in De Valera. In this way, he differed from all great Irishmen Sean could bring to his remembrance: from Brian Boy Magee, from Donal MacSean of the Curses, from Wolfe Tone, from Mitchel, from Fintan Lalor, from Parnell, from Davitt, even from Thomas Davis, gentle and all as he was, De Valera's national monitor and pattern. Douglas Hyde was the nearest to De Valera, for to him, from all he said, all life was sweet and varnished. Devotion to the church's curriculum kept De Valera on the steady path, avoiding hell, and reaching heaven, and all that. His kneeling on a stage, in front of a crowded house, as was recorded in the Press, to receive the blessing of a visiting cardinal, was, to Sean, a humiliating thing for the head of a Republican State to do. The pietistic Spaniard in him, Sean thought. But Ireland wasn't any longer a Republican State, either in theory or in practice — she was a theocracy, fashioned by the Vatican, and decked in the brightest sacerdotal array by the bishops of Maynooth.

Well, thought Sean, apart from his personal qualities, how does he manage to keep his grip on the leadership of the Irish people, swinging about with the greatest of ease, like a daring young man on an Irish trapeze? Perhaps because he is the last living Leader of the Easter Rising, and because he will never do a thing to make the clergy uneasy. He will do all things, rightly or wrongly, in the spirit of the good, never-wavering Vatican catholic. The one who, out of the smoke and the flame, came safe. The one-time soldier. With the church's *nihil obstat* written on his brow, this patriot is irremovable. His fight against the Annuities paid to Britain; his long contention with the Loud Speaker, J. H. Thomas, then Minister for the Dominions, are to his credit. His great bargain, after a bitter fight, by which the Annuities were bought for ten millions, ended the Economic War with Britain, and at the same time put a high and well-curled feather in De Valera's cap. His Irish Constitution added a pewter button to hold the feather in its place; not exactly a sparkling ornament, but stamped deeply with the seals in the ring of every Irish bishop. Underneath this pewter button, though De Valera can't see it, is a little red star.

One thing alone threatens De Valera — the rising of the people against poverty; the union of the north and the south, when Labour will become a hundred times stronger by the natural Republican and Socialist activities of the Ulster people. When this happens, all those to the left of his Party will swing into pace with the movement and De Valera will no longer feel at home in Leinster House. Then the orange sash and the green sash will show a red star in the centre of each of them.

Then will come the fight against the slums, reeking with rottenness. Down with them! And the tens of thousands of the homeless cadging a night's shelter from the sleet, the rain, the frost, or the biting wind; old men and young women, young men and old women, silent and patient too long; all of them strangers to life; dumb about it; wondering why some who passed by could chat so cheerily, or laugh so carelessly; wondering at Eire's gay-dressed cavalry galloping or trotting to a ceremonial parade of politician, social-climber, church dignitary and delegate; the Jesus Christ hidden from the worker by a multitude of tall-hats, the marshalled catholicism, not of Aquinas nor of Francis, but of Belloc and G. K. Chesterton.

Time was with the Socialists, and time would push away the anxious queues outside trimly-fashioned convents, waiting for a penny dinner, when pennies were more plentiful; or waiting to snatch a loaf of St. Martin's or St. Anthony's bread from a bustling nun, more interested in the bread than in the wretches seeking it. Time, armed with the power of the people, will push away the slow decay of tuberculosis, the choking fright of diphtheria, the soiling horridness of typhoid, the rickets that jellied the fibre in the bones of the growing child; all brought about by the ignorance of the many, the careless privileges of the few, indifferent to these many afflictions till some of them become afflicted themselves; heedless of the fact that the pyning pox can be equally hidden beneath the cardinal's robes as well as the rags of the beggar; ignorant that this disease destroyed Thomas Wolsey in his Cardinal's Palace, as it did Puffing Dick, King of the Beggars, in the over-hanging horror of the slums.

Often Sean wandered through the poor streets where these poor poorer houses were; sometimes going in and out of them, climbing down to see some of the thousands who lived in the basements, the poorest of the poor rooms in the poorer house. No tall-hat, no black tie with jacket, no white tie and black jacket with tails ever went down these stony ways, damp with the green of slimy moss, a decayed carpet honouring the feet of those decaying in the dimmer den below. Nor did anyone, even those happy with the keenest sight, ever see the scarlet or the purple biretta cautiously going down these slime-covered steps. Only when some soul found itself within the dim flicker of a last farewell to life, did some simple, black-coated cleric climb down to give a hasty anointing to the dying soul, indifferently fortifying it against the four last things — heaven, hell, death, and the judgement.

Frequently he wandered, hurt with anger, through these cancerous streets that were incensed into resigned woe by the rotting houses, a desperate and dying humanity, garbage and shit in the roadway; where all the worst diseases were the only nobility present; where the ruddy pictures of the Sacred Heart faded into a dead dullness by the slimy damp of the walls oozing through them; the few little holy images they had, worn, faded, and desperate as the people were themselves; as if the images shared the poverty and the pain of them who did them reverence. Many times, as he wandered there, the tears of rage would flow into his eyes, and thoughts of bitter astonishment made him wonder why the poor worm-eaten souls there couldn't rise in furious activity and tear the guts out of those who kept them as they were.

But Sean had more than hope now. He had had letters from a Raissa Lomonovska telling him about what was going on in the Soviet Union, enclosing photographs of the people and their new ways. Two of the pictures showed the children of the Caucasus and the Ukraine assembling to welcome the first Diesel locomotive that had come to the Soviet Republics. There they were — a crowd of them, thin-limbed, and scarcely dressed, infant survivors of a dreadful time inflicted on their bodies and their souls by the good, profit-loving Christians of the surrounding states. There they were; free now, and firm, gazing at the locomotive; not yet conscious of what this one locomotive would mean to them in the years to come. The first swallow to be followed by flocks that would brighten the sky.

Sprinkled among the children were some workers and a few Red Army Men, the soldiers dressed in their loose blouses, and wearing their old cloth helmets, decked out in front with a tiny star of red; poverty their companion and bedfellow, but resurrection and courage in all their aspect; a tremendous destiny before them all. There they stood, giving a firm welcome to Russia's first Diesel locomotive. They had just defeated a world in arms against them, and this one Diesel engine was their first reward from God. These of the Soviet Union were they who did not despise the day of small things, and this one small gain has since shown to what an amazing magnificence a single engine and firm hearts and steady minds can grow.

In the spirit, Sean stood with these children, with these workers, with these Red Army Men, pushing away with them the ruin they were rising from, the ruin from which all the people would one day rise, sharing the firmness of their unafraid hearts, adding his cheer to the cheers of the Soviet People.

The terrible beauty had been born there, and not in Ireland. The cause of the Easter Rising had been betrayed by the commonplace bourgeois class, who laid low the concept of the common good and the common task, and were now decorating themselves with the privileges and powers dropped in their flight by those defeated by the dear, dead men. And scarlet cassock and purple cassock were blessing them and their gew-gaws — the low-cut ball-dress, the top-hat, the tailed coat and the white tie, the foolish wig and gown, and all the tarnished decorations of a dead state. And Christ, the clergy said, was in the midst of it all. *Ecce Homo! Ecce Homo Noster!* Here was their Christ, like unto themselves — morning-suit, top-hat, gold cuff-links, and dud-diamond stud, with a neatly-rolled umbrella in lieu of a cross.

But steady, workers, here and elsewhere; steady, poor of the poorer places; your day is coming. The Red Star shines over the Kremlin, once the citadel of the Czars. Those who tried hard to shake it down have fled homewards, helpless against the might and good courage of a half-starved people. The Red Soldiers with their Red Cavalry are on the frontiers, are on the sea-edges of their vast land. Socialism has found a home, and has created an army to patrol around it. The Red Star is a bright star. No pope, no politician, no cleric, no prince, no press-lord can frighten it down now, or screen its ray from our eyes. It is the evening star, and it is the bright and shining morning star. It is the star shining over the flock in the field, over the mother crooning her little one to rest, over the girl arraying herself for the bridal, over the old couple musing by the fireside, over the youngster playing in the street, over the artist achieving a new vision in colour, over the poet singing his song, over the sculptor carving out a fair thing that he alone can see hidden in a stone, over the hammer building the city, over the sickle cutting the corn, over the sailor sailing the seven seas, over the dreaming scientist discovering better and more magical ways of life, over the lover and his lass in ecstasy on the yellow sands, coming through the rye, or sauntering through the indifferent business of some city street, over the miner bending in the deep tomb where the sun-embalmed coal lies low, over the soldier guarding his country's life, over doctor and nurse, forgetting themselves that they may coax back health into all sick persons and young children.

Morning star, hope of the people, shine on us!

Star of power, may thy rays soon destroy the things that err, things that are foolish, and the power of man to use his brother for profit so as to lay up treasure for himself where moth and rust doth corrupt, and where thieves break through and steal.

Red Mirror of Wisdom, turning the labour in factory, field, and workshop into the dignity of a fine song;

Red Health of the sick, Red Refuge of the afflicted, shine on us all.

Red Cause of our joy, Red Star extending till thy five rays, covering the world, give a great light to those who still sit in the darkness of poverty's persecution.

Herald of a new life, of true endeavour, of common sense, of a world's peace, of man's ascent, of things to do bettering all things done;

The sign of Labour's shield, the symbol on the people's banner;

Red Star, shine on us all!

THE TEMPLE ENTERED

THE bells were ringing an old year out and a new year in for Sean: he was on his way to the temple of drama, the Abbey Theatre, where he was an acolyte now, in full canonical costume. Among his thoughts was none of either success or failure. He knew nothing about these things. What he thought of was how much money he would get from the performances. He would soon be in a position to buy many books, and live comfortably reading them, for a considerable time. He found himself going through the streets without noticing the people passing, or the shops, hearing but faintly even the chatter from the public-houses as he passed them by. It was as if he was on his way to meet a girl. Well, this was Marlborough Street, and further down was the Abbey Theatre, renowned, people said, the world over. There opposite was the Pro-Cathedral, ·the Church of the Immaculate Conception. An ugly sight. A dowdy, squat-looking imitation of some Italian church, done up in a back-handed Greco style; a cheaply-fashioned souvenir of Rome. No indication that this was Dublin, and that an Irish church, except the stiff statue of St. Laurence O'Toole standing grim and uneasy-looking on a corner of the entablature. Inside of the church, not a sign of the Book of Kells, nor that of Lismore; or ever a peal from St. Patrick's Bell; or even a painted symbol of the Cross of Cong. All of it imitation, silly, slavish; pompous imitation of the Latin, Italian order of the Vatican. A cheap home for Our Lady of Eblana, a cheap and distressing vase for the madonna lily of the slums.

Here is the church, thought Sean, stopping to look at its brawny and vulgar façade, this is the church that refused to shelter the body of a dead Fenian for a night. St. Laurence O'Toole refuses to allow a ray from the smallest of holy candles to reach as far as the body of a dead Fenian. Here the top-hatted holy ones streamed sterilely in, on ceremonial occasions, to pay their sweet respects to Jesus. Here at this church Matt Talbot, a Dublin labourer, full-up of sanctity, stretched himself flat on the pavement to say preliminary prayers, then crawled up the steps on his belly to the big door closed against him, waiting prone on the stones till it opened to let him join in the first Mass, so that he might go merry to work; dropping dead one day as he hurried to another church in an effort to fulfil the obligation he put upon himself to pray without ceasing. But he hurried too fast this time, for his heart gave out before he got there, and he fell down dead. But he died with harness on his belly. Afterwards, in the mortuary, it was found that he was wearing a cart chain round the middle of his body, with another round one of his legs, while a rope was tied tightly round the other one, and all were spangled with holy medals. *A model workman and a model catholic*, the courtly knight, Sir Joseph Glynn, calls him, *and his life points out the only path to true peace for all who labour, a life of self-discipline lived in perfect agreement with the law of God and His church. Ecce hobo sapiens.* Blow, crumpeter, blow! So workers of Dublin, and the world, you know now what you have to do. Follow Matt Talbot up to heaven. You've nothing to lose but the world, and you've the holy chains to gain. Read this Glynn's *Life of Matt Talbot*, then read Stalin's *Life of Lenin*; and take your choice. Make the world safe for the bosses. If you do, you're sure to get to heaven when you die.

Think deep on these things, working-men. Why do you waste time demanding a living wage? Think of eternity, and remember there may be none there. Why do you want to bother about the health and vigour of your children? Pain and woe and disease may help them upwards. Why do you look for a comfortable home, with light and heat and colour in it? You fools! Consider Mutt Talbot,

and you'll realise that these poor things are but vanity. Worse than
vanity — burdens, clogs, stumbling-blocks, impeding your precious
way to heaven. Listen, you dockers and labourers of Dublin! When
a boat has to be unloaded in quick time so that she may catch a tide,
and you get an extra two shillings for the hurried job, don't take
them. Refuse this bonus as Mutt Talbot did, feeling with him that
idle moments waiting for lorries to come to be unloaded should be
set against the extra work. That was Mutt Talbot, that was! This
refusal of extra money, says the knight of Glynn, *was due to the high
sense of justice this man Talbot possessed.* Oh, how far short do we
come of this man's high sense of justice! Mutt always thought of his
poor boss. Look at all the boss had to do with his money — keep
a big house going, a carriage and pair, a well-dressed wife, and
high education for his little ones. If indifferent workers could but
see the truth hidden in time and eternity, they'd refuse any extra
reward of wage or bonus. They'd advance through life on white
bread and black tea to the glory of God and rich benefit of their
own souls, and so allow the bosses to enjoy their chicken and wine
in peace. Do these things, workers, and you'll all be lifted up to
heaven with sparkling cords made out of the gold of the rich men.
And the sight entrancing you'll all see there — Mutt Talbot and the
knight of Glynn shaking hands among the gallant and glittering
angels

—To hell with Mutt Talbot! muttered Sean, glancing up at the
cold statue of St. Laurence O'Toole, without the chime of a word
from him; we won't give in to the bosses as you, St. Laurence, gave
in to the Normans. If any saint is to be preferred, I choose St. Joan,
who, at least, prayed with a sword at her girdle. She was a fighter
who disturbed great cleric and great lord, and so signs on it, she was
burned before she was blessed.

This church was nicely set down, for it was but a minute's walk
from Dublin's fairest thoroughfare — O'Connell Street; a minute's
walk from fine business and great banking; and it was but another
minute's walk from the street where, in tumbling houses, fat-
breasted, big-thighed women, clad in brilliantly-coloured calico
gowns of crimson or green, sat at twisted windows, calmly drinking
down tumblers of luscious stout, frothing over the rim of the glasses.
A gentle shake of these gaudy gowns would show bare shoulders and
barer breasts, signalling seduction down to any likely man passing
by beneath; and many a wayward and unstable Mutt Talbot would
lift a wavering but flaming eye to the visions at the windows.

Here was the Abbey Theatre — a red flower in the slum; but a minute's walk from the church, too, so that judgement, heaven, and hell were but a short way from each other. Sean had entered the temple. He had passed under the glass-roofed awning, its iron standards and framework gilded discreetly, showing that, though austerity couldn't suitably don a golden shawl, she could decently wear a golden brooch in a black one. He remembered the first time he had stood in the tiled foyer through which so many fine souls had passed to watch Ireland finding at last her soul in literature and the drama. Sean had come in by the front way, and was now among the gods. To the left were the stairs going down to the stalls where Sean would sit now, to watch the play of another, and to see and help to guide the evolution, through acting and design, of his own. To the right was a door leading to the Manager's office and the stage, and in between these two entrances stood the tabernacle of all theatres — the box-office. Opposite, parallel with a stained-glass window, was a little narrow counter where the audience from the stalls drank coffee, ate biscuits, and discussed the play. Beside this counter, high up on the wall, hung Dermod O'Brien's painting of Barry Fitzgerald in the part of the King from Lady Gregory's *The Dragon*. A poster on another wall told in French when Synge's *Playboy of the Western World* was first performed in Paris.

Inside, Sean saw how small the theatre was, holding only half a thousand. It somehow looked smaller now than when he knew it so well as The Mechanics' Theatre. The freshness, the red-leather upholstered seats, the shields, bearing on them the armorial signs of Ireland's Four Beautiful Fields, and the black curtain with its gold stripes, showed up the points of the building, and brought them closer together. Again Sean was treading the poor, narrow stage, its expansion backwards forever prohibited by a slum lane-way running from Marlborough Street, where stood the Abbey Theatre itself, to Beresford Place, where stood the Liberty Hall, made so famous by the eloquence and flame of Jim Larkin, the Labour Leader.

He told no-one that he had known this old stage well, that he had even played a part on it; that one of his brothers had often done so; that he had watched, from the pit below, men, with hands tied behind their back, struggling to swallow boiling-hot suet puddings; in their haste knocking them from the table to floor, and so forcing themselves to stretch there, eating with voracity; for ten shillings reward was to be given to him who finished his pudding first. He remembered the drop-curtain, showing, in fading colours, the lovely Lakes of Killarney; now displaced by the dignified one of sable and gold, but showing signs of fading too. He had drunk glasses of diluted claret, sweet with sugar, with those who had played the principal parts in Boucicault's *The Shaughraun*, in a pub opposite the theatre; in a private room, too, for the pub proprietor had something to do with the venture. All changed now, changed utterly; and here he was now with plays of his own showing themselves off on the very same stage that he himself had trod as a growing youngster so long, so long ago. His brother, Archie, had played the part of Harvey Duff. Archie was a good black-and-white man with pencil or pen, a splendid carpenter, and a brilliant accountant, but there he was now, up in Liverpool, sweeping the floors of a Dunlop rubber factory. The lad's will hadn't been guided rightly into a fighting, fuller life when he left school; his talents had been left to perish.

The first night of his first play had gone very well indeed, and Sean had been congratulated by all the actors. But he was troubled with vexation of spirit when he was told that the play was to run for three nights only, and this vexation was sharpened when the Secretary of the theatre added the information that there was but thirteen pounds received for the night. However, the second night's receipts jumped to thirty pounds, and the last night to over fifty, which meant the first full house for the Abbey Theatre for many a long night. Sean smiled benignly at the Secretary when he was told the theatre would have no money in the bank till the guarantors sent in their guarantees; but, if Sean so desired, he could be paid from the cash received at the door, instead of in the usual way by cheque. Full of shy vanity, with a grand wave of the hand Sean told the Secretary he wasn't to bother, and that he'd willingly wait for the cheque.

When it came, it was less than four pounds. Less than four pounds! And he had bargained in his mind for twenty, at the least. And, if the receipts hadn't jumped up at the end, he'd have had but half of that amount. Dimly he began to realise that the Abbey Theatre would never provide a living. It was a blow, a bitter disappointment. The black stripes in the theatre's curtain were far wider than the gold stripes. Less than four pounds wouldn't even pay his passage to England for a chat about the Soviet Union with Raissa Lomonovska. It looked as if things would allow his talent to perish too. What he had got wouldn't even pay what he owed. The amount didn't extend even to the purchase of a book. What was he to do? One thing, and one thing only — go forward. He had put his hand to the plough, and he wasn't the one to look back. He would start a new play that very night.

So he had, and he called it *Cathleen Listens In*, a jovial sardonic sketch on the various parties in conflict over Irish politics — Sinn Fein, Free State, and Labour. It was a short one-act work, and was performed after a major play had ended. Another experience for Sean! The audience received the little play in dead silence, in a silence that seemed to have a point of shock in its centre. Not even a cold clap of a hand anywhere. They all got up from their seats and silently filed out of the theatre. He was the one and only playwright to have had a play received in silence by an Abbey audience; the only one to be deprived of even a single timid hand-clap. Indeed, it did look as if his talent, too, would have to perish in silence and with malice of after-thought. What would he do, for he was vexed, and a sense of humiliation discouraged him; what would he do? Go on, go on! Forever he would go on seeing through his own eyes, hearing with his own ears, speaking with his own tongue. No power of influence, no seduction of wealth, no affection for friend, nor would any love for woman draw him away from his own integrity. Let that integrity be right or wrong, it would be a true reflection of what he felt in his nature from the things he saw and the things he heard around him.

Going as a patient to the Royal Eye and Ear Hospital, with an ulcerated cornea, the head surgeon there, Mr. Cummins, had come over to him, gave him treatment, and then walked part of the way home with him, Sean leaving him opposite the doctor's own hall door, after refusing an invitation to come in and drink a cup of coffee. But that saunter through St. Stephen's Green was the beginning of a fast friendship which has lasted to this very day. A strangely fastidious man, a very sensitive soul, Dr. Cummins seemed to choose his friends cautiously; but he seized on Sean impulsively, and his efforts glowed with eagerness to make Sean easy in his company. It was an odd alliance. Joe Cummins, delicate in word and phrase and manner, sensitive to a high degree, but a true bohemian, all the same, on the one hand; and Sean, a rather rough and ready-tongued proletarian, well versed in Communism, and a revolutionary by nature, on the other. The calm and lovely serenity of most of the Dutch School of painting, balanced by the fragrant venery and graceful femininity of Fragonard, and the lace-like prose of Addison, balancing against the wildness of Van Gogh, the savage sarcasm and definite lust of Goya, the daring of Cézanne, and the tempestuous writings of James Joyce, mingled together and enjoyed themselves night after night in the doctor's surgery; and, long afterwards, when Sean left for England, he carried with him the doctor's warm rug against the chill of the long railway journey; though Sean had never pulled it from its strap, unable to reconcile the idea of himself with a rug around his legs.

The third work, a full-length play, was, from the Abbey Theatre point of view, an emphatic success, and Yeats halted in his meditations to tell Sean that he had given new hope and new life to the theatre. The house had been booked out for the first week, and the run of the play was extended for a week longer. Sean had come into his fortune of twenty-five pounds, after waiting more than a year for it.

Books, books, more books! And a step nearer to a trip over the waters to England. His choice of Barry Fitzgerald for one of the two chief parts had been more than justified. When Sean had mentioned his name, Mr. Robinson had demurred, had murmured the name of F. J. McCormick as a better selection for Boyle; but Sean had insisted on the selection of Fitzgerald, and the choice had been triumphant. After the Abbey season had ended a year ago, to give place to a long holiday, the Abbey actors had taken the theatre, and had put on Ervine's *Mary, Mary, Quite Contrary* so as to furnish themselves with something more in the way of money to tide the holiday over, and Sean had gone to see it, in a spirit of loyalty to those who had so generously helped him by their fine acting. He had known all who had played in it; all save one whom he had never heard of, whom he had never seen. This newcomer filled the part of the Anglican clergyman. The play began, and Sean sat easy wondering who was the new fellow that had joined the company. Sean soon sat up. This new fellow could act. This fellow was a great comedian. This fellow was an artist. Sean never looked at a programme in a theatre because of his bad sight, so he did not know the fellow's name. He would go behind, and find out. This fellow was the man for him. He had never seen him before; none of the actors had ever mentioned his name. Well, if they didn't, Sean would, and out loud, too.

When the play ended, he rushed round to tell all of his discovery. It was an unwise thing to do; a foolish thing, a stupid thing to do. But Sean was altogether ignorant of jealousies behind the curtain. He rushed across the foyer, through the doorway at the back, up the stairs, down the corridors where the dressing-rooms were, yelling, Who's the fellow that played the clergyman? Where's the chap that played the clergyman? Michael Dolan's dressing-room door was open, for it was a warm night, and the actor was busy taking the grease-paint from his face. He listened without a flicker of an eyelid to Sean's excited demand to know who and where was the fellow who played the part of the clergyman. A great actor, said Sean vehemently; a grand comedian; an artist born suddenly for the theatre.

—He's not bad, murmured Mr. Michael Dolan, rubbing quietly away at his face — when he happens to get a part that suits him.

—Good God, man, said Sean, it's long since the theatre's seen the like of him! And then there was silence, for Sean began to realise that such things spoken loudly were not wise or welcome. For the future, if circumstances called for it, he would praise what he thought was bad, and censure what he felt to be good — he would, like hell! But his ardent acclaim of what he thought was fine raised the first breeze of coolness between him and the Abbey actors.

Passing by his third play, a one-act work called *Nannie's Night Out*, a play no-one liked, except A. E., otherwise known as George Russell, who thought it O'Casey's best work; an opinion that didn't bother Sean, for he knew A. E. knew nothing about the drama, and felt it a little less; Sean, at length, found himself attending the rehearsals of his fourth one, a full-length drama. He was now taking an active part in a rehearsal for the first time. He had stayed silent and passive during these of his first two plays, and during those of his third play he had been in hospital with a sharp attack of bronchitis most of the time, finding the play well set when he came out, so that he had very little to learn or to do, except to persuade the timid Barry Fitzgerald that he could, and must, play the part.

But Sean's persuasion laboured on, for he saw before him clearly now a fine library and a visit to England, where his second play was doing well in the West End of London. He was buying furniture bit by bit, and still had a lot to get before he could be decently comfortable. He wanted to move somewhere else to a place in which he would find fairer comfort, greater space, and a steady quietness. He could do all this in England, but the expense would be great, and he hesitated. If the plays brought in double of what he had now, he would go. If the play on in London really settled down, and if this new play went well in the Abbey, he would hoist his sail, and go. A short farewell to Ireland; a hasty look round at places he had known for so long; a last thought of Irish gods and fighting men, and then he would go.

But he was anxious about the present play. He had fancied that

when he had fought his way to the Abbey stage, all his troubles
would end. Poor, guileless innocent! He had left old troubles to
embrace new ones. He had noticed an odd coldness and an irritant
nervousness in the manner of the cast. He sensed that something
was going wrong. A number of the actors were doing their parts
lazily, as if the play held no interest for them. Mr. Robinson, the
producer, was inclined to be irritable, and he was at times abrupt
when Sean ventured to make a suggestion. Then a whisper in Sean's
ear told him that Miss Crowe had decided not to play the part of
Mrs. Gogan. Sean went to her, and asked if what he heard was true.
She said it was. He asked why she wouldn't play the part, and was
told that *The part was not genteel.* Oh, Jesus! A Miss May Craig, an
actress little thought of, but very good, was got to fill the part, and
filled it to perfection. Miss Ria Mooney, chosen for the part of the
prostitute, was bombarded with barbed beseeching to rise out of the
part; for, if she didn't, she might no longer be thought respectable,
and might risk her future in this world and even the next. Fortunately for the play, she held on, and put more fire into the part
because of the opposition. F. J. McCormick was hesitant, and
seemed to be responding reluctantly to his part. Then, in the midst
of the anxiety, Gabriel Fallon, whom Sean had selected to play the
part of Peter Flynn, came stealing up to beg this part be taken from
him, and the part of Captain Brennan given in its stead. All this
made Fitzgerald more nervous than ever, for he had none of the
arrogant courage, and none of the jovial determination, which,
under different conditions, might have made a great man of Fluther.
And, finally, when Sean had ventured to suggest the kind of instrument needed to simulate a band leading the Dublin Fusiliers to the
boat, Mr. Robinson's outburst of Oh, shut up, for Christ's sake,
man! I've got enough to do to deal with the cast! settled Sean into
a wondering silence. To this day Sean isn't sure — for no word ever
came to him — that the cast, or any members of it, had heard of
the vigorous opposition the play was to meet with when it came to
the stage.

While he had been writing the play, Liam O'Flaherty had brought
David Garnett to the tenement house to see Sean, and had persuaded
Sean to tell of the play he was writing; so, round a blazing fire, Sean
had a vigorous chat with this clever and most amiable writer. Both
Garnett and O'Flaherty, probably out of politeness and goodwill,
had agreed that the play would be a work to be remembered. Afterwards, O'Flaherty's letter to *The Irish Statesman*, definitely and

emphatically condemning the work as a bad play, shoved Sean into taking a vow that never again would he reveal to anyone what he was trying to do; never again, except under curious circumstances, would he speak of work in progress. If he spoke at all, he would talk of something he but faintly intended to do. He would think it quietly out, do it the best way he could, and then send it out in the name of God and of O'Casey.

Coming close to the first night, Sean's eyes filled with inflammation, and in-growing eyelashes made the inflammation worse. Dr. J. D. Cummins, now an intimate friend, did all he could to lessen the searching pain; but on the night of the first performance, Sean found it hard and painful to keep his eyes fixed on the bright zone of the stage. The theatre was packed to the doors; the curtain went up; the play began. Though some of the actors didn't seem to strive very earnestly to swing themselves into the drama, most things went well, and the audience sat still, intensely interested in what they saw before them — the mimic, but by no means unimportant, portrayal of a part of Dublin's life and feeling. When the end came, the audience clapped tumultuously, and shouted applause. They shouted for the author, and Sean went on to the stage, quietly glad that the play had succeeded. He took the appreciation of those there nicely, though the flame of pain in his eyes pricked like red-hot needles. But all was pleasant, and the loud applause flowed from the serenity of agreement with, and appreciation of, the play. Tightening the belt of his rubber trench-coat tight around him, he went home settled in mind, happy in heart: the worst was over. He was very much the innocent gaum.

The next night he sauntered into a storm. Holy Murther had come again on a visit to the Abbey Theatre. When he entered the foyer, he was hurried up to the Secretary's Office, where W. B. Yeats was waiting for him. Listen to my tale of woe. There he was told that the theatre was in an uproar, and that the play could not go on, if something definite wasn't done; that missiles were being flung at the actors, and that it looked as if the stage would be stormed.

—We think it necessary that the police should be sent for immediately, so that the mob may be kept from preventing us carrying on the work we have set our hands to do, said Yeats. We want your consent, O'Casey, to send for the police, as you happen to be the author of the play.

The police! Sean to agree to send for the police — never! His Irish soul revolted from the idea; though Yeats and others reminded him that the police were no longer in a foreign service, but were now in Ireland's own. That the tricolour waved over their barracks, and that it even graced the big drum of their band. Even so, Sean couldn't see his way to ask them to come. No, no; never! But a wild roar heard in the theatre, seeming to shake the room where they all stood, told him to make up his mind quick; and swearing he could ne'er consent, consented.

The police were summoned, and the play began again — two plays, in fact: one on the stage, the other in the auditorium. Yeats tore down the stairs and rushed on to the stage to hold the fort till the constables came. The whole place became a mass of moving, roaring people, and Yeats roared louder than any of them. Rowdy, clenching, but well-groomed hands reached up to drag down the fading black-and-gold front curtain; others, snarling curiously, tried to tug up the very chairs from their roots in the auditorium; while some, in frenzy, pushed at the stout walls to force them down. Steamy fumes ascended here and there in the theatre, and a sickly stench crept all over the place, turning healthy-looking faces pale. The high, hysterical, distorted voices of women kept squealing that Irish girls were noted over the whole world for their modesty, and that Ireland's name was holy; that the Republican flag had never seen the inside of a public-house; that this slander of the Irish race would mean the end of the Abbey Theatre; and that Ireland was Ireland through joy and through tears. Up in the balcony, a section was busily bawling out *The Soldier's Song*, while a tall fellow frantically beat time on the balcony-rail with a walking-stick. Barry Fitzgerald became a genuine Fluther Good, and fought as Fluther himself would fight, sending an enemy, who had climbed on to the stage, flying into the stalls with a flutherian punch on the jaw. And in the midst of the fume, the fighting, the stench, the shouting, Yeats, as mad as the maddest there, pranced on the stage, shouting out his scorn, his contempt; his anger making him like unto an aged Cuchullain in his hero-rage; his long hair waving, he stormed in utter disregard of all around him, confronting all those who cursed and cried out shame and vengeance on the theatre, as he conjured up a vision for them of O'Casey on a cloud, with Fluther on his right hand and Rosie Redmond on his left, rising upwards to Olympus to get from the waiting gods and goddesses a triumphant apotheosis for a work well done in the name of Ireland and of art.

Then the constables flooded into the theatre, just in time. Rough and ready, lusty guardians of the peace. They filed into the theatre as Irish constables for the first time in their life; mystified, maybe, at anyone kicking up a row over a mere play. They pulled the disturbers out, they pushed them out, and, in one or two instances, carried them out, shedding them like peas from the pod of the theatre, leaving them in the cold street outside to tell their troubles to their neighbours or to the stars. Then the play went on, halting often, and agitated to its end. For the first time in his life, Sean felt a surge of hatred for Cathleen ni Houlihan sweeping over him. He saw now that the one who had the walk of a queen could be a bitch at times. She galled the hearts of her children who dared to be above the ordinary, and she often slew her best ones. She had hounded Parnell to death; she had yelled and torn at Yeats, at Synge, and now she was doing the same to him. What an old snarly gob she could be at times; an ignorant one too.

He left the auditorium where the people were watching the play, subdued and nervous, hedged in by the silver-plated helmets of the police, and strayed out into the foyer, right into the midst of a group of women squealers, members of Cumann na mBan — the Society of Women. They shot remarks at him from where they stood or lounged. They said he was a renegade, a friend to England, and that he would soon have a government pension. They said he had held up Ireland's sacred name to ridicule for the sake of the money he'd get for doing it; that it was he who, sooner or later, would feel the shame, and not Ireland. They said he was one now with those who had always hated Ireland, and that the Union Jack was his flag now, and not the Irish tricolour that he had defamed.

—Yes, said one, leaning against the wall, an' I'd like you to know that there isn't a prostitute in Ireland from one end of it to th' other.

Cathleen ni Houlihan was talking. Drawing her patched and fading skirt close around her, she was talking big. Through these women, she was talking. There wasn't a comely damsel among them. Sean noticed this with some surprise. They were all plain, provoking no desire in him to parley words with them, as a pretty face would have done, had one been among them. So after listening for awhile, and saying a few words, he left them to go up to the office to see how things were going. Yeats was shaking hands with an Inspector of Police who was introducing Sergeant Bantry Bay to the poet. The sergeant had developed into a mood of hilarious nervousness. He bowed to the poet, took off his hat, offered his hand, and when Yeats offered his, shook it vehemently, bending Yeats forward with the power of his hand's pull, blurting out a greeting that he must have been practising all the way to the theatre: *It is to be greatly regretted, sir, that I have had the honour and pleasure of meeting you for the first time undher such disthressing circumstances!* The Inspector looked silly to hear this greeting, and its unexpected eloquence stunned Yeats out of his senses for a few moments, so that he stared at the sergeant till he summoned enough thought to mutter confusedly, Yes, yes; quite. It is, it is.

Sean went home feeling no way exalted by his famous apotheosis. He was bewildered, and felt sick rather than hilarious. Slandered the people! He had slandered his class no more than Chekhov had slandered his. Did these bawling fools think that their shouting would make him docile? He would leave them to their green hills of holy Ireland. His play was doing well in London, and the producer, J. B. Fagan, had written several times to him, asking him to come over. Why didn't he go, and leave the lot of them? The land of Nelson and of Clive was beckoning to him more clearly than ever before; and he was near ready to leave the land of Patrick and of Tone.

A few days after he received a letter from Frank Ryan of the National University telling him that Mrs. Sheehy-Skeffington challenged him to a debate about the play. Would he take up the challenge, or would he not? He would; and he wrote to Frank Ryan telling him so. It was foolish to bother, but Sean felt that if he didn't take it up, it would be thought he was afraid, and his pride, stupid pride, couldn't allow that to be thought by anyone. He hadn't learned enough yet. He was still a gaum. When he got to the hall, he found it packed to the door, so crowded that those in the front were almost on top of him; so crowded that the air was gone, and a damp heat everywhere. That was one of the things he was never able to bear — a crowded, airless room always made him sick. And now that his eyes were full of pain, the sense of breathlessness would be worse, and thinking would be hard to do. He listened to Mrs. Sheehy-Skeffington speaking against what she called realism in the drama, and pleading very cleverly for the continuance of romanticism on the stage, especially in an Ireland fighting against many odds for her finest national conceptions.

But Sean knew well that those who had fought against the British had no interest in, no knowledge whatever of, the battling difference between romanticism and realism. What concerned them was the implication of fear showing itself in the manner and speech of the fighting characters of the play; and in the critical way their patriotism was ignored, or opposed by Dublin's poor. Mrs. Sheehy-Skeffington, a very clever and a very upright woman, saw it the other way, or thought she saw it so, and turned the dispute into an academic question, because — Sean often thought afterwards — she wished him to do the same, and so lift the question on to a higher plane than that of roars, fights with fists, savage abuse, and the tearing down of a theatre. But Sean couldn't, and wouldn't, get away from the everyday words and conduct of the common people, and what they thought of the things that had happened among them, adding to these things the thoughts which afflicted him about these same things too.

Ill as he felt with the heat and the thickened air, coupled with the neuralgic pain pressing on his eyeballs, forcing his thoughts into the confusing fear that he would speak badly, Sean watched the figure of Madame Gonne-McBride, seated like a quiet stone image this side of Mrs. Sheehy-Skeffington, and but a little distance from himself. She was clad in a classical way, with a veil of dark blue over her head, the ends flowing down over her shoulders. She turned slowly, only once, to glance at him; and Sean saw, not her who was beautiful, and had the walk of a queen, but the poor old woman, whose voice was querulous, from whom came many words that were bitter, and but few kind. This was she of whom it had been said that men could thrash out, on a dark night, a full barn of corn by the light from one tress of her hair. This was she for whom Yeats had woven so many beautiful cloths of embroidered poetry. She, too, was changed, changed utterly, for no ring of glory now surrounded that crinkled, querulous face. Shadows now were all its marking, shadows where the flesh had swelled or where the flesh had sagged. This is she who, as Yeats declared,

Hurled the little streets upon the great.

She had never done that, for her knowledge of the ways of little streets was scanty, interesting her only when they issued from their dim places headed by a green flag. She never seemed to have understood Yeats, the poet. Indeed, she could not, having little of the poet in herself, so that she never felt the lure of melody. She forever sat within the folds of, or stood talking before, a velvet green curtain, and never thought to take a peep behind. Here she sat now, silent, stony; waiting her turn to say more bitter words against the one who refused to make her dying dream his own. There she sits stonily silent, once a sibyl of patriotism from whom no oracle ever came; now silent and aged; her deep-set eyes now sad, agleam with disappointment; never quite at ease with the crowd, whose cheers she loved; the colonel's daughter still.

The sickness, suffocating, seized Sean when he got up to speak after Mrs. Sheehy-Skeffington had ended, and he was forced to sit down to wait till the pain in his head steadied into a droning discomfort; till the giddiness lost its power over his thoughts. He did not know, till more than twenty years after, that silicosis had, in shrivelling a lung, pulled his heart out of its place. Some said, Go home, and do not stay, for you look ill, and should be careful. But Sean barely listened to them, for he had come there to speak, and speak would; and speak he did. But it was a hard fight to get going, and his whole being was strained with the effort, and in his heart he despised, more bitterly than ever, the ones who made it necessary for a writer to defend a work so many hated and so few admired. Weary and scornful at the end of it all, Sean went home to his tenement in the little car of Frank Hugh O'Donnell. He felt very tired, and very sad. He lit the lamp, thanked Frank for giving him a lift, looked round, and saw a telegram that had been thrust under his room door. Must have come while he was out. Write to please the Mary MacSweeneys, the Countesses Markievicz, the Madame Gonne-McBrides! Jasus Christ, the very thought was laughable! He stooped, picked up the telegram, tore open the envelope, and read the message. It was from Fagan telling him that his play was coming off at one theatre, but another had been engaged, and the play would go on there; but there wasn't much of a chance of a new success, unless Sean came over for the first night, and so created a little publicity for the newer effort.

—I'll go, he said to Frank O'Donnell. I'll go over to help the play's entrance into a new theatre, and leave the wrack behind me.

When the shouting had died down, and the rowdier captains had departed, the turn of the intellectuals came to cheat Sean from any success he might be expecting. Sean saw another side of Ireland's enterprising malice and envy. He was learning more in a few weeks than he had learned in a lifetime. The intellectuals began to send letters to the Press, and to A. E.'s journal, *The Irish Statesman*, condemning and upbraiding the plays. Some of them were influenced to do this, Sean thought, because he had definitely refused to join them in a Club or Society which was to be organised to put the arrogant Yeats in his place. He would argue with Yeats, oppose him manfully, but personally, on any question of religion, politics, and even literature, if he happened to differ from the poet; but he wouldn't join any clique to do it, because he thought this opposition was born of envy of the great fame the poet enjoyed as the leading man of Irish Letters. He had never mentioned the matter to Yeats, for having done, or refused to do, what was right, or what he thought was right, he was satisfied in his own soul, and nothing else mattered.

Sean's plays were stoned with many criticisms from the intellectuals, so that he passed from one bewilderment to another. *The plays, said one, are naught but a series of Tableaux Vivants; O'Casey is purely a photographic artist. He is striving after a literary quality of speech which is entirely alien to the Dublin slum-dwellers; the plays have the structure of the cinema and the revue. They are a series of scenes rather than a play. The career of O'Casey induces fear for the future.* All this came from the bracing brain of Dublin's then first critic — Andrew E. Malone. Again, as if he felt he hadn't said enough, he goes on to add, *His plays are phases of Dublin life as abnormal as they are transient. O'Casey's humour is the humour of the music-hall without the skill of the music-hall or the sharpened point of its wit. Is O'Casey a dramatist, or is he but a combination of the cinema and the dictaphone?* That was written more than twenty years ago, and the Irish critics haven't been able to answer the question yet.

Following O'Flaherty's direct announcement (as pompous as anything Yeats could have said) that *'The Plough and the Stars' was a bad play*, came the young poet Fred O'Higgins's angry remonstrance and criticism, saying, *A new political quality approved by the arrogance of the Anglo-Irish is the only quality for which O'Casey is offered applause. His is a technique based on the revue structure, in the quintessence of an all-Abbey burlesque, intensified by 'divarsions' and Handy Andy incidents, with somewhat more original settings. O'Casey in his new play entirely lacks the sincerity of the artist.*

Another coloured bullet-bead was added to the string by a letter from Austin Clarke, another poet, who said, with poise and gentle dignity, that *Several writers of the New Irish School* (himself included, of course) *believed that Mr. O'Casey's work was a crude exploitation of our poorer people in the Anglo-Irish tradition that is now moribund.* Still another writer, R. M. Fox, referred to the plays as *The Drama of the Dregs*, adding that *The peasant plays have been followed by slum plays, but their reign will not be long, though as entertainment these slum dramas are permissible. But truth is wanted as well as entertainment.*

So Sean, at first bewildered by the riot, was now puzzled by the Irish critics, for, innocent gaum that he was, he didn't realise then that these fellows didn't know what they were talking about.

He wondered how he could have built on the revue structure, for he had never seen a revue in his life. He knew nothing about the cinema. If any of them had only mentioned melodrama, he would have cocked an ear, for he had seen many of these, and had enjoyed them all. They saw in Sean that of which they themselves were full — the cinema and the revue. Then first began Sean's distrust of, and contempt for, the Irish critics. Knowing all, they knew nothing. Two critics now began to shine on his thoughts — one Irish, curiously enough, and the other American. They were George Jean Nathan and George Bernard Shaw — the two Georges. He had got Shaw's two books of *Dramatic Criticisms* from America, paying twenty-five shillings for them — a big sum for Sean to hand out those days; but he found them to be worth the sacrifice. The books formed a gorgeous episode in Sean's life. Shaw's comments were on plays which — bar Shakespeare, Wilde, and Ibsen — he had neither seen nor read, and which, now, he would never see nor read, for they were all dead, never to rise again; but the criticisms lived on, and gave Sean a candle-light view of the theatre dead, and an arc-lamp view of the theatre living. Another book, Nathan's *The Critic and the Drama*, was a book of revelations to Sean. He was becoming less of the innocent gaum every page he passed. Here was a live man of the drama. As deep in what he wrote as he was gay. A wise philosopher, an undaunted critic, a lover of the theatre with cothurnus and sock attached to the glittering costume of the harlequin who carried a torch in his right hand instead of a lath. The Irish drama critics, even those who were poets, could now go to hell for Sean!

But, soberly, while he was here, he'd have to deal with the critics at home. How? By going his own way. That was the one thing to do, for there wasn't even a hint of guidance in what they said. They were no good. He would have to go a long way from the cliques of Dublin. But how could he escape? By living in the country or by crossing over to England. It was time he saw newer streets than those of Dublin. If he went to the country, he'd still be confined within the ken and den of Cosgravian and De Valerian politics, and well within the sphere of influence set up by Irish rosaries, Anthony's Annals, and all the crowding rolipoli-holiness of the Pope's green island; with Church of Ireland stained-glass windows shining timidly through the mist that does be on the bog. No, not that way. His future connection with Ireland must be somewhat similar to that of De Valera's association with the British Commonwealth — neither in it nor out of it. For him, the land of Nelson, Clive, and Canning in place of the land of Patrick, Tone, and Parnell. Not quite — Tone and Parnell would be forever very near to him.

Some little time after, the Abbey selected Shaw's *Man and Superman* for performance, and gave the play, in Sean's vision, a very bad production indeed. It had its comic side, for all the actors were subdued by the relentless enthusiasm of F. J. McCormick, who played Tanner, and seemed to be always hustling them off the stage. Barry Fitzgerald, who played the part of Roebuck Ramsden, could only timidly stare, and splutter out his part in an apologetic and bewildered way, like a man asking questions in a crowd speaking another language. It was a helter-skelter performance, and one would have felt no wonder if the characters had suddenly broken up, and joined together again, in a song-and-dance assemble. Ignorant and innocent gaum that he was, Sean, thinking now that he was among old friends, ran round when the play ended to tell the artists what he thought of it all. They were all shocked, and murmured Hush hush hush. Sean thought they would all roar out laughter with him over the production, but they refused. They kept silent, except to say Hush hush hush. F. J. McCormick came close to him, and said, 'I hear you've been criticising our rendering of Shaw's play. You've got a bit of a name now, and you must not say these things about an Abbey production. If you do, we'll have to report it to the Directors; so,' he added a little crudely, 'so try to keep your mouth shut.'

Bewilderment again afflicted Sean. Just fancy that now! After all Sean had gone through; after all his mouth had dared to say, it was to be kept closed at an Abbey actor's order. Sean went home, sat down, wrote a long letter, pointing out the bad parts of the production; why and how he thought them to be bad; added a note to Mr. M. J. Dolan, the then Manager, saying that the letter held his views of what had happened, and that he was at liberty, if he wished, to read the letter out loud to the Abbey Directors, have it printed in the papers, and show it to the world at large. This letter was shown to Mr. Lennox Robinson, who, in an ethereal voice, murmured, 'It's just like Sean!' The letter was then pinned up on the noticeboard for all to read. Some nights following, Sean was on his way over the Abbey stage to join the actors in the Green Room for a chat, when he was stopped by Sean Barlow, a scene painter, in an old-fashioned way; a maker of properties, again in another old-fashioned way, who asked what he was doing on the stage. On my way to the Green Room, replied Sean. There's none but the actors and officials allowed on the stage, said the bold Barlow, with a dominant note in his voice; and we'd be glad if you came this way no more.

No more? Quoth the raven, Nevermore. Never again. Nevermore. Ordered from the stage he had trod so many years ago and he a kidger, ay, mouthed the part of Father Dolan in *The Shaughraun* from its boards, ere ever the Abbey Theatre had entered its beginning; the stage on which his brother, Archie, had played Harvey Duff in the same play, and others in *Peep o' Day Boys*, *The Unknown*, *Green Bushes*, and *The Colleen Bawn*. Never again; nevermore. He turned away, leaving the other Sean victor on the field, and never after set a foot either on the Abbey stage or in the Abbey Green Room.

He'd hoist his sail and go to England,

> *Neptune's park, ribbed and paled in*
> *With rocks unscalable and roaring waters.*

DUBLIN'S GODS AND HALF-GODS

SEAN was now walking tiptoe among the gods, but he had begun to doubt the divinity of most of them. His reverence for the opinions of A. E. had begun to decline. He began to question in himself the once-held thought that Lennox Robinson was as near to knowing all about things theatrical and literary as any educated man could be. Lady Gregory was still herself in his mind; but Hugh Lane's reputation as one who could always tell a bad picture from a fine one was a wavering one now. James Stephens, the poet, was a hearty laugh in his mind, but a ringing laugh, one with the ring of bells in it, silver ones that sang merry tunes, tinged with the note of pathos, deep in the very centre of their chiming. Austin Clarke and Brinsley Mac-Namara didn't bother him in surmise or reflection; but Yeats stood majestic still. As he listened to the crowd of the lesser gods, listened long, he began to see that their sneering, lofty conception of what they called culture, their mighty semblance of self-assurance in the most of them was but a vain conceit in themselves which they used for their own encouragement in the pitiable welter of a small achievement. Some of these were imitators of whom Yeats said, when he was asked to praise them,

> *But was there ever dog who praised his fleas?*

He was learning by experience.

He had been told that Patrick Touhy was a great painter, and he believed it at the time. A. E., Robinson, even Yeats said so, so Sean believed it. He was delighted when this man, Touhy, asked him to come and be sketched. So Sean went several nights a week to the Metropolitan School of Art, where Touhy was a teacher, to sit for an hour or two, while poor Touhy's timid hand sought laboriously to set down the line and expression of Sean's face.

—Aw, chance a stroke, man! Sean would say, when he saw the timid hand holding the pencil, flickering, flickering over the paper without daring to touch it; niggling a little bit of a line here, then there, tormenting Sean with the idea that this man hadn't in him the courage and dash an artist must have, if he is to do work worth more than a smile.

He had agreed to give Touhy three guineas and autographed copies of his books for the drawing; but before it was finished, Sean saw that Touhy would never be among the named artists. Sean felt sympathy for him at first, but life was too much of a battle to give thought to one cowering before it; and the timid pencil in the quavering hand forced scorn into a fighter's mind. One of the loudest laughs Sean ever had was given when he saw Touhy dressed up as Macheath, with Sally Allgood at his side, gathered into the dress of Polly Peachum, on their way to the Dublin Arts Ball. There he was, stuffed into the most gorgeous of velvets, sword and all, a man clothed with timidity as with a garment. But Sally Allgood, as plump as he was meagre, fair smothered in a flowing tide of savage peplus, silk, ribbons, and lace, hooked her arm in his, and led him on to the wild adventure of the dance.

When he had varnished the drawing, Touhy sent a letter to Sean telling him to come and get it; but after he had seen what it was like when it appeared as a frontispiece to one of his books, he took no notice of the call to come. Looking at it close now, for before he didn't like to do this while Touhy was drawing it, he was staggered to see how badly it had been done. Later, down in Coole Park, Lady Gregory had got a grip on his arm to say more effectively, 'You must be tareful who you det to draw you. Touhy has made you look like a butcher.' Later on still, Augustus John praised it by saying, 'It was a damned fine drawing of someone else.' When he had settled in London, he got a letter from a relative asking him to what place they would send the picture, but he did not answer. The thing had no merit; he didn't want it; so he left it wherever it was. It was odd that the Ireland Sean knew had no great painter. Not one tended to

seal a soul to a picture whenever a soul came to gaze. Even Lavery
or Orpen didn't seem able to do this much. In Ireland there wasn't
even a shadow coming through the sun of work done by such men
as Renoir, Manet, Picasso, Cézanne, or Van Gogh. All the Irish
painters had halted at the half-way house of art; and most of them
hesitated to take the first step from the beginning; though each had
a mighty opinion of himself, backed by a very poor one of all the
others.

But Ireland was full of folly, seeking, probing even, for a good
opinion. He remembered once when he was in Coole, sitting by the
huge fire in the library, the great logs throwing up lusty golden and
scarlet flames, doing a fine dance on the coloured bindings of the
books marshalled around the walls, with Lady Gregory sitting
opposite chatting away; while she, at times, prodded the logs with
a brass poker into greater energy and glow. In her smiling chat she
had told him how shocked she had been to discover that Yeats had
read nothing written by Dostoievsky; how she had cried shame on
him for his neglect of so great a man; and how she had given him
The Idiot and *The Brothers Karamazov* only a week ago to take away
with him so that he might read them, and be delighted with the
images of a great and spiritual mind. Then she told Sean how Yeats
had written to say he had read one, and how great the work was,
and how he enjoyed it. Just then, Sean had had his third play taken
by the Abbey, and it was to go into rehearsal in a week or two.
When he got back to Dublin, he was told that Mr. Yeats wanted to
see him to talk about the play.

The next day he set out for the poet's home in Merrion Square.
This will be the second time, he thought, I have set a foot within a
house in this place which still treasures the secluded brocade and
perfume of the past. An awesome place, for the top achievement for
many years in Dublin had been a residence in Merrion Square. The
glory of living here was next to the glory of living in one of the Big
Houses of the country: a glory reached only by the lonely few. As
he came closer to it, the streets became more refined, as if aware of
their greater neighbour; and those that were closest to this elegant
dot of life began to assume an air of importance, and bravely tried
to look imposing.

He entered the Square, and halted to stand and stare at the
gracious houses. The Square looked as if it had been knighted by
king exclusion and queen quietness, separating it from the lumbering, trade-tired streets of Dublin. He entered it with a bow and a

murmur of Yer servant, Sir Merrion; for it was a holy place, to
poverty unknown; unknown, save by name, to the distant proletariat of the tenements. If a proletarian ventured to pass through it,
he would go quiet and quick, without lounging, or sending a dis-
paraging spit into its kennels. He would lift his passing feet carefully, and set them down intelligently, so as to provoke no noise
from the footway. He would pass through with the circumspection
he'd show while passing by a rich bed in which a noble or a bishop
lay sleeping; pass by slyly and rapidly, without commotion, eager to
get to a place where he could walk with ease, hands in pocket, and
spit in comfort, the poorer world before him, ready to fulfil his
hardier will and lustier pleasure.

How stately the houses looked with their gleaming windows, the
brightness of them muffled in the brief modesty of costly curtains,
concealing secrets of private life from the eyes and ears of the street
outside; their cleverly-painted, highly-polished front doors, each
side pillared stiffly, as if petrified footmen stood guard there to see
that no dirty hand was stretched out to soil a dazzling knocker, or
imprint a slum-speck on the bell-push, that shone like a brassy jewel
on a cheek of the opulent doorway.

—Here, the houses would quiver in pain, thought Sean, if a
hawker went by chanting, Strawberries, penny a leaf, penny a leaf,
the ripe strawberries! And the houses would swoon in shame if the
cry changed to, Fresh Dublin Bay herrin's, thruppence a dozen;
thruppence the dozen, the Dublin Bay herrin's fresh from the say!

Sean mounted the wide steps to the door which was Yeats's
dwelling-place. Two Free State C.I.D. men stood in the shadow of
the pillared doorway, planted there to prevent the assassination of
the senator-poet by some too-ready Republican hand. Guns guarding the poet, thought Sean, though he knew that the Republicans
had as much idea of shooting Yeats as they had of shooting Lady
Gregory or the Catholic Archbishop of Dublin.

—Are yeh goin' in to see himself? asked one of them who knew
Sean well; but as what he asked was half a statement, he went on,
I don't envy yeh, Sean, for I wouldn't like to be alone with him
long. His oul' mind's full of th' notion of oul' kings and queens the
half of us never heard of; an' when he's talkin', a fella has to look
wise, pretendin' he's well acquainted with them dead an' gone
ghosts. It's a terrible sthrain on a body whenever he stops to talk.
Wait till yeh hear, though, and his hand put down Sean's as it
stretched out towards the bell-push. Yeh know Jim Errishcool,

don't yeh? Yes, well, of course. Well, what d'ye think th' bugger's done, an' him on guard over Senator Fedamore's residence, some doors down? What d'ye think he done, disgracin' th' whole of us? Th' second time he's done it, too! Guess what th' boyo done?

—Fired at a shadow he thought a Republican?

—Aw, no, not that. What d'ye think th' goboy done but got acquainted with th' upper housemaid, an' when th' genthry were away, got into th' house quiet, an' lo and behold yeh, he gets th' girl in th' family way as cool as bedamned through th' medium of th' best bed in th' best bedroom. Now, what d'ye think o' that! A cool customer, wha'? Th' best bed, no less, for a fella only just up from th' bog, in Fedamore's own house, mind yeh, an' th' upper housemaid, too. They found th' bed all knocked about an' th' girl on it in a half-dead daze, cryin', an' murmurin', He's after nearly killin' me! An' th' boyo come on duty th' same night to take over guard, cool as you like. Now you'll be talkin'!

—Oh, well, he could do worse, said Sean.

—Sure I know he could, said the guard impatiently; but what about us? Everyone of us is misthrusted now. Th' way they look at us when they're passin' as if we all had th' same failin'.

—And I'm afraid we have, said Sean.

—We know all about that! snappily said the guard; I know we all have th' failin', but we all haven't got it in th' direct fashion of a fallin' thunderbolt overthrowin' an innocent girl!

When Sean stepped by the neatly-dressed maid, who held the door open for him, and entered the study, he was met by a blast of heat that nearly drowned him. He had entered a den of heat. Never before had he experienced such an onslaught of venomous warmth. The hot air enveloped him, made him sink into a chair, to silently gulp for breath; and it was soon forcing him into an unpleasant sense of sickness. On the chair, he wrenched his will towards feeling calm, towards trying to breathe easy. There it was, at the end of the room, the devil of heat, a huge, squat, black anthracite stove, belching out its invisible venom quietly, threatening Sean with an embarrassing display of faintness. Overcrowded or overheated rooms tended to make Sean's brain buzz, and his stomach feel queer, and already he could feel everything in his belly trying to turn over; the power of his will alone preventing it from happening.

And what was that sound of piercing shrillness, like the ear-splitting scream of a hundred fifes playing in a room at the same time, in dire disharmony together? Birds! A golden-barred cage, half filling a big window, swung there, swung and fluttered there with the shrill tuning of half a hundred canaries. Rich yellow ones, some of them streaked with creamier lines, some with dark satiny patches on them; active, alert, darting from side to side of the cage, from top to bottom, and back again, over and over again, never stopping, singing without cessation, singing, singing all the time, splitting the thick and heated air of the room with a mad, piercing melody of noise! These were the canaries that Lady Gregory had called Dose derrible birds! And through the heated air, and through the savage whistling, the noble voice of Yeats boomed out a blessing on the new play.

What was he saying, what was the man saying? Could Sean fashion the words from the booming, disentangle them from the violent chittering, mould them from the heavy air, and fold them into making sense within his own mind? No. Surely Yeats wasn't saying what he was saying! But Sean's will caught the words, and made sense of them, out of the heat, and through the mad fifing of the canaries; and he listened with an exquisite desire to laugh out loud, as he listened to the voice, the deep, fine voice booming out through the sweating air and the jeering whistle of the uncalmable birds; the majestic voice of Yeats, as he paced up and down the room through the moist haze, came booming to the din-dulled ears of Sean: O'Casey, you have written a great play; this play is the finest thing you have done. In an Irish way, you have depicted the brutality, the tenderness, the kindling humanity of the Russian writer, Dostoievsky; O'Casey, you are the Irish Dostoievsky!

Moving homewards, gasping into him the cool air of the street, faint still from what he had suffered in the red, ruthless heat from the anthracite stove, his shirt sticking to back and breast, Sean felt ashamed of Yeats and ashamed of himself. Wait, now, till he grew a little cooler. Sean had worked within the airless chamber of a boiler, helping to fix a furnace, but it never gave him the languishing feeling of sickness he had suffered in that room. Why was Yeats afraid of a cooler air? He had, Sean knew, a tendency to chest or lung complaints. But the heat in that room would be bad for one even in the throes of bronchitis. It will do the man harm. Now why hadn't he had the courage to tell Yeats that? Sean, when his second play was in rehearsal, had walked, with a temperature from bronchitis, and a sense of suffocation, from North Circular Road to Nelson's Pillar, in falling snow; had there taken a tram to St. Vincent's Hospital, and had never felt the worse for it. It wasn't a sensible thing to do, of course; but less dangerous than to live and sleep in such a torrid heat endured by the poet Yeats. It will do the man harm. And the piercing chatter of those yellow-clad birds — how can Yeats, the delicate-minded poet, stand that chirruping turmoil? He had no ear; he was tone-deaf — that was the reason. Now Sean realised that there were different kinds of bliss: what was heaven to one man might be hell to another.

Another Dostoievsky! An Irish one, this time! And Yeats only after reading the man's book for the first time the night before. If it hadn't been for his battle with the blast and the birds, Sean would have had a battle with laughter. Yeats was trying to impress Sean with his knowledge of Dostoievsky. That was a weakness in the poet. But why hadn't Sean the courage to tell Yeats that he knew damn all about the Russian writer? That was a weakness in Sean. It was a cowardly omission. He should have told Yeats he knew Lady Gregory had given him two of Dostoievsky's books only a night or so ago. And, instead, he had put a smile of appreciation on his heat-strained face when Yeats had said it. Christ Almighty, what a world of deceits! Sean's father would have said how he felt and what he thought without a hesitation. He had let his father's memory down. He'd try to be braver the next time. Some had said he was another Chekhov, others, a Dickens, and another Ben Jonson. He knew himself that he was like Sean O'Casey, and he was determined to be like no-one else; for better or worse, for richer or poorer, so help him God!

There was something lacking, even in the gods. None of them was destitute of human vanity and conceit. Sean remembered his very first evening (his last, but one) in A. E.'s house, how, when the company was leaving, after a long and abuseless spate of blather, James Stephens, the poet (who never, like the great little man he was, pretended to be what he wasn't; indeed, Stephens's weakness was, Sean thought, that he never fully realised the grace and grandeur of the delightful and dignified gifts he possessed), suddenly and hurriedly asking A. E., author of the *Homeward Songs*, for a Blood-and-Thunder novel, and A. E. had fished one out from his books without a search; he had plunged a hand in among the books, and out came the Blood-and-Thunder novel. No; these poets and dreamers hadn't fully embedded themselves in the Nirvana of literature and art.

And Lady Gregory, too. Returning with her once from Coole to Dublin, they had come from Gort to Athenry, and got out there to wait an hour and a half for the train from Galway to bring them on to Dublin. The two of them had eaten a lunch of ham and hard-boiled eggs, sitting on a bench in the dreary station. After they had eaten, Lady Gregory said she'd have a liddle rest, while he went to have a look at the town, returning in good time to be ready for the incoming train from Galway.

Athenry — Ford of the King. No king here now. Ne'er a sign of one even — bar the king of loneliness. Sean passed under a famous archway of which it was said that whomsoever it fell on, and buried beneath its ruins, would become the saviour of Ireland. Loneliness the king, and the wind his attendant. It blew cold and sharp through every narrow street. Like a scythe eager to cut down any sign of life that came to tease the loneliness around; or to disturb the town's drowsy restfulness. It came sweeping in from the levels of Clare-Galway bog and plain. The houses stood still, careless of stare, of pity, or of scorn. They looked old, oh, so old. And they looked neither sad nor sorry about it; they simply seemed set to wait for the end to come. They were lost in quietness. He heard a bell toll in the distance. The wind lessened it into the ghost of a chime. Somewhere in the town, maybe, someone had passed into a better quietness. The bell tolled, but the town did not stir. No sign of life anywhere, as if the bell tolled for the dead town. Resignation showed a passive power everywhere. It even looked as if eternity was dying down here.

Away over the bridge, above, the seepy silence seemed startled by a passing train; passing by swiftly, as if possessed by fear; passing by noisily, as if to give itself courage; straining to get away, as if in fear of being caught in the fearsome plight of life here, standing still to watch its own decay, and to wait for its own departure.

Sean heard a sound like a leaf's rustling. He turned, and saw a young girl coming out of the doorway of a sunken house. She had to mount four or five steps to bring herself to the level of the side-walk. Sean stood perfectly still to look at her. She was a winsome lass. A mass of brown hair gave a golden hue to a pale and trimly-chiselled face, with delicate ears, a straight and slender nose, digni-fying a saucy-looking red mouth; while a pair of blue, softly luminous eyes met Sean's admiring stare. She was dressed in a brown coat, open, showing a thin white blouse against which her young breasts pushed, forming a pattern that told Sean they were finely turned and tempting. When she came to the top step, Sean saw that her legs flowed finely into the delightful curving of her body. They had a charm that would entice a dead-tired man to take a long journey after them in the hope that a favouring wind would lift skirt and petti-coat higher, showing the legs off, and signalling Here is beauty. Her hand shot up to her head to recapture a lock of hair the wind had suddenly played with, and Sean saw that the hand was well made, though the skin looked rough, telling him that hard work was part of the girl's portion.

There the lass stood on the side-walk, facing him, framed in the muddy-yellow decay of the house behind her, like a lone cherry blossom thrusting itself shyly and impertinently forward through the ragged, withering foliage of an ageing tree. She was hesitating, maybe wishing him to speak, but he could say nothing. His mind had been too full of the loneliness and the ruin to be so suddenly called upon to reflect with words the wonder in his mind. He could say nothing. There she lingered, but his silence lasted too long. She lowered her eyes from his, turned, and went down the street, and disappeared round an alley-way a little lower down.

He looked at his watch: it was time to go back to Lady Gregory, back towards Dublin. He went slowly back to the grimy station, imagining what he would have said to the lass while she walked by his side, or stood where she had been, to listen. He would have told her he knew all the big men of Dublin, all the poets, and was a friend of Lady Gregory's, and of the great poet, Yeats. He would tell her that he himself was a dramatist, and even something of a poet. All the honours of acquaintanceship, all his achievements he would place in front of her to win her interest and secure her admiration. Neither for fame nor for money would he do this; no, not one of them would he summon to his aid for these things; but he would lay them all down before her so that he might look at a beautiful face, kiss a curving red mouth, and tune a lovely form into the circle of his supplicating arms. Whenever his mind wandered again to the lonely wretchedness of Athenry, he would see this lovely figure, this bud of womanhood, longing for life, standing, alone and radiant, in the midst of the houses, quietly resolute in sinking to their own decay.

He came into the station, and saw Lady Gregory sitting on a bench, her head lovingly close to a book. Coming over quietly, he bent over curiously to see what she was reading. Catching in her dulling ear a sound of his movement, she snapped the book shut, but not before he had seen that the book was called *Peg o' My Heart*.

—We won't have long to wait now, she said a little confusedly, adding as she noticed the look of bewilderment in his eyes, Ah, dat book? I fordet who dave it to me. I just wanted to see what tort it was.

Long afterwards, when Oliver Gogarty came on a visit to him in London, what he had known before was confirmed again. Gogarty had entered in a whirlwind of restlessness. He had flung down his suitcase, the impact had burst it open, and a book flew out on to the floor. Sean's wife and Oliver had made a dive together to get it, but Gogarty was a second too late; and Sean saw the title of one of Edgar Wallace's rich and rare inventions. Later on still, visiting W. B. Yeats in his Lancaster Gate lodgings in London, he found the poet busy with his last anthology of modern poetry. The poet shoved the books on the table aside, and entered into a hearty chat about the Abbey Theatre, the new Directorate, the sort of plays they should put on, and then about some of the glories of the Elizabethan drama- tists. During the talk, Sean's eyes kept turning to glance at a dis- ordered pile of books strewing the marble mantelshelf. Yeats noticed his glances at last, and cocked one of his own eyes towards them — for the other was covered with a thick green shade — and remarked that they were Wild Western Tales and Detective Stories. Yeats made no bones about it.

—When the mind grows tired, he said, reading so much excellent, and not so excellent, verse, I turn for shelter and rest to Zane Grey and Dorothy Sayers. One can read them while the mind sleeps.

—Dope, thought Sean. He uses them as dope to lull the mind to sleep, just as the one-two, one-two mind of a roman catholic keeps awake by reading the tuppenny booklets of the Catholic Truth Society. But Yeats is quite open and honest about it anyway; though Sean thought it odd entertainment for a poet. He himself had read several detective stories, but they seemed to tire his mind quicker than the deepest essay written by a John Locke; though the antics of Lord Peter Wimsey and his mother, of the new-fashioned mind, coupled with the mighty mass of grey matter in the head of Poirot (like Chesterton's Father Brown, beating his outward mind to solve a problem solved already by his inner one), were provocative of a quiet and comfortable laugh, now and again.

Ay, indeed; even the greater gods of Dublin had their frailties and their faults. They could sometimes build their little cocks of antic hay, and try to tumble about in them. The lordly ones weren't always quite so lordly with literature as they generally posed to be.

DUBLIN'S GLITTERING GUY

THEY tried to settle themselves comfortably on the hard-upholstered seat of the snug in the Blue Lion of Britain Street — Donal, Sean, and a young fellow named Edwin Droop Grey, who had contributed two poems, *Sparrows on the Housetop* and *The Eagle in the Air*, to A. E.'s journal *The Irish Statesman*. Donal took a slug from his bottle of stout, Edwin moistened his lips with his small port, and Sean swallowed a mouthful of his warmed claret. The snug was a tiny cubicle, smelling of a thousand beery breaths, tightly holding its occupants with dirty panelled partitions, a little window in front from which the drinks were passed from the bar.

—A. E.'s getting a little bent in the back, said Edwin D. Grey; and he looked old passing by us in O'Connell Street today. Curious guy.

—Dublin has her gods, her half-gods, and her guys, said Donal. A. E.'s our glittering guy. Dublin's logos, the word-final in painting, literature, poetry, philosophy, rural science, dreams, and religion. He's the fairest and brightest humbug Ireland has. There's a genuine humility in Yeats's arrogance, but there's a deeper arrogance in A. E.'s humility.

—And the other day, said Edwin, Dunsany, in an article, called A. E. the poet of the century. It's incomprehensible how Dunsany could overlook Yeats to hand the palm for poetry to A. E. What a mass of glittering monotony his poems are! All paralysed with a purple glow. Swing-exultation in them all. They make a mind dizzy. It's too much of a thing to be friends with the Ancient of Days; too big a thing to be the rocker of the infant suns; or to dip a forefinger into the fiery fountains of the stars; or to put on the mantelshelf of your room the Golden Urn into which all the glittering spray of planets fall. A. E. thinks he's God's own crooner. Listen:

> When the breath of twilight blows to flame the misty skies,
> All its vaporous sapphire, violet glow and silver gleam
> With their magic flood me through the gateway of the eyes;
> I am one with the twilight's dream.

—It's too magnificent, said Donal. Portholes of the eyes, would have been better. Think of the poem where he conjures up a vast expanse of coruscating battlements, blazing with divine beings, surrounded by imperishable fires in which other gigantic beings, crested and plumed with fire, appear; and, after them, starry races, stretching out line on line into the infinite; while Birds of Diamond Glory flit about from perch to pinnacle, among crowds of demi-humans and semi-gods, wearing tremendous tiaras, branching beams of coloured flames spreading out from their spines, with a steady pointed light sticking up from their brows, out of the Well of Indra. A wonderful scene. The great white way! And when he wants to get rid of them so that he may sing of his loneliness, he just says Gone!

—And they go, said Sean. These visions of flame-feathered and plumed masters, of blazing stars, of inimitable light, are as full of tawdry, childish decorations as those seen by French kids at Lourdes, Portuguese kids in Fatima, Irish kids at Knock, and Latvian kids at Kirkhala. And as superstitious, too; worse, even, for A. E.'s a grown man who ought to know better.

—And he sees but one colour, with its various shades, in the world, said Edwin. Purple is his pride, and the one aspect in the mirror of the day is a purple twilight. There's hardly a poem of his left bare of the word Twilight, or of the colour usually associated with that time of the day — purple mountains, lilac trees, violet skies, heliotrope clouds, and amethyst ancestral selfs. And what an acrobat he is! A daring old man on a flying trapeze! He swings from star to star, from planet to planet, as a kid swings from a rope tied to a lamp-post. And yet this great creator of greater things can write a thing like this —

>Your eyes, your other eyes of dream,
>Looked at me through the veil of blank.

—Monk Gibbon, the poet, says of him, said Sean, that he is such a high-blown mystic, his poetry should be read sacredly, one poem at a time. Otherwise, we won't be able to keep pace with the systems in their metaphysical universe. Each poem, Gibbon says, needs separate acceptance, separate meditation. As with his prose, A. E.'s poems should only be read at a time when our mood is already in some measure attuned to them. Trying to let Russell down easily, said Sean, as he let some claret slip down into himself. As if any poem, worth reading, doesn't need a separate acceptance, from *My Love is Like a Red, Red Rose* to *Dies Irae*; and a separate meditation, too, however different the meditations may be in spirit and in thought.

—He no longer lives as a poet in the hearts of the young, said Donal. They're laughing at the old humbug at last.

—I shouldn't go as far as that, said Edwin Grey, with a tinge of remonstrance in his tone. Not a humbug; oh, no. A. E. has his points; a quality of conviction, at least in what he sings; and a first-class painter.

—There I'm altogether against you, said Sean vehemently. He never was an artist in colour or line or form. Even though at one time, when he found himself short, as he told me himself, he could dash out of the house with a new-painted picture under his coat, and sell it for twenty-five pounds before he'd gone through two streets. No one who paints well could paint so many. His house is stacked with them. He was heard counting a harvest of them, once — forty-eight, forty-nine, fifty, fifty-one — there's one picture missing! I looked at them one evening, along with James Stephens. The pictures were stacked against a wall in one room, facing inwards, and A. E. brought them out, placing them, facing outwards, against another wall. Then he'd step back to wait for you to say they were all lovelies. It was pathetic and comical to see James Stephens going down on his knees to get a better view of them; but it was sad to hear him saying how grand they were; the misty trees radiant with light in the middle distance, and the rest of it. I could see little more than daubs in them, and remained silent, for I wasn't quite sure of myself as to how best to show why one picture was good, and another one worthless.

—You talk like that because you don't know, said Edwin Grey. I've learned a lot from Paul Henry, and I can tell you that A. E.'s pictures stand steady against the best that's being done today. You just have another and a longer look at them. The figures, saturated in sunshine, are deliciously ethereal, and you get from mountain, from flowing river, from the faery-like tint of evening skies, from the fugitive play of children and lovers, a Virgilian beauty that makes the transitory sister to the eternal.

—Jasus! said Donal, that's the kind of gush that gives the old bugger his reputation among the gulls who know no better. Him and his fairies! He even thinks that by putting in *ae* instead of *ai* into the word fairy he transfigures them into heavenly forms whose existence is undeniable. This grandee of incompetence is a danger to the young who desire to become artists.

—A. E., said Edwin Grey, you must remember, is a mystic, and lives embowered in the higher thoughts of the world's religions. A freelance saint, living an ascetic life, making it hard for us lesser mortals to fully enter into his vision of the invisible.

—A kind of ethereal faery himself! said Donal, with laughing scorn. Don't be talking rot, man! he went on, more hotly. Ask Orpen, and you'll know. Doesn't he tell us that A. E. paints two pictures every Sunday, one after a big breakfast of eggs and bacon, and the other one after a heavy midday meal? Ask Orpen. The fairies worried him; they were exactly like badly-drawn figures by Blake. But the fairies vanished when Sir Hugh Lane brought the French pictures to Dublin. Then every Sunday produced two slimy canvases by a would-be Millet. Each Sunday two came regularly, and aesthetic Dublin bowed its head, murmuring, How Wonderful! Then Millet got played out, and imitation Monticellis appeared on Dublin's house-walls, to be followed by Renoir, who was followed by Daumier, who was followed by Chavanne, till, Orpen says, I lost count. And all the time these Dublin aesthetes were bowing before A. E., they were shouting, Manet! Sure, he couldn't draw, much less paint!

—Maybe, now, murmured Edwin Grey, a smile of tolerant scorn dawning round his mouth, maybe, now, Orpen was jealous.

—Jealous? retorted Donal. Didn't Clive Bell call the ethereal ones, Dicky Doyle's Fairies? And didn't George Moore call A E., The Donegal Dauber? I'm telling you I wouldn't put a picture of his on a wall of mine, if I was paid a weekly rent for hanging it there!

—Ay, said Sean, you're right, Donal. And to escape from any criticism that might be born of thought, didn't A. E. proclaim everywhere he could find a listener that he never wanted to be known as a great artist, for such was but vanity; and that he had turned away from his vanity so that he might search for truth, undisturbed by the clinging fingers of beauty. He hid his want of inspiration, his pitiable lack of craftsmanship, in the statement that art was a self-indulgence which, if yielded to, would stint his life and hamper his homeward march to a lost divinity. The glorious art of painting, art of Titian, of Raphael, of Angelo, of Rubens, of Vermeer, of Constable, and Turner, a practice that would stint a life! And Fra Angelico who put the gold of heaven round his saints and angels! The fact is that A. E. realised in his heart that he could never come near to being a great artist; and so, in the foolish vanity of man's nature, besought himself to believe that his nature was too high, too noble, too precious to veil itself in art's indulgence. He was never offered the gift by the Holy Ghost, and therefore could never reject it. It is a gift given to few, and when once given can never be rejected nor despised without a soul's loss.

—Yes, said Donal, but did you ever hear tell of him telling George Moore that the gods came to sit on the edge of his bed so that he could sketch them? Didn't he say, if he told people that, he could sell every picture he could paint, and that they would think him a very wonderful person? The gods, A. E. said, swished in to sit on the edge of the bed while he sketched them. Cock your head a little to the left, Mananaan Mac Lir; that's too much — whoa, that's just right. And you, Angus of the Golden Hair, of the Ever-Sounding Harp, God of Love, I think you should stand in the centre of the room, a languishing look on your face, as if you were singing *When First I Met Thee Warm and Young*; and you, Louisiana Loo of the Long Hand, stand to attention, spear poised in the right hand, your left hand on your hip hip hurrah, as if you listened to the gathered Gaels singing *Go where Glory Waits Thee*.

—Oh, gentle and devout Fra Angelico, you could never be so surely arrogant! said Sean. In deep humility, out of the high imagination of your mind, you turned your men and angels into gods in colour and grace and happy simplicity of form. A. E.'s gods were as artificial as the light he often painted by, for artificial light was nothing to him, for most of what he painted never depended on the light the sun gave. His palette was typical of himself, indistinct, uncertain, to allow him to outspread a vision of thinly-tinted dreams. He splashed on the dove-grey, the light blue, and the pink, that coloured his empty heaven and his emptier earth, symbols of his own vague mind, vapouring everything in nature within lilac and pink and dove-grey so as to fit them into the tinselled universe conceived in the mirage of his own ancestral self.

—And no-one questioned him, said Donal; no-one ventured to deny his artistic greatness, and silence answered every doubt, every contrary opinion put forward by some braver fool. A. E. is a unique painter, they all murmured. He certainly is, for there was none ever like him before, and I hope to God there will never be again.

—Even Lady Gregory wouldn't say boo to the goose, complained Sean. Once, when we came into the Abbey Theatre Green Room together, she tightened her lips and shut her eyes when I pointed out to her the dull effrontery of an oil-painting of herself, hanging over a settee, done by A. E. Then noticing that I was annoyed, she caught my arm, gave it a good-humoured squeeze, a gleam in her bright eyes, a jovial twist round her expressive mouth, as she said, 'We won't look ad id; keep your eyes off id altodether. I know; bery bad. We leave id dere because we don't want to turt poor A. E.' So there it was left, swinging away on the wall in all its dull presumption.

—Amn't I after telling you that, said Donal. And as for the Art itself, is there e'er a one a body could call a painter left in the land, other than the boyos who put bright colours on the window-frames and doors of the haughtier houses? Donal answered his own question. Ne'er a one, he said, as he poured what remained of the bottle of stout into his glass.

—Oh, Gawd! ejaculated Edwin Grey in a tone of impatient resignation. Then he added languidly, I don't believe I heard the name of Jack Yeats once mentioned.

—He makes no appeal to me, said Donal.

—And so must be of no account as a painter, murmured Grey languidly.

—Oh, I'll say that in his early phase, said Donal defensively, each of his pictures gives a pleasant thought or two for a moment or two; but I've seen nothing to make you pause and wonder; nothing in colour and line that silently sings a lyrical song, like, say, Giorgione's *The Tempest*, or his *The Sleeping Venus*; nothing with the grace and power to hedge one in to looking at it for a long time, or tempt one back again and again to do it reverence.

—And his latest work? queried Grey, touching supercilious scorn into the sound of his words.

—That, said Donal, is even less to me than what he used to do. He seems to be poking the paint on to the canvas; a dot-and-dash kind of art; a morse medley of colouring; an unruly ecstasy of patchwork painting.

Sean said nothing. He listened. One for, one against — which was right? He would take neither side till he felt he knew.

The narrow door of the snug was shoved open, bringing in an evil air, hotter than the hot air of the snug. Through the open door, Sean caught a glimpse of sparkling mirrors in which appeared a multitude of dancing bottles, red-labelled, blue-labelled, and black-labelled, forming a tubular background to a number of excited faces, in which eyes winked, and mouths opened and shut, amidst a rowdy murmur as of many raucous chattering daws. Then a sturdy, plump woman wedged her way in among them, and with a muttered, Excuse me, gentlemen, flopped down on the little bench to the left of the snug's narrow window. She carried a basket which she put down on the floor at her feet, and Sean saw a few nosegays of violets left unsold from the day's sale. She was followed by a man of middle height, rather thin, but wiry, who held a brimming glass of whiskey in each hand. Kicking the door shut behind him, he handed a glass of whiskey to the woman and squeezed himself down on to the bench beside her.

The woman was nearing bulkiness in size, but Sean noticed her shape was clear and firm, and in places alluring. Her wide bottom covered two-thirds of the seat, but it didn't softly spread about, but remained firm in its rounded curves when she sat down. Sean saw, too, that the big globular breasts, scarcely hidden by a light-blue blouse, hadn't wobbled when she had flopped down on the bench, though it was plain that she wore no corset to keep them steady. Her head, bare of hat, was covered by a tossed mass of light-brown hair, a little dingy with the street's dust. It covered her head and the nape of her neck in clustered bunches, as if the thick curls were shy, and had crowded together in groups to hide themselves from staring eyes. A curiously pale face was wide and round, the full circle diverted by a rounder and a buoyant chin, topped by a thick-lipped mouth. Her nose was gracious and slender, looking a little uneasy in the rather jubilant width of her face. Over her blouse she wore a black shawl, bordered with lines of a deep yellow, and further set off with a fringe of the same colour. This she slipped from her shoulders, allowing it to fall into a cascade of yellow-bordered black cloth around her bottom and the back of her thighs. A brown skirt was tucked up and gathered in round her wide waist, and a stout, but invitingly curved, leg thrust itself brazenly forth, for all to see, from beneath a short petticoat of dark red.

A woman for a man to play with after an hour of loud song, when the taste of wine was thick on the tongue, when laughing hope was high, and the passions reckless. There was comfort in her, too; comfort as well as illusion in that wide, white, violate bosom. Here was the earth-breath, the great mother whom A. E. had so often searched for, and never found. A stalwart man, doubting his courage, might find new life, warmth, and power within the shelter of her strong, deftly-turned arms.

The man beside her was about sixty years of age. He was of middle height, thin, and wiry-looking. He had high cheek-bones, and his eyes were black and small, but bright and beady as a squirrel's. His hair, apparently once brilliantly black, like his eyebrows, had turned to a dull brown, heavily sprinkled with dim grey tufts. A long, thin nose cut the face clean in two, its butt almost jutting over a close and surly-looking mouth; but when he talked, the lips showed themselves to be red, and graciously well-formed. He was dressed in a thick coat of Melton blue, and a striped cotton shirt, and a white handkerchief was wound, cravat-like, round his neck. He wore heavy white corduroy trousers, so long that they showed but little of his thick-soled, heavily-nailed boots. His head was covered by a rough, brown tweed cap, its peak shoved to one side so that the wearer could get a full view of the lady. Though his rather bony hands were big, Sean saw that they had carried the glasses of whiskey cleverly, and one of them now clasped a glass with sinewy and supple fingers. Hands, thought Sean, that could hold a woman down tight.

—Looka here, said the woman, as soon as she had settled herself, I'm tellin' you he shouldn't ha' done it. No matther what you say, you're wrong, so y'are. It was an eyeopener to me. Julia, says I, Julia, thrust no-one afther that; th' Man above, yes; but anyone here below, no. Afther sayin' he couldn't do it, an' he wouldn't do it, he done it, regardless of th' feelin' of others. How are we goin' to look decent people in th' face ever again? We haven't got a single thing to stand up for now. Oh, Julia's a friend of his no longer. He's no leadher of mine, now. I'm tellin' you, De Valera should never ha' taken th' oath.

—Maybe you're right, maybe you're right, Julia, the man murmured thoughtfully.

—Here's health! she said suddenly, gulping down half of what was in her glass.

—Good health, the man echoed, drinking all of his and depositing the empty glass on the ledge by his elbow.

—Sacred Heart, it's hot in here! and Julia undid some of the upper buttons of her blouse, showing Sean that her skin was white, and seemed as soft as velvet.

—The dhrink here isn't up to the mark, said the man. You dhrink up, Julia, an' we'll go to my place where there's prime stuff waitin' for a hand to pour it out; and his glittering beady eyes wavered between looking at her face and at the white bosom peeping from the opened blouse. He pressed his sinewy fingers persuasively on to her thigh — Dhrink up, now, an' we'll go.

—I don't care what anyone says, muttered Julia, lowering the rest of her whiskey, he shouldn't ha' done it. He should ha' considered his followers' feelin's.

—Sure I know, I know, said the man. I know well how you feel about it. His hand went up slyly to her bosom, and fingered her blouse till another button was undone. It's aggravatin', right enough. He'll be sorry for it all one o' these days — you'll see.

—Eh, there, she suddenly said sharply, hitting his searching hand away from her blouse; don't start to open me up in public!

—Oh Gawd! came from Edwin Grey in a whispered moan. Let's go — it's too revolting!

—It's time to move, said Donal, looking at his watch, if we're going to go to Stephens's tonight.

They led the way from the snug, Sean following slowly. He longed to stay where he was, watching common life unfolding on the bench opposite; smoky life, catching the breath with a cough at times, but lit with the red flare of reckless vigour. It was the last time he would go to these gatherings. He liked James Stephens, loved him, really, and many fine people assembled there; but they were never themselves; they were ever on their guard; cautious and prepared, posing even, for there were few things in Dublin more conventional than the boastful, free-and-easy manners of its bohemianism. He bid a silent farewell to the black shawl with its rich yellow border, the pale, serious face, made jaunty by the twist of the big red mouth, the gleam in the grey eyes, and the bunchy recklessness of the curling hair.

Curious gatherings these of Dublin! Yeats's, and its very elect assembly; A. E.'s with its rather less select gathering of literature and timid politics; and Stephens's, with a few select, but many more of the lesser known, more homely, more honest-to-God, more happy than the other two conclaves. Sean strolled after the other two, thinking of how astonished he had been the first night he had gone to an A. E. *At Home*. When the room filled, desultory chat ended, and each settled himself for ordeal or treat. A. E. was climbing into his throne. This was a chair placed on a platform, and those present sat in a humble semicircle round this royal seat. A. E. climbed heavily, hoisting himself into it, the rotund belly and big backside eclipsing the throne for the rest of the evening. He ceremoniously lighted his pipe, while he waited for someone to start the talk rolling along like ole man river. It seemed plain to Sean that A. E. used the talk and the comments as a vocal rehearsal for what he would say in his Journal during the coming week. When he spoke, he did so as if his mind was the only one in harmony with the spheres. He became the policeman on point-duty directing the way through the avenues and lanes of this life, and those of the life to come. He had no music in him, for, like Yeats and Gogarty, he was tone-deaf. He poured out words in a steady, colourless torrent, full of sound, destitute of fury, signifying very little. It had struck Sean as strange how this man, so voluble in his own den, on his own throne, could be so silent when he was in Yeats's parlour. Sean had seen him there, sitting back in a fat settee, occasionally lighting his pipe with a casual air, as if to show an indifference Sean was sure he did not feel.

There he sat, silent, as if this talk did not matter, for importance and immensity were with him only who sat upon the fat settee. That A. E. uneasily felt that Yeats was beyond and above his rivalry was a sure thought to Sean, as he listened to the one and watched the other.

The three of them climbed up the stairs to James Stephens's flat, away up, up at the top of a high house in Fitzwilliam Square. The old kentucky home of Dublin's literary crowd. All the faces he had begun to know were there, together with a few he didn't know yet. There was A. E. right enough, holding forth on the arts; and Sean slipped to a chair in the background, for he knew, if A. E. spotted him, he'd be over to deluge Sean with the economic solution of ills, through his, and Horace Plunkett's, thousand-years plan of agricultural organisation policy. Oh, will you listen to him!

—*There's no doubt that magic is rarer in art than in literature*, he was saying with tremendous assurance. *In literature, Keats, Coleridge, our own Yeats, make a magical use of words. But in painting how rare it is. We can think of some, Turner and Monticelli. But it is Blake more than any other who suggests magic in his art. From him we get an excitement of spirit which far greater craftsmen are unable to communicate.*

—Ay, thought Sean, unable to communicate to A. E., for here his thought is rather of the magic of the medicine-man than of the artist. What an arrogant and conceited comment! Magic is rare in painting! We can think of some. It is Blake more than any other. Did this man know anything about painting? He couldn't know much. What kind of magic was he looking for? The pictured Christ that turned its eyes on the onlooker as he left the room would have made A. E. chant a *te deum*. He couldn't have meant the magic which beauty in colour and line and form raises in the minds of those who are able to see them; for in this world of strange and enduring magic there are hundreds of painters as good, or better than Turner or Monticelli, and very much better than Blake. And this man was accepted, not only as a critic, but as an oracle too. Oh, listen to him, now!

—*The painters Picasso, Braque, and Cézanne aren't good for beginners in the study of art*, rang out the arrogant voice. *Folk obviously inspired by Cézanne or Picasso should be sternly suppressed.* Evidently, to be inspired by the wretchedness of A. E.'s imitations was righteousness and peace; to be influenced by Picasso and Cézanne was wickedness and vice.

—Oh, holy God! mumbled Sean, he's on top of me now! A. E. had turned and had seen Sean; he made a bee-line for him, and planked himself down on a chair beside him. Then he poured the abstract chronicles of his *The National Being* into Sean's dulled and puzzled ear. Some demon or another, for a lark, to torment poor people, had bestowed on A. E. a brain that could vividly remember every phrase, every word of whatsoever he had written, and another demon had inflicted A. E. with a burning desire to pour all of whatsoever he had remembered into an ear unpleasantly situated to receive it by the fact that the listener hadn't a chance to escape. So Sean listened and ached and murmured in his heart, This man is not for me; none of these here are for me; you must go, Sean, go from them, for their people are not your people, neither is their god your god.

Suddenly, those present clapped their hands when James Stephens called on A. E. to join the crowd by reciting one of his poems, and in a fine burst of enthusiasm Sean clapped louder than the rest. A. E. murmured that it wasn't easy, after talking to O'Casside about things material for so long, to summon up the Divine Afflatus. The hands clapped again, a little more impatiently, either to give A. E. encouragement, or to show advanced appreciation of the beauty that was bound to come. A. E. was pleased, taking long breaths, puffing himself out, breathing solemnity and power into his psyche, amid a hush of awed silence. In the midst of the awed hush, Tom McGreevy's voice, like a thunder-clap, was heard saying, Give the poor man a chance — he has to pump himself up!

A titter, chokingly modified, rippled round the room, silenced altogether by Stephens's warning murmur of disapproval, and by the sudden rage of A. E. He rose roughly from his seat, snarling out that he wouldn't stay to be insulted; broke through the circle of friends by shoving his chair violently backward, and rushed swiftly from the silent room. No-one spoke, till McGreevy added to the already-given insult by saying, There goes the most conceited man in Ireland.

No-one was quite happy the rest of the evening, though James Stephens did his best to promote forgetfulness. So when Sean and his two companions left the house to walk home, their minds were fixed on the scene they had seen.

—McGreevy's right, said Donal. Under A. E.'s skin-deep humility is an insatiable vanity, a burning desire for acceptance. He filled his *The Irish Statesman* with his own articles under three or four different pen-names. He constantly talked to friends about the immensity of his booklet, *The National Being*, a booklet of tumbling words, weaving a useless and impossible pattern. He said that it had been translated into a number of languages; that it had appeared in India because Tagore wanted India to study it. He said his idea was used by Bulgaria, which, after the war, wasn't allowed to have an army; and that after the idea had been in operation for two years, a report on it was issued by the League of Nations. But these claims have died down, and were never confirmed. He told many that his *Thoughts for a Convention* created a great stir, for an editor had told him that the pamphlet had shaken the Unionist Faith in Ireland to its innermost tabernacle. Did anyone ever hear the like! The pamphlet hadn't rustled a hair of Irish Unionism's head.

—And look at what he said of Shakespeare, said Donal. Says he, *Shakespeare was the first supreme artist in literature who seemed to be absorbed in character for its own sake. And nothing is revealed in the Shakespearean drama except character. What did the genius of Shakespeare do for literature?* A. E. asks. And he answers, *More and more since his apparition have dramatist and novelist been artists of character for its own sake; and to be absorbed in character for its own sake is to be in a blind alley which leads nowhere.* And A. E. goes on, *Artists will revolt, and science which has been materialistic for a generation* (as if it was ever anything but materialistic!) *has become etherealised before the mystery of the atom; so the artist, always sensitive to spiritual atmosphere, may be inspired to draw literature out of the blind alley where Shakespeare has led it, to conceive of life as a part of a divine procession in which the personal dwindles, but the immortal may be exalted by a profound consciousness of cosmic purpose.*

—Terrible! said Sean. But then he couldn't stand Shakespeare's *Sonnets*, didn't like his plays, and no wonder, for Alexandre Dumas, Zane Grey, and others like them, were the literary nectar his gods gave him.

—And this was the kind of blather, said Donal viciously, that has dulled the ears, dimmed the eyes, and twisted the tongues of the younger thinkers and artists of Ireland. A. E. has scattered his divine processions, his ancestral selfs, his exalted immortalities, and his cosmic purposes as no sower would dare scatter his seed. Has all the mystery of the minds of all the great men and women of our race dwindled down into the mystery of the atom? Not a mundane mystery only, not a heavenly one only, but a cosmic purpose was to jump out of the activity of the atom. Holy and almighty atom, deliver us! Here was a man teaching his disciples to play the flute by simply blowing down it, ignoring the fact that they would have to use quick fingers to make the stops speak out a tune. Imagine the statement that, in a divine procession, the personality must dwindle. Imagine the personality of an artist dwindling when he wrote, painted, or carved a greatness into a stone. The long line of the greater painters, sculptors, architects, surgeons, and scientists are a divine procession, and the things they have done are their divine deeds, honouring God and glorifying man. We are all caught in the adventure of life through time and space, and to reap, plant, sow, mow, to cook a dinner well, to bring up children, and keep a home in order are divine deeds, calling for God's crowning and the sensible approval of man. Surely A. E.'s gospel is related to the mind of a man who secretly realises that in art and in literature greatness is not for him. And it comes ill from one whose talents were all derived, not from his own quality, but in imitation and in the practice of the far finer qualities of greater souls.

—The two of you are talking like a couple of barbarians, said Edwin Grey, his thin body quavering with annoyance. Your minds haven't yet risen high enough to understand the man. He is accepted the world over as a saint, a seer, the great philosopher of his day, a poet of the first rank, a painter of exalted imagination and of fine skill, a first-class economist, and a pioneer in agricultural progressive organisation. What did Monk Gibbon, the poet, say of him? This: *I have known one great man, one man alone, to rise head and shoulders above all his contemporaries.* Not this or that one, mind, but all of his contemporaries! And what does the poet, Katharine Tynan, say? This: *In Yeats, in Stephens, in Francis Thompson, I have not found the beauty of genius I found in A. E.* Good Gawd! are you two going to set your opinions against these two poets?

—Yes, why not? asked Sean.

—You would: in your pride, your vanity, your desire for notoriety, you would set yourselves up against finer ones than yourselves, A. E. was, as Con Curran, the writer and critic, in a sacred burst of enthusiasm, said, *He was a tribunal before which the ignoble dwindled.* He thought nothing of what men thought important; he sought obscurity as a companion; and he was intensely indifferent to fame.

—Ah, for God's sake, man! said Sean. A. E. hastened his death making himself known. In America, he had himself radioed from one end of the land to the other. He travelled from one end to the other, too, the sun blazing over his head one time, and frost under his feet at another. He rushed about everywhere, talking, talking, a Mr. Talkinghorn talking on things political, spiritual, artistic, philosophical, and rural, about which he knew as much as a new-born chicken; for what he thought he knew, he got from books stored in Plunkett House of Merrion Square. He never once had a sickle, a scythe, a fork, or a hoe in his hand. He never plucked a grain of corn from an ear; he never led out a horse to give him a drink; he never soiled his boots in the mud of a byre; and he never touched with his stout, pudgy finger the udder of a cow.

Indifferent to fame! Yet he is full of the way he talked to five hundred business men in San Francisco; how mightily he impressed them, though apparently none of them would, since none of them did, put down money to keep *The Irish Statesman* going. These were like the roaring catholic business men, so intensely concerned about the faith of poor catholic children, but diligently neglecting to give the money to maintain the schools in which to teach it to them. A. E. actually believed that he could hypnotise square-jawed business men who loved and praised the mingling of economics with the Aeolian poetry A. E. gave them. So they would, for there was nothing in either the poetry or the economics to alarm the business man. A. E. could safely say to them *Come with me, acushla, into the ancient hills*, for there was no danger that in the ancient hills their power would be questioned or their dividends cut. After telling us that Arizona reminded him of Zane Grey, he tells us that his *The Candle of Vision* is known everywhere. He lets out a cheer when he thinks that all scientists will soon become mystics, because Jeans, the astronomer, stated he believed in a divine mind; and he even plays with the idea that he may be elected an honorary member of the British Association, along with Yeats and other poets with an internal light! Internal light. Lady Gregory once said, in a merry mood, that A. E. hides a mystical light in a turnip; but the fact is that he hides a turnip in a mystical light.

—Vanity was the well-spring of his life, said Donal, lighting his pipe with emphasis; and Notoriety and Love of Fame were the two gods who constantly sat on the edge of his bed to keep him company. But he let his helplessness be known once when he was terrified to learn that the American practice of being up and doing hadn't the result he expected. He tells us that overdoing production in agriculture and industry, and with fewer people producing more than the world could consume, the Americans were staring at each other in surprise, for they found that, in producing so much, they had produced unemployment. More than they or the world could consume! This is the great economist for you! At that very moment, in the U.S.S.R., in India, in England, in A. E.'s own country, in America even, there were millions who weren't getting enough in either food or goods; and yet this know-all in economics told us that the Americans were producing more goods and more food than the peoples of the world could use or eat! This lover of truth wouldn't tell the truth; this destroyer of myths, this lover of humanity, wouldn't say that the production was greater, not than the world could use, but greater than the world could buy; that profits, about which he is silent, ensured that half of the world could go hungry rather than that profits should grow less. But he lectured on the depression, and a Harvard professor tells us that they listened to A. E.'s solution for the depression in Agriculture and Industry, and immediately began to organise the farmers on old-world lines, which terrified A. E. again — not because the method was a silly one — but because the farmers wanted five million dollars to set the scheme going.

—I still have the same reverence for A. E., said Edwin Grey languidly, that I had before either of you began to speak.

—Keep it bright and polished, said Donal a little bitterly; and do daily honour to him who hated fame and courted obscurity; he got Hughes, Sheppard, and another to make busts of his Olympian head. Indeed, during the Easter Rising, when the Hibernian Academy went up in fire, and the bust was lost, A. E. quickly sat for another, one in marble this time. Sarah Purser and Countess Markievicz both painted him, and F. R. Higgins, the poet, had a pastel done of him by a foreign artist; Yeats's father did him too; and there's the Gilbert Bronze, and the dry-point by Tittle, where he looks fat and gross, a thing that displeased many; and Rothenstein did him twice. A portrait by Dermod O'Brien; lithograph by Mary Duncan; wax portrait medallion by T. Spicer; bust by Jerome Connor; portrait by Estella Solomons; and one by Hilda Roberts. His bust by Sheppard blended in it the likenesses of Socrates, Ruskin, and all the sages of the world. A. E. used to refer to it himself mockingly as *Sheppard's Olympian Zeus*, but when one heard him say it, one heard a ring of prideful joy in the sweet mockery.

—Ay, and in America, went on Donal savagely, he hurried into a kinema to watch himself in a newsreel, as anxious as any mortal in Skibbereen to see himself as a public show. Zeus watching himself on a screen! A god veiling himself in the limelight. And how he rejoiced in telling that when Wilbut, one of Hoover's cabinet, held a meeting, the hall was half empty because everyone was flocking to another hall to hear himself.

—And what about his opinions of American cities and the people who live in them? asked Sean.

—I read it, said Donal. He said, *These cities are the last trap set for the spirit of man to draw him from nature and himself. The people who live in them are kind, but oh, so unhappy. They fly from one sensation to another and the way from body to soul is lost. If they close their eyes, they are in a darkness that frightens them. They cannot bear to be still or alone. They are thirsty for beauty, but cannot create it within themselves. When they meet a soul, truly living, natural and prodigal in itself, they are filled with wonder. They cannot help themselves, poor people. They were born into the mechanistic maze and do not know the way out. There was never anything in the world so pitiful as their souls.*

—The poor Yanks! added Donal sarcastically.

—Oh, it's maddening, said Sean. A. E. has always gone round preaching that, though we overcome material things, shortly after, material things overcome us. He was bitter in his cosy hatred of cities, so unlike Whitman, one of the great men he tried to resemble. There is as little (or as much) of what he calls spirituality in the country as there is in the city. He, himself, lived most of his life in a city. His home was in Dublin, and a very nice part of it too. All very fine to spend a few sunny weeks in the country, when everything was kind, and flowers bloomed in a haze of enchanting heat. But A. E. let well enough alone when the colder winds blew from the mountains and the bitter green sea foamed arrogantly over the beaches. In one of his books he tells of a young artist fleeing from the fog, gloom, cold, and mechanism of a city, as if the country never knew these things; could never be cold, never gloomy, never have a fog in the valley, or over the hill, never vibrate to the whirr of the combine-harvester and drill. The young man was fleeing from the blighting, mechanistic life of the city which he hated, but A. E., thoughtlessly enough, pictures him fleeing in a swell-upholstered, smoothly-running automobile. We see the young man, fleeing from mechanism, watching, through the window, the lemon light in the sky, the snowy fields, the cottages on the hillside; watching all from the centre of one of the finest mechanisms the mind of man has created. Away from the mechanistic city on the air-filled, rubber-tyred car, driven forward by the internal-combustion engine, conjuring up visions in the comfort of silent locomotion, soft cushions, and warm protection from the cold snarl of the snow. The young man, serene in the smooth-running car, comfortable against the cushions, wondered whether a time would ever come when all men would revolt as he had done, return to nature, and let that mother restore their lost likeness in soul and body to their ancestral beauty.

Could any reflection be sillier, more hysterical, or more hypocritical than this? Back to nature in a gorgeous car! Back to a lofty, roomy house, shaped like a Greek temple, with pillars holding up the façade, made of wood, and painted white! Oh, you mores, oh, tempores, how does your garden grow? Back to nature? How far now? To the skin-coat and the cave? To the tribe, or to the condition of feudal lord and feudal slave? Give up the tractor for the steel-bladed plough, or the steel-bladed plough for the deer's horn with which to scrape the ground? Give up the smoothly-running car, carrying the artist, for the sedan-chair, the horse, or shank's mare? Give up the electric glow in workshop and home for the candle or the rushlight? Give up A. E.'s own method in the co-operative creamery, with its fine machinery separating the cream from the milk, to make butter in the older, more natural ways of the bare hand and the wooden churn? Go back to the uncertain and hesitating probe, and abandon the Roentgen rays, making the surgeon's stab a sure thing, and so relieving pain and preserving life? Abandon the anaesthetic and germ-free theatre to go back to the old deal table, the meat-saw, and the tub of boiling pitch in which to plunge the stump and stay the bleeding? Smash all the delicate instruments denoting time, and go back to the days of the water-clock and the sundial?

Go back to nature! The yellow-bordered black shawl, the attractive face, pale as a new-born lily, with the luminous eyes, the big, red, defiant mouth, ascetic nose, crowned by the bunchy clusters of curling hair, the white bosom, pushing forward to be fondled, that had been flickering about on the screen of Sean's mind all through the talking, faded away now, for he was angry. It made him angry to think of these people murmuring from a chair, or shouting from a pulpit, Go Back to God; Go Back to nature! Go back to nature. We had never left her. Go back to God, go back to nature, without telling us how to do it. This is not the cry of the shepherd, but that of an hireling, afraid to face what God has brought to pass in the changes of a changing world. These people know, or ought to know, that the things done now, however mighty they be, will soon be lesser things behind the greater ones still to come. But they are afraid, they shiver before every forward step taken by man, and try to frighten him, too, with their meandering, delusive cries of back to God and back to nature. These were they who wanted life to die with a whimper, and were embattled, in Press, pulpit, and poem, against those who were determined, if life should die at all, that life should die with a cheer. It was utterly useless, and a little dangerous, to go about singing the song of Go back, go back to nature and go back to God, for it could never be done in the way they wanted it. The ways behind man were closed; the way before him was open, and forward he must go. If a God existed, then man was going to meet Him; he was not going to go back from Him, or slide away into a corner out of His sight. If God there be, then He is with the aeroplane five miles high in the sky, sailing over the North Pole, as He was with the first ploughman who fixed a steel edge to his wooden plough. If God there be, He is with the minds planning the bridge over the Severn as He was with the mind that flung a grass rope over a river to make a safer way to cross it; He is with the man of the combine-harvester sweeping over the prairie of waving, golden corn, gathering it and threshing it in big bundles, as He was with the lonelier one, heavily cutting his few stalks of grain with a sickle-curving flint-stone; He is with the scientist controlling or releasing the energy of the atom as He is with the anxious young mother kissing her baby to sleep. A wayward mother may bring misery and danger to her child, and wayward minds may bring misery and danger from the power of the atom; but, by and large, the mother will always be loving and true to her child, and the energy in the atom will be for man's redemption in the end.

—We leave you here, said Edwin Grey to Sean, when the three of them had halted on Binn's Bridge covering the canal, and within sound of the falling, gurgling waters on the lock. And remember even J. B. Priestley was constrained to admit that A. E. spent most of his time finding geniuses daily.

—And carrying them to the market in basketfuls, said Donal gaily — come on, if you're coming. Sean watched the two of them fading away down the Drumcondra Road, and turned to go his own way, thinking.

—It was said over and over, thought Sean, that adulation affronted A. E., yet no man of Ireland was ever more sicklied over with adulation than he; and he never seemed anxious to avoid it. He said he didn't like it, but followed it close, and was never far from where it was to be found. When the younger ones of Dublin discovered that A. E. had no real message for them; that he who rumour said excelled in all things, excelled in nothing but the vast intention of his own importance, they left him. The yogi contemplative felt lonely. Finding the adulation gone from Dublin, he sought it out in London; and finding it faint there, he sought it out in America. Desmond MacCarthy drawing a picture of A. E. in the last years of his residence in Rathgar Avenue, said, As years went on, fewer young men and women came of an evening to drink at A. E.'s fountain. When I inquired from friends visiting England, I was told — A. E.? I haven't seen him. Nobody goes there now.

Nobody goes there now. One would imagine that a sage, such as he claimed to be, would have welcomed loneliness as his salvation. Nobody came, so he was lonely. Socrates, Plotinus, Buddha, Plato, Confucius, were there, but he didn't want them. The great books of the Vedas, the Bhagavad-Gita and the Upanishads, were there, but they didn't go far enough for A. E. Alexandre Dumas was dead; Zane Grey didn't write stories often enough, and so he was lonely. He had no place for the yellow-bordered black shawl, the luring face, the snowy bosom; and so he was lonely. Humour might have saved him, but there was a sad lack of deep laughter in him. Neither had he song in him, for his ear was dead and dull to all music; and so he was lonely. All the glitter had faded. The glittering guy, so gay-looking in artificial light, looked drab and tawdry in the light of day. There was nothing of the child in him, so much of the kingdom of heaven laughed at and eluded him. He was too often with his own gods. He was never known to laugh at himself. He was never seen out walking with his wife. He was never seen out walking with a child. He would have thrown a yogi fit if a prepossessing whore, parading Grafton Street, had stopped him to ask if there was anything good in his mind. He was afraid of Yeats. He wrote never-endingly, he talked incessantly, he painted persistently, he travelled immoderately, and, finally, he left behind him a handful of pebbles, sanctified with a little gilt, that he took to be jewels.

As Sean ambled home, the lingering vision of A. E. burying his face in the earth grass when it was sunny, never when it was harsh and sharp with frost; or chanting his highly-coloured Sankey-Moody movie-emotion hymns; or watching, eyes shut, mouth agape, over the crest of a mountain, forms crested with many-coloured lights, gigantic forms that seemed shaped from some burnished and exquisite fire, went fading away to make room for Sean's own ungodly goddess, buxom and confidently aggressive in her womanly wisdom, her popular loveliness queenly cloaked in the richly yellow-bordered black shawl; and of the sinewy-handed, squirrel-eyed god beside her, dream-tipsy with the thoughts of the ecstasy and warmth hidden away from him in the swell of her white bosom beneath the blouse.

Gods of the earth, earthy, thought Sean; but none the worse for that.

THE GIRL HE LEFT BEHIND HIM

SEAN had passed away from two Jennies, one Bella, and this girl gave him the fullest experience of feminine good companionship he had had so far. She was a good-looking lass. Even now, glancing back after seeing many girls much more beautiful, his memory told him, with quiet insistence, that her big hazel eyes, her heavy mass of rich brown hair, softly-rounded chin, fine complexion, and full, white throat, made her a good-looking lass. Years before, he used to meet her on his way home from first quarter's work to breakfast, a sturdy slip of a girl, her long hair tidied into two long plaits, hurrying to a catholic elementary school where she was training to become a teacher. Then, in his cement-embroidered dungarees, his hobnailed boots clattering a morning tattoo on the pavement, she had attracted his attention; and he stared boldly into the soft hazel eyes, as he passed, seeking in them a soft, shy shelter in which to rest occasionally on the long, hard road that was stretching itself out before him. He had never spoken, and she had never tried to answer his soul's muffled appeal for the fanciful solace of a young girl's breast, and the red-lipped kiss of great encouragement. Yet a little while, and she passed by no more, for, a teacher now, she served another school far from where he walked.

Years after, they met again, during the beginning of an amateur drama club. She lived, not beside the Anner, nor on the banks of Loch Lomond, nor even by the pleasant waters of the river Lee; but in a most respectable, self-dignified little house. It was odd the airs these little houses gave themselves. They were stuck down in little narrow turnings off a bigger street, and each narrow way was given the delicious name of avenue. They faced each other grandly on either side of the road, a few more select than the others, having an upper storey, reached by a stairway that was really a ladder grown a little stouter with the years. The front room, or parlour, was a little wider, but less long, than the floor of a furniture van. In one of these, he had listened to a piano being played, and the instrument had looked as if it were terrified of its own music, for the sound of the notes played, crowded back, and smothered the new ones the piano was trying to give. The bedrooms were so small that a dim glance from one eye enfolded all that might be there. If you stretched out of the bed from the far side, you could put your head out of the window. The houses were pressed close, side by side, back to back, and front to front, each with its patch of back-yard surrounded by a low wall, so that a glance from both eyes could see them all boxed together, and, when people stood in them, they looked like cattle in their several pens. Yet the neatness, the cleanliness, the comfort of these midget houses were as much out of reach of Sean and his mother as lodgings even on the cold, cold floor of Edinburgh Castle, Buckingham Palace, or the Pope's private apartments in the Vatican at Rome.

Backed up by the stern respectability of their little grey house in the west, Nora Creena's father and mother were immediately against her having anything to do with Sean. And, indeed, as Sean discovered afterwards, Nora was scantily equipped with the courage to defy, or resist, the bitter respectability of these superb people; for Nora enjoyed all the peasant's awe in the tinselled glory of religion's parade, in supernatural nursery-tale of hell, and folk-invention of cherubim and seraphim that merged with the devil's face grinning from the show's centre, amid the coloured candle-light of religious fear. It had nothing in common with the child's delightful acceptance of coloured stories, which, however colourful, however violent, are always decent. There is hilarity and a comic certainty in a child's belief, and behind the sound of bells in the sleigh advancing, with its crimson-coated driver, are the painted cart, the green and yellow engine, the pink-faced doll, the gleaming gun, the silver trumpet, and the tasselled drum; the cart the symbol of harvest; the engine that of the good sense bringing goods everywhere that all may have a share; the doll of motherhood; the gun of war; and the trumpet and drum symbols of glory and the laurelled head.

But she was good to look at, gentle in manner, wistfully patient in listening to his talk, so the seasons through which they passed, using the city street or the country lane, spread enchanted hours before them, in fretted splendour overhead and tapestry of frost beneath their feet; or sun-dappled meadows, flushed with plenty, giving peace to timid cattle calmly grazing; or autumn weaving her russet, red, and golden mantle, covering the hedges with a lovely turmoil of gay and dying leaves.

He often wondered to which foliage of the autumn he should give the palm of beauty. To the oak, the elm, the beech, the birch? Certainly not to the chestnut, for its brown hues grew too coarse, and its fading leaves looked shabby and mean, stretched, drunkenly curling, on pathway and road. The common bramble? Ay, the touchy, ill-tempered, hand-biting bramble. Her stems are rich with purple, saluting the leaves where the green still lingers. Often on the same boastful stem there are the greenish-white of later buds, the pink smile of blossom, and the green, red, and black of the clustering berries. The leaves of the sycamore and maple are lovely, but never so gorgeous as the leaves of the bramble. This tough guy of the hedgerow dresses herself through the autumn as gay as a gay-hearted gypsy queen, thrusting her long, embattled arm through everything in her way so that bloom and berry may reign safe in the sun and the upper air. But autumn is all a revelry of decaying loveliness; the decorated garment of decline. Every field, meadow, and hedge a world of burning bush. Each dwindling tree, sensing the end of its summer hilarity, like a beauty preening herself with paint and powder before the final fading, slings around her cooling shoulders her gayest and most gorgeous shawl.

Sean deluged Nora's mind with the organ music of Milton's sentences so that they fancied themselves fighting side by side with Michael, and watched the resentful, squealing flight of the fallen ones; saw all of Satan's

> . . . *impious war in heaven, and battell proud*
> *With vain attempt. . . .*
> *Nine times . . . he, with his horrid crew,*
> *Lay vanquished, rowling in the fiery gulf,*
> *Confounded, though immortal. . . .*
> *Regions . . .*
> *Where peace and rest can never dwell, hope never comes,*
> *That comes to all . . .*

They heard the gallant words of Satan rejecting servitude in heaven for sovereignty in hell; shivered together with the shaking of his mighty spear uplifted in the mighty arm; and saw the black banner of evil streaming out from hell to the very rampart of heaven's jasper walls.

Sean lingered with her over the sad, sensuous, cynical innocence of

Omar Khayyám's rose-like meditations, knocking with him at the tavern door of life, shouting for its wider opening, so that they might

> *Make the most of what we yet may spend,*
> *Before we too into the Dust descend;*
> *Dust into Dust, and under Dust, to lie,*
> *Sans Wine, sans Song, sans Singer, and — sans End!*

He read the lovely cadences of Keats to her, trying to see things of beauty that would be a joy for the day; and often the pair of them heard Shaw laughing as he peeped from behind a tree, thrusting out a hand to guide a lover and his lass to Socialism; they listened to his merry and shrewd comments on children and their parents, on marriage, on war and peace, and on the things that mattered most to Roscullen in the heart of Ireland. And well she seemed to listen between kiss and kiss; listened, so that Sean, vain, vain man, thought the flame of his fancy was but a reflection of her own. He imagined for awhile that, in this glorious din of argument and beauty, she would decry the silly voice of warning; that she would henceforth wander as the wind which bloweth where it listeth; move among the brave to dance and sing with them when the softness of evening came, and stars were at their best; or when the moon appeared in graceful arrogance to drive all watchers from the heavens, and walk the sky alone; to walk within the limits of the sun, and cease to grope about within the shadowy glimmer of a holy candle. To stride along by the side of life, laughing; to fall with life seventy times seven; to rise again, and go on, rather than woo a crooked back and bending head from kneeling before the flimsy forms, in coloured clay, of men lost to Padua and Alcantara; to step aside from following fools, beset with fright that foxy-minded imps from hell, hid deep in every house and heart, sidling sly at every dark street corner, lurking even in every church, would, in an unguarded moment of a poor sinner's thought, snatch up their unwary souls and carry them off in a carpet bag to deposit them, safe and sound, into the itching hand of Satan.

Sean, suddenly, in the midst of an expected meeting, would get a pathetic and agitated letter saying that she could see him no more. Her words were mean with woe and the tale of reproaches, admonition, and threats from her people if she persisted in her folly of going with him. And these were too much for her. They would lay her low if she tried any longer to prevail against them. So for months he would see no sight of her, nor hear a word about her. He had then to hurry back to the constancy of his own companionship.

Then in the core of his heart, Sean knew that Nora Creena hadn't it in her to stand out safely against opposition. She wilted under the family's resentment and the priest's advice. He knew, too, that she would never force a way, nor stroll delightfully, through the embattled, or flowered, way of literature and life. He guessed that there weren't ten books, the number of the commandments, in the house where she talked, ate, and slept her life away; nor the semblance of a picture worth the time of glancing at it twice. Such books as she read were borrowed from the local library, a sound and very discreet loom and lure of literature. No need to make the sign of the cross on entering or leaving the building. The place was faint with the conquering grey breath of the pale Galilean.

She listened — how well she listened to all he said, to all he quoted; but Sean felt there was no real heed behind it. She would never plant a foot on any peak of Darien, never stray to any point from which the cross could not be seen; to where the bald unjointed chatter heard around it could be heard no longer. Our fathers and hail Marys chained her fast to where she wished to stay; she would never wander even as far as where she'd feel them binding her. For her the hunter of the east would never catch a sultan's turret in a noose of light.

Places far out in the country were chosen so that they might win a chance of escape from prying eyes; and, starting off early, Sean would walk there in his decaying boots, fearful of any cloud in the sky that would send rain falling to soak his boots into a sodden mass and saturate his thread-thin trousers. He had rarely a penny in his pocket to halve the heavy journey by tram, though she, in her sweet kindness, had often offered him the money, had tried to persuade him to let him share this simple thing with him; but, in his sour pride, he had always refused, bitterly, whenever she persisted in her persuasion. He had to submit to many humiliations that ground rage and bitterness into his soul. Several times, walking down a street near the rural edge of the city, they had met her younger sister coming towards them on the arm of her young man; and Nora, squealing out a Sacred Heart! it's Annie! would frantically wheel about, to run off in an opposite direction, while Sean, red with anger and shame, would have to trot away after her. He who was tense with the velvet-tipped doubt of Omar Khayyám, full of Shakespeare's exultation, rich in the grandeur of Milton, and under the blessing of Shelley's ardour and the beauty of Keats, had to hide miserably for fear of shocking ignorant respectability; denied the right even to pass it by in a decent and orderly manner, while the girl he admired, breathless with fright, trembled at his side. He who would face with indifferent effrontery castle prince or castle flunkey — here he was hiding from the midget majesty of a bowler hat. He used to be sick with rage for many a long day after.

But he enjoyed a brighter spell of life throughout any short hour that brought her by his side. Then she became a red, red rose, a westlin' wind bearin' home the laden bees, or a calm moon changing a mean land into a queenly world for one night only. But he knew, though she did not, that the moment the hour would turn into a life, the charm would end; for he realised that all they had read together, all she had listened to, hadn't added jot or tittle to her courage; hadn't toughened a fibre of her will to write a new sentence in her life, or criticise an old one. The Catholic Church had moulded the expanding universe into a doll's house for her, and there she lived by thronging duties pressed, with sorrows surging round, death shadowing her and hers, her future all unknown, there she lived in peace, in perfect peace; for Jesus she knew, and He is on the throne.

But it wasn't so easy for him, Sean thought, as he slouched homewards along the hedge-lined roads from Santry, Nora's kisses still happy and warm on his lips. He could not understand the stops, the ventages, the lowest, or the highest, compass in the melodious and malicious organ-tune of man's existence. What is man, O Lord, that Thou art mindful of him? *Thou hast made him a little lower than the angels, and hast crowned him with glory and honour.* Not much help there. What is he, who, *like a forward child, must be played and humoured a little to keep it quiet, till it falls asleep, and then the care is over?* Who and what is he who comes like water, and like wind he goes? A very superior being, thinks F. J. Sheed; for *Man is aware of his power to produce effects which have nothing whatsoever in common with matter.* What, nothing at all? But man being matter, and the effects coming from man, how can it be said that these effects can have nothing in common with matter? Because, says Sheed, *Man can think — thought is not reducible to anything that we can feel justified in calling material. It doesn't occupy space, it has neither shape, nor size, nor weight, and it is not perceptible to any of our senses; it cannot be made into something else.*

That's a queer saying, surely. May not a thought take the shape of a poem, a painting, a building? It may even turn itself into a war, national or civil. And hasn't catholic thought filled the sky with angels? How do we know that thought doesn't occupy space? How are thoughts sometimes carried over space from one mind to another?

And we give them definite qualities; we call a thought a deep one, a shallow one; there are great thoughts, high ones, low ones; dark thoughts and light ones too; and many a one has felt the sting of a sharp, fierce thought. What are they but the reflections of the mind that gives them birth, and the mind of man is made of first-class material — the brain. Does an electron, dodging about in an atom, have weight; what shape is it; can it be measured; and is it perceptible to our senses? But, then, it may have a mind, for all we know. *So this element, this utterly unmaterial thing,* says Sheed, *must be produced by some element in man distinctive from his body.* So this element, whatever it may be, with nothing behind it, or before it, is the soul. This is the everlasting I Am of each person. This thing, sans sight, sans smell, sans taste, sans everything, lives on forever; the nothing is a thing immortal. An element in a body, forming the little I Am, all that's left behind from all we knew, that doesn't occupy space, has no shape, nor weight, nor size, isn't perceptible to itself or anyone else, is a queer thing to go on living forever. And this is the soul of man, not the soul of man under Socialism, but the soul under the belief in the catholic faith. And this spectral thing that Sheed shoves out in front of the Communist, saying, No, son, your system won't work, for it doesn't take in, or account for, this strange and wondrous element, standing, like a tank trap, in the way of a proletarian march ahead.

The possession of a spiritual soul is the one thing that makes a fundamental difference between man and the lower animals, says Mr. Sheed. Seems from this that there is a corporeal soul as well as a spiritual one. However that may be, according to Mr. Sheed, the lower animals have been deprived of, or have never been given, the imperceptible element. God did not think it well to give them the power of thought, so in this way He separated them from man forever. Mr. Sheed seems very sure of himself, and of man, here. How does he know that animals can't think? And is he sure that the bulk of mankind make much use of this imperceptible element of thought? They seem to be beginning to do a bit of it now, and Mr. Sheed is getting a bit anxious about it all. Is he sure that animals, other than men, do no thinking? Who was it said, The more I see of men, the more I love my dog? G. B. Shaw tells us somewhere that a sheepdog understands his master better than most men can understand the story told by an astronomer. We had better be humble here. Sean remembered sitting in the kitchen of a friend when his host whispered to him to watch the big black cat, calmly sitting beside the fire between them, washing her face with graceful movements of her paw. Occasionally she paused to give a glance at the dresser where two herrings lay on a plate, while the woman of the house trotted round tidying things up serenely. To fetch something, the woman left the kitchen, and immediately the cat ceased her washing, listened a moment, then calmly walked over to the dresser, jumped on to a chair, and from the chair jumped on to the dresser, pausing a moment to listen before she bent to eat the herrings. A little later, her quick ear heard someone coming, for she raised her head, cocked her ears, then jumped from the dresser to the chair, from the chair to the floor, trotted back to the fireside, sat down quietly where she had been before, and once more, in all innocence, the graceful paw was moving rhythmically, washing the fur behind her ears. What a comic rogue that cat was in thought and action!

One time, Sean's brother, Mick, had a lovely, sturdily-built Irish terrier that became very friendly with Sean. He was a handsome animal, with a fine carriage and a proud mien; but Mick, when he was drunk, or trying to recover from the effects of drink, used to try to force the animal to crouch before him, after hard beating, so as to show to all who wanted to see how superior man was in thought and deed to the lower animals. Whenever he knew the dog was being beaten, and happened to be near, Sean hurried to the help of the animal; and many a row took place between Mick and him when he ventured to take the dog's part. One time Sean heard savage growling, mixed with Mick's curses, while he talked to a friend at the door, and hurrying upstairs he found his brother trying to land blows from a stick on the back of the dodging, snarling terrier, wild-eyed now, his back bristling, his lips curved savagely back to show his sharp, shining teeth. Sean caught Mick's arm, holding it easily, for the wild look of the dog had put something of the fear of God into Mick's mind; and the biting mood of the animal showed he was in no humour to crouch before his lord. Never had he done this before, and Sean loved the dog for his independence; for there was some of the fine animal's quality in Sean himself.

Keeping angry eyes staring at Mick, the animal edged towards the door which Sean opened for him. He followed the animal, and found him waiting at the back door. He looked up at Sean, plainly asking that a way might be opened for him to leave the house. Murmuring sympathetic words to the animal, snarling softly now, Sean with one hand stretched to open the door, while with the other he softly stroked the animal's rough strong neck. Sean opened the door

slowly, hoping that the dog would give him a friendly look, but he
never raised his head, nor ceased his quiet snarling; then, when the
door was open, he trotted out to the yard, jumped on the low, surrounding wall, and began to walk along it determinedly. Sean whistled
him lovingly back, but the dog went on; he whistled again, putting
an imperative tone of authority into the shrill notes, but, determined
and stately, the dog went on, and neither Sean nor Mick ever saw
the animal again. The dog had thought about it all, and had decided
to go and never come back. It was no flight; it was too determined
and dignified for that: it was, to Sean, a cold and calculated decision
to seek a newer and, perchance, a better life. Since Sean, the man
imaging God, couldn't protect him from violence, then this dog,
this lower animal, decided to rebuke Sean by leaving him. To this
day, the picture glows sadly before Sean's eyes; the pensive sky overhead, grey as a fasting friar's face, unmoved by a sharp, erratic wind
that stirred the dust in all the yards into eddying uneasiness; the
sturdy, arrogant church spire thrusting itself into the sober sky over
the shabby, shaking houses all around, like a wealthy parvenu, newly
nobled, rising to give advice to a gathering of charity children; and
by it all, walking steadily along the low wall, the dog passed on to
where he might find shelter and food without paying for them with
abuse and blows; or a place, maybe, where he could die without
them, in silence, self-respect honouring his own last breath.

We are told, canonically, that this insubstantial, everlasting element
is the bosom of pain, for without it the body would lose its power
of feeling. We feel pain because we are conscious, and we are conscious because we have a soul. All nice and comfortably arranged,
if you don't ask any questions. But the lower animals feel pain,
so what of them? All nicely settled too. Animals feel pain because
they too have souls, but their souls are not immortal. Sean was
taught that all souls were immortal; but here are souls which
die when the body dies. Dead souls. How, and when, were these
souls given to the lower animals? When Adam named them in
the Garden of Eden? How is it that while animals aren't conscious
that they have souls, we know they have them? Who told us
that now? Were they awarded souls only so that they might feel
pain? Not much of a gift, that! Are these souls graded? Are the
souls of the lowest among the lower animals equal in unsubstan-
tiality and precision of feeling? Is the soul of the mouse the same as
that of the lion? And how far down in the scale of the lowest
animals do souls go? Do they vanish at a certain point in the lowest

of the low among the lower animals of life? This element of thought, separating man from the animals, according to the theology of Mr. Sheed, having no shape, nor size nor weight, is the outward sign of the soul; so the soul should be as light and airy as the thought it manifests. But the church says, The soul is a substantial part of the body, and if this be so, then one is prompted to imagine that a soul is something more than smoke. Watch my smoke! Seeing, then, that the soul, though not, maybe, consubstantial with the body, is, according to Mr. Sheed's own church, a substantial part of it, that body which craves food, shelter, gaiety, health, security, then the element which — Mr. Sheed says — prevents a man from accepting Communism is the very element that will run about to seek it, and finding it, will embrace it as its own. How this good roman catholic writer trots along the road of life without an effort, truth and certainty gambolling along at his feet like docile spaniels! He lives in a world where no bell is cracked; no breeze is bitter; no sun to make him sweat, and no frost to nip finger or ear; where birds chant the Athanasian Creed; where the brooks are Aristotelian waters distilled by Aquinas, giving sweet drink to all who saunter by their banks; drink good for the body, saving the soul.

Easier to him than it was to a fine, brave, catholic theologian, Dr. McDonald, asking many questions that had been settled forever by minor minds, with their glib cathetical call of Supernatural Qualities. But what is a Quality? asks this anxious theologian, and how does it contribute to action? Don't ask me, mate, thought Sean; I'm one of the higher animals, but I can't answer you. 'Then in what sense is the soul a substantial form of the body? Or in what sense is the matter of which the body is composed — chemical ingredients, such as are found in the inorganic world — in need or capable of a substantial form? Is it that the soul acts as a source of energy? But is there any smallest fragment of the energy of the human body — nerves or muscles — that does not come into it from the ether, as to any other machine? Conscious sensation, you will say; but is there any sensation that does not reside in the nervous system, consisting entirely of material motions, which, no less surely than the movements of a blacksmith's arm, arise chemically? They tell us, now, from Rome, that this difficulty has been cleared up by the writings of John Peter Oliver; which, however it may have decided the question in dispute between Cardinal Zigliara and Father Palmieri, S.J., has left the real difficulty precisely where it was. In what sense, capable of being brought into harmony with modern biological science, is the human soul a substantial form of the body wherewith it is united?' Ask us an easier one, O theologian!

So Sean pondered deep in his heart on what he was and what he might be; whether annihilation's waste would be his when the end came; or whether what he was would flame with life eternally, as he wandered in winter by the tangled pauperism of the hedgerows, forlorn, save for an odd robin perched well within them, looking like the soul of a young saint, determined to be happy in the midst of desolation; or, in summer, when Nora had left him to journey home alone, when the hedges were jaunty with the trumpets of the bind-weed, sounding their tiny tucket to the sun; the dainty wild rose, not too delicate to be arm in arm with the less tidy and rowdier black-berry blossom; the scarlet pimpernel's tiny red star gleaming among the eager, careless growth, like the fiery thoughts of a brave man in a pushing crowd; and the speedwell's blossom so blue that it must have been dyed by God's own steeping.

Yes, in politics, he was a Communist; and in religion, a Rational-ist. From a casual friend he had once persuaded a loan of Lecky's *Rise of Rationalism in Europe*, but had read only the first chapter when its return was demanded, and he had had to give it back. A precious book, he was told; expensive, and one to be guarded against staying away too long from its proper home. Afraid the book might hurt his soul, Sean thought, for all Ireland dreaded the danger of a book. He had watched for a copy on the second-hand bookstalls, but none ventured there. A rare book. In the Public Library? Not there, not there, my child. Not in his locality, anyhow. He heard of a library in Capel Street, that held a finer and fuller collection. He hurried to the President of his O'Toole Club, Johnny Kirwan, Manager of Murray's Belfast Tobacco Branch in Dublin. Certainly, Johnny would sign the guarantor's form for him. Next day Sean found Johnny had changed his mind — he refused to sign the form. Why? Can't you trust me to care for the books? asked the puzzled Sean. Oh, dear, yes, Johnny could; it wasn't that; and after humming and hawing, Sean squeezed out of him that he was afraid Sean would read a book which might be bound to imperil his immortal soul. He'd buy Sean a book as a present; but Sean bowed, and told Johnny he could put the book where the monkey put the nut; and went his way, resolved that public libraries would know him no more, and that any book he might have in the future would be his own.

You see now, Sean, he argued with himself, the road you travel would never do for Nora. The rationalist would be pulling the religious forward; and the rigid religious would be dragging the rationalist back. She walked with him through the golden land; but would she trudge through the one of doubt and sorrow? Through that of sorrow — yes; through that of doubting — no. Revelation, coupled with tradition, gave insufficient answers to many questions he was asking. Ay, and as yet, to many questions, there weren't any answers at all; except those which refused to fit the answers, proved correct, confounding them. Was it right for such a mind as his to try to find an answer, rather than to abide with the answers found by others? Was it just vanity? Did it matter whether he moved forward, or stood still, when moving forward meant the shoving aside of some he loved? Mattering little or much, it was his way to go. He could no other. His nature had now led him to where he was; and the growth of past and present would inevitably shape his coming thoughts as growth brought forth blossom and fruit onto the blackberry and the acorn onto the oak.

Nora wasn't for him: she would forever shelter in the lee of a credulous respectability. He remembered well, once, when she was telling him she'd have to cease from seeing him, how savagely she had declared that if he failed to make a name for himself in what he was trying to do within six months, their sweet alliance must end forever. He remembered how resentfully his soul laughed at the threat, for his development was with life, and not with calendar or clock. The Holy Ghost was not a panting creature of time, yet here was a good catholic girl trying to goad him into a hurry. The Holy Ghost in a hurry! She was measuring the gay-coloured wings of the Holy Ghost, hiding eternity with their spread, with the pale wings, stable as dust, of the frail, flying moth of time. There were other months in the year as well as May in which to go gathering nuts.

Let her cling to the little house, with its tiny windows and door; its four small rooms, with their neat little beds; the windows graced with curtains. They were her due, and she did well to claim them for her own. They were genuine things, to be sought after by the sensible and satisfied. The lions had long departed from the Christians. Sean didn't despise them, either; he wished he could dwell in one of them, in peace, secure as this world goes; with freedom to go, if ever one of these tiny, gentle things tried to enwrap his soul with lies. But he would be safer, if need be, walking the roads, or crouching, like blind Rafferty, under a dripping bush, while the rain fell and the wind blew keen. Not for Nora the charm of embroidered cloths under her feet, but the firmness of well-glazed oilcloth, or the softness of a carpet, well woven, covering a floor. Not the red rose, with its agitating thorn, for her swan-white breast, but a black cross, nestling chill and steady there.

Never once had he mentioned the Bolshevik Revolution to her, though it was ever in his mind; never once had he tried by a word to attune her ear to an echo even of the march of the Red Guards, though he himself had followed, with quaking heart, the advance of Kolchak from the east, and the advance of Denikin from the south, till from where they were, Denikin said, they could see, on a clear night, through the windows of Moscow, the tight-lipped people getting ready to quit the city. The Press was full of the death and defeat of the Red madmen; then, suddenly, they fell silent; and Sean knew that the Red Flag was high in Moscow and Petrograd. O, silver trumpets be ye lifted up, and call to the great race that is to come! Yeats, Yeats, they are sounding now, though your ears are cocked in another direction. Sounding loud and brave, not for all ears yet; but for the many to hear; and Sean's were the first of the Irish ones to hear them. Christ the king was becoming a Communist!

He knew in his heart that Nora and he would never fix themselves together in the world. Freethought to her would be but blasphemy and ruin eternal. A big part of her life would become a mumble of prayer that he might recognise the truth, accept the faith, be converted, and live. Jesus! that would be death in life to him! After the first while, or so, her creed would again form her life, and then his crowded loneliness would end forever. Let her gentle, quiet nature live a quiet, gentle life; let his doubting, strenuous one live out its activity and struggle, however bitter and painful, any, or all, of it might be.

He stood still to watch the tired and shallow flow of the slow waters of the Dodder, near Rathfarnham; hard set at times to push a way through the thick and sturdy herbage, growing querulously far out from its banks, shoving a passage often to the centre of the river; so like the flow of Ireland's life. Above him, the evening had pulled a curtain over the sky of quiet rose and daring green, now patterned with the shapes of hundreds of deep-black rooks, like darkened souls flying off, half afraid of heaven; while in the east, a pale moon, shy and pearly, stole into sight like a shy lass stealing out to meet a wild lover alone for the first time in her life. And around in the sheltering herbage he saw dim forms of life commingling, each a lover and his lass embedded in all the loveliness surrounding them.

You say there is no substance here,
One great reality above;
Back from that void I shrink in fear,
And, child-like, hide myself in love;
Show me what angels feel. Till then,
I cling, a mere weak man, to men.

He felt that he could never be alone, however lonely he might be.

SILENCE

IT was everywhere round the place; round Maynooth College; as if heavy snow had fallen, covering every sound deep, so that there was no echo of any footstep, nor of a voice; no, nor the song of any bird: as if heavy snow had fallen, and no wind blew: silence.

One cold, windy day in Webb's second-hand book-store, that stretched drunkenly along a lot of Aston's Quay, Sean's hand flicked over shelves holding selected volumes, looking for something new. One caught his eye, labelled *Reminiscences of a Maynooth Professor*, for it reminded him of his visits to the College. He passed the book by, as having no interest for him, and went away with a volume of plays by Brieux, fortified with a preface by Bernard Shaw. A week later he was in Webb's again, and there was the Professor's book still staring him in the face. He took it down, and looked within to see the price. It was marked eighteen shillings, and Sean hastily put back the book on the shelf again.

Maynooth, a town in the County of Kildare, having a population of under two thousand, containing the Roman Catholic College of St. Patrick. One could as readily say, Ireland, an island with a population of four millions, containing the College of Maynooth; for this College is the brain, the body, the nerve and the tissue of the land, controlling two-thirds of the country, influencing it all. There stood the wide, heavy gateway, iron-hard as the discipline within; flanked on one side by the tower of the old Castle of the Geraldines, Lords of Kildare in the old time, and once nearly Lords of Ireland without division; and on the other by the Barracks of the Royal Irish Constabulary.

Ye Geraldines, ye Geraldines! — How royally ye reigned
O'er Desmond broad and rich Kildare, and English arts disdained;
Your sword made knights, your banner waved, free was your bugle call
By Glyn's green slopes, and Dingle's tide, from Barrow's banks to Youghal!

Behind the ruined tower, shrouded in ivy, rose the College, enshrining the voice of Ireland's ecclesiastical oracle, outside heard as the barking of Cerberus, inside as silent as the grave. And here, in this College, lived Dr. Walter McDonald, Professor of Theology for forty years; for forty long and lustrous years of thought and striving in the quiet room where he wrote, and in the quieter room where he slept at night.

Sean had visited the College three times, once in gay kilt, coloured shawl, and feathered cap. He had sat in the church while a young student had played sacred music (what is sacred music?) on the electrically-blown organ; he had watched the Mother Superior of the nuns sitting, frightened and breathless, on the altar steps, convinced she had a heart attack, while she murmured complainingly that she should never have ventured to walk so far, or stepped out so quick. He had tried to convince her that no heart could be hurt by such a short walk on such a level road; that if she had had a real heart attack, she could never have risen from the altar steps to walk back again, that the breathlessness had been brought on by her nervousness or need of exercise; and that she should try not to let her heart be troubled for as long as she could stand on her feet, and trip about her business. He had caught a glimpse of half a cow hanging from a hook in a hall, savoury meat for the sustenance of those soon to become Levites, dispensers of holy grace and truth to fallen man. Sean had looked, and had commented politely, at the long row of oil-paintings of past presidents hanging on the cloister walls — poor paintings of poorer men, one of them only prominent, as far as Sean could remember, for the part he had played in hounding to poverty and death the proud and gallant Dr. O'Hickey. Sean had played hand-ball in the ball alleys, and had taken tea afterwards in a big room of the College. He had watched groups of lusty young men on their way to the fields, some to play hurley, others to play football, a few of them, later on, to be canons, a smaller number, lordly bishops, one of them, maybe, a cardinal, but none of them a pope — no Irish need apply there; the Irish, notwithstanding their devotion to the Faith; their world-wide contribution to the priesthood of the world; their readiness to accept, open-mouthed, every word spoken by Italian cardinal or pope; the Irish were still reckoned as heathens, and their land was a mission field, and is still subject to the Congregation of the Propaganda. The land that did so much to re-Christianise the civilised world when it was peopled with warlike pagans after the break-up of the Roman Empire. The land of Columkille, of Colum-

banus, of Aidan, of Bridget, of Duns Scotus, and of a host of halo'd
followers, is still subject to a group of red-hatted Italians who are as
much interested in their Church in Ireland, and all that she has done
for them, as is Dan Muldoon the Solid Man, and care a lot less for
her than he does.

There were the students, hurrying to the playgrounds, loudly
restless, talkative, as if wishful to be forgetful of the life they would,
sooner or later, have to pretend to live. Occasionally, a nun would
flit up or down a path, hurrying head down, noticing no boys, and
boys passing on their way as if she had been invisible. Over all was
a strange silence, not a dead one, but a living silence, pale, venomous,
striking out the humanities from a man's heart.

A week or so later, the book was still on the shelf, and Sean took
it down, paid for it with a sigh, and went home with it under an
arm. What he read there jolted Sean into silence too. He said
nothing, but pondered the things he read deeply in his heart. He had
seen and heard many strange things during his long association with
catholic comrades at work, in the Gaelic League, and in the Irish
Republican Brotherhood. He had heard of a book called *Priests and
People in Ireland*, written by a Michael McCarthy; had heard Gaelic
Leaguers laughing at it, and he had laughed with them. Everyone
who could afford to buy or borrow it, read it; but ridicule was all
the praise it got. A great controversy raged in the papers about what
it had said, and the pictures of towering churches dominating miserable village hovels; but the battle died down, and, Sean heard after,
that McCarthy had left the country. Later on a book by Sir Horace
Plunkett, on the same kind of theme, caused another sensation; and
opposition, generated by the clergy, became so strong that it threatened to undo the work of the Irish Agricultural Society, so that many
had to plead excuses for the Knight's unworthy opinions about the
bad influence of the priests in all Irish activities. The catholics again
rose out, and filled the streets of the towns and the lanes of
the country with their outcries. West-Briton and Irish-Irelander
joined together to threaten the writer and mock the book; and
Sean, though he hadn't read a line of it, mocked the book with
them.

But here was a book that couldn't be mocked, neither could the
writer be threatened, for he was in his grave, having arranged that
the book should be published only after he had died. Here were the
cold, sober thoughts of no 'renegade catholic'; nor the criticisms of
a protestant and impatient Unionist: no; here were the spear-like

criticisms of a flower of the flock; of one writing from the very core of the catholic fortress, Maynooth; of a rebel confined to the bed of obedience. By God, here was a showdown of the mitred oracle of Maynooth!

Dr. Walter McDonald, the writer of *Reminiscences of a Maynooth Professor*, was born in the tiny village of Emil, in the parish of Mooncoin, famous for its hurlers, in the County of Kilkenny. He was the son of a small tenant-farmer, rather a hard-drinking, sit-at-ease fellow, who left his patient wife to do most of the work, surrendering her life so that she might sew, clean, wash, iron, and cook, while in her spare time she milked the cows, made the butter, cleaned the dairy vessels, and helped to prepare the food for the pigs and cattle. A refined woman, this hard-working country-woman, eager to wrap part of her life in literature, but forced to be satisfied with the coloured scarf of *The Arabian Nights* which she got in the house of the protestant Rector with whom she was friendly. She so loved the book that she hurried over ditch and fence, taking short cuts through the fields, the book under her petticoat (for the reading of such a book wouldn't be thought decent by her neighbours), so that she might for a few moments lie under a fence, to take an imaginative journey with Sinbad, or sit in the magic rays of Aladdin's wonderful lamp, before the others came up to lift her from loveliness into the dull ardour of field-work.

Dr. McDonald started school before he was five, a bitterly cold school for such a sensitive little fellow in body and soul. When he became a young man of eight, he went to another as a weekly boarder, a school seven miles from his home, and anyone leaning over the half-door of his cottage on a Monday morning early, would have seen the youngster trudging the lonely road, carrying a big basket of butter, eggs, oatmeal, and cake to serve him for the week's provisions. The long journeys on the hard indifferent road nurtured in the childish mind of the boy that resignation and patience which he was to carry with him — like the basket — all the days of his life. Happily he had a finer collection of literature than had had his mother, for the cultured condition of the island of scholars threw in his way *The Lives of the Saints, Robinson Crusoe*, some copies of *The Dublin Penny Journal*, a book descriptive of Irish scenery, and *The Five Champions of Christendom*, so that the boy caught a cloudy glimpse of what letters was like.

In his young boy-student days in the College of St. Kieran, learning was loved in Ireland, for, we are told, Latin and Greek were literally hammered into him, so that, oddly enough, he hated these languages for years. Wilful, obstinate boy, showing what an evil thing is original sin. This way was the only way to education. 'If you won't let it in at one end, I'll hammer it in at the other!' shouted an indignant father, laying on the lash to his squealing boy, as we were once told by *The Leader*. I'll learn you, with the holy help of St. John of Bossco! Seize that boy! Bring me my burnished cane and shining rod. Cane him, cane him, till his squealing voice creaks with pain! Cane him till pain forces him to honour God and coaxes him into a love of learning! They are tainted with original sin. That was the churchman's way of teaching then; it is the churchman's way of teaching now. Educate the young into slavery so that with many stripes from rod and cane we may hymn our way to heaven howling. Oh, sacerdotal sadists, your way has at last been checked by disbelief, and disbelief will go on checking it till kindly human reason will not suffer cruelty to live.

When McDonald left the mediocre men behind him at St. Kieran's, he found more of them waiting for him at Maynooth, such as Dr. Gargan, whose lectures on Ecclesiastical History were so poor that McDonald didn't like to speak about them; Mr. Hackett, who sat easy in his Chair, for he didn't seem to have any interest in Philosophy; and a Dr. O'Hanlon, whose *Notes on Canon Law* were 'elementary — such as one might find in any text-book'. Oh, God! Oh, great Maynooth!

The only enemies the College recognised then were the protestants, and little thought was given to the new Rationalistic spirit sweeping England, and which has since become such a mighty force in most protestant and catholic countries today. Though there was no danger of anyone in Maynooth becoming a protestant, some of them were agitated and disturbed when they could no longer avoid the arguments put forward so forcibly by the Rationalists. 'Indeed,' says McDonald, 'so imperfect was the system formulated even on the old traditional lines, that it was turned inside out not many years afterwards by Dr. Salmon of Trinity College, whose work on *Infallibility* still remains without a sufficient answer.' And, adds Dr. Coulton of Cambridge, remains so still. Don't worry, now; don't fuss — all's well, as long as the coloured symbol of the Sacred Heart hangs on the back of every door. These for the simple; the higher educated are saved by Archbishop McQuaid's declaration of excommunication on any catholic student who ventures to put his nose within the gates of Trinity College. But a wider and a deeper force is sweeping catholic and protestant countries today. The laity are busy building a church of their own outside of the animosity of worldly cardinal and wordly priest; a 'country where the State is the Church and the Church the people; a commonwealth in which work is play and play is life; a temple in which the priest is the worshipper and the worshipper the worshipped; a godhead in which all life is human and all humanity divine'.

And another bright light of Maynooth was Dr. Murray, 'more of an ultramontane than the pope, and a bigot, if ever there was one. Whatever view extended most to the exaltation and honour of the Holy See, the Church, or of God, the Blessed Virgin, or the saints, became, for that reason alone, to him more probable.' But they weren't all composed of Maynoothian fudge and froth. Wise and wary as she was, even Maynooth couldn't altogether keep person-ality from striding through her cloisters. Father Gowan came, by God's providence, at the beginning of Dr. McDonald's second year's divinity course to show the students the way of teaching and preach-ing the Christian Doctrine. He came in well-worn old coat and hat, strong shoes, between which and his short trousers the stockings showed; and though he never really appealed to those who judged a man by his clothes and his way of talking, he brought close to him the hearts of those who had respect for a good man. By God, a man in Maynooth at last.

Dr. McDonald was a happy and confident young man then, for he hadn't yet collided with any of the ecclesiastics. 'He knew no fear whether of professor or dean; and, if called upon, would have spoken truth, however unpleasant, to the College of Cardinals, for he had no notion that an honest, well-meaning man could be injured by anyone, and especially by any ecclesiastic.' He was very innocent then. His troubles began while he was teaching at St. Kieran's on *Certitude, and its Criteria*, a treatise as big as a strong man could uncomfortably carry, beloved and trusted by the professors of the divine way to life and eternal understanding. But it gave such a confused exposition of Certitude to Dr. McDonald that he flung it from him in anger, and never peeped into it again. Some time after, to renew his courage and faith, Dr. McDonald read Murray's tome on *The Church*, reading on and on till he came to the two hundredth objection to Infallibility, each of them lying in the book as neat and as precise as the pectoral cross on the breast of a bishop, and all so ineffective that Dr. McDonald, in a burst of anger, flung the great book out of the window.

Silence, Dr. McDonald, silence. Say nothing; keep all this to yourself.

'Oh, it's all very well to say,' said Dr. McDonald, 'that this or that is the traditional catholic view, and hence must be satisfactory, until its unsatisfactoriness has been burned into you. I say now, very solemnly, that the conservatism in which I was trained very nearly drove me out of the church on many occasions, and these good easy men who, for the honour of God and in the interests of religion, insist on these traditional views — making dogmas of what are but school traditions — are tormenting souls and driving them out of the church.'

School traditions adorned with the sacredness of dogma, with cardinal and bishop moulding new ones out of little wit and lesser knowledge, till every one of them, backed by monsignor, canon, and parish priest, comes to imagine that whatever any of them may say, on whatsoever subject, must be accepted without quavering, must be believed, acted upon at once, without misgiving; perpetuating their theology within the dribbling stage, so that the attention given to them by sensible men, in the light of what we now know, can be but the smiling attention given by the same sensible man to a child's nursery rhyme. It has its uses, for it is this sort of thing that sanctifies the orderly, money-making orgy of Lourdes, strange tinselled waste, and woeful issue of a sick child's slick dream; tipping rose-leaves out on running sores and eating cancers; setting its comic, codified cure, by dipping the sick into a well, thick with the scum of a thousand tumours, against the calmly measured scientific healing of millions, without the singing of a single psalm. God's gift of penicillin is worth ten thousand Lourdes.

Driving into a happier nonsense, Dr. McDonald tells us of how the bishops and the clergy were disturbed (like Dr. Johnson) by the swelling bosoms venturing forth from the low-cut bodices of the ladies. Before a Garrison Dance, to be given in Kilkenny Castle, to which many catholic ladies had been invited, the ponderous question faced the clergy as to whether these lasses could dance such a thing as a waltz, and wear evening-dress while dancing it. So they warned all whom it might concern that, at the first Synod of Maynooth, all such dances had been condemned by the pastors of the church; and the bishops called on all to whom God had entrusted the care of immortal souls to banish from their midst what was so often, if not always, an occasion of sin. So the Synod warned the ladies that it was a mortal sin to dance a waltz or a polka, in evening-dress especially; but the impudent lasses insisted that they, who had often done this before without thought of sin, knew better than the bishops. So the bishops sat round in a circle again, and thought and thought deeply on this vexed and sexed question, finally deciding that the ladies might go to the Ball, provided the dress they wore was cut merely into a V-shape at the throat; and that they might dance waltzes, provided the gentlemen held both hands of his partner in front.

Eyes front, gentlemen! Keep your hands steady! What if a gentleman, embracing a lady, allowed a wandering hand to slip down, and rest on her bottom! And what if the lady happened to like the feeling? Where would we be then! And what of the knowledge of sweet things seen within the movement of a low-cut bodice? What eager eyes would see, the eager heart would grieve for, and the gentleman's soul with the lady's soul would go dancing down into amour mortal sin. And what about when the Ball was over, after the break of day? What villainies of immortal sin might be committed on the slow way home! Illegitimate children swarming the streets of the town in their bare feet. But with deplorable recklessness, the ladies, ignoring the bishops' and the gypsy's warning, went to the Ball, and had a fine time of it.

What an odd bunch some of the professors were whom McDonald met in Maynooth! Murray, who denounced Parnell and the Land League as if it had been aimed at the Papacy; Dr. Farrelly, who added to the denunciation as ignorantly, for he was the slave of the cant of respectability; if he couldn't find a lord to fawn on, he fawned on any of the gentry he met — even in print; and Dr. McCauley, who disdained to listen to anything said by an uneducated plebeian like Michael Davitt, who had the temerity to set himself up against Mr. Gladstone, and all the education, wealth, and respectability of the British Isles; and Dr. Healy, after setting these gentlemen on, applauding all they said in denunciation.

> Soldiers of Christ, arise,
> And put your armour on;
> Strong in the strength a lord supplies,
> Or even a lord's first son.
>
> Worship respectable things,
> Keep thoughts well comb'd and trim;
> The one who this sage counsel heeds
> Will always be in the swim.

Pray to saints, kindly and grim,
But keep your bishop calm;
Make all his pleasure, every whim,
Your pray'r, your hymn, your psalm.

Oh, for a Bishop to be;
Or else a Monsignor gay;
Promotion sensible men will agree
'S the life, the truth, the way.

False pretence, deceit, and intrigue in Maynooth too. No! Oh, but yes; and since inferior officers in Maynooth are guilty of indiscretions, surely there must be rank blasphemy shown at times by the superior officers in Rome. Dr. Carr, one of Maynooth's professors, was out hunting for the Bishopric of Galway, and Dr. Walsh, the President of the College (afterwards Archbishop of Dublin), wanted Carr to get the job. At the same time, the notorious Papal Encyclical, *Quidquod de Parnellio*, condemning Parnellism, flew over to Ireland, to be read from every altar; an Encyclical engineered by the bishops and other enemies of Parnell and his people. The followers of Parnell raged, like the heathen, against it, even Tim Healy being constrained to call it 'an idiotic circular'. It hadn't any effect, and subscriptions to the Plan of Campaign, instead of growing less, demonstrably increased. And among those who sent subscriptions were five professors of Maynooth — McDonald, Hackett, O'Dea, Boylan, and O'Donnell. They sent the subscription in jointly, and through the public way of the Press. At the identical moment, the name of Carr had been sent foremost to the Vatican for selection to the Bishopric of Galway. Now what would Rome think of the name of Carr of Maynooth, when five of his brother professors had sent in, jointly, a subscription to a movement that the Vatican had lustily condemned? Well, what about it? What about it! Don't you see, man, that poor Carr's chance of the Galway job was lessened — endangered even — by this unseemly action on the part of five men on the College Staff? Strutting to their rooms, Dr. Carr, highly indignant, threatened them, one after the other, that they would hear more about it. And they did, too.

Immediately the Trustees of the College went into a huddle, and passed a resolution that members of the Staff must not take sides on public questions about which the bishops were divided, adding, cutely enough, that the resolution was not to be recorded on the minutes. Keep it quiet; must be known only to ourselves. Ourselves

Alone! All the bishops were united on the question of creating, whenever possible, an opposition that would trample into dust the heart of the Irish Leader. To make sure that the resolution couldn't escape into the Press, the Trustees decided that it was to be read privately to each of the five members of the Staff, and that a copy was to be given to none of them. Fair is fair. But fair is sometimes foul in Maynooth College. So, armed with a scrap of paper, Dr. Walsh (afterwards Archbishop of Dublin) came secretly by night, like a creeping Nicodemus, and read the resolution privately, by the dim light of a candle, to each professor in turn; all listening in silence, except Hackett, who asked for a copy, and when told he wouldn't get one, refused to listen to a resolution that wasn't given to him in writing. 'There was grit in the man,' murmured McDonald, astonished that there should be such a thing as grit nesting in the nature of a Maynooth professor. 'This was the first occasion', says Dr. McDonald, 'on which I knew — or felt — that an act so solemn as that of the Episcopal Body could be drawn up on false pretences. None of us could believe that we were reprimanded in this way merely for taking a side in a matter of public interest on which the bishops were divided. It was passed, we were sure, because Dr. Walsh and Dr. Carr — the Bishop presumptive of Galway — feared that Dr. Carr's appointment to the See of Galway would be endangered by so many of the College Staff subscribing publicly to a testimonial which the Vatican had discountenanced. The Papal circular was falsely coloured, striking at the testimonial without daring to strike openly, just as the Episcopal resolution struck at us, not for the reason assigned, but for one which had to be kept concealed.'

And these are the customers who lead the van in the curious, comic fight for 'the sacred rights of the individual'. The Gasquets, the Chestertons, the Logues, the Walshes, and the Hinsleys. These are they who allow and encourage their anxious dupes to festoon themselves with miraculous medals, Hinsley crosses — found as often on the mangled and the unreturning dead as on the living — and Winnipeg angels, guaranteed to bring young air-fighters back home safe and sound; or, at the worst, to furnish them with immediate entrance into heaven (on payment of forty-nine dollars first). These are they, too, who shudder into violent opposition the moment the faintest ripple of new thought appears in the catholic mind, on any matter, literature, art, education, or the social necessity for a wholesome change in the way the greatest part of the people live.

Like the Pope's government of the Papal States, after Napoleon's
defeat, abolishing street lighting as being too democratic and revolutionary. As the Vatican was in the days of Napoleon, so the Vatican
was in the day of McDonald, and as it was then, so is the Vatican
today. That's why the Dublin laddo in purple imposes excommunication on any catholic young man who ventures within the gate of
Trinity College, forgetting that the student kept safe outside will
meet, later on, opinions more dreadful than those of Trinity College
in the wider university of the world.

Rome, Maynooth; one sack, one sample. Intrigue, false pretences,
expediency, concealment, silence. And, unfortunately, the Protestant
Church in Ireland, and, indeed, many in the Anglican Church, too,
are rallying to become hardy non-commissioned officers in La Grande
Armée du Vatican; as Newman himself was, while life left him with
them, Cardinal Deacon and all, as they made him — a non-commissioned officer only. So it will be till honest and courageous men
in the churches stand out for a proper conduct in God's service; or
for no service at all.

Dr. McDonald soon fell in love with theology, as Joan of Arc had
first fallen in love with religion, and then in love with war. He began
to try to dress her more in the manner of the day, and, immediately,
he began to feel the fierce wind of opposition blowing against him,
battling to throw him down; but he stood up to the wind and the rain
like the man he was, and fought the bad fight, ensuring himself a
deep and honoured place in the dead silence of Maynooth College
and the Catholic Church in Ireland. Theology in modern dress
wasn't to the liking of the other theologians, the most of whom
fought her battle in the armour and dwindled plumes of the five
champions of Christendom. Dr. McDonald began to point out that
times had changed, and, changing, had brought new discoveries. He
asserted that even the most conservative would hardly deny that
considerable light has been thrown recently on passages of Scripture
(*Genesis*, for instance), as to which the theologians of a hundred
years ago were, surely, in ignorance; that even conservative school-
men could not complain of the statement that a hundred years ago
there was no little error in the schools of theology, even as to the
content of the deposit of faith; and, of course, that what was true in
one century might well be true in another. Dear me, will this man
never learn to keep his mouth shut! He went on to assert that it was
only the definite teaching of the church that might not be in error;
and that there was comparatively little defined, even as to the

content of the deposit of faith, and there was, therefore, a wide field for inquiry and speculation. Oh, Dr McDonald! not in Maynooth, Dr. McDonald! The faith me mother taught me is the faith for the men of Maynooth.

He saw that a good part of catholic traditional theology depended for its truth on natural science. He saw that the school of natural science from which it was derived was in many parts quite different from, and opposed to, what are now the received conclusions of modern physical science; he saw that theologians had got to choose between some of the received conclusions of modern physical science and an equal number of those of speculative theology. It was a long, hard road for Dr. McDonald, trying to harmonise the knowledge of modern science with a newer conception of themes of theology based on the revolutionary outlook of the modern mind. He fought his way out from the thicket of threadbare tradition to where he thought he could still see the light of heaven. He lets us know that he managed to get over the difficulties that arose, partly by satisfying himself that the conclusions of modern physical science, in so far as they were opposed by definite church teaching, are not such as commend themselves to a prudent man; and, in other part, on the ground that, when such conclusions cannot be rejected in prudence, even though they seem opposed to traditional or even official church teaching, the teaching in question may be regarded as non-definite, and may, in such circumstances, be rejected without disloyalty to the church.

But Dr. McDonald's new light on the faith dazzled the dim eyes of Maynooth and the Vatican, and the daring Professor was told to be silent, for they couldn't bear to look on this new thing that he had unveiled. *Cover her face: mine eyes dazzle: she died young.* He was watched; he was guarded from his own thoughts. He was soon to make the moan made by Cardinal Newman: *However honest my thoughts, and earnest my endeavours to keep rigidly within the lines of catholic doctrine, every word I publish will be malevolently scrutinised, and every expression that can possibly be perverted sent straight to Rome.*

Sent crookedly to Rome, he should have said, for these ecclesiastics, who are so deeply immersed in the love of God and charity for their neighbours, never hesitate to do a bad turn for a man of whom they are suspicious, for the man's own good. Just as what was done under false pretences to the five professors who stood by Parnell's policy to the extent of subscribing to the funds. And was later done to Dr. O'Hickey. So when Maynooth can turn to false pretences to furnish a crony with a job, what will the Vatican not do to preserve and develop its pride, its power, and its vast private property? So McDonald's book, *Motion*, was held up by the bishops. This McDonald wouldn't be content to let bad enough alone. A disturber of the peace. A raucous voice in the quiet city of God. So in a very smiling, friendly way, they told him his book must be submitted to the Holy See, instanter. No, no; no discussion. These No, No, Nunettes said No out loud and in whispers. The echo of No was heard everywhere, in the refectory, the lecture rooms, the dormitories, and went stealing through the cloisters. No discussion. Pass the buck to the Holy See. The bishops guessed that the No of Rome would even be more distinct than their own No, and that peace would be born again. And Dr. McDonald complains: *They shut us up in Ireland, and make us abide by the report of a couple of third-rate Roman theologians. The old, open church system has disappeared long since; now we are ruled by way of secret inquiries, conducted, no doubt, by good men, animated by the best intentions. We have got so much into the habit of these secret investigations that we look at public discussion as an evil; for no other reason, apparently, than because it is not secret; or, perhaps, because it gives too much information to the public and enables others besides ourselves to judge.*

Ah, there you have it, Dr. McDonald! Secrecy is the foundation on which their power is placed, from the modest presbytery of the village parish priest to the red-hatted consistories, congregations, and conclaves of the pompous, wealthy Vatican. Public discussion gives too much information to the public! This from a roman catholic priest and an eminent theologian, Professor of Theology in Maynooth College for forty years! Rest, rest, perturbed spirit. It will be hard for the brightest Bellocian logic or the loudest echo of Chesterton's vacant laughter, at the modern way of thought, to veil these opinions and this accusation against Maynooth and Rome away from the more seeing eyes of men.

One would imagine that a book by such an earnest theologian, on such a subject as the phenomena and effects of energy and motion in the natural world, compared with, or allied to, the action and effect of grace in the spiritual world, would have absorbed the thoughts, for a month of Sundays, of the theologians basking about in the sunny Courts of the Sacred Congregations; that, faced with so many instances of these analogies made by Aquinas from the physics of his day, they would have hastened to welcome the attempts of one of their very own, anxious to harmonise theological speculation with the newer knowledge of their own day. But no; for it was a dangerous thing to do — or so they said. The concept of Motion attached to things theological and religious might lead to the rejection of things familiar from babyhood, with which they were at home. New thoughts would commit them to uncertainty and discomfort. But surely these sun-bathed theologians of the Sacred Congregations should have paused when they came across Cardinal Mercier's opinion that *Vital activity is not an absolute commencement or creation, but a transformation;* and again, that *Vital movement is subject to the general laws of determinism*; and again, that *Vital movement is not spontaneous in the strictest sense of the word.* Perhaps, even in the case of St. Paul, there were some determining influences at work within him, before the thunderbolt of exciting grace struck him down on the way to Damascus. Such a man as he was could hardly have felt easy in his mind when he remembered his consent to the death of Stephen. Grace was there before it came.

The Consultors of the Sacred Congregation condemned Dr. McDonald's *Thesis*, and this is what Dr. McDonald thought of their report: *I noted that the document I received was drawn up by some Secretary, who had before him the report of the Two Consultors, from which he copied in the main. When I examined the animadversions, I had little respect for either his or their philosophy or theological attainments. Cardinal Mercier went further than I had gone, so that the admonition which I received should, with far better right, have been sent to Louvain. I felt, however, that the Holy See would think twice before sending them to that quarter.* Dr. McDonald had little respect for these theologians, though it is laid down that the knowledge required for degrees in theology must be *Not common or ordinary, but ampler; profound, exquisite, and varied.* There's richness for you!

Anyway, Dr. McDonald persisted in questioning the theologians of the Sacred Congregation, through letters sent to Cardinal Ledochowski, defending the parts of his *Thesis* which had been condemned. The Cardinal, tired no doubt of the insistence of the Irish theologian, and not being very well able to answer himself, sent a sharp letter to McDonald, and referred the remarks of McDonald back to the Irish bishops. First the bishops passed the theological buck to Rome, and then Rome passed the buck back to the bishops. The way, the best way, of course, of finding the truth that is to make men free. This manœuvre forced Dr. McDonald to believe that neither the Roman authorities nor the Irish bishops could reply to his questions without throwing over the Consultors of the Sacred Congregation of Propaganda. As his book had been condemned, though the very things singled out for special condemnation had been set down by other eminent catholic theologians without a word of censure, something had to be done to save the face of Roman authority; and so the Irish bishops forced forward the condemnation, but in a very vague way, so as not to mingle in the condemnation a number of others, whom it wouldn't do to condemn, for they were far more powerful than Dr. McDonald. So the bishops wouldn't tell Dr. McDonald definitely what he was to teach and what he wasn't to teach. The fact was that the Irish bishops and the Roman luminaries knew as much about God as anyone else, and a lot less than Dr. McDonald. Their God had become the God of Belloc and the God of Chesterton. So here they were, busy suppressing and silencing a man who, in the profound warmth of his honest soul, was trying to get closer to the God these others pretended to honour. They just looked upon Walter McDonald as a nuisance to Maynooth and Rome, with his anxiety to tell how the grace of God transmitted power and exciting activity to the human heart; trying to probe into the secrets of divinity, and seeking to find an analogy between the energy of matter and the energy of God's grace working in the human soul.

To definitely condemn McDonald, it seems, the Vatican and Maynooth would have had to condemn Cardinal Mercier, Satolli, Pecchi, Father Baudier, and Father de Regnon, S.J. When Maynooth at last got a professor who was a theologian, they didn't know what to do with him! So they concentrated on thinking what they could do to him. If he was let go on, he'd be stirring up trouble always. The fewer questions that had to be answered the better. Silence; oh, silence, for God's sake! Yes, but listen, Eminent Cardinals, Most Reverend Bishops, and Right Reverend Monsignors; listen: McDonald says that he ventures only to admonish the theologians who were arguing on principles of physics that had been altogether, long ago, discarded and thrown away by present-day scientists. Silence, we're telling you! Maynooth's the Peter Silentio of the Irish Church, for it is the spice of our spiritual life. We can't afford to let this fellow keep us wriggling in our episcopal chairs. In silence, remember, God brings all to pass. Only hell is noisy, and that is why Maynooth sits mum. And so must McDonald. It is far better to know more about the things that are Caesar's than to know about the things that are God's; for this brings danger; that brings security. So to silence the blower was the best, the just, the only thing to do; and silence him they did — for a day or so.

As it was in matters called religious, so it was in matters called political. The strife over the love of Parnell for a woman had begun in Holy Ireland, even the Theological Faculty of Maynooth couldn't keep out of it, for they as Irishmen would be vitally affected by the battle and its eventual outcome. The Liberals had declared that they could no longer co-operate with the Irish Party unless Parnell left it. Like the good catholic he was, Dr. McDonald then hated Liberalism, and thought Parnell should resign. But like the man he was, Parnell refused to do so; and at a meeting of the Irish Party in Dublin, he was supported in his determination by its members, Tim Healy shouting out that no-one should be let interfere with the man at the wheel. The bishops, it was said, weren't consulted; they were silent, but they were biding their time. Then, suddenly, they and the Liberal Party protested simultaneously, and many in Ireland thought that negotiations had taken place between the Irish Hierarchy and the English Liberals (the many who thought so were probably right); and that the bishops resolved to protest only when they were certain of support. Said Dr. McDonald: 'This was very galling to me, to find not only our nation, but even our Church, dominated by the English Liberals, and I made little secret of the disgust I felt. I couldn't restrain a suspicion that though the bishops claimed to speak merely in the interests of morality, this was not their only, not even their strongest motive. It was convenient for them to say so, as their pronouncement was thereby raised above hostile criticism. And some of them — their leaders — as I suspected, knew this well, and calculated on it; putting it forward as a very efficacious shield to cover the real, or, at least, more prevalent motive, which was political. Not, of course, that even these leading bishops did not think public morals in some danger; but that *their concern was much more to weaken or even destroy Parnell.*' Christ Almighty, to destroy Parnell! There are the Irish bishops for you, men and women of Eireann! What a gang they were! In his heart, Sean had known it all along, and he had always hated their hypocrisy, made more splendidly odious by the Tyrian dye of their purple magna cappas. He had heard of it all about Parnell; he had seen their trickery in the Gaelic League and in the Irish Republican Brotherhood; he had been in the fight against them when they had hunted down poor Dr.

O'Hickey; he had seen and heard their hypocrisy throughout the great fight Jim Larkin made to ensure a fair crack of the whip for the Irish workers; and now all that had been confirmed by one of their very own thoughtful theologians, the best they had ever had (since they kept him in his Chair for forty years, they too must have thought so), the best, probably, they will ever have again.

And this is one of the reasons why so many roman catholic countries are in revolt today — clerical domination in lay activities has gone too far to be put up with any longer. The prelate and the priest want to say, without the slightest contradiction, and under the dark cloak of their care for faith and morals, what the people's politics are to be. And so thought Dr. McDonald. 'The greatest danger to religion is likely to accrue from any serious attempt on the part of the clergy to deprive the laity of their political rights, under pretence that such rights counted as nothing when weighed against danger to faith and morals.' Wherever roman catholic power is potent, the minute anything new is put forward, something with which the prelates aren't fully familiar, in politics, in social amendment, or even in art and literature, these prelates begin to bark about faith and morals.

During the war, at a distribution of prizes in Maynooth College, Cardinal McRory (who had been a professor in Maynooth with Dr. McDonald) said, 'He couldn't help thinking of the charges so often made against the Church of Rome of ignorance and opposition to knowledge'. Yet this very man experienced this ignorance, this opposition to knowledge, when he was a comrade-professor with Dr. McDonald in Maynooth; and was one of the editors of a *Theological Quarterly* when Dr. McDonald, another editor, was harried out of writing for it by the bishops. Then touching on H. G. Wells, the Cardinal said, 'Lately in the papers appeared charges of this kind made by a writer of considerable notoriety in England, whose name I abstain from mentioning'. There we go — not open enough, or else afraid, to guide any of his flock to the name of Wells, lest their precious souls be lost. The Cardinal went on: 'I wish that writer could have come to see our distribution of prizes, to see the wide range of subjects and the vast field of knowledge covered by the Maynooth course, the great bulk of which had to be read by every student of the College'. There's a cardinal's idea of knowledge — reading over a great bulk of books! *Finnegans Wake*, one of them, maybe! Maynooth disposes of knowledge by bulk. Wholesale dealers in learning. Said the Cardinal: 'The Catholic Church is never opposed to knowledge, that is real knowledge, and that is not in some way injurious'.

There, thought Sean, we have the old, old bladher again that McDonald had heard so often. Real knowledge, mind you, which their greatest theologians had declared, again and again, to be old-fashioned, leaving the students, when they left the seminary, a laughing-stock to any able man who happened to discuss things with them. When this Cardinal McRory died, he was hailed by the secular Press and the Catholic Press as an 'eminent and distinguished theologian', though McDonald expressly says of him that while he knew something of the Scriptures, he couldn't be called a profound theologian; meaning that he knew very little about it. That is the way a lot of these cardinals and bishops get their reputation and authority.

Later on, Dr. McDonald wrote a review of a book in the *Freeman's Journal* (a Dublin daily paper of the day), called *Government of the Church in the Fourth Century*, written by another theologian, but one not on the staff of Maynooth. This review called down upon McDonald the wrath of the bishops, angering them into declaring with all the vehemence of a resolution that 'They deprecated Professors carrying on a discussion in ordinary newspapers of difficult questions of theology, which may easily be misunderstood, and lead to the disedification of the laity'. The laity! How the bishops love the laity! So they mustn't allow them to know too much. Imagine two professors saying, in public too, that the office of bishop wasn't once the exalted job the bishops reckon it to be now. Two bishops, highly annoyed, came to Dr. McDonald, one gripping his right arm, the other his left, and asked Why did he do this thing on them? It wasn't fair, it wasn't proper, nor was it at all expedient to say these things. It was wrong, decidedly wrong, to say that the presbyterians had some right on their side; for even though they might have, it was a grave mistake to admit it, and so give them an opportunity of crowing over the accepted beliefs of the catholic church. 'That', thought Dr. McDonald, 'may be good politics, but it isn't the scientific spirit, which does not hesitate to admit any error that has been proved. No small part of the weakness of Catholic Theology is due to this, that we persist in maintaining positions which have been long since shown to be indefensible, with the result that the adversaries of the Church, carefully avoiding us where we are strong, defeat us easily where we are weak, and are thereby able to crow over us, with justice and to our real disgrace. I might have discussed

Dr. Moran's book *ad nauseam*, if only I had made out that the episcopal office was from the beginning what it is today. That would be false; but, then, falsehood of that kind would not lead to the "disedification of the laity".' Falsification of facts is a common thing with those who stand as champions for the Vatican. Dr. Geoffrey Coulton has commented, time and again, on these seemingly irremovable characteristics of all Vatican apologists. He has even declared that if they will not hear the prophets of an outside creed, they should listen to their own, Newman and Acton; and now this courageous and honest man, Dr. McDonald, can be added to the number. Why, even in their own special matter of catholic theology, it is plain from what Dr. McDonald writes, that their professors are a poor lot, in spite of 'the vast field of knowledge' even the students cover, and the 'bulk of books' every student of Maynooth has to read. Swallow them down, lads.

A curious and impudent boast, thought Sean, when one remembers the millions of books on the Index; and that, backed by the bishops, the Censors in Ireland ban every book that has within it a single thought that might question the power their own invented tradition has given them; any idea that might bring discomfort into their own easy-going thoughts; anything that 'might be injurious'. Might be, not would be. Anything that they think shows the slightest sign of an arresting thought, and under it goes, banned for good. For fear souls might be lost, they say; but some have a hearty opinion that this fear is bred out of the fear of losing the monarchical power a bishop holds over his see. No wonder part of the catholic Press, in reply to an inquiry, said that it was part of Canon Law that anyone molesting a bishop was automatically excommunicated. Stepinac, stop!

The cardinals' and the bishops' divine love of learning, as proclaimed by the cardinal, who was afraid to mention the name of H. G. Wells, is indeed vindicated by the Trustees' choice of a church spire rather than that of a library during the day of Dr. McDonald. When he spoke for a library rather than for a church tower and spire, he was told they 'could get fifteen thousand pounds for a tower and spire, but couldn't get a fifth of that amount for a library'. But, he adds, the bishops by dint of propaganda pressed the money out of the people, and Dr. McDonald was certain that, had they used the same energy and eloquence for a library, they would have got the sum required.

How can we give a sizeable opinion about the result of all this wonderful love of learning on the part of the catholic students, most of whom later become priests, and mix and influence the thought and the culture of the laity? Surely, one way will be to judge them by what is called the catholic Press, so fulsomely blessed by the Holy Father. Well, what of the catholic journalist? Is there anything so timid, so commonplace, so ready to say anything calculated to bring a pat on the back from a monsignor, so ready to dodge away from fact or from truth, as the roman catholic journalism of the roman catholic popular Press? But when this cowardice, this false witness even, is to be found among the higher, more dignified professors, among the godlier sections of the catholic Press, need one wonder when it flashes forth in the commoner and more popular section of the Press? And why? Well, let Dr. McDonald — whose love for the Faith he held could hardly be questioned, and never was, by those who knew him — answer for us: 'A Journal kept in leading-strings will do little good to its members or readers, and very little to the Church, State, or College for which it works — in fetters'. Is he by any chance confusing the U.S.S.R. here with something else? In fetters! Do catholics really have to write in fetters? Dr. McDonald says so. Since you can't keep silence, Dr. McDonald, go on — we'll get you yet! 'If the Catholic Church has in her service hardly one (hardly one, mind you!) strong, well-conducted newspaper or periodical, that is the price she pays for keeping all (all, mind you!) journalists in bondage; no really strong man will continue to serve under the restrictions that prevail.' Still in the land of Egypt, still in the house of bondage.

Dr. McDonald, full of unwise zeal for the fair fame of his church, and for her holiness, advocated the publication of a yearly balance-sheet to show how the money, so generously given by the faithful, was used; smiling broadly at the sanctimonious dictum 'that while kings and their servants need to be watched, lest they convert the public funds to their own private uses, such a thing is, if not inconceivable, at least so rare as to be negligible in the case of churchmen'.

Publish a balance-sheet! What a startling and a shocking suggestion! To set the eternal church down beside a common, money-making business firm, the church that pulls a revenue from the living and from the dead! Bishops are far above the thought of money. And yet, if we read Coulton's *Five Centuries of Religion*, we'll be astonished at the effect money had on the monasteries as set down in the old Latin Records, where we find that even the good

St. Charles Borromeo was loaded with benefices in his early youth, and Cardinal Mazarin received the incomes of twenty-seven abbacies, not counting the pickings of a number of bishoprics. Cardinal and bishop and abbot seemed to have an itching palm for the gold pieces. In sorrow, rather than in anger, Dr. McDonald says, 'I verily believe that the Roman palaces of Popes and Cardinals have cost the Church something more infinitely precious than money; the history of the Papacy justifies the faithful in being on their guard against the maladministration of the Roman Curia. For if the Curia lost the hold on Europe it had in the Middle Ages, it is mainly because of misappropriation of church funds. Even Leo the Tenth held twenty-seven benefices, topped by the Archbishopric of Amalfi (the Duke of Malfi!). There would have been no Reformation, and no French Revolution, if Church and State had had the good habit of publishing their accounts.' Isn't this childish! Didn't Mr. Chesterton and Mr. Belloc set it down, with a thump, that, in England at least, the Reformation was due to the hankering of a king after the trim ankle, the seductive bust, slim legs, and bright eyes of a lovely lass? Is there anything more to be said? Can nothing silence this man?

Nothing. He even ventured to declare that the parents of children should have a say in the matter of managerial control, opposing a priest, who, giving a lecture, claimed a divine right and a canonical declaration for the dictated control of the schools by the priest. Didn't Cardinal Griffin imply recently, when dealing with the question of catholic teachers for catholic schools (and catholic teachers for protestant ones, and secular ones, too, if he had his way), that everything taught had a catholic importance, even arithmetic: catholic grammar, catholic geography, catholic orthography, etymology, syntax, and prosody.

These men, and the women who follow them, in the garb of the religious, or in secular clothing, want to dominate life from the cradle to the grave, greeting the present rise of the people against this madness with the wail of 'the repressive and oppressive movements of the people are interfering with, and strangling, the sacred rights and freedom of mind of the individual'. If the summer was icumen in, you'd hear the cuckoo calling. Back to the muddle ages, says Chesterton, rushing out of a pub after a quick one. Oh, a lovely time the common people had in the Middle Ages, bossed by pope, cardinal, prelate, prior, monk, and priest; and if the Roman Catholic Church only had now the power she had then, we'd all be revelling in the lovely sensation of ecclesiastical serfdom and slavery. This enlightened condition of things clung to life even up to the dawn of a more liberal day, for there were three hundred and fifty thousand ecclesiastical slaves bound to the monasteries of France alone at the time of the French Revolution.

At a public meeting Dr. McDonald advocated the entry into Trinity College of the catholics in an organised body, which, he felt sure, would preserve them from losing, or even weakening, a faith at once catholic and national. A whispered chat was carried on about this daring suggestion, and in the beginning of the twentieth century, under an English Liberal Government, a Commission was set up 'to inquire into the present state of Trinity College, and of the University of Dublin, upon the place they hold as organs of higher education in Ireland, and the steps proper to be taken to increase their usefulness to the country'. Everyone that had a thought left in his head got busy to try to bring harmony out of bitterness — but the bishops sang dumb. An effort to make Trinity College more like a Continental University was made by a College Committee, and a scheme 'for widening the Constitution of the College was drawn up and sent to the sitting Commission, first being signed by twelve Junior Fellows,. one Senior Fellow, and eight Professors of Trinity'. A Catholic Laymen's Committee corresponded with the Trinity men, and, in the main, agreed with the proposals put forward for a settlement that would shove the College of the Holy Trinity right into the centre of Irish life and thought. Four hundred and sixty-seven catholic laymen set down proposals, which, according to Dr. McDonald, 'were, practically, what had been agreed to by the Trinity Junior Fellows and Professors, with the sympathy of the Provost and by far the greater part of the College Staff, so that practical agreement had been reached, as regards a basis of settlement between Trinity College and the Catholic Laity'. Then the day after that on which the junior fellows and professors had been presented to the Commission, the roman catholic bishops, timing the thing nicely, woke and spoke, saying simply, calmly, and with a cool finality, 'The Bishops inform the Commission that under no circumstances will the Catholics of Ireland accept a system of mixed education in Trinity College as a solution of their claims'.

A roll of drums, boys! The divine voices had spoken, and the Commission, jerked out of its happy assurance, declared plaintively that 'As the Standing Committee of the Roman Catholic Bishops have assured us that the Catholics of Ireland would on no account accept any scheme of mixed education in Trinity College, we cannot hope to render the College acceptable to the Roman Catholic Episcopate by reasonable changes in its Constitution'. The gallant Four Hundred and Sixty-seven Catholic Laymen were swept away as so much chaff; gone with the wind raised by the bishops' blast. And yet these bishops are the boyos who are continually roaring out for the preservation of 'the sacred rights and freedom of thought of the individual'.

And, mind you, these Four Hundred and Sixty-seven Laymen were of those who had themselves received what was deemed to be a 'good education'; men who would be likely to give their sons a University education. They weren't 'The boys of Ormond Quay' whom Wolfe Tone longed to have at his side when he headed rebellion in Ireland; nor were they of the dockers, carters, and coal-heavers, who afterwards, under Jim Larkin, became the spear-point in the battle for the 'sacred rights of the individual'. No; they were those who had been toned down to respectability; professional men of good education and secure standing in both Church and State; and yet they were just pushed aside without comment by the bishops, as a Dublin policeman might push aside a Dublin whore who ventured to explain a point of duty to him.

As it was then, so it is now: there is no more chance of harmony now than there was then. For a catholic it is spiritual death to enter the College without the archbishop's permission. If he should, he suffers automatic excommunication. Ecclesiastical electrocution! A hothouse faith to have! And so damned silly, for however the catholic young man may jib away from Trinity College, sooner or later he has to plunge into the widespread world, a pressing, challenging world, and McQuaid's writ of excommunication doesn't run there, me man. There the north winds do blow, and there's free-thinking snow; and what will this robin do then, poor thing? The big mistake in Bunyan's book is the escape of Christian. There is no escape. Willy-nilly, like it or not, Christian must dwell forever in Vanity Fair. Even St. Bernard found that out, for Vanity Fair followed him into the monastery; and there was eating, drinking, dancing, and all kinds of merriment. And St. Benedict fared as badly, for austerity brought a quick decline in discipline, and seclusion brought no safety to the aspiring soul. The lure of the world without was within as well. Even Monte Cassino, now in ruins, came in for more than one swift, sharp condemnation, even from Dante, who thought that 'the walls that were wont to be a house of prayer have become dens'. Vanity Fair knocked at the monastery door, and the monks opened the door softly, and the revellers entered to make their abode with the holy men. There is neither shelter nor seclusion that can save us from the world. We live there and we die in it.

Sean sent his memory back to see Maynooth College again. Maybe this very Dr. McDonald looked from a window at him and his companions playing hand-ball; or listened to the skirling pipes when the band marched round the College grounds. Later on, when Dr. McDonald was gone, and Sean was in Maynooth again, he had looked over the many windows of the building, wondering which showed the room where the theologian had lived, had worked, perhaps had died. No word is given of how he died, or where he lies quiet and silent now. Possibly in the cemetery of the College he tried so hard to serve so well. Sean at his last visit had asked a passing student where McDonald was laid, but the busy student had hurried on, after saying he didn't know, and had never heard of him. He had disappeared from the College as if he had never been there. Even Chesterton's famous Father Brown wouldn't find him now. Wouldn't want to try either!

Ireland was safe now in the big hands of the bishops. The land was rocking in the sea with the dint of penance and prayer; rosary beads will festoon the land without division from one end to the other; holy pictures will be as thick as autumnal leaves that strew the brooks in Vallombrosa; scapulars will overlap every breast, like chain-mail of the Middle Ages, ready to quench the fiery darts of the evil one; the younger writers and poets will all be on edge to win a passing nod of approval from the prelate. The gael will be pickled in penance.

> Through the open door the hum of rosaries
> Came out and blended with the homing bees.
>   The trees
> Heard nothing stranger than the rain and the wind
> Or the birds —
> But deep in their roots they knew a seed had sinned.

Even the trees feel the malice of original sin. Even the trees; even so.

An article was written by Dr. Coghlan, attacking Dr. McDonald's book on *Motion*; an article cunningly written, with the words *To Be Continued* at the end of it, implying, of course, that there was more to follow, and persuading Dr. McDonald to wait for the additional attack. It never came, for Coghlan had shoved all he could into the first one, had taken advantage of the editor's absence to slip it into the Journal. The *To Be Continued* bluff was evidently meant to check

Dr. McDonald's reply, so that the editor would be back to prevent
its publication. The editor of the *Ecclesiastical Record*, Dr. Hogan,
refused to print Dr. McDonald's reply to Coghlan, to whom he
wrote, saying, 'Having allowed Coghlan's article to slip through, you
may take it from me that the series will not be continued. I must add,
however, that I certainly will not consent to have my Journal made
the medium of further controversy on the subject.' Short and sweet,
like a Christian ass's gallop! Hogan added, 'This, I daresay, will be
less an inconvenience to you, as you can get it into the *Theological
Quarterly*'.

It was a cynical reply, or so thought Dr. McDonald, for Dr.
Hogan knew only too well that Dr. McDonald's reply would not be
let into the *Theological Quarterly*. Later on, Dr. McDonald published
a pamphlet containing the correspondence with Hogan, and added
an onslaught on Coghlan's views on *Motion*, which, it was said, left
the wily Professor speechless. And sorrow mend him, for, says Dr.
McDonald, 'He made an attack which he felt sure I could not repel,
for he knew well that neither he nor I would be allowed to continue
the discussion in the *Irish Ecclesiastical Record* or in any other
publication subject to ecclesiastical control. There was nothing the
bishops wanted so much as to stifle discussion on the *Motion* question, in regard to which they were uneasily conscious that neither
they nor the Roman authorities had covered themselves with glory.'

The bishops' 'prime aim was to stifle discussion'! That is their
prime aim everywhere, and about everything. Only what they themselves say is to be the sterling currency of thought. And yet these
gay lads on altar steps, on platforms, in pulpits, at cocktail parties,
proclaim, chant, assert, and demand full recognition for 'freedom
of expression, and the sacred rights of the individual'. Well, we can
hazard a guess as to what would have happened to H. G. Wells if
the Vatican had had supreme control of things as they once had —
he would have gone up in smoke!

And they ask, preach, even command tolerance in others than
themselves. 'The Federal Council of Christian Churches who have
persuaded President Truman to withdraw the American Envoy,
Myron Taylor, from the Holy See, are guilty of intolerance', said
Cardinal Spellman. This is a kettle black as hell calling another one
as black as night. Catholics are canonically forbidden to have a peep
at a protestant wedding, or a protestant christening, however friendly
they may be with the parties concerned; a dead protestant isn't
allowed to lie side by side with his catholic wife in a consecrated

catholic cemetery (according to the catholic press); the humblest roman catholic clergyman isn't allowed to join directly or indirectly in any national celebration or ceremony at which anglicans and non-conformists participate, even though it be but to say the Lord's Prayer, sing a *te deum* or *de profundis*, and say a creed common to all. Why? Because catholics 'expose themselves to the danger of losing their Faith by taking part in the services or prayers of a false religion'. It would seem that if one of another faith wagged a finger at a catholic he would immediately shed his faith, quicker than a snake would shed a skin.

So neither Dr. O'Hickey nor Dr. McDonald was allowed to put forward a fair case in their own defence, but were subdued into silence by the vanity of the bishops and the dodgery of a pope; Archbishop McQuaid imposes immediate excommunication on a student entering Trinity College; the parish priests walk about in mortal dread of their bishops; Dr. Coulton, of Cambridge University, could say in his book, *A Premium on Falsehood*, dealing with the deliberate mis-statements made by Cardinal Gasquet on historical facts, 'Meanwhile the Gasquet policy is successfully continued by Belloc, Father Thurston, and other less-known writers. It is almost demanded of them that they should twist the truth, and they do that job to perfection.' Dr. Coulton, in the same publication, gives a list of roman catholic Journals, *The Month, The Tablet, The Universe*, and others, which refused to publish letters from men replying to letters criticising them, which had appeared in the Journals; some of them refusing, not only letters from non-catholics, but even from catholics anxious to get at the facts, just as their own theologian, Dr. McDonald, tried to do.

Indeed, Sean himself had more than one experience with this kind of people. One was a professional catholic lecturer. He once wrote to Sean asking for a subscription to a catholic charity to meet the needs of abandoned children. The subscription was sent, and back came a letter glowing with thanks and praise of Sean as an angel, the thanks flowing on into high praise for Sean's work, which the writer loved. A few months later, when the Abbey Theatre was having a Play Festival, lectures on the dramatists were given, and at the one on Sean this boyo attacked the 'angel', calling him an atheist, an anti-catholic and an anti-Christian, adding a postscript as to the vulgar, low, and uncatholic nature of Sean's work. Insincerity and dishonesty are nothing to most of these professional catholic apologists — lay or clerical — they take them in their stride. And these are the persons who go about yelping for tolerance and fair play!

Dr. McDonald frightened and angered the Maynooth authorities by arguing that Latin ought to be abandoned as a serious study for the students. What Chesterton cheered (or was it Belloc?) as a bond, uniting in love, understanding, and thought, the whole catholic world, Dr. McDonald calls a millstone round the necks of the students of catholic seminaries. The bishops, in Ireland and elsewhere, share Chesterton's enthusiasm, dreading the more critical line of thought that the use of the vernacular would bring into the minds of the faithful. 'The fact is,' Dr. McDonald points out, 'that Latin is used only with reluctance in all the offices and tribunals of the Holy See; where, if you want to get business done quick and satisfactorily, you must speak or write in Italian — the natural language of the place. None of the Irish Bishops are at home with Italian, and so are frightfully handicapped when they go to Rome on business.'

—Good God! ejaculated the Bishop of Belloe, would you criticise propaganda itself! Ah, now, you wouldn't do that, would you, Dr. McDonald?

—Yes, and criticise greater than Propaganda! History proves that laws have been better made and better observed since subjects became free to criticise them; and there would be ever so much less to record, with shame and tears, if there had been more criticism, reverent and fearless, of those who occupied high places in the Church, even in the past.

—Dr. McDonald! Silence, sir; silence, Dr. McDonald!

—What are we to do? Are we to go on, silently, though convinced that things are rotting before our eyes?

—Silence!

A Doctor of Divinity wrote an excellent work on Ecclesiastical History, which won a Doctorate from the Faculty of Theology; and later on he made an application for a vacant Chair of Theology, but was quietly shoved aside by the Visitors, for the book he had written stirred up fear within them, and they thought it wise to cool his ardour by leaving him out in the cold like the king at Canossa; their cowardly rejection of a fine mind in favour of a mediocre one forcing from Dr. McDonald the bitter comment of 'If you wish to succeed, oh, my students, you should take care not to write at all, or to write good commonplace; above all, not to write anything original, however excellent it may be'. So signs on it, the stigma of the commonplace is plain on almost everything written and said by the present-day leaders of the Roman Catholic Church. One has but to listen to the speeches or read the pastorals of the bishops, or skippily scan the simpering, pompous columns of the roman catholic Press, to realise to what a low imaginative and intellectual plane the present-day catholic mind has fallen, when dealing with things, spiritual and temporal, as related to their faith. From the leading articles in their Press to the book, *The Road to Victory*, by Cardinal Spellman, all that is said, all that is thought, sinks down, as foretold by Dr. McDonald, to the level of the commonplace.

A sad thing happened soon — Dr. McDonald was told by his doctors that he had but a short time to live; but facing it bravely, as he had faced everything else, he set about writing the last will and testament of his thoughts. When the world was deep in the dark of the war, he wrote a little book called *Ethical Questions of Peace and War*, causing the bishops once again to roar out Silence, in their own quiet, sacramental way. Here, he showed them up when they were bursting with love for Ireland; he showed them up as fools and cowards, just when they were posing as patriots. The word that wasn't with God went round that the book was to be left severely alone. It was not to be written about, not even to be mentioned, except in private, with door closed and windows shut, and all light extinguished. The catholic *Month* said, in a short notice, that 'Dr. McDonald's book challenges all, Bishops, Politicians, Professors and Editors; challenges beliefs which are almost axiomatic among his brethren; challenges them mostly by name, and no doubt the lists will soon be thronged by eager combatants'. Well, wait till we see.

Dr. McDonald sent a copy of his book to the *Irish Ecclesiastical Record*, but the Journal never answered; he sent a copy to the *Irish Theological Quarterly*, but it took no notice; he sent one to *Studies*, but it sat silent. Dr. McDonald was told that the editor of this Journal was very angry with him for the attack he had made on Father Lehmkuhl, S.J., and through him, on the moralists of the Jesuit Society for teaching folk how to defraud governments; and the editor threatened some terrible things in the next or another number. The clock went on striking till it struck twelve, but no attack came from the editor, or from any in the Society of Jesus.

Why did they spare him? Dr. McDonald asks, 'was it some remnant of a grace of courtesy, or of an ancient friendship, that bade them now suffer eclipse themselves rather than see my reputation injured? It would be nice to think so, but I do not think it true.

Since then there was no answer to my challenge, it can have been only that it was felt there was none to give; that the Professors, Politicians, Editors, and Bishops had put themselves in a hopeless position, making use of rotten arguments, bogus history, and indefensible ethics. To get at me they must hit at Rome; and no one who knows the higher ecclesiastics of Ireland would ever deem them capable of such folly as that. So all they could do was to belittle me, and keep silent about the book.'

During the course of the World War, Cardinal Logue broke out into a cold sweat one day, a warm one the next, when he heard that a Professor of Theology had been teaching that it was lawful at times to revolt from what had up to then been legitimate sovereignty, and that in this way the great French Revolution could be justified, and also that of New England under Washington. The Cardinal had learned all this from McDonald's book on *Peace and War*. The Cardinal threatened to make visitation of the College, and punish severely all who had taught doctrine so much opposed to Catholic Tradition. But changed things in Ireland made the cautious, cunning, ignorant Cardinal stay where he was in Arrah-na-Pogue Coeli, silent, sad, and anxious, for he didn't know the hell what might happen next. And as it would not, and could not, be denied that this principle was a development and new, Dr McDonald said, 'I take some little pride in being the first Catholic Theologian, as far as I know, to proclaim the principle that political sovereignty, which was quite legitimate and morally unassailable up to a certain stage of its duration, may at that stage become illegitimate, making it lawful for the subjects to throw off the yoke then, if they can, without doing greater mischief thereby'.

And this is the condition Dr. McDonald finds his country in at the time when he is getting ready to depart forever: 'History has already judged some of these cases of conflict, that, for instance, over the case of Parnell. Many good judges now admit that it was a mistake not to have come to terms with Trinity College; and more still are becoming convinced that all isn't right with the Managerial question; the *Irish Theological Quarterly* hasn't set the Liffey on fire since it was taken under the protection of the bishops; and the new Code of Ecclesiastical Law has left us with the old abuses of patronage, finance, and even of punishment without real trial. Parish priests may now be deprived of their benefices almost at the episcopal will, while bishops are being appointed with increasing disregard for public opinion; and should the regulations for the United States be adopted here, as is to be expected, the bishops can appoint their own successors practically, and the government of the church will pass more and more into the hands of a ring. For having stood up against all that, reverently and modestly, to the best of the weak power allowed to one in my position, I do not apprehend any severe judgment when I pass into the beyond.'

A pathetic, a brave, and an honourable farewell. All these cool, studied accusations are made, not by a secularist, but by one of their own theologians; one who was Professor of Theology in the core of Irish catholicity for forty years. And yet Miss Maisie Ward neglects this great, brave man, this great Questioner, to write down the life of the chirruping Chesterton. Oh, folly, folly to crown the jester and shove the seer aside; to colour with flags the shallow ship sailing shallow waters, and tug the great ship, asking a deeper sea, to a hidden harbour, there to rust alone.

The questions the Questioner asked are with us still, unanswered; and, now, even unasked. There they are in the lonely room, where he pondered deeply in his heart about them; or in the place where he slept, thinking, thinking, before sleep stole him away from his thoughts. 'There is danger in them, but comfortable Bishops, Cardinals, and Consultors — who became what they are because they never had a difficulty — will not see the danger coming, as their predecessors could not see the Reformation, and as the counsellors and parasites of the Bourbons could not imagine a Revolution. Congregations and Commissions would have us depend almost altogether on tradition, and shut our eyes to difficulties that strike us in the face.' A prophet come to judgement, by God; and the judgement given hidden in the grave!

Was St. Paul right in his outlook on pagan Greece and Rome? Were these poor idolators as inexcusable as he represents them to have been? Was Samuel ethically right in pressing Saul with Jehovah's supreme displeasure for not having put to death even the women and babes he had taken from Amalec? Are we bound to the arguments for the existence of God set forth in the *Book of Wisdom*, or by St. Paul in the *Acts of the Apostles*? Did the human writer of *Genesis* mean to teach that the world was made in six days of twenty-four hours each, that the Deluge was absolutely universal, and destructive of the life of land animals everywhere; that any species that survived, did so by being brought into the Ark; that all men of the time were present at the building of Babel, and it was there that diversity of tongues arose?

'We know that there have been answers which satisfied our fathers: as that God could have placed fossils in the earth to try our faith. He could, of course, but did He? Can one now rely on such a possibility for an explanation of the difficulty? These are but a few of the questions that torment, and will continue to torment, honest students of the Bible.'

'So too in the early history of the church, and especially of the papacy and of episcopacy: when there were no monarchical bishops anywhere, can we believe that there was one in Rome? Did Cyprian and Fulgentius, who recognised no "bishop of bishops", believe in the primacy of the successors of St. Peter, as that doctrine is now set forth in the Vatican decrees? Did St. Augustine, with his belief in the necessity of divine charity, recognise the sufficiency of attrition to remit mortal sin? Or, if charity was necessary, did he think mortal sin first remitted by the sacraments? Were, in fact, sacraments of the dead instituted and administered for the remission of guilt, or only for that of punishment, and for the giving of graces to lead a purer life in future?'

'And, then, grace and virtues; supernatural qualities? But what is a quality, and how does it contribute to action? How does grace operate, and when is it given: before, or after, justification? Can human souls be supernaturalised in part — in the intellect, while the will remains in its natural state? Where does the supernatural begin in the roots of faith? Can faith be lost without formal mortal sin? And what is the testimony of modern life in this respect? What is mortal sin, indeed? How does it stand with regard to charity — in its commission and its remission?'

'When trouble arises, as it will, over certain Church definitions with anathema attached, the standard and great test may well be', says Dr. McDonald, 'that decree of the Council of Vienna as to the human soul being a substantial form of the body. That the Council taught it to be in some sense I take as evident from the words of the decree; as also that the definition is one of supreme authority, claiming infallibility. Is it infallible? Is it even true?'

On these questions and many more such, Dr. McDonald tells us he found peace on lines no little divergent from the tradition. 'I have done my best,' he says, 'and the results will be found, in great part, in the unpublished books I leave behind me. I should dearly love to see these volumes published, but I must pass away without hope of that. They might do a little to withstand the Revolution which the official guardians of our religion will not see coming, or will endeavour to keep out with broomsticks. Good men, animated by the best of motives, but so short-sighted, and so cruel, too, in their religious blindness to such as cannot shut their eyes.' The Revolution has come, and the broomsticks wave; but though they have the shape and order of croziers, they are broomsticks still.

In spite of creeds and things of faith defined, every thoughtful Christian, like Dr. McDonald, must catch his own peculiar glimpse of God; even that Christian who sees nothing where he seeks to find Him, and then, as an honest man, becomes what the creed-coveting crowd call an Atheist.

Few of the younger catholics have heard of the man, McDonald, and the older ones never mention his name in the presence of others. His name is never mentioned either in the religious or the secular Press. No one seems to know why his books have never been published, or even where the MS. of his work is to be found. There is a sombre and a secret and a sinister silence about this man who so modestly and so reverently questioned God. In Dr. Hyde's *Mise agus an Connradh*, the name of every Irishman, known and unknown, is mentioned, even that of Dr. O'Hickey, the life-long friend of McDonald, yet the name of Dr. McDonald is absent. Since the Irish Vatican prelates allow this, encourage it, even enforce it by their own supreme silence, then it must be thought that they consider this man was a dishonour to their core of catholicity, Maynooth College. Yet they held him there, with odd persistence, for forty years. They let him die silently, they lowered him into the grave silently, and left him there to disappear from Irish thought forever. If an eye looks in that direction, if a thought strays there, they raise the shout of Great Is Chesterton of the Roman Catholics! And silence falls again.

Here are the heavy iron gates of the College, St. Patrick's Roman Catholic College of Maynooth. Silence. It is everywhere around the place; around Maynooth College; as if heavy snow had fallen, covering every sound in sleep, so that there is no echo of any footstep, or of a voice; no, nor the song of a single bird; as if heavy snow had fallen, and no wind blew. Nothing but silence. Even the echo is silent. Outside the gates Honesty and Courage stand. Honesty in her white robe, Courage in her red one. Do you hear the shout of them rending the silence!

McDonald!

INISHFALLEN, FARE THEE WELL

IT was time for Sean to go. He had had enough of it. He would be no more of an exile in another land than he was in his own. He was a voluntary and settled exile from every creed, from every party, and from every literary clique, fanning themselves into silence with unmitigated praise of each other in the most select corners of the city's highways and byebye-ways. He would stay no longer to view life through a stained-glass window, a Sinn Fein spy-glass, from a *prieu-dieu*, or through the thigh-bone of a hare. He would go beyond these, and view life through his own eyes. From where he would go, he'd look back now and again to see how the figures looked with a more distant sun shining on them. Oh, steer my barque from Eire's isle! He would be sorry to leave behind the few friends he had there. Each of these had binding cords to hold them there, while he had none.

It had often been recorded in the Press, by those who could guess shrewdly, that Sean was a slum dramatist, a gutter-snipe who could jingle a few words together out of what he had seen and heard. The terms were suitable and accurate, for he was both, and, all his life, he would hold the wisdom and courage that these conditions had given him. Wheresoever he would go, whomsoever he might meet, be the places never so grandiloquent and rich, the persons never so noble in rank and origin, he, O'Casey, would ever preserve, ever wear — though he would never flaunt it — the tattered badge of his tribe. Not that he thought of praise or blame for it, but simply because he had to bring his life around with him. But he would sew on to that badge, soiled with the diseased sweat of the tenements, a coloured ribbon or two of his own making, and, maybe, fix in its centre (like the jewel in the toad's head) a ruby or an emerald, giving the poor badge a gleam as good as that of any ancient order of chivalry, or that which goes with the posing piety of the Papal Court.

One thing that was good — he would never be in contact with any controversial literary Dublin clique. One of these cliques, not long ago, had tried to entangle him into an effort to undermine the literary influence and authority of Yeats; and he had been shocked to watch this mean and reprehensible envy of the poet's literary standing bubbling up in the minds of educated and cultured, but lesser men, who had been so safely and so comfortably nurtured in cradle and in school.

Yeats didn't praise them enough; he saw through them, but said nothing. Some of them were the fame-fleas that A. E. wanted Yeats to recognise with a little, or, maybe, substantial praise; pointing out that the poet had praised what others had sung or said, forcing from the lordly Yeats the little verse,

> You say, as I have often given tongue
> In praise of what another said or sung,
> 'Twere politic to do the like by these;
> But was there ever dog who praised his fleas?

Masked pompously he was, in style and manner, but under all was the poet immortal who will be remembered forever. Friendship with Yeats was something Sean couldn't reach yet, for the poet was almost always hidden from view by this group of Gaeligorian guards who, now and again, wrote an article for *The Irish Statesman*, or sent an occasional poem to the Journal to fill a vacant corner. Wherever the poet stood, there they stood too, and followed meekly where he led, though secretly hating the man's true greatness. All that one could see from the fringe of this guard was the noble head of the poet, wearing now the mask of Sophocles, then the pompous one of Plato; again, the mask of contemplative Robartes, and, anon, the wild, warlike one of Red O'Hanrahan; and, to Sean, the deep, medieval voice, seeking impressiveness, however it might sound in laughter, or whatever it might say, always seemed to be murmuring, *Regina, Regina, Pigmeorum, Veni*. Though Gaumalfry followed him everywhere, Sean felt sure that Yeats, without his guards, could be simple and childlike, ready to gambol seriously, and would be inclined to gossip about, and laugh at, the follies and fripperies of men. So Sean kept away from the poet and his guards, for he was captivated by his own work, had been made a prisoner by himself, and his captivity had set him free.

Sean always felt a rude desire to laugh whenever he found himself among this group of guards; he felt that most of them realised this; sensed a sound of silent laughter somewhere. He remembered once when he went to the house of Yeats, in Merrion Square, to see *The Hawk's Well* played in the drawing-room. The room was full of them, dressed in their evening best, the men immaculate in shiny sober black, the women gay and glittering in silk sonorous, and brilliant brocade, all talking animatedly and affectionately together, like teachers and children waiting for trams to come to bring them away on a Sunday-school excursion. Sean tried to attach himself to the conversation by listening, but there was nothing to hear. No-one spoke to him, and, right or wrong, he felt that they were uncomfortable with a tenement-dweller in their midst. Yeats suddenly caught sight of him, came quick to him, and guided Sean to the front, where he wheeled over a deep and downy armchair as a seat for Sean.

—You'll be able to see well here, he said.

Yeats had read in a big book all about the Noh Plays, had spoken about them to others, and had seized on the idea that he could do in an hour what had taken a thousand years to create. And so with the folding and unfolding of a cloth, music from a zither and flute, and taps from a drum, Yeats's idea of a Noh Play blossomed for a brief moment, then the artificial petals faded and dropped lonely to the floor, because a Japanese spirit had failed to climb into the soul of a Kelt.

Passively funny was the sight of Mr. Robinson doing a musician, and Mick Dolan, the Abbey actor, acting Cuchullain, so serious, so solemn, his right hand, extended, holding a spear, saying so surlily-amiable, I am named Cuchullain; I am Sualtam's sin. No; charming and amiable as it all was, it wasn't a Noh Play. Poet and all as he was, Yeats wasn't able to grasp a convention, grown through a thousand years, and give it an Irish birth in an hour. Zither and flute and drum, with Dulac's masks, too full of detail for such an eyeless play, couldn't pour the imagination into the mind of those who listened and saw. The unfolding and folding of the fanciful cloth couldn't carry the stage to the drawing-room. No, the people's theatre can never be successfully turned into a poetical conventicle. A play poetical to be worthy of the theatre must be able to withstand the terror of Ta-Ra-Ra-Boom-Dee-Ay, as a blue sky, or an apple tree in bloom, withstands any ugliness around or beneath them.

There was a buzz of Beautiful when the cloth had been folded, and the musicians had taken their slow way from the room; and Sean wisting not what to say himself, added Very. There was grace and a slender charm in what had been done, now that he had had a long time to look back at it; but it wasn't even the ghost of the theatre. Sean tried to murmur a few remarks, but no head turned to listen, and the chatter went on as if he had been a wraith invisible. Only one spoke to him — a Miss Estelle Solomons, a tall and stately young lady, shielding herself in a shining purplish-blue silken gown, moving a gold-covered shoe in and out under its hem, as she talked to Sean. Though Sean never saw her again, he remembered her as a clever and charming young woman.

But in this crowd, outside of Yeats, there was no friend for him. He could foresee that much. Most of them had gathered here, not to see the play, but because Yeats was Yeats. As Sean stood, watching, trying to listen to what they said, he wondered how they would feel, what would happen, if Fluther, furiously drunk, came tumbling into the room, looking for someone to fight him.

—Any two o' yous, any three o' yous; your own selection; anywhere yous like — here or in th' sthreet!

An ignorant, ignoble savage, shouting that He wouldn't let that poet fella make little of Fluther's religion; lost to, and separate from, these elegant ones here in Yeats's drawing-room. And yet, Fluther was of the same family; bone of their bone, flesh of their flesh; a Christian, too, never missing Mass on Sundays. What headlines his visit would make in the morrow's newspapers! Fluther runs wild in Yeats's drawing-room; Shocking scene; The poet tries to reason with him; A number of dress-suits ruined; Six constables remove Fluther Good!

Yet there was life in this Fluther that these elegant persons lacked; and life in them that Fluther hadn't got. What a pity, what a shame, they couldn't share their gifts between them. Fluther had his rights and he had his qualities. Fluther, on Sundays, sober; his old suit brushed, a faded bowler hat set rakishly on his head, a newly-washed shirt showing over the top of his waistcoat, coming up the poor street, would be surrounded by children, some preceding, some following him, and all crying out, Sing us a song, Fluther; give us *Th' Weddin' o' Glencree*! And, shy and self-conscious, Fluther would set his back to the wall of a house, remove his hat, and sing the song for them. When it was done, Fluther, to regain his confidence, would say, I've a wing (penny) left; come on all of yous. He would lead the way to a sweet-shop, buy the sweets, and share them equally. Once, Sean saw him go back to the shop, and say, I want to give the chiselurs three each, an' I'm three short; and, for peace sake, the shopman would hand them over. But the children would never pester him; never beseech him to sing a song, till they saw him wearing the clean shirt and the bowler hat, and saw that he was sober.

And, bar Yeats and a few others, Sean was as far away from these elegant people as the doughty Fluther. Far farther, for he was nearer to Fluther than he was to them. There was something of the wildness of Fluther in Yeats himself; and Sean could clearly see Lady Gregory listening attentively to Fluther shyly singing his *The Weddin' o' Glencree*, if he happened to come to Coole; for this was Fluther's one shy way of giving a bow to the glory of literature and song.

No, this trifling group of the drawing-room would never deliver Ireland from what was coming — they thought of themselves too much. Knowing so little, and still lacking confidence, Sean was silent. There was no chance of a growing carnival of thought here. There was nothing in the fervency of their talk; no honour to Yeats in it; he was simply circumscribed with hesitant murmurs of Beautiful: it was as if a tired and unbelieving priest was murmuring the last words of *Missa est*.

Sean thought he could sense two systems of censorship sprouting out in Ireland. One was the group gathered here in Yeats's room, among the richly-heavy blue curtains, the seductive settee and cushions, the gleaming glass, and shiny silver; a censorship of brittle badinage and dainty disdain for anything written different from what they wanted, or were used to, because they had tried it themselves. The other was a prelatian-led crowd of ding-dong dedero devotees, roaring out opposition to everything outside of what Father Tom, Dick, or Harry thought proper to put in poem or book. Holy water would soon be raining down for forty days and forty nights, and the sooner Sean got into the ark of England the better, if he was to escape the deluge. It was time to go.

Almost as long as Sean could remember, the life of Ireland was lived in a hall whose walls were roof-high stained-glass windows, nationally designed; but these were giving place now to glass that gave back the colours of pietistic twist and glossied tantrum. The window where Wolfe Tone had shone in his sky-blue coat and bright epaulettes of a Brigadier, now showed the wan figure of Bernadette raptly listening to the Bells of St. Mary's; in the one which had Robert Emmet in his gay green coat, carrying a plumed hat in his hand, stood now the black-clad, smiling-faced Father Malone in his new Sunday hat. Here was Father Dempsey ordering Mat Haffican to behave himself; and over there, the huge one of sickly-yellow and muddy-black glass, showing Matt Talbot, the tenement labourer, on his knees at full steam in prayer; the rusty steel chains he wore round his middle eating into the flesh of belly and back, changing into a bonny ring o' roses O. Opposite this was a big one of Chesterton and Belloc, entitled Comrades since we were Boys, supported by the impediment of nicely-trimmed alto-relievo figures of the Middle Ages. Chesterton's Father Brown was there too, taking a rabbit and a blue cross from his clerical hat; beating his noble brow to get some sublime intuition about a head severed from a body by a sabre stroke into coherent thought. And over, under, and around them all, were panes and panes of figures of friars in grey, in black, and in white; a robal army encompassing all things Irish that journeyed from the cradle to the grave.

The bishops began to climb into the saddle after the death of Parnell. Then came a vicious disunity, and the bishops got their chance to dominate both parties. The clergy didn't mind when William O'Brien called Tim Healy 'a disgrace to human nature'; and they never turned a hair when Healy replied, accusing Dillon and his followers of 'selling O'Neill's county, Tyrone, to an English party for £200 per annum per seat'. But when Lamb of Newry and Dr. Kenny ventured to say, 'they would not take a Catholic University, if the present Hierarchy had anything to do with it', they were soon squelched by the episcopal statement from Maynooth of 'We cannot tolerate the use of such language. We trust this admonition will be enough, and that we will not be forced to an exercise of our spiritual authority for the prevention of this very great evil.' Aha, excommunication for them who spake against the bishops! Silence! Discretion is the bitter part of valour.

The Orders will be let loose over the country to tighten up the faith of the people; the Civil Service will become the Third Order of St. Formulus; the Knights of Columbanus will become the soldiers of the Legion of the Prayer Guard; the Pope's Brass Band will be developed into a symphony orchestra, Armagh conducting, with Dublin as the first fiddle; the gay rustle of a girl's skirt will be hushed by the discreet rustle of the priest's cassock and the friar's gown; and, like the cleric in Sierra's *Two Shepherds*, the priests will drag the people of Ireland into heaven by the scruff of their necks.

It was time for Sean to go.

All outward trace of the distant grandeur Sean's youth had known, from afar off, had gone into the mothering dust. Yesterday was as if it had never been. Gone were the ladie ardilauns, alone and unhappy often, in their swelling mansions, having as many rooms as cells in a beehive. Gone forever was her daintily-made thought of charity of bringing tenement women to her gorgeous gardens to sip tea, trembling; to be presented with a geranium in a pot as they got up to return to their home sweet homes. The return from Fingal! Gone the majesty, and even the interest, of the scarlet, blue, and gilded covering of the plaster-made lion and unicorn, hanging haughtily over the shop-front of butcher, baker, and candle-stick maker who enjoyed the privilege of being a spasmodic provider of goods to the king's Lord Lieutenant. Gone were the Arabian nights of dance and delicate Erosian devotions in Dublin Castle, where rows of debutantes, half hidden in clouds of brocade and tulle, waited for entrance with military or naval escorts in scarlet and blue and gold, topped by helmet or busby, over-topped with spike or plume; and after the bow and the greeting, when the streets flowered for a moment again with silks and tulle and muslin medley, they waited wearily in queues, wearily waited to have their photographs taken in Lafayette's or Chancellor's, striving to make a moment immortal through a picture of fading shadows. Gone the home and colonial governors, carrying away their gnomish glitter with them — the Abercorns, the Wimbornes, and the Cadogans; their absence blotting away the yearly dotting of Ireland's name with the honour of baronet or knight. Gone indeed were the cometic visits of king, queen, or prince, prancing through a pompous fairy thoroughfare of steady light and fluttering flags. The Balfours had said goodbye to Ireland, and the Clancy name had come to take their place. All had faded out of the land of prayer and dreams, and most of them had crept out of the world itself. All the display, the pertinent confidence, the complacency of show and tangled tinselry, the everlasting words writ on parchment and sealed with coloured wax, had all been subdued into dust, blowing about, restless, no-one knew whither or where. Even the memory of them was growing cold in the clasp of the mothering earth. The braid, the bugles, and the blast of their blessing had all gone.

These pantomimic figures — the harlequin-viceroy with his sceptre-shaped lath, the columbinian grand lady, the clownish office-seeker, the pantaloonian judge with his policeman hanger-on, had run from the stage of Irish life, frightened off by the rage of rifle-shot and machine-gun fire; the chorused clang of violent opposition that had developed out of the first shot fired at Bunker's Hill. Earlier, even, than that: the Levellers' fight for what is on the way now; earlier still: the sign of things to come in the curse given by the peasant serf outside of his lord's castle; and his brother's bony hand in rage buffeting the thick stone of my lord abbot's monastery wall, which he prayed would fall on the abbot, killing him stone dead as a reprisal for robbing him of his labourer's fee, and of assisting the lordly ones in keeping the peasant a slave; though the angry peasant fell quick to his knees when the abbot came out on his caparisoned palfrey, out through the wide gateway, with his cavalcade of nineteen horsemen, his hawk on his wrist, his dozen of dogs, and his string of servants, on his way to the Manor House; the peasant getting to his feet when the abbot's out of earshot to fling a complaint, in the rage of his poverty, after the glitter of God's man: *What doeth gold in your bridles? It may not put cold or hunger away from your bridle. It is ours that ye so spend in pomp and vanity.*

So the abbots and the lords took, and so they spent, though tongues cursed them and hands hammered the stone walls. But the hands have grown stronger since, and will grow stronger still.

As of the first, so of the second phase of Sean's life — it had almost all gone. The singing lark in the clear air had left the sky, and the cawing crow was there now. The minstrel boy went to the war no more, and the harp that had once roused Tara's halls had corded strings that gave no music. The Gaelic League had dried into a skeleton, and was carried round to be exposed at every feast with the green flag wrapped round it. The boys in power mouthed an odd tribute to the Gaelic, then hurried home to dress themselves in the bits and pieces scattered here and there by the English Garrison when they had lived in the country. Even in religion there was little to distinguish the Irish catholic from the English one. Bernadette, St. Vincent de Paul, and The Little Flower were the popular triad in Ireland today, with St. Anthony of Padua runner-up. Not a church from one end of the land to the other seemed to show a sign that the church was an Irish one. They were all lick-spittle imitations of churches in other lands. Was there a sign in any of them of an Irish touch in the painting and sculpture that called the faithful to remember things past? Was there a sign of art, even, in any of them? In all the badges, the symbols, the aids to piety that had been delivered out of heaven to this saint and to that, God seems to have forgotten that Ireland existed.

All the Irish significance had gone to the grave with the older saints, and Bridget, now, couldn't hold a candle to Bernadette; though there was something silly, sensational, and tawdry in Bernadette; while about the name of Bridget clung the essence of charm, of poetry, and a realistic love of life. But now Kildare's holy shrine was dark and empty, while Lourdes was a blaze of candles carried by crowds. Oh, the trains, the yellow, the blue, the white, the brown, that race, tirra lirra, along to Lourdes! Racing along, carrying their rotting crops of humanity, to where a hymn and a prayer are to prosper them back to health. The woe and the waste of it all! Lourdes, where hope is swallowed down by misery to be vomited up again, more miserable, and lost. Where Lazarus is offered a crumb, but can never crawl near enough to get it. Where miserere jingles little bells of expectation, and never hears them sounding. Where belief plays her last joke on the dying. The church's great sweep of misery and woe. You may be the lucky one. Take your chance and keep the bells a-tolling. If at first you don't succeed, try, try again. Keep smiling — someone has got to be cured. The Coney Island of misery, agony, and woe. And when the festivity of death ends, and all gather to go home, wending slow through voluptuous chants of *Ave Maria*, the untouched ear can hear the sickly growl, sombre and low, with a hiss in it of *She never cured me, She didn't cure me*.

When all the lights from a hundred altars had been darkened; when the priests had divested themselves of their sacerdotal grandeur; when the swelling hearts of the ailing had been emptied of desire from very weariness; and the treasures given for the Virgin's glory were being counted; go the sad souls back to the vigil of the lonely couch, the biting sigh, the broken prayers, born of the broken hope of going forth broken and coming back whole. What could not this ill-spent energy do, this waste of transport, this garnered wealth do, if all were devoted to those efforts, those saintly efforts, to conquer the direr ills of man, sending more young to the grave than Lourdes can cure in an eternity of time. Disease can never be conquered, can never be quelled by emotion's wailful screaming or faith's cymballic prayer. It can only be conquered by the energy of humanity and the cunning in the mind of man. In the patience of a Curie, in the enlightenment of a Faraday, a Rutherford, a Pasteur, a Nightingale, and all other apostles of light and cleanliness, rather than of a woebegone godliness, we shall find final deliverance from plague, pestilence, and famine.

And all the other centres of sacerdotal healing are envious of Lourdes: Fatima, in Portugal, Kirkhala in Latvia, and poor little innocent little Knock in Ireland's sweet Mayo; for only Lourdes has succeeded in forcing a way into the limelight from heaven. A stream of water flowing out of it, a stream of gold flowing into it. A gigantic bazaar of tapers, holy images, holy water, in a storm of prayer, with frightened souls embedded in bodies braided with tumours, phthisis, scrofula, and cancer, hoping against hope for an impossible pardon, bringing solace, joy, and good fortune to the holy Fathers of the Assumption. The battle-ground where Father Sempé fought with

the Abbé Peyramale; fought like tigers for the possessions of Bernadette, one tugging her to the old town, the other tugging her where
he saw a new town rise up, till Peyramale was dead, and the old
town with him; so that spires and towers and great churches rose
up in the new town, under the guardianship of the Fathers of the
Assumption, guided, day by day, by the care and strict cunning of
Father Sempé, all heavily embossed with godly pomp, pious pride,
and wealth no single bank could hold. Oh, St. Patrick, St. Patrick,
dear saint of our isle, what were you thinking of when you let little
innocent little Knock be ousted by the impudence of Lourdes!

There had to be a song about it, and so there was: *The Song of
Bernadette*. Poor Werfel, panic-stricken, flying from the brown onslaught of Nazi gun and tank; flying breathless, with the screaming
crowd, promised Bernadette that if he came safe, he'd visit Lourdes,
and sing a song to her. He didn't wait to think why God should
single him out from the thousands of fleeing Christians, hundreds of
them good catholics, letting them die, while He was busy finding a
way to deliver Werfel. It was a tall request, a terribly selfish one, too,
and highly impudent; but it was a success, and Werfel was piloted,
safe and sound and high and dry, to the promised land to sing his
promised song to Bernadette. This Adeste Fideles to Bernadette has
been sung and chorused by millions of catholics, in seminary, in
college, in the cloister, on the street, in the market-place. But somehow there is something wrong with it; something mean, paltry; and
something crawling that nibbles at a noble, resistant resignation.
There is something like the moaning of a sick slave in it; and through
the sounds of its sickly chords there is a bitter tuning that some say
is the sigh of the thousands who died unaided; who suffered so
monstrously in the concentration camps; who were executed in
heaps; who prayed, too, but got no answer; who promised, but
weren't let live to keep their promise.

It would seem to be something elusive, or delusive, in God to
suggest that He would sacrifice so many to save one for such a song.
If it had been for a Shakespeare, now. Ah, a Shakespeare! Or a
Tolstoy. Ah, a Tolstoy! Or for a Strindberg, an Ibsen, a Yeats, or a
Joyce! But for this thing of a song! Was it indeed God who gave this
song to the world? Did God, or the Blessed Virgin, bring this man
safe from the flood of fire — leaving all the rest to die as best they
could — in order that this song might be made, and that it might be
extended into the slimy glory of an orgiastic film? Its poor pietistic
preaching brings new wealth and fresh power, maybe, to the good

Fathers of the Assumption, and, through the Fathers, to the Vatican Congregation of Propaganda; but it adds not one tittle to the glory of God in the deeper thoughts of any Christian's heart. It plasters rouge on the Virgin's face.

So let the blue trains run, and the red and the white ones, and more if they be needful, this year, next year, and all the years that follow; bringing the selected delegates, representing the diseases of their countries, to the Lourdean parliament of death, where speeches are pitiful prayers; resolutions, pain; and amendments, a moaning hope, held too long, turning now into a brooding vacancy of rejection.

There they go — the red trains and the brown trains, tcheh-tcheh-tcheh-tcheh-tcheh-tcheh, straight down through France, passing through fair valleys, by fruitful vineyards, going quick, but not quick enough, tcheh-tcheh-tcheh-tcheh, diving under tunnels, rushing through town and village, straight on to Lourdes, white train and yellow train, their carriages carrying the incurables, Muldoon the Solid Man's son and Mick McGilligan's daughter among them, on to the Maid of the Grotto, tcheh-tcheh-tcheh-tcheh,

O Maid of the Grotto, heal us,
From thee all skill and science flow, all pity, care and love;
All calm and courage, faith and hope — oh, pour them from
above;
Tcheh-tcheh to Lourdes, to Lourdes, to Lourdes.

Sean felt that if he stayed in Dublin, life would become embarrassing to meet. Dublin was too close to everyone. All its streets led into the one square where everyone met, where hands were shaken, shoulders clapped, and drinks taken to every other person's health. Sound and happy association, with one reservation — that when one was on the way to a good creation, he might be waylaid, left by the wayside, to die there, unfortified by the rites of the church. He remembered what he had gone through with his last play: Mr. Robinson agitated during rehearsals; silent sullenness stiffening the dialogue spoken by the actors; Lady Gregory anxious, and talking to Yeats about what might happen; and gigantic whispers wandering from one room to another in the Abbey Theatre, making the sullen more sullen still. 'I refuse to say the word Snotty,' said F. J. McCormick, while someone, in the background, murmured For righteous men must make our land a nation once again; 'and I', said Miss Eileen Crowe — having first asked her priest about it — 'refuse to say the words "Ne'er a one o' Jennie Gogan's kids was born outside of th' bordhers of the Ten Commandments"', a chorus in the background chanting,

> Oh, sure you're right, allanna, for decent people know
> That every girl in Ireland, as things at present go,
> Is the soul of truth and of melting ruth,
> With a smile like a summer at dawn;
> Like the colleens that trip up and the colleens that trip down
> The sweet valley of Slieve na Man, amen.

O Yes, O Yes, and there was Mr. O'Brien, the Abbey Director, running round moaning, 'The Song, The Song! That'll have to come out; Yeats, you've got to be careful.' And the lights in the pubs went higher and higher, and everything in them was agog and aglow. And Mr. Michael Dolan, the theatre's Manager, writing to Lady Gregory beseeching her, with tears in his eyes, beseeching her, of her charity, now that the theatre was booming, to have nothing to do with this play; for the language, oh, the language in it goes beyond the beyonds; and the song at the end of the second act, oh, the song at the end of the second act, sung by the girl of the streets, is, is unpardonable; and we don't want to give any enemy of the theatre Anything To Grasp At. And Mr. Michael Dolan, eaten up with his zeal for the good name of the theatre, went on assuring Lady Gregory that there would be real difficulty in getting the Company to play in it, so he begged her ladyship to have a care. He had had a hot argument with O'Casey over the recent performance of *Man and Superman*, when O'Casey called the production a very bad one, and then added a letter to prove he was right; but this, of course, had nothing whatever to do with Dolan's dislike of, and fear of, this new play of O'Casey's, which, in his opinion, would do harm to the dear little, sweet little theatre of Ireland.

And all this time Mr. O'Brien, the one and only catholic Director on the theatre's Board, was going here and going there, asking all whom he met, 'Would the Song be cut out? You know, the song at the end of the second act, the one which tells about the woman's objectionable preference for a sailor — will it go; will it tarry; will Yeats do the right thing, and have it removed?' And the whispers of the pubs quivered like things infirm when they touched on the beyond the beyond language of the play; and some said this, and others said that if the play was allowed to go on the public stage as it was, it would have been just as well if St. Patrick hadn't come to Ireland at all. The song in it was bound to slip over the seas, and destroy the reputation of the Irish Race. Now, just imagine it! After five hundred years of work here and intercession in heaven, just imagine St. Patrick (I won't mention the name of Bridget in the circumstances) hearing that song for the first time in London or in New York; and then, when St. Patrick rebuked the English or the American saints for allowing this song of bawdry, to hear that it was first sung in holy Dublin, See of St. Laurence O'Toole; and that a catholic actor had sung it out loud, and shamelessly! So even a blind man could see clearly that something must be done.

All the time, in the foyer, a Mr. Holloway, who had superintended the architectural change in the theatre, under Miss Horniman, spluttering spit over anyone stopping to listen to him, kept saying, 'This play was an abominable one, for there never was a street-walker in Ireland since reliable history began to be written; and, if the truth had to be told, he'd say every girl in Ireland was an angel's whisper. Look at poor O'Brien, there, going by, his honest heart sore troubled with the echoing in his mind of that song at the end of the second act in O'Casey's play! The implicity of that song is appalling, and it'll go down the ages against us, if it's allowed to be sung.'

Sean looked around the room at all the furniture he had. All of it would fit into a small container — settee, desk, chair, filing-cabinets, and books; and he could get them over to England a day or two after his own arrival. He would leave all the rest — the linoleum, curtains, bed, saucepans, crockery, and oddments — to the lady below him. Then his customary footfall would never again be heard in a Dublin street. And the lamp — he'd leave that too; for he felt that, in England, there'd be electric light wherever he chose to live. A tip of a switch, and the room would flood with light. That in itself would be a great step forward. Lead kindly light, amid the encircling gloom — electricity was now one of his gods. More light, murmured Goethe with his dying breath. Let there be light! said Faraday; and there was light. How much richer, how much more like a god, than the bishop in his gaudy dalmatic, does Faraday look in his dalmatic of light.

Sean realised now that the theatre, called the Abbey, as a whole was against him, and that it would be a good thing to put a greater distance between it and him (though it was very ironical to look back to see that some of these very actors, who had so strongly protested against the play, afterwards — when the tumult had died down — carried it all over the United States to their own advantage, bringing back many dollars which happily made their future a little less uncertain for them than it had been). At present there wasn't even the width of the Liffey between the theatre and him; soon the expanse of the Irish Sea would separate them. To go a fair distance away was the best way to check a developing difference. But seas between us braid hae roared, sin auld lang syne.

He packed his few last personal things into his one suitcase; the suitcase that had gone with him to Coole, and was now to shepherd the things that would allow him to strut respectably through the streets of London. There was nothing to keep him here: he had no part in Cosgrave's party, or in De Valera's policy; nor had he any in the Labour Movement bossed by William O'Brien; no, nor any part in the Protestant Church of Ireland, or that of the Roman Catholic Mission here; though each and all of them had had a part in making his life as it was now, and in streaking it with many colours. He would soon be crossing the border of his own life. To London! To art galleries and picture shows. He would learn a lot more about painting. He would see something of what Van Gogh, Cézanne, Renoir, and Manet had done, for, as yet, they were but glittering names to him. London! He wouldn't have to listen to A. E. any longer, who couldn't comment on a painting unless it had a label. And Augustus John's *Galway* — he had seen it pictured in a magazine; but now he'd see it as John had done it — life-sized and magnificent. This magnificent man as well as magnificent painter had come into the Abbey Green Room once, fleeing from Count McCormick who was beseeching John to paint him; and Sean had asked the artist why he didn't do it, to be answered, brusquely, Because there is nothing to paint!

Yes, London would mould him into a more fully-developed mind and man. The booming of Big Ben would deafen his new-listening ear to any echo from the bells of Shandon. Though he felt curious, and a little anxious, about meeting things he did not know, he felt relief at leaving behind the things he knew too well. The Easter Rising had pulled down a dark curtain of eternal separation between him and his best friends; and the few that had remained alive and delightful, now lay deep, with their convivial virtues, under the smoking rubblement of the Civil War. It was getting very dark in Ireland, so his flight to London would be a leap in the light.

He strapped the suitcase tight. Any minute now the jaunting-car would come to take him to the station where he was to take the train for the boat. He went to the window, and looked out — a cold, windy, harsh March morning. Early on a wild March morning. An old song strayed into his mind:

And as I stood upon the quay, a tear fell from my eye,
For divil a blessed soul was there to say, old friend, goodbye;
They were glad to see me sail, far away from Inisfail,
Early on that wild March morning!

The weather meant a rough passage, but he'd stick it calmly, however roguishly rough it might be. His day in Ireland had been a long one, but the long day was over at last; a long day over; long day over; over at last.

He would leave Yeats on his Island of Inisfree, standing pensively àt the door of his small cabin of clay and wattles made; or moving, slow and moody, between his nine bean rows, thinking of peace where there was no peace; for Ireland's red-rose-bordered hem was muddy now, and ragged. There was no making love to Cathleen, daughter of Houlihan, now, untidy termagant, brawling out her prayers. He would leave Lady Gregory watching wild swans rising from the lake, or walking in her Seven Woods of Coole; and the lesser writers, too, conceiving little things of verse chipped from the touch of little things timidly seen and carefully handled; and his brother, Mick, with his dream of an endless queue of pints waiting to be swallowed.

Here comes the car. Sean swung his suitcase up on it, and climbed into a side-seat; and away they went on the first trotting steps to England. England? Well, Sean was going into a land enslaved to ill-doing and left alone by God, according to Father O'Reilly, who, at a meeting of Maynooth Union, whose members were priests, is reported to have said but fifteen years ago: 'The character of the English mind ought to be understood in Ireland. It is a fleshy spirit, bent towards earth; a mind unmannerly, vulgar, insolent, bigoted; a mind whose belly is its god, yet which cannot endure the word belly; a mind to which pride and lust and mammon are the matter-of-course aims of life; a mind where every absurd device, from grossest Darwinism to most preposterous spiritualism, is resorted to, and hoped in, to choke the voice of eternity in the conscience; a mind to which the idea of a churchman possessing real, efficient, and spiritual authority over his flock would be unspeakably ludicrous.'

A bad place to be going to, certainly. But while this reverend cleric was speaking, down south a farmer had become certain that his handsome young wife was possessed of a witch, and got the local reverend cleric to say Mass in the house to deliver her. But the intention failed, and the farmer, with the help of neighbours, set about it himself, burning her with a red-hot poker, forcing her to drink things made from herbs gathered over the mountains; and when these sensible and holy acts didn't do, carried her down in her shift, and held her over the fire till she was roasted alive; and then buried her away in a lonely place of gorse and thorny briars. A week later she was dug up, displaying purple marks round her throat, and with the muscles of her spine burned away. And, after the inquest, neither lay nor clerical would give a hand to bury her; so the police had to do it by the light of lanterns, and in the dead of the sympathetic night.

The outside-car swung along down Dorset Street, where Sean had first seen the peep of day; past George's church, in the pocket of which had lived the Dalton family with whom he had trod, as a youngster, the stage of the old Mechanics Theatre, now known the world over as The Abbey; down Cavendish Row where the Dispensary had been from which the gentle Dr. Oulton had come to cure Sean of a fever; down Sackville-O'Connell Street, catching a good glimpse of the Post Office, where Padraic Pearse had sounded the horn that roused Ireland out of her sleeping. In this very street, on the top of a horse-drawn tram, when a little boy safe beside his mother, he had swept into the galaxy of illuminations, lit to honour an English queen; and, years after, had been almost suffocated in this very street by the surging crowd escaping from the batons of the police. In this very street.

The car turned down Abbey Street and swung into Beresford Place, trotting past Liberty Hall, once the sweltering, weltering University of the Dublin workers, now a dead tomb held by an enemy, with Ichabod written all over it, for Larkin had gone, and its glory had departed; down Tara Street, surely the drabbest and dirtiest street in Dublin, looking as desolate as Tara itself; wheeling into Brunswick Street, passing the Queen's Theatre where Sean had seen his first play, *The Shaughraun*; past the ancient Concert Rooms, where the National Theatre performed some of its early plays, before it had a habitation or even a name. It was this street that had been Sean's *via dolorosa*, through which he had passed, three times a week, year after year, for fifteen or more of them, with his mother first, then on his own, to the Ophthalmic Hospital to seek ease for aching eyeballs. Ah, here was Westland Row Station — the last spot of Dublin that would feel his footfall. It was from this sad site that the coffin holding Parnell came slowly out, borne by strenuous, tearful men, hesitating to part even with the dead body of their persecuted Chieftain. Oh, God Almighty, the life he was living now had almost all been spun from what he had felt, had seen, had touched in these few Dublin streets!

He was on the deck of the mail-boat, feeling her sway and shyly throb beneath his feet; watching the landing-stage drift far away, getting his last glimpse of Eireann — separated for the first time from her, and never likely to stand settled on her soil again. It was bitterly cold, with a·fierce, keen wind blowing, and soon it was sending sharp sleety hail and salty spray into his face, stinging it deeply — Ireland, spitting a last, venomous, contemptuous farewell to him.

Well, everything of any value he was carrying away with him: the moral courage and critical faculties of his father, and his love of good books; the gay humour and dogged resolution of his mother, and her love for, and understanding of, the bright colours among dead, drab things; the remembrance of the warm clasp from the Reverend Mr. Griffin's firm, white, delicately-shaped hands; the love of his comrade workers, catholic and protestant, with whom he had fought and starved and fought again; all the fair things he had learned during his sojourn with the Gaelic League; the affection and goodwill of Lady Gregory; the reluctant godspeed from Dr. Cummins; a fond recollection of brother Tom; pity for his sister Bella, and a little less of it for Mick; and, above all, a strict and determined confidence in himself. Jewels he could never sell; jewels that no thief, however cute, could take out of his hands.

> Sail on, sail on, thou fearless bark,
> Wherever blows the welcome wind,
> It cannot lead to scenes more dark,
> More sad, than those we leave behind.

The ship turned giddily to right, to left, plunged with upturned bows, dipping them again as quick, for there was more than a half-gale blowing. Sean had been anxious about sea-sickness, but he felt no discomfort. He was a good sailor. He faced resolutely towards where the ship was going. Sweet Inishfallen, fare thee well! Forever!

ROSE AND CROWN

This is the porcelain clay of humankind

To the Young of All Lands,
All Colours, All Creeds:

Shadows of beauty.
Shadows of power;
Rise to your duty —
This is the hour!

LONDON APPRENTICE

HERE he was now, planting a foot for the first time on the pavement of London; planting it firmly, with a confident air and a fluttering heart. Sliding with the hiss of steam and the throb of pistons into the heart of the

> Great flower that opens but at night,
> Great city of the midnight sun,
> Whose day begins when day is done.

A London apprentice now. Listen!

> Oranges and lemons, say the bells of St. Clement's.
> When will you pay me? say the bells at Old Bailey.
> When I grow rich, say the bells at Shoreditch.

How different was the view now from that of the lovely coast of Wales, lacing the land's edge from Holyhead to Chester. Coming within the grip of the city, he had been wondering through miles of the journey at the dismal wretchedness of the houses, apparently trotting away from him as the train ambled to the end of its journey; trotting away from him so that he mightn't fully see the abject royalty of their miserable appearance. The train had run through a long, drab gauntlet of houses, some of them fat with filth. The magnificent, wealthy city of London, with her gilded Mayor and red-robed Aldermen, was entered through long kennels of struggling poverty and disordered want. Sisters to the houses he had so often seen, slinky with shame, in the shabbiest streets of Dublin. There were the lacerated walls, the windows impudent with dirt, the poor, shrinking clothing, reluctant to be washed, hanging from poles thrust through the windows, fixed to the sills. Just like the hidden parts of Dublin. 'Faith, her privates we. One didn't land in London through a lane of roses.

Euston! Alight here as many Irish had done before him; a short visit so often extended to take the emigrant's rest of life. England; Sasana! Euston; a sprawling untidy place, dim and dark; tormented with many sounds — the clatter of trucks, the patter of hurrying, fussy feet; babble and squeak of passengers not sure of the right train or the proper platform; the sibilant hiss of steam; the sturdy smell of smoke; the soothing, sickly scent of oil; porters hurrying,

251

guards sauntering amid the rustle of paper and magazine, bought by
people who would never read the half of them; women sitting semi-
alert on benches, waiting for the hands of a big clock to tell them
when to move; streams of men, women, and children, dropping
from the train that had just stopped, pouring along under the grimy
roof like an underground river towards an open sluice-gate, to divide
into rivulets and trickles, spreading fanwise to different parts of the
mammoth city. Each one an individual, a soul-body; something
separate from each so like itself, conceit concealing that each one
is a simulacrum of the other;

> Albert Johnson is my nayem,
> England is my nation;
> London is my dwelling-place,
> And heaven my destination.

Heaven! Meanwhile, we must be satisfied with the smoke and the
grime of Euston. 'Seen at night, or through a mist, Euston Station
is one of the most impressive sights in London', said Aubrey
Beardsley. Well, seen by night, or through a mist, there may be many
things appearing impressive, be it either man or dog or eunuch; and
the picturer of his own horrible delusions added, 'Euston Station
has made it unnecessary to visit Egypt'. The slimy, fruitful Nile,
sun, sand, date-palm, and bedouin — none are needed. Pharaoh
porters about here.

To Sean, who stared at the building before he hid himself away in
a taxi, the entrance looked surlily bewildered, as if it had been set
down in the wrong place, as indeed it had, for ancient Egyptian
architecture does not wed itself with English life. Though it forced
itself into the appearance of a temple, here was no shrine at which to
pray for a safe journey from one place to another. The ponderous
pillars holding up its tremendous back looked like a monster's heavy
feet standing in a jungle clearance, the whole brute staring in front
of itself, not knowing which way to turn.

There was James B. Fagan hurrying towards him, having caught
sight of the red muffler encircling Sean's neck, the insignia Sean had
written to say would reveal his advent to London. Sean's play had
been transferred from the Royalty to the Fortune, a little theatre
directly opposite the towering, bully-like Royal Theatre in Drury
Lane — Falstaff and the little page. The play was to open itself out
in the new theatre two nights from now, and Sean was to be kept
hidden till then so that familiarity with others should not mar the
appearance of the slum dramatist on the first night in the Fortune;

enhancing publicity by standing on the stage, grinning, bowing, and saying a few sweet words to the applauding audience that had filled the house for the first performance.

Embedded in a taxi, he was bowled off to the Kenilworth Hotel, Bloomsbury; hustled up in a lift to his room, while Fagan waited below, like a warder, till Sean had freshened himself with a wash, and was ready for Fagan to take him off silently. He was to be kept like a peril in an oyster till the first night of the play had passed into time that neither he nor Fagan would ever touch again. After a light meal in Fagan's flat in Great Russell Street, Sean was again embedded into a taxi, and taken, like a prisoner out for an hour's amusement, to the Duke of York's Theatre to see Jean Forbes-Robertson playing in Chekhov's *Uncle Vanya*. The theatre he was in was no different from the big ones of Dublin. That was all he learned from this outing. Things were so different with him now, so new, so far from what he had been used to; his future was so uncertain, his mind so buoyant with jostling thoughts; and he was hushed so deeply back to the rear of the box, with Mary Grey and James Fagan in front of him, that to this day he cannot remember a single thing about the play, the acting, or the production. The one memory remaining is the name of the play and the name of the leading actress, and these were fixed in his mind by the lovely coloured lights of red, yellow, and white, flashing over the entrance of the theatre, telling out her name and the name of the Russian play she acted in. The first London play he had seen, he hadn't seen at all. A long wait in the box when the play was over to ensure that the crowd had gone, in fear anyone among it should have recognised Sean, and have shouted out the hot news that O'Casey was here. Then a quick retreat into a taxi again, and so to bed.

He was to be shown off, a new oddity, an odd wonder; a guttersnipe among the trimly educated and the richly clad; the slum dramatist, who, in the midst of a great darkness, had seen a greater light. Fagan was constantly pulling Sean away from his own thoughts, trying to listen to the part of England speaking to him, trying to see the part of England passing him by. He was pulled here, pulled there; brought, bowing, before young men and women, before elderly men, before anyone who could write about him in the daily papers and in the weekly journals, so keeping the romance of his arrival in London before the people in order that the beautiful sign of House Full should garnish the front of the theatre nightly.

He was photographed getting into a taxi and getting out of one;

photographed in the theatre, and in the flat where he lived; photographed talking to policemen; brought face to face with those whose pencils could dash down a swift impression to appear fresh and full-blown in some paper the following day, or in some periodical at the end of the week; some, grinning and ghastly, showing themselves in a paper on the Lord's day. Coriolanus O'Casside hurried here and there by Menenius Fagan, to show himself, to say what a good fellow he was. He was tired of it before it had well begun. Very boring, for Sean in his heart didn't care a damn what anyone thought of him. Once, when a photographer handed him a huge, green, cardboard shamrock, telling him to fix it in his coat, and look gay, Sean let loose on him; and James Fagan, going white, heard for the first time the savage and profane vernacular of the Dublin navvy.

Having written the play, he was now busily employed selling the tickets for the show — or so it seemed to Sean. Once, after a smiling interlude of an introduction by Fagan, Sean was led to a teashop by the eager and delicately mannered Beverley Nichols, young, oh, so young, and, oh, so ambitious, whose white hand was already fidgeting with the latch on the doorway to fame; trying to lift the heavy iron without hurting his fingers. Sean hoped some day he wouldn't mind hurting his fingers, for it was on lads like this one that England's literary life depended. The teashop was filled with young men and women, weary-looking and pale-faced, seeking whatever nourishment cakes and buns could give them, adding the stimulant of tea to roughly orchestrated cymbal-clash of crockery, toned down by the bass of shuffling people, some rising to end a meal, others sitting down to begin one.

Sean flung off a heavy sky-blue overcoat, reinforced within by a warm, brilliant lining of black-lined red squares, bought in Moss Brothers, second-hand for four pounds, through the advice and bargaining of Fagan, who was afraid the east wind would do Sean harm — for Fagan had a fine kindliness deep in his heart under his anxiety for the prosperity of the box-office.

Sean looked at the figure sitting at the other side of the table, and wondered what was really beneath the nicely pressed suit, the handsome shirt set off by a handsome tie. He noticed the figure carefully placing a pair of soft, quietly yellow kid gloves on the chair beside him, taking no notice of the turmoil around him. He looks, thought Sean, like a canary among a flock of quails; or a daffodil on a morning without any of the March winds about. Never saw a hobnailed boot in his life, not even in a shop window. Mignonette among the nettles.

A toff! Still, such signs were deceptive. Sean had known friends in Ireland, customarily as dapper as this lad, who had turned into hurlers and footballers as fierce and gallant as any who had raced around a Gaelic playing-field. Deep down, untidiness was often envious of a satisfying neatness.

Be nice to him, for his articles are widely read, Fagan had advised. Rather good-looking youth, Sean thought, but ne'er the sign of a furrow from thought on his soft-complexioned face. Intelligence without the practice of deeper and dangerous thought. Too young yet. *Nichols was educated at Marlborough School and Oxford University*, Fagan had whispered, but this only put Sean wondering now if Oxford created souls; God made a start, and Oxford finished and polished the job. Not God nor Oxford, but only man himself could develop his own soul. He had but the haziest notion of what Oxford was or what Oxford meant, and he was too full of his own thoughts to care what the name of Oxford meant when it was added to the name of Man. (Later on, Sean came to know that great men of his own day came out of Oxford and Cambridge; men like Trevelyan with his History under an arm; the warrior, Coulton, leading a vivid word-pageant of Five Centuries of Religion; Rutherford with the atom an ornament on his watch-chain; gentle-soul'd Gore, of Oxford, holding high his lantern of Lux Mundi, to lighten men's feet along the narrow way; and Frazer marching into the kingdom of the knowledge of good and evil waving his lovely Golden Bough. But no man has a reason or right to be proud of any Institution, though many an Institution has a reason and a right to be proud of many a man.)

The handsome lad began to question Sean as to what he thought of the painted ladies, bright young things whose outlook on life was a squealing, giggling contempt for it all, bar what they lived of it themselves; what he 'thought of the crimped young men, the poisoned critics'; all the wilting, hectic generation which many had come to take for granted — as if this generation of gaudy gomerils had come from first creation, and would extend to the end of time — though some of them weren't aware even of the way to breed. Nichols asked Sean what he thought of the 'brilliant young dramatist, Noel Coward, who had specialised in the portrayal of this particular stratum of life. What did he think of this utterly, absolutely artificial crowd?'

Wasting his time and mine talking of things that didn't matter much, thought Sean. Aloud, he said: They couldn't be absolutely artificial, for even the worst of them are of human flesh and blood subsisting. They may not laugh as others do, or ponder as others do; but none of them can evade the pinch of human pain, and, sooner or later, sorrow will singe their souls, and then they become as others are — splendidly mortal. Careless conduct, high-handed hysterical laughter, and devil-may-care devotion to their own flighty flock can never cover them completely from the searching hand of life.

These, thought Sean, of whom Nichols speaks so inquisitively, who dazzle his thoughts so that he can think of none else; these are but a few false notes in the sad, sweet, silent music of humanity. They think they dance through life, but the dance denies its own merriment. With all their sour fragrance, their hiccuping laughter, their contraband carelessness, their jigging on the tomb of their own dead endeavours, they will descend one day soon into as much dust as a new-born baby's hand can hold.

A story of grand school and grander college was tailed on to this sparkling young man, yet Sean thought it strange that this son of Lady Beaufort's bounty never mentioned a name to him that was known in any art or any science. Not a word from this gem-like lad about England's greater children; Shakespeare unmentioned; Shelley apparently forgotten; Milton ignored; neither could Sean see a sign of a scene from a Constable or a Cotman livening the iris of his boyish eye. Not even a word for the working millions of England's men and women, whose labour made it possible for his cleverness to live and go about gay. He didn't know. Sean wondered if he cared. Refusing to brave the rougher airs of life, he had left the elegant airs of the colleges behind him. He brought with him neither airs from heaven nor blasts from hell.

What was this young fellow's England, and who lived there? From his own unjointed chat, slyly inserted between questions, it was a small part of London inhabited and inhibited by a bunch of frolicking fools, who slapped Time in the face and spit on his beard in an effort to frighten age away, not knowing that age was but crossing the crest of the hill to go down the other side of life, where new flowers grew, and charm abounded as rich and delightful as those loved and handled on the younger slope left behind for ever. These frightened young people, afraid to fight fear with courage, fought fear with fear. Well dressed, extremely well dressed, clever, with fair homes, some of them gaudy with goods, idle, yet knowing no want, these youngsters were already of life's down and out. These young, desperate things had abandoned life before even they had learned how to fight for it.

We are all artificial at times, thought Sean, edging thoughts into his mind between the mechanical answering of the questions put to him by Beverley Nichols. I am being artificial now, for two currents of thought run through my mind, mingling in orderly confusion, and betraying each other: the one bidding him, for the sake of his play, to go easy, and be nice to Nichols whose articles were so widely read; the other prompting him to tell this lad that to work for a few years in a factory; to work, too cold, too wet, too warm, in a field-farm; on a railway platform or permanent way; to come to this hot, hasty restaurant even, and take whatever meals he could get for a year and a day, would give him a good chance of receiving a revelation from God informing him that life, even the life of London, wasn't accounted for by a flippant generation whose members wouldn't crowd two streets of a tiny town.

But Sean held his peace, till the fine figure had jotted down in a note-book all that Sean had ventured to say; had carefully placed the delicately yellow gloves on the confident hands; had settled the dignified trilby on the confident head, and they had risen to take body and mind away from the centre of the tired hurry of the restaurant, the pale faces, and the walls ribbed thick with hanging overcoats and dangling hats.

—Goodbye, murmured Beverley Nichols, as they stood on the path outside, while red buses reared and roared by them; I hope we may soon meet again; and a carefully-gloved hand touched Sean's bare one for a moment. Then the young man departed, carrying himself nicely within a top-coat cleverly caught in at the waist, and flowing from the waist around the slender legs; walking along the rumbling, rancorous street as if he were sauntering down a gilt-edged garden path.

Then Sean said, Jasus! And thought, what a world without there is for this lad, but he stays at home!

The plays proved to be a passport for Sean into the big, big houses. Houses that were big-doored, with many wonderful windows opening on to fairylands of blossom and of tree; houses with wide stairways, smooth floors coddled with cosy carpets; gleaming wood of chair, table, and bureau of Louis Quatorze's fancy and Louis Quinze; Georgian make of Sheraton, Chippendale, and Hepple-white, that fair dazzled the eye. Houses that were patrolled by men free to wear jewelled orders dangling from their coats; and women, coarsely created or finely formed, clad in all the arrogance clever and imaginative minds could weave around them, moved hither and thither over the accommodating carpets with indolent energy, gems nodding drowsily to life on the yellowing and crinkled skin of the old, or sparkling saucily and invitingly on the bosoms of those presented with the ardour and audacity of youth, their beauty often blurred by the sparkle of a white and saucy breast.

Precious stones; precious, but still stones; lovely to look at, to handle, even to wear; but not good enough to honour, worship, and obey. With all their sparkle and beauty, they were dying things, and the people who honoured, worshipped, and obeyed them, were dying too. *The fire-born moods have fallen away.* Mighty baubles, alight with smiles underneath the glow of electricity and candelabra; and, yet, with all their luminous gallantry, like the gay girls who wore them, doomed to remain of the earth, earthy. Were they richer, any more lovely than the common stones that could be gathered from a lonely beach? Pebbles, black, mottled white, or ribbed with white lines; pebbles, white, stained with whorls of sable rondelles; pebbles, red, marked with brown, or tinged with amber; loveliness trodden under foot by the elder when the great sea sparkles, but causing children to pause at play, to stoop, to pick them up, and wonder what god had dropped his jewels. Pebbles that are coaxed into quietude by the summer sea, and tossed and tumbled by the yelling and the roaring tides driven by the winds of winter. Even in all the humility of their massed production, each is as great a miracle, each is as lovely as their costly companions, glittering vaingloriously underneath the gaudy glow of electricity and candelabra.

Sean passed by and touched with his fingers the treasured furnishings in sandalwood, teak, mahogany, rosewood, and walnut, ivoried often, and inlaid with ebony, mixed with mother-o'-pearl; bowed and shook hands among the gracious, showy assembly of silk dress and displayed jewellery; sat on a reponned red couch or a golden-ribbed chair, and eyed it all, finding it elegant, often gracious; delightful at times, dignified at times, but always sadly ridiculous because it was moving towards its end. Kindly they were, eager to share by show with him all their mighty nonsense; but no silk or satin, no sibylline shine of riches could shield him from feeling that this life was nearing its end. The twilight of the goods had come. He wondered what were the real thoughts that silk and satin bannered away out of sight, what troubled outlook on life touched the heart beneath the jewelled bodice and the lace that fringed its edge. They had great possessions. Come, sell all that thou hast, and follow me; follow us; follow the people. Follow, before the fight develops into a bloody tug of war. Already the jewels on the breasts of the beauties, the orders on the coats of the men, were looking awry now, for the little streets were hurling themselves on the great houses. Within them now but shadow shows were seen: all the miracles were happening outside. With all its costly pageantry, its jewelled assertiveness, its air of everlasting confidence, this life was losing its nerve; it was all afraid; it had begun to stumble. Even Beaconsfield's six hundred baronets (the noble six hundred) couldn't save things now. Six hundred of them in their dark-green costumes — the appropriate dress of *equites aurati*; each with his badge and his sacred collar of SS; belted and scarfed; his star glittering; his pennon flying; his hat white with a plume of white feathers; the sword and the gilt spurs; on a hand of each the thumb-ring and signet; each holding his coronet of two balls.

Noble fellows, all, but utterly ineffective now. The Egremonts and the Mitfords were sliding down the hill. Steel and cement were ousting the rococo and the ormolu; the classical portico and the gothic spire were sinking into cordial insignificance. There was no greatness that couldn't be excelled by greatness elsewhere. There could be *infinite riches in a little room*. There had been more majesty in his own one-room tenement home than all the glory in these places gathered together. Shakespeare had often come there, had sat by the fire. He had brought Mistress Quickly with him, and Doll Tearsheet leaning on the arm of the panting Falstaff. And Dickens had shared many a meal with him. Keats's Grecian Urn stood on the dusty mantelpiece with its leaf-fringed legends unfading; the young lad and younger maiden, running; one for ever loving, the other for ever fair. And Shelley's Prometheus laurelled the dim room with defiant patience, waiting for the knee-benders of the earth to pass to the dark, to the past, to the dead; till, veil by veil, evil and error fall. Hardy came, too, and sat him by the tenement fire, and sighed, mourning misunderstood Tess of the D'Urbervilles and Angel Clare's dead decisions. And there, too, on that settee, poor Jude the Obscure died disconsolate and alone, while Hardy's darkling thrush, aged, frail, and small, sang its defying song out on the sill of the window. Painters came, too, to show him dim glimpses of the glory he was yet to see — Giorgione, Constable, and Goya, telling him to look away from Irish eyes of painting, smiling into miserable vistas of yellow-roofed, white-walled cottages, with their brown piles of turf beside them, bunches of gorse by the wayside, and the skies full of Yeats's purple glow; all of one piece, one manner, one misery, destitute of colour and line and form.

No great music came sounding into Sean's ear, for the clef was to him an undecoded hieroglyphic. The chant of an odd bird, the lowing of cattle, the whistling of the wind, the patient patter of falling rain; the brave, meritorious tinkle of the Abbey Theatre orchestra, were all the sweet sounds that the ear of Sean knew. Oh, and the folk-song, the folk-song, the gay and melancholy strains of the Irish folk-song, on fiddle, on harp, and fife. And no folk-art is there but is born in the gay disregard of gain, and in the desire to add a newer beauty and a steadier charm to God's well-turned-out gifts to man; and so, out of the big love in his heart for all things comely and of good shape, the great poet Yeats exclaims:

Folk-art is indeed the oldest of the aristocracies of thought, and because it refuses what is passing and trivial, the merely clever and pretty, as certainly as the vulgar and insincere, and because it has gathered into itself the simplest and most unforgettable thoughts of the generations, it is the soil where all art is rooted. Wherever it is spoken by the fireside, or sung by the roadside, or carved upon the lintel, appreciation of the arts that a single mind gives unity and design to, spreads quickly when its hour is come.

Yeats, a vic, you never spoke a truer word.

When Sean had had time to look around and to hear what was said, he discovered that the city was packed with playwrights. He would be hard set to find a place for the sole of his foot, for, according to what he was told, the city steamed with drama-genius. And which were the greatest of the great? he had asked; but no-one replied to his question. There were so many, they murmured, it would be hard to choose. So many; so great. But by listening cautiously and constantly, he found that the two names most often mentioned were those of Noel Coward, a young man, and Edgar Wallace, a middle-aged one. Top dogs. Turning plays out by the baker's dozen monthly. Came natural to them. What kind of plays? he had asked. Oh, just plays, you know, plays; assorted plays; serious plays, sunny plays, sad plays; all sorts. The finest dramatic literature (to judge from what was said) given to the world was flooding the London people with deepest emotion and best of good cheer. Managers were working overtime producing the famous plays, and book merchants tired publishing them. The garlanded playwrights were the envy of all pup upholders, for they wore the best clothes, ate the best foods, drank the best wines, travelled in the best equipages, and shook hands heartily with the best people, calling them by their pet names. How'r you, Duke Jack; hope you're well, Baroness Babs. They balanced neatly on a newer peak of Darien.

So Sean was eager to see the theatre curtain rise to reveal the stars; to share what Nathan, in a preface to a book of plays, says is innate in all good drama — 'probity, the passionate undertone, the brave resolve, the hint of spiritual music, poetic sweep, the surgery of human emotions, and the warm golden glow'. Up, up goes the tawdry curtain, and Sean saw *Cat's Cradle*, *Easy Virtue*, *The Queen was in the Parlour*, *Kid Boots*, *This Woman Business*, *Journey's End*, and *Rose Marie*. Of all he saw, of all he heard, he could remember nothing; not a word, not a gesture, save one thing only: the chorus of *Rose Marie*; the extraordinary beautiful slide and slip, shimmering with colour, of the girls in the chorus of that immensely mortal musical play. Of all the rest, he could remember nothing; not a word, not a gesture. Not a rag left of all the finery worn in the theatre of that day; nothing that memory could give a salute to; not a thing. They had left not a wrack behind. How easy it is to write a play to be staged; how hard to write one to be remembered!

And yet fanfares of welcome and praise were blown by many of the critics for these poor, pottering things. Agate, the critic of *The Sunday Times*, heralded fast and furiously a number of them — *The Combined Maze*, *The Old Ladies*, *As Others See Us*, and *Journey's End*, calling them, in much excitement, great, wonderful, exquisite, and enduring. Sean had seen them all, and had sighed, and was silent. There wasn't a human heart-beat, no, nor even a human footstep in one of them; not a knock at the door; not a sob in the silence; not a stone flung through any amiable window of thought.

Most of the playwrights were out hunting the golden will-o'-the-wisp, *Ingenium*, which, Mr. Agate explains in his book, *My Theatre Talks*, means 'the power to attain success'. So there they were, running hither and thither, using all the thin nets of their talents, trying to ensnare the flying West End butterfly of *Ingenium*. A name in coloured letters of glowing lights sent shivers and exultation through the hopes and down the spine of every anxious playwright. If he could but get his name there, he could fancy, as he walked along, that his name should be called wonderful, a prince of space and light and time. A garland of glowing jewels adown the dowdy street as if a flock of gaudier toucans were roosting on the ledges of the walls. Here are the shining crests of the playwrights who have caught the elusive mothley called *Ingenium*. Look and live; without seeking ye can find me here. The lights of a playwright shining upon us, giving us pride in the greeting of a great one. His lights shine before the sons of men. Lights to the jew and the gentile. But these lights are often false flatterers, deceiving the name that dwells within them.

Surely, though, occasionally, a figure comes the way of this drab street, one from the homeland, or from far across the sea, and hangs a lantern boldly on an outer wall; and the light lights, not only this one street, but every street in every town of England; a light that does not fail; a light not lit with hands, eternal in the world's ways. This light lasts; that one shines more gaudy for a day or two, but the hand of time quenches it; it is seen no more, and is gone from the ken of man for ever.

Why is the English Theatre so low in mind, so scanty in fancy and imagination, and the play-acting so fond of fasting from manly action and a lusty voice? Let him who spoke thirty years ago, speak again. Go on, Mr. Yeats — we're all listening:

All exploitation of the life of the wealthy, for the eye and ear of the poor and half poor, in plays, in musical comedy, at the cinema, in Daily Mirror photographs, is a travesty of the life of the rich; and if it were not would all but justify some red terror; and it impoverishes and vulgarises the imagination, showing a life that is all display and hurry, passion without emotion, emotion without intellect, and where there is nothing stern and solitary.

You're speaking the solemn truth, Mr. Yeats: go on, son of my heart, go on:

The Theatre grows more elaborate, developing the player at the expense of the poet, developing the scenery at the expense of the player, always increasing the importance of whatever has come to it out of the mere mechanism of a building or the interests of a class, doing whatever is easiest rather than what is most noble, and shaping imaginations before the footlights as behind, that are stirred to excitements that belong to it and not to life; until at last life turns to other things, content to leave specialised energy to weaklings and triflers, to those in whose body there is the least quantity of herself.

Leave your hand in mine, poet from the first, friend at the last; you took the words out of my mouth. The people of Ireland and the clique that hemmed you in from them never knew the man you really were. One word more before you go, sir:

All the arts when young and happy are but the point of the spear whose handle is our daily life.

Ah, Yeats, a ray from the red star had pierced your ear, although you didn't know it then; but you began to feel its stirring stab before you went away and left us lonely; left the land barren of a life anyway equal to your own.

The Committee of the Garrick Club, in British kindliness of heart, made Sean an honorary member for a few weeks till he had settled down. Fagan towed him into it. Full steam ahead, Fagan went forward everywhere, while Sean followed him like a dinghy tied to a ship's stern, till he began to feel that London was being hidden from him by the size and shadow of Fagan's big body. Some great man of the theatre, Bancroft by name, Fagan told Sean, had died on the day Sean entered, and, as a sign of grief, a great wreath of brass and silver-gilt, its brightness blasted by a big black bow, had been thrust forward for all members to see, and seeing, honour. Sean noticed that most of the members, when they passed by the silver and brass, gave a grin, ornamented with no reverential nod; and it seemed plain that the thing failed to reverently link the day of radium, of speed, of the golden bough, with the day of Dickens' mute and Mr. Mold. Bancroft? Who was he? Sean asked one or two of the members, but neither was eager to talk of the dead man, one of them murmuring that he had been a great actor in the days that were past. A dead actor down under the dusts of years ago. Sean had never heard of him before, and had never heard of him since. Bancroft's ghost would never appear in the mist of memories like the ghost of Macready, or Garrick's ghost, or Kean's either.

A big house kept the Garrick Club together; big, a little pompous, bubbling with dignity like a percolator. Balconies stretched their way along under the windows of the upper story, bulging out into a bigger one over the front door. But no page from England's shameful and gallant story was written on its façade for Sean to read; it didn't look like a bit of England at all. No sign here of Kelt, Saxon, Norman, or Dane. A pile of stone, mortar, and bricks that told a visitor nothing. No scent from Constable's cornfield; no smear of salt from England's surrounding sea; no beer-stained snatch from Bardolph or from Corporal Nym; no whiff from Hogarth's hellish Holland's gin; no wave from England's life lapped as far as even to the lowest step of the entrance of the Garrick Club.

The building was an imitation of another one, of something from another life, from another land. Not knowing much about architecture, Sean could but guess that it imitated something found in Italy. It had the look of a building taken out of a crowd of others over-populating Naples, or on the road to Rome. Latinity in the bowels of London. Latin buildings, Latin saints, Latin headings to the Psalms, Latin literature; Verjil for ever! The fountain-hid of culture. King Billy looking like a fat Caesar on a Romanly-caparisoned horse in a Dublin Street; a Latin horseman with Latin armour, sword, and shield, remembering the cavalrymen who fell in the first World War; Charles the bawdy put into Latin dress, with a Latin laurel crown shading the shocked swing of his face. The Roman finger is thicker than the Englishman's thigh. No sign anywhere here of the Trumpet Major, the Lincolnshire Poacher, or the Shropshire Lad. One would imagine that, in one way or another, every important building in London should whisper a word in every ear that this is England.

A very handsome place inside, spacious and well furnished. Attractive dining-room where a fine and well-cooked meal could be had for a very reasonable price; and well the room looked when it was serving the members, the white table-cloths half shy of coloured blossoms leaning over the rims of vases like wee fairy lassies watching from crystal windows and wondering at the life they saw around them.

Fagan introduced Sean to a number of the members. These bowed, murmuring something as loud as the tick of a watch in a leather-lined pocket; bowed and went their ways; forgotten: all but two, a playwright and a play-critic — Arthur Pinero and James Agate, standing, polished and prim on the dining-room floor, with Fagan courtesying before them and waving a consecrating mitt in the direction of Sean. Before coming to England, Sean had read, with a shock at the heart and head, a book, *The Old Drama and the New*, written and composed by William Archer, the drama critic, in which he had tossed the old, The Elizabethans, into the lowest circle of hell, and had exalted the new, Robertson, Pinero, Sutro, and others, into a higher heaven. This book was the first thing that cracked open Sean's belief in the London drama critics; for of them Archer was of the highest, and he had written the worst book on the theatre ever opened under the nose of man. And here was the dramatist whom Archer had lifted into a higher heaven than the higher one, swept and garnished for his imitators. Here was the hero of drama of whom Archer had written: *I re-read Pinero's plays with renewed and increased admiration. How insignificant are the blemishes upon the splendid series of comedies and dramas with which he has enriched our literature! If we had a rational system of repertory theatres, there are at least half a dozen of Sir Arthur's works that would be constantly before the public eye. When history views things in their just proportions, he will stand out as a great master of the essentials of drama. Sir Arthur Pinero, in spite of certain weaknesses, is an original dramatic genius.*

Jasus, boys, pause, now, to take breath. Sit down, sit down, golden lads and girls, and listen:

A remarkable fact is that some of the most highly esteemed dramatic criticism in the language has been written by men who had no clear conception — or perhaps a clear misconception — of the real nature of drama. Are there, I wonder, colour-blind painters and critics of painting? One is sometimes tempted, in these days, to answer the question in the affirmative; but I am sure they are not, and can never have been, so numerous as drama-blind dramatists and critics of drama.

All this was not written in a hurry. It was included in Lectures given at King's College by invitation of the London County Council, afterwards to be published in book form. So Archer must have read all he wrote a dozen times, slowly and carefully, taking thought for what he should set down in the permanency of a book. He had not to form an opinion and pour it out to harden in the pages of a journal between the descent of a curtain at eleven and the starting of a printing-press at twelve midnight. He had had time to carve it all out in the hardest of stone. And here it is, icebound, like a fossil dead for twenty thousand years.

So this was Pinero who was standing before Sean? How old-fashioned the little figure looked in its cut-away coat and dark-grey trousers; the expansive collar and the padded tie; the gleam of a watch-chain caressing as it crossed the neatly buttoned waistcoat; all setting off the timid face offering a look of pertness to the public gaze. Looking like something too long bedded in lavender, now sharing the scent of its withering with the figure it had tried to preserve. Another fossil, still above ground, and faintly visible in the light of the visiting moon.

A little aside stood James Agate, appraisement in his every glance at Pinero. No grace in this man, in build, in face, in raiment; no power either. Heavy, clumsy-looking, but with a cleared brow, like a refined son of a refined Caliban. A complexion like faintly-ruddied lard; smooth skull, with diminishing eyebrows, and a mouth lower at one end than the other; small eyes, having in them neither glint of humour nor gleam of passion. Everything heavy about the man: the head seeming to press heavily on the shoulders, the trunk on the legs, the legs on the ground, and even the clothes he wore — more modern than those of Pinero, and natty enough — seemed to ruffle stiffly when he moved, like a pliable suit of armour: the bulkiness was all.

Fagan had spoken a lot about Agate to Sean: the most important drama critic in the theatre world; most important to get him friendly; most important to humour him; to keep him well on your side; to let him have his way, even when he went against you. He could make or mar a playwright. Hannen Swaffer was next important. Hannen Swaffer, an haitch, an ay, an en, another en, an e, another en — Hannen. Looking at Agate, Sean thought he'd rather be marred by this man than made by him. If you can only get talking to Agate, went on the most important voice, and interest him, you're secure and settled for life. Especially if you know anything about ponies. The Savage Club is another haunt of his.

Sean would not grapple this fellow to him with any hook of steel, for if a good play wasn't enough for a drama critic then to hell with him. No, he wouldn't connect by a thread a button of his coat to any button on Agate's. A small man in spite of his bulkiness; a small inhabitant of a smaller world. Big and all as he was in corporal size and steaming reputation, he hadn't an arm long enough to encircle the waist or even the neck of life; his longer arm would but stretch round the neck of a bottle. Talk of ponies, and he'd give a good notice. Ponies! Sean wondered if these thick and clumsy legs had ever crossed the back of horse or mare; certainly they had never crossed the back of a Pegasus or a Pooka.

Crown the critic with cow-parsley who coolly wrote that the playwright had got to write for duffers. He had got to write down to the lowest common feeling of the crowd. The play, *The Silver King*, is the type of play best suited to a general audience. Shakespeare is only popular in the theatre because he deals with the same themes as *The Silver King*. Deals in the same themes — a fine phrase for Agate. Sign of the sunday times. As Agate was in the beginning, so he was to the end: the same today, yesterday, and tomorrow. Except for the greater plays, already half worn away from the touches of praise given through the years by others, which plays he praised because he could not else, he suited himself to those plays which caught at the hearts of the duffers and roused the lowest common feeling of the richer common crowds. He fought the bad fight, he kept his dim and dowdy faith free from any touch of a great morning or dreadful night of the drama. *De mal en pis.*

All in the Garrick Club was comfortable and some of it cosy; use was here and satisfaction. No complaints. All was attractive save one room, one room only — the library. Fagan wanted to look up dress designs for the period of his play, *And So To Bed*, so he gave warning to one of the staff that the library was to be prepared for a visit. Strange, thought Sean, that he had to warn the staff to prepare the library. Sean went with him and found that the library was kept locked till some member demanded an entry. They went in. There was a fire smouldering in the fireplace, 'to banish some of the dampness', Fagan said. 'The library isn't used a lot,' added Fagan; 'that's why it smells a little musty.' Musty — the library! It seemed to be a lovely library too, and Sean mooched around, pulling a book out here, pulling a book out there, till Fagan called him over to look at designs he had found in a book, full of the frills and furbelows decorating the boozy bodies of Charles the Second's aristocrats. What a fuss Fagan was making of his poor play. Silks, satins, velvets; specially painted scenery; viols da gamba, lutes, and harpsichords; even the very snuff-box used by Pepys himself, with Edmund Gwenn and Yvonne Arnaud to muster life from a moribund play. Mr. Pepys comes out of the Garrick Club and goes into the theatre. So Fagan gets the member of the staff again, the lights are turned out, and the door is locked till at some future time another playwright may seek a remedy from a book to render first aid to a dejected play. Gloom in the library and sweetness and light everywhere else. The playwrights separating themselves from life without and from the records of life within.

The members of the Garrick Club have shut themselves away too much, too securely, with their own beady baubles of treasure and thought; farther away from England than if they had been buried in a foreign land. Their minds are safely hidden away in their heads. A new life is needed. It will come when the doors swing open to hail the noisier entrance of Covent Garden porters, salesmen, and lorry drivers, who will add consequence of power to the dignity of the stately rooms from the vigour in the sons of the Lincolnshire Poacher, the Trumpet Major, and the Shropshire Lad; who will shake open the musty library into lasting readiness to serve the seeker after rare things; who will, in the evening time, or during a leisure hour, stroll in to listen to human, homely talks about how England builded her honours of song, story, picture, fane, and cosy homestead in the past, and of all, or some of, the schemes in the mind of scientist, thinker, and artist, to weave and build from these a finer form and a higher glory. Mr. Churchill and Marshal Montgomery say a lot now about 'the English way of life'. Well, let it be an English way of life: the way of Purcell, Constable, Darwin, Shakespeare, the morris dance, and Johnny, My Own True Love.

Perhaps those who shell themselves within the Garrick Club belong to a different pattern of life; a different pattern, perhaps, but the same thread woven from the same loom of life; and the pattern will cease to grow if they cut themselves off from the parent thread.

The arts have always lost something of their sap when they have been cut off from the people as a whole. The old culture came to a man at his work; it was not at the expense of life, but an exaltation of life itself; it came in at the eyes as some civic ceremony sailed along the streets, or as we arrayed ourselves before the looking-glass; or it came in at the ears in a song as we bent over the plough or the anvil. It is possible to speak the universal truths of human nature whether the speakers be peasants or wealthy men, for,

Love doth sing
As sweetly in a beggar as a king.

You never spoke a truer word, Yeats. Call up now to the tight-closed windows of the Garrick Club; call to England and the whole world; call with a loud voice, saying that you were often bewildered, that at times you buzzed about after vain things; but you believed; your ear caught the sounds of the people's cry, you heard their songs, and your heart replied fully, and your mind replied a lot.

THE SILVER TASSIE

SEAN stood in the office of a business man in whose fancy the sombre blackness of coal glittered more than the onyx, jasper, and chrysolite of heaven's architecture. It was a big, dull, thoughtless room, deprecating any emotion other than one connected with the sale of coal.

Hush! This room is sacred to the transubstantiation of coal into the shimmer of money. In front of a big, dusty window stood a wide table-desk of the dullest brown Sean had ever seen. It stood where it was, like a rock of ages, steadfast, and, apparently, immovable. No wisp of poetry, no wistful tinkle of a folk-song had ever entertained its lonely bulk. Ink, pens, blotting-paper, a ruler, and office writing-paper, each in its proper place, were piled on its pompous top, as if invoking animation out of the stillness, saying silently, Use us, and make the big desk hum. To tinge the common hue of business with the colour of art, two pictures of a costermonger and a costerwoman, by Jack Morrow, had been hung on the wall; badly done, they went on withering, colourless and cold, pictures that must have been dying while they were being painted. In a glass-doored bookcase, handy to the great desk, were two books on the value and quality of coal, flanked on one side by a huge brass-bound, brass-buckled family bible, intimating that with the things that belong to Caesar, the things belonging to God may be very near and very dear to the business man. Under all, a red and blue rubber carpet covered the floor, the red dull, the blue duller.

There the boss sat at his desk in a wide, leather-seated swivel-chair, a portly man as firm in his seat as the desk was on the floor. A large head, bald on the top, but sprayed at the sides and back with sturdy tufts of iron-grey hair. A broad, ruddy face like a big cheese turning rusty, with small, shrewd, beady eyes; eyes that were never dimmed for more than a moment or two by any thought of worry. A thick soft nose, and under it a broad, thick-lipped mouth, which laughed, or shouted vehemently, any reason for laughing or shouting invariably equalling the others in futility.

Knowing little of art, literature, or science; self-centred, not only in the earth, but in the very universe, he sat there, humming; yet possessing a charm and forcible personality that seemed clouded with a knowledge of all things; a friend of artists, with a charm that was irresistible in a restaurant at a luncheon, or sitting, sprawled before an intimate fire with a friend or two, or persuading a doubt-ful business man that his way was the best way; a volatile mind that could gather coloured thoughts round trivial things, and present them to any company ordered into the frame of a confused and hilarious picture: a molten mass of brazen energy without a hope of taking an ordered form. A great soul lost in the flood of its own hilarity.

There he sat idle in his swivel-chair, a wide-brimmed black hat slung carelessly on the desk beside him; there he sat, a big, hooked pipe dangling from his red, fleshy lips, his stout, short fingers tapping out some inconstant, uneasy tune on the top of the hardwood desk.

He had nothing to do; the miners were on strike, and no coal crept up the river in big-bottomed barges to herald the income of heartening cheques in return for the toil of writing a letter after breakfast, one after lunch, and another before the office closed for the evening. The fires of the nation were going out: the big-topped desk could do no more.

Idly, the strong, fat fingers tapped the desk-top, and the thick, fleshy lips moved moodily to the humming of an air. Then the hum changed to a whistle, then words began to trickle through it to an air Sean had never heard before. He cocked an ear to listen; the words came huskily to his ear, uttered thoughtlessly, unemotionally by the moody crooner:

> *Gae fetch to me a pint o' wine,*
> *An' full it in a sulver tossie;*
> *That I may drink before I gae*
> *A service tae my bonnie lossie.*

—Ay, Sean, me lad, it's a woefu' state o' things: th' flooers o' th' forest are a' wede awa'. There isn't as much as a bean in th' locker, th' day.

> *But it's no' the roar of sea or shore*
> *Wad mak' me langer wish tae tarry;*
> *Nor shout o' war that's heard afar —*
> *It's leavin' thee, my bonnie lossie.*

Sean was startled. Aaron's rod had budded. A riotous and romantic song had drifted up from the solid rancour of the big, impassive desk, that was to hum in his mind for many months to come. He hummed it in his tiny flat in South Kensington; he hummed it in the dead of night, strolling down the Cromwell Road. He would give the title of the song to his next play. He would set down without malice or portly platitude the shattered enterprise of life to be endured by many of those who, not understanding the bloodied melody of war, went forth to fight, to die, or to return again with tarnished bodies and complaining minds. He would show a wide expanse of war in the midst of timorous hope and overweening fear; amidst a galaxy of guns; silently show the garlanded horror of war. However bright and haughty be the burning of a town; however majestic be the snapping thunder of the cannon-fire, the consummation is the ruin of an ordered, sheltering city, with the odious figure of war astride the tumbled buildings, sniffing up the evil smell of the burning ashes. The ruin, the squeal of the mangled, the softening moan of the badly rended are horrible, be the battle just or unjust; be the fighters striving for the good or manifesting faith in evil.

And he would do it in a new way. There was no importance in trying to do the same thing again, letting the second play imitate the first, and the third the second. He wanted a change from what the Irish critics had called burlesque, photographic realism, or slices of life, though the manner and method of two of the plays were as realistic as the scents stealing from a gaudy bunch of blossoms.

He was working on the last act when Mr. Lennox Robinson suddenly paid a visit to his flat in South Kensington. Not to linger, he said, but just to ask about the new play. There were rumours in Dublin that the play wouldn't be given to the Abbey Theatre. The rumours aren't true? You will give the play? Oh, that will be joyful! Yeats and I were sure the rumours were false. No, I can't stay for a cup of tea. Just called because of the silly rumours in Dublin that your play would not be given to the Abbey. Mr. Robinson held out an aesthetic, tentative hand. Goodbye, Sean. Sorry I can't stay; so glad you'll give your play to us; and off he went to the air, it seemed to Sean, of *Danny Boy*.

Rumours? Sean couldn't believe it. If there were, surely he would have got letters asking if they were true, and he hadn't received a line. He was puzzled. The Abbey seemed to be eager to get the play; he was eager to give it, and so all was peace. He calculated the play would run in the Abbey for at least three weeks, maybe four, and the royalties he'd get would about cover the expenses of the birth of his child. Oh, that would be joyful, too!

Later on, while a play of his was running in the London Court Theatre, and Sean was in the office chatting about the poor houses, the Commissionaire came in to say that there was a bloke called Yeats outside who wanted to see him. Before he had ended the sentence, the stately figure of the poet stepped in as if it was marching to the tune of *Old Comrades*. He would sit down only for a moment. No, wouldn't take a whiskey and soda — doctor's orders. The company in the play were good, very good. He came to ask O'Casey if he intended to give his new play to the Abbey. Rumours in Dublin said O'Casey had decided to ignore the Abbey, which would be a pity. O'Casey had come to the Abbey when he had been most needed, and a refusal of the new play would cause irritation. The rumours untrue? O'Casey will give the new play? Oh, that will be joyful! He could assure the other Directors that the Abbey would get the play. No, he couldn't stay longer. Friends were waiting. Goodbye; and the great man stepped out as if marching to the tune of *Your Tiny Hand is Frozen*.

Sean had promised the first glimpse of the play to Sir Barry Jackson, had sent him the manuscript, and had forgotten about it. Then one day Sir Barry came bustling into the house when he and Eileen were busy trying to make the debts they owed meet and marry the money they had in hand. Sir Barry was in a hurry, a panting hurry; he sat down on a chair in a hurry, first setting down a burnished bowler hat on the table in a hurry, and arranging a pompous-looking umbrella to a stately stand in a corner in a hurry too.

—You've written a fine play, he said; a terrible play! An impossible play for me. I dare not put it on — an English audience couldn't stand it. There's the script. I'm grateful to you for letting me read it. His hand shot out for the burnished bowler hat. I must go now. The play would lacerate our feelings; it would be unbearable. Goodbye; and he hurried out to his waiting car, and vanished: a plain man in a plain van rushing from life. The next morning, the plain van slid up to the door, and the plain man slid into the house, and hurried to the stately umbrella still standing in the corner. My umbrella — I forgot it yesterday; and the plain man vanished into the plain van again, and Sean saw him no more.

With, in some ways, a difficult cast, Raymond Massey, the producer, had a hard task with a most difficult play. He had never seen in the theatre before a scene like the second act; neither had Sean, so he could be of no help to the producer. But Massey's strange patience, his skill and experience, came to his aid, so that the second act, helped hugely by Augustus John's serenely-coloured church window and sinister, savage gun, stood out oddly, eerily, and effectively, throwing confusion and some panic into the minds of most of London's drama critics. Over all and through all went C. B. Cochran's quiet, strange, and mysterious influence. So dapper; so pompously simple in his way of walking; so unassuming in his way of talking that few would say There goes a Man of the Theatre. But there he was, a Man of the Theatre from the sole of his small foot to the dignified crown of his bowler hat. Every glance of his discerning eye; every sound in his eager ear; every word from his firm mouth; every gesture of his hand, had something to do with the theatre; the greatest supervisor, most imaginative and courageous man, of things low and things high in the English theatre An England consciously thinking the theatre more than the life or death of a sparrow would have made Cochran independent of the Backer. Had this man had a theatre and no necessity to coax the coming of coins into the box-office, out of a few mistakes would have risen pride, elegance, and fun, making the English theatre of today share the glory and gusto of the theatre in the generous days

of Shakespeare and his comrades. The Clowns were always on one
side of Cochran, the Tragedians on the other, and he had the
imaginative eye and cunning hand to weave lovely patterns round
the pair of them.

On account of the child's size, the doctor in charge of Sean's wife
decided, after consultation with a colleague, by an operation to make
the birth immediate; so, to be out of the way, Sean was packed off to
spend the night with a friend. The next morning, a telephone call
told him a big boy had been born, and that Eileen was eager to show
it to him. He hurried off, opened the door of the house in Woronzow
Road, entered the hall, and saw a large envelope from the Abbey
Theatre lying *solus* on a table; too big to hold an advisal of a coming
production He opened it, and read the letter from Lady Gregory
and the letter of condemnation, peppered with pompous advice,
from Yeats. Curse o' God on them! His anger grew at every line he
read.

He went upstairs, saw his wife, congratulated her on the birth of
her big boy, looked at the laddo, touched his cheek, and said
nothing about the play's rejection. He would have to wait till she
was safe; till she was up and about; and then he would send a salvo
of words that would shake the doors of the Abbey and rattle the
windows.

He read the letters again: the one from Yeats was the one to be
answered. Sean could not but believe that the play's rejection had
been decided upon before the play had been sent. To answer Yeats
would be a dangerous thing to do. Yeats in his greatness had influence everywhere, and the world of literature bowed before him. But
answered he must be, and answered he would be, even though the
strife meant the end of Sean. His mind tore through the letter again.

*The most considerate thing for us to do is to suggest that he with-
draw the play. My letter gives an opinion, doesn't absolutely reject.
He could withdraw the play 'for revision' and let that be known to the
Press. He should say that he himself had become dissatisfied and had
written to ask it back. If he disagrees with our opinions as to its merits,
he can wait a little, and offer it to some London Manager. If the
London Manager accepts, then our opinion of the play won't matter to
him at all. Or, on the other hand, if no Manager accepts, or if he
doesn't offer it there, he can keep it by him, revising, or not revising,
as he pleases. I want to get out of the difficulty of the paragraphs in
the Press saying that the play has been offered to us* (and hard both
you and Mr. Lennox Robinson asked that it should be offered to

you. S. O'C.). *I have not told anyone what I think of the play, and I will get Lennox not to give his opinion. You have, perhaps, already written to Casey* [sic]*, but even if you have, I should like you to write making this suggestion.*

This to Lady Gregory and then to Sean. Obviously, Yeats was sure Sean would shake at the knees when he got this opinion; would hasten to sit down and write for the play back; would light a fire with it the first thing the following morning. Would he? He thought and thought it out: He was fenced in with money anxieties; he had now a wife and a child to guard and keep, and a rented house which needed many things more before it could become a home. Indeed, but for what his wife had brought into it from her own flat, there would have been barely enough in it to suit himself. Before they were married, she had sublet her flat; had got no rent from the tenants; and only by last-minute efforts did she manage to get her belongings back again. When he and she had come to the house they were in now, the sitting-room had had but a carpet on the centre of the floor, with a broad border around it varnished by Eileen herself; one chair, John's pictures, one of a Gitana, the other of Sean himself; a coal-scuttle and fire-irons; so that, while he sat on the floor before the fire, she sat on the chair, and wept. But not for long: they soon saw the grim humour of it, and laughed merrily over the barren way the room looked. The little they had was oozing away; now, since the child had come, what was left would depart in a steady stream; and, if *The Silver Tassie* didn't bring in enough for a further year's life, then the nights would be full of anxiety's light and the days would be gloomy and glum. Still, he had been in worse circumstances before, and had come out of them. But then he had been alone — his mother didn't count, for she had the faculty of being able to live on air, and laugh. Yeats's rejection of the play was a blow on the heart.

Casey could write for the play, and say he wanted it for revision — that was the meanest moment in the letter of Yeats. It was a bitter suggestion, and made him live with anger for a long time to come. A fight was the one honest way out of it. Almost all the literary grandees would, naturally, be on the side of Yeats, and most of the Press that mattered would, directly or indirectly, make a bow to his decision. This was inevitable because of Yeats's reputation as a literary genius; and what made it harder for Sean was that the reputation was a suitable crown for the man's achievement. But fight he should; and fight he would.

Well, here he was surrounded by Yeats's opinions. *You are not interested in the Great War; you never stood on its battlefields, never walked its hospitals, and so write out of your opinions. You illustrate those opinions by a series of almost unrelated scenes, as you might in a leading article.* Oh, God, here was a man who had never spoken to a Tommy in his life — bar Major Gregory; and to him only because he was an artist as well as a soldier — chattering about soldiers to one who had talked to them all; infantry, cavalry, and artillery; who knew most of the regimental marches; who, when a kid, had listened to them telling, in their halting way, stories about Canada, Hong Kong, India, Gibraltar, Malta, and the wilds of Shorncliffe Camp and Salisbury Plain. One who had known soldiers since he was a kid of six; whose uncle had been wounded on the field of Balaclava; whose brother had gone through the Boer War in the Dublin Fusiliers; whose elder brother had worn the khaki in the first World War; who had walked with the Tommies, had chatted with them, had sung songs with them in the hospitals of St. Vincent and of Richmond; who had followed the Great War from its first declaration, through the Russian Revolution, to its final end by the surrender of Germany. And now he was being told by one who wouldn't know a Life Guard red from a Horse Guard blue, that he wasn't interested, directly or indirectly, in the Great War! *Not interested* to one who had talked and walked and smoked and sung with the blue-suited, wounded men fresh from the front; to one who had been among the armless, the legless, the blind, the gassed, and the shell-shocked!

Among the things that dramatic action must burn up are the author's opinions. Do you suppose for one moment that Shakespeare educated Hamlet and Lear by telling them what he thought and believed? As I see it, Hamlet and Lear educated Shakespeare, and I have no doubt that in the process of that education he found out that he was altogether a different man to what he thought himself, and had altogether different beliefs. D'ye tell me that, now, Mr. Yeats? Well, I don't know; but one thing's certain, and that is if Shakespeare became a more educated man while writing *Hamlet*, then it wasn't Hamlet who educated him, but Shakespeare who educated himself. But what proof — beyond an opinion — has Yeats that what he says was so? As he sees it — of course; but it doesn't necessarily follow that everyone, or anyone, will see it the same way. A man altogether different, with altogether different beliefs when he'd finished the play from what he had been before he started! Here, the poet is suggesting, or trumpeting, the opinion that he was as intimate with Shakespeare as he was with the number on his own hall-door. There are as many opinions about the character of Hamlet as there are lines in the play. Even Shakespeare wasn't sure himself, for we are told: 'The variations of an early copy from the play of *Hamlet* in its improved state, are too numerous and striking to admit a doubt of the play having been subsequently revised, amplified, and altered by the poet'. Of one thing we can be certain, namely, that what Shakespeare makes Hamlet say was not what the living Prince would, or could, have said, but what Shakespeare wanted him to say; that the play is largely a biography of Shakespeare's thoughts.

Sean carried the letters of Yeats to Macmillan's. He presented them to Mr. Daniel Macmillan, remarking that if the firm wished, after reading them, he would allow the contract to be withdrawn. Mr. Daniel read the correspondence through. He handed it back to Sean, saying, This is, of course, a matter between Mr. Yeats and you. It does not concern us. We do not agree with the criticism. We think the play worth publication, and we will publish it. We make our own decisions, and this controversy cannot alter our intentions.

Very kind, very manly, and very encouraging to Sean, for he had had a half fear that the criticism from Yeats might check, might even prevent, the play's publication. This was his first victory over the potent, almost impregnable, influence of Yeats. So he hied himself off to C. B. Cochran, and put the correspondence before him. Beyond saying to Sean that he should never have given another party the option of a production while the play was under consideration by a London Manager, Cochran was undisturbed. Sean was taken aback by Cochran's indifference to the denunciation of the play by Yeats; for denunciation it was rather than a criticism. But the two decisions — Macmillan's to publish the play, Cochran's to produce it defended the flanks of Sean's effort. Had Macmillan's withdrawn from their promise of publication; had Cochran decided to abandon production, then Sean's defence of the dramatist's right to experiment would have been a hard one indeed. It was very curious, this rejection of the new play, for Yeats had known it wouldn't be done in the old way. In the Court Theatre, Sean had told him it would be different from what had gone before; that the second act would be an impression of the World War, and that the play would be written in a new manner; but Yeats had made no comments on Sean's rapid and excited account of the new idea: he sat silent there, listening. Yet during his stay in London, at that very time, Yeats, speaking before the Irish Literary Society, had enthusiastically mentioned the receipt of a play from a young dramatist which contained the promise of a new idea in Irish drama. The first act showed a group of young men making bombs in an underground cellar. They had been confined to this work and to this room for a long time, Yeats said, and the act was an expressionistic effort to show the psychological reaction of these young men to their peculiar circumstances. He went on to say that this act foreshadowed a new direction in Irish drama, and regretted that the rest of the play had been very bad; adding that O'Casey had built the bridge across which the coming Irish dramatists would pass to a new technique and a new art. But the poet had, apparently, waxed faint and furious to find that the first dramatist to cross the bridge was the dramatist who had, according to Mr. Yeats, built the bridge himself. It was very curious. Though the play might not be what Sean thought it, it was far above three-fourths of the plays appearing on the Abbey stage, and it stood up, fearless and steady, to the higher standard of the theatre.

Sean sent the letters written by Yeats, with his own replies, to St. John Ervine, who sent them to *The Observer*; and to A. E. for publication in his *The Irish Statesman*. The first journal published them; but a letter came sailing over the sea from the lordly A. E. saying that he wouldn't, couldn't, and shouldn't publish the correspondence in his journal for fear of a possible action for breach of copyright. Brother Yeats taking an action for breach of copyright against Brother A. E.! It didn't make sense. The man who had sung about 'the golden heresy of truth' was hedging. A few days later the Irish Press informed the world and Sean that Dr. Yeats declared a serious breach of copyright had been committed by the publication of the correspondence, and he was about to take legal action through the Society of Authors. So Sean got another letter from A. E. saying, Aha, I told you so! All Sean could do was to write to the Press to say that he was indifferent to the threat, even if Dr. Yeats decided to lay the dispute before the League of Nations.

The dispute, fostered delightedly by most of the Irish Press, jumped over to the English Press, wafted itself across the Atlantic, and spread excitedly over American papers, big and small; while many European journals carried the story further, and tossed the names of Yeats and O'Casey into minds which had never bothered about them before, and would hardly ever bother about them again, many of the comments showing Sean that the name and reputation of Yeats were much more important than his arguments.

One dignified Irish paper opposed the coloured clamour. Spraying itself with the hood of literature over one shoulder, and that of civil law over the other, the *Irish Times*, accompanied by the Borris-in Ossory Thing at Arms, hastened first to the pinnacle of Christ Church Cathedral, and then to the entablature of the Bank of Ireland, where, after the Thing at Arms had blown a funfare, she proclaimed to the listening ears of Ireland, the following proclamation: Whereas the essential feature of the correspondence about O'Casey's play is its portentous gravity; whereas Yeats and O'Casey discuss the play as if its goodness or badness really were a matter of vast importance, showing that they are unable to grasp two facts: Nobody in this generation — certainly not O'Casey — has written, nor is likely to write, immortal literature. O'Casey's two acted plays are good and striking plays, but no better than a thousand that have been forgotten. If they survive for fifty years, they will survive not as plays but as historical documents.

So the manicured hand, in a kid glove, of the *Irish Times*, tossed the controversy in her waste-paper basket, and turned to better things — the church services, the racing lists for the Derby, the differences between De Valera and Cosgrave, and the price of fat cattle.

It was very important to Sean, touching the security of his life, his wife's, and the kid's in the cradle in the room beyond him. They were all depending on what the play would bring in to allow them to live decently for one more year. The first honest home he had ever had, simple as it was, stood silent and shaking. The previous ones had been dens to eat in, to sleep in agitation, tormented with flea and bug; raucously restive, dark, menacing, and ugly, save where the glow from his mother's life made them bearable and good. His life pressed more heavily on him than ever, for his anxiety was threefold now — for himself, for his wife, newly fledged with mother-hood, and the babe, newly fledged with life. The play was very important to him.

Some months ago Lady Gregory had written to say how glad she was to hear he had a little house and little garden of his own; and how pleasant it would be for him there, to sit in the sun among the flowers. The flowers! Sean hopping and happy among the holly-hocks. The syringa tree was wearing its bridal-robe of snowy blossoms, and the lilac her purple gown of modest royalty; the pansies were tumbling out in groups, brown and blue, white and speckled; and the little lawn — about as big as the floor-space of his last tenement room — looked green and buoyant. But there was no peace among them for him. Even the rose of Sharon or the lily of the valley would be no solace to him now. He could eat no pleasant bread amid their scents, among their coloured blossoms. Their ways were ways of pleasantness no longer.

While clenching his spirit into the fight against the Abbey Theatre's determination to stereotype a writer's manner and style, and, through them, to fight the wider literary influence of those who believed that at the name of Yeats every knee should bow, Sean received unexpected reinforcement from the mind of Bernard Shaw. Out of Passfield, where the great man was staying with the Webbs, came a fiery letter, saying: *My dear Sean, what a hell of a play! I wonder how it will hit the public. Of course the Abbey should have produced it, as Starkie rightly says — whether it liked it or not. But the people who knew your uncle when you were a child (so to speak) always want to correct your exercises; and this was what disabled the usually competent Yeats and Lady Gregory. Still it is surprising they fired so very wide, considering their marksmanship. . . .*

If Yeats had said 'It's too savage; I can't stand it', he would have been in order. . . . Yeats himself, with all his extraordinary cleverness and subtlety, which comes out when you give him up as a hopeless fool, and (in this case) deserts him when you expect him to be equal to the occasion, is not a man of this world; and when you hurl an enormous chunk of it at him, he dodges it, small blame to him. However we can talk over it when we meet. Cheerio, Titan.—G.B.S.

But although Bernard Shaw stood by his side, Mrs. Shaw tried to prevail upon him to restore the sword to the scabbard. On her pressing invitation, Sean and Eileen went to Whitehall Court on the 21st of June 1928 to have lunch with her and her husband, so that, Mrs. Shaw wrote, 'they might talk freely (about our friends? — No — about the play!)'. Over a charming lunch Sean soon discovered that the ray of support from G. B. S. was being deflected away from his conception of the scurvy way the Abbey had handled his work to the ending of the dispute; towards the silencing of Sean; and towards soft persuasion to be used on Yeats to induce him to change his mind, and allow a production of the play in the Abbey. From doctor and saint he heard great argument about it and about: but evermore came out by the same door as in he went. Through the delicate fume of the conversation, Eileen's silvery voice suggested the compromise of Sean submitting any further letters to Shaw, who, if he disapproved of a paragraph or sentence, could edit it into a more suitable and tactful expression. Mrs. Shaw vigorously applauded the idea, G. B. S. approved, and Sean sat silent. Mrs. Shaw and her husband would come to lunch with the O'Caseys in a couple of days to push the plan further ahead. Some days after, a letter came from Mrs. Shaw to Eileen to say they couldn't come to the O'Caseys because they were *Just starting off abroad for a holiday and have got so terribly tied up with all the silly odds and ends we have to get done before we go. We have taken our sleepers for Sunday, and are remaining in Passfield till Thursday. Then there will be an orgy of business and packing!*

I am the more sorry for this as I do feel Sean wants a lot of looking after just now. He is going to be very naughty and fierce and resentful — and he is a terribly hard hitter!

That idea of getting G. B. S. to see his letters to his 'friends' is a grand one. Do keep him up to it. Any letters addressed to 4 Whitehall Court will be forwarded at once, and I will send you an address the moment we are settled, and Sean must write about all he is doing, and G. B. S. will answer quickly, and try to act as a lightning conductor! Directly we come back, we will go to lunch with you, and see Breon, if you will ask us again. Yeats didn't come to see us about the play, but about the Irish Literary Academy they are trying to get up. He never mentioned The Silver Tassie. *It was I who insisted on talking about it, and he was rattled, self-conscious, and reluctant! Our very kindest and most friendly thoughts to you both.—C. F. Shaw.*

Well, so near, so bad. Sean couldn't welcome this kind of help. He had no wish to have his letters edited, even by such a man as Shaw. Yeats had hit as hard as he could, and Sean wasn't inclined to hold his punches. He had refused the counsel of Uncle Yeats, and he had no intention of taking the counsel of Auntie Shaw. He would fight alone; one alone and not a second. He would fence in his own sour way, thrust, parry, and cut with his own blade of argument, in his own way, not according to rules perfumed with the stale musk of custom; but according to the measure of his own heart, the rhythm of his own mind, logical now, savage and sudden a moment after: in this fight, he would face any opponent, and thrust straight at the side where the heart lay.

But Mrs. Shaw, in her heart, resented Sean's independent critical outcry, and remembered it against him.

THE FRIGGIN FROGS

WATCHED by Mrs. Yeats, helped by the sun of South Europe, Yeats was spared for another spell with Time. Mrs. Yeats still held death away from him; and the summer saw him again in Dublin; heard his voice in the Senate; and his hand, less vigorous now, still held the Abbey Theatre back from falling flat before the cleric and the clown. Sunning himself in his charming little house in Rathfarnham, in the midst of wife and children, the poet lingered in a quietness he had rarely known before; for even in the stilly nooks of Coole's gardens, roused only with rustling of linnets' wings, Yeats had always been agitated in the explanation of mysteries his own ruffling mind imagined, shaping them into living shadows following where he went.

Coming to Ireland for a brief visit on money gained out of New York's production of *Within the Gates*, Sean had got a kindly letter asking him to come to lunch and spend afternoon and evening with Yeats in Riversdale. He crossed a plankway, forming a bridge over a little brook, and came to the house to be received with a quiet, gracious welcome from Mrs. Yeats, who left him to chat with the poet for a few minutes before lunch. Again they talked of the Abbey: how tiresome the customary Abbey play was becoming; how the Theatre needed new life through a newer type of play; and how several new Directors had been added to the Board to create a richer variety of opinion; but Sean's grouping of thoughts about the Theatre, past and present, were rudely scattered by a vehement and sudden remark from Yeats.

—O'Casey, he said, bending towards him, you've succeeded in your last play, *Within the Gates*. The co-ordination of mood, dialogue, and technique there is a success, where, I think, it is a failure in your *The Silver Tassie*.

—Oh, thought Sean, forcing his thoughts on to what Yeats had said so suddenly, *The Silver Tassie* is still in his mind. He's excusing the rejection of one play by his praise of another. Aloud, he said, Do you really believe, Mr. Yeats, that *Within the Gates* is a successful achievement?

—I do, he said, emphatically; I believe it to be a most successful achievement in your newer manner.

—I wish to God I could believe it too! came from Sean in a burst of frank fervency; and he was amused at the signs of hesitation surprise, and doubt that flooded into the poet's expressive face. Sean learned then that Yeats wanted the Abbey to do *Within the Gates*. He objected. He wouldn't refuse, but set out the difficulties of production by the Abbey company, and showed the poet that the Abbey stage would never accommodate the play's action. Besides, the play was clumsy in parts, and, some day, he would try to amend it. He made it clear that never again would he send a play to the Abbey; but that the Abbey was always welcome to do any play of his they wished to do. He suggested *The Silver Tassie*, a play far easier to put on the Abbey stage; that Yeats could have the other, if he insisted; but that *The Silver Tassie* was a far easier venture. The poet was silent for a few moments, and then said he would put the question before the Directorate.

After lunch, a young and vigorous man, Captain McManus, of the Free State Army, came on an evening visit. Yeats at once proposed a game of croquet. Yeats, by far the best player, his daughter, next best player, on one side; McManus, a fair player, and Sean, no damn good at all, since he had never seen a croquet ground, much more played a match, on the other. Sean heard Yeats murmuring to McManus that he could show O'Casey how to play as the game went on; but, in spite of efforts towards tuition, O'Casey did very badly, and the poet and Anne won by a very large margin. Yeats was elated, McManus a little crestfallen, O'Casey glad to get in out of the sharp wind blowing from the Dublin Mountains, but a few feet away from the croquet pitch; though, when she had seen him shiver, Mrs. Yeats had thoughtfully made him wear his overcoat. His first and last game of croquet. A game in which Yeats played like a champion. The only game of croquet Sean had ever played; the only one he would ever play, played with the poet Yeats.

Sean noticed how stiffly Yeats slid into the comfortable chair by the cosy fire. He was bright, though, and aimed at gaiety; had he nested sooner here and longer, letting restlessness ooze out of him, he'd have had a chance of a longer life. He couldn't, for there was in Yeats an irresistible leaven of childlike desire for glitter in imagination and masqued activity. He loved to *pace upon the battlements and stare on the foundations of a house*. The battlements, the battlements of a tower; the winding stair to the same battlements, with Sato's gift, a changeless sword on a table, forged before Chaucer saw the light o' day; and the poet's crook o' th' knee to an old and gallant ancestry. There he was, ailing, but in his insight still declaiming:

I declare this tower is my symbol; I declare
This winding, gyring, spiring treadmill of a stair is my ancestral stair;
That Goldsmith and the Dean, Berkeley and Burke have travelled there,
Swift beating on his breast in sibylline frenzy blind

Signs and symbols! Seeking substance from shadows, shining or shrieking. The poet had played with his toys too long. Aristocratic toys, self-fashioned; a few coloured with a wild philosophy, all tinged with beauty, some even with a gracious grandeur; but he had played with them all too long. More than half of life had passed him by while he was unsheathing and sheathing Sato's sword, staring over decaying battlements, or restamping out a dim impression of a long-forgotten ancestral crest. Young mortality. Ancestry had long since lost its handfast hold of man's mind. Man was no longer bothering to claim big house or battlemented castle, but was claiming the whole earth for his ancestry. Yeats was tired, and so the morioned head, the sword at hip, the spurred heel, had given place to the soft slipper, the comfortable chair, and the cosy fire.

But the poet, when he wished, with a light spring could jump down from the battlements to the earth again. The bold Yeats! Here he was now, talking laughingly about the censorship. In the beginning when Yeats and the intellectuals saw censorship was bound to come, they planned how to make it ineffective. Before a book could be banned, the Censorship Board had to come to a unanimous decision that the bloody book deserved it. The cunning mind of Yeats moved that a protestant clergyman be included on the Board, Yeats and the intellectuals feeling certain that a protestant divine would, *pro natura antagonisticeomnibus*, oppose any opinion expressed by the catholic members of the Board. They were wrong: any incautious mention of a girl's gown, or any whisper of a crack in the concrete solidarity of a creed, caused the reverend gent to close his eyes, tap the table, and cry hem! He was worse than any of the others.

—An odd man, thought Sean. No; let Yeats try ever so hard, he could never have been an aristocrat. With his castle, his crested spoons, his sword of Sato, he was no more an ancestral aristocrat than James Joyce; or even than Fluther Good when Fluther was singing his song about *The Wedding o' Glencree*. The poet was too passionate. Too dispersed in thought. The bigger weakness of Yeats was that he could never hammer his thoughts into any harmony of unity. Joyce did; Yeats couldn't. Image after image did a ballet-dance in his mind; when he chose one as perfection, he lost it among the other dancing images, and when he found it again, he saw that it had changed into another form and a different fantasy. And yet he could stamp on the earth as firmly and as rudely as any Joyce could. He was one who could sail for a year and a day in an argosy, and then go for a voyage of a week in a tramp steamer. Born into the proletariat, Yeats would have made a magnificent docker.

When the evening had dwindled into a darkening dusk, Sean bade farewell to the poet; an affectionate farewell, with a tight grip of clasped hands.

Some time after Sean's return to London, the Abbey Theatre produced his *The Silver Tassie*, seven years after it had seen the lights o' London. When it appeared, Joyce's terrible clap of thunder, that frightened the primitive man into frenzy, shot into the startled ears of Eireann; and all Eire's sacred frogs began to croak, Brékkek Kékkek Kékkek Kékkek Kóax Kóax Kóax! A reverend member of the Dominican Order had issued a premature warning in a semi-canonical proclamation, saying: *There have been tentative announcements in the Press recently of the forthcoming production of* The Silver Tassie *by the Abbey Theatre. The Abbey once rejected this play to which it now offers the hospitality of its boards. Dublin is to have the opportunity of drinking deep* (Drinking, drinking, drinkinkin, ing, inking!) *from* The Silver Tassie. *I fancy Dublin is a little too wise in nineteen hundred and thirty-five to put its lips to a cup that possibly may have been filled from a sewer.* (Guinness is good for you.) *The Play has been published, and is in our hands for cold inspection. It defies analysis. It is a vigorous medley of lust and hatred and vulgarity. I have no hope of conveying any adequate idea of its deliberate indecency and its mean mocking challenge to the Christian Faith. The fracas over* The Playboy *was but a flash in the pan, a child's cracker, in comparison with the hostility with which the Abbey is confronted if it persists in defying Catholic principle and flouting that reticence which is characteristic of our people. Plain etiquette will not tolerate horror, indecency, or blasphemy, on or off the stage.*

Sublime is the warning, so, quick! we have but a second! Here's a hot inspection for you, from a truly, ruly, reverend gentleman too. Here's one destined to drive out the indecency of poverty, the blasphemy of disease, the dull despair of dirt, the horror of war, with the midget-magical sword of Plain Etiquette. Stainless steel. Drive these things from the Abbey stage as a preliminary, and then drive them hellter-skelter out of the world: One, two, three — go! Hearseman, pass by!

But the heated hostility, desired by the cleric and sedulously prophesied by him, made no appearance to disturb the production. The Reverend Gentleman had a quiet guard; not a mouse stirring. But there was a commotion within the theatre, behind the scenes. One of the Directors got the shock of his life. He came rushing out of the theatre, horrified that such a thing could be. The ripe ribaldry of O'Casey's play was a severe shock to his finer feeling. He exclaimed to all that he felt an outrage had been committed. Two of them now fierce in the fight: the cleric and the Theatre Director, layman, — to God and Ireland true. Two true now. The Director, in a burst of holy indignation, told O'Casey where to get off, for he was keen and tempered to uphold *Catholic cleanliness and wholesome entertainment in a theatre which our Catholic Government is subsidising. Insane admiration here, and the half-witted culture of New York and London's admiration for O'Casey's vulgar and worthless plays, where they are always failures, filling O'Casey full of a fantastic opinion of his own importance, though he is best at his gutter level in controversy with Mr. Yeats, who has replied, after silently enduring years of the foulest abuse, with this gesture which forces our audience to endure* The Silver Tassie, *even though it was only for a week.* He sought out those in authority, and demanded that all the impudent, naughty words be cut out of the play, for, as he says, *The onus lay upon the other Directors and the Producer to respect the suggestion I had made about the cutting of the play, and act accordingly. Their duty was clear, and I did not wish to be unduly insistent in pointing it out to them further. At the same time, I did not altogether leave out of consideration what I felt must be the reactions of the players to the offensive portions of the play; but since the publication of my statement, Mr. F. J. McCormick has made an explanation on behalf of the players that these reactions were such as might have been expected, and that he, himself, were he a free agent, would not, as a Catholic, have appeared in the play. On Friday last, I expressed my regrets to the players that my statement should have involved them, and I now take the opportunity of saying that I wholeheartedly accept Mr. McCormick's explanation. I felt it necessary to explain that some steps had been taken to mitigate the offence of the production so that it might not be taken as a lasting disgrace to the Abbey Theatre.*

Get out the harp, Pat, and play. The catholic Harp, man. We're all pupae in the Papal flag. Let me alone, though I know you won't,

I know you won't; let me alone, though I know you won't, impudent Jimmy O'Dea!

But, whisper again, boys and girls, whisper: While eager to cut things out of O'Casey's play, he didn't like the same thing happening to his own. Oh, no, boys and girls. Earlier on, he had complained to the Abbey Directorate that actors were leaving out words from authors' plays, as was explained by the Theatre's Secretary reporting to the Press that 'Owing to representations made by the Director at a Board meeting, instructions were issued to the Company that no word must be left out, no sentence changed during a performance'. It is usual, when cuts are thought to be desirable, to ask the author about them; but here was the lad bouncing about demanding cuts without even letting O'Casey know that such a thing was in his mind.

Reinforcements were hurried up to the Director. The Irish Press, secular and sacerdotal, bawled a blast on the play. *The Cross*, magazine of the Passionists, hands on hips, declared, *It is a poisonous draught from a dirty cup. There was a time when the Dublin men had the courage of their convictions, and were not afraid to make effective protest against anything that outraged their feelings. In these good old days, as anyone familiar with the history of the Abbey Theatre can recall* (out in the dear, dead days beyond recall!), *there was a famous week when riots took place every night during an offensive performance, and five hundred police were needed to keep order in the Theatre and its vicinity. But times have changed, and O'Casey's* The Silver Tassie, *with its dreary monotony of blasphemy, vulgarity, and filth, passed off quietly without the need to call in one single officer of the law to preserve order. We have no hope of arousing the decadent Directorate of the Abbey Theatre to a sense of its public duty. But the Abbey audience that could contentedly sit through such a performance is certainly worthy of examination. What witless fools are in our midst, that could sit, open-mouthed and empty-headed, and gape at the guttersnipe's rhapsody presented on the stage for their delectation! The people that could applaud such blatant blasphemy had not even enough intelligence to see that they were throwing bouquets at one who was dragging them down with him to wallow in the mire.*

Well, boys and girls, what do you think of that delectable denunciation by a Father of the Passionist Order, a Brother of St. Paul of the Cross? And a Scholar too, for he is the Editor of the magnificent magazine; a learned man; a Doniel come to judgement. How genteel and reticent the comments are. Sparkling with the divine courtliness of the St. Paul of the Cross community. Deeply disappointed, too, that disorders hadn't afflicted the performances. Delicate detonations of phrase worthy to be framed and placed on the white walls of the Marian League of Art.

Here is the report from *The Irish Catholic*, full of a pure and holy purpose: *If* The Silver Tassie *withstands the test of fire to which it has been subjected within the last ten days* (ten days that shook the world), *then, though it would not thereby be proved genuine silver, the base metal of which it is composed is at least equivalent to asbestos. Personally we believe that the effect of the flood of correspondence will be the exclusion for all time from the boards of any Irish theatre of Mr. O'Casey's precious production. Galway and the Catholic Young Men's Societies have been in the forefront in bringing about this highly desirable result. The bitterness of the atheist heart is seen by the judicious in all that Mr. O'Casey has got put upon the boards — it gives its repulsive and morbid tang to whatever comes from his dramatic pen. Those who relish the rank sort of fare that Mr. O'Casey provides ought to be denied by law the opportunity of indulging their debased tastes.*

Let us take a thimbleful of stimulant now as a sursum cordial against the effects of these blows from Balaam, by quoting the famous American drama critic, George Jean Nathan: *If* The Silver Tassie *with all its admitted deficiencies is not one of the most honorable experiments, then I am not the man to have been engaged to write this foreword.*

Another holy snarler, *The Standard*, otherwise *The Eagle*, came out like this: *It was a revolting production in which the Church was mocked, the name of God insulted, immorality flaunted as a matter of course, and the foulest language of the gutter used before audiences overwhelmingly Catholic. As a play — though this seems beside the point now — the production is mere trash. Nothing even remotely approaching the dirtiness and stupidity of this wretched attempt at drama would be permitted to be shown on the screen. This play gives us a golden opportunity of improving our stage, and of reconsidering the value of our literary heroes who have been set up for our admiration. Mr. W. B. Yeats is no literary leader for a Catholic country.* (Remember Parnell!). *No matter to what poetic heights he may soar, he will never lift us to the heights to which we aspire.* The eagle's whistle! Excelsior!

Cu Uladh, President of the Gaelic League (the one who, when the Treaty was signed, rushed out to hang a notice on the railings outside his office thanking God, in pitiable Irish, for the sake of freedom;

then, when De Valera disavowed the Treaty, rushed out to bring his blessing in again), came out with *The Abbey Theatre at its worst, which seems to be at the present moment, is intolerable and must be swept aside. I have not seen, thank God, this latest horror, but I remember some years ago going to see* The Plough and the Stars, *and having to leave before the second act from a fit of nausea.* And this *item indignatio* adorned himself with the title of Ulster's Hound, the title of Cuchulann, greatest hero of the Red Branch Knights. Sean could only murmur, as big Joe Brady, the Irish Invincible, murmured on his way to the scaffold, Poor oul' Ireland, poor oul' Ireland!

The crinolined, Roman Catholic *Tablet* ventured out with no direct opinion about the play. Sitting safe among her cushions, perfume on one side of her, smelling-salts on the other, she gracefully fluttered her fin, snowy-white, streaked with yellow, and simpered, in reply to a question put by a reader, *To this inquiry we cannot make an answer worth having; because we have neither seen O'Casey's play nor read it in print.* The Silver Tassie *is known to us only by what we have heard and read about it. While refusing to give a critical opinion of our own, we are at least entitled to say that Irish Catholics, both priests and laymen, for whose honesty and intelligence we have deep respect, deplore O'Casey's play, not only in itself, but as a very blatant sign of a very evil tendency in Irish dramatic circles. Mr. Louis J. Walsh has a strong article about this tendency in the October number of the Irish* Rosary. *He thinks that the temptation for an author to write down to what he regards as Abbey standards is tremendous for a poor or over-ambitious man; and he believes that there is a definite malignity in the whole Abbey outlook.*

Louis J. Walsh! Well, he wasn't poor, but he was ambitious. A competent solicitor, but an incredibly bad playwright. The title of one of his plays alone sounds his requiem: *The Pope in Killybuck.* Walsh had sent it to Sean for commendation, with a letter gleefully adding that he had modified it when it went north so that it might meet a welcome in protestant Ulster. The play was too bad to bother about, so Sean sent it back, but kept the letter, which frightened Walsh because of what he had said in it, so that he demanded it back. Give me back, give me back what I wrote unto you, for what I have written I have not written. A nest of frightened people. Fear and a sly expediency are the immoral fibres spreading viciously through Ireland's soul.

A roman catholic secular paper, *The Evening Herald,* had a leading article about the production. The article was headed by the notification of The Feast of the Day — the Beheading of John the Baptist. Holy humbug hanging on to God. It said, *It is strange that the severe criticisms which appeared in the Dublin Press (before production) of this play were not sufficient to satisfy the producers of the utter unsuitability of this blasphemous and sordid play. It is time a check was put to such productions that appeal to morbid minds.*

Brékkek Kékkek Kékkek Kékkek Kóax Kóax Kóax. Croak away! In the midst of the frogs, one blackbird whistled a melody for Sean. One Roman Catholic, Robert Speaight, the prominent English actor, in a letter to the Press, denounced the attack saying, *The play is an outcry from a passionate and embittered mind. But it is much nearer to Christianity, because it is nearer to life, than the complacent criticisms levelled against it. The soul of the bourgeoisie has betrayed itself. This surely is the essence of the bourgeois mind — that it cannot look tragedy in the face; for O'Casey has seen into the heart of the horror of war, and wrenched out its dreadful secret; that the co-heirs with Christ destroy one another in the sight of the Son of Man.*

Sean sauntered away from the frogs, getting away from their croaking to busy himself with other work. He would forget them for a time — the journals, the bawling priests, the shouting members of the Catholic Young Men's Societies, the very wise and stout-hearted defender of decent literature, including Shakespeare, of course, Dr. J. Murphy, representing the University of Galway grey (representing the same community, oddly enough, long after and later on, when the poet Yeats was finally laid to rest within the reach of the strong arms of famed Ben Bulben). Let them all alone for the present. Like Graham Greene's Father Rank, in *The Heart of the Matter*, they didn't quite like observant men. They saw too much, and what they saw, they saw too clearly; and when they saw, they said. And that doesn't please the papal priest or the papal bishop, as Dr. McDonald saw so clear and said so promptly. The day of blinkered blessedness was nearly over. God is numbering them off on the rosary of the years. The light of other days is light no longer.

Twelve years later, *The Silver Tassie* was performed for two crowded weeks in the Gaiety Theatre, the largest one Dublin has in her pocket; and, throughout the performances, not a word was spoken, not a drum hit, not an ecclesiastical curse was uttered by sunray, lampglow, or candlelight. The holy hibernians were hibernating. The play could rest in peace now.

But no! Nearly two years later, Sean gets a letter from Mr. Ward

Costello, an ariman in the last World War, now a student of drama at Yale University, Connecticut. He wrote to say that he had defended O'Casey during an attack made upon him in a lecture given by Mr. Lennox Robinson to the University's students of drama, with Marc Connolly in the Chair. The young student asked Mr. Robinson 'if *The Silver Tassie*, since it had not been produced by Yeats because of his prejudice, had been produced, or considered for production, since his death?' And 'Mr. Robinson had answered with a flat "no", adding that it was a bad play; even though Lady Gregory had changed her mind about it'. The old lady had said Yes, when the Huntingdons brought her to see the London production of the play.

Perhaps this was the last stroke of the bell tolling for the demise of the play? But no: *The Silver Tassie* is dead, but the damned thing won't lie down. This very month of October, nineteen hundred and fifty-one, a revival of the play in the Queen's Theatre by the Abbey brought on more thunderclaps of resentment. Miles na gCopaleen, in *The Irish Times*, quotes the critic of *The Evening Herald* as saying, 'It's a poor play The second act, set in the trenches [by the way, the scene is Not set in the trenches, but behind them; the trenches are out on the horizon, as the script plainly says: but this is but a minor part of an Irish critic's splendid critical equipment], finds O'Casey having a shot at expressionism — and in the process being weird, vague, and lamentably wide of the mark. For the majority of play-goers this act is in exceeding bad taste. The litany to the gun is the crowning piece of offensiveness.' Bring out the hackbut and battle-brand! Miles na gCopaleen, after the sermon, gives the priestly curse: 'In the Queen's Theatre, the Abbey makes its début with as loathsome and offensive a "play" that has ever disgraced the Dublin boards. The second act is a perfectly plain, straightforward travesty of Catholic Church ritual. The rest is bunkum and drool.' The toll has changed into a tocsin!

The Irish critics have made all the use they could of the Abbey's first rejection of the play, and have pursued it with curious and persistent hatred; but it still refuses to lie down. Peace, be still, heart of O'Casey: It is only Ireland that abuses the play now. Everywhere else, the play has been accepted as a fine and courageous experiment in modern drama, and only the other day the drama critic of *The Times Literary Supplement* said of this very play, this very act, 'If the voluble rapscallions of Dublin tenement life are unforgettable, so, too, is the pre-presentment in universal terms of the horror of war in the expressionistic act of *The Silver Tassie*'; an opinion oddly different from that of J. J. F. of *The Evening Herald*. For reasons too short to explain, Sean preferred to embrace the opinion of the English *Literary Supplement* rather than that of the Irish journal.

But Yeats was stretched out, alone and motionless, in a grave, thrust away in a farther corner of France. The battler was gone from the field. His bow was broken, and the scattered arrows lay where they had fallen; but

> *Here, perhaps, a hundred years away,*
> *Some hunter in day dreams or half asleep*
> *Will hear his arrows whizzing overhead,*
> *And catch the winding of a phantom horn.*

And, now, his young shield-bearer, F. R. Higgins, has followed him: the riverside is lonely, and the street where the Abbey is; the plains of Meath and the fields of Connacht lack a lover.

> *Cold, cold!*
> *Cold tonight is broad Moyburg.*
> *Higher the snow than the mountain-range,*
> *The deer cannot get at their food.*

The frogs were happier now; louder: Brékkek Kékkek Kékkek Kékkek Kóax Kóax Kóax.

FEATHERING HIS NEST

THE General Strike in 1926 had emptied the Fortune Theatre. The packed houses had given way to audiences of ten and eleven nightly; so Sean's first play was taken off, and the second one, *The Plough and the Stars*, was put into rehearsal, its first night to be given in the New Theatre. A few days before this, the young girl playing the part of Nora fell ill, and Fagan got another young Irish lass named Eileen Carey, who had been in the cast of *Rose Marie*, to take on the part. She came to settle the arrangement while Sean was in the Theatre's office, talking to Fagan. In she came, neatly and delightfully dressed, and a lovely lass she was; a very lovely lass. Sean's Irish eye was as keen in the choice of a pretty lass as the American eye of George Jean Nathan, so he stood staring at her for a long time. He had rarely seen a lovelier face or figure anywhere in this world, and didn't expect to find anything better in the delectable world to come. She was nervous; Sean saw she was sensitive, for the talk about wages embarrassed her, so he helped by demanding that she get the same as had been given to the girl whose place she had taken — for Fagan had offered her five pounds a week less, reproaching Sean when she had gone for adding to the expenses of the production. But Sean was well pleased to be of service to such a delightful girl whose voice was clear and musical and whose bright eyes betrayed a natural but hidden intelligence.

The poor girl accepted an almost impossible job, for the rest of the company were now perfect in part, movement, and position, while she had to begin, teasing them and silently asking them to show her the way through the play. And scant sympathy and little help she got from them in her efforts to come level with their knowledge and experience of the play. Had Sean had then the knowledge he acquired afterwards, he would never have allowed the young lass to undertake the uncongenial and thankless task; but she bore it all patiently and doggedly, and played the part till the other young actress was fit enough to take it on again. There was, too, an affinity of race between Sean and her, for she was as Irish as the heather on Howth Hill. But there was nothing in her of Harry Lauder's Scotch Bluebell, and, indeed, Sean didn't believe there was such a lass in Scotland either, down in the Lowlands or up in the Highlands. He could see that she had many undeveloped gifts; that she was a fighter, that she was of the earth, knowing that there was a deep blue sky over it; that, though she was nervous now, and a little shyly hesitant, she had courage and a determined spirit, mingling with a true kindliness — gifts that can form, and be, only what we call the kingdom of heaven within us. And time has proved that he made a good guess. Emerson has said that a pretty face is a great gift to a woman, an attractive figure a greater one, and a charming manner the greatest of all; and when one gets these in a *trio juncta in uno*, then one has been promoted in life by the gods themselves; especially when their grandeur is subdued by a gloriously human sense of humour. There's nothing lovelier in life than a lively laugh. Eileen had faults; a lot less than he had himself, for these were many; but faults are trivial things in a nature worthy of all men to be accepted.

During a lot of this time the General Strike had spread itself all over England, and Sean had been amazed at its quietness. At first, he had thought, Now is the accepted time, now is the day of salvation; but no voice spoke, and quietness seemed to brood all over

England. Three million of men out on a militant strike, and it looked as if they had all gone to bed. He couldn't help comparing the dense quietude of this effort with the exhilarating uproar and daring intensity engendered in Dublin by the Lock-out of nineteen hundred and thirteen, when every worker was a warrior and any who blenched were banished from the fighting tribe. Everyone was in the struggle, from the Viceroy of Ireland to the raggedest urchin of the slums who had reached the years of talk and a prentice understanding of events. Then every vantage point had its machine-gun, and the Viceroy was praying to God for help.

The excitement, as far as Sean could see, was all on the side of those who wished to maim the strike; with those who had more than they needed, with those who depended on those who had more than they needed, and with those who depended on those who depended on those who had more than they needed. The Two Nations of England were lined up for war, the one against the other. *Two Nations: between whom there was no intercourse and no sympathy; who were as ignorant of each other's habits, thoughts, and feelings, as if they were dwellers in different zones, or inhabitants of different planets; who are formed by a different breeding, are fed by a different food, are ordered by different manners, and are not governed by the same laws —* THE RICH AND THE POOR; and Sean wondered if Disraeli had meant this when he set it down, and, if he were here now, would he get a Vavasour to lead his baronets, with their coronets of two gold balls, against this menace of men out to fight for the right to live; to fight the men wearing the Mons Star who were threatening the safety of the unearned incomes.

Those who had more than they needed suddenly displayed and paraded a remarkable burst of Christian charity and kindliness. They had cars, and they insisted in placing them at the services of those who preferred to walk. They slung placards on their windscreens saying, Ask me for a Lift, and were much upset and annoyed when a lift was refused. Young aristocrats and university men, oil-spattered and smoke-grimed, helped by soldiers, stood on the footplates of engines and tried to drive them hither and thither; and rushed here, rushed there, rushed everywhere to keep the essential services going; even the younger sons, who, as Disraeli says, *Should be the natural friends of the people, though they are generally enlisted against them. The more fools they; to devote their energies to the maintenance of a system which is founded on selfishness and which leads to fraud; and of which they are the first victims.* So the eldest sons stood with the fathers and the young sons stood with their elders to oppose the menacing workers who had spread a pall of quietude very like death over the whole land; revealing to all but themselves that without labour there can be no life.

All the Unions had been called out by the Labour Leaders in support of the miners; for by coming out to help a comrade, they had but come out to help themselves, and Jim Larkin's slogan flashed through Sean's mind, An injury to One is the concern of All. They silenced England that their voice might be heard and the needs of their wives and children known. As it had been, so it was still:

> The golf links lie so near the mill,
> That almost every day
> The labouring children can look out
> And see the men at play.

The strike began on May the 4th and ended on May the 13th, a nine days' wonder. The Trades Union leaders found fright in their hearts when the stillness began to brood over the land; they feared for the fat salaries their jobs gave them; they feared to lose the happy assimilation of friendship with those who had more than they needed; their wives had cast off the hodden grey and had put on fine linen and silk, and they had no desire to go back to the hodden grey again; and Sir John Simon, after a search through many old books of parchment, discovered that the strike was illegal. Parchment, sacramented with sealing-wax, declared against the workers. The leaders called the strike off; the men, all but the miners, went back beaten, and Sir John Simon put the precious parchment back into the safe again. So the homes fit for heroes to live in that had been bobbing up and down on the waves all round the coast, disappeared over the horizon; for it was all a mirage; and there never will be any houses fit for heroes or humans to live in till the heroes and humans build the houses themselves. The hour had not struck.

The miners held out, and Sean sent a subscription to their funds, with a message of a comrade's support of their fight, adding another to the man for Labour who stood for the workers' cause in the by-election of Leith. It was this support that first showed Sean that free thought didn't altogether go unchallenged, even in England. He received a rather indignant and advisory letter from William Blackwood, the great friend of Harry Lauder. William Blackwood was a prominent man in the Northcliffe publications, editor of *Answers*, and he had used every possible appeal to induce Sean to write an article for the periodical, but Sean wasn't interested enough in the publication to do it. An election took place in Leith, and Sean had sent a letter of courage and good hope to the Labour candidate. Some time after a letter came from Fleetway House, signed by Billy Blackwood, saying:

'What is this I hear about you? Namely, that you have been putting your name to election literature of the most seditious kind.

'I happen to mention the other day to a well-known literateur that I had the honour and pleasure of your friendship. He thereupon went off the deep end, cursing you loudly and bitterly for taking part in the recent Leith by-election, and allowing your name to go on some pamphlets which were distributed by the tens of thousands all over that section of my beloved land affected by the election. This morning he sends me a copy of the document, along with a note urging me in impassioned language to ask you to refrain in future from lending so distinguished a name as yours to the Anti-christs and Bolsheviks of Britain!!

'Joking apart, my own idea is that probably you never saw the document in question, and, in any event, I am not sufficient of a politician to be concerned by it either way. But I think seeing your name on such a virulent Red pamphlet has been rather a jolt to some of your literary and dramatic admirers.'

And Sean, thinking over it once only, sent something like the following:

'A leterateur, a literateur — what the hell's a literateur? How does it look? What does it eat? Where does it live? I know some of these "Literateurs" — nancy boys in art whose hands will never stretch to pluck bright honour from the pale-faced moon. . . . And they can go to hell, and tell them that from me. I know very little about politics, but enough to save me from the stupidities of the H. of Commons. As there are "tied houses" so there are tied men, and your literateur is probably one of them: a one whose humanity is as broad as the cheques he gets for the work he does. And he can go to hell, and tell him that from me. And I will probably go on jolting my literary and dramatic admirers; let them wash their own feet and comb their own hair, for they won't get me to do it.'

He had offended Fagan too. Fagan had given him the typescript of his play, *And So To Bed*, to read, and so Sean had, and had flung it aside on to a table, forgetting about it in the excitement of his lady's loveliness and the roar of London, blazoned with business; for he had become one more among the city's crowds rushing hither and thither, waiting at the crossings till the mighty surge of oncoming traffic, bullied by the big red buses, was suddenly stayed by the upraised hand, white-gloved, of a big policeman, who stood, or moved right and left, with a calmness astonishing in the midst of so many impatient, panting, go-ahead, on-ahead vehicles, crouching in alertness, waiting for the stately, white-gloved hand to come down, to shoot forward. So Sean watched, waited for the hand to go up, and, when it did, shot forward in the midst of the crowd to the other side of the street, separating to this side, or that, to allow an opposing crowd forging forward to get to the side of the street he had just abandoned. So he forgot the play.

The telephone rang at his flat, and Fagan's voice, a note of reproach in it, begged him to take a taxi, and bring down the play to his office at once. So Sean did, hurrying down with it, slapping it into Fagan's hand, and saying, jaunty with the sights and sounds pressing on him everywhere, and buoyant with ignorance, There it is, Jim, and don't waste my time any more by making me read such trivial plays. Fagan said nothing; silently told a stout, smiling man beside him who this excited fellow was; gave the play to him, and bid him a smiling goodbye. Then Fagan said quietly, You might have waited to say what you thought of the play till my friend had gone: that was Edmund Gwenn, who is to play the part of Pepys in my play, that was. Sean was thoughtless still. He had plagued Fagan in other ways, for Fagan had insisted on becoming his father and friend, watching over him, telling him what to do, where to go, whom to meet, till Sean was angry and resistant. He got a blank invoice from a Bond Street tailor, and, disguising his handwriting, had entered thereon a bill for a plum-coloured velvet jacket, black satin trousers, a yellow-flowered waistcoat, the lot costing seventy-five guineas, which he told Fagan he wanted to wear when he was going to answer evening invitations by personal presence, making the producer shake with nervousness that Sean would put him, with his ignorant, exhibitionist ways, to an open and a shut shame. Again, Sean bought a gaudy little watch for three shillings, got a plush case for it, and telling Fagan the price was twenty-five pounds, asked him very seriously to lock it in the theatre safe till he made up his mind as to whether or no he'd buy it. A few days later a bill for the amount came to the theatre demanding the twenty-five pounds without delay, or the immediate return of the watch. This Fagan had read, for the bill came unsealed, and he, immediately, without Sean's knowledge, returned the watch. When Sean learned of this, he became artificially angry, and demanded that Fagan should never interfere with his affairs again. Afterwards, the papers recorded that the dramatist, O'Casey, had bought a baby elephant, and was taking him out for walks in Hyde Park; so Fagan got frightened, and left Sean alone, asking him no more to meet particular friends, or to come to his flat for a meal. So now Sean could sit on his own chair, and eat at his own table, and look about for a friend or two of his own choice. Yet Jim Fagan meant well; he was gentle — a little too gentle — and he had a very kind nature.

So, surrounded by these things and many more, Eileen and Sean went on building a nest. They entered a little three-storied house, including a basement, used as a dining-room because it was near to the kitchen, when the streets were knee-deep in snow. It was a simple Georgian house, one of a long terrace, with two decent rooms, a tiny bathroom, and a huge kitchen, with an old-fashioned range in it big enough to do as an altar for Stonehenge. And, by God, it burned the coal as fast as one could shovel it in, but took its time to heat the water. There was an oven in it would roast half an ox, my ox, your ox, his ox, her ox; but you would have to put a turkey into it on the very first of January if you wanted it cooked for Christmas. Going down the basement stairs, one had to hold tight and pray fervently to prevent a broken neck. After a short time in residence it was found that the tank holding the household water leaked badly, and, when examined, it was seen that the tank had been stuffed in many places with rags to keep the bulk of the water from flooding the whole locality. But these things took time to discover, and, first, the home had to be furnished. They were, he and Eileen, full of the necessity to make the home comfortable, bright, and original. It was delightful and easy to picture it as they thought it should be. They would search for cretonne, for prints, for chinaware, for curtain-stuff, for chairs, tables, and divans till they saw what their hearts desired and their minds understood to be suitable. Life was singing a song in their hearts. They spent days in Heal's and holidays in the print shops of Charing Cross Road. They were for ever handling things they couldn't buy. Lifting lovely things, then hurrying away when told the price of them. The house had been taken on a lease which swallowed nine-tenths of what they had had. Now they were discovering that the house demanded more, for a new tank had to be bought, the roof had to be repaired, a man had to be employed, according to the lease, to keep the little garden in order, the house had to be kept insured; again, by order of the lease, old pipes had to be stripped from the outer walls, and new ones put

in their place; and Sean began to wonder if he would have enough
money left even to buy spoons for the two of them. Jasus, it wasn't
half as easy as it had looked!

But they had to do something; so they hurried off, hurried to
Harrod's, buying there a fender, fire-irons, a polished-steel bucket in
which to put coal, an oak chest for linen, and a hearth-brush with a
brass back. Leaving the chest behind, they carried all the other
treasures back in a taxi. When they had settled the things in the big
front room, they looked around, and saw on the floor a square of
brown carpet, meeting a wide frame of stained flooring, for their
money didn't allow them to carpet the room to the walls, the stained
margins and the empty room making the carpet shrink to a smaller
size; a single armchair by the fire and curtains on the big window,
and that was all — a bare room, looking like a native, naked but for
a loin-cloth; a room declaring an imminent departure rather than a
hurried entry; and Eileen, after a glance around, plumped into the
chair, and wept. But not for long: shortly after, the room's repellent
glare changed to a comic look of an appeal for help, and Eileen and
he laughed loud and long, saving themselves from the folly of self-
pity.

Eileen had let her flat before meeting Sean, and they were now
waiting for her furniture to set the home fair for living in, for he
had but a few things, mostly books, which wouldn't even furnish a
decent room for his own use. She had got no rent from the tenants,
and couldn't get any reply from them when she asked them to return
the furniture she needed herself so badly now. By a lucky chance,
she managed to get the key as they were about to flit to another
place; but she found the furniture in a woeful state, for they had
planked hot saucepans on divans, carpets, and chairs; the carpets
were torn and stained, and the kitchen-ware had never been cleaned
from the day Eileen had handed over to them. It was all very
vexatious and discouraging, but a great many things were salvaged,
lovely things in mahogany, fine cutlery, much linen, and a beautiful
Bechstein piano; so Sean, in the end, found himself in intimate
touch with a few of the elegant things of life. To this very day, he
doesn't know what they'd have done had not Eileen brought as her
dowry the furniture of her four-roomed flat. With all my worldly
goods I thee endow; an easy endowment, indeed, for all he had
were two pictures, a chair, a desk kept together by the mercy of
God, a cheap divan, a crowd of books, a spoon, knife and fork, a
kettle, teapot, and a few articles of delfware. But they were kept

going to supply the bare essentials, ekeing out payments with the few royalties he got now and again for performances of his plays. None of the fitments of either flat, his or hers, would suit the requirements of the house they now had. To supplement the hot-water system, they installed a gas geyser to help the panting, gurgling pipes coming from the range, which were choked, and now almost useless. The geyser was easy to work (so it was said), a thing that a child could use; foolproof (so it was said). Eileen strolled to the sparkling copper geyser to sample its first bath, while Sean chatted by the fire with a friend, Billy McElroy, roguish, bombastic, laughable, and a wonderful personality. The two of them heard things hissing, the hissing changing to a dull thump at times; but they put no pass on it. Then Eileen came in to say she couldn't get the geyser to work. Sean looked it over, tried to light the jets, but, after a long effort, gave it up. He told Eileen that she must forgo the bath for that night, and returned to his friend by the fire. Suddenly, the whole house rocked to a foul explosion, fretted by the mocking tinkle of breaking glass, and from the noise's centre came a frightened scream from Eileen. She had managed to get the geyser to work. Sean ran to the bathroom — Eileen was staggering about, moaning that the child within her had been killed. The bathroom window, frame and all, had been lifted clean out of the wall, and now lay shattered down in the street below. Sean got Eileen stretched out on the bed, and, rushing to the telephone to summon a doctor, he saw his friend tiptoeing down the stairs, saw him placing his big-brimmed black hat quickly on his head; saw him open the door softly and close it quietly after him as he hurried away home. But Eileen was none the worse for the accident, beyond a few weeks of anxiety about her baby and unpleasant buzzing in her head; but the restoration of the window made quite a hole in the little pile of money remaining, for neither Eileen nor he even guessed that they might have claimed the cost of replacement and of the doctor's fee against the incompetent, and even dangerous, fixing of the geyser. Eileen had come out of it unhurt, and what claim could thankfulness have against anyone?

The little house was one of two stuck together, as if the one couldn't stand alone; so were they all on their side of the road, each a clump of two joined together with a space of little more than four feet between each clump, the back gardens hemmed into their own privacy by low walls. A small garden, its length three times that of its width; in the centre a narrow strip of grass that residents called a lawn, surrounded by a border holding flowers, dominated by a

graceful white syringa, a fragrant lilac bush, and a delightful labur-
num. Eileen and he had bought prints of pictures by Van Gogh,
Utrillo, Renoir, Manet, and Segonzac. Eileen had framed the
pictures in her own way, refusing to make use of the conventional
gilt frames. She had narrow frames made to tone with the chief
colours in the prints so that, when the pictures had been hung on the
walls, they looked like coloured panels which formed decorative
parts of the walls themselves. And she dispersed them in a new way.
She didn't hang them so that a big one took the centre flanked by
smaller ones at either side. A big one might be closer to one side
than the other, and a smaller one would flank it far away on the
opposite side, but not on the same level. Between them, not in the
centre, but nearer the smaller one, would be a vase of blossoms; and
well the gay simplicity looked, forming an added picture of harmony
and divided lines to the coloured dignity of the pictures.

The only gilt frame in any room was the dark gold one surrounding John's beautiful *Head of a Gitana*, one of the loveliest expressions
of graceful delight in paint Sean had ever seen. Taking lunch with
Augustus John in a restaurant in Chelsea while the artist's exhibition
was on in a gallery opposite, Sean had shyly and timidly offered John
a tenth of what he had for a picture, for all of them as marked were
wildly above anything Sean dare chance. Without a word, Augustus
John had written a note to the manager of the exhibition directing
him to give Mr. O'Casey any picture he might choose; so Sean had
run straight over to the gallery, had made his choice, and had been
rewarded by John saying, when he saw it, You made a good choice,
Sean. So he had, and the picture is still the O'Casey centred jewel
hanging upon the wall. Supplementing this treasure was the royal
portrait that John did of Sean himself, in blue-green coat, silver-
grey sweater, with a gayer note given by an orange handkerchief
flowing from the breast-pocket of the coat; the face set determinedly
in contemplation of things seen and heard, the body shrinking back
tight to the back of the chair, as if to get farther away to see and hear
more clearly; a sensitive and severe countenance with incisive lines
of humour braiding the tightly-closed mouth — a princely gift from
a great artist and a most generous man.

But when all had been done, when the simple, little house had
begun to look fine, like a quakeress wearing a bright bandeau round
her head and a daring locket on her bosom, they discovered that the
district was a very expensive one to live in. They knew nothing, or
next to nothing, about marketing or about the domestic ways of

life, and had to learn by rough and punishing experience. Piously and vehemently, Eileen and he, now and again, hurried off to do the marketing in Kilburn, but the strain of the journey and the burden of hiking back all they bought, impaired their ardour, and so they plunged again into the dearer market of their own district, and the flabby little bag of money at the bank became far flabbier still. Then their first baby's birth had been a costly affair, the doctor taking fifty pounds, plus the cost of a nurse who stayed with them for six weeks. When he remembered what it cost a woman to have a kid in the tenements, he realised more fully than ever the terrible difference between one birth and another. And the Income Tax Collector, a kindly man, was coming to the house on the track of fifty pounds owed to the Revenue, which sum Sean hadn't got, but which the Collector thought must be found somewhere. Sean had tried to interest the kindly man in the bees in the garden, but the Collector didn't care about bees. He said he didn't know a thing about bees; how they lived, or how they were brought up, or a ha'porth. He knew a bee could sting a man, but that was about all. He was glad to hear that they were so useful to man in the pollination of flowers, a thing he hadn't known before. He knew, of course, that bees were thrifty things, laying up a store for a rainy day, and so a lesson to us all. He had other calls to make, but hoped he'd get the fifty pounds before the week-end, for he couldn't wait indefinitely, and went his way.

He got a letter from Lady Gregory saying how glad she was to hear he had a home of his own, with a garden too, a thing he would very much enjoy. Well, though he got in this home the rejection of *The Silver Tassie*, and all the anxiety and trouble that went with it, he had spent many enjoyable hours with the bees and the flowers, the only ones, bar those enjoyed during his days in Coole, he had ever been able to handle and watch without feeling they were not for him to pluck. He had had many still and happy hours with the spiders too, covering shrubs and bushes in the autumn with their beautifully balanced webs. He had wondered at the spider's speed, at its patience, waiting, sphinxlike, for the prey to come; at its frenzied haste, whenever a huge insect like a bee became enmeshed, to envelop it completely with silken threads, lest its frantic struggles should tear the web to pieces. Sean could never understand why some hated the spider. He knew one man who hated them so that he hunted them out, plucked them from their webs, and gloatingly plunged them into water to drown, or, if he could conveniently manage it, into hot water to be boiled; and, oddly enough, this man was a rabid pacificist; a conchie who had served a long time in jail rather than stick a needle into another man. He remembered how he himself had felt grieved in his heart when September's heavy rain ruined many of the lovely webs. Now he would have to go. He'd leave these things behind him. They'd have to sell the remainder of the lease, and live on what they got for another year. Looking at his bank book, he found that expenditure was two hundred and seventy-three pounds, against three hundred and twenty-nine pounds on the credit side, so that he had fifty-six pounds left to face the roll-call of payments which would be advancing on him soon. He'd have to sell out and go.

Yeats's denunciation of *The Silver Tassie* had done Sean's name a lot of violence. The Nobel Prize winner, the Leader of English literature, was a judge against whom there was no appeal for the time being. Sean's flying start had been rudely curtailed of its fair proportions, and he would have to start over again, and fight the battle anew. He would have to hand over his little grey house in the north-west to another. The sale to a Film Company of one of his plays had stayed the inevitable away for a few years. He had got a thousand pounds for it — six hundred down and four hundred in six months' time. One night of fierce wind and heavy snow, when the house shivered in the midst of the glow from all the fires they could afford to light, a Mr. Mycroft came driving up from Elstree to offer the money for the making of the film. Out of his speedy little car came Mycroft, covered with thick flaky snow, a genuine *deus ex machina* when funds were gone and hope was waning. Pressed to stay the night because of the fierce wind and the falling snow, Mycroft refused, anxious to get back to report that consent had been given, and that the Company could go on with its terrifying plunge into experimental art; so out and on Mycroft went through the fierce wind, under the falling snow, fervent as a dashing courier carrying home the news of a gallant victory against heavy odds. Hysterical vanity of film production, hasty excitement in the production of the theatre, like hungry hens rushing headlong for a handful of scattered corn. Hysteria in the production of a mediocre film, clownish excitement in the production of a mediocre play; the more mediocre the play, the greater the excitement; the more mediocre the film, the greater the hysteria.

But Sean found that a lot of the film money would have to go into preserving the sanctity of an original peppercorn lease, and keeping the house merry and bright for the present landlord. The Estate Surveyor, a Sir Someone or other, with his clerk, and the heir to the estate, came to check up on the state of the properties, and, in due time, came to where Eileen and Sean were finding it hard to live. Outside, round about, with a man to examine the roof, like druids in modern dress, the three of them circled, the clerk jotting down items at a whisper from Sir Someone; through room after room, the three of them marched, halted, looking up, looking down, looking round, the clerk again jotting down items in a notebook at a whisper from Sir Someone. When they came to Sean's room, they gave but a faint echo to his lusty good-morning; Sir Someone was quiet; the clerk quiet and deferential; the heir excited, thrusting his face forward towards Sir Someone to say, Quite a nice little property, sir, which caused the Sir Someone to quietly leave the room, possibly having caught a glimpse of Sean's sardonic grin as he watched the ritual.

Property is theft, said Proudhon, but he must have been doting. Property must add to righteousness, for it is supported and sanctified by bishop, priest, and deacon. Some talk of morality, and some talk of religion; but give me a snug little property, sang Maria Edgeworth; and she was right. This lad had a snug little property, and he was beaming. And Tennyson chorused:

> Dosn't thou 'ear my 'erse's legs,
> As they canters awaäy?
> Proputty, proputty, proputty — that's what
> I 'ears 'em saäy.

Even horses know the importance of property, so who was Sean to question the demand to fork out what he needed for himself and family, to plaster ceilings, pipe walls, repair roofs so that a nice little property of another might remain a nice little property still. But nice and all as it was, it would soon have to see the last of Sean and of those who were his.

From this nice little nest of property, so beloved by the heir who owned it, which had filched a lot from Sean's limited means, he had flown to two organised meals only: one, an Annual Dinner of the Critics' Circle; the other, a lunch given to Jim Brady, the celebrated New York Theatre man, by C. B. Cochran. And these two were quite enough for a lifetime. He had been selected by the critics to respond to the Toast of the Drama, and before the date fixed for the event he had had three different reminders not to forget to be in his place to respond when the toast was given. He was there all right, and, when the time came, spoke too damn wisely and too damn well. He criticised the critics for their jaunty adulation of trivial plays, the actors for their devotion to, and admiration of, their insignificant parts in these trivial plays, and the playwrights for writing down to the leading actors and actresses by scorching out of their work any good or important element in the secondary characters so that the part of leading lady or leading gentleman might add perceptibly to their own importance by the lessening of the importance given originally to the other characters circling around them. The speech didn't go down well, though it was politely honoured by a timid and hesitant handclap. But Sean was bucked up afterwards by the distinguished guest of the evening, Lord Cromer, telling him that it was easily the best speech of the evening. But the critics weren't at all pleased at having their colours lowered, even for a time, to a half-mast flutter; and so, signs on it, Sean has never had, for over twenty years, a whisper of an invitation to come within talking range of any annual gathering of these gentlemen: they didn't like the flash of criticism within the orbit of their own united circle of comment. Had Sean been less ignorant and innocent then than he became afterwards, he wouldn't have given 'the best speech of the evening'.

There was a big crowd of chaps only at the theatrical lunch given by that great man of the theatre, Cochran — St. John Ervine, Noel Coward, Archie Selwyn of New York, old Jim Brady, Branker, afterwards lost in a flaming dirigible, and many others. Sean never cared for stag parties, and it wasn't long till he was longing for the sight of a pretty face and the swish of a woman's skirt. Never to him could a place be comfortable or fully human without a woman. But here the stags, the men, felt free, and let themselves go. The silent censorship of delicate-minded woman was absent, and unfettered language flowed free from some of the mouths. It was romantic nonsense to imagine that women couldn't swear as well as a man. There was no docker of the tenements, no labourer of the slums, proficient in what is called vile talk, who couldn't find a woman his equal in the same tenement or the same slum. Old Brady made a speech that was lurid with the lightning of bad language. But it was stage lightning badly lit. The words were forced out of a pretended intimacy with profanity. They were not natural. The poor man didn't know how to use them, and so they sounded horrible in their deformed obscenity. There was no health in them. He should, before using them, have taken a long course of lessons from some lusty seaman, some ignorant navvy, some lowly docker. For the first time in his life Sean felt uncomfortable at the sound of bad language because it was unsound. The difference between it and that of a woman of the slums was that the old man's language made his blood go hot, while the language of a woman of the slums would have made his blood run cold. Neither was it the profanity which, in general circumstances, often gave off a glow, or a great humour. Cochran made a speech as neat, as orderly, and as respectable as his own appearance. A very good speech. A quiet man, Cochran. Under the neat quietness a deep well of artistic emotion. What a will he had for the theatre! But his way was blocked, turn him how he might. Had he had the way as well as the will, the last forty years of the English theatre would have been fretted with many stars. Well, these two feasts were a long way off now. The last glimpse of the luncheon which lingered in his memory was of Archie Selwyn, the New York producer, impressed mightily by the thought of Jack Buchanan and Evelyn Laye strutting majestically on a New York stage in *Bitter Sweet*, pacing up and down the room feverishly, exclaiming *Jack Buchanan and Evelyn Laye together; in the one show. My God, what a sensation!* He seemed to think that the combination would be so tremendous that God Himself would leave heaven to make a personal appearance among the audience.

Sean tried heavens hard to imagine *Bitter Sweet* to be a good and charming musical play, principally because his wife was acting a part in it, so presenting an importance to him another play of its kind could not have. The first night cost him thirty-four pounds, for Eileen sent tickets to many friends, anxious, of course, that the show should be received well, if not tumultuously. Sean went a second time with the doctor, Harold Waller, who had brought their first-born into the world, and who had become a great friend of the family. (Sean seemed to get on well with doctors. There was Dr. Cummins, of course, whose friendship he would remember to his dying day; again, Dr. McGuinness, who had attended him for bronchitis, and whom he met in London; Dr. Waller, who gave up a West End practice to be chief of a maternity hospital in Poplar, a son of the clergyman, Waller, who had been the friend of Livingstone; and Dr. Varian, of Totnes, a Dublin man and a fine fellow.) Dr. Waller, who knew a lot about it, thought the music bad, and Sean, try how he might to think the contrary, thought the wording worse. There seemed to be nothing in the first week's glow to predicate a success, but wizard Cochran worked a miracle, and by lusty nursing made of this poor thing a tremendous success for himself and for Mr. Coward.

They put off the day of decision, but they knew that the day was coming when they would have to leave the pleasant little house. He remembered how many good hours he had had with his boy, Breon, watching him begin to crawl on the grass, then make primitive and violent efforts to get to his feet, enacting over again man's first painful evolution from a four-footed animal; then the thrill of seeing the tiny boy plunge forward recklessly into the steps betokening the coming man who must stand alone and walk his own way through life; who had had his own birth, and would have his own development, his own sorrow and joy, his own wife and children, his own old age, and, finally, round it all off with a sleep. Many good hours had been spent in Regent's Park, but half an hour's stroll from the house, one side of the Park running round the Zoo, where wild horses could be seen in their paddock (though they looked very much like tame ones), and the wild goats jumping about on their rocky heights. At times, the air was made uneasy by the scream of a tiger or the roar of a lion.

Occasionally, half-way on to the Park, he turned into the church-yard of the parish church of St. John's Wood, opposite Lord's Cricket Ground, and sat him down to watch the nurses and nannies — too tired to go the further way to the Park — airing their bottoms on benches, a pram holding a baby beside them, and older charges, eminent in being fit to run, tearing about on scooters, or riding sedately on tricycles along the paths bordered by grass and measured by decaying tombstones that were frantically trying to keep their heads from sinking under the ground. Some of the sturdier young-sters, risking the fire of adventure, careered away on their tricycles to the uttermost ends of the churchyard, and, with toy pistol in hand, shot all who passed without the railings, and a few that ventured nearer within, returning to their nannies breathless with the risks they had taken and the difficulties they had overcome. Voyaging further into life among the dead. Here, indeed, were the quick and the dead. Near to each other, yet wide apart, but near enough. The graves had no meaning for the youngsters within, or for the hurrying citizens without. The ardent young ones blew their toy trumpets, shot their toy guns, careless of the rebuke of the silent dead. The living dust was vivid, asparkle, bounding about; the dead dust had ceased to shine, even in the memory of man. The dead thrust down here had been forgotten: they had died too far away in time for men to bother about them, for even the dead grow old. No stone should show where the deep dead lie.

Did Yeats ever chronicle himself as sitting and sounding out thoughts in a churchyard? Sean failed to think of any reference to such a crowded isolation. Death would have been too like death to him in a graveyard. And yet the explanation of it was here and it is that there is none; except that that one who has died ends his importance, while this one newly born begins it. If Yeats were passing by here now, even as those citizens hurrying along the street outside, he would act as they do, never turning a head to look within. They leave the buried dead to take care of themselves and answer their own questions. Not among the dead, but among the living, Yeats sought an answer to the riddle of death. Old mortality had no interest for the poet; he sought out the newer mortality within a room, having heavy curtains on the windows, making himself a part of a circle of clasped hands; the lights extinguished, the hymn sung, and a diamond-tipped pencil scratching out words upon a window-pane. But all he could gather from his quivering search as an answer was the echo of his own thoughts.

Sean's own sturdy lad was gallivanting about among the graves. He and his companions were making fun of death; playing tig around him; hide-and-seek between his legs; tiring him with their tireless movements, their present laughter, and their noisy cries. Death is helpless to prevent them; unable to force the sombreness of the scene before them. Life is too busy, too gay, to be bothering about bones hidden beneath the soil. *Weep, for ye are but mortal,* death tries to say, but he stands there mute. He is silenced by life. He is disregarded, pushed about, dishonoured in his own domain. He is as powerless as his own dead battalions. The little bugles blow the call of life, the little drums beat the march of life, and Death has to stand still and listen.

Yet for a little while longer, till sense and regard for life come creeping into the mind of the common man, Death, getting savage and resentful, may choke a little child with croup here; sling another under a swiftly moving car there; or thrust another little one, astray from her place of safety, under the slimy waters of a city canal; but young life in street, park, and playground laugh and mock him into quietness again. So there they go, dodging in and out among the dead, the tombstones thrusting themselves despairingly up to insinuate their importance to the notice of the passer-by, an identity and presence that have long since ceased to be. No name of a

chimney-sweeper on any tomb: all seemed to have lived and died in
good circumstances: golden lads and lasses all. Vanity of death, for
even the name-remembering stones are crumbling too. The dead
disappear from view; they fade from the memory of those who knew
them; from the memory of those who loved them; and when these
die too, the dead, who went from life before them, go from life
altogether.

What does the hurrying sun think of Yeats's eight and twenty
phases of the moon, the great Yeats, with some majesty even in his
medley? What do the dead here and the living beyond think of
Yeats's grouping and groping of life through various incarnations?
The poet, so restive against discipline concerning his own art and
thinking, would bring the whole universe within a discipline of his
own. He points a finger at the dead and shouts Come forth! But not
a mouse stirs. The laughing secular sun, the superstition-breeding
moon, the evening star, the bright and early morning star, and all
the graces and the airs within the universe, declare the monstrous
insignificance of the dead.

What did this old church here think of them? The old church of
either St. John who baptised towards repentance in the river Jordan,
or St. John who saw in Patmos a rabble of sights surmounting all
that Yeats himself saw in the room of the Golden Dawn. The church
probably never thought at all; it was beyond thinking, and it looked
to be ageing. It was trying to stand up and look important, but there
was an air of deep decline about it. Time and thought had made it
shabby. What did it stand for; what was it for; what did it do? It
seemed to be a sentry guarding the dead, but looked like a sentry
asleep at his post. Custom kept it standing; custom kept its door
open. It looked lonely, and seemed to be aware of its loneliness. Am
I nothing to all ye who pass by? Not much.

The day is long gone when what you wearily symbolise now was
the power of the city, of the whole land, of the whole known world:
faith unquestioned and power unchallenged were yours. When the
monks were masters. Monastery, nunnery, church, college, chantry,
and chapel watched over the land, and rooked it of all it had. The
Pope was Lord Mayor of every city and town in merrie England. To
please the people the Grey Friars came over in rags, and, on Corn-
hill, built themselves homes of clay and wattles made. They were
living as the followers of Christ should live, and the people were
delighted; but not for long: they soon moved into a monastery in
Newgate Street whose church was made of dressed stone, with a

nave three hundred feet long and sixty-four feet high, the friars
sitting down to tables of polished pine from which they took the
best the land could give, adding wine of the better vintage from the
lands where the good grapes grow; while Dick Whittington filled
out a fine library for them of fine books, which a few of them read.
Pile the weight of wealth and power and mighty buildings on top of
the grave of Jesus, driving him deeper down. All gone now, and
young lads of the Blue Coat School used to run and step and leap
over where the Grey Friars sleep as do the golden lads and girls in
this very churchyard of St. John's Wood.

England was made merrier with Austin Friars, Black Friars,
Canons Minor and Canons Regular, so that a buzzing swarm of busy
bedesmen turned the land into a realm of litanies and lice. And the
bells tuned them into time and authority. The bells bullied the people
about from the cradle to the grave. They belled the baby into the
world and belled the dying man out of it; they belled the bride to
her bed; they belled the workers to field and workshop, and belled
the time for him to straighten his back and give over for the day,
charging fees most of the time, according to the bigness of the bell
and the time he took in tolling.

This old church in St. John's Wood, this spare relic of a powerful,
busy past — how lonely it looked, and how shamefacedly it seemed
to be aware of its unlamented loneliness. Ichabod. Am I nothing to
all ye who pass by? Not much now. The Christians who have more
than they need, with those who depend on them, gathering crumbs,
have crucified Christ afresh, and have buried him down with the
dead men. You do not mean much to us now. We are busy with
other things. You have no bearing on our thoughts today. You
rarely had, except to frighten us with myth and legend. A meagre
myth by now. We know the herald angels didn't sing, and we are
not sure that Christ was born in Bethlehem. Some say he was. They
say: What is there for the man of today? Let us go even unto the
little town of Bethlehem. Who goes there? And what shall we find
when we get there, and how many want to go? Bethlehem is little
more than a little toy for Christmas now; brought into play for a
little hour, and put away again. Butlin's holiday camp is the popular
rendezvous now. Yeats would sail the seas to come to the holy city
of Byzantium. His holy city. Flecker would go the golden road to
Samarkand. His holy city. Eileen's is New York. And what was
Sean's? Moscow. Not a holy city, but an able one, a flame to light
the way of all men towards the people's ownership of the world;

where revolution stands in man's holy fire, as in the rich mosaic of a red wall. But he would not soon forget the lot he owed to London, or the warmth and good-fellowship of New York.

Well, for the moment, he'd have to bid goodbye to the vision of Yeats rushing round Ireland's market-place; his quick mounting of the political pulpit and the quicker dismounting of it; his divining the accurate way in which the Abbey Theatre ought to go; and his sudden rushes away from all to put an eye and an ear to the key-hole of the ivory door of death, to try to catch a glimpse and hear an odd sound of what was going on behind it. He'd have to leave his spiders, some of which he nearly knew by name, his charming little garden, and the pleasant district of St. John's Wood for some place they couldn't think of yet; not Rapallo or Capri or the Riviera; just some place out of London that might soften the worry of what they were going to do to make both ends meet. All the gallant recreation they had cadged from what they had had, was a few weeks' stay in a boarding-house at Margate.

Came a friend of theirs, whose daughter and her husband had held a cottage in Buckingham, and who had now abandoned it, to tell Eileen and Sean that they could have this wee house for as long as they liked to live in it. Another grand myth, lifting up his heart for a day, then sending it down deeper than ever for a year.

ROSE AND CROWN

SEAN was astonished to see the moon shining just as bright over London now as he had so often seen her shining over Dublin. So clear, so elegantly, too, that he almost thought she must have left Dublin, and all Ireland was a dark night now. But the rain fell here, on the evil and the good; the sun shone out on the just and the unjust English; the same blue sky tented London as once had tented Dublin; and, now, the same moon, so beloved of him in Ireland, shone silently and grand in the English night-sky. The English were known to God! But she did not shine quite so lovingly: when the moon shone over Dublin, a reverie could easily conjure all the wider scenes and all the famous forms of old long since into the streets again. Swift's fine face, furrowed with heaven's venom against ill things done, growled indignant with the earth beneath him as he ambled through Hoey's Court, or strode through the scaling streets home to Patrick Street; Emmet came thoughtfully out from Trinity College, his mind tense with the flaming idea of revolution; and Grattan slowly mounted the wide steps of the Parliament House, bent on delivering his nation from the cut-throat casuistry of Castle-reagh.

All the fame of Dublin City from the time the first worried warriors crossed the river at the Ford of the Hurdles, to the recent days when desperate Irishmen from corner, from pillar and post, sent shot after shot into the Black and Tans, can gather to pass by, or stop to talk in a corner of an Irishman's mind. But London was too barbarously outspread for the moon's magic to gather together in comfortable compass all the brave things done, and all the figures of fame that had given her high history and made the world wonder. The famous shadows in armour, in cuirass, in buff jerkin, in red coat and blue coat, in top-boots and knee-breeches, in top-hat and cut-away coat come into the glimpses of the moon, come here, come there, pause wistfully among the people, try to speak, but cannot; they remain hidden, for rare is the Englishman who has them memoried in his mind. A city set too wide apart to assemble them from one reverie in a single mind, linking the Roman to the Kelt, the Saxon to the Norman, the English unifying all, from the battles of Boadicea to the time of the flaming building, the toppling of the masonry, when the Fascist foe came to destroy, and found death waiting for him.

The moon of England now shone over the innocent elation of Stanley Baldwin, for the last election had proved to be a red-letter day for the Conservatives and their commercialised cronies. The Stock Exchange had hung out all their best banners, the Archbishop of Canterbury was quietly deleterious with joy, and the home of every company promoter, landlord, and tied tenant, had roses round its door. It was another restoration. The old order had the upper hand of the new. All right-minded persons declared that it had all been prophesied by the sages of auld lang syne. This was confirmed by many who had heard the lions roar round Trafalgar Square; by others who had seen the statue of Achilles in Hyde Park wave his sword, saying On, Stanley, on; by some who had seen and heard the granite gun of the Hyde Park Memorial go off with a real loud bang; and by one, a newly appointed clergyman, who said he had distinctly heard the statue of Prince Albert murmuring, most devoutly, Thank God, the Conservatives are in once more; once more in the dear homeland. There were, to be sure, Conservatives, bright in mind, young in heart, who, though they didn't yet believe that all things should become new, realised that a lot of old things must go; young Tories who had possessions, but were not bound to them, body and soul; who said God was speaking better than Baldwin; who heard the changes of Time chiming; and who carried the gonfalon of conscience into Conservatism's centre.

The Old Conservatives trotted into the House dancing, as they well might, led along by the sound of music from lutes, flutes, pandemonia, and euphoneya. All right-minded people, all honest folk, all God-fearing persons had been safely separated for ever from Bolshevism. Scudamour, Artegall, and Britomart were safe. Now they could light the lamps and leave their doors open. Conservative men could see clearly, feel fortunate, and speak freely; each Conservative lady could go forth with the walk of a queen. The Bolshevists could be left alone to slay themselves; to disentrail themselves; or, be left alone, with laughter, for each to exile all, or all to exile each to bitter cold and faraway Siberia. Soon, the men of gadsir behind Stanley Baldwin would hear the fall of a self-destroying Communism.

> As down the cliffe the wretched gyant tumbled;
> His battred ballaunces in peeces lay,
> His timbered bones all broken rudely rumbled,
> So was the high aspyring with huge ruine humbled.

It was odd that this stout, stolid man, sensible soul, thought his return to power had sliced the workers of the world away from the influence of the Soviet Union; from their own needs; from their old loyalties; from evolving life itself. Strange that the mind of Baldwin thought it could stop the change in things; that it could not conceive of life outside of itself. Drumbeat and bugle-blast! The Communist Manifesto had been jailed in the thick-ribbed, everlasting ice of sad Siberia. The quietly cocky Baldwin was too short to see over the heads of his crowding Conservatives. He wouldn't even try. No tiptoes for him: he would stand flat and firm on the ground. For this relief much thanks. Now thank we all our God with hearts and hands and voices. The workers now couldn't squirm into a strike; instead they would have to whistle while they worked.

At a gathering in a great Conservative Mansion, Richer England's tapestried tavern of the Rose and Crown, where the wines were rare and the fittings gorgeous; where the vast rooms were flounced and friezed by the gorgeous gowns of many ladies, floors pattering elegantly with sandalled shoes of crimson satin or filigree of gold, the air swooning with the moist sweetness of effectionate perfumes, and all was lit up by jewelled orders looking alive on the coats of costly men; Baldwin took Sean by the arm, setting him down on a settee beside himself, to ask him what of the night of De Valera, and of Ireland. What could Sean say to this poor man who knew as much about Ireland, and cared as much about Ireland, as the Archbishop Hinsley, or a monk of Caldy Island dead for a hundred years? Sean glanced at the wide, innocent face, blandness blazoned on it, the wide-open, guileless eyes curtaining the cunning mind of policy that had been ripening to a perfection of power for seven hundred years and more, and was now turning sere and tinted with decay. There the figure solemnly sat, set to pretend to listen to what Sean might have to say, coining its face to a heightened seriousness, but communing to itself of chances for further power and future prestige.

For all this man's headship, thought Sean, his courtly uniform (though less eager for it than many Labour leaders), his brotherly love for power and privilege, his soul's for ever hovering over the boiling pot; his mind jingles with the jingle of coins falling into a till. In him, there is no music, no flow of earthly line or cosmic curve, no sense of the divine anger or the diviner gentleness of words. He

Trembles before the flame and the flood,
And the winds that blow through the starry ways,

and so has no part

With the lonely majestical multitude.

This Baldwin is akin to De Valera. Two most honest and kindly men, yet neither having in him a spark of Blake's deep-desiring vision, or Walt Whitman's expansive one of brotherhood. Separated but by a few pages of history, they could easily meet and mingle; could haggle, hand in hand, in the same market; might feel no disquietude kneeling at the same altar; and, dying, stepping together, could enter heaven confident of a welcome home; while, passing by, a soul like Wolfe Tone might wonder who they were and where they came from.

—Tell me, now, said Baldwin, blandly, about this man, De Valera; of what he is to Ireland, and what you think will be the result of the relations between us and him.

—He would have to play with this poor soul, for an' he would, Baldwin could not understand him. That he had little interest in what might be said, was plain to Sean. Out of a dutiful patronage, Baldwin was politely noticing a new writer invited to an assembly in a grand salon. I will hand a cordial to the dead, thought Sean. Whatever De Valera may be to Ireland, said Sean, aloud, he is so by chance, and not by nature. He is no part of the Ireland revealed to the world, or of the hidden Ireland either. What De Valera is does not matter much, for he is a man of a moment. Ireland, sir, will be with the world when I am gone, when De Valera's voice is silenced, and when you are no longer the bright head of the English State.

—Quite, murmured Baldwin, halting to crumble tobacco into his pipe, light it, and take a few preliminary puffs. Quite; but the question that puzzles me is, Will Ireland help? Is she going to forget past worries, now that she possesses all she wants? Is she ready to forget the inglorious past, and stand with us for the King and Empire? Is she going to stop looking behind her, and look in front for once?

—Ah, sir, said Sean, you make too many implications; you ask too many questions of me, and you ask too much of Ireland. Ireland's past is not altogether inglorious. To forget is a hard thing to ask, for it isn't within a people's power, or a person's power, to wilfully forget. To forgive — yes; but it is not possible to forget. As far as I remember, sir, not once did Jesus ask us to forget injuries done to us; he commanded us to forgive our brother, but not to forget what a brother had done, because, as a wise soul, Jesus knew that to forget was to ask the impossible.

Sean had fancied he had seen a shiver pass over Baldwin when he had heard the name of Jesus. It didn't seem right that such a name should be shot into a political discussion. It startled the Prime Minister. If Jesus was to be followed at all, he should be followed at a very respectable distance; and, if his name was mentioned, it should be only when the subject was a suitable one, and the place propitious. Baldwin's face went into a pucker, but he pulled himself together with a smile, and said, Well, then, O'Casey, will Ireland be content to forgive?

—When she forgets — and she may forget — then she will forgive.

—But you have just said that to forget was impossible, and Baldwin's face went into a pucker again. You puzzle me, he added, taking the pipe from his mouth to say this more emphatically.

—Looka, sir, said Sean, touching Baldwin tenderly on the knee, nothing is impossible in Ireland — provided De Valera doesn't make it so.

—Aah, said Baldwin, venting a murmur of agreement, now I begin to understand you! The Seltic Twilight, the enchanted island where the impossible always happens; the Land of Tir nan Nogg, where the unexpected is found whenever one looks long enough.

—Ay, said Sean, and even when you don't look at all, sir. I'm pleased to see you begin to see the darkness through the light; for Ireland is the harp in the air, the murmuring messenger from the isle of the blest, the land of clouds that lifts the silver shield high to re-echo in God's ear the Irish songs of joy; the land where a star dances on every moving plough.

—Yes, yes; I know. A spiritual land, O'Casey, never engrossed with the things of the world. A wonderful people, if only agitators would leave them alone. A people ever soaring after the things of the spirit.

—Ay, sir; ever rushing on and on and ever soaring up and up and up; a people who
> *Wing all their thoughts to reach the skies,*
> *Till earth, receding from their eyes,*
> *Shall vanish as they soar.*

It is the Lord's doing, Mr. Prime Minister, and it is marvellous in our eyes.

—Yes, yes, indeed; very marvellous. Baldwin took a few meditative puffs, then resumed his valiant chatter. Yeats, your poet, knows his people. The Selt is well outside of the world of men. That's why your heroes are so universally renowned. You do well to remember your heroes — Daniel O'Connell, T. P. O'Connor, and Timothy Healy.

Ay, and mister McGilligan, the famous father of Dublin's wonderful Mary Anne, added Sean.

—Him, too, added Baldwin; all good Irishmen. You do well to remember them.

—Never fear, said Sean. They shall be remembered for ever.

—You certainly know a lot of Irish History, sir, said Sean, letting his eyes shine with approval.

—Not really, O'Casey, replied Baldwin; and Sean saw that the man felt flattered; a Prime Minister has little time for study. But I know some, O'Casey; I know some. I've actually heard of Tara. And the great man actually smiled.

Carson went lumbering by; a great hulk of a man, his weight driving his polished boots well into the pile of the costly carpet. A heavy, jowled face, cut by deep fleshy clefts, enlightened by a scowl, dull eyes staring about him and seeming to press out beyond the rims of the lids. This was the man who had made a covenant with God that he would never let Ulster put her nose across the border. He looked bulkier in his black suit, with its tails swinging awkwardly, and his wide, firmly pressed black trousers. He paused on his way to stand before a huge portrait by Lawrence, blotting the picture out, and framing himself between gilt borders half a foot wide: sable and gold. The man who had wilfully separated the orange from the green. Ulster's king of harms. The one who slammed protestantism into a corner and made little jack horners of militant Ulstermen.

How dissimilar, yet how like, was this man of the Nassau orange and blue, who had never been an orange-man, to his comrade King's Counsel, Timothy Healy, who was never an Irish Irelander. Both bullies, both men of a loud mouth, both using parties for their own ends; both wrapping themselves in the power of their several religions; both loyal to a king because it was expedient and profitable to be so; both determined to take no risk that would dim the polish on the knockers on their trim hall-doors. The one of Dublin or of Cork who had never sung a Gaelic ballad; the other of Belfast who had never sung an Orange song; both were often busied calling on God to witness to the sincerity of their ingenuity of looking after themselves. The one whose love of country had lifted him into a lordship, the other whose love of country had lifted him into its governor-generalship.

Here Carson stood, embedded within the brilliant and costly Conservative society, framed between gilt borders half a foot wide; he stood looking down towards Baldwin and Sean, courtly gentlemen and glittering ladies passing to and fro behind him, the music of a waltz, played by a band in the big room opposite, saluting the ponderous, deeply carved figurehead of Ulster's protestant totempole. He came nearer, keeping himself between the golden borders, and bent forward to say, I hope he's giving you good advice, Prime Minister?

—The best that money cannot buy, responded Sean for Baldwin; and the bulky face seemed to become oulkier with surprise at the answer to its question; the bulky figure hesitated, then moved on without another word, and the handsome figure painted between the gilded borders loomed out again.

—What grieves us, said Baldwin, after a pause, is Ireland's constant refusal to be friends; her refusal to appreciate what we have done for her; her bitterness in all things and on all occasions. What makes Ireland so bitter towards us, O'Casey?

—The winds, sir.

—The winds, murmured Baldwin, bewilderment wrinkling the placid face; which winds, what winds?

—The four winds of Eireann, sir: the white wind from the south; the black wind from the north; the brown wind from the west; and the red wind from the east.

—But I don't understand — the black wind, the white wind — what do these winds mean?

—Some say, said Sean, that the black wind signifies the Dominican Order, the brown wind, the Franciscans, the white wind, the Carmelites — three powerful orders in the Roman Church, and very powerful at present in Ireland.

—Aah! Now I understand, O'Casey. Of course, of course; the clergy. But you mentioned, I think, a red wind — that doesn't mean Socialism, does it? It couldn't, of course.

—It does, though. Since Bunker's Hill, when it blew from the west, the red wind has always blown from the east: first from France, when the Bastille was stormed; then from Russia, when the red flag was raised in Moscow and Petrograd; blew strong first, then died down; blew strong again, when De Valera's Party sent delegates to the U.S.S.R. to win support for the Irish Republic; died down when De Valera, raised to power, peered out at the world through a bishop's ring. You may remember, Mr. Prime Minister, that Yeats in the midst of dream-dances and dream-kisses, stared through the collar-bone of a hare,

> At the old bitter world where they marry in churches,
> And laugh over the untroubled water
> At all who marry in churches,
> Through the white thin bone of a hare.

But De Valera, safe and sound man, prosperous in the grace of God, looking through the gold circle of a bishop's ring, sees life steadily and sees it holy; and so the red wind from the east has died down in Ireland to a tantalising breeze.

—Yeats was a great poet, I'll admit, said Baldwin, somewhat dubiously, but I'm not sure that his influence on Ireland was altogether a good one. He said and wrote questionable, very questionable, things at times.

Sean granted himself a deep inner laugh as he looked at the toby-jug face of the Prime Minister. Baldwin, thought Sean, thinks that Yeats is a great poet. What a kind concession! But ne'er a ripple of satisfaction would pass through the soul of the poet if he heard him say so; for scant would be the attention given by Yeats to either praise or blame from Baldwin.

Sean laid a hand softly on Baldwin's arm, said soothingly, aloud,

You must try to be indulgent with the queer and questionable things sometimes said and written by W. B. Yeats, sir. You must always remember:

> *That Yeats had been he knew not where,*
> *And Yeats had seen what he could not declare,*
> *Yeats had been where the cock never crew,*
> *Where the rain never fell and the wind never blew.*

—There is that to be remembered and considered, of course, O'Casey. Poets claim a liberty of speech denied to ordinary men like me. They have the prerogative of being whimsical, as long as they don't go too far in saying things tending to disturb, or even dismay, law and order. The poet must strictly confine himself to his particular art. It is injurious for any artist to enter into, or bother about, the world of men. You agree with me, O'Casey?

—Cordially, sir, said Sean; but they will persist in doing it in spite of the danger. Even Shakespeare does it; even he.

Baldwin looked at Sean, puzzled and a little startled to hear that Shakespeare might possibly be ranked among the rebels; but, after some hesitation, seemed to decide that the remark had better be left unchallenged. Giving his pipe a few vigorous puffs, he resumed the talk, the homely and kindly face fixing on itself a more serious look than it had before. The priests, he said, at least, are pure. They manage to keep Ireland steady; they are to be trusted — don't you agree, O'Casey?

—Yes, said Sean, they are to be trusted. They have been your good friends in the past, and will be so again in the future. They laurel your law and order so long as they think that may be the way to a peak of promotion. But they haven't always managed to keep Ireland steady, sir; they thought to do so by destroying Parnell, and succeeded in destroying the country with him for many years; they condemned to excommunication the Fenians who would make Ireland one, but the Easter Rising burned up their curses, and slapped the bishops in the snot. There is in Ireland, sir, a political catechism as well as the one coined by the Council of Trent.

Sean saw that Baldwin was becoming bored or getting uneasy. He was fidgeting with his pipe; looking at it as if he were wondering was it really his. Then his gaze left the pipe to watch the gay, commanding figures passing to and fro from one room to another. They were easily understood, but what was this Seltic figure sitting beside him trying to say? Sean's belly filled out with the ecstasy of secret, mischievous laughter, as he saw the look of quiet perplexity on the stolid, kindly face of the Conservative leader. Discussions with an Irishman went dodging in and out, twiningly, like the old interlacing decoration in their coloured and ancient books. Like the silky mist sprayed by a spider over a despairing prey; a rational man would be lost in its teeming words if he didn't struggle, break through, and run. Here was this fellow, O'Casey, snug on the laps of the best people, handling the tapestry of riches and power, yet he was as bad, as inattentive to sense as the rest of them. Hadn't these Selts eyes to see and ears to hear? Couldn't they realise that while the heavens declared the glory of God, the earth showeth the handiwork of the Conservative Party? Baldwin made a stir as if to rise and go.

—What we're anxious to know, O'Casey, is why isn't Ireland willing to help. But I have to go now — I want to have a talk with Carson. We'll meet again, I hope.

—Hold on a minute more, sir, said Sean, laying a gently detaining hand on Baldwin's arm. The night's young yet. Wait till I tell you: If you were to put that question about help to Ireland herself, she'd say she helped you too damned much already, in battlefield from Crécy to Tel-el-Kebir; sowing your potatoes, and reaping your corn; building your docks in Liverpool, carrying your railways across Canada; evangelising the British pagan; and giving you an example of literature in the prose and poetry of Virgil.

—Virgil? echoed the Prime Minister, so startled that he whipped the pipe out of his mouth. Not Virgil, the Roman poet?

—The same, sir, the very same. Though a Roman citizen, like Paul, Virgil wasn't a Roman. As the one was a Jew, so the other was a Kelt. Ferghil, the shining one, and this Kelt influenced literary thought and manner till the great James Joyce came to shove him out of the way. Yes, sir — a link with Tara rather than a link with Rome.

—This is the first time I heard Virgil called a Selt, O'Casey. It amazes and amuses me. Your race seems to have left its mark on the whole world. Well, we've had a very interesting chat, and I'm sorry I have to leave you now.

—Oh, much more than a mark, sir, said Sean rapidly, forcing Baldwin to sit still and listen uneasily out of English politeness. Sure, you haven't heard the half of it. Wait till I tell you: the very broad arrow you stamp on your governmental goods and weave into your prison garments is the broad A of the Keltic Druids. We've left marks everywhere; from where we are to the faraway land of the Calmucks. Khan is the same as the Irish word for a headman; taisha is the Mogul term for the head of a tribe, and, today, De Valera is termed the taoiseach, the leader of the nation, the tribe. Ha, man, you don't know the half of it. The silent thunder of wisdom rumbles round everywhere a Kelt is walking. If he wants to, a Kelt can have the wisdom of Fearceartais; the intelligence of the bardess, Etain; the clear truths of Mor Mumhan; but he must sell to them all he can spare, and part of what he cannot spare, in time and pleasure and property, if he is to achieve these things so that they become an interwoven part of his nature. Then the word of knowledge will fashion fire in his head, so that he can foretell the ages of the moon, and reveal the spot where the sun rests. Thus it was that the Druids who taught magic to the Persians became the spiritual ancestors of Omar Khayyám.

—Really? mused the murmuring Baldwin, half crouching towards Sean, for, out of English politeness, he disdained to shake off the gently detaining hand of Sean resting on his arm; really, now? I never heard that before. The Seltic race must, indeed, have been an amazing one. It is amusing to think of them being responsible for Omar Khayyám. The Prime Minister was well bewildered now by Sean's narrative telling of the Keltic power by influence over the solid and the fluid world. Sean's remarks had seemingly split into many sparks which were whirling around in the toby-jug mind of the Prime Minister.

—But a Prime Minister, unfortunately, went on the murmuring mind, has no time to spare for the contemplation of the flights of the spirit; but is forced to confine himself within the problems found in the world of men. The stocky, self-satisfied figure straightened up, and Sean's hand slid from the arm. I must go now, for I want to have a word or two with Carson.

—Lookat here, sir, said Sean fervently, rising to deliver the parting shot, if you want to find things hidden and know things unrevealed, you couldn't do better than study the musings of Michael Robartes with John Aherne, the twins, embodying the two minds in one person; give and take; ebb and flow. Fully embattled with the knowledge retained, you can look at the world with the eye of a saint, and when that eye gets tired, you can look at the world through the other one with the eye of a drunkard. You'll watch the

Sun and moon that a grand hour
Bellowed and pranced in the round tower.

And listen: when nature falls away from you, you may in re-creation be a bird of song, hammered out of silver, perched upon a golden bough to sing to lords and ladies of Byzantium.

—A sober English bird would suit me better, said the Prime Minister, with a sober wave of his pipe; and it is time enough to be that same, he added, smiling contentedly at uttering what he thought was an Irish idiom. Goodbye, for the present, O'Casey; and the Toby Jug was off to set itself upon a caparisoned table for homage and admiration. A kindly man, a shrewd one, conscientious, according to his lights; but utterly deaf to the terrible drum-beat in the march of life. As it is with Labour, so it is with the warm-hearted and younger-minded Conservatives — they are barricaded behind the sleep-shod minds of their ministers who saunter slow in thought, and never risk a run.

There goes the leader of the Party that had within its circle not only the fire, the earthquake, the big wind, but the still, small voice as well. Things done had been useless; things to be done in the future would be useless, if they were not done in the world by the Conservative Party. And Baldwin led them, while the Bulldog Drummond of the Party, Churchill, sat sulking in the conservatory. God's children without the wings. A lot of rare talent was being wasted in both parties. Tens of thousands of Irishmen had worked in their factories, toiled in their fields, sat on the benches of their judicature, taught in their universities and colleges, gone down full fathom five in their fighting ships, strewed the British battlefields with their bodies, and yet these fellows didn't know a goddamn thing about the land these tens of thousands came from. They knew a lot about every coloured ribbon save the ribbon that was green.

A word with Carson! With Carson, who had betrayed his native land into a diminished Ulster; and had betrayed Ulster for what he could get from England. Who instead of encouraging Ulstermen to come out of a corner, had frightened them into one. Carson should have led his men over the border with a bang; fifes and drums hilarious; the crimson banner of Derry to the right, the orange and blue one of Nassau to the left, and the gallant green flag, embedding the golden harp in its folds, carried high in the centre. Oh, it was cowardly to shrink back and not thrust forward. Courage the Ulstermen have, but courage they have not shown. Occasionally, by a shower of bolts and nuts, aimed at the heads of the philistinian catholics, they have fostered rowdyism, but rowdyism is nothing more than the restlessness of a cankered cowardice.

London was Carson's damasked mistress, jewelled delightedly; full of wealth, portly with good fare, and free with gifts to those who kissed her cunningly; Belfast his wife, a puritan maid, trim; jading prayer trickling from her lips rather than the ripple of a song; afraid of charm; idealising those who go grim for God; offering fine linen indeed, but bearing no purple to go with it; and dealing even the linen out with wary eye and sparing hand. And for London's lure, Carson, instead of putting fight into Ulstermen, took all the fight out of them. In mass formation, bunched together, they could be hilariously brave, but not so confident or sure when scanty numbers were calmly coerced into melodious deportment by a contagious roman catholic crowd.

In Dublin, when on his way to work before six o'clock of a morning, Sean had seen the little Dublin contingent of a few hundred Orangemen marching through the deserted streets, men of the Orange Order, the Purple Order, and Knights of the Grand Black Chapter; all sash-clad, spangled with insignia of bible, sword, and crown, led by a miniature fife-and-drum band, headed by the Nassau banner of orange and blue; stepping it out for the train that would hurry them to Belfast in time to join their Ulster brethren in the mad march of bigoted elation on the day of the 12th of July; through the still, deserted streets of Dublin, brawny protestantism marched, a big Ballaghaderreen policeman halting on the sidewalk to stand and stare and wonder who and what they were; the shops shut, the doors closed, the blinds down, heads up, they marched bold and blatant, through lanes of catholics in a sighing sleep or snoring, the timid souls went on with nothing to daunt them but the chilly air of a summer morning. Oh, the canting Christians of the Christian isle that God made well and man has murked with his mad religions! The isle deluged with Christian calls to charity, where no green sash could strut the streets of Belfast in the light of day, no orange sash strut the streets of Dublin — though both decorations, as folk-art, are poor and paltry, less promising or pleasant than the gaudy paper hats hailing Christmas night's hilarity; but they are sincere, however ignorant and bigoted those who wear them; and, to that extent, they are sacred.

Jesus, how these Christians love one another! Jesus said Love one another. We heard you. We do our best. Here, lads, bring them up to him so's he can have a good look; bring up the head split open, the bleeding eye, the bruised arm, the broken jaw, the limping leg, and let Jesus have a good look. All in the day's work, sirree, and we'll do better one day. All in fair fight and no favour. Knock them out and do them in's the slogan of apostolic love. Line them up so's they can be seen proper. Papist bastards on your left, sir; protestant

gets on your right. Their own mothers wouldn't know them well. A
sight to be seen. We offer the work done, sir, as a token of our
esteem. Whoever did it to the fellow with half his face gone deserves
a noble prize. Altogether, lads, now, in harmony:

> Faith of our fathers, we will love
> Both friend and foe in all our strife;
> And preach thee, too, as love knows how,
> In kindly words and virtuous life!

And so do we. The hymn shows it. Father Faber's mouldering
fable. Speak your mind! Jesus did, and was crucified. He speaks it
still, and still is crucified.

The ministers of the Rose and Crown have never known, and
know not now, anything about the ways and means that have made
the Ireland of today. Knew nothing, know nothing, about her folk-
art in story, song, music, legend, and dance; know nothing about her
struggles to perpetuate her life with something else besides a potato;
know nothing even about the later things that tingle the Irish nerves,
fire the Irish blood, provoking one section into wearing an orange
sash, and another into wearing a green one. One or two of the
ministers may have a faint remembrance of having heard an echo
somewhere of a melody by Moore, but why it was composed, or
what it was all about, they cared little and knew nothing; though, by
standing on a chair in their house of Downing Street, any of them
could have seen the Union Jack flying from a tower of their castle
set down tight in the centre of Dublin city.

Yet the predecessors of these men ramped over the land for
hundreds of years; shot, hanged the leaders of the Irish who couldn't
agree with them, and jammed the jails with the rest; when every
tenant-farmer in the land lost the right to live; when hunger rose up
with them in the morning and went to bed with them at night; when,
at one go, in one place, seven hundred people were flung from their
homes, poor mud-made homes at that, but homes all the same, by
an absentee landlord, because the tenants couldn't give him enough
for an extra fit of whoring; when peasants were bound to pay six
pounds an acre rent and work for their landlords at fippence a day;
when an English earl was forced to exclaim, *If the military force had
killed half as many landlords as it had the revolting Whiteboys, it
would have contributed more effectually to restore quiet*; when in
eighty-five years eighty-six coercion acts were passed to keep the
Irish peasants toeing the landlordian Christian line; when to have a
pike, a lance, or a knitting-needle constituted an offence worth a

term of transportation for seven years; when everyone or anyone found walking the roads, or standing at a corner, an hour after sunset in a proclaimed district was liable to the long holiday of fifteen years' transportation; when every judge to be a judge had to be a landlordian lover, and, finally, all were made to act as jurymen as well as judges; when the catholic peasant of the south and the protestant peasant of the north of Ireland spent their lives sowing their own graves that stretched from the river Lee and the river Boyne to the shores of Lakes Ontario and Erie and far beyond them; when every government minister, every privy councillor, every magistrate, was a landlord, or a landlord's brother, or a landlord's friend; so that the threat, as recorded in the holy bible, made by the king of Assyria to the people of Israel that he would reduce them to eating their own dung and drinking their own piss, fell upon the catholic peasant of the south and the protestant peasant of the north; while the perfumed voice of Lord Beaconsfield applauded, and Lord Salisbury declared, with a clapping of cold hands, that very soon the Kelt in Ireland would be as scarce on the banks of the Shannon as the Red Indian on the banks of Manhattan. But these powerful boyos inserted a clause in the eviction laws which redeemed their terror, and justified their severity in the eyes of God: they declared that no eviction could take place on Good Friday or on Christmas Day, and that the roof of a house must not be sent tumbling down till the tenant and his family had had time to get out.

The sowls of the ministers of the crown were salvaged by this act of grace, and when it was first proclaimed it was said that all the red roses of England went white with the sense of their deep purity and perfection. Oh, generous genuflexion to the glory of God! No family could be thrust from its home on the day that saw Jesus born or on the day that saw Jesus die! Ballyhoojah, ballyhoojah, ballyhoojah!

Baldwin and Carson were going to and fro on the cordial carpet, walking up and down on it, as if it were the earth; and there goes Churchill astrut on the same deistic daïs, solidly set on himself, impetuous for the renewal of old, unhappy, far-off things and battles long ago; visioning himself in buff jerkin, halberd in hand, and morion set tight on his corybantic head; an officer of the king's guards, a bulky and ageing D'Artagnan of the Conservative Party, a little scornful of the officers of the regiments of foot. A man of many splendid qualities which seemed to be at ease only in thunder, lightning, and in rain, in a plunge back to an old world, rather than a step forward to the new life.

Mayfair had marooned itself by its loud victory in the last election. They had packed the House of Commons with too many clumsy bodies and too many dead heads. They were in great glee. During the progress of the election, the broadcasters had announced with ribald monotony, with voices paused and poised in exquisitely official adulation, *Conservative gain, Labour defeat, Conservative gain,* and Baldwin looked as if he had succeeded in commanding the sun to stand still in the heavens. They could pray or praise now in Westminster Abbey or St. Paul's with acclamation. The Labour Party were·gamins in the street again. But the leviathan of Conservative rule, of law and order, had a fatal weakness — it hadn't one representative from the workers at the desk, in the field, factory, or workshop. The skin of the Conservative fruit was shining and gay-coloured, but rotten at the core; the skin of the Labour fruit was jagged and thin, but its core was sound, and needed but another day to be perfect with vigour and sap.

Nor was there any worker in this beautiful big house either. No miner, no farm worker, no clerk, no shop assistant, not a single railway guard, driver, signalman, or porter: no visitor from among those who kept the life of England going. Not one in this imposing residence, showing how rich the rich were, with its gilded ceiling, carpeted floors, luscious furniture, costly pictures; with a stairway up which a column could march without touching the banisters; with silver ware for the morning meal, and golden ware for the meal at night; where every woman wore a gown costing enough to keep a worker's family going for a year without privation. And in and out through the caramelic splendour went Baldwin; while Churchill walked under the figure-filled ceiling, within the aurora of the glowing chandeliers, trenchantly treading down the cringing carpet, his forensic head, sunk down between his shoulders, thrust forward, as if seeking out some policy or opponent to puck. Earlier on, Stephen Gwynn with Sean beside him had spoken, rather diffidently, as if a word or two with the great man was a sly adventure; but two Irishmen were too many or too few for the politician, for, though he slackened his step, he kept moving, sending back a few mumbled words heard by God only; then he went on to where the warriors were, disappearing behind the moving curtain of silk and satin worn by the ladies of the land. He was right to pass on quick, for there was no answer for him with O'Casey or Gwynn as to what would happen, or what was to 'be done.

Sean had yet to meet a government official who knew anything about Ireland; or even one who wanted to know anything. Indeed, what do they want to know about Wales, either? Only today, the Labour Prime Minister, speaking to a meeting in Llandudno, was asked to receive a Welsh National deputation to discuss the question of an independent parliament for Wales. While he was putting on his hat running to his car, the Prime Minister flipped into the face of the deputation the remark that he hadn't time to meet such a question, much more discuss it. Though the Englishman George Borrow thanked God the Welsh kept their language, the English Prime Ministers think of it as puff puff; and the lives of the Welsh people are of no more importance to any one of them than a wave of a ministerial hand from a Downing Street window. But Attlee hasn't come to walk under the gilded ceilings yet; at present, like a nice little boy, he is just squinting in through a window at the gay goings on in the big house.

Yet it would serve these portentous and prime ministers to know something of the lands, different from their own, that they govern. Had Churchill known the little he should have known about Scotland, he would never have hailed Harry Lauder, singing 'Keep richt on tae the end of the Road', as Scotland's national bard at a great meeting in Dunedin, presided over by the Lord Provost of Scotland's capital. God knows there are many to choose from; but Churchill chose one who is none. Stalin would probably know better about him who had a claim to be called a national bard of Alban. Scotland's history and Scotland's art is more than a tartan tie, or the waggle of a kilt. And what have we ever been told by these governors, pastors, and masters about the Commonwealth countries perched on the rim of the world? Not a damned thing. We know the Australians and New Zealanders as great cricketers, great breeders of sheep, great exporters of wool; and there the story ends. Indeed, not to journey too far away, what do these ministers know about the people in the counties of their own fair land? Curse o' God on the much. They don't appear on the stage; they don't show themselves on the films; they are shunted on to a siding over the wireless, and tolerated for a brief half-hour in song or story, like a child brought into a gilded drawing-room to display a childish gift, and then hurried back to the hidden haunt of the nursery. It is hard to believe that either Churchill or Attlee would bend away from their business even long enough to listen to a Northumbrian playing *The Bonny Tyneside*, or listen to one singing for the ferryman to come and bring him to his sweetheart over the rough waters of the river.

They're too big for that diversion. With them it was always over the sea to Paris, over the sea to Amsterdam, but never over the sea to Skye. And yet it is these singers and pipers, allied with the dockers of the quaysides, the men and women of the farms, the workers in the big and lesser cities, who made England in the past, and will remake England in the future. The General Strike showed this, for it struck England like lightnings from the hands of Zeus. England within a few hours became a waste land. And remained so till J. H. Thomas, frightened into respectability by Sir John Simon's revelation from heaven that the Strike was illegal, sought the counsel of the lords and ladies, becoming one with them as a faithful butler to an old family dizzily bedizened in a web of inherited quarterings of their coats of arms bestowed at first-hand by Billy the Conqueror or Billy from the Boyne. He chose the red carpet to be under his proletarian feet rather than the red flag to fly over his head. He chose well for the time being; putting, as he thought, the workers away in drawer or on shelf, like little tin soldiers, leaving the rebellious and blackened miners to fight alone a gallant rear-guard action. Though he looked hale and was excited at having done the decent thing by the Rose and Crown, the moment he had handed over the workers to the chill clutch of defeat, that moment he had fallen, had died, as Courage tossed his name out of the book of the people's life.

Here he was in grand form, tailed coat, white waistcoat and tie, stormy with a sense of his own importance. He did not walk about with the silent solidity of Baldwin, or the restless, stoical step of Churchill; but came in and went out in spurts. *I'll hear no word against Thomas — he has played the game*, as a gracious and intelligent lady said tersely to Sean, in reply to a critical remark of his. Indeed, he had, and he was playing it still, even now; even here. It was Jimmy there and Jummy here; a companion of honour, breathing the soiled air blown from fans, the whole world a promise before him. The workers out in the rain. Oh, never mind — they're used to it. But shove as Jimmy Thomas might, he couldn't find a place in the arustocratic frieze in which to fix himself. He could edge in here and there sideways; but there was no niche for an eyes-front pose. He was permitted to climb the wide-awake stairs, lounge in the drawing-room, but not allowed to sit down at the family fire. A useful, handy man to have about the big house. And dream himself, if he liked, into being one of the family; and dream it he did, in his tailed coat, his white waistcoat, his quite right white tie. He enjoyed a lackey's privilege for pulling the family out of a bad crisis. He was allowed to run up and down the imposing stairway, sit down on the gilded chairs, eat out of the finest of porcelain, and even from the gold ware once or twice, so that he could see and handle and understand the exquisite and kindling treasures he had saved from the mean defacement of a rest in the proletarian pawnshops. All the church bells are ringing, Jimmy. Ding-dong ding-dong-dell; for you and for me and for everyone else.

They were to ring again, louder than ever, later on. A day after, or, maybe, later, the bankers, making their rounds of the strongrooms to count the bars of gold, got the shock of their lives. The cupboards were bare, their hearts stood still. They ran and hurried the Prime Minister, Ramsay MacDonald, the Chancellor of the Exchequer, Philip Snowden, and Jimmy Thomas to the place where the gold hath lain, nothing now but wide and empty spaces.

—Look for yourselves, they said; you can still see the marks on the shelves where the gold bars lay.

—Distinctly, said Philip.

—We cannot go on and on and on and down and down, said Ramsay.

—Not bloody likely, said Jimmy Thomas.

—Listen to the bells, said the bankers.

No joy in them now. A single stroke; a long silence; another stroke, slow, sad, shivery. Out of the deep we cry unto thee. The bells were tolling. Britain was about to be buried. Sad sounds. The Crown is crushed, the Rose is withering. England's golden day is going, England's golden day is going, England's golden day is gone. For whom the bell tolls. The church bells are tolling for you and for me.

And they mourned in that place which to this day is called The Place of Retrenchment; they mourned there with great and gleeful mourning, rending their garments and throwing dust over their heads and into the eyes of the people; for their souls were brought low, even to the dust; and their bellies cleaved unto the ground. It was a pitiable sight to see; all the world wondered. And the gods took pity on them, and, as a token, sent a voice roaring out of heaven, saying, Get up, get up, boys, and get a move on! So they rose up, comforted, and took counsel together to end the exceptional and menacing emergency.

—We must do something to avert disaster at the earliest possible moment, said MacDonald.

—We must explore every avenue to see what can be done, said Snowden.

—We must leave no stone unturned in order to solve the problem, said Jimmy Thomas. We must balance the budgit. Let's go and have a chat with our buddies, the bankers.

And they hurried to where the bankers were gathered at the gates of the cities, in the churches, in the major manors of Mayfair, in the sanctuary, and in the courts of the lords. And they held up their hands, saying, Is it peace? And the bankers held up theirs, saying, It is peace, provided ye do what is just and lawful, following the commandments of the governors given by God to the Bank of England, true liegemen in financial verity and honour to the Rose and Crown. Honour their commandments, keep their ways, and they shall promote thee, that ye shall possess the land for ever. And the three suppliants bowed down, saying, We're only too anxious to do those things that are righteous in your eyes, to the greater glory of the Crown and the Rose.

—Expenses must be cut down by fifty millions, said the bankers. As an earnest of faith, hope, and charity the unemployment benefit must be reduced. It is costing the Rose and Crown twelve millions a week. It must be cut.

—It must be cut, echoed Ramsay; quick, said Philip; soon, said Jimmy Thomas.

—We must all make equal sacrifices, said the bankers. We must slash everything, except profits; for these be incentives, and keep the Rose fresh and the Crown sparkling. Profit is the great incentive in every Christian country, though there is patriotism, too.

—Patriotism isn't enough, said Ramsay.

—Not half enough, said Philip.

—Not worth a damn, said Jimmy.

—We must have a National Government, said the bankers.

—Representing the people, said Ramsay.

—The whole people, said Philip.

—And nothing but the people, added Jimmy.

And so for the sake of the Rose and the Crown, these three men made great sacrifices, without the murmur of a moan. Ramsay retired into the position of Prime Minister; Jimmy into the job of Minister for the Dominions; and Philip into the rich robe and coronet of a Viscount.

Sean first met Ramsay MacDonald at a lunch in the flat of Lady Gregory's daughter-in-law, where Lady Gregory was staying at the time. Among those present were the then High Commissioner for Eirinn and his pretty and clever wife, Josephine MacNeill. The company had come together as helpers in the effort to get the Lane Pictures back to Dublin. Sean turned the pictures towards the wall to demand from Mr. MacDonald more revolutionary action in the policy of the Labour Government. He said that the Labour leaders had put on a Tory overall to keep their clothing clean. He urged MacDonald to advance into the fight' by forcing the larger enterprises out of the hands of private ownership into the full possession of the people; but MacDonald had laughingly set the appeal aside as the wild vision of an idealist. Sean had insisted that, ideal or no, it was what the Labour Government were bound to do by their baptism, at which they had renounced all the works and pomps of Capitalism; by their faith in the workers; and by their abounding hope for the future; adding that even this achievement would be but a beginning; but the learning of the first few letters of Socialism's alphabet. But MacDonald had turned the pictures right face forward again, and lost his hearing looking at them.

MacDonald was a handsome fellow, tall as one of the old Gaels, who carried himself about with great dignity and grace. His head was splendidly formed, his face finely-moulded, with just the touch of ruggedness that made it manly. A charming manner flowered from his nature when he was faced with friends, or with those whom he thought to be his friends. Had he had but the deep carelessness of Walt Whitman, he would have lived, he would have died, a great man. But the odd narcotic vanity unbalanced him, craving admiration and a twinge of envy from all who knew him in person or by picture. I am Ramsay MacDonald, Prime Minister of England, was the slogan of his later life.

He trod on silk, as if the wind
Blew his own praises in his eyes.

Lux Britannica. The title of Prime Minister was his lady-love, his Lily of Laguna. *The Conference is to be opened by the Right Honourable Ramsay MacDonald, Prime Minister of England,* was, for him, the unrolling of many flags, the beating of many drums. He sacrificed the workers, his own ease of mind, and, at the last, his life, that he might hear the title announced in public and in private, and sense it being murmured by the undulant mind of the nation. But within the man there was no fruitful force behind the thundering title. He wore the kilt without the claymore. He had handed over the claymore to the Tories the time he handed over the power lent to him by the united front of the working-class. He was lost among his friends. They smothered him elegantly with their scented odours, their soothing organdies, and their sleepy silks. He escaped from the taint of coal-dust, the smell of factory oils, the decay that made agriculture fruitful; his ears slept away from the discordant clang of railway wagons clashing together; the bang of the hammer and the buzz of the saw: he shrank away from all that had moulded his life into the service of man; and with these he gave away the fierce fealty of those who go forth to work, to their labour until the evening. For a tinsel dream he gave away his glory. He shrouded himself within an iridescent bubble.

The three were rewarded: one became Prime Minister for an hour; a second was allowed to wrap himself up in the phantasy of a Viscountcy for an hour and a half; and the third became a Minister of the Crown and Rose for a day. Then they died, and their names are on no banners now. All for nothing! The incomplete revenue of the time was but a summer shower, but the three made it an excuse to scramble for shelter into the bright pavilions of the Tories where there was warmth and wine and fine feeding. But they and those were punished for taking from the workers part of their daily bread given them of God. The deluge came later, when the bright pavilions came tumbling down, to be swept away in the swirling surge of war, leaving the Tories to find political homes in barns, or slumber, bruised, on the benches in the parks.

Of the three, MacDonald was the one, despite his weakness, his corroding vanity, who preserved within his nature some of the salt of dignity which never lost its savour; and, in a limited way, he held on to the vision of colour and form. He appreciated the variegations of art, and intently watched the latest work done by the younger painters. He was a genuine patron of the drama, and could easily lean on an elbow when talking about a book; qualities that most of his comrade Cabinet ministers needed to quicken their tempered outlook with the sudden snatch of a song. Sean had a deep and distant affection for him, but could never manage to get to talk with him alone. MacDonald always protected himself with the company of others, knowing that Sean knew and deplored the way he was going. Sean wanted to warn him, to use all his feeling of affection to coax the man to keep heart-deep within the might of the masses. MacDonald was willing to see Sean in the House, on the terrace, or in the foyer of a theatre, when surrounding company kept him safe from questioning or appeal. He would never come to Sean's home for a talk and a smoke by a friendly fireside. He promised to come, but he never came. Sean wrote to him, even pretending sympathy with the Prime Minister's difficulties of governing, in an effort to entice him to where an Irishman and a Scot could sit together quiet, and talk things over. This is his reply:

CHEQUERS
PRINCES RISBOROUGH
BUCKS
February 19th, 1932

MY DEAR O'CASEY,

I was so glad to have your letter. You understand so many things which the ordinary person does not. I would like very much if you would come and see me here one week-end when I am down, and I shall write to you when I get back from my holiday. Thanks to an upbringing something like your own, I am getting better by leaps and bounds.

With kindest regards to your wife and yourself, I am

RAMSAY MACDONALD

But he would not come. *We must meet soon*, said one of his letters; but he never came. He was joined to idols, and had to be let alone. And snappy Snowden and sunny-jim Thomas valeted and worried him well on his way.

Consummatum est. Here were MacDonald and Thomas, elate and hysterically calm, above the richness of the carpet, under the starry chandeliers, with Churchill and Baldwin and a fine flock of great ones murmuring in the ears of the two men, Well done, good and faithful servants; enter ye into the joy of your lords. They were all so excited that they heard the trumpets of the workers but *as horns of elfland, faintly blowing*. So happily trimmed with triumph that they couldn't be mindful of even their own poet singing of

> *The vast republics that may grow,*
> *Titanic forces taking birth*
> *In divers seasons, divers climes.*

Yet Sean's heart knew that MacDonald's heart was not in what was done. The echo in the glory of cheering workers, lost now, lost for ever now, would dimly simulate itself and sound sad in his ears every day unto his last day, his very last hour. In an attempt to break the workers, he had but broken himself. Even Winston Churchill, guerdon of the Conservatives, hurrying along, and contemptuously shoving MacDonald aside, saw in his divided way that MacDonald's harassing of the workers served but to harrow his own soul, for he set down in a book that *MacDonald, the Prime Minister, had severed himself, with the uttermost bitterness on both sides, from the Socialist Party which it had been his life's work to create. Henceforth he brooded supinely at the head of an Administration which, though nominally National, was in fact overwhelmingly Conservative. Mr. Baldwin preferred the substance to the form of power, and reigned placidly in the background.*

Supinely brooding! Churchill didn't know, probably didn't care, how a man might feel having viciously abandoned what had been his life-work to create. How pitifully a soul may suffer when it has betrayed its heart's desire. Churchill, too, was lavishly concerned with himself. He, too, had his own tormenting vanity, a belief in a Cassandrian power of prophecy that no-one paused to listen to. He carried it about with him like a hump on a camel's back. Although he calls and calls upon the people, his prophecies were directed towards the white ears of those who dwelt within the porticoed houses and walked beneath the gilded ceilings; beings *who had been formed by a different breeding, were fed by a different food, are ordered by different manners, and who are not governed by the same laws*: who go about, who act and think as if they had not been born of mortals as others were, but had been carefully lowered from heaven in arks made from golden bulrushes, strengthened with precious stones, to grow up, well watched, till they had ripened enough to become the owners and guardians of the earth's domains. Specials from Providence: who parade the rich places of the earth, whose tattle in the salons, according to Beaconsfield, *Has in it something humiliating. It is not merely that it is deficient in warmth, and depth, and breadth; that it is always discussing persons instead of principles, and cloaking its want of thought in mimetic dogmas, and its want of feeling in superficial raillery; it is not merely that it has neither imagination, nor fancy, nor sentiment, nor feeling, nor knowledge to recommend it; but it appears to me, even as regards manner and expression, inferior in refinement and phraseology; in short, trivial, uninteresting, stupid, really vulgar.*

Gracious, intelligent, and even noble as some of these silk-clad chatterers were, they could not, in market or exchange, be other than the guardians of profits, rent, and interest, the frantic defenders of the cohesive power of public plunder. MacDonald and Thomas now wandered among them, not as equals, but as favoured servants allowed into the drawing-room for a period to admire its stately grandeur. This is what you have preserved, you two; have a good look, and go. MacDonald was above it all, and did what he did only out of the craving of vanity embedded in his inner nature. He was sick and ailing. He left it, and set sail in a big ship for a far country;

but his heart failed him, and there on the ship, he died, never again to show off his vanished face.

When workers march, mayhap they'll pause a while where he lies low and lonely. The boy and man lie buried here: the man who left them, and the bonnie, ragged lad of Lossiemouth. Buried here's the gallant bird that lost its comely look; the disc of gold that nearly turned to lead; the thistle's purple plume that took to rust; the Scot who dropped his claymore and his targe; the chief who in the last frenzy of the struggle sank down under the burden and heat of the fight.

Oh, workers, pause a while where lowly buried is the one who listened long to the parrot screeching till he was deeved to deafness; who listened too long, and left the views

> That were peculiar to us
> Afore his vision narrowed
> And gar'd him think it time
> The Claith was owre the parrot.

Oh, workers on the march, pause here awhile, and lay a wreath of part-forgiveness on the lonely grave. Bring forth a piper of his lordly clan and bid him play a brief lament for a clansman's weakness; forgetting the grey-haired man who did not stay the strife; remembering only in the minute's pause the gallant ragged lad of Lossiemouth.

BLACK OXEN PASSING BY

AFTER the threat of an action for breach of copyright, which was never carried out, Yeats fell silent. He returned to the attack no more; no longer stood on the defensive. Perhaps the comments made by Mrs. Shaw when they lunched together persuaded the silence; maybe it was the letter written by Bernard Shaw to Lady Gregory, criticising the conduct of the Abbey, shamed him into it; or a decision to ignore Casey as a contemptible item in his life. Perhaps, like Aeschylus who delighted to begin a play with an awful silence, Yeats liked to end a discussion with another awful silence. Whatever the reason, the poet decided to stay in his room with the blinds down. To Sean it seemed that the great man was determined to be interested in, to listen to, to dispute with, those only who were content to be so many coloured buttons on the poet's dinner-jacket.

Up went the London curtain on *The Silver Tassie*, and, in spite of the fact that Laughton was badly miscast, and had a bad cold, that a few others were as bad as he, in spite of a few mishaps, the play was a hit; not at all in the conventional sense, but in a moral and a complex sense: using a Joxerian expression, the play gave the patient, wondering public a terrible belt in the kisser. It caused many of the critical minds to turn their usually serene and complacent comments into a shout; for comments were so many, so angry, and so conflicting, that only a bawl of an opinion could be heard through the din; an opinion, though heard, was not listened to, for each who saw it, wanted to yell out his own. They didn't want such a play; they didn't wish for it. They wanted war with the flame died down in it, and the screaming silent. This thing was so different from the false effrontery of Sherriff's *Journey's End*, which made of war a pleasant thing to see and feel; a strife put spiritually at a great distance; a demure echo, told under candlelight, at a gentle fireside, of a fight informal; a discreet accompaniment to a strident song, done on a lute, played low; the stench of blood hid in a mist of soft-sprayed perfume; the yells of agony modulated down to a sweet pianissimo of pain; surly death, or death exultant, fashioned into a smiling courtier, bringing himself in with a bow; a balmy breath of blood and guts; all the mighty, bloodied vulgarity of war fore-shortened into a petty, pleasing picture. Here is shown, according to the famous G. J. Nathan, 'a ladies' war. A second view of *Journey's End*, widely acclaimed as a masterpiece, emphasises my original conviction that there is a humorously falsetto note to the exhibit, and that the late war, as the author sees it, apparently needed only a butler to convert it into a polite drawing-room comedy.'

But this play of Sean's was a very different thing. It tried to go into the heart of war, and, to many people whom it blasted with dismay, it succeeded. The curtain fell on the last scene amid a chorus of boos. The critics were confused, one saying this, and another saying that about the play, failing to analyse it faithfully or well, which was no wonder; for, if the author had been asked to analyse it himself, he would have failed as badly. One kind and effective thing the critics did for him. Almost unanimously, their criticisms implicitly declared that the play, with all its faults, was a work well worth producing by the Abbey Theatre; and that the play, far from taking away its high fame, would have added another spot of honour to the Theatre's reputation. And Sean knew that their comments had, unintentionally, delivered him from the thickest of the dangers that had come upon him through the contemptuous rejection of the play by the Abbey Directorate. He had but to wait a few years longer.

Sean O'Faolain ran home to tell Da Russell that 'it was to be feared that before he had exhausted the possibilities of the technique he knew, O'Casey had turned to technique that proved beyond his powers. Showed in other words that this play is not good theatre as we understand the term in these islands. O'Casey and the producer found the result of this experiment in a new technique a little beyond the capacities of the modern stage. The second act suggests that Mr. O'Casey finds the conventions of the modern stage insufficient for his purpose; though, as I suggest, he has written far too little to say so with any authority. The producer was clearly at a loss. The second act he must have found easy game; that sort of stuff has been done more than once before. Augustus John designed the scene, the chanting was handed over to a special man, and, anyway, there wasn't enough sensible core to the rigmarole for anything much to be obviously wrong. It was clear that neither money nor trouble was spared to fashion Mr. O'Casey's noveletta into a stage play. O'Casey must not be angry with us because we do not flatter him, as his easy English critics do. His talents are undeniable, but, so far, as all agree, they have not produced a play without the stamp of the workshop on it, and this one as much as any.' The Wild Irish boy soothing O'Casey's last moments.

In the quiet domestic turmoil of living from week to week, Sean got a letter from Lady Gregory saying she was in London, and would like to come to see him, his wife, and their baby. He was greatly troubled, and wished that Lady Gregory had forgotten him. He would not let her come. He would say hard things about Yeats and Robinson that would hurt her. His wife begged him to let Lady Gregory come, for she was eager to get to know the woman of whom he had so often spoken affectionately and well. No; he would not let her come. Eileen begged him again to change his mind, saying his refusal to see her would hurt Lady Gregory more than anything he might say. But, no; he would not let her come. So Lady Gregory went back to Ireland without a word with him; without a last affectionate handshake, for he never laid eyes on her again. This refusal was one of his silly sins. He still thinks angrily of himself when he thinks of her, or hears the name of the gracious, gallant woman. He should have listened to Eileen.

Sinclair wanted to do *Juno* in Belfast, and Sean wanted the money that might come from the royalties. He had now no connection with the Abbey Theatre, and so gave a hearty consent to the production. Then came a telegram from Sinclair telling him the Abbey had prohibited the performance, alleging that they alone had the licence. Sean maintained they had no claim to the play, but the Abbey solicitors pointed out, in majestically legal terms, that the contract, lasting for a year, could be extended to another one, by acquainting the author of the Theatre's wish, when the first year's contract was about to end. This, they said, they did. This, said Sean, they did not do. Sean pointed out, too, that, the year before, the Abbey had pencilled in a production of the same play in the same theatre in Belfast, which, later on, they had cancelled. Now when he had succeeded in getting the chance of a production there, they got busy to prevent it. The controversy became bitter. Sean got McCracken & McCracken of Dublin to act for him, and, with their help and Lady Gregory's interference, the Belfast production was allowed; the Abbey confining its claim to Dublin, with Sean agreeing to this permission to run for one year more. All the past things, according to Lady Gregory, 'were meant kindly, if Sean but knew'. Perhaps they were, but it seemed to him that the Abbey wasn't acting fair. According to their own admission, his plays had done a lot to help the Theatre out of financial insecurity; it had had a percentage out of the London production of his plays; but this querulous attempt to prevent him from making a little money, badly needed, didn't tend to breed within him a kindly feeling for the Abbey and its odd and wondrous ways.

But this wasn't the end of the irritation. Soon after, Sean began to realise that royalties due to him weren't arriving. Some had been due quite a time. He wrote to the Theatre politely pointing out that these royalties were due. He got no answer. Blessing a second one with a curse, he wrote again. He got no answer. The Theatre was as if it was not. He wrote the third time, and a letter came back to say that the cheques had been sent long ago, and must have gone astray; but new ones were on their way to him. Again the halt happened; again he wrote to the Abbey; again there was no reply. He wrote to Lady Gregory, and she replied to say she would write to the Abbey. But over in Dublin, on a holiday with his wife, he had to go personally to the Abbey to get the payment of royalties due for months. He began to feel more acutely than ever that the Abbey was bent on making things unpleasant for him. When he returned to London, the halt in the sending of royalties began again. After a long and irritating wait, he wrote asking for them. He got no reply. Several letters followed at decent intervals, but no notice was taken of them. At last he registered one, and sent it off, but that went into the well of silence with the others. Then he placed the matter with McCracken & McCracken, the Dublin solicitors. They questioned the Abbey, and got the old answer that the cheques had been sent, and that they must have gone astray. The solicitor asked why the registered letter had not been answered, but there was no reply to this question. Finally all was paid to the solicitors, the Abbey saving Sean the solicitors' fee by paying it themselves.

Odd things appeared in some of the English Press: 'One wonders what will happen to *The Silver Tassie*. Mr. Yeats suggested some slight alterations in one or two of the scenes. These O'Casey refused to consider. "You must have it whole, or not at all", was the reply. So the play went to America after a very brief run in Dublin. Mr. Yeats and I were members of a house-party in Wicklow when the play was produced in Dublin. I shall always remember him sitting by the fire on a wet Irish night, declaiming verses from his own work in that impressive and sonorous voice of his. Then he turned to *The Silver Tassie*, and recited the opening lines, which were not happy. We saw the difference.' A Peter Pan picture. They were all false statements. The play had had no run, very brief or very long, in Dublin. The play had not gone to America, for it hadn't yet been done in London; and in a letter to Sean himself, Yeats said, 'he never told anyone he suggested slight alterations in the play, or alterations of any kind; and that he could not imagine himself declaiming verses at any house-party; and that he could not recall seeing the critic on a wet Irish night in Wicklow, or anywhere else'.

Then the American *New Republic*, writing about Yeats and the Abbey Theatre, went on to say that 'The Abbey Directorate, led by Mr. Yeats, was definitely changing its outlook and ideal; a change clearly shown by the quick rejection of O'Casey's play, *The Silver Tassie*, because of its continuance of the cult of naturalism'; whereas the contrary was the case, for the play was refused, not because of its naturalism, but because of the play's lack of it. By a twisted version of the controversy, O'Casey's unnaturalism was being used in defence of Yeats's continued desire for realism. And it was all very annoying.

Sean must have replied to some, or one, of these misrepresentations, for in a copy of a letter sent to Mrs. Shaw, in 1931, he finds himself saying, 'I do not know how much I must read into your advice "not to be too belligerent". God be my judge that I hate fighting. If I be damned for anything, I shall be damned for keeping the two-edged sword of thought tight in its scabbard when it should be searching the bowels of knaves and fools. I assure you, I shrink from battle, and never advance into a fight unless I am driven into it. I give you a recent instance: The Abbey Theatre are going on a tour through America; notices appeared in the Press, mentioning the plays, which included *Juno*. I wrote to Mr. Robinson about this, and he replied that he had asked the Chicago Lecture and Concert Association months ago to get into touch with my American agents. I left the matter there, and said no more. Then I got a letter from my agents, Samuel French, Ltd., saying that the Lecture and Concert association were asking for *Juno*, and that they had asked for an advance of five hundred dollars; this was refused, and the demand was reduced to two hundred and fifty dollars; this, also, was refused, with the statement that all the other dramatists were satisfied to do without an advance. I rang up the Authors' Society, explained the situation, and was strongly advised to press for the advance. The intimation (that the Abbey had selected *Juno*) came so recently that I had no time to write about the matter, and so to avoid any suspicion that I wished to hurt the success of the tour, I wrote to the agents telling them not to bother about any claim to an advance of royalties. So, in face of a possible misapprehension, I shrink even from insisting on a very modest demand.

'On behalf of James Joyce, before me now, is a letter I received this morning, which tells me that someone has translated a story into German, and has had it published in a German paper over the name of this writer. Joyce declares that he never wrote the story, and that his signature is a forgery. And, worse than all, the thing is altogether beneath the genius of Joyce. Now should I sing silently in my heart of the meanness of this deception against an artist; or should I give this man the comfort of indignant sympathy from a comrade in the evil that has been brought upon him? I shall not keep silence, and the song in my heart and on my lips shall be in harmony with the indignant song of Joyce.'

It was bad enough to have the great Yeats trying to deflect him from doing what he wanted to do; bad enough to have the envenomed clergy spitting anathemas at him; and now he had the dulcet, sour assurance of Mrs. Shaw piping out a tune for him to dance to. Thank you; he would do his own tap-dance, and to his own composition too. Uncle Yeats and Auntie Shaw were equally anxious that when he roared, he would roar like any sucking dove. When he turned to the right, he was to say what Uncle Yeats wished him to say; when he turned to the left, he was to say what Auntie Shaw wanted him to say. A gilt-edged security censorship. Uncle Yeats and Auntie Shaw would join hands for him to sit on them, so that they could give him a soothing, little swing swong wrong. A nursery cursery for Sean the proud. To them the things that are theirs; to Sean the things that are his; for better or worse; for richer or poorer; till death shall call out Silence.

The time swung along from one year to another, like a monkey swinging from branch to branch of the same tree. Yeats's great black oxen trod the world, pushing away older life to give space to the newcomers. Sean's next play, *Within the Gates*, hearsed within an atrocious production, had appeared on the London stage; had run home to hide in a corner of a silent room. From a home in Buckingham, Sean had set out to America to help in a production of the play in New York; crossing to Belfast first to spend a week in Mount Stewart. Sailing back from Belfast again to Liverpool; and from there away, away to the New Island, the name given by the Irish to the United States that gave a few great riches, and gave to many of them the serenity of the grave. Home he came from America, very tired and strangely thrilled, to sit and think and recover by an electric fire in a new home formed from a flat in Battersea. There one day a letter came to him from W. B. Yeats. He recognised the writing: from the poet, right enough, the great Yeats. He was bade to come to take dinner with the poet in his lodgings at Lancaster Gate. At last, Yeats had stretched out a hand of friendship; and the heart within Sean rejoiced greatly. Then here's a hand, me trusty frien', an' gi'e's a hand o' thine! Seas between us braid ha'e roared sin' auld lang syne.

At Lancaster Gate, Mrs. G. Yeats was there watching over her famous husband. Pushing death away from him with all the might in her little hands. Anxious that he should not do too much. When dinner was on the table, she left the two men alone to eat it, and Sean felt the lack of her quiet charm and her good looks. Yeats was stuck in the centre of strife, selecting poems for his *Oxford Book of Modern Verse*, and shortly after dinner, he tried to win Sean into an hour's fight with him. The room seemed to be thronged with poem-books from all persons; while on the mantelpiece lay a pile of Western Tales of cowboy and Indian chief, sliced here and there by a detective story, which were there, he told Sean, to ease a mind tired and teased with a long concentration of thought on the imagination of others. Twice, he asked Sean's advice on selections, but Sean shut his ears, saying, with finality in his voice, that he could not suffer himself to give a judgement on a poetical piece. Yeats desisted, sighing and saying, it was hard work, but his ear was true, his ear was sure; the tone of his murmur seeming to indicate that he wasn't so sure as his words declared.

They turned to talking of the Elizabethans, whom Yeats evidently loved, and was glad that Sean shared his delight in the careless splendour of their poets, who made even violent death majestic in a mass of jewelled words. The stern intensity that Tourneur and Webster showed in velveted revenge, plumed murther, and rotten lust that ermine covered grandly. Mighty souls decayed to shivering flesh and chattering teeth. Two minds whose thoughts were phosphorescent lightning, to whom the world became a great revolving skull in which life tried to live, knocking its energy against bony walls; out of whose eyeless sockets life looked out on nothing, to shrivel back, to look, and see the less within. Where the Jew of Malta bows to the Duchess of Malfi, and Vittoria Corombona stands indecently triumphant on the pedestal of Liberty's statue.

And yet, in spite of all their weary boniness, their mire of lacerated flesh, their spilling wildly of the shrill, sad scent of death, a sombre rosiness lights up their caverned despair, and simple blossoms, wild and wanton, steal and wind around their tomby places. Brocaded butchery of power sinks to the tender:

> Call for the robin redbreast and the wren,
> Since o'er shady groves they hover,
> And with leaves and flowers do cover
> The friendless bodies of unburied men.

What better mourners could a dead man have than a robin and a wren, decking his buried dust with animation and broidering it with a song; fluttering over his dense, deep sleep, disturbing gently the everlasting silence of the dead. Finer salute to what was, and is not now, than the cold mumbling of cardinal-bishop or cardinal-deacon, black-robed as a Jesuit or scarlet-clad as a Secularius. A quiet trumpet sounds elation in the chirruping *de profundis* of the birds, for the dead live on in their work left behind with the living.

The teeming thoughts of Yeats turned suddenly into himself as a tremulous stoppage of breath started an outburst of coughing that shook his big, protesting body, stretching his wide chest on a rack of straining effort to rid itself of congestion, or end the effort by ending life. His hands gripped the sides of his chair, his fine eyes began to stare and bulge, showing the storm within, as he leant back and bent forward to sway with the waves of stuffy contortion that were forcing resistant life from his fighting body. The whole stately dignity and courage of the poet was crinkling into a cough. He has caught an everlasting cold, thought Sean. His own black oxen are treading him down.

These Elizabethan poets pulled a bell to tell of criminals, hidden and revealed, hiding in ermine and scarlet taffeta; the horrid things they did, nagging at heaven to get rid of the lot of them; as if the slimiest and most villainous souls of Paradise Lost had come to town to be converted into duke, cardinal, and courtier. Cardinals who 'made more bad faces with their oppressions than Michael Angelo made good ones'; and lords, who, when they laughed, were 'like deadly cannons that lighten ere they smoke'. No worse than Hogarth's later gin-mad men and maids; no more mischievous than those later ones who gambled their estates away in London, Bath, and Tunbridge Wells, impoverishing their tenants, ruining the land over which they claimed an immortal, menacing ownership. And do today.

Sean longed to cross to the coughing Yeats, and lay a warm, sympathetic hand on his heaving shoulders; to say silently so that Yeats could hear, God knows, if power were mine, you would be for ever young; no cough would ever come to warn you that the body withers. But custom held him back; the fear of offending his structured dignity by resting a kindly hand on another's shoulder. Afraid of the outward and visible sign of an inward and invisible sympathy.

—I get this way at times, the creaking voice of Yeats apologised behind his curtain of coughing. I have had congestion of the lungs.

Here, in Elizabethan drama, was not one particular court of Calabria, but all courts caught in a poet's mirror, where kings and dukes, spunned in flatteries, walked; and toadies tumbled in their haste to lick the shoes more costly than their own; where

> The poor rogues
> Pay for 't which have not the means
> To present bribe in fist; the rest o' the band
> Are raz'd out of the knaves' record; or else
> My lord he winks at them with easy will;
> His man grows rich, the knaves are the knaves still . . .
> While divinity, wrested by some factious blood,
> Draws swords, swells battles, and o'erthrows all good.

Ay, and you can see the same things today, if you only look out of the window.

There's a man, Sean went on thinking of Yeats, who never saw it; and, if he did, censured the crowd because they came uncultured. But his is more than a bare name; one who will never shake hands to say farewell to reputation; who sought the society of queens and kings over the hilly lands and hollow lands of thought; and thought them brave and precious; never descrying that their careless grandeur and perfumed manners were milled from the sludgy life the people lived; from whose satin-bound laws, but a day ago, came the decisions that he who snatched and ran, who stole two pounds from a dwelling-house, or five shillings from a shop, or picked from a pocket a coin but one farthing over a shilling, must suffer death by hanging; and when a kindlier man brought in a bill to substitute transportation for hanging in cases of theft from dwelling or shop, six bishops voted against it, led by his grace, the Lord Archbishop of Canterbury. Oh, brave old world!

Here is he whose dreams of his loved one were wronged by

The cry of a child by the roadside, the creak of a lumbering cart,
The heavy steps of the ploughman, splashing the wintry mould;

so that he turned away that he might not hear. A buccaneer among shining shadows. So different from Lady Gregory, who would run out to see why the child cried, or why the wheel of the wagon creaked. And yet his poems belie the man, belie him badly; for there was no braver man among the men of Eireann than W. B. Yeats. In every fray of politics, in every fight for freedom in literature and art, in every effort to tempt Dublin's city into the lure of finer things, the voice of Yeats belled out a battle-cry.

Some have said that Yeats was an actor, enjoying himself posing about in trismegistic mask on a painted stage. A charming fellow, they said, wearing his cabbalistic cloak well; but genuine only in making his acting look genuine, though done in a world painted into the panels of his own deceptions. But beneath the masque, under the cloak, was the man of powerful integrity; vain and childlike, fearful of what might be a humiliation; brave before rich or poor; courteous, even to those who lingered to bore him; a truer rebel than truest politician; and eager, like the upsprung husband of Malfi's duchess, to fashion the world right.

—The scene where the echo sounds is fine, said Yeats, when the cough had loosened its grip; where the echo tells the lover-husband, out of his own words, his wife's end and his own. It is beautiful, is it not, O'Casey?

—It is very beautiful, and it is very sad.

—Yes, Webster, murmured Yeats, though not too deep for tears, is far too deep for laughter. Others may bind the brow of life with laurel; Webster binds her brow with crêpe. The incense in his temple's burning brimstone.

—But through the choking mist, said Sean, burn many coloured candles.

—We are afraid of sadness, the poet murmured; we have it in life, but we fear it in the theatre. You mustn't be afraid of it, O'Casey.

—I'm not, if it tinges, or even startles, life, like a discordant note in a lovely symphony. I'm not when it has nobility. But when it comes brazen through hunger, disease, or wretchedness, then I hate it; then I fight against it, for through that suffering there can be no purification. It is villainous, and must be destroyed. Even Webster condemns the sorrow his own imagination created. He, too, was one of those who longed to fashion the world right.

—You're a Communist, O'Casey, aren't you? His face came closer, and his bright eyes peered and pierced, as if he would read Sean's thoughts ere any could be fashioned into words. It is astir in the world today. What is this Communism so many place their hope in, so many fight for, and so many speak about, as if it were a new *lux mundi*?

A shock to Sean. He never imagined that Yeats would smite his mind with such a question; and he wondered if the poet was really interested in any answer to his question. Was the interest in Communism, or was it but Yeatsian curiosity eager to peer into the mind of another? Even were the poet genuine in his question, what was he to say to the white-haired man who so often took up a current question to look at it for an hour, and then let it fall from him when interest faded?

—Communism's no new *lux mundi*, he said. Its bud-ray shone when first a class that had all, or most, of what was going, became opposed by a class that had little or nothing. It has grown in power and intensity till today it floods half of the world's skies. We give it the symbol of a red star. Earlier it was called the sword of light; Prometheus; Lugh of the Long Hand.

—Ah, O'Casey, these things, symbol or myth, do not belong to the crowd. There is danger here: would you set the rabble in power against the finer and fuller things common to great and gracious people?

—No, Mr. Yeats, not against them; but set the rabble, as you call them, down among the finer things of life, and give them the chance and power to help create them.

Yeats shrank back into his chair; shrank into himself, and saw the little streets hurling themselves against the greater ones. So Sean thought, and so he seemed to see that Yeats didn't like the sight entrancing.

—The finer things aren't so common among your great people as you think. There are many of them who have never read a line by Yeats. Some of them know no painting but a few handed to the family hundreds of years ago, hanging on the wall still, not as a graceful glory, but merely as a rich endowment. They journey each year to the Royal Academy Exhibition, where they are rarely puzzled, and can cry Hem! before the pictures. Many of them today do not even know the clock, and are constrained to cry out with Falstaff's What time o' day is it, Hal? Most of your great people, Mr. Yeats, are so ignorant of, and so indifferent to, fine things that Lady Gregory and a few more stand out as remarkable or even unique.

Yeats sat silent for quite a time, staring into the gas-fire, not altogether relishing what Sean had said. He coughed again, then the fine head moved closer towards Sean, and he said, What is this Communism: what is its divinity—if it has any; what is its philosophy? Whatever the State, there must be a governing class placed by wealth far above fear or toil.

The mind of the poet was probing again: what did that mean, now, what does this mean? Why should Sean worry this white-headed man with thoughts alien to his nature; this man who was a warrior among mere fighters, who had given to life more than he got from it? He got to his feet, laughing. Ah, Mr. Yeats, he said, the divinity in our philosophy is but the things the massed energy and individual thought can do. All of us will be above the common fear of life, and work will be a desire in us as strong as hunger or love. Our leaders will be above the rest only in the measure of more vivid minds and more enduring energy; used for the fuller security and higher benefit of all. Communism isn't an invention of Marx; it is a social growth, developing through the ages, since man banded together to fight fear of the unknown, and destroy the danger from mammoth and tiger of the sabre-tooth. All things in science and art are in its ownership, since man painted the images of what he saw on the wall of his cave, and since man put on the wooden share of his plough the more piercing power of iron or of bronze.

—It isn't enough. What I've heard of it, O'Casey, doesn't satisfy me. It fails to answer the questions of What is life, What is man? What is reality? It tells us nothing of invisible things, of vision, or spiritual powers; or preternatural activities and energy beyond and above man's ordinary knowledge and contemplation.

—Aha, said Sean, what philosophy does? Even Christian theology leaves us prostrate and puzzled. You yourself have read many philosophers who failed to answer your questions; failed utterly, or you wouldn't be asking them now. Communism deals with man as man, a glory great enough to begin with. Think deep as you can, think long as you may, life depends on low reality.

—But the Catholic Church, which has a vision, however we may disagree with it, and a divinity, though we may not believe in it, has a social philosophy, O'Casey, just as Communism has.

—Well, said Sean laughingly, the Roman Church builds her social contract on the Rearum Noharmum Harum Scarum Rerum Novarum, but we build ours on the Communist Manifesto: this time it is our philosophy that is built on a rock, theirs on a hill of sand. All the glory that was Greece, the grandeur that was Rome, sprang from corn and oil and wine. We cannot safely go a day without a hug from Demeter. All the poetry of Shakespeare, Milton, Shelley, and Yeats was first embedded in the bosom of Demeter.

They talked about the Abbey and its newer plans; of the new Directors appointed on the Board to broaden its outlook, for Yeats thought the time had come for a braver display of European drama; the poet mentioning Hauptmann's *The Weavers* and Toller's *Hoppla!* He asked Sean to tell him of any new play the Abbey might do.

The cough shook the fine frame of the poet again; the breast ebbed and flowed spasmodically; and the fine hand grasped the arm of the chair with tenseness. Odd that Yeats couldn't see that no divinity, Gaelic or Christian, came with balm to refresh with health the corroding chest of the poet. Sean stood silent, watching the shock of lovely silver hair bounce up and down to the rhythm of the racking cough, and waiting for the hoarse harshness to decline into a deceitful peace. The last mask—a mask of pain.

—It hampers me, this, he said, in little gasps; comes on so often, so often.

—You mustn't let anything disturb you, said Sean, trying to put the affection he felt into his voice, and hoping Yeats would sense it; nothing but the vexing necessity of resting. We need you, sir. Your very presence, without one thing done, one word said, is a shield before us all. I have tired you. I shall go now, and leave you in peace. Goodbye. No, no; don't stir—I can easily let myself out; for the poet was rising to give three steps from the door in courtesy to his guest.

—We shall talk of this again, said Yeats, stretching out a hand in farewell. Thanks for coming to see me, O'Casey.

Sean left him staring at the gasfire, crouching in the big armchair. His greatness is such, thought Sean, that the Ireland which tormented him will be forced to remember him for ever; and as Sean gently closed the door behind him, he heard the poet coughing again: broken by the passing feet of his own black oxen.

A LONG ASHWEDNESDAY

SACKCLOTH and ashes, silence and anxiety everywhere, but for the indifferent gaiety of the little fellow at play. Eileen was having a hard time of it. She had married Sean knowing he hadn't much, but hardly guessed she'd walk beside him to a time when he'd have nothing. The pretty mouth was tight again, determined to fight it out. The play agents, Samuel French, Ltd., had offered three hundred pounds for the world amateur rights of his Irish plays, provided a prompt copy of each play was given to them; and Sean and Eileen, who had never seen a prompt copy of a play, were now busy in the bungalow making out three of them. He had seen the theatrical symbols of R.C., L.3.E., that had spotted the editions of *Dick's Standard Plays*, so often read when he was a young fellow forcing a way to his heritage of literature; but he had never paused to ask himself what they meant; and, now, busy typing, cutting, and pasting his plays into a new form, he was adding these damned symbols into the script, things that should never be admitted to the published edition of any play. It was a sickening job; worse for Eileen, for she had to preserve interest in the work for the sake of what it would earn, while he hated the task, though forced by circumstances to go through with it. In a letter to Sean, Bernard Shaw had kindly advised against the sale, but there was no way out of it. So Eileen and Sean toiled on, he cursing, she in a brave and quiet way, for Sean couldn't shake off the belief that Yeats and the Abbey Theatre were mainly responsible for the tension of his affairs: so he and Eileen toiled on. Oh, that he could forget these matters that with himself he too much discussed!

Some days before, Lady Keeble had written to him asking him to her home in Oxford where there was to be an exhibition of verse-speaking by first-class members of the English stage, and Sean had written to say he couldn't go. Then a telegram had come to say that H. G. Wells would call to bring him to Oxford, and that she would take no excuse. In the stress of the work in hand, Sean had forgotten letter and telegram—Lord, I am not worthy of this work, Lord, I am not worthy; may I never have the hope to know again the infamous glory of this positive hour. In the midst of the typing, cutting, and pasting, a jingle came to the door-bell, and Eileen, returning from answering it, proclaimed that a Mr. H. G. Wells was waiting to take him to Oxford, and H. G. Wells walked into the room to face Sean in trousers, shirt, and slippers, sleeves rolled up, sweat on his face, tackling the job of the prompt copies for the Firm of French. And God said, Complain you to the wind, to the wind only, for only the wind will listen. In came H. G. Wells, his broad face smiling, his chubby hand stretched out for a cordial grip. A rather stout, shortish figure, looking like a classic undertaker whose services were given only to the distinguished or very wealthy. He was dressed in black from top to toe, a black tie nicely connecting the two ears of a stiff collar, modifying the gayer note of their white colour; black kid gloves covered the plump hands, one of them holding firmly to a black bowler hat. So neat, so prim, so precise in dress and manner was he that there seemed to be almost a *noli-tangere* touch about him. A figure of evolutionised respectability stood before Sean, in no way expressing or even implying the shape of things to come. Not H. G. Wells, but Mister H. G. Wells stood before him. Indeed, Sean thought, God put some odd shapes around some of the greater souls. Sean found it hard to imagine that such an insignificant-looking torch should give out such a great flame; a flame that had shown the way to so many tribes of thousands out of encircling gloom, led them bravely over torrent and crag to where they could be brave to speak, strong to climb, and where they could see to do; so much more effectively than the gentle Newman, leading his tribes of thousands to where angel-faces smiled for a moment, then left him and his thousands far from home and lost and wandering.

In came H. G. Wells to hike Sean off to Boar's Hill, Oxford, where distinguished persons had gathered together to hear the trained and true recite verses from poem and from play. But Sean could not go. Why not?

—I've come out of the way to get you, said H. G. Wells, laying a genial and encouraging hand on Sean's arm, while Eileen stood by, silent; Lady Keeble sent me a telegram commanding me to call here and bring you with me. So, you see, there's no escape.

—It was good of you to come out of your way, Mr. Wells, and I'm sorry I can't go with you.

—Lady Keeble will be very annoyed, said the still, small voice of Wells, the hand on Sean's arm slowly sliding away from it; very much annoyed, and I shall be very disappointed. Do come; you will meet many distinguished people.

—No, said Sean, I can't go. I'm in the centre of a job I hate, and, if I broke away now, it would be almost impossible to begin again. I will stick to what I'm at till the thing's done. And why hadn't Lady Keeble asked Eileen, thought Sean, and why didn't Wells ask her now, as she stood near them, listening to what was being said? He didn't relish leaving her alone with her boy and a host of anxieties. Besides, she was as intelligent as any distinguished person on Boar's Hill, and, probably, far more lively. They must get some money somewhere, before they could comfortably listen to a voice reciting verse. No, he would not go. Through a dark cloud of fears the time redeem, the well-read vision in the lower dream; to put new money in the fading purse, the time redeem.

H. G. Wells slowly fixed the black bowler hat on his head, and murmured a cold goodbye. Sean's mind, full of the job he was doing, only half comprehended that the great man was annoyed, and paid no attention to Eileen's whispered, You ought to go. He and Eileen went with Wells down the long narrow drive to the gate where a fine, big, black car waited to bring the two of them to Oxford, Sean funnelling excuses into Well's ear telling how he'd written to Lady Keeble, saying he couldn't come, afterwards sending a telegram that he couldn't go, emphasising the fact that he must have some money, and to get it, he must finish the job he was at; that debts were waiting to be paid, and that he couldn't stir from where he was till things improved; but Wells walked straight on, never answering a word, never turning his head to glance at Sean, never repeating the cold goodbye, but climbed into the stately black car, motioned to the driver, and was driven off; and, though Sean and Eileen waved a sorrowful farewell, never turned his head to see it. They stood there till the car swung out of sight, Sean with a heavy heart realising that though he hadn't made an enemy, he had lost a friend; and, though he wrote several times later on to H. G. Wells, suggesting a meeting, he got no reply, and never saw H. G. Wells again. O Lord, teach us to stare and not to care, Teach us to stand chill. Pray for us winners all the hours of our life.

Ah! A Vancouverian letter from Barry Fitzgerald, on tour with the Abbey Company throughout America. A resplendent tour as concerning the journey; into Pennsylvania, up to Montreal, from one side of Canada to the other, down south-eastwards to Florida, over the Rockies, which, when Fitzgerald saw them, made him cease to 'wonder why God rested on the seventh day'; struck dumb by the vision of Manhattan, the buildings surely being 'a new wonder of the world' though he thought that some of them 'showed a dis-position to go wrong at the very top'. But things weren't going too well with the Company. Another smudge of ash on Abbey foreheads. The letter said that the audiences in the Universities and Women's Clubs weren't so friendly as those in the commercial theatres. 'In Philadelphia *Professor Tim* met with a heavy reverse, and even the great McCormick was brought hurtling down by many shafts of criticism. The University papers dismissed *Juno* with an airy wave of the hand, while they submitted *Professor Tim* and the shallow Robinson comedies to a profound and respectful analysis.' Aha, Barry has his knife in the Universities! According to the letter, Fitz-gerald and Maureen Delaney got the best notices, in spite of the fact that two players, Eileen Crowe and F. J. McCormick, 'had been heavily starred in the preliminary notices and handbills prepared by Robinson. In the handbills, Lennox Robinson says, "There have never been any stars in the Abbey Theatre during its long history, but if there were stars", and then follows a long and glowing descrip-tion of the work done by McCormick and Crowe.' Fitzgerald adds that the rest of the players, himself included, thought it a lousy way of breaking through the traditions; but, he goes on, 'we have been secretly comforted by the fact that McCormick has failed to live up to the reputation made in Dublin'. Indeed, Fitzgerald says that, in spite of good parts and plenty of publicity, 'McCormick has been a decided flop. I'm sorry for Peter, because he feels it keenly, I think.'

Oh lord, here's a laughing between the porch and the altar, for what is actual is actual, not only for one time, but for many times, not only for one place, but for many places. This was more anxiety, for if the American audiences thought the Abbey plays poor and the acting bad, then Abbey plays — and his were among them — and Abbey acting would excite small interest in the years to come; but Sean comforted himself with the soothing assurance that these growls were fostered by the jealousy which afflicts actors, so often envious of a line of praise given to another. Fitzgerald wrote of a plan for another tour the following year — good news to Sean. A business tour, this time, confined to the commercial theatres along the eastern coast, 'leaving the universities and small towns crying in the wilderness; a strictly business tour, without cultural cod-acting pluming it'. Fitzgerald thinks that the Dublin public are 'off him', for in press-cuttings sent to him from the Irish papers commenting on the tour 'my name is never mentioned, in spite of quite good notices', and Barry wonders if there be 'some religious prejudice, for Dublin is very catholic now'. Less catholic, Barry, more clerical.

It wouldn't be long till there would be no cultural cod-acting in the Abbey itself, either, for death had pushed Lady Gregory into the bog of stars, and Yeats was now fighting hard for breath. When the subsidy was given with the demand that the new Director must be a roman catholic, the first flush of decline touched the Theatre. There was a wariness creeping into the Theatre's conception as to what plays would make a profit and what plays would not, and the episcopal crozier was tapping at the stage door. It was to thunder on it when the Theatre ventured to put on his own *The Silver Tassie* a few years ahead; break it down and loosen the bonds that had riveted the Abbey to what was brave, fantastic, and provocative in the art of the drama. But not yet, for Yeats was still to the fore to press his back against the door's yielding. But he was soon to die, and the younger poet, Higgins, stood in his place till he, too, suddenly shuddered into the grave. Then came the rush to lay down the red carpet to the box-office, which has become the chief prop of the building: the stone the builders rejected has become the head of the corner, with the Manager, Mr. Blythe, within, singing his troubadour song that the successful play was the play that filled the house. Pull down the final curtain on all or any cultural cod-acting. Be fair, Sean, be fair! The Abbey was having a difficult time; playwrights were working with the keener eye on the Censor; actors and actresses, at the first chance, swept headlong down the suction-pipe of the films, and were joyously lost in the golden dust-bag of Elstree or Hollywood.

Sean worked off and on at a new play, *The Green Gates*, a title he afterwards changed to *Within the Gates*. He had written a lot of dialogue and rough drafts of themes, and now he was trying to knit the wild themes and wandering dialogue into a design of Morning, Noon, Evening, and Night, blending these in with the seasons, changing the outlook of the scenes by changing the colour of flower and tree, blending these again with the moods of the scenes. The dominant colour of Morning and Spring was to be a light, sparkling green, that of Noon crimson and gold; Autumn's crimson was to tinge itself with violet, and Winter and Night were to be violet, turning to purple, and black.

At this time, he had become a little interested in the film, and had thought of this play as a film of Hyde Park. He thought the film world was dangerously indifferent to the life of England and her people. He thought of the film as geometrical and emotional, the emotion of the living characters to be shown against their own patterns and the patterns of the Park. It was to begin at dawn with the opening of the gates and end at midnight as they closed again to the twelve chimes of Big Ben striking softly in the distance. He had written to Alfred Hitchcock to come and have dinner with them, so that they could talk it over, and Hitchcock had agreed. Hurrah! Eileen got out the handsomest tablecloth they had, and laid the table with their best dinner-set, one kept for state occasions, or for particular friends, with a bottle of wine looking like an awkward jewel in the table's centre; for Sean and Eileen had secret visions that this coming talk might bring money worries to an end for a long time.

Sean had his own ideas about films. To him the camera was the king of the kinema. It was the actor in all the film did, or tried to do. Actors however great, actresses however glamorous, were but minor correlatives of the kinema, like fancy buttons on a coat or a pretty buckle on a belt. Good acting by man or by woman could never create an art of the kinema. No power on earth could turn the shadowy figures on a screen into living men and women. By and large, the films, without a doubt, had become the lowest form of entertainment, an insult to infant and adult man, even to him who had painted pictures on the wall of his cave. Chime their church bells as they might in film after film, they'd never win a casual glance from the passing Jesus, or induce the meditating Buddha to lift a shuttering eyelid, or Mahomed to give a stir enough to cause a crease in his cloak. Let them multiply their succulent close-up kisses as they will, they'll never show off love as Shakespeare did or Rostand either; let them crowd their streets with gunning gangsters, they'll never this way show the rapidity and excitement life has within herself. All their agitated screens that flow from Hollywoods and Elstrees to flicker and flap all over the country are little else but lurid ornamentation on a great big scab.

Hitchcock was a hulk of a man, unwieldy in his gait, seeming as if he had to hoist himself into every movement. Like an over-blown seal, sidling from place to place, as if the hard earth beneath couldn't give him a grip. Seated at table, though quiet in his movements, he seemed to be continually expanding, while Mrs. Hitchcock seemed to contract, a stilly mind sitting silent but attentive, registering every gesture and every word. His sober lounge suit, straining at the buttons, seemed to want to let itself go, while her gayer dress seemed to tighten round her body, imprisoning the impressions her mind formed from the experimental talk of the evening. Hitchcock liked all the suggestions made by Sean, but Sean noticed that his wife kept a dead silence, merely answering quietly an odd question or two put to her by Eileen. Hitchcock blazed up about the power of the camera — it could take into itself all in heaven, on the earth, and in the sea under the earth; there was nothing beyond its scooping eye. But Sean felt that the camera could do very little. Keep moving was its cry, like a parrot-policeman. It could not pause to take a breath as the stage did; it had to keep on the go, or perish: a still wasn't still life; it wasn't dead life; it was nothing. The film's sad moment couldn't spare a second for a sigh, its comic moment a second for a laugh. At its best, the film is something outside of man; at its best, the theatre is something within him. The film is a sword without a blade, a banner without a staff, an arrow without a head.

Hitchcock left, bubbling with excitement over what he and Sean had proposed; leaving a hearty invitation to come to dinner some day the following week, of which Mrs. Hitchcock would let them know, so that the discussion might go on again; but Mrs. Hitchcock departed smiling and silent, slowly silent and sure. Sean never got the invitation, never heard from Hitchcock again.

Madame Adami came to set down the score for the songs in the play, and for the plain-chant to the verses in the second act. For days before, Sean had felt a severe, continuous pain in the place where his heart was said to be, but he ignored it, and went on, singing, with his work. Half-way through the lilting of the airs for Madame Adami, the pain suddenly burst into a flame of agony, and his chest shot out and in as if the heart was going to do a high jump out of his body. Madame Adami fled from the room. Lie still, keep quiet;

phone for the doctor! Lie like a dead one, while the heart pulses madly on. Having lost its rhythm it is frightened, like a little child lost rushing hither and thither for its mother. My heart's in the Highlands; my heart's bowed down. Do not say that life is waning, or that hope's sweet day is set. Maybe soon he'd be a picture without a frame; the summer's saying goodbye to the rose. Goodbye, blackbird! Oh, give me back my heart again.

Eileen's heart was a hive of buzzing fears, and Sean, though tortured with pain, was uneasy too with the desire to laugh at the sudden change in the life of the house, the common household duties suddenly flooded over with anxiety and time-consuming care. Run along, hurry up, phone him quick — the doctor! Bar the door, shut to the windows, and keep death away; hot haste everywhere in the midst of an alarmed quietness. The repressed and dread expectancy that death may be coming up the steps to the door. Knock knock knock. When lilacs last in the dooryard bloomed. Oh, Sean, oh, Eileen! Our child, our little boy. Stifle the thought. And Sean laughed at the renewed vision of Madame Adami flying out of the room.

Death! What is a death but a fading leaf falling in an infinite forest of life! It should be sad, it should be always sad, even when the old, having used up all that life could give them, sink sleepily into darkness; but death should never put uncertainty into the life it leaves behind. Why should a sad thought in a sadder mind be forced to cry out, How are we going to live now? Why should death, which is hard enough, act harder still by bringing hardship in its train? Why should it matter a damn to the widow and the orphan as to what they shall eat or wherewithal shall they clothe themselves? Why should one be dependent on another for bread? To Give us this day our daily bread, there is often no answer. The prayer doesn't travel far enough. Not here, there is not enough silence, and there is too much noise near heaven for God to hear. Not that Eileen or her boy had had much from him. What he got from his work had, as 'twere, to be dragged out of infinity. Hardly enough to keep them; never enough to free their minds from the jagged prods of anxiety. If he went tomorrow, it's little she'd have to lose, but even that little might be missed by her and her boy. There wouldn't be enough to pay the doctor looking down at him. Certainly, Eileen with him would never be like Madame de Guermantes, able to buy and wear such a red dress that made her look like a blazing ruby.

He must remain perfectly still, the doctor was saying, the cautious eyes still peering down at the outstretched Sean. For how long — an hour or two? For a fortnight; just to lie as he lies now. Only the barest and most cautious of movements. He lay for a few minutes after the doctor had left. What if his heart was as bad as they thought, it could never be much better, and the setting of the score would finish the play. Up he got, and in he went to the room where the piano stood, and where stood Madame Adami cloaked and hatted just ready to go. He lay down on a divan, and before he gave in to the battling heart-beats in his breast, he sang the songs and chanted the plain-song till all the scores had been set down for the book of the play.

An X-ray was taken in the local hospital, but the plan showed a scarred lung hiding the heart, so the heart was hidden away, and no thesis could be written about it. He must see a London specialist, but how to get there without the burden of travelling in a bus was a problem. Lady Londonderry very kindly solved it by sending down a car which carried Sean like a grandee from his own hall-door to the doorstep of the London specialist. Then the fight began, for, after a few questions, the specialist caught a grip of him, flung him on to a couch and started an all-in wrestling tour of Sean's body, thumping, twisting, and pulling him about, till Sean thought that if there hadn't been anything wrong before, there was bound to be something wrong with his heart now. He was paying dearly now for the early luxury of his life. But Bertram Nissè was evidently a specialist in spirit and in truth, for nothing happened but a few gasping laughs from Sean as he was whirled about on the couch.

Pulled out of the hurly-burly of pummelling, Sean was wired to the cardiograph and his heart-beats were measured and timed with the quietness and confidence of electrical surveillance; and the end was that while his heart was not a first-class one, it was not what he would call diseased; O'Casey had a heart of his age. When this was said, there was a long silence, for Eileen and Sean had convinced themselves over such a long time of waiting that the heart was diseased, that, when the doctor said it was not so, they couldn't suddenly adjust their minds to the declaration, causing the specialist to ejaculate, You don't seem to be glad of the good news. Then the silence was broken by a laugh from Eileen and Sean — not because of relief, but because of the extreme care they had taken to prevent Sean stretching even a finger too suddenly.

But, added the doctor, he mustn't do any kind of strenuous work; must live for a few months on green herbs and water; and must, above all, separate himself from worry. Well, the rose of life was still held in his hand, but Sean could see some of the lovely petals falling. He who loved to trundle a barrow filled with grass or weeds, to swing a hook into undergrowth, or an axe down on a sturdy log, must sit still on a deck-chair, and listen to the humming of the bees; walk between the violet and the violet, walk between the various ranks of varied green. Well, it was better than an illness changing the universe into a corner wherein we crouch; but it was one more smudge of Lenten ash on his forehead. If the wings were no longer wings to fly, they would beat the air with effort; they would never fold themselves to stay still: for ever patient and for ever active.

No worry? But he had to worry about his family, about his play, and about the way things were going in Spain. There Saint James of Compostello, shoulder to shoulder with Franco, was herding a crowd of Moroccan Mahommedans into arms to keep the Christian Faith all alive-o in Madrid and Salamanca; the Koran was now part of the Cannon Law. England's Government was doing all good men could do to ensure fair play was rampant, opening the sky for Hitler's and Mussolini's bombing squadrons to make a bloody blot of Guernica.

Shattered a bit by his illness, Sean took thought as to how he could get his play produced. He had waited a long time, knowing that if he didn't get something from the play, the family would be in a cleft stick of poverty. It had been published, but no sign came that any commercial manager was interested in it; no lordly amateur like Barry Jackson thought even to give it a passing nod. It lay there, embalmed in the book. The English way of life didn't go the way of experimental drama. While the leaders of English Christians were attending the Public Schools, and the mightier universities, they tensed their minds to have a drink or two with Chaucer or Shakespeare; but when they came home they swam about in the blue lagoon of musical comedy, or sat down to enjoy the tremendous thrill of watching agitated gentlemen on the stage vying with each other as to which of them would sleep with a certain lassie when night must fall.

Had C. B. Cochran had enough of money to play with, the work would have had a production of rich colour and emotional movement, for Cochran was the bravest man England's theatre has had for a century and more; the bravest and the best. Dapper from his dainty bowler hat to his spatted boots, grasping an elegant walking-stick, Cochran had all the light, glow, and colour of the theatre within him, like the kingdom of heaven in the soul of a saint. A Master of the Revels, if ever there was one; the king's revels and the revels of the people. It was he, and not Lilian Baylis, who should have had a theatre to nourish and display, for he had more courage in a new look at things and more imagination towards the projection of the drama into the minds of men, without his cloak, than Lilian Baylis had with her cloak of pretence flowing out from her shoulders, and flicking everyone in the face. Everyone bowed the head, if not the knee, at the mention of the Baylis name; and stars of the London stage, straying into a conceited generosity, would, occasionally, play a star part to emblazon the Baylis name, and give their own a lime-light glow of love for drama; indifferent to the other poor actors around them giving all they had for nothing, or, indeed, paying a fee to be permitted to play. Stars asking a paltry pound a week from Baylis (Baylis was willing), would, a week later, ask a hundred from Cochran, and get it, too. A god-testing lady, this Baylis, for when-ever she needed money for the Old Vic, down she flopped on her knees, saying, Dear God, now's the time for some dough; so open up the old everlasting purse, and shower it down. And down it came, clinking down to fall on her lap as the gold of the god fell into the lap of Danaë; ay, and more than enough, for she died with a tidy superfluous sum in her private back pocket.

The Baylis Theatre, known as the Old Vic, was said to be a world-famous place, dedicated to the production of Shakespeare's plays, but chiefly maintained to beatify the name of Baylis for ever amber. Sean was guided there first by J. B. Fagan, who had charge of the London production of his play; guided there in a taxi-cab, with Mary Grey and Fagan, silent and reverential all the way from Bloomsbury to Waterloo Road. The play staged that night was *Romeo and Juliet*, and Sean was shocked at the poverty of the audience (their numbers, not their clothes), the acting, and the scenery. Beyond the fine portrayal of the Nurse and Mercutio, there was no reason to give even a cold clap of the hands. The scenery had the faint bluster of things children at play take from a rag-bag, with-out a child's imagination left to make them glow; colourless, though colour wasn't costly; it was just that the children playing on the Old Vic stage wouldn't be permitted to deploy a daring, or even an eager imagination (if they had had it) by the mother Baylis; for not having any herself, she repudiated it in another. The whole play was flat and flimsy (bar the part of the Nurse which stood out from the others like a tulip half-hidden in a pack of chick-weed), a performance that penetrated far into nullity and put Shakespeare in front of it as a beggar for the charity and goodwill of the passers-by. Several times Sean went to see Shakespeare in differing moods, but the performances were all sullen, bold with poverty and impudent in pretence, like crutched cripples playing at football. So they went on, dragging one year after another in the performing of Shakespeare's plays, spacing them out as a farmer spaces out his regular rotation of crops.

Some time near now, the television authorities asked Sean by letter and telephone and courier to write and speak a three-minute script giving short and pithy reasons for the formation in England of a National Theatre (there had been an argument and discussion in the Press about it, and Sean had written heatedly in favour of one in *Time and Tide*). After much hesitation (for he didn't like the idea of televising himself), after argument about it and about, he consented, spending quite a time in bringing together what he thought were cogent reasons to force forward the idea of a National Theatre within the short space of three minutes. Finally, half satisfied, he submitted the script, which was not only accepted but praised for its brevity, and, he hoped, for its wit. Then he spent anxious hours waiting for the time to come when he'd stand forth for a National Theatre on the little screens of ten thousand television sets, to be, at the end, rewarded with a fee of three guineas. The day before the event, a telegram came, saying that mother Baylis had lodged a vicious protest against the proposal with the television authorities, and that Sean must now, during his appearance and speech, make it clear that the Old Vic was England's National Theatre; or, if not, the delivery of Sean's ideas would have to be cancelled. Shortly after the telegram, a motor-cyclist came snorting up to the door, the rider hurrying in to confirm the telegram, and to beseech Mr. O'Casey to agree to the terms of mother Baylis. Sean had never written a word against the Old Vic; he hadn't mentioned it in his address, for his idea of a National Theatre was something wider, more responsible, more productive of colour, line, and form than anything yet done, or yet to be done, than the drab dramatic heraldry displayed in performance or production by the holy house in Waterloo Road. Sean told the envoy that what he had written had in it what three minutes gave him to say; that the television authorities had accepted it; and that nothing could be taken therefrom or added thereto; so the envoy departed sorrowing, saying that the address could not be given, mother Baylis's authority thereby depriving him of a much-needed fee of three guineas. To this day, it is inexplicable to Sean that mother Baylis should have been allowed to countermand a request by the television authorities by ordering that O'Casey should chant a paean of praise to her, or keep his big mouth shut.

Sean knew that the more he tried to put into a play, the less chance he'd have of a production in England, so he had to decide whether he would model a play so as to squeeze it towards triviality, or persist in experimental imagination, and suffer for it. On the other hand, if he did get a production of an experimental play, he would be forced to submit to a rag-and-tag one, one that would be cheapened so much that half the life would be gutted out of it. The English critics, by and large, would measure the play by its furtive, underhand performance, so giving the play no chance of a better and deserving production in the future. Not only that, but a furtive and fidgeting production in London echoed loudly in New York, which wrapped the play in a web of failure, encouraging the American managers to falter in having anything to do with it; while the English critics, immersed up to their buttocks in love for the tawdry and trivial, are only too ready to give an imaginative play a kick down rather than a hand up.

So Sean, grubbing the infinite for a few faint pounds, was forced to risk a paltry production which brought to light all the darkness his poor heart had feared. After a struggle with Herbert Hughes, who wanted to torture simple tunes with elaborate musical decorations, Sean handed over the mystery of his playwriting to Norman McDermott, who reduced whatever lustiness there was in the play to an agitated and timid tinkle. An ugly woman was shooting an arrow into the sky. On the very first night of the production, Sean saw in the theatre's foyer the bunch of crêpe hanging there, telling him and all who came that the play was dead. After Herbert Hughes's share had been deducted from the advance, and after various expenses incurred during rehearsals had been paid, Sean had less than twenty pounds to call his own. Indeed, were it not for the kindness of Lady Astor, who gave him and Eileen a room in St. James's Square, with a fine breakfast thrown in, the O'Caseys would have been in a dire condition indeed. It would be a long time before he could retire at this gait of going; before he could lay down the pen, take up the pipe, and plank himself down in a deck-chair all in a garden fair; or smoke quietly in a valley of growing stars. No; better live on lively through the burnt-out ends of fiery days. Live in the world's garden, but not rest in it, for there are things to be said and things to be done. We chat with truth and sing with truth, and act with falsehood.

> Blessed sister, holy mother, spirit of the garden,
> Suffer us not to mock ourselves with truth.

A GATE CLANGS SHUT

RUNNING from London, fleeing from poverty as aforetime Milton fled from the plague. A man can flee from a plague, but never from poverty. It kisses him sourly when he wakes in the morning, and goes to bed with him at night; lies between him and his wife if he happens to be married. Sean was in a bad way, for little had come in since his battle with Yeats over the play, *The Silver Tassie*, which had been rudely placed under anathema by the poet. His work, accepted before, had now to force another way forward. Sean had to start all over again, separated from even the passive approval of Yeats and his admirers. Reviewers who hadn't yet found a way of their own copied the condescending criticism of Yeats. Even Dr. Starkie, one of the Abbey Directors, putting a hand to his better ear, caught the Yeatsian echo of, 'O'Casey is losing his dramatic fire by remaining in England; he is separating himself from his roots, and is beginning to write of things in which he has no interest'. So Dr. Starkie answered the echo by sending one of his own into the attentive air, saying, 'O'Casey has left the scenes of his impressionable years, and has lost the power to see intensely'.

A most unfair and cleverly-stupid statement to make. Sean had begun to write the play before he had been a year in England, and it couldn't have been possible to lose in less than a year the impressions of forty. Again, a good deal of this time had been infused into the London production of his older plays, so that maybe a lunar month remained for him to lose his 'power to see intensely'. Again, again, both Yeats and Starkie had spent far more than a year away from Ireland themselves, yet no-one accused them of having lost the 'power to see intensely'; indeed, Yeats had gone to school in England for quite a time, had lived in London as a young man for many years, and, afterwards, had paid many visits there; yet no-one had so far accused him that because of this he had 'lost the power to see intensely'. Again, again, again, Yeats himself had been inspired to write the lovely lyric, *Innisfree*, by the sight of tinkling water running down a window to keep things cool in a shop on the Strand of hot and dusty London.

So Sean and Eileen and their boy fled from London, after selling what remained of the lease of their London house; fled from the frying-pan of city poverty to the furnace of poverty in the glad, green country. A friend of Sean said he'd a cottage in Chalfont St. Giles, he didn't want it, and Sean could live in it as long as he liked. Live in my heart and pay no rent. So off they hurried, Eileen first, and Sean to follow as soon as the furniture was stored. Then a message came from Eileen for a quick despatch of seven pounds; the last tenant hadn't paid his telephone bill, so the postal authorities wouldn't allow its use till the bill had been paid. Poor Eileen, in a hurry and anxious to have a talk with Sean, signed a form acknowledging responsibility, and, though Sean wrote to, and argued with, the district manager, he couldn't get a refund of the money. A bad start.

How charming the cottage looked from the road, the road that came from Amersham and went to London, with the Chiltern Hills encasing the country round, and tucking everything in nicely. Near London, too, for the great city was only nineteen miles away. So near and yet so far: the last bus from Amersham left early for London and London's last bus left early for Amersham, so one couldn't let a friend spend an evening with one, unless he was put up for the night, and a London friend had to say goodbye at seven, if he couldn't put you up, and you didn't wish to walk the nineteen miles back to the Chalfont home. Lively chat had to cease, good company break up at seven, if the one wanted to be carried back to London or the other wanted to be carried back to Chalfont. Western way of civilised life.

It was an attractive road, hedged in with hazel, hawthorn, and bramble, which, in summer, held up vast bundles of wild bryony and wild clematis, giving place, in autumn, to masses of old man's silvery beard and myriads of beady berries, green, yellow, orange, and crimson, of the woody nightshade. And on this road stood the Misbourne Cottages, two of them, looking like dolls' houses that the manor, Misbourne House, had originally built for the amusement of the children and the use of their workmen. Misbourne House, now filled with a rich, retired business man and his family, stood, important and aloof, safe from foul contact, among its gardens, lawns, and its tennis-courts. Western way of civilised life.

The cottages were surrounded by a trim privet hedge, and, at the

gate of the one Sean and his family were to live in, was a lovely
white lilac-tree. Surely, the lilac is a rich feather in the cap of God's
creation. A tiny garden of grass formed a mat in front of each
cottage, ornamented with a round bed in the centre holding a red
geranium within a circle of dreamy petunias. To the side, separating
the cottage garden from the tradesmen's and workmen's entrance to
the Big House, was a brick wall, sprinkled lavishly with slimy moss,
with many ferny plants jutting from the crevices. Supporting this
was a grassy slope which bordered a narrow path leading to the dry
closet jutting out by itself from a side gable of the cottage. A towering, gaunt pine-tree stood uneasy in a corner of the little garden,
looking as if it had been kidnapped when young, and was now trying
to break through the hedge and join its companions in a wood. The
front door opened into a space, half hall, half room, forming a
dining-room, and from this room all the other places sprang. On
the right was a small room, evidently meant to be the parlour, just
big enough to hold a few chairs, a small table, and a stand by the
window on which to place a flower-pot, or rest a book. Here, at
night, Sean read and worked, stretched out flat on his belly, with an
oil-lamp beside his head, a practice that gave him a bad lump on his
elbow, caused by the hard floor's friction, which gave a lot of
trouble before it disappeared. At the back of the half-hall was the
tiny kitchen where all cooking was done on an oil-stove, for the
cottage had neither gas nor electricity; to the right of the kitchen,
stairs, as steep as a ladder, led to a loft which took the place of a
bedroom where the boy, his mother, and nannie slept; outside of
this room, along a narrow passage, was a cubby-hole big enough for
a stretcher-bed, and here Sean slept stuffily, for there was no window
in it; opposite was another cubby-hole in which was a bath so big
that one wondered how it got in. Oil-lamp and candle had to say let
there be light when the sun went down, though gas and electricity
mains ran along the road but a few feet away from the garden.
Chesterton would have enjoyed it a lot, and much more, if candle-
light and lamp-glow had been but the glimmer of a rushlight — shades
of the golden medieval age.

After some months of a bruised life, the landlord put in enough
electricity for a few lights, Sean paying half the cost of installation.
The rent was a pound a week, and when they had been there for a
time, Sean was presented with a bill for twenty pounds, four for his
own tenancy and the rest for the tenancy of the last tenant who had
gone suddenly to God knows where. The landlord expected that

Sean, out of kindness to landlords, would pay the amount owing cheerily-o; but Sean, in the hardness of his heart, refused. Eileen, who had a passion for cleanliness, used the bath daily for herself and night and morning for the boy, till after the fourth day's use, the bath remained full and wouldn't empty itself for anyone. It was soon shown that this would never do, for the waste water, when released, poured down into a sump-hole, and when the sub-soil became soaked, the bath stayed full, and one had to wait till the waters subsided, which might take a week or ten days. Consummate cleanliness had to stop, and a bath brightened from a monotonous certainty into an exciting hope.

The entire back of the house had no window, for it formed the gable-end of the big hothouse of the manor, making the whole house hot and stuffy on a fine day, and so a previous tenant had planted a meat-safe in the alley to the side of the house, providing a cooler place a step away from the closet. The closet itself was a simple affair, consisting of a rough seat from wall to wall, with an exposed bucket beneath the hole, and a box of sand with a shovel handy to be used discriminately after a visit had been paid to it. In the winter, a visit at night was an adventure, carrying a candle which couldn't be lighted, if a breeze blew, till the closet had been entered and the door shut.

How many miles to Babylon? Three score and ten.
Can I get there by candlelight? Yes, and back again.

A western worstern way of life. One night, groping his way along the alley, Sean slipped, and shot out a hand to the wall to save himself, immediately becoming conscious of slimy, wriggling things soiling the flesh of his hand. Lighting the candle, and shading the light with his coat, he saw the wall to be a mass of wriggling, twisting slime. Hundreds of thick-bodied snails, oozing their phosphorescent sweat out of them, and as many more corpulent slugs, were sliding damply up and down the wall; crowds of white, yellow, and pinkish worms crawled about between them; and myriads of fat woodlice and other vermin darted hither and thither when the light of the candle flame fell upon them. A Walpurgis night of vermin. A hideous, crawling, wriggling world, active in the silence and the dark. Sean turned the candlelight on to the meat-safe, and there, too, on its legs, on its sides, and probing at the perforated panels, were the snails, the slugs, and the woodlice. Sean took the light away from the animated ooze and ugliness, and stood in the darkness, shuddering, for darkness could not now hide from his eyes the sight of the mean, unwholesome medley of squirming, slimy life. Eileen and he poured pounds of chloride of lime over the detestable wall, to purify the place, but, in spite of their efforts, night after night the wall was curtained with this noiseless medley of moist rottenness, crawling and twisting about in its own unhealthy and unholy slime. He felt sick. Today, when it crosses his mind, the wriggling façade appears again, and Sean shudders.

And all this medley of wriggling dirt is part of God's creation; part, too, of Massingham's solacing and gay exhilaration of country life; part, too, of A. E.'s devotional delusion of the charming little furry things playing about in the tall grass when

> *Withers once more the old blue flower of day.*

Sean was beginning to see even here, but nineteen miles from London, that country life wasn't always lovely; just fields of golden corn or bearded barley; or the pungent honey-scent of haymaking; or the lark's loud song. He had come face to face for the first time with a few, out of thousands, of the farmer's enemies. And loathsome things, indeed, a lot of them were; and the fighting farmer couldn't be content, like Sean, to hide, shuddering in the dark: he had to meet them, fight them, destroy them all. These things were enemies of man; enemies of him who walked the paved cities as they were of him who walked where the elms grew and the plough, horse-led or tractor-driven, turned the furrows in readiness for the waiting seed. Later, he was to learn a lot more about the enemies of cultivation, visible and invisible, the mass-produced creations of God, boring and nibbling away the vegetable and animal wealth conjured into existence by man's animated mind and the endless energy of his toiling hands. He had heard of tubercular cattle, had seen an animal swelled and panting with anthrax, a horse twisting and stiffening with tetanus, a hen running round, gasping, its throat eaten away by the pip. Here, on the Amersham road, a farmer, before his face, had dived towards the ground, had caught a turnip-fly that had been busy with millions of its kind destroying the turnip crop.

—There's the blasted little bugger! the farmer had said, holding out the squashed speck on the ball of his thumb.

Then there was the rust in the corn, the rats in a thousand barns, the blight on the gooseberry, the mould on the apple tree. Here, and everywhere, a new exorcism was needed, and was being put into practice. A day ago, the roman catholic journal *The Universe* had reported that a boy in Washington, whose name was not given, had been, his parents said, possessed of an evil spirit, which dragged the mattress across the floor while the laddo slept on it, and sent him somersaulting out of a heavy chair whenever he sat in it. This couldn't be allowed to go on, so for thirty days a Jesuit priest, name not given, wrestled with the evil spirit, praying and fasting while he fought the evil thing, each effort bringing a violent outburst from the laddo that must have shook the windows out of houses along the street, till, at last worn out, the evil spirit went away, all witnessed by a stout protestant clergyman, name not given, who must have felt queer when he saw the demon disappearing into the stenchy curriculum of poor things damned. All broadcast from a news-service by NCWC Co., the paper said. So these dusty fables, blown about by a sour wind from the middle ages, rise like dust and blur the eyes of some, but settle again soon, to be lost in the ashes of the last stake that flamed around the last screaming heretic.

Man is busy now with a new exorcism — the expulsion of disease from man and animal and plant, defending the holy tissue of the flesh from pollution of virus and of bug; the exorcism of fear from man's way of life that he may stand up and speak out and laugh loud. Exorcism that calls for no candle, bell, or book, cassock or stole; a church where the altar is a table, the god a microscope; the ritual a bold imagination, a peering eye, a ceaseless searching mind; so that health may be sanctity, energy prayer, and the achievements of men and the play of children most acceptable praises to God.

To get rid of all that weakened or brought rot to the body; to sanction pain no more; to coffin nothing but what had lived a life to the full, a life that had no disappointed breath for a sigh at the leaving; a life that sank down, pleasantly tired, into the rest-rewarding earth. To give to the commonwealth of man the strong heart, the clear mind, the keen ear, the enduring lung, the bright eye, the stout limb, and the cunning hand — oh, Jesus, wouldn't these things be grand for man to have! Oh, Jesus, wouldn't these be achievements measuring as holy with, and higher than, Salisbury's Cathedral and Westminster Abbey!

Chalfont St. Giles was almost all owned by three families, the Nashes, the Tripps, and the Lanes, all inter-connected like the interlacing of an old Keltic illumination, while in the village and on the little heights around, stretching up towards the Little Chalfonts, dwelt the notable, the less notable, and the least notable. The village and neighbourhood had three religious and three social sects: the gentry, those who thought they were gentry, and all who caught a glow from working for them, went to the dignified Anglican Church; the business people, the higher artisans, and those who worked for the business people, went to the Congregational Church; and the rest, deprived of any chance to pretensions, sought God through the Methodist impromptu prayer and the rollicking, rallying hymn.

The village of a string of cottages, a butcher's, a newsagent's, a general store, a small post-office, and a chemist's, had two claims to glory: a stump of an oak-tree, right in the way of traffic, where, when it was flourishing, Milton was said to have sat himself on sunny days, and the cottage where he fled to when the plague beset London. Here, it is said, he wrote *Paradise Regained*, and here in this doddering house, looking as if a sneeze would knock it down, some pens and papers, with a few pictures, were set out to bring back to shadowy life a poet long since dead. Everyone in the village knew the cottage, but Sean never met a soul who knew the man's work. Mr. Nash, the business lordeen of the place, talked once of Edgar Wallace, but went silent when the name of Milton smote his ear; went silent and went away, never speaking a word to Sean again. To all the district around, it was as if Milton had ne'er been born. And no wonder, for to the poets elect of today and to those who garland these poets, Milton's name is one to be forgotten by the wisely-cultured moment. Emotion no longer minded him. The voice that sighed or shouted, the voice that sang with music, was not in a state of grace. Milton found no favour now with the Muses chattering among the cocktails, now in darkness, and with danger compassed round. Even the fine poet Eliot whispered into the ear of the embarrassed Milton, who was being silently pushed about by the quietly excited crowd — You'd better go, John, for your voice is gone and your vesture's queer. You were too prone to mix with the things poets keep away from: the voices of men throughout the wheeling years but make the present poet's ears ache; for all he worships now's the single self. England hath no longer any need of thee. They no longer serve who only stand and wait; no longer, no. I pray thee, get thee gone; get cracking, man, and go. And no-one said hello; and no-one asked who's he; and no-one said goodbye.

After a year, they moved into a bungalow, which, though of no great shakes, at least was cleaner than the horrible cottage, and was big enough to hold the little furniture they had collected. So when they had settled in, the first question was the choice of a suitable school for Breon, now going on four, and a fine, sturdy, upstanding lad. Eileen came down at week-ends from her work on the stage in

London to sport with him and teach him how to read from nursery rhymes and little books she got for him — a task at which Sean was useless. The boy needed companionship, for, though Sean played a lot with him, and played well, it was a strain, and not quite satisfactory for either of them. He had played with the little girl and boy of a Cockney couple living in a cottage a few yards away, but the father went to work in a garage miles away, and so, amid many tears, the children had to say goodbye to each other. Where was the boy to go to school? Sean, who had gone nowhere and had had to seek knowledge everywhere, didn't know; didn't know anything about the method of educating a child. He left everything to Eileen, who decided on a lower middle-class one with modern manners and cheery guidance rather than one whose rule of life was the rule of fear. But it should be a catholic school, for Eileen since her marriage had been a practising catholic. Having written for it, along came the handsome Prospectus from the Holy Cross Convent School, Gerrards Cross, for boys and girls up to ten. Fine building among trees, charming grounds, spacious rooms, good equipment, and fine fees too. And Sean's funds were very low. But Eileen was very confident; never mind; the nuns would be glad, when they heard the father was an author, to take a reduced fee till a play of his got going on a stage. They would be anxious that the boy should be brought up in the faith, seeing that his father hadn't been born into it, and had never caught it to himself; and such a fine little lad, too; you'll see, Sean. But Sean stayed doubtful. Eileen had been brought up in the lap of the faith, and had learned all she had forgotten from what was taught in the Ursuline Convent, Burgess Hill. Taught primarily to repress the natural vivacity beaming from her nature, an active, imaginative, and humorous mind hidden in a silly repressive gentility, till she escaped their consecrated clutches, and found a fuller life in the theatre. All these precious convents did the same service to their pupils: you must grow up into a ladylike person at all costs; refined, reticent, ignorant of life, of its valour and its vehemence. But Eileen was quickly coming to herself: she was developing the rash and lovely confidence which the nuns had dulled; she had a bright eye for paintings; she was at home and hilarious with children; she hadn't the faintest smudge of the snobbery so sedulously plastered over the souls of the pupils in the higher-class convents; she saw through people, and her humorous penetration often burst into a cascade of laughter at the follies of men and the antics of women. She had a ready ear for conversation, and she was becoming a good judge of plays. But Sean still remained doubtful about the nuns being willing to think of a soul before a fee.

The appointment was made. Eileen dolled herself up and little Breon wore his best tucker and bib, all shrouded over with mackintoshes, for the rain was falling furiously. The bus came, and off they went, three in one and one in three — for the Convent; Breon excited, Eileen cool and confident, Sean trying to look hopeful. He was to remain outside; he might disturb things if he came in; say something to rattle the sweet sisters. Spoil it all. Sean could see by the furrows gathering on Eileen's pretty brow that she was thinking out what to say to the same sweet sisters, potent help of Christians. Here they were out to bring the boy up in the way he should go. Which way was that, now? The catholic way, Genevan way, Mahommedan way, or the Buddhist way? These were but a few of the hundred ways carved out under the feet of every stepper-in to life. Eileen chose the catholic way; a way as good or as bad as any of the others. Sean hoped that when the boy grew up he'd take and make his own way. The right way to Sean was the desire to see life, to hear life, to feel life, and to use life; to engender in oneself the insistent and unbreakable patience to remove any obstacle life chanced to place in its own way. The way of the world; the way of all flesh: no-one could show Breon the way through these ways; he would have to find a way for himself. Life's way of yesterday wasn't life's way today; and life's way today couldn't be life's way tomorrow; so neither Sean's way nor Eileen's way, nor Swann's way, could ever be Breon's.

The bus stopped, and they stepped out of it. Here was the Convent of the Holy Cross surrounded by a wall; a fairly high one, too. Private residence of the potential saints. A big black iron gate, semicircular bars topping it, within the semicircle the name of Holy Cross Convent in large letters of gold, with all the ironwork and the name crowned by a golden cross: barriers to keep out the Fluther Goods. Hardwood and ironwork without and within.

Open your gates and let us through, not without a beck and a boo;
There's the beck, there's the boo; open your gates and let us through.

Fine grounds, too, now serenaded by the sough of towering pines as their wide tops were sent swinging to and fro by a strong wind; the serenading sough accompanied harshly by a bass droning discord of cawing rooks darkening the soothing sough of the wind-swept trees; while, from the sodden, hodden-grey sky, the rain fell with a rapid drum-beat on leaf, on grass, on pavement, lulling the earth and all that grew there into activity and freshness.

Eileen opened the heavy gate, and passed through, and the gate closed behind her with a clang. Sean watched the mother, through the bars, going up the rain-soaked drive, taking her boy to look indifferently at the cunning light in Christian eyes, and the tightened lips of divinity in man when money was in question: taking another step towards the glowing tedium of life's quick-march; then he hurried to a telephone booth twenty yards away from the Convent gate, pushed the door open, and went in to shelter from the teeming rain. From a side window, he still saw the stout wall, the iron gate, and the golden cross on top of it. A strong enclosure; fortified place; *ein' feste Burg*. How these important Christians fence themselves in! The whole appearance of this Convent called out, Come in with circumspection, and well clad; or keep out. One couldn't come in to the presence of a bishop or a community of nuns with a song as you could to God. Imagine Fluther Good, if he happened to be a father, going up this drive, his heavy hand holding the light one of his son; Fluther's shoulders squared, his walk a swagger, his lips forming the words of *The Wedding o' Glencree*; on his way to interview the reverend mother.

—How much, ma'am, for this little fella? How much? Jasus, ma'am, that's a lot to charge a chiselur for his first few lessons, an' makin' him into an ordinary, ordherly Christian man.

No; the little sons and daughters of the Fluther Goods were a long way from the Convents that flourished a golden cross; a long, long trail from the catholic way of this catholic Convent. The catholic way? Is there a widening way to wider thought there; is there the fearless peering into life; is there the loving, immeasurable sweep of the imagination in art, science, and literature in the catholic way? No, there isn't; not according to Newman, Acton, Duchesne, Dr. McDonald of Maynooth, and many more eminent men who suffered and were abused for standing up to truth, giving her honour, and making this daughter of Time their dear sister. The catholic popular Press is so shamelessly pietistic that no youngster honoured with a little intelligence would be caught dead reading it. In one of their journals there is a weekly sprig of verse so dismally silly, so senti-mental, so amazingly kiddish, that even *Casabianca* would look superb beside it. Their libraries seem to find few places for works on art, literature, or science. This is shown in a letter written by Mabel Jones, Librarian, Catholic Truth Society, Liverpool, who says: 'Apart from the classics (which are not in great demand unless a film popularises it) the bulk of novels by non-catholics, which are fit for distribution among catholics, are of ephemeral interest, and are likely to be left dead on the shelves unless great care is taken in their selection. Generally speaking, most of the writers of more serious novels nowadays hold a false philosophy of life, and a dangerous unchristian theory of morals. Thus, with some exceptions, the catholic library is reduced to mystery tales, adventure tales, and love stories of the lighter kind.' Mystery tales, detective fiction, and light stories of love, are, then, the high and holy books most catholics read, bar an odd classic when it has been suitably prepared for them by the film magnates.

Present-day Christians seem to be curiously attached to the detective story. Indeed, it is odd how even some of the theological lights among them aid the common catholic in his quest. G. K. Chesterton was their fiery godfather in this respect, and made a little, moon-faced catholic cleric a prime spyer-out of crime. The moment moonface began to beat his head, one knew, at once, that the criminal was as bad as caught. Then there's Monsignor Ronald Knox spending some of his spare time with a corpse in a culvert; and the quasi-theologian, Miss Dorothy Sayers, making the Lord Peter Whimsie into a noddle policeman, catching criminals as a good cat catches mice; and Dr. Alington, Dean of Durham. Then there is another gentleman of detective fiction, a collegian, who has used his detection talent to harmonise the gospels. He might have spared himself, for a scholarly catholic cleric told Sean that Ronald Knox's essay on *Watson of Watsonia* 'was written as a skit on the compilers of the Higher Criticism of the Bible', whose efforts to prove that the bible was written, not by one, but by many, were shown to be baloney by Knox, for the discrepancies in Doyle's books were as blatant and as many as those in the bible, so that it could be proved that Doyle's stories were written, not by one man, but by many. Maybe by thousands. So we can all rest easy, now, when we read the bible. Knox has made it all quite clear by having a little fun with it, though the Monsignor seems to forget that Doyle claimed no divinity to be hedging in every word he wrote. Indeed, Monsignor's thesis seems to have in it a hint of hiding himself. There seems to come from it, what, if someone else, other than a catholic, had written it, might be a glint of irreverence, making God out to be something of an absent-minded beggar. By implication, it seems to give a picture of the deity trying to remember what had been done, and when it had been done, a couple of million years before. Let me see now: What date was it now when the world was shaped from chaos? Come out, come on, come up here. Were Adam and Eve moulded by hand or made by a *deus ex machina*? There certainly were men in the world before Adam, says the catholic *Universe*, but they had no souls. When did they begin to get them? On one Hallow Eve or on a bright May morning? We do not know because we are not told. Biblical criticism, the turning tapsalteerio of testaments that had been divine authority for centuries, is no joke, and To be, or not to be, is a serious thought. There is pathos in the Christian's praying to Him whom he thinks his Saviour to deliver him from the pains of eternal death; in the Brahmin's praying to the purple-tinted God, O Shiva, grant that I may never be born again; and in the poet-tent-maker's wistful farewell, Where I made one — turn down an empty glass.

They were a damned long time in the Convent, thought Sean, for he was beginning to feel cold. The damp came through into the telephone booth. Looking out of a window on to the world. The rain still fell in sheets, racing down the glass windows of the booth as if the glass itself was melting. There wasn't a soul in sight, and the little common in front of him was desolate and deserted. A bench on the common, looking as if none were alive to sit on it, seemed to be sensing that the world was dead, and that never again would there be a lover and his lass alive to come and rest there. The trees bent over swiftly in the windy gusts, struggling back to their upright pose with labour and great creaking when the gust subsided, ceaselessly chanting the song of their soughing. Only an odd crow, heavily flapping its wings through the wind and the rain, lightened the hodden-grey sky, as it cawed resentfully, and winged a clumsy way to the rooky wood, looking like one of the nuns, caught up by a divine wind, and getting carried to heaven without her consent. Indeed, when in their black habits, the nuns looked like a flock of crows, cawing carelessly, too; for they all hummed the same tune in the one key, on the one note, throughout time, in the hope that they might hum the same tune, in the same key, on the same note, throughout eternity.

Thinking a way out of the world to heaven. The city of God. No mean city, by all accounts. O Paradise, O Paradise, who doth not long for rest: so the roman catholic and the protestant sing together, No one does really; certainly not for the rest death brings. All are ready to stick it out here as long as they can. The Christians aren't quite sure about the place above. No-one has yet succeeded in suiting the manner of after-existence to man's nature. The Christian conception of it is neither pleasant nor inspiring: a dreadful monotony of eternal praise was more than one would wish to inherit. Such a never-ending job would make of immortality a life not worth living. It is said that eternal praise, eternal contemplation, was what God had in store for the saved. Had he? How come? Was it some conceited cardinal, some conceited bishop, or even some conceited saint, who, making God out in his own image, thought out this way as the way of God?

What did Sean really want of any after-life to take the place of the robe, the harp, the crown, and the eternal confinement in a prison of praise? Well, for a beginning, he'd like a thousand years of life to get to know the peoples of the world so as to be able to enter deeply into their sorrow and their joy, and to encircle them with his arms like a girdle encircling the waist of a motherly woman; and as a step beyond a beginning, another thousand years to study and enjoy the world's plant panorama from the lichens clinging to the deadening wall to the towering redwood trees of California.

The dampness was beginning to circulate through his blood, and stamp his feet how he would, they grew more clammy and numb. He opened the booth door and went out into the teeming rain to stroll, stamping, to the Convent gate. He looked up the drive but saw nothing but the rain dancing about the neatly-gravelled paths; then, when the rain was streaming down him, he saw them, heads bent, running down the drive, the little fellow laughing as he stretched out his legs to keep pace with his mother.

—Let's hurry, said Eileen, when she came up with Sean — I'm dying for a cup of tea.

The little bus swept them away from the holy Convent, redolent of God's passionate plan for man and the history of the pound note, the secluded building canopied by cawing crows, a dear little, sweet little rookery nook; Eileen chatting away excitedly to Breon, her shapely little mouth clenching into tightness whenever she claimed a pause to rest in silence. That night, when Breon lay in a cosy corner of sleep, Eileen told him all that had happened: the nuns had encircled them smiling, beguiling, giving a welcome to mother and child; welcome as the flowers in May; come into the parlour, dears; stormy weather. Oh, sacred charms of childhood, unto Christ so dear; and, if you bring a proper fee, there's nothing left to fear. Not a thing. One and twenty welcomes to the little lad. A sturdy little fellow. He would be a charming addition to their school, a nun said. And an interesting one, too, considering his father to be a writer, said another nun. Under God, children are the one surety of God's Church continuing, said a third nun, laying a partly-blessing hand on Breon's head. You both must stay for tea, murmured the reverend mother, both stay for tea, murmured a nun behind the mother, stay for tea, murmured another behind the nun. Polly put the kettle on, we'll all have tea. Thank God for tea! What could the world do without it? How did it exist without it? Nobody knows.

I'm sure he'll be happy here, said Eileen, if we can only manage about the fees. Just now we have to ask you to let them down a little, only for the time being; for less than a year at most, perhaps but for a month or two, till a play his father's written struts the stage. The cock-robin confidence died down at once. The sisters grew silent as those who had stood on a peak in Darien. Their hearts stood still. Oh, no; no, Johnny, no. The hands patting the child's head hid away under the folds of the black habit. The good nuns, and they were all good, receded to a safe distance; on retreat. No, no. There was nothing to do but go. An old nun led the mother and child to the door, and bade them a curt goodbye; a never-ending goodbye now. Shut the gate after you! Clang!

While the prudent nuns went on measuring the worth of minds by the fees they brought, Breon took his first step towards organised community life in Longdene School, owned by a young quakeress, a green-shirt of the Social Credit Party, the little lad unconscious of any educational gain or loss, with Sean sure he was better where conditions placed him. And if it were a loss,

> His loss may shine yet goodlier than their gain
> When Time and God give judgement.

Here in the midst of Jordans, where William Penn lies buried, in the heart of the country where religion paraded the sombre black suit and the steeple-crowned hat, a part of England rich in the dust of those odd quakers famous in their longing for the grace of God and good business; here, quietly, unmolested by either heaven or hell, Breon passed through five energetic years, growing daily in the grace of boyhood and yearly in the wisdom of the oncoming man, learning by experience that the clang of a closing gate is but the clang of another one opening.

A FRIAR BY THE FIRESIDE

AWAY in a house in the deep green country, Sean nodded in his chair set near to a flaming fire, for the night was cold, and even the air of the room felt frosty. Midnight had passed by, and he was sleepy, but he knew that if he went to bed, sleep would go, for his mind was too tired to sink deep into it. Besides, the bed was far off and the bed was cold, while the spot by the fire was seductively warm, inducing a condition of wakefulness that was half-way towards sleep. He had extinguished the lamp, for the oil had wasted and the light had flickered; but the brilliant flaming of the fire gave enough light to show everything in it resting quietly among their own shadows. The whole house was asleep, and he was half-way towards it, nodding sleepily by the flaming fire.

> We're all nodding, nod, nod, nodding,
> Yes, we're all nodding good years of life away.

Father Clematis of the Cuneiform Order of Unimpassionate Canons Irregular had been to tea and supper, and had left a few minutes before twelve to give him time to mutter his Office before the last midnight chime had struck. A pleasant, chatty young man, ordinary though, whose main distinction was the habit he wore. His company was no gain, for he had entered the Order young, before life had had time to give him kiss or clout. No humour either; not a single spiritual or temporal laugh within him. Sean had seen hundreds like him in Maynooth — ordered and priested before life could give clout or kiss. Still, the lad seemed lonely, and, as he had evidently enjoyed his visit, Sean forbore to question his own foolishness in wasting time that might have been given to thought for work in progress. He was reluctant to say anything that might hurt the young friar's feelings when matters touching religion came up between them, so Sean had to keep the flag of conversation flying at half-mast; and so his mind had grown tired thinking of what not to say. And there was another reason for keeping away from anything likely to disturb the friar's mind: Sean could easily see that he wasn't made of sterner stuff; that though he might think of things, even be agitated, he would never have the gusto, the determination, to demand an answer from perplexing thoughts in his own mind, or questions put forward by the keener mind of others. Sean had known another mind like this one, but a much keener mind, that of a catholic layman, who, for a long time, had been a laughing absentee from Mass, who had expressed very liberal opinions, and had often quizzingly rejected both the theory and practice of the Church; but had neither the depth nor the resilience to carry the freedom of not knowing where life led when death came; not full enough to go on bearing the occasional foolishness and risky hilarity of humanity without a monthly assurance from a confessor that his sins had been forgiven, and that he was mounting monthly nearer to God; though, maybe, remaining as foolish, more foolish, in a harsher way, in sanctioning things and beliefs more ridiculous than had before given him any laughing pause.

For the first few visits, Father Clematis had worn the ordinary dress of a secular priest, but, afterwards, came in his rust-red habit and girdle of blue. Though to Sean the uniform didn't hide the man, to the roman catholic the habit was a grand uniform of vocational grace; the man was hidden in it, a tweedy carapace confining passion, pride, and all other characteristics, good and bad, of the common man. Sean couldn't help feeling that in its wearing on these occasions, there was something of the show-off in the young rust-red friar. A show-off, a show-off, a show—

Oh, we're all nodding, nod, nod, nodding—

A tap on the window-pane from a stem of the black-blossomed climber, Sartre resartus pedicularis, roused Sean with a start from his nodding. Curtains had not been drawn, and he could see the sky, thrilled with a multitude of frosty stars. Stare at the stars. 'These priests and Religious Orders, monks and nuns, are the Stars', says Mister Bing Crosby. What is the stars, Joxer, what is the stars? These is the stars, man — the priests and the religious orders. 'These', says Bing Crosby, 'are the real makers of history', says he. 'The rest of us run a business and make some money,' says he, 'and after a while we're gone, and the money's gone', says he; 'but', he says, 'they are building kingdoms of spiritual values, that are going to rule and influence generations years and years away', he says. And make some money along with the spiritual values, too, I says. 'Day after day they work patiently, shaping the characters', he says, 'of girls and boys, who will be the mainstays of this good American way of life of ours, which is founded on a belief in God. Look at any American coin,' says he — 'In God We Trust: on each and all of them', says Mister Bing Crosby. 'The Father O'Malleys and the Sister Benedicts are the stars in the film of real life', says Bing. The Bing Boys and the Bing Girls. And yet, I says, the highest percentage of crime among boys and girls, here in England, is among those who go to the roman catholic schools, and the lowest among those who go to the secular ones. And, I says, since our ideal in life seems to be in 'founding a little business, and making some money', then, it is a wise thing, I says, to put a spiritual slogan on the coins. We can depend on coins; they'll never let us down, and there's great value in a pious ejaculation on a coin, so there is, now. A week's holiday, without pay, from forced labour in Purgatory, maybe. Holy Night gives place to the Holy Nickel. Outside the blue-black birdies sang.

> Holy nickel, sanctified cent,
> Bless each proper lady and gent
> In every city and every clime,
> Now, tomorrow, or any damn time;
> Bless them all without reason or rhyme,
> Holy dollar and dime!

Well, there had been a Religious, a Star, sitting at Sean's fireside, a star that had a very dim twinkle. He pretended: he dismissed as nonsense what appeared in the weekly roman catholic Press, which he said, he never read, couldn't read, and wouldn't read — nearly adding so help him God (as other clerics did, too); but Sean knew that if challenged to say this openly in the pulpit, or print it in the Press, the young friar would slink off and hide where no challenger could find him. The young hand waved aside all of what he called the long-forgotten animus of ecclesiastical authority to punish spiritually and corporally any schism and every heresy; forgetting, or hiding, that the canon laws regarding these conditions of thought, flowering in the middle ages, were as fully in flower as canon laws in the Church of today. The young waving hand went on to decorate the voice saying, We rule and are authoritative only in matters concerning faith and morals; hiding the fact, or forgetting it, that roman catholic moral philosophy covers everything a reasonable man may think about. There is no important, and hardly any unimportant, activity of daily life that it doesn't grip, direct, or try to choke. 'It is notorious', says G. G. Coulton, the Cambridge Professor, quoting Schulte's *Ueber Kirchenstrafen*, 'that even voting at a political election has often been treated as a question of morals by the Church' (*and didn't Sean know it!*). Recently, Cardinal Griffin seems to have added mathematics; and a letter from a roman catholic in the *Spectator*, 1902, said quite gaily and off-hand, 'The real reason why religious persecution is unpopular today is that nobody is strong enough to persecute'. Still, the Church tries it on by condemnation in its Press, and by refusals to allow any defence from an attack; by inducing its more ignorant members to shout reports of blasphemy and obscenity in novel or poem they have never read, or play they have never seen; doing all they can to endanger the livelihood of anyone daring, even implicitly, to criticise anything they have said or done.

Our Community got where we are now, Friar Clematis had said, settling himself comfortably in the armchair by the blazing wood fire, got it through the goodness of God and the intercession of Holy Saint Joseph. We needed a centre of spiritual force somewhere in this district, a place not to be too big, but to have a generous chance for expansion; and a place not to be too dear. A retired officer owned it; he was provoked into putting all he had into a bogus company by a rogue of a company gambler. The end was a pistol shot; the house was said to be haunted, was offered for a small sum, and the Community bought it.

—An easy cop, said Sean, unconcerned in how they had got it, or what they had given; for his mind was tired, and he was full of sleep.

—Oh, no, not easy, said the friar complacently; we had indeed a long search, and it was only through the intercession of our Patron, St. Joseph, that we found our home at last. We must have trudged a hundred miles before we set eyes on the haven we hold now. Then he had gone, leaving Sean nodding, a nod knocking the walls away, letting the country roads flood into the room; and the fire become the rising sun at morn and the setting sun at night.

And it was as if Sean had been with them when they went forth on their journey to find a home. Out they set with a concerted sign of the cross behind them, the Prior, Father Auricula; Father Campanula, carrying a veiled image of St. Joseph; Brother Bugloss, and Father Clematis; seeking a place here, seeking one there, but finding none that would do. They wandered far and wide while the winter was on, cold winds sending the skirts of their habits flapping around their legs; along the road, sometimes hardfelt with frost, with never a bird in the sky or the sound of a bird-song from the empty hedges; finding no spot to suitably honour St. Joseph, ever praying him to help in finding, somewhere, something their scanty means could furnish.

Through the spring they journeyed, buds in the hedges and on the trees, singing a song of a summer to come, but they found no shelter for the saint's indwelling; the days shortened into the sudden hush of autumn at her own leaves falling, as the friars trudged up the road and down the lane, seeking to the right, to the left, a sojourning place for the image of St. Joseph, and finding none; journeying till backs were bent, feet went forward sore and aching, and thigh-pits flamed red with the friction of sweat; down road and up lane they trudged, around this house, that garden, without one drink at an inn to soften their dust-dried tongues, with hardly a word spoken, so that time wouldn't be lost for prayer to be said; sometimes thinking fearfully in their sinking hearts that Saint Joseph wasn't listening, or that he had decided to let the poor people sway along in their own perverted, pagan way. Then, one day of an opulent summer, they circled a house and they circled a garden till they came to a gateway, and, as the Prior's hand stretched out to open it, they felt that their journeyings had ended, and that St. Joseph had brought them home at last.

—This is where we come in, said Father Auricula.

The place was in the heart of a dark wood of Mauriaceni pines infested with original sins that burrowed under everything. At night one could hear the barking of excommunicamuses, the sharp chirruping of nihil obstats, and the shrill squeals of the greyem-green birds, silenced only now and then by the baying of protestans britannicuses which had their lairs everywhere: a dreadful medley and confusion, though all said it was all part of God's curious Kingdom.

It was dusk, and the garden darkened as they stood in a bunch, ready to pump out prayers that this house might be theirs so that it could be used in the expansion of Holy Church. Here, in this group, was the lust of the Church, garnered into its vast psychology, day by day, for nigh two thousand years. And Sean was as if he were there, close by the friars in the midst of the garden where the orthoagonies and the heteragonies bloomed in the day and the dusk, where many dear little bees sucked heaven's honey from one kind, and big bastard bees sucked hell's honey from the other kind, and all was blessed and blasphemous buzzing; there Sean stood, watching, listening, and hearing the sound of secret strife.

—Expose the image of St. Joseph, whispered Father Auricula; and Father Campanula whipped the white veil from the image, and the Saint shone forth in his robe of glistening crimson, edged finely by fine gold, his white beard tinged into mauve by the dusk, a brown staff held forth in his right hand as when he guided his young Spouse and young Child safe into Egypt, as recorded by Luke, but by no-one else, ready now to guide the Cuneiformians to a safe and lasting home.

Looka the face at an upper window of the silent house! A face so pale, a face that was twitching, a face so pale that the face formed its own flickering light, a face staring down at the shadowy friars praying among the orthoagonies and the heteragonies of the garden; and Sean sensed the sound of a silent strife that would make the possessor the dispossessed and the dispossessed the possessor. A deep green streak in the dusky sky gave a green glow to the window, and there in its centre shone the ghastly white face, whiter now because of the sad green light around it, with its eyes, hollow and glittering, peering out into the dusk, and through the dusk to the friars hidden in the purple peace of the garden. Looka the gaping mouth in the face at the window! But the friars looked not, but bent down lower as the gaping mouth, black in the white face in the green-lit window, gave a sigh, gave a long, sad sigh, filling the still air with a silent stir.

—Keep your thoughts on St. Joseph, murmured the Prior; there are many enemies near; contemplate the holy image: Oh, Holy Saint Joseph, Patron of the family and the home, be with us; give us what we seek and what we need and send us soon to serve thee here.

—What we seek, what we need, and send us soon to serve thee here, echoed the friars.

—Veil the image again, and let us go, said the Prior; we leave our petition with the Holy Saint: in this spot, in this place, around this house; and nowhere else; and none other house. He crossed himself, and added, Let us go!

The friars turned about, went out by the gate, and took to the road again, a sharp, sudden pistol shot echoing loud at their heels, following their footsteps pattering purely along, away, away, a woe away; and Sean watched them go, their rust-red habits black now, as the friars, sheltering close together, forged into the purple dusk of the late evening, hugging the image of St. Joseph away from any evil that might be there; for

> Self-slain soul, in vain thy sighing:
> Self-slain, who shall make thee whole?
> Vain the clamour of thy crying;
> Toll, bell, toll.

Then the door of the house flashed open, and a maid came rushing out, calling; calling; she ran through the garden, calling for help, and ran out by the gate and down by the road, calling. She had looked in at the doorway, and had seen it lying there; her heart had tightened with fear, and she had run from the house, calling. And in his mind's eye, Sean had seen it, too, lying there, coffined in its own clay for evermore; stretched out in the curious way the dead lie who leave life violently; but twist themselves in their agony or their fear how they may, they lie the same way in the sad solidarity of death. There it lay amid solid and respectable furniture, well made, lasting, rudely sneering at the lighter and more imaginative furniture of the age; christianly comfortable, made for life next to everlasting, full of the pride of permanency. The deathly face seen at the window was a face no longer, for it had become a white mask of hardening clay, dwindling into indifference as the maid ran along down the road, calling, and the bunch of friars went pit-a-pat through the purple glow to where they waited, a day's march nearer home, till St. Joseph had rung the bell, lit the candle, read from the book, and made the place fit for the friars to live in. And so the dead stayed where it was till uniformed brothers came to see, to connect the wound with the gun, and both with the hand that fired it; till other brothers came to lift it up and carry it off and hide it in the bosom of that mother who never denies a child, but willingly shelters all away from the heat o' the sun and the furious winter's rages. A pistol shot pronounced a blessing.

—So the Community got the place cheap, had murmured the young friar; St. Joseph didn't fail us, a happy thing for us. *Quam bonus Israel!*

—A happy thing for them, murmured Sean, in his own mind, wondering why this young fellow had such an odd idea of heavenly aid, and why he never once ventured a word of sympathy for the stretched-out figure that had brought such fair fortune to the Cuneiformians by rushing out of the world in a wrong, wild way. He had peered at the friar, looking past the habit to the man within: a man to whom all life and history must be explained by a collection of dogmatic decrees, 'which', according to Leo the XIII, 'impose themselves upon all catholics, and which no man is permitted to call in doubt'. Embedded in a decree, like a caterpillar in his cocoon. And the bishops drum their way about, denouncing doom on all who disagree, or venture a doubt.

> Fat bucks of bishops in a barrel-roofed room,
> Yell'd out, roar'd out threats of doom —
> Bell, book, and candlelight standing on a table —
> Pounded with their croziers in a frenzy of fume,
> Hard as they were able,
> Boom boom boom.

Excommunicamus, if you dare presume,
Bell, book, and candlelight will bring you what is due,
Bring you what is due and hoodoo you,
If you dare presume,
Doomday doomday doomday doom!

After two thousand years of thought, discussion, supernatural grace, and pious practice, all they can do to save man is to bind him tightly into one chair, and to bind God rigidly into one throne. Here by the fire, in a rust-red habit, with its blue girdle, sat a laddo who believed that he carried authority of life and death wherever his body happened to go; an ordinary mortal, who, because of what was called the laying-on of hands, pointed out the way of thought and action to everyone else, as if born to it as he was bred to it; with little knowledge of the way of thought himself, timidly obedient to every convention, every custom, honoured by common brethren, within and without his own community of faith. Sean had met many men in various walks of life who had assumed authority while in actual service — the doctor at the bedside, the scientist in laboratory or lecture hall, the foreman watching the rise or fall of a crane's jib: all these become common men in the give and take, the ebb and flow, of social life; but not the priest: he alone had a crystallised sense of authority that he carried with him everywhere, from the altar into all the odds and ends of social life. Pretend as he would, in casual talk, in quip, in serious conversation, the sense of rigorous, ritualistic authority over all life and all things clung to the priest, so that he could never be at one with the common man. Perhaps the one fireside beside which a priest might feel fairly free was the fireside of an agnostic, for here he needed neither sense nor show of his grace-engrafted authority; here was equality, here man spoke to man. Here the clerical pursuivant of grace abounding found he had no claim on anything but his own wit, knowledge, and geniality; here he was safe from any false honour.

Ritualistic grace seemed to have emptied everything else out of the young friar. He took no notice of pictures or print on the wall, never looked at the books on the shelves, never tried, or even asked anyone else, even to tinkle a simple song on the piano. Even primitive man, wrestling with life in a smoky darkness, painted pictures on the rugged walls of his cave. Sean tried to lead him to book, picture, folk-tune, but the friar leaned back from them all. They were all dangerous, a snare in each of them, though the friar loved the movies. But a thought outside the thought of the Community would leave him almost lost. It is a most dolorous sight to see a timid priest acting the bravo, providing for entertainment a quip, as innocent as a cowslip's bloom, about a bishop; knowing well that if he advanced any opposition to a bishop's or abbot's will, he would feel an episcopal fist striking his snot; and, if that didn't learn him, a crack from a crozier would lay him low. Crooks are no longer for rescue, but for authority; to thrust down rather than to pull up a soul to safety.

Nor any kindling thought for children. No light in the friar's eyes for a child. The brevity of life should be brought within the child's vision at an early age. Death should be forced up close to the young and encouraged to stay there. And the cane to guide them, to flail them into a fear of hell, lest worse befall them. In the priest's ear was the echo of the tale of how a little one, guilty of some 'mortal sin', was roasting in a red-hot oven in hell, the youngster turning and twisting itself about in the fire, screaming to get out; beating its head against the roof of the red-hot oven; stamping the little feet on the floor of the red-hot oven. A bad child, but God had been very good to it. He saw that it would probably get worse, would never repent, and would have to be punished much more in hell. So God in his mercy took it out of the world in its early childhood so that it would suffer nothing more painful than eternal imprisonment in a red-hot oven. A most gentle way of doing things. This is a fragrant roman catholic storiette, quoted by Dr. G. G. Coulton in his *Infant Perdition in the Middle Ages*, taken from number ten of Books for Children, this one named *The Sight of Hell*, written by a Father Furniss, C.SS.R., with the dewy *Permissu Superiorum* on its cover, and published by Duffy, Dublin, around the time when Sean's mother was a young woman about to be married. Its echo is heard still in the cry of the clerics yelling for the whip and cane to be used with precision and power to keep young hearts in the knowledge and love of God and of his son, Jesus Christ, their Lord. Gentle and kind is he. Oh, Father Furnace, how well you warn each young one of a personal *dies irae*. Here, now, was a young rust-red friar, sitting by Sean's fireside, talking about the boy, and asking why Sean and Eileen were so anxious to keep their lad healthy; why bother about what is mortal — the body? Why, indeed? Why trouble overmuch about a child's health when all that care has done may, in a moment, be a mangled mass under a passing car? And Eileen listened with wide-open and disapproving eyes by the corner of the fireside.

A raven suddenly perched on the roof of the Priory; and an evil bee of love invaded the Prior's cowl and then buzzed about in his bosom. He paused to pluck a rose as he passed, and the gay petticoat of an Annabel Lee fluttered Father Auricula into an indiscretion. A heart too soon made glad. The moth's kiss, first; the bee's kiss, now. The Community hung silent on the hook of consternation. The two primitive ladies who had given their best room for a chapel went frantic for fear of a scandal. Hush! The Prior was brought back to Headquarters for judgement, and, it was said, Father Clematis had been ordered to join a Mission in China. The silence lengthened, and the O'Casey fireside knew the rust-red friar no more. Hush, hush.

Where are you, Walter McDonald? You're needed now. They're making a show of everything, of everything; making a show:

> And we're all nodding, nod, nod, nodding;
> We're all nodding at work or when we pray.

STAR OF THE COUNTY DOWN

WHEN all was dismal, through the good and generous help of George Jean Nathan, the famous American drama critic, a contract was signed for a New York production of Sean's play *Within the Gates*, with an order to come to the United States — all expenses paid — to help in the rehearsals. Just before, he had had an invitation to come to Mount Stewart, the Irish home of Lord and Lady Londonderry, and stay a week there. So off he set from Heysham, straight for Belfast, from there in a boat dipping and rising a lot in a three-quarter gale, with two women in the next cabin far gone in seasickness, their wails and their abuse of each other preventing him from sinking into a satisfying sleep.

—Jasus, Annie, said a wailing voice, I'm in a bad way. I know it; I'm in a bad way, really — are you listenin'?

—Oh, shut your big mouth! came back an answer in a louder voice, an' let me concenthrate on me own disthress. You would insist on comin' to Belfast to slip down to Dublin to see Mr. De Valera. You made your voice a buzz in me ear of sayin' I must see De Valera before I die so often that I was thricked into bein' spellbound. Who the hell's De Valera that anyone would want to see him!

—It was you yourself, Annie Fitzsimons, that persuaded me I must see De Valera before I was a day oldher, an' all because you wanted to see him yourself. I'm near dyin' this minute. I'll let you know, Annie Fitzsimons, that my intherests aren't your intherests. De Valera's led me into a nice quandary of jumpin' up an' dippin' down. If we dip down a little too far, what's goin' to happen?

—You went sailin' in an' came sailin' out, said the loud voice, afther buyin' th' tickets without a single thought of askin' them responsible if the like of this might happen, knowin' that neither of us was ever on the sea before. Sacred Heart, isn't this terrible!

—It was you yourself led me into this, said the wailing voice; an' I'll hold you responsible, Teresa Tierney, with your De Valera's the one for Ireland; a holy man, a thrue pathriot. Well, now you know th' kind he is, an' you can have him all to yourself for Annie Fitzsimons. If I live to land, will I slip down to Dublin, to see him? I will not. Jesus, Mary, an' Joseph, amn't I to be pitied this night!

—It's meself doesn't give a damn whether you go down to Dublin or not, said the louder voice, for it was you was always sayin' you'd set foot on the land of Eireann before you'd die to lighten th' misfortune of bein' born on a foreign sthrand. Didn't you numb me ear with your ceaseless, ceaseless registration of De Valera as th' genius of the Gael? Now, looka where your lordly ideas have landed us! An' if we do strike land, what are we goin' to do when we think of havin' to go back again? To go through the same again. Have y' any answer to that one, Teresa Tierney? I wish you well of your wish! Amn't I convulsed thryin' to prevent me organs from shootin' outa me like a jet from a fountain! Stewardess! Oh, when I go back, if I ever do, what'll I say to me poor husband when he sees the state I'm in!

—An' I asked the sailor comin' aboard how'd it be, an' he said that I'd feel no more than a gentle rockin' of a cradle. What way can they be sailin' th' ship with its hoppin' up an' jumpin' down! In God's name, call th' stewardess, Annie Fitzsimons. It's plain that life's only a sideline on this ship.

—I'm tired callin' her, said the louder voice, though I'm sinkin' fasther than yourself. Call her you. Rockin' like a cradle! Why hadn't you th' sense to cross-question th' sailor-fella about th' manner o' rockin' he meant?

—For God's sake, don't ask questions, for I'm feelin' near th' end of things! Annie Fitzsimons, between the waves of agony goin' over me, I ask you what'll happen if we foundher?

—We're both well foundhered already. Ask your great De Valera what'll happen if we foundher! Curse o' God on the persuasion that got me into this disasther! Stewardess!

—Stewardess! echoed the wail as Sean, between the whistling of the wind and the pitching of the ship, slipped into a slumber that silenced the voices, waking only when the siren blew on entering Belfast Lough, giving him time to put on his best shirt and jersey, have a fine breakfast in the ship's restaurant, before the elegant car slid on to the wharf to take him through Newtonwards and along the margin of Strangford Lough to the home of his hostess, Mount Stewart, in building, the star of the County Down.

There it was, lovely and languid, embossed by beautiful gardens, sheltered by many trees, fading into hilly lands and hollow lands, fringed in the distance away south by the blue peaks of the Mourne Mountains sweeping down to the sea. Wide grounds so extensive that it seemed that to cover them it would take, even on a horse, a full day's journey. For those who walked, there were peaceful huts of a restful shape here and there, the floors and walls tiled with broken pieces of chinaware, some a rich blue, some more modestly so, others lightly coloured, and more still tending to whiteness, but tinged with the blue of their brothers. These pieces formed the floors, cunningly woven together, and on the walls were panels showing portraits of old Keltic saints, each done with the same pieces of blue chinaware, each piece of a different shade of blue from the rich, dark, full blue to a faint flush of it in those pieces tending towards whiteness, and woven more cunningly together than the tiling of the floors. In this summer-house was a panel silhouetting in blue the figure of St. Columkille, in that one the figure of St. Bridget, in another, maybe, that of St. Aidan, the time the Keltic Church preferred Glendalough's seven churches to the clamorous call of Rome, seeding itself in the mind of the popes. Chinaware patrons of places in Eirinn and guardians of Mount Stewart and the Londonderry arms, lovely to look at; but guardians no more, for their prayers, so long effective, were potent no more since God's ear was now cocked to hear the slogans and songs of the marching peoples.

> The Communes are comin', oho, oho,
> The Communes are comin', oho, oho.
> Who still are asleep, let them lep outa bed,
> An' run to catch up with the columns ahead,
> There's the richest of wine an' the whitest of bread,
> For the Communes are comin', oho, oho!

The Communes are comin', and the Big Houses are in the way of their march. The Big Houses must go with the times. The People are debouching from the public roads into private property; the

vassals and serfs are clattering into the marble halls; plucking
flowers from elaborate gardens to put into vases of their own;
writing their common names in the big Visitors' Book on the big
mahogany table in the big manor hall: Tom, Dick, and Harry,
Annie and Sue. A miner sits on a gilded chair; a cotton-spinner plays
boogie-woogie on the grand piano, prelude to Beethoven's Symphony in C or Mozart's Clarinet Concerto in A major. Clap your
hands over your ears. What was a feast is becoming a famine; what
was a famine is becoming a feast. All heraldry, simple, quartered, or
cross-quartered, has merged itself into one field of crimson, and has
become a red flag. A new age is here. Christ stepping down from
a spurious kingship has become a carpenter again. God save you
merry, working men, let nothing you dismay. Rejoice and be glad
that this day is our day; this year, our year; the future is ours for
ever.

And Mount Stewart was one of the Big Houses forced to flee the
new and robust life. They were the triumphs of vast wealth and
withering poverty. Then, all the wealth was gathered in by the few
and the only wealth the worker had was the spittle he spat on his
hands to give him a firmer grip of spade or hoe. Mount a hill and
look around and fail to see where Mount Stewart ended. Here were
meadow and farm, orchard and garden, majestic trees and thick-set
shrubbery; lowing of cattle, bleating of sheep, neighing of horses,
high-stepping animals as handsomely endowed as the family that
owned them; and a mighty wolf-dog cantering from hillock to valley,
through the gardens, into the big house one way in and out of it
another; massive in body and so gentle in manner; a shaggy beauty
that sometimes tempered man's nobility to a seemlier modesty.
Here were flowers from many families; roses that one would wish
could turn to marble and stay for ever; many flowers Sean knew well
already, and many more he met for the first time, never to learn their
names; antirrhinums, mazed with their own colouring, defending
the house from evil spirits; purple and crimson fuchsias that would
make gorgeous fringes for a high-priest's fullest vestments; all the
browns and yellows of France's marigolds and England's too;
begonias in great masses, decking the ground with pink, orange, and
crimson rugs, looking like magic carpets of the East that had grown
tired of sky-travelling, and were having a rest on the duller earth,
their elephant-like ears ribbed through the green with the colours of
the flowers themselves. The spacious gardens were packed with a
chorus of blossoms that found no place for the gentle murmur of

the primrose, which, earlier on, had clothed the hedge and bank with a carelessly thrown-on yellow gown of spring; and in the garden's centre, a great gathering of crimson flowers formed the firm red hand of Ulster, defiant and sullen, but looking pathetic in its glowing loneliness. Rich dark-yellow apricots dangled in hundreds from the sunnier walls of the big house; apricots

> which, like unruly children, make their sire
> Stoop with oppression of their prodigal weight;

apricots so luscious that their delicate savour would make any Duchess of Malfi sigh for a helping of the dangling fruit. Further on, long and deep thickets of hydrangeas bordered the Lough, the blue of their blossoms echoing the blue of the sky above them, while on a paved courtyard, in huge green-painted tubs, orange trees grew with fruit the Irish sun couldn't coax to a size much bigger than a crab-apple, but whose tiny golden globes gave a twinkle to the bitterness of the black north. Not so bitter either, for the north was bitter only when the north wind blew. The whins could be golden in Ulster, and the hawthorn blossom heavy; the thrush's song could be merry and the blackbird's could be loud, and purple heather could clothe a clumsy hill with cloth of glory, each tiny bell of the mass formation offering a fairy flagon of honey for the prodding bee; ay, and more, for Alfred, the Saxon King of Northumbria, said of Ulster,

> I found in Ulster, from hill to glen,
> Hardy warriors, resolute men:
> Beauty that bloomed when youth was gone,
> And strength transmitted from sire to son.

But protestant Ulstermen have failed to fuse the past with the present. As soon as they are out of earshot of the hammering of the shipyards, the rhythmic clacking of the spinning-mills, or away from the sowing and reaping of the fields, they see the cannon-smoke and hear the musket-shots of Boyne's battle. The god-confident protestant David is always going forth to fight boastful catholic Goliath, and, indeed, the wee sling and a few wee stones are part of the rites used in initiating a newcomer into the Orange Order.

Down to the south lies the spot where St. Patrick is said to lie buried, and, a little to the north, is Saul, where, it is said, he said his first official Mass in Ireland — two sacred places that no-one cares a damn about, though one might think that many a miracle would be hopping round here quietly. France's Bernadette and Italy's Anthony are honoured more by the Irish than their own

St. Patrick. His grave is said to be covered with bramble and briar by any occasional traveller accidentally coming to it; and hardly a hand in Ulster, or in any of the other three beautifields of Ireland, has ever planted as much as a primrose on the spot where Patrick's buried. No-one goes near it, though thousands parade to the grave of Wolfe Tone; and Downpatrick is better known as the place that saw the hanging of *The Man from God Knows Where*, rather than the burial-place of the land's apostle. The whole county reeks of ecclesiological memories that have been long forgotten. The town of Newry in the twelfth century saw a horde of kings and chiefs giving a charter to the Cistercians by which they got half the county from the king, McLoughlin, as his own proper gift for the health of his soul, and that he might be partaker of the benefits of masses, hours, and prayers that were to be offered in the monastery till the end of time. The end of time came quicker than they then thought; but the gifts made a long list of the people's lands and their riches to the holy brotherhood: the lands of O'Cormac with its lands, woods, and waters; Enachratha with its lands, woods, and waters; Crumgleann with its lands, woods, and waters; Caselanagan with its lands, woods, and waters; Lisinelle, Croa Druimfornact, Letri, Corcrach, Fidglassayn, Tirmorgonnean, Connocul, and many more places with all their lands, woods, waters went away from the people to the monks in honour of the Blessed Virgin, St. Patrick, and St. Benedict, given by the King of all Ireland, who also said that with the lands he threw in the mills as well; and added pointedly, I WILL also that, as the kings of Iveagh and of Oriel may wish to confer certain lands upon the Monastery, for the health of their souls, they may do so in my lifetime, that I may know what and how much of my Earthly Kingdom the King of Heaven may possess for the use of his poor monks; while Giolla MacLiag, Archbishop of Armagh, with the *Staff of Jesus in his hand*, which was the Crozier of St. Patrick, nodded approbation, with a pleased grin on his gob; and all the nobles, with their tongues in their cheeks, of Dufferin, Racavan, Lecale, Donnegor, Kinnelaerty, and others, signed the assessment, or clapped their hands, and cursed silently and severely the circumstances that had made them give up so much of what they wanted to hold; Giolla Odar O'Casey, the Abbot of Downpatrick, gave a congratulatory blessing to those who had provided such a nice and decent chance for God to get up early to enjoy the freshness of a morning, or walk about at his ease in the cool of the evening through the lands and the woods and by the waters that a holy king had given to the poor monks. Not a damn word about the poor people.

Where are all these lads, so manly, so imposing centuries ago? Gone. Even the dust they became has vanished from the sight of men. Basil Brooke is now, not only chief of Down, but lord of Ulster, co-adjutor with Churchill and Attlee in the affairs of the Realm.

Where now are Cuchullan and his brothers of the Red Branch? Gone, too; gone into dust ages ago. Not altogether gone to dust: their heroism is told still, and their great names are listed in a lot of memories, though the clang of their bronze chariots galloping by has gone into the clang of the hammers in Belfast shipyards; the handsome women in the sunny place of the clan's household, busy embroidering, turning the spinning-wheel, are changed to the clacking of the spindles in the many-windowed mill; and all is embossed, all is ordered by the blustering brilliance of the orange lily. But these in the mills and those in the shipyards are the clansmen and clanswomen of Lecale, of Iveagh, and of Oriel, as Irish as the O'Casey, Abbot of Downpatrick, or as the O'Loughlin, Archbishop of Armagh, with a grin on his gob as the woods, the lands, and the waters of the people passed away to the monks. And clans of mill and shipyard will have their own again.

Now a cry has gone forth to save the broken turrets of the Big Houses, restore the towers that are dropping their stones, replace the wide gates that are hanging loose, scrape away the damp mosses clinging to the weakening walls, and give back a lacquered life to the gentry who live in them. Let them become the pensioners of the State; tax the workers so that the gentry may be there for the workers to go and see how they live; and come away civilised. Many of them have been gracious and charming, but these are but the glittering scales of civilisation, easily scraped away. Civilisation goes far deeper down than either grace, or charm, or big house. There isn't much in the well-made silken gown or well-pressed suit, the stately walk, or the delicate handling of silver spoon and costly cup and saucer. Easy to be charming, even to be courageous, where these are plentiful; but their charm cannot come near the dignity and the courage so often found with the earthen floor, the vulgar earthenware, and the ragged skirt and trousers. 'A building', says an architects' Journal, 'is part of a way of living.' A building to the many is a home, and a home is more than a part of a way of living; and it is these buildings called homes that must be made gracious, comfortable, and enduring. Apart from these homes, the public buildings, the school, the factory, the hospital, the store, the theatre, and the church, owned by all, used by all, will manifest the temporal and spiritual march of the people, all participating in design and form of the newer shape of civilisation; each national community preserving in them the essences of their own racial utterances in art, from the pile-dwelling days to the day of the steel-boned building, the jet-plane, the motor-car and motor-coach.

The revolt against the Big Houses has come even into the hearts and minds of the younger members of the grandee families. Those who have any outlook on life, any intelligence, no longer want to breakfast in a room big as a concert hall; no longer want to be ruled by a string of servants; no longer wish to sup soup from a golden plate; no longer desire the many inconveniences of being chained to a big estate. When life began to answer them back, and they couldn't give a clear account of why they lived in this burdensome way, they began to look like things lost in a museum; the house and the things in the house themselves had become objects of a life that had passed away for ever: there was to them a touch of ridicule, with aspect laughingly pathetic, like a sedan chair borne seriously round Oxford Circus, or a hansom cab tinkling through the streets of New York city. Gone and almost forgotten, too.

And what was under, always under, this graciousness and charm, seeding and fruiting in the Big Houses of the land? The very common-place things of worldly goods and worldly power. The first anxiety of the gracious charm of the Lords of the State was, as Dickens says, 'the safety of the preserves of the loaves and fishes'. With all their grandeur flaming, the elegant crowd were out after, as they had to be, as the workers were, their 'bread and cheese'. 'Not heaven or any of its delights were the incentives of the peasants of the Middle Ages, but, as always and everywhere, for a sufficiency of bread and cheese', says Coulton, in his *Five Centuries of Religion*: and in all the manorial houses the richly-dressed, stately-mannered persons were after the same lowly fare, though disguised and garnished under ornate dish, soup-tureen, and sauce-boat. And what a base of misery kept up this lacquered superstructure of charm and graciousness! The misery of millions in every land, of black and white men moaning. Sean had seen much of it himself in Ireland, though the worst of the evil had been then broken by the people, headed by the noble-hearted leader, himself a landlord, Charles Stewart Parnell. Misery conjured up among the millions was every-where, in every land. One of their own class, General Gordon, of a great Scots clan, one of whose ladies gave an immortal regiment to the British Nation, says of the robbery of Egypt by the English rich, 'Duke of This wants steamer—say six hundred pounds; Duke of That wants house, etc.; all the time the poor people are ground down to get money for all this. If God wills, I will shake all this in some way not clear to me now.' And again, 'They weigh the actions of ignorant natives, Zulus, Kaffirs, and Pondos, after one and their own code, they act towards the natives after the native code, which recognises the right of the stronger to pillage a neighbour. Oh! I am sick of these people. It is they, and not the blacks, who need civilisation!' A rather shocking indictment of the charming lords and ladies who poised those charms on the heads of poor people, black and white. 'Punish the natives if they don't act in the most civilised manner, but if it comes to a question of our action, then follow the custom of the natives—viz., recognise plunder as no offence whatever.' Gordon's actual words. Is this the reason why Gordon's name is never mentioned? Was this why he was left alone to disappear from life in faraway Khartoum? Do the charming ladies and gentlemen recognise themselves in this mirror held up in the hand of Gordon? No, of course not; why should they? If they do, they swiftly turn their faces to a curtained glass. But the natives are recognising them for what they are—from China to Peru. And not only black men, for Gordon asserts that few anywhere suffer the conditions endured by the Irish peasants. So shocking were the sights he saw there, that he drew up a plan for compulsory purchase of the land from the landlords, warning the Government that 'no half-measured Acts which left the landlords with any say to the tenantry of these portions of Ireland will be of any use, for the state of our fellow-countrymen in Ireland is worse than that of any people in the world, let alone Europe'. And General Sir William Butler adds, 'These were terrible words, coming from such an authority, coming from one whose knowledge of human misery was unquestionably greater than that of any living man, but they fell on ears that wouldn't listen'. The gracious ones, the charming ones wouldn't listen; and didn't listen till they were made to listen. And as it was in Ireland, so it is everywhere else: the charming ones, the gracious ones won't listen till they are made to listen. To preserve all they have they would be content to make of the world a commonwealth of woe. But not all then; not all now: Shaftesbury is a name worthy of a place on a people's banner when the children march; Disraeli, for all his hatred of Ireland, thought of the people; and Gordon; and now there are young and warm-hearted Tories asking why so many should have so little, so few so much.

But now these selfish ones are being challenged as never before; by those who have never gone to Lyonesse, but who have magic in their eyes; by a truth far greater than any share of truth they may have had in the beginning; by a dignity no less than theirs; by a kindliness that makes each man and woman, through labour, a golden digit in the sum of man. Jesus of the life that rayed out courage and new thought, gallant Mahommed, pensive and holy Buddha, help us to skip aside from the danger of having too much!

Sean himself belonged to the generation that had looked up to class privilege as God-begotten in a natural law, ordained to stay put for ever; honoured and almost worshipped by the quiet people. The rich and noble lay safe in the sweet shade of the green bushes, fed and attended by their true love, the quiet people. But they have lost their love. So confident beside the green bushes they never saw, never felt, her go, and woke up one morning to find the dear one gone.

> When he came there, and found that his true love was gone,
> He stood like a lambkin that was all quite forlorn;
> She's gone with some other, and forsaken me,
> So adieu the green bushes for ever, said he.

But now Sean had to turn aside from higher thoughts, and bend low over his own affairs (how quick the austere mind lands down on a lower level when faced with need of bread and cheese!). The last penny was leaving the bank, and he had nothing now. Lord and Lady Londonderry had generously given a guarantee to Sean's bank on his behalf for two hundred pounds to let him go to America with an easy mind. Nothing was given out on the guarantee, for Sean began to get American largesse in the shape of royalties before Eileen had parted with the last of her fifteen pounds; but that fact took nothing away from the kindness of his two friends. Indeed, it might well have been that when they gave the guarantee, they bid goodbye to the sum it guaranteed, for things of this sort are often quickly used, and as quickly forgotten by those who have benefited by them.

Goodbye to the Keltic saints reposing so snug in their pretty summer-houses; to the ripening peaches on their sunny wall; to the Red Hand of scarlet flowers in the garden's centre; goodbye to his generous Irish friends; goodbye to the serene face of Strangford Lough, for he was off to Philadelphia in the morning. The people of

America held his destiny tight in their hands. If they failed him, he was a goner. They needed bread and cheese, too; but if they didn't give him, Eileen, and the baby she was soon to have, a share of what they had, he, Eileen, the boy, and the baby would be goners go bragh. The Americans had to work themselves for their bread and cheese, and he couldn't expect them to weep or work for him; yet his one hope now was that America might stretch out a helping hand to an O'Casey. America's busy, teeming, intricate whirl—shut not your doors to him. A penny for the young guy.

SHIP IN FULL SAIL

BOUND for New York, for the Manhattan of Whitman! A huge ship, unwieldy-looking, seeming too massive to move, rising up from the Mersey like a futuristic town, with her short masts—really derricks—her big-bellied funnels, wider than many of the English roads to take buses and lorries along, her sides peppered with port-holes; the whole aspect of her shouted to all who looked that she had a mighty confidence in herself, her broad sides and sturdy bow asking what wave on God's ocean could topple her over. Like the world at large, she was divided into classes—steerage, tourist-class, and cabin-passengers. The last—which shall be first—had two decks to themselves on which to promenade and play; the tourist-class had more than half of a deck below, and the steerage had the bit that remained. Yet the steerage travellers numbered a huddled hundred to each of the other's ten; so, even here, passengers were divided into the nice sheep, rougher sheep, and the goats. The white-coated stewards, dashing about with the smoothing-iron, were running up and down the gangways, silent, in rubber-soled feet, settling the passengers into their cabins, thinking out the tips they'd get at the journey's end. Sean had been warned that the chief steward must get two guineas, his own steward a pound, the waiter at his table another one, with other tips, suiting the amount of work done, to him who provided a deck-chair, to him who handed out books from the library, to the barman who served the drinks, and to the quarter-master supervising the deck-sports. It seemed to Sean that he should have taken the fifteen pounds and left the five with Eileen. No deck-chair, no book, no drink for him; nothing beyond the bare necessaries bringing him safe to New York City. He must have been the poorest cabin-passenger that had ever set foot on a White Star liner. A record established, never to be broken. He was amazed at the quantity of luggage brought aboard by the passengers; some had a ton of it. The men dressed differently six times in a day, and the women seven times, or more. A friendly steward showed him the cabin of a couple when they were rushing around in shorts on the sports-deck, playing deck-tennis: clothes were flung about everywhere, across chairs, on the floor, over the beds; good clothes, too, much of them costly, flung about like litter left behind on a camping-field. Enough of it to clothe a slum family for years. These self-busy ones never asked a single question about the stuff in the steerage; never once thought of them. Occasionally, a few cabin-passengers stared down at the deck where the tourist-class paraded the limited space provided, but none gave the tribute of a look to where the steerage mammals prowled about their closely caged-in quarters: they were but part of the cargo.

The stewards slipped along the corridors in their snow-white jackets and black trousers, half ghosts, half men, hiding themselves under the passengers' orders, rarely giving themselves a glimpse of the sea, inhaling the testy smell of the cabins from port to port, answering all questions, asking none, linked to the bodies of the passengers but not to their souls; their whole life upon the ship the waiting upon a wish. Once only had Sean caught a steward looking over the ship's side at the swell of a subsiding gale, and heard him say, with a shudder, Deep troughs, sir; must be thirty feet down; seem to want to coax a man down to them; and shuddering again, slide through a doorway back into the ship to be safe with the will of the passengers. The friendly steward brought Sean stealthily down to their quarters, down very low in the ship's belly, where the top of the ocean was but a foot or two below the lower rim of the port-hole, so that, even in a light swell, the port-hole had to be closed, or the sea would come pouring in on top of them; almost airless, too, with tiers of bunks leaving but a head's space in which to preen themselves into the natty, white-coated figures one saw gliding around the ship.

The liner made a curving cut up Cork Harbour, going slow, for there were shallow banks on either side that might ground the big ship. Sean looked about for Spike Island, where John Mitchel had been as a treason-felony prisoner on his way to the convict settlement of Bermuda, and where he had met the gentle, scholarly Edward Walsh who taught the convicts. Walsh was a harper and a

Gaelic scholar wasting his sensitive life away teaching the convicts how to add two and two together, his golden hair grey, his beloved harp dusty, his heart hanging hazily on to life, working that he might have bread and water with a taste of meat on Sunday. Out came the tender carrying another crowd away from the western holy land to The New Island, as the United States was called by the Gaelic speakers. They streamed into the ship, and but two, who were priests, came to the cabin-class passengers; the rest were lost, a few to the tourist-class and a crowd to the steerage. Away round the cliffs of Kerry to Galway for another crowd, a 'great port' which the people had made with their own hands out of their pipe dreams. It was dark night now, and the tender came with a green light and a red light sparkling on port and starboard. Again the gangway fell; Galway passengers came aboard, three priests, a bishop, and a solicitor to join the cabin-passengers, a few others joining the tourists, and the crowd again pouring into the steerage. All the descendants of the clans were streaming like silent sheep into the steerage of the White Star liner.

> Goodbye, acushla, goodbye, me darlin',
> I can no longer stay.
> The good ship she is waitin',
> Grief must be abatin';
> Goodbye, me darlin',
> I'm off for Amerikay!

American soil is rich with the dust of the descendants of Irish king, chief, tanist, poet, bard, and artificer. Many and many a son of Conn, and many a blue eye of Clan Colman, lie deep in the earth of New York, of Indiana, Butte of Montana, and Texas in the deeper south; forgotten. And more go freely. Let the singers who stay chant how they may about the lure of Ireland, the brown of the bog, purple of heather, blue of lake, red of fuchsia, white of lily, the gold of the whins; the goers will go timidly or go galloping to where they think the corn to be nearer to the groping hand. The few among the tourist-class, the fewer among the cabin-passengers, may return; but the ones in the steerage have muttered a kiss-me-arse goodbye to Banba of the Streams.

Flying from history, too; from fine history lapping Ireland round in greatness, with many a remembrance giving glory even to that which has none; glory not needed with Burren of the kings, Tir Fhiachrach Aidhne; Gaura in Meath, where Oscar fell and the

Fianna were broken; the cromlech covering Aideen's grave, Oscar's sweetheart, on the head of Howth; Tara and Emain Macha, and Cong where Ireland's last king lies stretched;

Peace and holy gloom possess him,
Last of Gaelic monarchs of the Gael,
Slumbering by the young, eternal
River-voices of the western vale.

And what is Rory O'Connor, dead these many hundred years, to those hurrying into the steerage, or to the better places of the ship; what is he to them, or they to him? Nothing.

Clear as air, the western waters
Evermore their sweet, unchanging song
Murmur in their stony channels
Round O'Connor's sepulchre in Cong.

Galway itself, while stout William of Orange, helped by his stouter officers, was shoving Ireland into England's bag, sheltered the Irish Tirconnell and the French Lauzun who had fled from Limerick, laughing at Sarsfield when he said he would hold the town; Lauzun telling him the town walls could be battered down with roasted apples. There, shrunken into saviours of themselves, glittering in their rich uniforms, they paddled in the sea when the sun shone, and played bagatelle when the rain fell; while Sarsfield fought with the men, the women, and the children of Limerick; fought so heartily that William was thrust back, who, disillusioned, packed his troubles in his new kit-bag, and returned to England, leaving General Ginkel to carry on, which he did, right worthily, by packing up too, and getting as far away as he could from Limerick, while Lauzun and Tirconnell paddled away in the sea round Galway. So, signs of Irish regard for Sarsfield's gallantry, Patrick became a common name for the boys born in Ireland from that day forth. But Churchill, later Marlborough, greatest grandfather of the present one, battered down the walls of Cork, and took the city, forcing the Irish to abandon the fight for the Stuart King, who left them to recover from the war in the worst way they could. Christ, Ireland has had a rough time with God and Man!

The big ship swung round, and set her course for Boston, in a calm sea, with the Aran Islands fading away into dark dots, then vanishing from ken, leaving the men of Aran behind among their tiny homes, their patient cattle, their pitiful potato patches made from handfuls of earth pilfered from grasping crevices in the brine-soaked rocks and from kelp gathered dripping from the sea, and carried home on their backs to fertilise futility—a suitable life of austerity for the workers in the heaven-loved Aran of the saints.

The passengers settled down, some to play shuffle-board, some deck-tennis, others parading round the promenade deck and around, at a great pace, while the crowd stretched themselves stiff on to deck-couches, covering themselves with thick rugs, so that the ship seemed to be on the way to Lourdes:

> There they lay all the day
> On the broad Atlantic low;
> Long they pray—keep thy sway
> Gentle, mighty ocean O!

On the first evening of the voyage, the Chief Steward had asked Sean if he would like to have his meals at a table presided over by an officer, or would he prefer a place less conspicuous, and Sean had bewildered the Steward by asking him if he could have them with the crew. Less than a hundred miles from the Irish coast, the sky darkened and the wind blew, setting the ship to a jauntier motion on the sea's surface. Sean noticed the crew taking things from the main deck, tarpaulining the hatches, and fastening loose things firmly. There was a scurrying among the ones reclining, who flung their rugs away, and hurried off to their cabins, and the hardier promenaders walked the deck no more. Sean found that but he, a priest, and a ship's officer remained on deck watching the rise of the sea and listening to the gathering howl of the wind. The deck he stood on was forty feet above the sea, and was surrounded by thick glass so that the wind gave no feeling of its strength, the breaking sea not strong enough to smash the glass, so he could face it all, and enjoy it all, with acclamation at the wonder of its fierceness. As far as the eye could reach, wave after wave, in close battalions, came rushing towards the ship, the waves following those about to strike her pushing the ones in front, as if in a desperate hurry to strike the ship themselves. The cleaving prow of the huge vessel cut through the surge of the piled-up mass of agitated waters, which, after a ponderous pause, roared over the deck, everything on it disappearing under the swell of the green-and-white tumble of waters, so that Sean seemed to be standing in a glass-house tossed about in a surging greenery of waves, the tops of them shattering asunder to slash viciously against the thick glass through which Sean looked, often now but a screen of streaming water between him and the tumult outside. Then, as the stream rushed its hasty way down the glass, and vision came again, he saw the deck below buried under a passionate surge of wave for a few moments, till the ship rose out of the trough, and the waters poured away through the scuppers down to the leaping sea again.

Hour after hour, Sean watched the waves and listened to the wind, feeling a thrill whenever a mountainous wave rose up level with the upper deck, poised itself for a moment, and then fell, like fronds of a horrifying fern, in a downfall on the main-deck, hiding everything below from all watching eyes under a tumbling millrace of wriggling, rushing, greenwide waters.

What crowds of glimmering ghosts floated aimlessly about underneath all these waters, from the years of the famine to years of the first World War! How many of the Irish, fleeing the famine in the coffin-ships, fell into their keen, cold, undulating grip, and found their never-ending silence there! Swing him over the gunnel—one, two, three, while some storm-a-long tried to mutter a prayer he couldn't remember. Now! And down went McGinty to the bottom of the sea. Many an old man, old woman, chattering child; many a lusty youth, handsome maiden went down engulfed in the proud, pouring toss of the billows. Billows? Somewhere in a letter, the fine poet, W. B. Yeats, rebukes a poet for calling a wave a billow, adding the news that another fine poet, T. S. Eliot, wouldn't permit the word billow to enter *The Criterion* for fear of smearing its odorous and austere integrity. But these seething masses of waters, rearing up, with menace in their aspect, before they came tumbling down on the quivering ship, were more than mere waves. These bulging breasts of sea, gigantic and fierce, as the eye searched into their smothering depths, made the nerves thrill and the body shudder, for in them was no rest, even for the tossed-down dead. Each oncoming mass had in itself its own half-hidden tempest. It was within these sly, green billows that many a soul went tumbling, scrambling down through the fierce ebb and flow and sway of the deep green sea. Many a lass whose name was Mary; many a blue-eyed Irish boy; many a Nora creena, many a larboard watch ahoy. Many a frantic lad saw, for the last time, his true-love's gasping, last farewell: Adieu! she cried, and waved her lily hand. Sean could see sweet faces, fair forms lunging round, helpless in the swelling sway of the tumbling sea: Propertius's Cynthia; Yeats's Dectora, sadly mingling with the common ones outside the longing, lasting memory of verse.

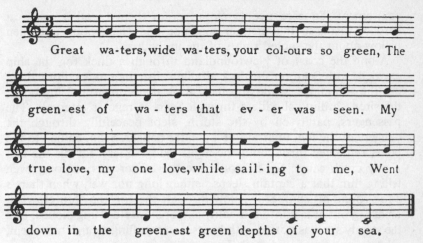

Great wa-ters, wide wa-ters, your col-ours so green, The
green-est of wa-ters that ev-er was seen. My
true love, my one love, while sail-ing to me, Went
down in the green-est green depths of your sea.

I'm coming, quite fast, on a ship sailing south,
To print all my love with a kiss on your mouth,
She murmur'd; I heard her, and waited in glee;
But the ship and my true love sank in the green sea.

She lies fathoms down, lapp'd in mother-o'-pearl,
Lies quiet that once was my high-hearted girl;
And over her all the wide, green billows roll,
Chanting a green keen for her sea-shrouded soul.

Sean noticed a heavy iron door, grimly bolted and locked, in one of the lobbies. A door leading to the steerage, through which cabin-passengers weren't allowed to pass, though Sean saw none making an effort to try. He did; a steward left it open for him, and down he went, like another Dante touring Inferno, with the circles growing hotter as he descended. Down to the steerage. The corridors were crowded, the little lounge was packed. The throb of the engines here was palpable, pant pant pant, and the place quivered with their movements. No privacy here, no room to stretch away a bit of boredom. Here were Galway, Mayo, Roscommon, Cork, and Tipperary, standing, squatting in the stairs, crouching on the floors, wedged together, while Sean, crouched on the floor, too, talked to some of them. Sean surmised the many miseries that must have fruited here while the storm was on; and no priest from the cabin-passengers came here to share the discomforts of this part of their flock. No; comfort was the priests' guardian angel, poker their amusement. Squeeze people closer, cram them together, make a herd of them, so that neither soul nor body has room, and then bellow about the sacred rights of the individual!

Along the coast of Newfoundland through a thick fog the ship crawled, with Sean on the deck all night, listening to a sailor calling out the soundings, while an officer took them down in a log-book, the siren shrilling shudders through Sean at regular intervals. The passengers, paralysed by the storm, slept peacefully through the dangers of the fog, unafraid of a greater danger. Sean, chilled to the bone, remained throughout the night ready to leap for his life-belt if any crash came; for he could see the officer was anxious, even telling him that a captain sleeps neither long nor well when there's a fog round his ship. Slow, slow through the fog the ship crawled, breaking out at last into a dreamy sky of slowly-drifting clouds, and the steady sea was dotted with boats, some puffing steam from them, others spreading a wide sail. The passengers came pouring out from the saloon, hurrying over to the gunnels to peer away into the misty distance.

—There she is, said a puffed-out man, staring through a pair of binoculars; there she is, at last, stout and taut as ever.

—What is it? ventured Sean; what do you see?

—Statue of Liberty, said the puffed-out man.

America's Lady of the Lamp. He couldn't see her, but he knew the golden words she nourished on her lap:

> Give me your tired, your poor,
> Your huddled masses yearning to breathe free,
> The wretched refuse of your teeming shore.
> Send these, the homeless, tempest-tossed to me:
> I lift my lamp beside the golden door.

Little sparkle in the words now; well worn and nearly rubbed away; the refugees musta worn their welcome out. America now had huddled masses and homeless of her own, and there were a lot more than a hundred most deserving cases of poverty in the United States; thousands of very poor, unhappy souls. The words on Miss Liberty's apron had lost their meaning. But wait a minute, think a little, boy. Wasn't he, in a lot of ways, a refugee himself, coming to the United States out of necessity rather than out of love? He was already half-homeless, and would be homeless altogether, if he didn't succeed in getting American dollars to carry home with him. There was no denying of it. Like a budding hero, he carried a drama

with him as a banner, hoping to astonish the Americans with a work
of art; but down in his heart he knew he was here to collect funds.
He was a refugee, for Ireland had cast him forth, England couldn't
afford to keep him, so he depended on America now to provide him
with a sufficiency to keep him and his family for another year or
two. An unpleasant fact, but a solid, sober one.

Sweet Miss Liberty, Belle of New York, and Man of Manhattan,
hear my prayer, and let my cry come unto ye!

A new land, honoured nowhere with a Greek temple or a Roman
road; no medieval monastery showing itself off as a tasty heap of
ruins; no Norman castle to let us fancy seeing bowmen from the
walls shooting arrows into the bowels of people living round it;
no Ides of March, or anything else like them, to remember. Here,
instead, were the cloisters of Emerson, the limitless habitat of Walt
Whitman, the battlefields of Washington, and the rush and rendezvous of modern mechanics; all the lure of freshness and of power.
They were enough, and had in them many miracles for the
future.

He would meet new people, and see new things. He would see the
Hudson River, Grant's tomb, Bunker's Hill, maybe, and Brooklyn,
the camp of the dead brigade; for the first time he would set a foot
on foreign soil, though for him no land was a foreign one, since all
were peopled by the same human family. But it was like the squirrel
meeting the mountain, and having words with him. Well, if a squirrel
couldn't carry forests on his back, neither could the mountain crack
a nut.

IN NEW YORK NOW

As the great ship was being tugged to the dockside, Sean felt so
agitated by what was before him and what he had left behind him,
that he was a little giddy, and his heart beat so that he pressed a
hand to his side to steady it. Here he was on the fringe of New York
with but a few pounds in his pocket, while Eileen at home, expecting
a baby in two months' time, was moving to Battersea with fewer
pounds in her pocket, if there were any left there now. He was about
to descend on to the land of Babbitt, the go-getter, land of the rush
and roar of business, with a gangster at the corner of every street,
according to the films. He had read a volume of Mencken's *Americana*, and knew there were strange men and things north and south

of the Mason–Dixon line; but he knew, too, that there were odd men and things east and west of the place where the river Shannon flows; so Americana didn't frighten him.

But he felt very lonely. In spite of the close connections between the U.S.A. and Eire, he knew little about the fullness of American life. He knew why the Flag had its stars and its stripes; knew some of her past; had heard of the Pilgrims, of the Covered Wagon, the Ride of Paul Revere, of Pocahontas, of Johnny Appleseed, and of Daniel Boone; and, of course, he had read of the last stand made by General Custer. He knew something of Washington and a lot about Stonewall Jackson, whose Life he had read, for his admiration had first gone to the South for no other reason than that John Mitchel, the Irish rebel, had stood by the men in grey, and had sent his sons to battle for them. He had been suckled on American culture, for the first fine book from which he had taught himself had been fashioned in New York; an old book, called *The Comprehensive Summary*, for use in American schools, containing flashes from science, mythology, and biography, with paragraphs of history from that of the Medes and Persians, down to Bunker's Hill, Yorktown, and Saratoga; and in its broad bosom lay a fair and full copy of the American Constitution. A kid's book that he had learned by heart, leading him a little way into the past and present knowledge of life; a book he had kept close to him till it had fallen away, page by page, with the dint of use. It had been a godsend. He wondered was there any record, any remembrance even, of it in America today? He would love to hear it was still alive in some American memory.

He had heard the names of Harvard and Yale, which had but a faraway sound of Oxford and Cambridge. He had read some American literature, past and present, and had contributed a few things to *The American Spectator*, a magazine that had told him there were minds in America that were flushed with courage, with wit, and an unreluctant will to show up political hypocrisy and intellectual sin. He knew something about Nathan's American theatre by what the critic had written about it. It was a brave and a dignified theatre. No-one was asked, for all its grandeur, to take his shoes from off his feet when entering, nor obliged to genuflect, nor even to salaam; but each had to behave himself. Here thought went back to the past, and here thought stretched forth to the future. Here Edmund Kean and Coquelin had laid different tributes on the same altar, and Shakespeare's and Molière's shadows coloured the glass of the windows gay. Here was heard often the hush of awe, but the hush of awe was always fringed by the silvery bells of laughter, for here the jester laughed beside the man about to die saluting Caesar.

During all his life Sean had spoken to but four Americans — John Anderson, a drama critic, who had come on a visit when on a holiday in Europe; John Tuerk and George Bushar Markell, the two men responsible for putting on his play in New York; and Claire Luce, an actress and a very lovely lass. Going down the gangway, he felt very lonely, not knowing whether he was about to enter an indifferent maw, or going down to rest on a friendly arm. Not for long, though: in the Customs' shed, two men were waiting for him — Dick Madden, Sean's American agent, and George Jean Nathan, the famous drama critic, waiting for him with hands outstretched.

Nathan standing in the huge Customs' shed full of flurried passengers teasing white-coated stewards with anxiety and question, who were busy bearing bundles and cases from the ship to the shed, so that they looked like swarms of varied-coloured fowl cluttering and cackling around white-plumaged cocks, indifferent to their outcry. Here, among the great boxes, the corpulent trunks, the elegant suitcases, among the chattering passengers, the cold-worded Customs Officers, keen in their readiness to poise and pounce, Nathan stood looking at nothing, seeing everything, his luminous, wine-coloured eyes glancing at Sean, to see, maybe, if there was a chance of him being something more than a bore; and Sean thinking what in the name of God he would say to this famous critic now standing before him, a soft slouch hat on his finely formed head, set safely on a thick crop of dark hair, slightly tinged with grey here and there; a greatcoat, so full in the shoulders that it fell round him capewise down below his knees, a curving wrinkle of humour, now in repose, trimming the corners of a full, sensuous, handsome mouth.

Nathan in his cape-coat reminded Sean of Augustus John standing calm in Victoria Station, where Sean had gone to wish the great artist god-speed to France; standing there within a throng of excited passengers running hither and thither, porters hurrying this way, that way, laden with luggage, a slow voice from a loud-speaker directing passengers where they were to go, accompanied by the hissing of steam or the shrill yell from the siren of a train departing: there the painter stood, straight and pensive as if he stood thoughtful beside deep waters of a standing pool, his searching eyes dividing nature's cruder patterns into finer forms, her reckless colours into lovely tones and tints on road, in tree, flower, jug; or in figure at play, resting by a sea, or working close to a caravan. As John stood then, so Nathan stands now, half adream in the agitated crowd; almost motionless, his one wakefulness, maybe, a hope that this O'Casey will be something more than just bearable company, standing there, with the surge of two thousand years of drama forming the kingdom of heaven within him; watching with anchorite concentration, week after week, cascades of theatrical fireworks, pale or brilliant, rising over the New York stage, and breaking out into ephemeral brightness under the battens, watching in the hope that out of the falling, fading lights, a lasting star may at last shine out from the falling dust, and mount higher to hang itself in the heavens.

Beside Nathan stood Dick Madden, handsome, tall, able, and eager, a pouncer to set any client well before the public *belle vieu*; smartly dressed, and proud to have attached Sean's *Within the Gates* to the great wheel of the theatre, now praying that the play would be a New York hit.

Sean enjoyed himself and Sean saw many things, though his visit to the States was but as a lightning-flash graciously lingering just a few seconds longer. The streets were deep and Dantesque, dizzying the mind when one looked up to the tops of the buildings towering up as if they sought a way to the blue sky and the sun ashine therein; and the whole city in its aspect and its agitated life grew into a rosy, comfortable, and majestic inferno; life so busy and stimulating that all but the sick in soul and very sick in body forgot the time they would come to dust in the cool of the tombs: a grander-patterned background than many of the grand ones Sean had threaded in his hasty way through life.

The wide wonder of Broadway is disconsolate in the daytime; but gaudily glorious at night, with a milling crowd filling sidewalk and roadway, silent, going up, going down, between upstanding banks of brilliant lights, each building braided and embossed with glowing, many-coloured bulbs of man-rayed luminance. A glowing valley of the shadow of life. The strolling crowd went slowly by through the kinematically divine thoroughfare of New York, each of them like as if he were a child in a daydream, wandering, open-eyed, through a city conjured into a gem-encrusted glow by the genie of Aladdin's wonderful lamp. Veneration for the god of the kinema, who, by day, slept under the drabbest coverlet man could make, a naked tangle of wiry web over the doxy-minded god; and, at night, stood up in a robe of scintillating jewels for all to see and to admire. Honolulu, honolulu! Lost Angeles has come to town, and glory whines around.

Honolulu! And names of the demi-gods of the films hang in the gigantic glitter, their faces, too, silently calling on the millions to come and splash about into the ecstasy of seeing themselves in the amazing magnified mirror of the lady of shallow, and worship the lord gaud of Sobbaoth.

What is the great crowd seeking, the young, mostly courting couples, prowling so aimlessly, yet so steadily, along the Great White Way? They seek the Muses, though they know it not, for these restive lights are to them

> a bank whereon the wild thyme blows,
> Where oxlips and the nodding violet grows.

They straggle along seeking beauty which is yet a shrinking seed within them. They seek for what they know not, though they feel their need of it, and sometimes sense a twinge of near arrival within this blaze of bastard culture. Roman catholic and protestant mingle and mate with the uncomplaining, muted midgets caught in the glare of the Great White Way, unaware that outside its dazzling destitution, away in the darkness ahead, shine faint, enkindling rays from the stars of art, literature, and science. They have been told and yet they do not know; for the tale came too late, or it was told too low for them to catch the whisper. They have had no help to get away from the fairy tales of infancy, lovely in their day, but turning slyly silly when men reach the age of misunderstanding. But many of the common people are now making for something more than the savage contentment with coloured bead and strip of coloured calico. They ask for something better than these things no higher than flimsy rhyme and fainting fairy tale, without the shrewd jingle of the one or the longing beauty of the other. Even this gaudiness, blaspheming light, wherein they wander webbed, is an outward sign of inner seeking all they feel they need. The people are beginning to realise the longing for good shaping of things; in the streets they pass through; in the buildings banking the streets they pass through; in tablecloth and crockery ware; in the homes they have to have; in pictures they see, music they hear, the simple vessels they handle; in all things whatsoever which mingle man with life: a share in all the greatest the community can imagine, in all the greatest the community can do.

Many are getting rid of the dismal daydream that the good in life is something similar to Christmas in Killarney with all the folks at home. First, they are seeking and fighting to keep taut and even that umbilical cord stringing all men together — the bread line. They have long prayed for their bread, now they fight for it. May Jesus Christ be praised! They are organising to alter the mad method of life among them and bring it into order, as Lycurgus did in Sparta in the old time before them: 'Where the State was overloaded with a multitude of indigent and necessitous persons, while the whole wealth of the land had centred upon a few. To the end, therefore, that he might expel from the State luxury and crime, and those yet more inveterate diseases of want and superfluity, he got them to consent to a new division of land, so that they should all live together on an equal footing; merit to be the only road to eminence, and the disgrace of evil, and credit of worthy acts, their one measure of difference between man and man.' There's a lot in this, my people, a lot in it.

Whenever Sean got a chance of sliding aside from a daytime rehearsal, he wandered through the streets of the city, looking up, ahead, behind, left and right, looking everywhere his eyes could go. He thought curiously of the Dublin guttersnipe stitching himself into the gay and hurrying pattern of New York city. A figure with a lean and hungry look threading himself through the streets, so firmly, maybe, that he might be there for ever. Far easier to weave oneself within New York's life than within that of London, for this city's life is too sloven, too outspread, and too voluminous to weave any conforming pattern a human mind could frame; the world-weaving activities here created but a bewildering tangle in London's life. Even the poets and prelates reposing in Westminster Abbey are buried out of sight in the impenetrable, smothering tapestry of London city. So he went around New York watching, wishing he could spend a decade with the life and its background around him. Once, on Thanksgiving Day, he was caught in a great crowd in Times Square that had watched a procession of bands and contingents carrying gigantantic effigies made of blown-out balloons; and this great crowd was now crossing east, crossing west, great flocks of people, whenever the tremendous traffic paused and seemed to present them with a chance of moving. In the street's centre stood a huge policeman shepherding them this way, that way, so that they might go in safety. He was perspiring and impatient, waving the people across with angry gestures. Once, when a flock wanting to cross hesitated to answer his impatient gesture, Sean was astonished to hear his voice roaring out in the rich and lilting accents of an Irish Civic Guard:

—Christ! Are yez goin' to cross over, or are yez goin' to lay down there, an' die!

One thing that struck Sean hard as he scanned the streets, on the level and high up, was the fading away in New York — more than in other cities, far more than in Moscow — of the orthodox, institutional conception of the Divine Idea. There had been too many mitres planted on too many musty heads. Here, the churches seemed to shrink away into eroding corners. They seem to have ceased to be essential parts of American life. They no longer give life. It is the huge buildings of commerce and trade which now align the people to attention. These in their massive manner of steel and stone say, Come unto me all ye who labour, and we will give you work. Work! Labour the *aspergas me* of life; the one great sacrament of humanity from which all other things flow — security, leisure, joy, art, literature, even divinity itself. Passing through the bustling streets, it seemed to Sean that the churches crouched silently into solitude, thrust aside by the bigger buildings, standing erect, monumental pride in their height and form, coldly ordering any church within their view to Get away, old woman, you have had the time of your life, and have no more interest for the beautiful people. No use of you yelling out now, 'Hello, out there; if your heart's in the lowlands, this is where you will find comfort, sucker, and care'; for the passers-by hear you not, or, if they do, heed you less.

The newcomer to New York City, American or foreigner, doesn't spend a glance on St. John's of Morningside Heights, or on St. Patrick's in Fifth Avenue, or on the Russian Basilica on Fourth Avenue, or thereabouts; but makes for Rockefeller Center, where he can get an eyeful worth seeing; he comes to gape at man's newer magnificence in building, a newer Babel, significant of order instead of confusion; the fuller fruit of Stonehenge. New York's mother-church of commerce and trade, not honoured by the head bending, for here the head must be thrown back to sink within the cavity between the shoulder-blades to see its summit. Here the visitors come, here the visitors go; and even New Yorkers themselves, having seen the building day after day, still glance up at its wonder as they hurry by. Many times Sean wandered round it, finding its back parts as well-proportioned as its front face, flashing with the clean austerity of stone and glass. In the midst of the crowds going in, coming out, the lifts going up, coming down, the never-ending groups of sightseers, the building stands aloof, as chill and as lovely as an Alpine glacier, as sparkling, too, when the sunshine glints on its glass, imposing a sense of cold awe on every soul who sees it. There it stands, majestic, with the brassy figure of Prometheus, having snatched fire from heaven, lying at its base, like a tawdry brooch which the building, resenting an attempt to disfigure it, had shaken from its breast to the indifferent pavement below. And Sean sat down on a bench to brood.

He bent his thought on the difference between this strident, confident building and the languorous loveliness of Westminster Abbey, or Salisbury Cathedral that Constable painted from the midst of the luscious meadows around it; built first on a hill, where winds blew constant and boisterous, and the lord of the adjoining castle owned the one well, and charged the clergy so much a bucket for its waters; the wind and the water so plaguing the bishop that he appealed to the Pope, and got leave to change to the valley, where few winds blew and where water was plentiful. As one hefty bishop said to the Chapter's Dean, after they had come down from the windy hill of Old Sarum to the sheltered valley — 'A body would need a brassy bottom to stand the wind there.' A different wind, but a keener one, indifference, blows around their bottoms now. And so the bishop hied him down to where the big cathedral stands today, lingering out a life that the castle had lost centuries ago. There was Salisbury Cathedral, here was Rockefeller Center. Here is life; busy, and often very vulgar in its entertainment, thrust out over the people by broadcast, cinema, and theatre; but it is life, and always capable of growth. But death always glosses the cathedral with gloom: the tomb of this bishop or lord, that poet, thon statesman, meet you as you walk the way of the aisle or nave. Sculptured tombs, once gay with armorial colouring and dizened with royal gilt; but with the colours gone now, and the gilt grown rusty. In a book about the Cathedral we are told that: 'Here the first Earl of Salisbury is buried. Here the effigy of the warrior lies wrapped in chain armour, his head exquisitely turned to the right [an earl's head would hardly be turned exquisitely to the left], his left arm bearing his shield, lovely with the six golden leopards of Anjou, his right arm fallen by his side, the heavy armour fallen from it; more wonderful than the life. Nothing in the world is grander or more touching than this exquisite statue; there is nothing in the world to surpass it, and little to equal it.'

More touching! A mother suckling her babe, for one thing, is far more touching than this memorial to this fellow, probably a bloody ruffian who won his 'golden leopards of Anjou' by slaying as many people as he could. And Angelo's David is a far, far finer figure than this one. Odd how, even in this day, some wanderers through life swoon into a mad praise over chantry, tomb, and cloister. A dead idea that nothing new can be as grand as anything old; souls who live their leisurely dreams, supine, in the 'twilight of grey gothic things', moss-grown and mouse-ridden. Cathedrals in which is shown no tomb of those who built them with their labour, or who furnished the wherewithal to build them in the sweat of their face toiling from sunrise to sunset, their hard lot a massed measure of wealth for lord, lady, abbot, and bishop, to whom, always, the steel tip of a lance was more fervently sweet in the sight of God than the steel tip of the plough. A few shattered pieces of glass, saved from a heap left lying on the ground by the puritan destroying angels, have been gathered into the big west window, and there one can see the shield of Gilbert of Clare (whoever he was) with its three red chevrons on a gold field; and the blue one scattered over with the golden fleurs-de-lis of St. Louis of France, the crusader, brother of Henry the Third; and the red one figuring the three golden leopards of Henry the Third himself. Not far away, stretched out stiff, embalmed in marble, lies the giant Cheyney, standard-bearer to the bold Richmond, whom the crooked-back Richard, in the battle of Bosworth, sent spinning from his horse with a thrust from his lance; so that from what can be seen in the windows, on the floor, and all around, one is assured that the kingdumb of heaven admits no one lower than the rank of knight; now, not even knights, for them were the days when knights were bold.

Out in the cloisters the footsteps of Sean and of his younger son rang hollow as they strolled along, while heavy rain fell beyond their shelter, copiously soaking the green of the cloister garth. Here the canons of the Chapter used to seek refreshment, reading their pious books, so that they might be the better able to arrange the life of the world by the method of theological legend and divine myth. Behind them, on the cloister walls, decaying wooden crosses, brought from the graves of Englishmen who fell in the first World War, were hanging dolefully, to associate, in some magic way, the souls of the dead with the reputed holiness of the place. The names and ranks of the fallen were painted on the wooden trinkets of woe: all officers; the graves of the well-known warriors; the rank and file and all that appertaineth to them could go on lying where they first fell. Grey stone, green grass, grey rain, and an old man with a young one walking on the grey-blue pavements of the cloister, some of the slabs covering the long-ago canons of the cathedral. Lonely and slow, the two paced the cloisters, a man of seventy and a lad of fifteen; slow, each thinking his own thoughts. Did the old canons here ever bother to say Anima Christi, sanctifica me. Corpus Christi, Salve me. Sanguis Christi, inebria me? Ignatius Loyola's aspirations — far less musical, less courageous, less penetrating than the Deer's Cry, the appeal put up by whomsoever, under the name of Patrick, went down the slopes of Meath to face the Irish pagans. A lad of fifteen and a man of seventy; the old picturing in his mind the old, forgotten life led here, dead down now; the young lad curious, consciously indifferent, his grade of life separating him for ever from it and casting it away.

And many more, too, of the old and the young. A roman catholic, writing of this cathedral of Salisbury, says: 'On a market day, the city of Salisbury is at its best; but it is curious that the lively English crowd, so cheerful and yet so sober withal, altogether avoids the cathedral, which is then, as always, in its magical if icy silence. In the fifteenth century the cathedral would have been thronged, the shrine of St. Osmund all surrounded with worshippers, the lofty nave filled with a multitude that gave it all its meaning. The Wiltshireman does not tread the aisles, he avoids the place, it frightens him. It seems to belong to the gentry, and though the doors stand open wide, never will he enter in.'

Seems, sir? Nay, it does, and always did, belong to the gentry. Though the gentry and the churchmen fought each other, they always united to keep the common people down. How low we've fallen, implies this crier after long-forgotten things; how high, with all our faults, we've risen from it all, thinks Sean in his searching heart. In the heyday of these ecclesiastical activities, how did the Peter the Ploughmen, their wives, and children live? While the lesser sons and daughters of the gentry entered nunnery and monastery to have a good time with wine and women and bawdy song, Peter the Ploughmen toiled on ceaselessly, poverty their whole being and misery their companion, with death and the black plague plying their bulldozer spades to make graves for tens of thousands of them within sight of their own poor doorways.

No cathedral equalled this building of New York in its height, its cool beauty, its significance for the present world — not even Wren's St. Paul's or Angelo's St. Peter's. It was the new displacing the old; the old that had lost its meaning and its use. Within, it had the means of flooding the people in stupid song, stupid story. It could send out a message, saying, over the wireless: 'By the courtesy of the Louisiana loo loo Motor Corporation, you are about to listen to the Voice of God'; and then some pip-squeak of a cleric would minimise God to his own conceit of himself, mangling even the terse beauty of biblical phrases in a dreadful disdain of the divinity of man's diction and thought; but, still, through the rowdy conceits of cleric, of crooner, of clown without wit or verve, came pushing forth the voice of God through the words of eminent men of science, of drama, and in the sounds of Beethoven's and Mozart's music.

Sean sat on the bench, and thought how lively, how lovely the place looked: a warm and brilliant sun shining on the gigantic façade of the building, turned the glass to gleaming crystal. Some rectangular pools, curbed by stone, ruffled by tiny but restive waves, gave out a minor gurgling song; like lily pools they were, with waters too restive to allow the growth of the lotus or languorous lily; and a vivid blue sky hung over all — blue and grey, grey-green and silver, giving a grand picture of colour and tone to the receptive mind. Secular serenity as serene as any ecclesiastical church or cathedral. Once, all the stately buildings in a town were church and monastery; here all the stately buildings are secular — the Empire State Building, the Chrysler Building, the Singer Company's Building, and the railway stations, whose booking-halls are as lofty and fine as a cathedral nave, and much more useful. Is it better so? Are we brighter, safer, merrier, having wider minds and greater knowledge than we had when the Churches and their Canon Laws constricted life within the terms of their congealing catechism? Yes, a lot merrier, safer, having greater knowledge and wider minds, with an amazing chance of splendid development in the future. God wants to be with us now.

It is odd — mostly entertained by roman catholic apologists for their own reasons — how many prate of the days when the Church ruled the roost, as if then all was jollity, sweetness, and effulgent light; whereas, in fact, those days were riddled and ruined with venomous puritanism; hatred of dancing, of music, of painting, of sculpture (except the sculpture of saintly figures and the sculpture of the tomb), and of any natural beauty in woman. Hilaire Belloc in his *Europe and the Faith*, says: 'Two notes mark the thirteenth century for anyone who is acquainted with its building, its letters, and its wars: a note of youth and a note of content'. Again, dealing with the effects of the three hundred years following the Reformation, he says: 'With all these, of course, we have had a universal mark —

the progressive extension of despair'. Even the English *Church Times* said a few years ago: 'Medieval spring, summer, and autumn had many delights when the church's holidays were holidays; when the people not only worked hard, but prayed hard, and played hard'. There were, then, says G. G. Coulson, a hundred holydays in the year; on these the people could do no servile work; the landlords, lord and abbot, refused to divide, and so the holydays were dark indeed to the workers. As for 'playing', almost all of it was done under a shower of denunciations from the clerics. St. Jerome, with his lion, an authority quoted throughout those times, bawled out against all the frolics and joys that flesh is heir to; and St. John of the Cross warned us that 'the spiritual Christian ought to suppress all joy in created things, because it is offensive in the sight of God'. The sea, the rock, tree, fern, and flower, offensive in the sight of God! Oh, lord! But there's worse than these; oh, ay. The whole period's frantic with the abuse of woman, who, to the clerics, was far more dangerous than the American blue-tailed fly. Odo of Cluny, a big-shot Benedictine in those days, says: 'Looka, boys, though girls have no power to add to their looks, they powder and puff and dye their faces, or fiddle their hair into fanciness, give the glad eye, and vary their dress by divers other far-fetched methods; how much better it would be, all this while, if they were intent upon the upkeep of their souls!'

Ha, ha, ladies of *Vogue*, who go contrary, and how does your garden grow? Are you looking after the garden of the body rather than the garden of the soul? Know ye who sit on a cushion and sew a fine seam, and feed upon strawberries, sugar, and cream, that beauty is but skin deep. So says this great Benedictine of Luny, adding that: 'If men could see below the skin, as the lynxes of Boeotia are said to see into the inward parts, then the sight of a woman would be nauseous to them. All that beauty consisteth but in phlegm and blood and humours and gall. If a man considers that which is hidden within the nose, the throat, and the belly, he will find filth everywhere; and, if we cannot bring ourselves, even with the tip of our fingers, to touch dung, wherefore do we desire to embrace this bag of filth?' Why indeed? God only knows. Not a very amiable fellow, this. Yet there is fire in dung, and tremendous energy that gives rich sap to the corn and to the fruit-tree. Sean had fearlessly handled it himself in the freeing of choked drains, in the cleansing of septic tanks; and many a delicately-handed surgeon removes rottenness, giving health again to a body racked before with pain and illness. Odo's thought is not a godly, but an inhuman one. Odd that Belloc and Chesterton never seem to have known the sweetness and light of their own authorities. Odo wasn't a bird alone; there were thousands of little Odos saying the same thing. Much better than the man from Luny is Solomon's Song of a lad for his lass and a lass for her lad: 'Thou art all fair, my love; there is no spot in thee. Thy two breasts are like two young roes that are twins, which feed among the lilies.' Or the nursery rhyme of What's a little girl made of, what's a little girl made of? Of sugar and spice and everything nice — that's what a little girl's made of. Poor, pitiable men groan and agree. It seems men can't help hugging them, whether men like it or no. Men are like the hermit student brought up in the desert, who, when he walked to the town with his abbot, and saw women dancing, asked the old man what they were; geese, replied the abbot. When they returned the young hermit fell into a flood of tears, refused to eat, and when asked what can the matter be, what can the matter be, shouted out so that all in the monastery could hear, I want to eat of the geese I saw in the city!

It is laughable to think of Chesterton's or Belloc's vision of medieval days as a happy time of 'Dance, and Provençal song, and sunburnt mirth!' A time of plush and Christian perfume. And how! Even today, in the *Catholic Encyclopaedia*, a writer on dancing is in a funk about what he should say concerning the vicious denunciation of the sport in the meddle ages by the clerics. He hems and haws it off by saying that: 'Undoubtedly, old national dances in which the performers stand apart, hardly, if at all, holding the partner's hand, fall under the ethical censure scarcely more than any other kind of social intercourse'. Hedging. Speak your mind, speak your mind! Come unto these yellow sands, but don't touch hands. Keep your distance, Harry. Don't let trousers touch the skirt, or there might be trouble. This is an Alice, where art thou dance!

> Oh, what shall I do, love, and what shall I say?
> Shall I tumble down flat, shall I hold you at bay?
> I'm frighten'd a lot of that buzzing, big bee
> In your impudent bonnet of bonnie dundee!

> I've lost sense of time and I've lost sense of date,
> I can't tell even now if it's early or late;
> I'm longing to hug you, while anxious to flee
> From the sight of your bonnet of bonnie dundee!

> Be cooler, be calmer — don't clutch me so tight;
> If you want to do things, learn to do the things right.
> Oh, I've tumbl'd; take care — you'll do damage to me,
> With that impudent bonnet of bonnie dundee!

All these old boyos dreaded the dance — St. Augustine, Salim-bene, Aquinas, even Abelard, and many others. In the *Summa Angelica* rules are laid down for wholesome dancing: No one must dance for a considerable time. The dance must be of an honest kind. The dancer's intention must be good. St. Antonino can think up no case where a dance can be free from sin; and G. G. Coulson says Antonino was a good chap, full of the milk of human kindness. 'Chesterton wrote an article in *The Dublin Review*', Coulson goes on, 'defending the attitude of the meddle-ages' clerics on sports, basing his arguments entirely upon a single passage from St. Thomas Aquinas, which he has evidently not sufficient Latin to construe correctly. It is odd that the Editor of the *Review* or some theological friend should not have intervened to save him from such a blunder. I have appealed to him in the *Review of the Churches* to name a single orthodox writer from St. Thomas Aquinas to the year eighteen hundred who understood St. Thomas in the sense required by Chesterton's argument; but Chesterton reserved his defence with a dead and dumb silence.' Even Sean's own St. Patrick's Purgatory gave a friar a vision of 'a great thick circle of iron set with needle-pointed nails on which a group danced while a rain of red-hot coals and sulphur fell on their naked bodies, dragons gnawing at their bowels'. Happy-minded fellows these, weren't they! Even Petrarch, even he, immersed in the puritanism of the medieval Church, denounced dancing too. Even he, a poet! Says he, 'From dancing we get nothing but a libidinous and empty spectacle, hateful to honest eyes and unworthy of a man; take lust away, and you will have removed the dance also'. No

> Swing your Kate, swing your Sue,
> Swing your girl and she'll swing you,

for Petrarch. Apart from one Pope and Bernard — who permitted it on a stout string — and St. Francis, who is said to have loved the troubadours, they all dreaded and denounced dancing. Music, too; oh, yes, music, too, just the same. The medieval clerics couldn't stick it; couldn't stick 'the rush of the bellows, the clashing of cymbals, and the harmony of the pipes'. Even were it not Mozart at his best, it must have had funny moments, and fun didn't glorify

God. Surely God must have been amused; or is it a ukase from the
clerics that God must go without a laugh from one end of eternity
to the other? In one of Dunbar's poems there is the big idea that
God can laugh, for he tells of a gay goodwife's sly slide past Peter
into heaven when Peter's back was turned;

And God lookéd and saw her lettin in, and laughed his sides sore.

Many young girls were amongst those who circled around Sean,
coming to see the great Metropolitan Church of New York's secular
buildings. Many of them were pretty in figure and face, a number of
them delightfully so. In a younger state of life, if they had let him,
Sean would gladly have swung with any one of them in any round or
square dance, and violently risked hell as a consequence. As for ugliness
under the skin, man had as much of it as any woman; as Sean's own
doctor said once, laughingly, 'We all carry a cesspool about with
us wherever we go'. We do that, but we won't despise each other
because God has been pleased or contented to make us just in that
way. If Church prelates, past or present, had even an inkling of
physiology they'd realise that what they term this inner ugliness
creates and nourishes the hearing ear, the seeing eye, the active mind,
the energetic body of man and woman, in the same way that dirt
and dung at the roots give the plant its delicate leaves and its full-
blown rose. This outlook on woman, as strong among the clerics of
today as it was in the middle ages (unaware of it as he sat on the
bench, Sean, because of his play, was to suffer a deluge of it from
the clerics a little later on), is just sinisterly silly. The woman, for a
start, is half the human race; and a woman's hand, however bawdy
in its touch it may sometimes be, can salve a wound, cool a fever,
and bring courage again to a disconsolate man. The swish of a skirt
in this world is more useful, more encouraging to life than the swish
of an angel's wing.

All of these young lassies, passing by, were probably in jobs;
working-girls; most of them gracefully dressed, each with a splash
of colour on dress or bodice or hat, made brighter by the brilliant
sun shining. Colour: a sign of the changing of time. Not now were
the workers all dressed in the law-imposed drabness of russet
clothing, as in the earlier days, up to, and far beyond the time of
England's queen, Elizabeth; when colour was the ornamental bene-
fice of the noble and the gent. In spite of the darkness in America
yet; in spite of the poverty there; of the sad things happening in the
South; in spite of the deep depression that F. D. Roosevelt and the

people were trying to fight away through a fair deal, life was moving in all the forty-eight States of the Union.

The theatre, too; oh, yes, the theatre too: the House of Satan to the clerics. To this day, in his own diocese, no priest is permitted to attend a performance in a theatre. He can go to the kinema as he will to enjoy there the many succulent shows of sex, garnished with tendentious words, and leave the place elated. But the theatre is taboo. A great, if earlier divine, and a powerful preacher, Massillon, says: 'You ask me if theatres are innocent amusements for Christians: In return I have but one question to ask you. Are they the works of Satan or of Jesus Christ? There can be no medium in religion. You have but to decide whether you can connect the glory of Jesus Christ with the pleasures of a theatre. Could Jesus Christ preside in assemblies of sin, where everything we hear weakens his doctrines? Where the poison enters the soul by all the senses. Every Christian should keep away from them.' The theatre is neither the work of Satan nor of Jesus Christ: It is the glorious creation of Man. Does that frighten you? Where have we left to go to? Only the kinema. From the earliest days, up through the monks and friars, down through Gerson and Massillon, and so to the *Roman Catholic Encyclopaedia*, the clerics shake their fists at the tavern, at music, at any fairness in woman, in any brightness they add to their dress, and at the theatre. Are we to live like white bones scattered under a juniper tree, without even the song at or as the white bones sang in Eliot's poem? Shall we close our eyes so that we may not see a lady on a white horse, rings on her fingers and bells on her toes? Shall we close our ears so as to fail to hear the music that follows her wherever she goes? Aw, hell! And Sean rose from the bench and went his way, as the dusk fell and the evening came quick.

On that same calm evening, when the moon rode high, George Jean Nathan guided him towards the one hansom cab left living in the world. There it stood, wisting not of the new world's ways, cab, horse, and driver, embedded in time that had stood still for them; close to the kerb of a sidewalk in a measureless street running past a threatening towering hotel, racing on ahead of life, and pushing its way out of the past of a year ago. There they waited, an *ill penseroso* of forgotten days; jarred in a jellied time within the surrounding epic of living steel, concrete, and stone. A dreaming ghost of Fergus Hume's *Mystery of a Hansom Cab*. The serious critic and the serious dramatist, the man from Indiana and the man from Dublin, climbed into the cab for a jaunt through a park in the moonlight. Away they went through Central Park to the tune of clop-cloppety-clop of the hansom's horse, valiantly keeping his tail up; the beetling buildings surrounding them looking like stony titans watching two of their titan children taking an evening airing in a huge old-fashioned pram with its big hood up like the horsey's tail; the buildings, ebony where the moonlight shone not, quietly candescent with a primrose silver shade where the moonlight fell; cloppety-clop now through a patch of gloom, then through a glade marred delightfully by a crop of rugged rock spurting up through the delicate grass, glazed over with soft moonlight and sad, shining like a light from a lantern carried by a god looking for a lost and lovely goddess.

The horse, the cab, and the driver sent ghosts of the past sidling up to Sean; shadows of the time when men's eyes sought the jutting bustle, and whose ears listened for the frou-frou of the trailing skirt; when the inverness cape was set on their shoulders and the double-peaked cap was set on their heads; when men rode bicycles that could be mounted only if one had the spring of a leopard; when Madame Patti sang *Home, Sweet Home* under the gas-light glitter, and when Sherlock Holmes stole through the streets to solve some mystery; time of the transformation scene and the harlequinade, of roses from Picardy, and the Martini-Henry rifle; with two old children enjoying it all; a joyous jingling hour of life; a big, red berry on life's tree. A joy-ride: the pair of them were young again, and heaven was all around them.

WITHIN THE GATES

THERE is nothing in life so dusty and dismal as a curtainless, gaping stage yawning out at those sitting down in front of it, and to those treading about within the poverty of its boastful emptiness, during the harassing transports of a rehearsal. In one of these dark places, within a first-class New York theatre, the rehearsal of *Within the Gates* went on under the guidance of Melville Douglas, a stalwart chap, handsome and able, and, after many struggles, began to show itself off from among the dusty shadows. These times are very harassing to all, but most so to a dramatist whose conscience ranges a little outside of himself and his own interest. He has to think (though he tries not to) of the actors who work so hard for weeks, and yet may walk about idle again, after performing for a few nights, even, maybe, for one night only; and of him who furnishes the money for the play's production, however wealthy the man may be; but especially if the producer be one who has just managed to scrape enough dollars together to lift the play to the stage. Grey hairs grow fast during the rehearsal of a play, brazen with imagination and experiment, on the commercial, or any other kind of stage. And the finer the production the greater the anxiety, for, in a bad production, the dramatist is almost assured from the start that the play will be a failure. So Lillian Gish, Moffat Johnston, and Bramwell Fletcher, with many others, were busy on the play's behalf; went on gaining ground over difficulties, till, at the dress rehearsal, it broke out into an unsteady but glowing cascade of speech, movement, colour, and song. Sean was glad; let it succeed, let it fail; at least the play would justify its full and defiant appearance.

During the whole period between emptiness and dusty posturing, in dull working-kit, to the breaking out of the play into colour and song, there was but one disturbing incident. One day, Moffat Johnston, who was playing the bishop, came to Sean, very worried, to say that the designer had arranged the crucifix he was to wear so that it would dangle, not upon his breast, but at the base of his belly. The amiable actor was very uncomfortable, and many others of the company were distressed, too. Sean assured him that the symbol was meant to hang on the bishop's chest, and there and nowhere else it would be worn. He went to the designer, Irish by descent, and, by all accounts, a roman catholic, and told him so. The designer angrily said he had so designed the symbol to hang between the legs, and there it was to hang, or he'd have nothing more to do with the production. Sean said the symbol would hang in the place where the script had placed it, but he was told that the design was more important than the play; Sean, responding to the angry face glaring at him, said, The play was the living body and soul and the clothes that covered them, while the designing added coloured buttons, braid on the sleeves, and, maybe, epaulettes on the shoulders; but however important and lovely these things might be, and often were, without the play they couldn't be summoned even into existence. The script says the symbol is to hang on the bishop's breast, and there it will lie till the play comes off; and, in a high rage, the designer ran from the theatre, and they saw him no more.

At intervals, or whenever he could sneak away from rehearsals, Sean sauntered the New York streets, trying, in a once-over, to get some idea of what New York was like. The great city is indeed an animated place; a glittering go-boy, with a grace and dignified strength that makes the go-boy grand. Many have said that the city is a place of confounding noise, and some have said that its clatter kept them from even one decent night's sleep during their stay in it. Sean slept there as serenely, more serenely, than he sleeps now among the quiet hills and valleys of Devon. The road to Plymouth running outside his house, with the sounds of its passing lorries, vans, private cars, varied three times a day by the more musical tumult of noisy children just let loose from school, makes more noise than any Sean heard, even adding the siren-calls of the rushing police-cars, in the abiding places of New York City. Then, in summer, all the day, and on into the evening, ears are entangled in the cease-less calls of the cuckoo cuckoo; and, later on, when the cuckoo has got tired, there's the bark of a dog here, there, and over yon, crow after crow from many a cock; and, in the night, the eerie squeal of the screech-owl out on the prowl for prey. Again, in the first fresh-ness of morning, when all but the farmers sleep on, the chant of competitive birds shrills out as soon as the sun sends his first finger of light into the low sky; and sleep, except for the hardy, becomes a contest in a restive bed. A countryman soon gets used to a town; a townsman finds it harder to get used to the country.

The first natural thing Sean enjoyed in New York was the spark-ling blue sky overhead, giving a clear and buoyant air in which to breathe alertly. The desecration came along some of the Avenues, from the sombre, crudely woven steel and timber of the Elevated Railway, running from one end of Manhattan to the other. The trolley-cars came swift behind it. Sean watched for well over an hour one night these strange-looking cars swinging around Fortieth Street, or one near by; watched them clanking along, clod-like on their iron rails, bringing home to his ears sounds common on the quayside of Dublin's docks. Long and low, solidly framed, door-way and body, dull-coloured, borne heavily along on cumbersome swivel and wheel. It might almost be that, out of this one, clumsily clanking around the corner, Walt Whitman would step down jauntily, lilting one of his many songs of Manhattan.

The New York subway in harmony of structure, comfort of use, or brightness of aspect, limps a long way behind the London Under-ground, and a longer way behind its remarkable cousin in Moscow; and the pale, mauve lights, indicating a station, show all the apolo-getic timidity of a poor relation to the prouder and more opulent activities of the city. So, too, are the buses running along Fifth

Avenue, looking like expanded perambulators carrying the family as well as the baby. It is the taxi which commands the streets of New York; fleets of them, like gay-plumaged swallow flocks, red, yellow, green, brown, white, and black, ground-bound birds skimming along the road's surface as if swiftness were all; a thrust-forward tension in each of them, even when they come to rest; a sway upward and forward as the lights suddenly call a halt to the swift going, an agitated purr of an engine delayed; and, as the shadow of green appears in the lights, a slim, sliding spring ahead, and the eager bird is on the swift wing again. It seemed to Sean that the American taxi, in its indolently slim form, is a daughter of the gondola transfigured into the muse of energy, while the English taxi, in its stiff, box-like stand, is the son of the sedan chair.

One day, he sped in one of these swift cars to a great synagogue, the Temple of Rudolph Sholem, if he remembers aright, whose pastor was Rabbi Newman, a young man with a pretty wife, three children, and a passionate love for plays and literature. He had invited Sean to come to speak to his people when they had gathered together for a Sabbath Service in a building so long and wide that a microphone stood by the rails of what Sean thought to be the chancel. After the chanting of psalms, led by the Cantor (identical with Caintaire in Gaelic, signifying a singer or chanter), the Rabbi spoke a few words of introduction, and Sean, greatly harassed by shyness, found himself speaking to a great crowd of Jewish people. There was no conceit in his stand, for he would far rather have been down among them, speaking to this man, that woman, as time and strength allowed. Conceit is a mother of many evils. Oh, Jesus, Oh, Buddha, Oh, Krishna, let a core of humility be in every conceit of energy necessary to life or dear to the heart of man!

Sean spoke about the curious resemblances existing between the Jews and the Irish — apart from the wild legends of the Irish being the descendants of the lost Ten Tribes, or that the first to land on an uninhabited Ireland were a granddaughter of Noah, her husband, Fintan, who lived for five thousand years, and fifty companions, who came there to try to escape death from the flood. The Irish were always eager to make themselves out to be as old a race as the Jews. Maybe they are, too. But, apart from these, there are many points in which the two resemble each other. There is a likeness between the old Gaelic poetry, in rhythm, emotion, and manner, and the poetic literature of the Jews; the Irish country people like bright, even gaudy, colours (Sean had a gradh for them himself); the one power of the Irish was their wit and nimbleness of mind, like the Jews; and, like the Jews again, the Irish were a scattered race, and had suffered great persecutions in their time. Spenser, the Elizabethan poet, gives an appalling picture of Ireland in his day; and, later on, in 1846–47, famine swept millions into the grave and millions more to the kindlier shore of America. So Sean went on, probably the first Irish-man who had publicly spoken in a synagogue.

When the service ended, Rabbi Newman told him there were many Irish men and Irish women there who wished to go by Sean, shaking his hand as they passed him; so for a long time Sean stood astonished, shaking hands with an Irish woman married to a Jewish man, or an Irish man married to a Jewish woman. He heard the name of almost every county Ireland had, including Connemara and his own Dublin, so that by the time his hand began to ache, all Ireland had paraded before him. Greatly — perhaps foolishly — moved, Sean had to murmur in his heart that the world's best blessings would swarm round the Shield of David and the Harp of Eireann.

The play was presented to a large audience, went well, though reviews the following morning were sharply divided; some were hot in their praise, others cold and caustic. It was a beautiful production in every way, and any fault shown on the stage was in the play itself. No voice, clerical or lay, was raised against its mood or its manner, and after a number of weeks' run, a tour of the play was planned, beginning at Boston. While the play was on in New York, coming up to Christmas, Sean left New York for home to be with his wife who was soon to have the other child. Two children now for them, but the tour was almost bound to bring Sean enough to make one more year reliable. Hurrah! Silence for a while, then the news that the Bostonian clerics were out in force against the play, and that the Mayor had banned it. Sean was being tossed about once more in the old sturm of style. Oh, God, here it is again! Wesleyan and Jesuit had joined hands to down the play.

'While I was in Maine', said the Wesleyan bishop, Charles Wesley Burns, 'my preachers in Boston held a meeting, and, when I got back, I was told they had voted to protest against the play because of what they had been told by Father Sullivan; and so I added my name to the protest.' The coo of the Wesleyan pigeon was aligned with the croak of the Jesuit raven. Point counter Point. Keep the kingdom of heaven respectable, please. So a bishop of a big church, eminent in the great city of Boston, decided a question of art and morals, not on first-hand news, not even on second-hand news, but on third-hand evidence: he decided to protest because of what his preachers told him of what Father Sullivan had said. Father Sullivan, S.J., representing the Boston College of Roman Catholic Organisations and Head of the Legion of Decency, followed the bishop with, 'Any religious affiliations [curious phrase — religious affiliations] would protest against the sympathetic portrayal of immorality, and all right-minded citizens, too, would protest against these things described in the play, and even more so the setting forth of the utter futility of religion as an effective force in meeting the problems of the world.' Sweet Jesus, will you listen to this! He thinks the futility of bishop or priest is equal to the futility of religion. Do not the thoughts of this Jesuit themselves show how ineffective his part in religion is, anyhow, in meeting the problems of the world? Is it immoral for a young woman to desire motherhood? Or to want to earn a living without having to prostitute herself to her boss? Or even to go away with a young man who loves her, and who was the one who showed understanding and regard for charm and vivacity? Isn't the whole play a cry for courage, decency, and vitality in life? Is it any more an act of immorality for a man and a woman to come together without a permissive chit from a priest than to make golden corn a flaming martyr before the eyes of hungry people that profits may be kept steady and sincere? Bum priests blathering.

Sullivan was joined by a brother Jesuit, the Rev. Terence Connelly, S.J., the 'noted dramatic critic'. Worse and worse. Here he is starting — he's off: 'The whole play is drenched with sex. The love song in the play is but a lyric of lust and a symbol of death. O'Casey has written on immoral subjects frequently in the past, but in art, as in life, the end does not justify the means. There are degenerates who delight in looking at raw human flesh, and in art there are those who demand life in the raw. But normal human beings swoon at the sight of human flesh exposed. They require the silken curtain of the skin to tone down the sight, and give the human flesh the normal colour that is the symbol of life. O'Casey has often written on immoral subjects. It appears first in the incident of the betrayal of Mary Boyle in *Juno and the Paycock*.' Even Juno; even she! Never a word, never a public word about the well-known and very able roman catholic writer Graham Greene's *Brighton Rock*, in which Brighton becomes a city of darkest night and darkest morn, too; in which everything and everyone seems to be on the road of evil. Talk of James Joyce! Joyce had humour, Greene has none; and in the darkest parts of Joyce there are always bright flashes of light; here the very light itself is rotten. Even the blessed sun 'slid off the sea and like a cuttlefish shot into the sky with the stain of agonies and endurance'. Here the roman catholic girl of sixteen and the boy of seventeen, respectively, are the most stupid and evil mortals a man's mind could imagine. One more quotation, and, if the clerics want to stick their noses deeper, let them get the book: 'She was good, but he'd got her like you got God in the Eucharist — in the guts. God couldn't escape the evil mouth which chose to eat its own damnation'.

Stand up there, now, Terence Connelly, stole and all on, if you want to wear it, till O'Casey has a word with you; a word he wanted to say when the row was on, but couldn't, because influences were used to prevent its printing. Isn't it amazing that such things should be said but a few years after a war had flung millions of men out of life and had so mangled millions more that they had just enough life left in them to hang on to it for a few years longer! Just as they did in the middle ages, so they do now, like this lord high admirable crichton of morals and art, going about to damn any who see and hear better than they; damning all as if they were bosses of the universe, cosmopolitans of the cosmos, dukes of divinity, and blights of the world, with the right to decide what man shall think, say, do, and imagine at all times, even to the time and the manner in which and by which any man or woman whatsoever shall proceed in slow motion to the hymeneal bed, or, in perversity, shall, on the other hand, fling themselves, as it were suddenly, with ravening speed, on to a couch without prim and purposeful preparation for the roister-doistering deed of love. It's funny, when one thinks of it, that a permissive chit from a cleric makes all the difference in the world, presenting those who get it with what Bernard Shaw said was 'the maximum amount of temptation with the maximum amount of opportunity'. Aw, let them blather! Neither life nor art cares in its creations a damn about them. Look at the God-laurelled ghosts in literature hovering about and laughing at these black-clad figures spitting on the musky petals of the rose — Tristan and Iseult, Abélard and Héloïse, Romeo and Juliet, Paolo and Francesca, Parnell and Kitty O'Shea, Jennifer and Dubedat. Let them rave: the musk of love will ever cling to the rose of life.

'The curtain of the skin has been put there by God to tone down the horrors beneath' — as another cleric said: By God, it hasn't! It has been said that the skin — far from being there to save man's feelings — is there to protect the delicate and vital tissues beneath

it; not one, but two of them to make assurance double sure. Whoever created the human skin (or any other kind), or however it came
to be evolved, it didn't come into existence to save man an emotional
shock, but to save him from a physical one; to protect the amazing
network of vein and artery and tissue beneath it, which the poet
Osbert Sitwell so poetically (and so rationally, too) calls *The Scarlet
Tree*.

And here's a frill to the stupid remarks of the learned Jesuit:
'Normal people swoon at the sight of human flesh exposed'.
Wouldn't it indeed be a hapless thing when man was plunged into
an accident on rail or road, in factory or in mine, or in the deliberate
mangling of the battlefield, if normal fellow-beings, running to help
and deliver, swooned down dead at the sight of flowing blood or
human flesh exposed by the lacerating infliction of an accident,
or the deliberately-imposed injuries of the battlefield! Or, again,
wouldn't it be frightening if a surgeon about to separate flesh from
quivering flesh so as to take away some poisonous interference with
healthy life, fell flat in a swoon when he caught sight of what he was
doing! Salute to Florence Nightingale and all true nursing sisters who
nurse men out of plague and fever, and bind up wounds with courage
and with skill. Silliest idea of all is that of God plastering silken skin
over a body to enable normal people to live in harmony away from
the sight of all that throbs beneath it. A comical association of a
theological aspect of the biological reason of protection. And, anyway, who are Fathers Sullivan and Connelly to denounce the body
when God Himself found it good enoughsky? D'ye call dis religion?
No, no. D'ye call dis religion? No, no. D'ye call dis religion? No,
No-o! What is it, then? Dope! Is it any wonder Bernard Shaw wrote
down that he had 'never yet met an intelligent Jesuit'?

But the Wesleyan bishop and the Jesuit priests didn't quite get it all
their own way. The students of Harvard stood by the play, as did
those of Radcliffe, Wellesley, and Tufts Colleges. A letter to Sean
from Richard C. Boys of Lowell House E-42, Cambridge, Massachusetts, said: 'We are in the midst of the furor created by the
banning of your play in Boston by Mayor Mansfield. Realising the
stupidity of such an action, we have circulated petitions to the prominent colleges of the Boston area, and the response has been great,
and in two hours last night four hundred signatures were obtained
in Harvard alone [Atta Boys!]. Part of the Petition runs, "We
protest that the action of Mayor Mansfield in banning *Within the
Gates* on grounds of immorality and irreligion is not warranted . . .

and we urge a reconsideration of the Mayor's decision. If religion today has not developed in its many adherents a moral and religious attitude capable of withstanding the 'insidious attack' allegedly made in this play, it is a criticism, not of the play, but of the religion, which should be able to stand against the gates of hell. It would appear, furthermore, that the play does not attack the essence of religion, but only those external and ossified fripperies, which, in the play, as so often in life, are presented to the communicant as true religion.''' (Atta Boys, again!) But the Jesuit janissaries had their way, and the play was banned. The lads and lassies from Harvard, Radcliffe, Wellesley, and Tufts Colleges came in special trains to see the play performed in New York City. Other places, frightened, followed Boston, banning the play, disrupting the plan of the tour so that it had to be abandoned, and so Sean's additional reliable year went vanishing into the stuff that dreams are made on. Abandoning the crackling fire around the figure tied to the stake, the clerics' do things now in a more refined way. Cunning boys!

Apart from the Wesleyan bishop Burns, and Fathers Sullivan and Connelly, who are most honourable, very learned, and fit to stand, heads up, among first-rate men; let us look at the average and a half of the roman catholic clerics who walk the world, teach in the seminaries (as described by their own Dr. McDonald, for forty years Professor of Theology in Maynooth College, Eire), or sit by their fireside in their presbyteries as parish priests or as catholic curates; those who set themselves up as anointed authorities on what should be read in a book, or what should be seen and heard in the activity of the theatre. Looka that chap walking along before us — just like ourselves. As a young fellow, he has gone (probably) to Maynooth where he has read 'a bulk of books' — à la tra la Cardinal McRory — listened to lectures, tried to crook himself away from the touch of any passing skirt; till, finally, he has said certain things in front of a bishop and the bishop has said certain things in front of him; then with many gestures, touches, and genuflections, he receives the authority to serve the sacraments to the faithful, which, even in the rigidity of his own limited community, doesn't give him the authority or the education to be an authority on the art of the theatre. Thousands of these laddos swarm the world, having gone through a systemised ceremony, filled their minds with a smattering of Latin (and in the matter of Latin, not only parish priests and their curates, but the starlit scarlet cardinals of Rome; for, as Dr. McDonald, so long Professor of Theology in Maynooth, tells us, when a petition or document in Latin goes to Rome, the first thing done is to translate it into decent Italian so as to make it easy for the Curia to read); and then scatter over the world, to settle down and inflict their infallible awethority on men concerning literature, art, drama, science, morals, height of bodice, length of skirt, politics, and God wot else; if there weren't spirits near enough and capable enough to keep them in their small corners. It's a big beneficium clergicorum they are after; and not only that, but curselorum, too, ay, and rato-lorum as well. They had them all once; but man's wiser now; and the venomous denunciation of *Within the Gates* brought no restoration nearer.

What splashed from the play over the Jesuits wasn't filth in any form, but hyssop, purifying hyssop, though the clerics didn't like the sting of its cleansing criticism. There is no more of venomous vice in the young woman of the play than there was in the young woman, Katerína Maslova, of Tolstoy's *Resurrection*; a book which, probably, the Jesuits never read, though a reading of it would do them more good than the reading of their Breviariums. But to a lot of clerics, as Tolstoy said, 'What they consider sacred and important are their own devices for wielding power over their fellow-men'. They tried to wield this power over Sean by making it more difficult for him to live; but dark difficulties have often proved to be brighter angels, and, in this instance, he doesn't grudge the throe, for their enmity towards the play hás made them, not more, but less, and him it has made, not less, but more.

PENNSYLVANIAN VISIT

SEAN went on a week-end visit to the Pennsylvanian home of the play's backer, George Bushar Markell, a descendant of the Dutch colonists, accompanied by the play's producer, John Tuerk; good-natured and amiable men, putting themselves out a lot to make things pleasant for the foreigner. It was a great trip in Markell's swift-moving motor, away up to hills first cousins to the Appalachian range. The car swept by fields full of Indian corn, woods, and pasture lands, and for a time along the bank of a river in spate, but Sean could only now and again snatch a glance at the new and gigantic country through which the car was speeding. Never before, save once when strolling through the wood of Burnham Beeches, in Buckinghamshire, in late October, had he seen such a tapestry of autumn tints in field and wood, a wild and drunken display of summer's fading. Nature in a desperate and colourful song, setting aside for a moment the surety of death. Such a display could be equalled only by the tabard worn by a herald from the king of kings, lord of lords, and only ruler of princes; a mantle given by the Fall, and that the Fall would shortly take away, leaving the trees in a patient, penitent nakedness that would quicken again in the spring, to swing into a revel when the summer comes icumen in again.

When the car had climbed for a long time, they came to a simple and cosy house set in the shoulder of a hill. It was fitted in front with a Dutch porch where a huge telescope stood on a tripod, which brought the farther hills and the valleys around them close to the gazer's nose. At the door to meet him and give him welcome was Mrs. Markell, a woman something over thirty, very handsome and lively in her manner and her movements. Before a meal had ended she was calling him Sean and he was calling her Gertrude — certainly a very amiable one-way manner in the American way of life. After the meal, Sean was brought down through a long and wide garden to see the swimming-pool; a very practical one, wide, deep, and long enough for an honest swim. It was a plain pool lined and banked by concrete, with concrete huts in which to dress and undress when the sun made swimming desirable. It had nothing Hollywoodian about it; it was there for use and not for show. The garden that led to the pool shocked Sean. They walked through a garden of tremendous growing tomatoes; tens of thousands of them, ripe, luscious, and full of goodness; thousands dying, too, within a tangled mass of leaf, blossom, and fruit, each as big as a full-blown grapefruit; some of them in the full scarlet flush of maturity, some others a day or two away from it, touched still with a golden yellow; but most of them slinking into a pulpy decay to hide from man's refusal to make a kindly use of them. So hard to come by at home; as plentiful here as blackberries on a bramble-covered English common. Here they were, lost, their richness trickling sulkily away into the indifferent ground. So many that Sean's boots crushed their crimson as he went along;. so many, and all lost to the mouths of men; so many, yet not even a Jack Cade starving here to meddle with and munch one.

That it may please Thee to give and to preserve to our use the kindly fruits of the earth, so that in due time we may enjoy them. They are here, they are here, O Lord, but we do not enjoy them: a glorious pride of edible wealth wincing here and vanishing. Look down, look down, O Lord, and tell what you think about it. Fruit here in multitudes, and no man here to pluck them; no man; though Bushar Markell no more than Sean himself could do a thing about it.

The hospitality of the house was gentle and full-hearted. Roosevelt, the President, was to give a fireside chat over the wireless in a national hook-up the evening of Sean's arrival, and he, full of the New Deal and of what it might mean to America, and, indeed, to the world, was very eager to hear what the President would say, ignorantly assuming that every American loved the man and his Fair Deal. He asked if he could hear it, and promptly the wireless was tuned in for the President's speech. Sean listened eagerly, said Hear Hear and Clapped Hands at several points made in the speech, never noticing the sombre silence of his friends. Weeks afterwards, when he had gone back to New York, he found out that his friends' feelings towards their President were anything but friendly. They had been staunch Republicans all their lives, dreaded the New Deal, yet no one of them had shown a sign beyond a simulation of interest in what the American President was saying to Sean's fascination and delight. It was a quiet and grand gesture of courtesy, giving silent sanction to a chat they nearly hated, so as to cause no embarrassment to a favoured stranger.

A remarkable thing, one that made him wonder, a thing he had never seen before, was a miniature waterfall pouring down the chimney of the sitting-room. There it was, in the midst of a painted background, with real plants backing its reality, cascading down in silvery streams, real water tinkling through stones, and vanishing away, with a melodious gurgle, through the bottom of the grate. It was unfamiliar, funny, and attractive, for within the chat of the evening one heard the tinkle of falling water and its gentle gurgle saying goodbye going away; but it never caused discomfort to the ear, nor did it disconnect in any way the easy flow of conversation. There was method in the madness, too, for when the sun was strong, the cascade kept the room adorned with a cooling sense of breeziness; and, if the weather suddenly changed to coldness, the waterfall could be made to disappear by the pushing of a button.

Another wonder worked more usefully in a basement, where a mechanical-stoker kept a furnace going with rhythm and precision. A huge hopper was filled with coal; when ash accumulated, a raker started to rake all superfluous ash away, and when the fire sank the hopper mechanically refilled the furnace, so while the household chatted, took their meals, or slept at night, the robot boyo in the basement kept working away, keeping up an even and comfortable glow that suffused the house with a soothing and satisfying warmth.

In the sitting-room was a lovely mahogany or walnut cabinet over which stretched a bright steel rod. This was called, if he remembers aright, a theremin. By placing the hands near the rod, drawing them away to certain distances, bringing them nearer again, various tunes could be played on it; and Sean's host, with rapid and graceful movements of his hands, played *Home, Sweet Home* and *The Star-Spangled Banner* for him. In a basement room was a workshop in which Sean's host did many things; he painted pictures, and made things from wood and metal; but, apparently, got tired after a while at whatever he happened to be doing, and so the place was strewn with lost achievements. Bushar Markell had been born into wealth, and there was no need for him to take life seriously. A great pity, for many things he had done showed him very clever with his hands, and, had necessity forced him to work for improvement of his talents, he might have done many good things in woodwork or in metals. Sean had noticed this detention of talent in a number of persons who had been born into a comfortable allowance. While the sensation of a new effort was fresh, they enjoyed themselves, but knowing no necessity to be thorough, the monotony of practice tired them out, and they abandoned any chance of profound or even competent workmanship for an easy-chair, a book, a girl, or a game of bridge. Wealth often takes away chances from men as well as poverty. There is none to tell the rich man to go on striving, for a rich man makes the law that hallows and hollows his own life.

The second day of Sean's visit was one of shelter from a flooding curtain of rain, that came pouring down in broad sheets stretching away far farther than any eye could reach; so heavy, so constant, that the splashing of it over valley and hill gave forth a melodious, watery hum, and all around, tree, hill, house, seemed to be aswim and asway in a flooded world. There was no thunder, ne'er a flash of lightning, no breeze blew; only the rain teemed down silently save for its own sound; falling as if it had begun when the world started, and would go on to the world's end. A heavy, grey sky leaned sullenly on the tips of the hills; never a sparkle appeared in the pouring rain to chasten its steady gloom, and, looking through the telescope, Sean saw slaty floods chasing madly down the mountain roads. He had never seen anything like it before, save once, many years ago, in Dublin, standing beside Jim Larkin, the Irish Labour Leader, under the portals of Liberty Hall, headquarters of the Irish workers' militant movement, the movement that had stitched a red flash forever into the green, white, and orange of the Irish Tricolour. Throughout the night they had stood there, in the open doorway, watching the rain, the lightning, and listening to God's concertina, the thunder, in full play. The square in front of them was lit from end to end with vivid, rapid-following flashes of lightning, so vivid, so frequent, that it seemed there were many mingling and whipping through each other, like a weave and warp of furious streaks of bluish light, knitting themselves together throughout the sky at the same moment; flashing the great Customs House before them in a sea of flickering light; farther off to the right, the thick and thinner masts of the ships moored to the dockside, sticking up and wavering in the bluish glow, like conductors' batons guiding the rhythms of the storm. Only for a few brief seconds, and at long intervals, did a sudden darkness ease their eyes, to give way again to the flash and the flow of the fervid lightning; so expansive as if light were enveloping darkness, and filling the firmament with luminant aggression. And through it all the rain falling, falling, diminishing at times to a heavy shower, then rushing down again with vehement speed, slashing itself even into the portal where the two of them stood: watching God having a little play-about in the streets of Dublin. Jim Larkin, Sean, and the big Barney Conway, big-bodied, big-hearted; barely able to read and write, but a grand talker, a fine story-teller, who, had he had a suitable education, would have been one of Ireland's great men; the three of them stood, silent there, watching a storm in Dublin, as he stood now with two other friends, on the side of a Pennsylvanian hill, watching another one, watching the rain, silently falling, save for its own sounds, flooding the valleys, tumbling down steadily from the low, dark-grey sky through the disheartened air, saturating everything that stood or crouched without a shelter, bending the trees with persistent pressure, having and holding the visible world within its splashing power.

So Sean stood, so many years ago, within the doorway of Liberty Hall between two friends, Larkin and Conway, watching a Dublin storm, just as he stood now with two new friends, within the portals of a house in the Pennsylvanian hills, watching the fall of the pelting, blinding Pennsylvanian rain, bringing to his mind a night-long vigil, in the throes of a great lock-out, through a storm of lightning and of rain, standing between two great comrades in the doorway of Liberty Hall: life staring back at him again, reminding him of old and happy, far-off things, and battles long ago: far away and long ago.

WILD LIFE IN NEW AMSTERDAM

DURING rehearsals Sean became acquainted through Dr. Pat McCartan (who, years after, came to Ireland, and stood against Sean T. O'Kelly for the Presidency of Eire, making a great fight, but losing, which was a great pity), then carrying on the profession of physician in New York, with a Judge Lynch, who, for some curious reason, had a liking for Sean's plays, and had showed his effusive admiration by embracing Sean when they met for the first time. This Judge Lynch and Dr. McCartan had a friend living in a residential suburb on the fringe of New York City. This family group consisted of husband, wife, and one living son. They invited Judge Lynch and Dr. McCartan to dinner with them one night, and kindly extended the same invitation to Sean, again through Dr. McCartan; and he, falling for the warmth and kindliness of Lynch and McCartan, agreed to go. After Judge Lynch had received therapeutic treatment from Dr. McCartan for a stiff neck and painful shoulders, in the Doctor's surgery, the three of them popped into the Doctor's car, and shot off to visit the friend. A swift journey in a swift car through the darkness to a big house in the midst of many dark shapes which Sean's peering eyes took to be trees, and they sauntered into the brilliantly lighted home of the host, the wife, and the one son. A quick introduction, a quick lowering of a glass of rich-coloured sherry within a murmur of informal phrases, and then to dinner in a big room, resplendent with a wild display of walnut and mahogany reflecting the gleam of glass and the glitter of silver; thick carpets embedded boots at every step; candles lighted the outspread magnificence of the table, flanked with flowers, and spired with many slender, tapering bottles of differing wines. A rich household, redolent of plenty, developing into a warehouse of rich and selected goods. A residence fit for Arnold Bennett rather than a home for Walt Whitman. Courtesy here, touched with a taint of vulgar grandeur. The host was a portly man, shrewd-faced, with a round head, bald, ornamented with a few tufts of hair; he hadn't very much to say, though he surveyed those present with a look of Aha, I'm here, see, while a pudgy hand fiddled and diddled with a fine watch-chain crossing his superior belly. His wife, too, was stout, taller than he, and had, for all her gallant dress and genteel manner, a half-hidden look of a mother about her. An Artegall changed into a bourgeois gentilhomme with a lady Britomart revelling in reduced circumstances, according belaccoyle to strangers. Dunged deep with a complacent regard of themselves. Sure of themselves, they silently pointed out to the visitors that they were in the presence; that they were surrounded, hemmed in, by substantial things in which the family had its being. They sat down in the midst of good things; they could raise their eyes, and see plenty before them, circumspect, costly, and thoroughly polished. The five guests sat at the round table with the family, the son on his mother's left, Judge Lynch on her right; Sean next to the Judge, then the spearman; the father sat opposite the mother, either at an end of the table; Dr. McCartan sat on the right of his host, then a man, a stout protestant, from the County Down, bringing the circle to the son again. The spearman was an American whose livelihood began by the hunting and killing of big cats (jaguars and panthers) with a spear having a ten-foot shaft and a one-and-a-half-foot blade, then advanced into the job of bringing out the sons of rich parents, wild with a lust for adventure, to do the same thing, but more safely with a rifle. Ahunting we will go, and ahunting we will go! He was a rather short man, but trim and hefty, with twittering eyes, a somewhat restless manner when spoken to, and a brown pointed beard gave a sharp look to his face. He had chaperoned the host's young lad on a safari through weeks of prowling and probing in a jungle of South America, pushing through tanglewood tales, so that the led lad could possess for ever within his Id the idiotic ecstasy of having killed one of the world's big cats; so, heads down, noses pointed forward, eyes left, eyes right, through the dangle of the orchids and the tangle of hibiscus, one day, the growling came into their ears, the jungle jangle parted, and the beast leapt. Puff! And when the smoke cleared, there was the laddo, rampant, behind the body, one hand resting on his hip hip hurrah, the other holding the rifle, the butt alongside the lad's right foot resting on the dark and tawny stripes of the snuffed-out animal. And so to bed.

Sean gazed at the coloured photograph showing the lad with his foot on the tiger, the spearman standing by to look respectfully over his shoulder, the lad at the other side of Sean asway on his feet, so dizzy was he with the pride quivering within him; the mother a little way off, smiling towards her raptured son, the spearman murmuring, He got his cat, right enough; first shot, too, plumb in the head; good hunting. So, for evermore, the lad would have something to weary his comrades with; something within setting him aside from ordinary folk: a one who shot a great cat in the tales of tanglewood. Rather a weedy lad, something over twenty-one, a gentle grin showing his weak nature, and his whole aspect showing that the glow of his limited mind was almost too much for him. Sick with ecstasy at others getting to know of his astonishing achievement. Hardly able to eat, so full of himself. Sean saw that the father knew it and felt it by the assertive way he ignored the lad, and kept his attention on his guests; he was disappointed in his son. The mother, nearer to charity, tried to shield the boy from being discovered, and, while pretending to listen to the table-talk, would, at times, swiftly bend towards the boy to whisper something to him to bring him within the circle of diners; and Sean saw the boyish, grinning face change to a foolish gravity and the head give a cursory nod, as if the hunter was acknowledging a trivial remark from a timid, trying woman. The civilised tigress watching over her civilised cub: we aren't very far from the animals. Oh, the wild wish to see our children shine! The curse of money begetting the force to put a life where its power is in the way of a larger life. Taking up time and thought needed for finer things. How high the cost of equipment, the big fee for the hunter-charman, the expense of carting this lad to a faraway jungle and of bringing him safely back a wriggling hero, with a picture of himself, his right foot stamping unsteadily the lovely body of a big dead cat; his mind remaining a mind that would never peer into anything higher than a boy's annual. It was odd; the father knowing what his son was not, but tolerating the idea of a special worthiness, though in fear that strangers saw through the contradiction, puffed out his own importance, as if to assure himself that his own impressiveness was more than equal to his own importance and his son's defects. The mother seeing the sham in her heart, silvering it over, as the oyster iridescently nacres an irritation, with a sham of her own, accepting the myth, and decorating it with gravity and praise. The spearman complacently assuring himself that he had lifted the limited lad into an eminence, deeply doping the lad with a ridiculous glory, and affording the parents a chance to take a tormenting interest in a son never to be so clever as his father.

All wore dinner-jackets, save Sean and the spearman, who was dressed in rough, wide tweed trousers and a rougher tweed coat, befitting a man whose important part of life was joined to the jungle. The dinner was eaten within a radiant sparkle of all things; sparkle of glass and silver, of mahogany and walnut, with the more graceful glamour of snowy tablecloth and richly laced table-mat and napkin; and the sparkle of vivid conversation carried on between Judge Lynch, Dr. McCartan, and the man from God knows where in Ulster; talk of things that had happened to them, of things they had heard, mostly incidents from colloquial history, sprinkled tartly with stories about Yeats, the poet and the man; the host at the table's head nodding knowingly, the hostess, at the other end, sending simmering smiles around when the others laughed, the spearman trying to enter into it all, and the laddo content to remain drunkenly alone in his daring achievement of killing the cat: all within the gleam and glitter of glass, of silver, of walnut and mahogany. They talked away, the host nodded approval, and his wife accomplished many a smile of amusement, when Sean was startled by hearing the Ulsterman say slowly and sharply: 'The Irish wud be a grund people but for the inseedious releegion of the romun catholic church ruining thum'.

Sean saw an uneasy look flash over the lean, almost ascetic face of McCartan, and a murmuring Hush hush; oh, hush, came from the gleam and the glitter of glass, silver, walnut, and mahogany.

—That's a matter of diversified opinion, came from Judge Lynch, in a conciliatory murmur; as a matter of fact, the catholic faith has never put any obstacle in the way of an Irishman's advancement.

—I'm tulling you different, said the voice from Ulster; it brings puverty ond eegnorance everywhure it fastens on the minds of people. Thure's one thing stupping the Irish, one thing only: the clinging of thum tae what hus no wurrunt from the mind of mon, or the ravelations of holy scruptures.

—That's a debatable question, came in a sharper murmur from the Judge.

—It's no' a debatable question, I'm tulling ye! It's the prime on' pure truth! Ulster's voice was loud now and the face was flushed. On', looksee, St. Puthrick, himself, was eegnorant of three-quarters of the beliefs common to romun catholics the day; on' thut's no' a debatable question with ony open mind, either.

—So protestants say who don't know a word of historical truth;

and the Judge's voice, too, was louder as he thrust his stiff neck forward over the table towards the Ulsterman. Will you deny that St. Patrick did penance for the Irish on the cold, windy top of Croagh Pathrick, and that he got his holy mission from Rome?

—Looksee, that's only two of the old wives' fables you Romanusts use to strungle God's truth! Croagh Pathrick! If he wasna' a fule, what for would he want to climb to the tup of a wild ond windy hill to say a prayer when he could do it better in his own buckyard or his own frunt room? Besides, uvery mon must confuss his sins, not to a priest, but to God. If ye confuss your sins — surch the scruptures, mon.

—Oh, God, thought Sean, Connemara's Croagh Pathrick and Belfast's Cave Hill are at it again, and, of all places, in New Amsterdam!

Dr. McCartan leaned back in his chair and sipped from a glass of wine uneasily. His lean face assumed a dreamy look as he murmured for all to hear, I remember one day in Dublin, when Yeats and Gogarty were going down Sackville Street——

—Wait a munnit, Pat, wait a munnit, said Ulster's voice with a note of annoyance in it, tull we suttle this question of reeleegion once fur all; thun we can listen to your blether about Yeats ond Gogarty going down Suckville Street. This question concerns truth on' mon's eturnal future, on' is not to be compurred with Gogarty on' Yeats goin' down Suckville Street. What has God's truth to do with Yeats on' Gogarty goin' down Suckville Street? Naethin', mon. But He has with this question: th' question we're suttlin' is God's own question, I'm tullin' you!

—St. Peter's our man, a saint; the rock on which our church stands. What's yours piled up on? On a shameful attachment of a despicable English king for a loose lady of his court! Judge Lynch was getting hot and bothered.

—Lussen, mon, lussen.

—I've listened to you long enough, almost shouted the Judge. Henry the Eighth and a harlot! It gets me down how any decent mind can take it. The only two saints in the protestant church, Henry the Eighth and his harlot — it makes me laugh; ha ha!

—Gentlemen, gentlemen, change the subject, please, persuaded Dr. McCartan.

Hush hush, murmured the glitter and gleam of the glass and the silver, of mahogany and walnut wincing; hush, oh, please do.

—Ours is the one church that is universal, and your shouting doesn't shake it, said the Judge, shouting himself; there in the beginning, it will be there at the end; yessir:

> A great while ago, our church began,
> With a hey, ho, the wind and the rain;
> In God's all-important and permanent plan
> There's no place at all for the protestant man
> Except it be out in the wind and the rain —
> So rid yourself, Ulsther, of peppermint malice,
> Extra ecclesiam cum grano salis;
> Top of the morning's to Biddy McCue,
> There's nothing but hell-terror awaiting for you;
> Stark naked and shy and all flusthered with pain,
> A flaming soul lost in the wind and the rain!

—Och ay, ye can laugh the day, said Ulster, pushing his tumbler farther back, so he could thump the table; but wull ye laugh whon ye get tae the pearly gate — gin ye mount sae high — what wull your ain Pether say tull ye thon?

> Oh, Roman lad, you're out of date,
> You're all too early, all too late;
> Aha, the ruein of it.
> Ye didna' hulp the sawls in need;
> We ken the real plant frae the weed,
> On' scorn the blether in your creed,
> Gang off frae here, on' gang wi' speed,
> Aha, the ruein of it!

What d'ye say, O'Casey, mon? he questioned suddenly; adding, as Sean stayed silent, Go on, O'Casey, speak your mind; say the richt thing, like a mon. Go on; you know the truth as well as ony man. You're an onlightened mon, as I om. Truth is waitin' on tiptoes fur ye tae speak out.

—Oh, said Sean, trying to shuttle the argument off, the wide-open spaces are needed when a row starts between Wittenberg and Knox on the one hand, and Maynooth and the Vatican on the other. In these disputes, we are like frightened birds jostling each other in the dark.

—We're no' birds, said Ulster angrily, on' we're no' frightened; we huv our intullects, ond we're well abune the birds. Ye know the scruptures, O'Casey. Well, then, quote thum, ond you'll be nearer the murk.

—If God be what He ought to be, must be, if He be God, said

Sean, then He has no time to bother about the Anglican Thirty-nine Articles, the Westminster Confession, or the Trentian Creed.

—This is no laughing mutter, O'Casey, said Ulster; we're talking now about the affairs of God ond not about affairs of mon. I want to know if God is a catholic or a protestant: answer thot, wull ye?

—He's neither, said Sean laughingly; relationship with Him isn't sanctioned by the push-button of an opinion. He may be more than He is claimed to be: He may be but a shout in the street.

—That remark's derision! ejaculated the Judge. It wasn't right to use it. A shout in the street! What d'ye mean? What kind of a shout?

—A lomuntable remurk, O'Casey, said Ulster; on' irresponsible. Tull us what kind of a shout God could be.

—When God is a shout in the street, said Sean, the shout is never a creed.

—It must be a shout of something for a purson to believe in; a church for all ond God's world for us all untull the end, said Ulster.

—It might be a shout of people for bread, as in the French Revolution; or for the world's ownership by the people, as in the Russian Revolution; or it might just be a drunken man in the night on a deserted street, shouting out Verdi's *Oh, Leonora*, unsteadily meandering his way homewards.

—Now maybe you realise the lamentable result of denying tradition and sacred authority in order to decide for yourself? said the Judge, stretching the stiff neck further towards Ulster across the table: God is reduced to a common shout or song in the street!

—Not common shouts or a common song, said Sean.

—I want no guessing, said Ulster irritatedly; I want the full facts of the whole truth. Thot's my faith, the releegion of a protestant: the full facts of the whole truth.

—Gentlemen, said Dr. McCartan, rising, we have to go. He bowed gracefully to the hostess; thank you for a very pleasant evening. Come, gentlemen, we've a journey to go; Ulster a farther one, and the night is ageing.

They moved towards the door, the host following, McCartan between the two arguers, arguing still, muttering moodily:

—Your thochts are born out of confusion of mind, mon.

—Out of clarity of mind, you mean.

—Confusion of mind, I'm tulling ye.

—Clarity of mind.

—Confusion.

—Clarity.

Sean lingered behind hoping the Ulsterman would be gone before he got to them. He thanked his hostess, and on his way out, he stopped to look at a photograph of a clear-faced, handsome young man hanging on the wall.

—A handsome lad, he said; who may that be now?

—He was my son, said a quivering voice, my elder-born. Everyone said he was a very clever lad, and everyone liked him. He died more than a year ago of some fever, of pneumonia; oh, I don't know what — he just died on me!

Sean turned to look, and saw the plump body quivering and tears running down the rouged cheeks. She, too, had the immovable pearl of sorrow in her breast. Just as he had seen long ago Lady Gregory looking at her son's picture, while the tears ran down her face. Cover his face; mine eyes dazzle; he died young. This vulgar woman, agog with her possessions, for all the way she strutted proudly through them, would, Sean saw, willingly give up the gleam and glitter of silver, of mahogany and walnut, could she but have her son again; the son thought to be so clever, the one everyone liked. Oh, my son! Would God I had died for thee, my son; oh, my son! How many mothers have anguished the air with the same cry! His own mother over her dead Tom. It is time that this cry at least should be silenced the whole earth over.

Bring me a grain of mustard seed, said Buddha to an agonised mother who had brought her dead child to him, beseeching him to restore it to life; bring me a grain of mustard seed from any house anywhere in which those who live in it have never suffered sorrow through the death of a loved one; and I shall restore your little one to health and strength. And the woman had searched and searched for many months, but could not get a grain of mustard seed from a house that hadn't suffered through the death of a loved one.

Jesus, Buddha, Mahommed, great as each may be, their highest comfort given to the sorrowful is a cordial introduction into another's woe. Sorrow's the great community in which all men born of woman are members at one time or another. Here, the better had been taken and the lesser left. We all make mistakes at times. He took her hand, and gently pressed it, and said, My dear, dear sister, here a mother loses a son; there a son loses a mother. We are all the same when equality brings us grief.

> Oh, known and unknown of my common flesh,
> Caught in the common net of death and woe,
> And life which binds to both.

He went out to mingle with the muttering immensity of Calvin and Bellarmine disputing whether the banners borne by heaven's seraphim, cherubim, thrones, dominions, virtues, powers, principalities, archangels, and angels were the yellow and white of the Vatican or the orange and blue of protestant Nassau.

HEARTS AND CLUBS

THERE are a great number of critics and reviewers in America, and Sean got to know a lot of them in New York, Boston, and Philadelphia. Busy chaps, all; but friendly, and anxious to be good to a foreigner. No time to be formal; let's get acquainted: This is Tom, that's Harry, and here's Dick. Indeed, friendliness is the badge of the American tribe. All right by Sean. They were very different from their critic brothers in London. Nothing a foreign dramatist visiting there can do or say can push away the friendliness of the Americans. They almost hoist him up on their shoulders and carry him around everywhere. They have the happy, human quality found in critics the world over of differing casually or violently from one another; but they unite as one big man to try to make a foreign dramatist feel the warmth and good nature that is generally believed to live and flourish in a home. Every drama critic whom Sean met, those who liked his work and those who didn't, linked an arm through his, and gave him friendship. They confirmed it with a meal in this critic's home, or in that critic's club, or, more casually, but none the less heartily, with a sherry egg-flip at a busy bar. Sit ye down, and I'll trate ye decent; so they said, and so they did, too. There was one snag in all the kindliness: it hemmed one in; there was but a bitter chance of seeing the plain people of the city, or finding out how they lived, what they thought, and where they worked. Only when Sean could sneak away from the clutching hand of friendship could he go alone to wander where he listed.

This lilting kindness of American friends, especially of the drama critics, struck him the more forcibly because of the coldness and curious reserve blossoming from the frosty nature of the London critics. He had thought that this icy blandness was inevitable in the nature of criticism till he went to New York. Never had he paid a visit to a British critic's home other than Bernard Shaw's; never had he had a meal with one of them, either in restaurant or club; never

had he ever even had a sherry or a small port with one of them; never had he even sipped a single cup of strong or weak tea with one of them in a Lyons corner shop. It was curious, now, when one came to think of it; for even as they did, so he, too, belonged to the theatre. It couldn't be because of the many faults within him. There were many for sure, but none that would be likely to inflict torment on the poor critics. He wasn't, he believed, a bore — the worst fault anyone could have. He had hardly been twelve days in America before he seemed to be friends with all the New York critics; he had been twelve years in England, yet had never sat opposite to one of them in a bar; never stretched a leg under a table of theirs; never had a single drink side by side with one of them; never even sat beside one of them on a bench in the park. Indeed, he has now been in England for twenty-five years, yet never a one of them has blown him a kiss or given a wave of a hand from a distant point: bar Bernard Shaw. He had had meals with him, long chats, and many good moments. They had laughed together, Shaw drinking milk, Sean lowering a modest glass of wine; good fellowship and a dear liking right to the very end; unto this last. With this one only. None of the others had ever given a knock on his door, nor had he been asked to give a knock on any door of theirs. He wondered why? Too full of himself, maybe? But he was as full of himself in New York as ever he had been in London; fuller, in fact, for there he threaded himself through and in and out of a friendly tapestry. To Sean, the London drama critics seemed to go about like reserved sacraments,
The hope only
Of empty men.
Well, goodbye, and God be wi' ye! Till we meet again. Never, now.

At a meeting in London, Mr. Tom Hopkinson, ex-editor of *Picture Post*, is reported to have said, 'Anyone who has seen American films, read American books, and visited America, was aware of a streak of brutality in the American character'. Is this idea of American friendliness that had enveloped Sean, then, an illusion? Just a mirage of souls, unAmerican, and long dead? Does this 'streak of brutality' (because of what was done in Korea) run through the American nature like a tiger's stripe? No, not any wider nor more conspicuous than the streak of brutality in other peoples. All nations in tensive times and peculiar circumstances have a streak of cruelty in them. Look at the Indian Mutiny when the English fastened the rebel Sepoys to the muzzles of their cannon, touched the guns off, and filled the air with flying bits o' bodies; or — for Sean hadn't to go back far to find another example — look at the time of the Black and Tans, the Auxiliaries; and even the decent, common English soldiers, when fear assailed and assoiled them; then many an Irish nostril was stung with the cindery smell of a burning town, and many a lintel of an Irish doorway was splashed with the blood of a first-born. Just to show there's no heat here, look at the time the Black and Tans, the Auxiliaries, and the decent British soldiers were gone, hardly half-way over the sea on their way home, when the Irish Civil War began, and the catholic Irish showed in executions and torture (the gentle Yeats voting for a Flogging Bill) that they were as good as any other at rifling life and liver and all out of temples of the Holy Ghost. The indictment of one nation over another in this way is foolish, for when greed of gain or of office becomes an uppermost idea in a soul, or when the blood's afire with fear, the arm will be raised and the fist will strike, let the fist be black, yellow, brown, or a Christian white one. To Sean, the Americans weren't in the remotest degree like those seen in the films, or like those read about in American books; and these very films and very books are as welcome as the flowers in May to the English and Irish cinema-goer and reader as they are to the American people. We are all tarred with the same brush. In war, judgement flees to the brutish beasts, and men just lose their reason. All men, not merely Americans. And there will always be a strain towards war, international and civil, while the lust of profits is allowed to mar the mind of man. As Nietzsche says somewhere: 'Merchant and pirate were for a long period one and the same person. Even today mercantile morality is really nothing but a refinement of piratical morality.'

And often, not even refined. The English tycoon rapes life as readily as the American tycoon. The Jolly Roger is the banner of competitive business. Free enterprise brings war to other countries, and strews poverty and disease about everywhere in its own land. But the American people, as people, are not as they represent themselves to be in their own films and their own books. To Sean, the peculiar streak in the American nature (apart from them being presidents, tycoons, judges, critics, workers, democrats, republicans, communists, or any other walk of life or mode of thought) is that of a lavish and delectable generosity. They may be cautious as critics, venal as judges, ruthless as tycoons, but, in their personalities, in their inner natures, they all have this glow-like streak of generosity in them. They seem to be unable to help themselves against it. A warm-hearted pushing crowd.

One thing only that Sean met in America frightened and harassed him: the Women's Clubs. It was a flutter of the heart to have to say yes, for the sake of the play, to an invitation to come and speak at one of the gigantic gatherings. He felt as Moses did when asked by God to go to Egypt and speak on behalf of the chosen people. But go he had to, for these Clubs bought bunches of tickets for a play, and were very powerful. Go he had to, though his head was a bulging vacancy. At one of these gatherings, two other speakers were, thank God, present; one, Mr. Williams, who wrote detective fiction; and a Mr. Stone who wrote a life of Van Gogh. The women came in thousands to hear the three famous fellows, and you could hardly find stir or breath. It was a monthly Club lunch, and this one happened to be a birthday number. Desperately dejected, Sean put on a cheerful and confident gob, and inwardly prayed, atavistically, that he might be given something to say to these good women. He lifted himself from his worried want of thought at a thunderous outbreak of clapping, and away in the distance he saw a giant cake, resting on a four-handled barrow, each handle resting on the shoulder of a sturdy waiter, carried into the room to be paraded about, while all present sang 'Happy Birthday to You'. It was, he was told, to be given to one of the New York hospitals. When the cake had gone, the lights suddenly went out, and at the far side of the vast room, curtains shot aside, and he beheld the American flag fluttering in a floodlight. All stood up while a woman standing beside the banner sang in a rich soprano *The Star-Spangled Banner*. Emotional nonsense! He didn't know about that, now. He himself had enjoyed emotional tension at the display of romantic Ireland's green flag; later on, at the tricolour of republican Ireland, and, a little later, at the fluttering of the international red flag calling on the workers of all lands to unite together. Nationality was something deeper than even life in a man's nature. There seems to be something eternal in the feeling one has for the land in which one moves, or has moved, where one lives, or has lived, where one has, or had, one's being. Good it must be, and it will persevere, though the Roman Catholic Church cautiously regards it as a heresy, bringing about the 'deification of the state', a belief, the Church says, that sprang from the mind of Rousseau, and the higher thought of the French Revolution; though, surely, as Shaw points out, nationalism was beginning to show its mind in the lifetime of St. Joan. What the Church fears is that nationality will bring a national Church into existence, as happened in England in the time of Henry the Eighth. The Pope and his cardinals wanted the Church to become another expanding universe, with the bishops sailing about on supersonic clouds guiding us in the right use of literature, science, art, contraceptives, politics, and parsing. The Welfare Church! Outside of her, all things tended towards evil. The Renaissance was a bad start. The Rev. P. J. Gannon, S.J. (another Jesuit), says in the roman catholic magazine, *Studies*: 'The Renaissance was followed by the most disastrous revolution in European history, though it was euphemistically called The Reformation'. And a shout from Mr. Hilaire Belloc tells us 'Europe must return to the Roman Catholic Faith, or perish!' Down, down to hell, and say Belloc sent thee thither! Dither.

Yet when all Europe were of the one and only Faith, there was the same disunion, the same discords, the same murder that gentlemen say are plaguing us now. From the moment, and before, that Christianity became a consolidated force with the Pope at the head of it, seeking temporal power and crescent wealth, the holy roman catholics were stabbing at each other's powers, clawing at each other's ambitions, filling Europe with battle, murder, and sudden death. On and on and up and up it all went, so that even in 1918 they were hard at it, according to one of their own authorities. One example: Donald Attwater, author of *Catholic Eastern Churches*, tells us in *Studies* that: 'After a period of incredible confusion, Poland in the autumn of 1918 assumed sovereign authority over Galicia, lately an Austrian province. Civil war followed immediately. The war was pursued with detestable bitterness and unscrupulosity on both sides. When one reads of the rapes perpetrated by Catholic Poles in the churches, monasteries, libraries, and so on, of their fellow-Catholic Ukrainians, one can hardly be surprised if certain Ukrainian priests so far forgot their Christian duty as to preach in their sermons the extermination of the Poles, as the Polish Government, truly or not, alleged.'

Catholics destroying catholic churches, monasteries, libraries, and so on; and gutting their fellow-catholics, too! The roman catholics' delightful manifestation of the Sacred Heart all burning with fervent love for men! A contradiction in therms.

Here they were sitting down, the song sung, the fluttering flag gone again behind the heavy curtains, the lady chairman knocking with a mallet on the table for silence; *mater silentii*; and Mr. Williams rising to address the audience. He spoke of detective fiction as an art, as being, at its best, on as high a plane as any other art; of its many difficulties as to plot and characterisation; and that inspiration played as big a spurt in its composing and creation as it did in any poem, play, or novel. He said the nickname of Whodunnit given to detective fiction was conceived by star-crossed envy engendered in those who couldn't achieve success in the creation of convulsive consternation of the prime detective story. He remarked in passing that one of the great divisions between them and the Soviet Union was that while the detective story was an integral part of Christian western civilisation, communistic Russia but held this art in very remote remembrance. He emphasised the great development of the art since the rather primitive efforts of Sherlock Holmes, adding that the art today was bursting with experiment that was sure to furnish new wonder and delectation in the time to come. He spoke as if to the manner bread, and proved that crime and murder were substantial parts of Christian conceptions, and equally so in man's place in nature. Then he sat down again, enveloped in upstanding and determined applause.

Then Mr. Irving Stone got up and spoke of the labour and the research that went into the writing of the lives of great men. Something no-one could imagine. The research and the creation concerned with the setting forth of an orderly story was a work of years. The reward was the making of a great man to live again. So Mr. Stone furnished all present and correct with the synoptic account of the work he did in fashioning Van Gogh into life again; that odd, strange man who gave an old chair an honoured place in the universe, robed an old jar with the purple of the iris, sang a pictorial song of golden corn growing, and gave to roses the whiteness of priestly hands breaking the sacred bread.

While Sean was silently murmuring Lead kindly light, lead kindly on, and lead me outa this, he heard his name called out by the Lady in the Chair, and up he stood to enlighten the minds of America's mothers, sisters, daughters, sweethearts, and wives. He opened his mouth, and taught them, saying — but he had nothing to teach them. He expounded unto them a parable — but divil a parable Sean had to expound. Why was he uneasy at the risk of speaking badly, of boring his audience? Looking at it in the deeper way — conceit. Anxious to shine, be God! To show off, be a big fellow; hear others clapping him. At home, De Valera was preparing to withhold the land annuities from England — doing the big fellow; in England, J. H. Thomas was preparing to circumvent De Valera — doing the bigger fellow; and in Europe, the Furor, Hitler, was strutting around Germany doing the biggest fellow of all, a deed that was to deluge the whole Continent with a mangled mass of Jew and Gentile in one red burial blent.

Sean was here just because his name had appeared in the papers. Probably each woman here was as deep in life as he was himself, and knew a lot more about it. Women were nearer to the earth than men; they had their feet deeper in the soil. Men went lightly over the ground; women trod firm. They are closer to common things, and so have a more ready and lasting knowledge of life. Men shout dogmatically, they gesture, and run here, run there; women stay more still, speak more quietly, and say more in their silence.

Now, for an hour or so away from their silence, they had come to hear him because his name had appeared in the papers. He couldn't believe that many of them had gone, or would go, to see his play, and that the sale of his play-books would jump a lot after the meeting had ended. Still, he had to do it. Ay, but how? Irving Stone had talked about the apparent failure of Van Gogh, and, indeed, the great artist must have been dead tired with a sense of failure when on that memorable day he rose from his chair by his brother's side, went out, and shot himself sadly in the garden. So Sean talked of failure that might be a success, and success that might well be a failure; urging that no-one should be cocky in what was declared to be a success, or despondent in what seemed to be a failure. No-one, but Time, knew definitely. Time was the boyo who placed the final crown on the head, or gave the final kick in the pants. Be apprehensive always of success; never be afraid of failure. There was always honour in failure as a result of doing one's best. We can never be sure that failure isn't success in a shroud. And, anyway,

> Vivas to those who have failed,
> And to those whose war-vessels sunk in the sea,
> And to the numberless unknown heroes equal to the greatest
> heroes known.

And Sean's flag fluttered laxly, went behind the curtain, as he sat down tired.

ONLY FIVE MINUTES MORE

WITH rehearsals over and the time coming to go, go back to the Rose and Crown, the tempo of Sean's running about quickened. Only a few of the dozens of invitations to go to places and speak unto the people could be accepted; mainly because he didn't feel constrained to speak to the people; mainly because he felt he had little to say to them. He wasn't one who contented himself with the Salvation Army's method of saying any kind of nonsense that floated into their minds; their building up of a beautiful life, here and hereafter, with a phrase of 'Out of self into Christ, into Glory. Simple, isn't it?' as he heard a Salvation Army officer say once. Damned simple, right enough. Turning everyone into a quick-change artist. Becoming in the twinkling of an eye guided missiles shooting into heaven. He came across a group of them on a street in Philadelphia. There they were, large as death, ensconced under a huge umbrella, coloured red, yellow, and blue; there they were spouting out their spick and spam way of eternal life. Their glory was vanishing now. Like all the bursts-out of evangelical heat, this one, too, was beginning to cool quick. Just like the energy and enthusiasm of the first friars, black, white, and grey, launching them-selves among the poor to save them from the Reformation; whose love of poverty soon lay buried under a gigantic and splendidly built rubble of riches. So, too, the Wesleyan outburst of all-embracing piety to set aside the lukewarm decline of the Anglicans, fell, itself, into the same dead state; so badly that we can read in *Americana* the wail of a Wesleyan faithful few, keening:

The Church that God through Wesley launched
Two hundred years ago,
Is going now beneath the waves,
Down to eternal woe.

Piety has become a possessing pose. In one of the *Capuchin Annuals* (1942) there's a grand picture of His Excellency, The Most Rev. Paschal Robinson, O.F.M., Apostolic Nuncio to Eirinn, show-ing him in all his gallant costume of richly made undress cassock, piped and braided, with his lovely chain holding on to his jewelled pectoral cross; a gorgeously dressed cavalier of the Roman Church, and very nice, too. This gent didn't live in a slum or shack, ate things higher than pulse and beans, refused to sit and work in fire-less rooms, and never roamed about in the cold with bare feet blue. None of them do. Not till they are dead. This one, this Excellency, the Papal Nuncio in Eirinn, died a year or so ago, and in his last gasps ordered that when he was dead, he was to be dressed in a coarse garb, his feet bare, and set so as to stick out from under the shroud to show there was no deception. Tramp tramp tramp, the boy is triumphantly marching up to heaven in his bare feet. A grand example to the workers to embrace poverty for the good of their souls. Workers of all lands, don't bother about wages, don't bother about thin clothing, broken boots, scanty meals; remember the dead Nuncio in his bare feet. Christ, how many saints would the Ireland Sean knew have given to God, if saintship rested in pinched faces, empty bellies, and bare feet!

Easy a minute; easy a minute, now: it's damn easy to go about in your bare feet when you're a day dead. And a nice change, too, when, like this excellent Nuncio, you spend all, or most, of your life well housed, well fed, and covered cordially with crimson or purple array; with handsome, rain-proof shoes for the street, and violet or scarlet satin slippers for wear when the poor feet pass over thick and soft and gay-coloured carpets. No, Mr. Monsignor; it's a bit too late for the bare-feet blues when the time comes to stick your toes up.

Hurry up, hurry up, on the way, through Connecticut and Rhode Island, all the way to Boston, in a Pullman car, sitting in a cosy armchair that can swivel round to face where one desires to look, its comfort coaxing a soul into a conscious rest; and with many choice foods to shorten the journey, a magnificent negro setting them out in front of one with skill and courtesy; all the way from Alabama; Sean asking him as he served, would he like to be back home in Alabama.

—No, suh, he said; I'se all right here. There's noding in Alabama, noding for me, suh.

This little Alabama coon didn't want to go back home to Alabama. Nothing there for him. Nothing in Ireland for Sean; nothing for this great negro in Alabama; exiles, the pair of them. How often had he sung the song when a lad,

> Hushaby, don't you cry, mammy's little baby,
> Mammy's liddle Alabama coon.

The crosby touch when crosby was being hushaby'd himself, and just as solidly sentimental.

Only twice had Sean met souls from Alabama — this splendid negro now, and, many years later on, another; this time a white from the same State — by accident. Outside of his home, Sean was watching a long convoy of great American tanks, lorries, and guns, the lorries packed with G.I.s, toiling along the narrow Plymouth Road, all in a hurry to get to the front, but stopping often to squeeze through a narrower part; crawling along a way never meant for these huge thunderers of Thor. In one of the lorries, a steel-helmeted American sat astride the tail of a lorry; a young lad, who glanced about from right to left, wondering.

—Eh, boh! he shouted to Sean, where are we; what's this place called?

—Tot-nes! shouted back Sean. It's in Dev-on, in a south-west corner of England. Where do you come from?

—From Alabama! shouted back the boyish soldier.

—It's a hell of a long, long trail from here to Alabama! yelled back Sean, as the lorry jerked away.

—It sure is! came back the voice of the boyish soldier, and a sad note seemed to be in the sound.

On the way, well on the road,
The leaden road to Okinawa,
To splutter in war's muddy mode,
The soldier rode, the sign-posts show'd
The leaden road to Okinawa.

The call has come, I'm made obey it,
If I knew a prayer, I'd say it,
Along the road to Okinawa.
Oh God! if God but only knew
What we poor bastards tumble through,
He'd strip off all this sulky woad
From Yank and Jap, and disembode
Us from the glamour of the road,
The leaden road to Okinawa!

To lose oneself, becoming wholly
War's tatter'd, bloody roly-poly.
Farewell to arms, to legs, to seeing,
Farewell, maybe, to all my being.
No more now than a skimpy toad,
Made up in shit-like sulky woad,
I make my way along the road,
The leaden road to Okinawa.

Oh Jesus, it is only fair
That we should live as long as there
Are years to live before we're old,
And not be thrust down in the mould,
Before a grey rib stabs our hair.
But on and on I'm firmly tow'd,
To give death all I haven't ow'd
Till all my fresh, young blood has flow'd,
And laid the dust along the road,
The leaden road to Okinawa.

Two men, one a negro, anxious to keep away from the cotton fields, or from a job in Mobile; the other, a white, eager to get back once more to Alabama; and God deciding. Nothing in the State for one, everything in it for the other.

Sean passed through Boston in a taxi, seeing nothing but tall buildings whirling by, blurred in the flabby greyness of a thick fog; but remembering that here Emerson had been born, who, transcendentalist (big word) and all as he was, stretching himself up to the sky to handle what wasn't there, still kept tiptoe on the common earth beneath him; the taxi speeding on to a big hotel, where cordial Pressmen gave him a cordial dinner, talking through the hours of what was and what was to come to the theatre, little realising what was to come to the world. On, then, in the early morning in Horace Reynolds' old grey mare of an automobile, to Cambridge, where Sean was to speak to the members of the Harvard Poetry Society on the Elizabethan Drama as pictured in Archer's *The Old Drama and the New*, the worst book ever written about drama, new or old; and the silliest. It was to be an informal chat in a cosy little room to about fifty members of the Society, but Sean was frightened when Horace Reynolds told him in soothing bits of information, as the car rattled along, that a lot of interest had been aroused in the lecture; that many wanted to hear it; that they had to take the large Hall, and that, instead of the quiet, simple fifty, hundreds and hundreds would be there. So Sean had to give one ear to hear what Horace was saying, and the other ear to hear himself praying for deliverance. Sean, standing on the professorial rostrum, gave his lecture, and, of course, was applauded. The audience could hardly do anything else out of politeness. Indeed, one middle-aged professor told Sean afterwards, *sotto voce*, that he wished he could lecture in that way; knowing quite well, if he did, he wouldn't hold his job a week. A hurried look at the buildings, a cosy hour with the younger students in their club-room, heightened by tea and sherry, and lowered by many questions that Sean couldn't answer, but answered all the same; and a trot round the modern library, rosy-red and inviting, confidently exclaiming in its layout and attractive façade that all older universities needed knocking down so that sensible premises could take their place, more suited to the outlook and needs of our changed and more attractive and secular life. Dinner then with the amiable Horace Reynolds and his charming wife, Kay, with their two lively and handsome children, John and Peggy, looking him over, without Sean having chance or time to show them he was something of a kid himself still: both married now, and Peggy a mother. Oh, we grow old, Master Shallow, we grow old! Later on, he was to entertain in Devon several of the young students when they had grown into combatants of the war against Nazism.

Swing low, swing high up on to the train again, and off to New York, sleeping roughly in a bunk as the huge train pounded its way along, char-char-charrity-char, with a clatter across a level-crossing, a roar diving into a tunnel, and loud, sibilant hiss penetrating opposing winds as she whirled by another train going the opposite way; and into the great cathedral of the New York station at five in the morning, to hurry down to the splendid underground restaurant where a wash and a fine breakfast armed them for another day's excitement. Off the next day to speak at a club in Philadelphia, to meet at an exhibition of stage designs the lass, Kitty Curling, who had played Mollser in the Abbey Theatre production of his *The Plough and the Stars,* and who was now an American wife and mother of a baby. A rapid talk of an hour with a group of Pressmen, after the lecture, and on the train and off again for New York, chut-chut-chuttity-chut, a clatter over level-crossings, and a roar of a dive into a tunnel, waste o' time waste o' time waste o' time, chut-chut-chuttity-chut, for he had spoken and spoken, yet had had nothing to say. Oh, God, he must have been born to be a bishop! For once in a while he was feeling a sense of sin. He was doing all this to swell, by one or by two, the numbers that came to see his play; a swift-flowing, tightening, sibilant hiss as they passed a train whirling along the opposite way; chut-chut-chuttity-chut, waste of energy waste of energy doing what he couldn't do well, maybe what he couldn't do at all. A dot of Irish humanity rushing around, carried about in taxi and train to impress itself upon the American people. Ravelling himself out of the American fabric by trying to knit too much of himself into it, and all for the sale of a few more tickets that he might still go haltingly on through life. But needs must when the devil of echonomic memory of past poverty drives one to where one doesn't want to go. If these speeches got him into touch with the people, they would be grand things; but the one sure way of being intimate with humanity is to work with them, go in bus, elevator and underground with them, or sit chatting with them by their own firesides. Lectures built up on facts should be given by scholars and experts; by those who have the faculty for teaching, having fitted themselves for the job; chats by those whose imagination would turn history into a song and theology into a ceremonial dance.

Chut-chuh-chut-chuh-chuttity-chuh, over levels, under tunnels, through culverts, the train steamed into New York again, a wash, a meal, an evening's chat with George Jean Nathan, a sleep, and off again, in a taxi this time, to the Bronx, with Dr. Herring, President of the Bronx Rotary Club, to speak to its members. A great gathering in a big room of a big Bronx hotel, ready for lunch. Men and their wives assembled for their monthly meeting, gay, and in a gavotte mind, withal taking themselves very seriously; looking upon themselves as the leaders of the Bronx people, which in a sense they were, for they were the professional men and business men of the place; the better-off inhabitants. Indeed, from *Americana* we learn that a Pennsylvanian member said of Rotarians that 'Rotary was more than a luncheon club; it was a Posture of the soul'. (Now that the Vatican has banned any priest from membership, and warned its lay members to keep out of it, it is plain that the Vatican looks on Rotary as an Imposture of the soul. Even the innocent Rotarians banished from the Civitas Dei.) Well, here he was in the midst of the Midianites, eating with them and chatting away, till lunch was over, and the birds began to sing. A big green broadsheet was handed out to everyone, splashed all over with the words of the songs. He had it before him now. In the right-hand corner were pen-sketches of heads of pretty, neatly-hatted young ladies. In the centre, the title of The Bronx Rotary Club; and to the left of this, Welcome Ladies, leading into the festivity of the Bronx Rotary Greeting Song:

Hollo, hollo, everybody — Bronx Rotary is greeting you today,
Hollo, hollo, everybody — we're glad you're here,
We hope you'll like your stay.
                              Words by Andy Keogh.

First a song, led by the men grieving at being married to the women, then a verse by the women grieving at being married to the men, to the air of *The Man on the Flying Trapeze*; the men's verse going:

Once I was happy, but now I'm forlorn,
Since I've been married my liberty's gone,
No more do I go out and stay until dawn;
Gone are the girls of my dreams.
Oh, the dame that I wed is so stubborn,
And I try all I can her to please,
But I'd give all I have for the freedom
Of the Man on the Flying Trapeze!

They gathered this way monthly to sing and eat, and, if the chance came, to sling a speech from a guest at the assembled fathers and mothers badged with the Rotary spirit. Here they were, the smaller of the bigger men of New York City, doctors, dentists, solicitors, teachers, contractors on a small scale, and shopkeepers; active, hard-working, and important people, forming a vast part of the American public opinion; very simple and courteous to their guests. None of them spoke to him about his play, and Sean was suspicious that none had gone to see it. His name had appeared in the Press, and the leaders of the Bronx social life had been eager to show him off to their comrades, much in the same way as they might go to see a strange animal in their own Zoo. They sang loud, with a rough-edged harmony, but the songs didn't seem to echo in their hearts; looked as if they had to exhibit a gaiety and a confidence the state of things denied them. Few of them, perhaps, had any sense of a secure tenure of profit, even of life. They were striving in the deep middle of a deep depression; so they sang songs that brought to them no genuine thought of love, or adventure, pain, or doubt; less than a child singing a song of sixpence. But they were determined to be gay, fixing themselves, for the moment, in the daring hilarity of a song. Here we go again, Let me suffer and let me sing:

> Dear Old Girl, the robin sings above you,
> Dear Old Girl, it speaks of how I love you,
> The blinding tears are falling,
> As I think of my lost pearl,
> And my broken heart is calling,
> Calling for you, Dear Old Girl!

Nothing in the way of poetry; little in the way of verse; but, apparently, the best they could do to emotionally speak their minds. And who is big or grand enough to say it is awful? Perhaps there were some of the men there who had shed tears over the death of a Dear Old Girl. It wasn't impossible; or some woman who mourned the loss of a Dear Old Boy. No American folk-song flitted into their singing; like that about the little black bug from Mexico — the Boll Weevil; or Some got Drunk and some got Boozy, an' all got struck on Black-eye'd Susy; or the Nova Scotia one, *The Tree in the Wood*, that Sean had so often chanted himself among national groups in his own Dublin; or *The Dying Cowboy*:

> Oh beat the drums slowly,
> And play the pipes lowly,
> And play the Dead March as I'm carried along.

Bring me to the valley
And lay the sod on me —
The poor dying Cowboy who knows he's done wrong!

One would be too near to their inner thoughts; maybe they knew none. Gay and irrepressible chaps and lassies, but haunted all the time: with home problems, with State divisions, with the growth of the unemployed, with the state of trade. Sean couldn't help feeling that there would be less disillusionment, fewer disappointments among these decent people if they hadn't to hurry about so much in search of bread; if life were but a little more certain; if today could tell even half of tomorrow's tale.

Only five minutes more, and the great liner would swing away from the giant dock. Life had given him one more grand experience: he had touched down on American shores, and had scored a try. He had made a good few good friends who would stand to him through a trying time, though he didn't know it then. He carried away with him many desirable memories, the strangest one 'The fervent blessing of an old priest' from Dr. Morgan Sheedy of Altoona, Pennsylvania; the life-long friend of Dr. Walter McDonald, so long a Professor of Theology in Maynooth College. Land of riches and of poverty, farewell, in whose sky hung the purple star of generosity. A young land, a little nervous of its own power, not quite sure of what to do with it; flexible in its moods and kindly in touch to strangers.

The siren blew, warning friends of passengers to leave the ship. Sean shook hands with George Jean Nathan and his friend, the lovely, regal Mimsie Taylor. Farewell! He was tired, very tired, from the strain of speaking publicly so often, without enthusiasm, without the desire to do it; for his words were not the ready ones, but the words thought of and handled before they ventured out to speak for themselves. Yet, withal, had he not had a beloved wife and child, with another on its way, waiting for his company, he would have stayed here where Ballyvourney spoke to Kiev, Budapest to Mexico, Edinburgh to Athens, Jerusalem to Rome; where the thoughts of all lands with their differing moods commingled. Well, farewell to all of ye, and my blessing remain behind me.

The five minutes had passed, and the liner swung out into the harbour, with Sean leaning over the side watching New York drawing away from him. It was a calm day, crispily cold; the evening was falling over the city, and Sean saw it fading in the half-light of the dusk, its towering buildings darkened, and a myriad lights from hill and valley of windows gleamed like friendly eyes watching him go: a city that is the outcome of many civilisations — of Stonehenge, of Peru, of Mexico, medieval Europe; melted down, remoulded, and cast out into the modern America; before all men, with all its faults, tremendous, terrible, inspiring. Many thoughts about many he had met were embedded in his memory for ever: the long, lean figure of Eugene O'Neill in the latest of Daks, with a warm, welcoming smile softening his sombre face, the deep-set eyes of the great dramatist burning with a light like what would glow in the eyes of a battle-scarred crusader staring from a rocky, sun-browned hill at the distant city of Jerusalem; his wife, Carlotta, caring for him, a dark flame of loveliness; the clever, voluble Sinclair Lewis praising the goodness of the corncob; the sturdy Elmer Rice quivering with rage at the thought of what Nazism would do to the world; Richard Watts calmly raking through heaps of sandy stagecraft in the hope of finding a nugget, or, at least, enough gold dust to make a ring for a lady's finger; Lillian Gish growing younger as the rest grew old; Brooks Atkinson talking of Roscius and roses, or rushing from the theatre at curtain-fall to send a review skimming on to the prattling printing-press, his charming wife easing his impatience while setting elegant and comfortable hospitality before a guest; the open door of George Nathan's hotel home, and the cosy armchair within waiting to seat Sean safely; the kindly and bustling workers behind the scenes with whom Sean often had tea below the stage; and many more, and all. All fading into a sea mist now. Oh, Honey, fare thee well, fare thee well! Is America a land of God where saints abide for ever? Where golden fields spread fair and broad, where flows the crystal river? Certainly not flush with saints, and a good thing, too, for the saints sent buzzing into man's ken now are but poor-mouthed ecclesiastical film stars and cliché-shouting publicity agents,

> Their little knowledge bringing them nearer to their ignorance,
> Ignorance bringing them nearer to death,
> But nearness to death no nearer to God.

Nor to man, either. Golden fields would spread fair and broad when all men were one; spread fair and broad in all lands; and saintship would be left to private enterprise. America, like all other lands, was a land for men and women and children, and that was enough for Sean; for where the people are is the land that never hath an ending, that never hath an ending, that never hath an ending.

The buildings now were but faint silhouettes, fading into the lights of multitudinous windows; soon all these, too, would go, and there would be nothing but a sullen sky above and a grey and choppy sea below to keep him gloomy company.

Hail and farewell, America! It was unlikely he would ever walk the streets of her cities again; so an Irish blessing and an Irish good-bye to America's people who shall never have an ending, never have an ending, never have an ending.

SUNSET AND EVENING STAR

*You cannot prevent the birds of sadness from
flying over your head, but you can prevent them
building nests in your hair.*

CHINESE PROVERB

I'm gonna wash 'em all outa ma hair.

*To My dear Friend Hugh MacDiarmid
Alba's Poet and one of Alba's first men*

A DRIVE OF SNOBS

BACK to London, New York lingering beside him still (Oh, linger longer, do), his hand still touching Rockefeller Center, his eyes still luminous with the myriad windows lighting up New York's night; here he was driving back with his boy, Breon, and their maid, Marion, back to their new home, a flat in Battersea; back with presents, nylons for his wife from Tessa, his agent's wife, more nylons from Lillian Gish, a padded silk bed-jacket for her from handsome Sylvia Sydney, a grand black-and-white silk scarf from George Jean Nathan, a set of pop-up books for his boy from Mimsie Taylor, a lass as lovely as his own wife, and that was saying a mouthful — a phrase he had learned in London, but which he had never heard in America; and his pockets jingling with enough dollars to keep things going for another year.

> Home is the sailor, home from the sea,
> And the hunter home from the hill.

Home safe from terrible dangers, too, as this letter, one of several, can show:

Hudson Theatre

Mr. SEAN O'CASEY

Now Mr. O'Casey, I attended your play, *Juno and the Paycock*, last night. I felt very discrossed also discoroged with it could you not make it any better than you have it, if not you are getting a warning to stop it at once or can you not make it any more pleasant for the Irish people who are delighted to hear something of their own country.

I have seen many plays throughout New York but I have never seen anything like what is in the Hudson theatre. Its rediculus and why dont you think so too you must remember that these disgraceful pictures and plays are condemned and *Thank God*. You are getting a very keen and good advise now before you go any further with your work, dont you think you would be better to be bricklaying than ridicaudling the Irish, you are going to be Jumped upon some night and you and your gang are not safe. The most prinsible thing *Stop the cursing and swaring* for the players good. This is only a warning.

KELLY, BURKE, AND SHEA

Heaven having a blast at him! He would have to amend his The Bells of Mary's were bullying. He'd have to thank God for the race

459

and the sod, for Kelly and Burke and Shea. The members of the
Legue of Dacency were out defending western Christian culture.
Sign your name, Kelly, sign your name, Burke, sign your name,
Shea — this'll put the wind up him! O advocates of heaven. Their
letter was a *cry di curé*. Comrades of the great war against profunity.
Oh, sweet and salient natures! A chosen three, who carry great green
banners in St. Patrick's Day Purrade, and are blessed by father
Spiellman as they go bye byes. Henceforth he, with Erinn, would
remember the days of old; he'd give three hours a day to mend the
harp the minstrel boy tore asunder; he'd seek out mother machree
and love the silver that shone in her hair, so that, at the last, having
kept the faith, his name might be written down from everlasting to
everlasting in the Book of the Green and Golden Slumbers.

The O'Caseys had taken a five-roomed flat in forty-nine Overstrand Mansions (the forty-niners), facing Battersea Park, on the
south side of the Thames. All the homes here, along Prince of Wales
Drive, were flats in groups of mansions, York, Prince of Wales, and
Overstrand, the line of them extending from one end of the park to
the other. A. de Blacam, who, some time ago, used to write a daily
column for De Valera's paper, *The Irish Press*, excited himself and
his readers by proclaiming one morning that the great democrat,
G. K. Chesterton, had lived for years in forty-eight Overstrand
Mansions (next door, be God!), plump in the middle of the workers
and the poor. He did in me neck! Occasionally, he may have caught
a glimpse of a poor woman or a poor child coming from the poor
quarters to enter the park for a play or a rest; but no fuller revelation
of the worker's life comes before the eyes or enters the mind of the
select residents of the flats in the select mansions of Battersea. These
hoity-toity persons were far more selective of their chance acquaint-
ances than were the proper persons of Park Lane in the hey-day of
its historical hallowed-be-thy-name period. The livers in these flats
were of the higher-low middle-class, a step or two down from the
grade of the middle-class who lived on the other side of the river in
the Borough of Chelsea; so they had one more river to cross before
they entered the land of Canaan. Battersea was, almost wholly, a
working-class borough, and so the families of the mansion-flats
shoved themselves as far as possible, bodily and spiritually, to the
edge of the district. All they knew of the workers was the distant
glimpse of sooty roofs they got from a few of the higher windows at
the back of their flats; or, during an election, when they went to give
their votes for what Disraeli called 'The barren thing — Conserva-

tism — an unhappy cross-breed, the mule of politics that engenders nothing'; though the workers' district barely loomed into view from where the votes were cast. The name of the Borough rarely appeared on the notepaper of the residents, who hid the humiliation of Battersea under the simple postal symbol of London, S.W.11. Peek-a-boo, I see you, I see you hiding there! In conversation the name was never mentioned: it was as if they had innocently crossed the border of Chelsea, and had settled in Battersea without knowing it. They were not to blame: that was their life, and they lived it.

The first floor of the flats had a balcony going right across the façade, the second floor a concrete jut-out on which one could stand, but couldn't sit, and the upper floor had no balcony at all; so the rents sank as the flats mounted. As well as this distinction between the flats themselves, there was also a distinction between the blocks, Overstrand being ever so slightly more genteel than the York block; and York was careful to await an advance from Overstrand before assuming acquaintance with Overstrand, for fear of a snub; for it is almost unbearable for one snob to be snobbed by another.

Once a Mrs. Black, living almost next door to him, wife of a civil servant, was presented at Court. She dipped the knees in a curtsy to kingship, and returned to the flat creaking with exultation. Her kingdom had come, and she entered gallantly into it; for that night, in her court dress, feathers and all, her husband in white tie and tails, with a few select friends, she sat down in the flat's dining-room to a five-course dinner, done to a turn by a qualified chef, served by a footman in coloured coat and plush britches, and eaten by candle-light; a first-class offering of thanks to God for his regarding of the highliness of his handmaiden, who had now been magnified in the sight of all her neighbours.

There was a Mrs. Green, too, her husband, Ben, their two children, Peter and Pauline, all rigid with fear of touching person, place, or thing beneath them, and quivery with desire to acquaint themselves with persons, places, or things they thought to be above them. Once a month, mother, son, and daughter went to ride in Richmond; and all the morning before departure there was a running-up-and-down parade of hard hats, whips, and jodhpurs (a lady goes apace apace, a gentleman goes a trit trot trittrot); though, as a matter of fact, each was taut with a constricting fear of canter and gallop, from the time they got on to the horses to the time they gladly got off again.

—No, said the mother once to Sean, they had never been in a stable; they mounted of course in the yard; and she was shocked when Sean told her a horse would never know what to do with her till she had spent a good deal of her time in a stable with him; till her nose had got used to the smell of dung and horse-sweat. Yet to those whom she believed to be her equals, she was a very pleasant woman, loved her children, and took good care of them. But no thought for other children troubled her, or any of the other residents. They all spluttered with indignation when the Battersea Council organised popular entertainments, flooding the park with poorer children, neatly dressed or tattered and torn, jostling the middle-class kids out of their way, the over-populated bodies of the rougher children transferring surplus vermin to the fresh and vacant bodies of the better-kept kids, making their flesh become delightful feeding-grounds for louse and flea. A-hunting we will go, a-hunting we will go, a-hunting we will go! No-one could blame them for dividing their children from the louse and the flea; they were to be blamed, though, for raising no word against the conditions which inflicted these dangers and torture upon the children of others. Again, when a rough-and-tumble crèche, a roped-in patch of grass, surrounded by shade-giving trees, was founded so as to give working-class mothers a snatch of rest from their labours, by leaving their toddlers in charge of a woman there at tuppence an hour a head, the residents, as superior rate-payers, signed a complaint and sent it to the Borough Council, complaining that the crying of the children, in anger or in play, disturbed them, and that the crèche utterly destroyed the order and serenity of the park. And this was the rendezvous chosen by Chesterton in which to laugh and sing and clap hands with the workers!

Mrs. Green sorted out her mansion-house flat into a greater eminence by giving all the corks drawn from champagne bottles emptied enjoyably by her and her husband, to the tune of a bottle a month, an honoured preservation. She fixed all the corks into a finely-made walnut frame, windowed with fine glass, enclosing a soft bed of cramoisie velvet on which the cosy corks lay; each cork crowned by its own patch of tinsel, green, gold, or silver, with an ivory-tinted card below each one telling the name of the wine and the district where the vine grew and the vintage year in which the wine was pressed from the grape; with the year, month, and day the wine was drunken. There they swung in their costly case on the wall of the dining-room, like dried-up, shrunken heads of enemies to be honoured and gloated over at seasonable times; honoured as Queequeg honoured, and departed from, the withered head he carried about with him, as told in the story of the White Whale. Wine of France and milk of Burgundy. No corks here damp with English ale or brown with the stain of Dublin's potent porter. No, sir. Fine bouquet, delicious aroma, Mrs. Green; various vintages, but all excellent. You are honoured in your corks. There is nothing whatever vulgar about corks: they are graceful, and full of meaning. Quite: a soul is safe in a champagne bottle.

Here in the medley of middle-class dressing for dinner, of creaking jodhpurs; of grades in flats and grade in car; in assembly of champagne-bottle corks; in one-maid or two-maid establishments; in first-class or second-class convent school; in carat-weight of collar-stud or cuff-link; here, among all this middle-class tension and torture, *The Irish Press* was declaring triumphantly that Chesterton was living with, and plunging about, among the workers and the poor!

And yet these people were important to England and to life; intelligent, mostly kind in a limited way, and anxious about the future of their children in a mistaken way. Too anxious that they should get on in the world; anxious that they shouldn't do any new things, but that they win respect from others by doing all the old things that were fading out of life. The lady of the jodhpurs' son, Peter, was attending a school whose system was a preparation for the manner and method of a public school, imitating the public school in all it did, while the public school was itself imitating all that had been done by itself through all the years gone by forever, ignorant of, and indifferent to, the new throb in the world's heart, the new beat in the world's pulse. Once, when Sean was sitting on a park bench with Mrs. Green and her son, the mother complained to Sean that Peter didn't want to accept from Mr. Lemon, the head-master of his school, an invitation to spend a week's fishing with him during the holidays. Fancy, she had said, thinking of refusing such an invitation from such a man; and Peter, head hanging down, had mumbled, I don't want to go, mother; I'd hate it. To which she: You mustn't say such things, Peter. Mr. Lemon's your Headmaster, and, even if you do hate it, you'll have to like it; and you'll have to be nice to him, very nice to him all the time; all the time — do you hear? Don't you agree, Mr. O'Casey?

—Well, Mrs. Green, I can't see how Peter can hate and like a thing at one and the same time. You are asking too much of him.

—He'll have to like it, said Mrs. Green, emphatically; have to learn to like it. Mr. Lemon's his Headmaster, and quite a gentleman.

Sean, knowing that nothing he could say would change Mrs. Green's attitude of mind, and anxious to make it as easy as he could for Peter, put his hand gently on the lad's shoulder, saying, Never mind, old boy; do your best. We old fellows are very trying to the young. You'll get used to him, and like him after a bit.

—No, I won't, said the lad, a little bitterly; I know I won't; I'll simply hate it all the time, all the time.

—All the time, all the time, thought Sean; tormented all the time. No choice for the kid. Lemon showing him how to fish, and the lad too nervous to take notice. Evidently a Headmaster wherever he might be. Aloud, Sean said, It won't be so bad, after a bit, Peter. You feel at ease with me, now; but if I asked you to come for a week's fishing with me, you'd be saying to your mother: I don't want to go; I'd hate it.

—No I wouldn't, burst from Peter. I'd simply love to go with you!

There was so much energy in the boy's exclamation, so much sincerity in the look he gave to him, that Sean, for the first time he could remember, was at a loss for a word to say.

Sean felt sure that no one out of all the middle-class residents in Battersea had ever thrust a foot into a working-class district. And here was where and this was how Chesterton lived among the workers and the poor of Battersea Borough. Never in his life, Sean believed, did he smell the smell of a slum. In her life of him, *Gilbert Keith Chesterton*, Maisie Ward flips in a remark made by a journalist that G.K.C. was 'cultivating the local politics of Battersea; in secluded pubs, he drinks with the frequenters, and learns their opinions on municipal milk and Mr. John Burns'. She doesn't halt to say what the frequenters said to Chesterton, or what he said to them; nor does she record any conversations held in the secluded pubs of Battersea; and, as a matter of fact, Battersea pubs are no more secluded than pubs anywhere else. These visits — if they ever occurred — were evidently part of those tip, touch, habits which coloured his whole life. Rushing round, he tipped Shaw, Dickens, Browning, John of Austria, breathless with running all the time; and as he ran past life, he shouted gee gee up to the white horse, dismounting for a while to chuck the roman catholic church under the chin. There's the brave horseman, there's his two min; there he goes out and here he goes in; chin chucky chin chucky under the chin. He never waited a second to sit down in any room of thought, contenting himself with peeping round the door, throwing in a coloured puff-ball of braggart doctrinal remark that went round the room of life till it fell into dull dust when some curious finger chanced to touch it. A whiff of his love for the workers is felt in his 'As far as personal taste and instincts are concerned, I share all your antipathy to the noisy Plebeian excursions. A visit to Ramsgate during the season and the vision of the crowded howling sands has left in me feelings which all my Radicalism cannot allay.' His instinct was to run from the worker, man of the lower-class, when the worker was noisy. Lover of the worker's soul, let me from thy presence fly. He didn't like the noisy children just let loose from school. He never did. And his deep love of God, expressed in his deep love of humanity, is shown in his 'The guide showed me a cross given by Louis XIV to Mlle. de La Vallière. I thought when reflecting what the present was, and where it was and then to whom it was given, that this showed pretty well what the religion of the Bourbon regime was and why it has become impossible since the Revolution.' In Chesterton's mind, the symbol couldn't come to rest in the hands of a whore. And Blake and Whitman were two of the higher souls this laddo tried to touch! Maybe, the king didn't give her the cross in levity; maybe, she didn't take it so. How did Chesterton know? Even if he gave it in levity and she took it in the same mood, what was that to him? The poor king and the rich whore — if Chesterton's religion was as true as he so heartily and so superficially made it out to be — would have to answer for it, and not Chesterton. It is difficult enough for us to judge the things of time; it is beyond us to judge the things of eternity.

In another way, we get a glimpse of his childish mind yielding to a visible dream of violence, for Maisie Ward tells 'His love of weapons, his revolver, his favourite sword-stick, remained with him all his life': till death did them part. Chesterton's bow of burnished gold, his arrows of desire. Bang bang! Not a hoe or a spanner, not a fiddle or a fife; no, a sword-stick and a gun. The cross and the gun; an up-to-date union. A film critic reviewing a film said 'We saw at once that the face of him who carried the cross for the Saviour was the face of Hopalong Cassidy'. And here we are again, for in a lot of ways Chesterton was the hopalong cassidy of the roman catholic church. No, this was no man for a symbol on a workers' banner. One could ne'er imagine this man striding along between Feemy Evans and Fluther Good. He knew far less about the workers than did Yeats or Lady Gregory, who mingled with them at a hundred feiseanna, sat in their homes, chatted with them, and recorded many things about them as their works do testify. In

Battersea and Beaconsfield, Chesterton dwelt among the jodhpurs, worn, not for riding, but for display; among the gatherers of champagne-corks; among those who graded life by size of flat and cost of car. His dive into a workers' district was similar to his dive into the country, when he went to live in, and wander through, the rural life of Beaconsfield, a village tongue-tied to London, with as much of the country in it as Wandsworth Common, Hyde Park, or Kensington Gardens. He figured finely in the drive of snobs. Decent people, important people, kindly in a limited way, intelligent, though over-anxious for their children to keep the perishing rules: these were his peers; and to associate him with workers or with the poor was but to upset the man's nature with a rosy libel.

The residents round, possessing no gardens, made Battersea Park one, and regarded it as their own, nearly as private as those green squares in cities where residents round them are provided with private keys, admitting themselves, and rigidly keeping everyone else out. The flower and the tree belong to you and to me, but no-one else. Breeds without the law and without the railings. A broad path led to the sub-tropical gardens, and one passed through this into a wide, concreted, circular space, in its centre a bandstand, and surrounded with benches. On fine days, these benches and this circle were crowded with nannies, minding the children of the flats, or with middle-class mothers minding their children when their nannies were off for the day. The wide circle round the bandstand was usually crammed with children riding round on bicycles, tricycles, rolling hoops, or playing ball — an animated scene of wild innocence and joy.

Opposite to the path leading into this circle was another leading out of it, bringing one to the park's centre and towards the green sward that ran along parallel with the Thames. At this exit from the circle stood two enormous chestnut trees, their pink and white flowers flooding the circle with floral candle-light when a spring day grew gloomy. Sean often sat here watching his boy, Breon, careering round on his bicycle with Mrs. Green's children; or sat with Eileen busy now with sewing things for the coming baby. Here, he met a Mrs. Mellor, minding her young and intelligent son. He had noticed that she usually sat in a spot with a vacancy on either side of her, seeming not to wish to mingle in talk with the other mothers there. She looked sad and anxious, as, indeed, she might well be, for she told Sean, who had sat down beside her, that her husband, Editor of the *Tribune*, was seriously ill in hospital. She mentioned, half hopefully, that when her husband recovered, he would visit and work in the constituency he hoped to represent for Labour in the next election. A woman, Sean thought, bravely trying to live a middle-class life on scanty resources, determined to give more than she could safely spare to her little boy. How hard it was for all of us to bring them up in the way that they should go!

Here, too, he came across an old codger of seventy-two who was well in with all the more superior members of the flats, who admired him as a real, respectable working-man, one who knew his place, and fitted himself into life a long long way from theirs. They had given him gifts from what they possessed, and for which they had no further use, so that all he wore, inside and outside, from his socks and shoes to his bowler hat and walking-stick, had been worn and carried by a flat-resident some time before; a life going around in cast-offs. Whenever he came towards a lady watching her playing child, he swept off the bowler hat, and sat down near her, if, by a gesture of movement, she invited him to do so; leaving always a deferential space between his lesser body and the lady's loftier one, gracious to him so long as he kept his reverential distance. Once when Sean was chatting to Mrs. Green, he appeared, came near; off came the bowler hat from the grey pow, and Mrs. Green moving nearer to Sean, invited him silently to sit down and rest. After some words about his own health, which was fair, thank God, he asked about the health of Mrs. Green's children, Miss Pauline and Master Peter; and, on being told they were fine, the old fellow burbled out a handsome Thank God for that, Ma'am. Suddenly Mrs. Green crossed over opposite to an acquaintance who had just arrived in the circle to give her child a chance to play; and Sean and the old man were left together. He had eyed Sean's untidy get-up and battered cap curiously, concluding, Sean assumed, that there was nothing there that could suit him; but as Sean had been talking amiably and easily to Mrs. Green, he surmised Sean must be one that had been accepted, and so would make a safe buddy.

The old fellow leaned back on the bench, and crossed one leg over the other. Never before had Sean seen these old legs crossed. While sitting with his lady-friends, the old man invariably sat upright, his legs demurely kept together, divided only by the walking-stick thrust down between them. Now the bottom of a trouser-leg was stretched high over a shoe, and Sean saw he was wearing a pair of vivid purple socks. The old face was almost handsome, gentle-wrinkled, still young-looking, the white hair and whiskers alone calendaring his age; a face, though, made too soft and pleasant by the torpor of submissive manners. Never another sky for him now but the sunset and evening star, brightening into a star of the night.

—You know Mrs. Green? he asked Sean, looking sideways at him, a little puzzled at his status still.

—Well, said Sean; her mother, father, uncles and aunts as well.

—Oh? came the comment; a puzzled query. A very kind lady; very kind. Her children, too, are very genteel and respectful, treating me as if I was almost a gentleman myself.

—Yes, said Sean; a kind lady. Her little family is all her world.

Master Peter and Miss Pauline came by on their bicycles, jumping off in front of the old man to ask him how he was. The old bowler hat was lifted in a minor tribute as he said he was well, thank God, and inquired after their health, which being satisfactory, they said goodbye, mounted their bicycles, rode off, and the old bowler hat was carefully replaced on the old head.

—A very kind lady, he murmured. She thinks of me at times. He took off the hat, extending it towards Sean so that he could get a fresh look at it. Her husband gave me this; yes, indeed; her husband's hat.

—It still is, said Sean. Whenever Mrs. Green looks at it, she knows it's her husband's hat. You know it, and I know it, for you've just told me so. If you tell it to others, they'll know it, till all Battersea will know it as Mrs. Green's husband's hat. He patted the thin, bony knee of the old man. Don't be too grateful, friend. Your humbleness and respectability deserve more than an old hat from Mrs. Green's husband.

—I should be grateful, and I am, he murmured, glancing curiously at Sean. I know my place, sir, though the kind ladies here treat me almost as an equal. Though poor, I was brought up proper to remember my place, and to be humble and respectful to my betters.

—Reared up in some Institution, thought Sean, and taught a damaging docility. His place in the universe, or his place in nature? Of no importance. What matters is his place among the kind ladies and gents. Ah, my friend, he said aloud, it isn't good to be always humble. The lower-classes are busy casting humbleness aside, and are shedding their respect for those who rob and rot them.

—Oh, no, sir! I hope not, sir, looking at Sean in a puzzled way, as if to try to discern Sean's place among the ladies and the gents. They will only destroy themselves. Our class can do better by knowing their place and keeping it. Ruin themselves, they will, if they go on like that, sir; or talk about being as good as their betters. Oh, a bad sign, sir; a very bad sign! God never meant us to be equal.

—All will be equal one day, said Sean, but each will differ from the other; but difference is very different from inequality.

—I dunno, sir, said the old man, bewildered by the talk. He sat silent, casting sidelong glances at Sean. Who was this fellow, talking this way, upsetting things? Yet he had often seen him talking so free and easy with Mrs. Green, Mrs. Black, and Mrs. White. God help him — odd things were happening these days! He got up from the bench, fiddled with his tie, tapped the pavement with his stick; glanced at Sean, then at Mrs. Green sitting opposite, chatting away with her friend. God help him! Treat the people above you as you should, he said, faintly, and they'll do the same to you. I must be going, now. At this time, I make a little cup of tea for myself. I don't need much. It isn't right to ask for things beyond us, or wish them either. I must be off. You must know I'm right, sir. He looked dazed, fumbling with his tie and tapping the pavement with his stick. I must go, he went on; I never miss a cup of tea about this time. It does me good. I look forward to it. Goodbye, sir.

He made off towards his tea, his eyes searching out Mrs. Green opposite, chatting to her friend. She saw him, and waved a lily-white hand in farewell; and off came the bowler hat in a grand sweep of reverential gratitude. Sean saw Mrs. Green pointing him out to her friend; telling her, doubtlessly, of the grand old working-man, so rare and so unlike so many of his class and station; and Sean knew that the old codger had won another client. The two ladies still kept looking after the old, upright figure, very likely wishing to God that all working-men were like this worthy old man, a real gentleman in his own humble way; yes. But workers were getting less and less like him. The old faithful retainer had become but a mummified memory. The bowed head before a master existed no longer, even in a picture. They had become conscious of their power, and as this consciousness grew, they saw less importance in those to whom they had been for so long such a comfort, such a stay. They were breeding importance within themselves. Yes, ma'am, a pleasant sitting-room, a wireless-set, my own bathroom, and every second evening off: sounds fairly fair. I'll think over it, ma'am, and let you know as is convenient. Of course, the first week'll be only a trial to see if you suit me, ma'am. You want to know by tomorrow? Oh, well, if you're in such a hurry, ma'am, you'd better look for someone else — goodbye.

The old man paused where the two trees stood, canopying the old bowler hat with chestnut blooms as they would canopy a crown concocted out of jewels; as they would carelessly canopy tinker, tailor, soldier, sailor, richman, poorman, beggarman, thief. There he paused, his head below the murmuring foliage, his feet touching fading petals on the ground; an old mind trying to bud old thoughts; an old man standing in the shadow of the trees as if he stood hesitant in the valley of the shadow of death. Here, he paused, turned, and looked towards Sean. Sean waved a hand; the old man took no notice, but turned and went his way, and his old world went with him.

CHILDERMESS

ANOTHER child was on its way into the world. A world weird and wonderful. Well, it wouldn't know what was being forged in front of it. Here was the new life pushing a way out into smoke, into fire, into shouting; woven within the walk of Ribbentrop among the roses of England and the lilies of France; within the hearing of the cocksparrow chirrup of Chamberlain charming away war, and the distant humming of waiting panzers, impatiently ready to make a rush at life. But new life is careless of what may front it, and so a new life was pulsing its way out of a peaceful darkness into a marring and menacing light. A difficult time for man and woman; difficult in the way of doing the right thing by life and making both ends meet. It is an expensive thing to bring a life from the womb into the world. Was then; worse now. The middle-class now die and are born beyond their means. Unto us a child is born, unto us a son is given, is an alarming announcement today, giving to the tenor of the joy-bell the ugly minor note of the knell.

Through the stir of middle-class emotion, and by a middle-class doctor's advice, Eileen had booked a berth in a London wist-not nursing-home, many miles from the Monument, the fee being twelve guineas a week, not counting extras, of course. Adding the doctor's fee of fifty guineas, Sean saw in his mind the mighty sum of a hundred pounds demanded of him, with other costs lurking in dark corners ready to come out when the bigger bill was paid. The uncertainty of how the common claims of life are to be managed is the laocoön with which man is for ever struggling.

Sean had no respect whatever for London nursing-homes, nor for the middle-class emotion that kept the contemptible things going. The knights and dames of low degree had to have their tiny honours. Sean had visited three of these places to see sick friends, and had been stabbed by amazement at their drabness and dirt; how unsuitable they were for the needs of the sick. On entering, he had run his fingers along the ledge of the dado, and had shown them covered with thick dirt to the friend that was with him. The rooms were heavy with old air, and wore a weak look, as if they, too, were sick; and all he saw seemed to whisper cynically of uncleanliness and of clumsy, uncomely methods of management and care. He was to have his surmises habited by proof. Eileen entered, and became a patient. Sean went to see her settled there. As in the others, here in this nursing-home the glamour was gloom. Rowland to the dark tower came. The hall rimmed with dust; no sign of surgical cleanliness or of that quiet alertness felt where doctors and nurses are. The Home was joined on to a crowd of similar buildings so that there was little air in the room, and whatever air crept in was immediately swallowed up by the dusty-thick curtains blotting the window, and the dustier and thicker carpet smothering the floor. Brown curtains, a browner carpet, brown dado, sovereign effects to hide the clinging dangerous dust. A grey-green bedspread covered the couch which was soon to see the birth of a new life. In a glumly-grey jug on a bedside table, a massive spike of crimson gladioluses flamed a challenge to the bum-pomp of all the room's pattern: a present from a friend, and no indication by the nursing-home of any desire to brighten and sanctify the room.

Various kinds of ailments were tethered to this place; there was a patient down with double pneumonia, a lady trying to wriggle out of mental dementia through having nothing to do and taking too much drink to pass away God's good time, a duodenal-ulcer case, and another of appendicitis — not a merry or a wholesome throng to greet a new-born babe. Britannia, mother of jellabies, stretching out her generous hand to teach children of Africa, Asia, and the West Indies, shoves her own children behind her, and squanders the priming force of her people. The thought given to the mind and body of the English child is the thought, not of a cultured leadership, but one as low as that given by a rude council pow-wowing under a cowhide wigwam. Childless with all her children. The middle-class are to blame. Caught in the glare of their snobbery, they strain, not after knowledge, but after Eton; not after human development, but after a nameless name; suffering indignity and danger, rather than give up a few pieces of silver, a good address on their notepaper, and a badged blazer for a son or a daughter. Ad ardua sed disastra.

The two housemaids seemed to have the minds of backward ten-year-olds; they were untidily dressed, clumsy, and incoherent when asked a question; giggling rather than answering, mouths sloppily open; a grin without a gusto. Cheap labour out of some Institution, thought Sean. Besides the matron, whom Sean never saw, there were two nurses — one for the day, one for the night; each, from what was said, eager to find another place. Won't find it easy, thought Sean, for they didn't soothe his idea of what efficiency and carefulness should be. Clearly the place was being run for profit; not clean or competent profit, but profit grimed with a corpulent greed. Eileen agreed with him, but hushed him whenever a protest in his mind rushed forward to the tip of his tongue. Many a time he had sat at Eileen's bedside, fuming at the way things were being done — the wobbling walk of the housemaids, the dirty tray of slopped-over tea, the dirty window, the whole aspect of continual carelessness; fuming so plainly that Eileen stretched out a hand to touch his arm, and whispered — quiet, Sean, you will only make bad things worse with a temper. Then he would close his eyes, sever the tension by a great effort, and sigh for the cowardice of his human heart. Children brought to birth in a dust-bowl. The Little Johns and Maid Marions, whose people had enough to pay for decent attention, were getting the worst in the world. No complaints. The middle-class would stick anything to preserve the wan and wasteful manner of their status, burying under it the best of their intelligence, energy, and sense. They chloroform themselves with snobscent. The moment a boy shapes himself into the world, while he is giving his first cry, his parents dwell in Etonsville; if a girl and an anglican, then Roedean — Roedean, oh, girl! If a roman catholic, then a posh school of the Sacred Heart or the Ursulines to learn all she needeth to know of how and when to ape the gentility. Cease to be human, learn to be swell. They shove aside even the sacred name of hospital and hang out that of nursing-home, so that they may feel themselves of a loftier mien than the mass of men, even in sickness and in pain. Sheltering a stranger, entertaining a guest — so hangs the holy name of hospital; and to the Christians all sick persons should be guests of Jesus. He is on His way to visit a sick woman — no, a lady. What hospital? No hospital, man; a nursing-home. Does Jesus, then, turn his nose, too, up at a hospital? Oh, no, not exactly that; but the sick lady's a lady and thinks herself something of a nob snob, and must stretch herself higher than the ordinary commonality of the country.

When I was a lady, a lady, a lady,
When I was a lady, a lady was I.

The sacrifice of children on the altars of Eton and Harrow to a will-o'-the-wisp conception of grandeur is as superstitious as, and sillier and much more subtly dangerous than, the sacrifices offered at Stonehenge to the Sun.

Eileen and he went for walks in the afternoon to give her exercise, waiting, waiting for the event to happen; all along the streets nearby, fearful to go too far lest the thing might come upon them in the twinkling of an eye. Down and up a bit of Knightsbridge, glimpsing Hyde Park, but never venturing in; in and out by Lowndes Square, out on to Cadogan Square and Cadogan Gardens, till they knew every number on every hall door. Round and round the village, round and round the village, as they had done before. Down the opposite way for a change; slow march down Sloane Street and around Sloane Square, and around again, bringing back to him memories of his first fast days in London, his memory helped by the desire to creep away from the fear that was with him now, walking with Eileen. She was silent, dwelling in her condition, and so helped him to slip away from the fear of a too sudden birth. Here, in her daughter-in-law's flat, he had met Lady Gregory, and had set out with her to see T. P. O'Connor, M.P., at Morpeth Mansions, within the shadow of the roman catholic cathedral; going to enlist his aid in the recovery of the Lane Pictures; aid promised, but never given. Small blame to O'Connor, for he was then three parts in the grave, and was now being suckled from a bottle. No more chablis, no more sauterne; no more running after a skirt; no more fiery words, cheers, and the roll of drums, at the yearly Feast in Liverpool in honour of St. Patrick, Ireland's senior saint. Green grew the rushes here no longer for T.P. After getting to know Sean, he had appealed to him to go in his place to the feast in Liverpool, promising him 'lashin's of eating and drinking', and had waxed very angry when Sean refused to go. Born in Athlone, Ireland's centre, here he was now — a man who had healed everything Irish in him, except his humbug. An abortioned soul from the O'Connor clan. What a wild difference there was between this Irishman and the other Irishman, Shaw!

They rang the bell of the flat's door, and O'Connor's nurse, an elderly woman without a uniform, opened it and showed him and

Lady Gregory into the sitting-room; left them standing in the room's centre, pausing at the door to say, 'I'll wheel him in to you in a minute. Not any exciting talk, mind, to curdle his stomach — I don't want to be up half the night with him.'

After a swift look around, Lady Gregory and he subsided on to a crimson-coloured couch, sitting side by side, stunned when the look of the room had hammered itself into their eyes. It was ghastly and almost terrifying: red couch, red carpet, red curtains, red-seated chairs, and on the wall opposite, protected by a redder canopy, pulled to at night, looped back now, the picture of O'Connor himself, painted by John Lavery in his worst mood. The heavy, commonplace face, looking as if a dead hand had limned it, stared out with a simper at anyone daring to look at it. Me, the O'Connor, privy councillor and chief perennial of the Scotland Division of Liverpool. Flanking it on either side was a wooden corinthian pillar, heavily gilded; surmounting the picture was a gothic gilded roof, like a baldacchino; and underneath were four wide and shallow steps, covered with crimson carpet, leading the looker up to a platform from which to get a face-to-face view of the face in the painting. Around the fireplace was a thigh-high heavy brass fender, ledge upholstered in red leather. Lady Gregory, seeing the stunned aspect of Sean's face, laid a soothing hand on his arm.

—Don't look at id, she said. Tlose your eyes and dink only of the Lane Pictures.

So this room represents the boyo who yearly acts as Ireland's Ambassador, showing forth Ireland's culture and civilisation throughout the centuries of her independence and the hard and bitter centuries of subjection to an alien power and still more alien culture; yearly shows forth the features of Ireland in Liverpool on St. Patrick's Day!

—Tlose your eyes, Sean; dank Dod de curtains aren't green.

The truculent-looking nurse, her brawny body stiff, her face set firm, wheeled the hero in and placed him close to the carpeted steps going up to the picture: the real McCoy was now before them.

—Not too much talk from you, now, said the brawny one, bending down over the chaired giant, or I'll have to be stiffening your heart with tonics. At the door, before departing, she turned to say D'ye hear me — all of you?

It must have looked a comical sight — Lady Gregory and Sean sitting on the crimson couch in the crimson room, their eyes half shut, slanting down towards the red carpet, trying to hide from the picture on the wall and shade their eyes from the razzle-dazzle of the gilding; the over-blown body of the privy councillor seeping over the framework of the chair, the round head lolling on the bulging chest, the little eyes pushed back into the head by fleshy folds, the big pudgy hands clumped on the chair-arms, unable to grip them, the thick voice, with the hint of a gasp in every sentence, telling them that it would speak to this Minister and to that one, and that the Lane Pictures would shortly be hanging on the wall of the Dublin Gallery. A room in Huis-Clos, from which Sean, in his mind's eye, could see the bulky steeple of Westminster Catholic Cathedral looming in the background, hearsed in this pathetic figure and halting voice; Lady Gregory nodding her sage old head at every promise of help trickling from the wide and twitching mouth of this dying old humbug, able still to convince far greater minds than his own of his amazing influence and the depth of his sincerity.

—A mistake, Lady Gregory, he was saying, his poor tongue and shaky lips hesitating over the words; it will be rectified, believe me.

—A lousy, rotten, god-damned robbery, if you ask me! burst from Sean, and Lady Gregory's soothing hand was touching his arm again.

He could scarcely contain himself listening to the blown-out blather of this Irish leader who had always led everything from behind, knowing that O'Connor was at his old game of humbugging Lady Gregory as he had the Irish people who had sent him, year after year, to the British Parliament to represent himself. Now all this self-interest had shrunk down into the recessiveness of a wheel-chair. Here was the soft-wood face trying to be the same again, carrying the adulation of power to the very verge of the grave. Here were the remains of one who had declared during the Gladstonian and ecclesiastical opposition to the great Parnell that 'Parnell had done too much for the Irish people to go back on him now. Ireland is socially, enthusiastically, and fiercely on the side of the Irish leader'; and the very next day, the scut recanted with a shout, signing a declaration that he was with the priests and against Parnell. Well, today, none of the young Irish remember O'Connor; most of the young Irish remember Parnell.

Sean's surmising was cut off by the entrance at the door of the old boy's caretaker. She stopped at the door for a few moments, looking in at them and listening to the talk; then she suddenly strode into the room's centre, and catching the handbar of the weal-chair, she whisked it round to face the door.

—You've talked enough for one day, she said, tartly. I don't want to be up half the night with you. Say goodbye now, and come along.

—Send me signed copies of your plays, Sean, he said, departing.

—He will, said the old Lady, swiftly, before Sean could reply, for de sake of de Lane Pictures; and the chair-imprisoned privy councillor, father of the House of Commons, vanished, and was never seen again by either of them.

He had signed the plays, and had sent them to the dying fossil; signed as if to a friend, for a scut who had helped to hound the noble Parnell to his grave. Oh, what a rogue and peasant slave he was to do it! One of the worst things his life had ever done. A tare in the tapestry. Right in the place, too, where he had woven the name of Parnell with reverence and with love.

—We'll go, said the old Lady, to the roman catholic cathedral, and look within id to forget de derrible room.

They had gone before to the Tate Gallery, had sat on a bench together, for she loved to look around wide, long, lofty, secular buildings, or those consecrated to what men called religion. Here they had sat for a long time, quiet, forgetting about the coloured misery of the dying pictures in the Turner Room; the hell of a golden glory. Here they were now, gazing into the womb of the catholic cathedral, full of a flourishing dimness revelled in by thousands, with the lighted tops of candles twinkling patiently away in the far distance where the altar stood. Her old head was slightly thrust forward gazing toward where the Host must be resting somewhere between the twinkling lights of the altar. Sean guessed that she slyly welcomed into her mind a venturesome idea of the Real Presence, and that she might have been reconciling her own minor idea of the mystery with the major one of the roman catholic church manifested by the exposition of the Sacrament in twice ten thousand churches. Here, then, according to the Christian Faith, Jesus was looking at the old Lady and she was looking at Him; very reverently she was looking, but calmly, for she was a venturesome and courageous woman, of good standing, combining the spirit of Martha with the spirit of Mary; the grace of useful commonsense with the rarer grace of a gay and a vivid imagination. With these thoughts about her was mingled one of his own on the contrast between the seductive gloom of this big building and the glare of the little red room they had just left.

They came out, and waited for a suitable bus to carry her home. One came gracefully along and purred into a stop beside them. She gripped the handle, but the step was high and the ageing body was stiff; she stood rigid for a few moments, a hand gripping either handle, and Sean wondered if he should give her a handy hoosh up; but she tightened her lips, gave a pant, then a spring, and the stiff body lighted on the platform, her two feet landing together with a bang. She shot down into a seat, tucked in her black dress so that he could sit comfortably beside her, smiled and patted his hand, as if to say, Here we are, and we're bound for the Rio Grande.

Lady Gregory had married when he was being born, and it took many a long year before they met, before even he was prepared to meet her. Each had travelled his or her own different way, very different ways, yet, in the winter of her life, in the late summer of his, they had suddenly met, each facing towards the same direction. The pattern of life she was weaving, and the one he wove, mingled and stood out bravely in the tapestry of Irish life. The Lane Pictures should be facing out from the tapestry both had woven, but she is dead, and the pictures are as far away as ever. She can no longer trouble government officials, at home or abroad, with her vexatious babble about them. De Valera never thinks about them; Costello never bothers about them; neither does MacBride; nor do many at work or at rest in Kathleen ni Houlihan's Four Beautiful Fields. The younger ones growing up, one day, may, he hopes, stretch out a stronger arm, and take them back from the thieves.

Both gone now — the poor old parliamentary humbug and Lady Gregory herself. It was odd and a little sad that in the thousands of years that were in the future's flow, she would never be seen again, her charming lisp would never again mingle among the sounds of people speaking. Had she a place in the Universe now? In the memory of some, she had. A fleeting immortality; the leaves falling one by one from the tree of remembrance till the tree is bare, and the tree is dead. What is beyond us outside the world of what we see, hear, smell, taste, and touch, we don't know. Not one of the philosophies that has tried to hem us in or bring us out has told us, or can tell us, anything outside of ourselves and our world. Science has told us a lot, will tell us more, and we must wait for science to tell us all. One philosopher has said that science, having driven values from the Universe, shows itself to be nor good, nor beautiful, nor just, nor holy. To Sean, science was all these things. It wasn't content with a guess, however good, just, or holy the guess might be. A philosophy that set out to solve a problem created another of its own. Whenever he had read, or tried to read, a system of philosophy, he had always heard the echo of a song, a song he had often chanted himself when going round in a ring in a Dublin street:

Oats and beans and barley grows,
Oats and beans and barley grows,
But you nor me nor nobody knows
How oats and beans and barley grows.

The two of them, Eileen and he, now were concerned most nearly with the strange energies of the body, and with the life a body was soon to bring forth to the world they knew. More children, with little thought for them, and less room. Round and round the two of them travelled, past the Court Theatre, where she had acted in a play of his, and where both of them had first seen Shaw's *Back to Methuselah*; fainting memories just now, for they had new events to record, bringing hope and not a little fear. Up and down again, past a school where in a tiny closed-up yard the children could but ape the action and spirit of play; down and up, Eileen's steps growing slower, an odd spasm of pain smiting her, sending them back at a quickened rate to the nursing home. Half-way there, Eileen would say with a laugh, False alarm, and round and round they would go again.

One day in the hall of the home, about to go out, he saw a look of disquiet on her face, and, answering an inquiry, she said she didn't feel too good; then suddenly bent down in a violent spasm of pain.

—I won't go out, she said; I feel it may come on me any minute now.

I will greatly multiply thy sorrow and thy conception; in sorrow thou shalt bring forth children; thy desire shall be unto thy husband, and he shall rule over thee. A fine Dadlantic Charter! The king put into the parlour, the queen put into the kitchen. Woman has brought forth children with pain, and her husband has ruled over her for twice a thousand years; but things are changing, and, and now only, the church is busy bouncing this bonnie law about. The pain, subjection, and sorrow have declined with the years, and will be entirely banished in some year to come. The agony and sweat were still with the woman, but not so dangerously now, though shouts were still needed to prevent a woman being forced to go through this furnace of pain and danger too often. There must be a good rest between one ordeal and another. He for one would oppose the celibate clerics who frightened women into having a child year by year till she was battered into dumb agreement with her devitalised life and the ghastly problems of attending to a horde of children. One of the ghastliest pictures he ever saw was one in a roman catholic journal showing the Pope with a father and mother and their twenty children; and another of Cardinal Spellman, a grin on his face, standing before a kneeling Pole surrounded by his wife and fifteen children, who had travelled to New York by air, though the journal said they were utterly penniless. It was said that the Cardinal had emptied his wallet of a wad of notes, and had given them all to the old Polish ram; the journal adding that the Cardinal had entered New York without a make. Left himself without a dime! Your need is greater than mine. And how! Now what sarcastic voice whispers that it wouldn't be long till the Cardinal's wallet would be as full as ever with the finest and fairest of dollar notes? Since then the Cardinal has given ten thousand pounds to Ireland's St. Vincent de Paul Society; Dublin's Archbishop has given a thousand; and Cardinal Griffin two thousand towards the rebuilding of Southwark Cathedral; three plates in the trim hands of three prelates, one carrying a thousand, the second, two thousand, and the third, ten thousand. Pie from the sky. God's Episcopate is doing very nicely, thank you. Gold and silver have I none — it's all in notes, crisp and fresh from the bankery. There's more, lads, where these came from. Do they work overtime?

Sean would like to see a celibate cleric stay with a pregnant woman day after day, hour after hour, during the last three months of her trial; to try to help her along, entertain her with chat, go for walks with her, bring change of thought through a game of cards: it would learn the cleric a little; teach him that birth wasn't just a thing to make a joke about from a pulpit. It's easy for them to rant to women about their duties to their husbands, or to praise the big families. Some day the clerics will get their answer: like the woman coming out from a Mission to women, conducted by a friar of orders white boosting bigger catholic families, shouting at them to reproduce catholic life quicker and oftener; the flushed and angry woman coming out from it all with an angry ejaculation of — Jasus! I wish I knew as little about it as he does!

A houseful of children! No glory left in that boast now. We have begun to realise that children need not only life, but liberty too. For too long the children have been buried alive in church, in school, in the home. As Bernard Shaw has said, 'The most grotesque, wild, and costly absurdity in our social order is the strictly enforced reservation of large tracts of country as deer forests and breeding grounds for pheasants whilst there is so little provision of the kind made for children'. Sean knew himself of a discussion about a playing-field for the young in a country town lasting for twenty-five years; and, today, the field isn't yet ready for the newer young born into the locality. The child is surrounded with enemies who imprison it in a corner called a school, or a corner called a church; it is a great concession when it is let loose on the playing-field. One great blessing enjoyed by the kids of the poor is that they spend a great part of their lives on the streets; the parents have to let them, for there is no room in the house for them. They get many a blow, but a blow is nothing to the stealing of curiosity and conscience from the mind of the child: those, says Shaw, 'who devote themselves to the very mischievous and cruel sort of abortion which is called bringing up a child in the way it should go; perverting that precious and sacred thing the child's conscience into an instrument of our own convenience, and to use that wonderful and terrible power called Shame to grind our own axe'. How conceited we all are to wish our children to be like ourselves! She's very like her mother; he's the dead spit of his father! Put into the same kind of schools, made to read the same kind of books, pray the same way, think the same way, and make it a custom, instead of a religion, to honour the God of Abraham, Isaac, and Jacob. And such schools and such books! The books are getting better now, most of the schools getting worse. Hundreds and hundreds of them in Ireland and England, packed with children, though fit only as the dwelling-place of the rat, the cockroach, and the woodlouse. No; children, as Bernard Shaw says, 'should look up to their parents, not as an example, but as a warning'.

> Childer, beware, childer, take care!
> They're eager to make
> You waddle through life like a duck, like a drake;
> To turn each new soul to a shivering fake,
> For ever too frail just to open its bake;
> Quack-quacking consent to men and to movements well out
>   on the make.

Bent down in a spasm of pain, Eileen stretched out a hand to touch Sean, and said, don't get frightened. It will be all right; don't worry.

He hurried back into the hall to shout up the stairs, Nurse, nurse! The only nurse there came slowly down the stairs, an impatient look on her face as she asked, Well, what's wrong now?

—The woman's in her labour! said he, fearfully; bring the matron.

—The matron's out, and won't be back till night-time.

—Phone her, then; phone her, woman!

—She didn't leave word where she was going; I don't know where to phone. You are both too anxious. Try to be a little braver. It won't happen today, or tomorrow either. She took Eileen by the arm. Go off, now, for a nice walk with your husband; and saying so, she turned back, and went up the stairs again.

They stood hesitant in the gloomy hall, then began to cross it to go out; but she bent again in a greater spasm of pain than before.

—Go home, she said to him, go home. Go home — I'll manage all right; and she ran from the hall and made for the room, with its dull bed, duller curtains, and dullest of carpets; while he, running up the stairs, caught the retreating nurse harshly by the arm.

—Get the doctor, woman, he said, fiercely, if you can't get the matron; and go to her yourself till the careless and negligent bitch comes back!

A look of alarm flooded the nurse's face, and she rushed from him into the room of delivery. She was of little use, and Eileen had to bear the most of it alone; the frantic rush in the stripping of herself; the flinging of herself on the bed, the deep crescendo of ascending pain that seemed to be engendering death entering through a riving body, with ne'er a drop of chloroform to modify the biting torment of the struggle, and ne'er a voice near to say a word to cheer her on; for the air-tight box of bandages and drugs was away in a cupboard in the housetop, so that by the time it was hurried down and opened for use, by the time hot water and towels had been gathered, the courageous woman had delivered a boy herself. A young girl inexperienced, just beginning to realise and comprehend the seriousness of her own life and the lives budding from her; so sensitive that she shuddered at the thought of any child in pain; a lass who had had her first-born in her own home, a clever, sympathetic doctor beside her, a capable nurse at his right hand to help; now having her second one alone, surrounded by hasty confusion, with nothing ready, and with those who were, perhaps, competent to help, away in other places doing other things. Fortunately, she was vigorous and healthy, and had a curious quietness in serious circumstances and time of stress; so throughout all the pain that stormed over and through her, she kept her alert mind set on a determination to deliver the boy safely: a brave girl fought incompetence and carelessness to a standstill, and gave successful birth to a big and healthy boy.

Their one idea now was to get away from the nursing-home as soon as possible, for she had discovered that the babe, when taken from her after a feed, was often in the charge of a maid with a thickened mind, and that the child was set to sleep in the operating theatre, reeking with the smell of ether; added to the suspicion that the ether was helped by an opiate whenever the mite happened to be restless enough to disturb the nurses.

They fled from the curse-home on a cold, grey day in January, the strong tail of an east wind teasing their faces, tilting at the dust in the kennels, and chiding the scraps of paper thrown carelessly aside by passers-by; grey and cold, with a sky of a deeper and heavier grey hanging down overhead; no comfort without, but joy within that they were getting away from a place that was a menace to the health, and so to the life, of their child.

Some kids never escape — kids in orphanages, institutions, and foundling homes, not to mention those sent to industrial schools because, it is said, their parents are unable to control them. What a time the most of these must have! Never free for a second; always under discipline, for ever watched. He remembered visiting the home of a worker whose two boys had returned after serving their time in an institution. Every time a question was asked of them, they sprang to their feet with a yessir or a nosir, waiting till they were told that they might sit down again, a voice behind Sean proclaiming that it had never met such good-mannered children before. When they got used to life outside their institution, however, they changed so as to become the most ill-mannered and ill-natured boys in the locality. There was the institutional school in Ireland, housing kids from five to ten, doddered by a group of nuns, kept in a gloomy building, well away from the convent where the nuns lived. At night the dormitories were locked and bolted, and all were in charge of an old woman who, herself, had been an inmate all her life. The building took fire; the kids were locked in; there was no light; and before the miserable help of the local fire-brigade came carrying ladders too short, thirty-three of the kids were burned to death in the dark. There was the gentle roman catholic Brother who caught hold of a child tricking at the gate-way of a college and locked him up in the great hall, so that, when night came, the youngster in a frenzy of fright managed to climb up to a clerestory window, open it, and fling himself on to the pavement below, crippling himself for life; the gentle Brother pleading afterwards that all he meant to do was to frighten the boy, careless of knowing that to try to frighten a child is to try to injure it, not only in body, but in soul, too. A second gentle Brother, this an anglican one, who, helping to dish out dinners in Dartington Hall to the evacuees, demanded of a boy why he was a little late for the meal, and, on being told that the farmer kept him late helping on the farm, shouted that that was no excuse, and shouted louder that the boy would get no dinner that day; ignorant that the boy's explanation was no excuse, but a reason for his lateness. Still another gentle Brother, a roman catholic one again, who lugged a lad of fourteen — the working age — from an industrial school to a hotel that wanted a Boots, and asked the Manager what were the hours the lad would work, and the pay he would get; on being told that the hours were seven in the morning till eleven at night, and the wages would be ten shillings a week, the Brother replied emphatically that ten shillings were too much for a start, and ordered that the boy should be given five shillings a week for a year or two to prevent him from getting too hot in his leather. There was the widow who couldn't keep her children properly on her widow's pension, the Authorities said. She had kept them perfectly clean, fed them as well as her means would allow, dressed them as best she could: there was no complaint whatever against the woman's efforts; yet in a frenzy of tearful protest by widow and children, they were wrenched away, and handed over to an Institution by the Irish Authorities, who paid the Institution three times the amount received by the widow in the form of her pension. Had she had so much herself, she could have kept her little ones in clover. There was no yelp on the part of the clerics against this interference of the State with the rights of the parent. Indeed, they quietly commended it. The State can do no wrong when it serves priest and prelate.

Oh, the sacredness of family life! So they say, so they sing, so they even shout. Yet, as Shaw proves, most parents who can afford it get their children away from them as far and as long as possible. Tidy incomed protestants and catholics hasten their kids off to boarding school, seeing them only for a few weeks a year during the holidays. Oh, the tiresome holidays! The famous Roman Catholic writer, Evelyn Waugh, has told the world, over the wireless, that he 'sees his children only during the holidays; that he never carries them on his shoulders, or plays ball with them; but that when they come to years of coherent speech, he associates with them'. A very important person, a model da. The higher schools, public and private, the high-school convents of the Sacred Heart and the Ursulines, are crammed with imprisoned kids; away from their people, outside the family,

living a community life, so dreaded and damned by the clerics whenever they preach to the poor. The domestic hearth has often been
a cold one. Imposition on the child, with God's bells ringing it in,
from morn to night; from cradle to maturity, till the newness and
freshness of a young life becomes a worn-out thing. Do what I have
done; say as I have said; think as I have thought; read what I have
read; look at what I have seen. Follow your leader. Example is a
perpetual buzz in the ear of a kid, loud as the buzz of a may-bug.
The last thing to be done is to let a child see for itself, hear for itself,
think for itself, and, when hands are old enough to be used steadily,
do for itself. Sean knew a father who, according to his own tale,
kept everything readable he thought to be vulgar (even *Treasure
Island*), and persistently read to the lad bible stories only. The result
was that the lad, whenever possible, made a dive for a Comic. Now
the bible stories are fine, however fantastic some of them may be,
but, as Shaw points out, the bible is not enough.

The sage says, 'The real bible of modern Europe is the whole
body of great literature in which the inspiration and revelation of
Hebrew Scripture has been continued to the present day. It cannot
supply the need of such modern revelations as Shelley's *Prometheus*
or the 'Nibelung's Ring' of Wagner. There is nothing in the bible
greater in inspiration than Beethoven's ninth symphony. Only a
foolish one would substitute *The Imitation of Christ* for *Treasure
Island* as a present for a boy or a girl, or for Byron's *Don Juan* as a
present for a lover or his lass. And the most dangerous art in the
effort to help the young to discover a form of art that will delight
them naturally, is the art that presents itself as religious ecstasy. For
religious purposes, Ivanhoe and the Templar make a good enough
saint and a good enough devil.' Of course they do; and, when the
boy and the girl get a little older, there is the second Saint Bernard
waiting for them with wisdom, wit, and laughter; waiting, too, to
hear them take three solemn vows against poverty, obedience, and
a chastity that belies life, forcing a woman to pose as a portrait of
good works and skin-deep satisfaction, and young men to form a
faction against the first clause of the creed of life, and to hunger
secretly and silently for a woman's favour, for, as Langland tells us,
'There are no hardier, hungrier men than men of Holy Church'.

Childermass — the Mass held in honour of the Holy Innocents,
slain, according to the fable, by Herod in the year of one. Time now
to think about the unholy innocents born into the world each day
of a passing year; think more about them than we do. There is more

care given to hens, more diligence in the gathering of their eggs, than there is in the care, and gathering up, of our children. Rachel has now another crowd of children, but she no longer weeps, though they are injured and degraded in slum, school, and even, at an older age, in the high-toned colleges of our land; till at the age of three score and ten, they are still frightened children, afraid of the light whereas once they shivered in the dark, thunderstruck now that the old woman tossed up in a blanket ninety-nine times as high as the moon, carrying a broom to brush the cobwebs from the sky, has been replaced by the scientist who has brushed away the cobwebs as well as the woman, and has shown us the mighty nothingness of expanding space filled with a multitude of blazing suns; or, in Ireland, its effect may be a simple and consummate love of making money, for, as the poet, Kavanagh, tells us, 'In Ireland nothing else save money talks'. The voice of God declares the rise of shares in the Stock Exchange, and the price of fat cattle in the market.

Don't run off with the idea that this Childermess is celebrated here only and in Ireland, too. One of America's biggest and best-known publishing firms has printed a folder telling us that over two million of American children do not go to school; that outmoded equipment and obsolete text-books are in use in many schools; that many buildings are in sad disrepair, and that classrooms are overcrowded and teachers underpaid and overworked. The folder further says that during the last ten years, three hundred and fifty thousand teachers left the public schools because of bad conditions, and that fewer and fewer students are entering the teaching profession. It says further that the U.S.A. spends one and a half per cent of its National Income on education, while Britain spends over twice as much and the Soviet Union more still. One father, looking into a school attended by his son, found at the edge of a fine residential district a school where the children had to go down flights of stairs to the washroom which was without flush toilet, soap or towels, and which served the whole building. There is more in the folder of the same sensible wail, showing how governors, spiritual pastors, and masters value the worth of the kids to the nation; though these very kids will be the nation in another hour's time.

Millions will grow up to be unable to read *Moby Dick*, *Treasure Island*, or *Little Boy Blue*. Won't know enough arithmetic to be able to count their blessings. Won't dare to have minds rising higher than the philosophy of donald duck, or be warier in the ways of art than the words and music of crooning swing king bing crosby.

We must think of the kiddies. We do, of course — at Christmas especially. That's the kids' festival above all others; cakes and wails. Christmas beer and bells, and the kids love bells. Ring out, wild bells. Ring out the old, ring in the new; ring out the false, ring in the true.

A lesson there for all of us, Mick. Yeah. Lay the red carpet down for the Child and the children on the one day of the year. Tinsel the stable couch with colours that fade when the night must fall. The Crib. Oh, come, let us adore Him. Where 'r you pushing, you young scut? What are you pushing for? You want to see the kings and the cow? Well, you'll wait till your eldhers have had a look at them first. If you were my kid, I'd learn you to respect your eldhers. I'd warm your little arse for you! Where were you reared at all? Oh, come, let us adore Him. Shout out your praise and your prayer, Mick; shout them out to the little lay figure lying on the yellow straw filling the manger in a lowly cattle-shed. Bring in the holly and the ivy, the mistletoe, too; and line the walls, and hide the dirt with the green leaf, the red berry of the holly, the white one of the mistletoe. Blast you, you little pusher, where 'r you shoving? Want to see the cow? Didja never see a cow in your life before? Don't you see hundreds of them walkin' the streets every damned day? Doesn't it look grand, Mick? Yeah. Just like what it musta looked like once in royal David's city, long ago, wha'? Looks like it was all real. Yeah. Oh, man, looka the shepherds in their velvets and their ermines. Them's the kings, you thick! Of course; I know well, know well, no hell no hell, now! Oh, boys, a stable for the King of Glory. Oh, lowly Lord. Glory to God in the lowliest! It was a stable, you thick, because there was nowhere else to go; there was no room in the Inn. There are tens of thousands of kids born daily in lowlier sheds than this one, and no kings either, nor a star to light them up, or even a single shepherd bothering a head about them; only a wail from a mother wondering what she was going to do now. Nunna that kinda talk here, Mick. God rest you merry, man. They are looking after the childer. This very day, in churchtown, in churchtown, a handful of kiddies are getting presented with half a dozen of newly minted pennies in remembrance of the gold presented to the little Jesus. Shining like gold themselves, the pennies are. Lullay, lullay. We must all cherish the childer. Suffer the little ones to come to me — remember? We remember all right. They are the newly lighted candles on the altar of the world. They are the nuts gathered by the church in the month of May. Here we come gathering scuts in May

— remember? Precious jewels, precious jewels, His loved and His own. Oh, yes, we must cherish the childer. The kiddies' day, Mick, the kiddies' day. And why, then, aren't your own kiddies here? They aren't here because they were bold and misbehaving, that's why. They'll have to be better childer if they want to have a gawk at the crib. They're be themselves at home while the missus 's at Mass. Dtch dtch! And you left the kids at home alone, with nothing but their toys? No, no toys neither. No, no toys for them this Christmas morning. No, not till they learn to behave themselves properly. Deliberately sleeping it out this morning, and neglecting to light the fire, get the breakfast, and bring up a cup of tea to the missus and me to stave off some of the cold of the first taste of the day. No, no toys for the like of them. I made them warm with a fine hot larruping instead. I can tell you they're feeling a sorry little pair today. If I teach them nothing else, I'll teach them to think of others before themselves. I'll learn them reverence for their parents, for the Holy Child, and for the Holy Child's day. They'll remember next year and be more careful. Hard? How's it hard? 'A good larruping's better than a cuddle', said an eminent Judge t'other day. 'Snatch a doll from the hand of a child of six', said Monsignor Wiseman, 'and at thirty it'll know the greatness of self-denial.' I'm a catholic, same as you, and I don't give a curse what the Monsignor said — I wouldn't do it. I'd be damned rather than do it. Hush, that's not the kind of talk for here. I won't listen, Mick; I won't listen, I won't lis . . . Don't be 'Micking' me! I tell you the one who'd jerk a joy from a child of six is nothing less 'n a savage lowser. If I met such a one even up above, I'd give him a hot one in the snot that would make heaven a place of pain for the time being! Your talk's edging into blasphemy, Mick; I won't listen. Young souls must be laundered into good beginnings. Original sin, remember! *Ad roddium salvationem juvenilia est:* The rod is youth's salvation. Youth must be kept under; corrected continually. Sin must be bet outa them. Original sin, remember! All God's chillun got stings.

There is no end, no end to the jamboree of injustice to children, the worst of them veiled in the pretence that all is prompted by the love of God and the child. In a booklet about Matt Talbot, one who called himself a 'slave to Mary', and to prove it wore steel chains round his belly so that they rusted into the flesh, we are told that this Matt said 'The kingdom of heaven was promised not to the sensible and educated, but to such as possessed the spirit of little children'. Put the kids in irons, and make them more presentable to

Jesus. Here's another example of it culled from a Christian catholic journal: 'The mysteries of a complicated alphabet were expounded to me by a black-robed ogre with the aid of a leathern instrument, applied to my palms from time to time. I dared make no complaint to my father, who, strangely blind to the genius of his lovely boy, would have belted me with a great black belt, remarking with an utter lack of sympathy: "If you won't take it in at one end, I'll wallop it in at the other".' So we see that weals on the arse and weals on the hands of a little child are, after all, but the small matter of a joke. Biff! Whoosh! Wallop! Purify the kid's vile body with a wealth of weals. Monsignor James Redmond, Liverpool Diocesan Chancellor, warned his listeners that magistrates weren't empowered to order punishment by the birch to boys who had turned fourteen, adding that if parents only gave the much-needed corporal punishment, he would guarantee that juvenile delinquency would end within a year. Another cleric tells us that cruel children (ignorant, apparently, that all kids are thoughtlessly cruel) should be birched, for, he says, when they hurt others, it is reasonable that they should be warmed up themselves. Exorcising cruelty with further cruelty. Why is that little child screaming? Oh, they're only knocking hell out of her under the mantle of Mary. The sign of the three kindles of piety: the whip, the cane, the crozier.

So, well within the borders of Battersea, Eileen and he went on with their life, now widening out into a family; receiving friends from Ireland, from Manhattan, Massachusetts, Pennsylvania, Minnesota, and California farther away, to say a few words, and to let the great Republic shake hands with the little one, standing unsteady yet on one foot only; old comrades from Dublin who had gone with him through the great Lock-Out of nineteen hundred and thirteen, grey now, and wrinkled, like himself, but eager to go over again the scenes of battles long ago, filling the room with their own husky laughter, mixing with the slender, silvery laughs of Eileen, when they told Dublin stories of man's ridiculous conceit, or woman's comic frailty. Souls so different from the jodhpurred souls of Battersea's middle-class, so different from the soul of Tay Pay O'Connor, M.P., yet no different from his own or Eileen's, and very little from the soul of Lady Gregory or the soul of W. B. Yeats.

All mingled with the growth of their two sons, Breon and Niall, Eileen smiling and delightful with all comers against the background of a vanishing bank account; and through all these friendly and human activities, the casting of bread upon the waters in the writing of a first biographical book — *I Knock at the Door*. Those who came, came, and in their going, went not, but left impressions clinging to the life of those to whom they came; came, and went not, the time T. S. Eliot was passing through his *Ash Wednesday* in prayer and meditation within the desert in the garden and the garden in the desert, in and out between the blue rocks, going in white and blue, colours of Mary's mantle and Mary's frock, hoping to hear and hear not, to care and care not, to be still among a thousand whispers from a you tree; they came, and were distrained to waver between loss and gain, for this was God's disposal, saying, The land thou tillest shall be plundered with thistle and with thorn, and in the sweat of thy face shalt thou eat bread. Sweat-stained bread. Tommy Tucker must sing for his supper. The life God gave cannot be silent, cannot be still; it has too much to say, too much to do to live; and he who runs away to hide, deserts the life that God gave. God has decreed the whole earth to be a forced labour camp, and so we must work before we eat. He has put wings to time, and so we can build from toil and time but a little corner in a little room for a little thought. To sit still and care not, in desert or garden, is a vain thing, and may but ripen a soul into drying dust that cannot be spat out like withered apple seed. The blue isn't always bright, and the white must at times be blemished in the cares of life and the keeping of a household going; the slender hands grow rough in time with the washing and the work. In the voice of many speaking, in the whirl of the world's changing, the word is heard; and the whirl of the world's changing is the word, and the noise of men is the word growing louder. Among all who come and go, who is there fit to say that in men's anxiety, their bargaining, their lovemaking, their laughter, there is no sign of the blue of Mary's mantle, the white of Mary's frock, or the red-like crimson of Jesu's jacket?

Sweat-stained comrades of building-site, railway-line, and ship-lined dock, you did what you could to make on-coming life safer and sounder, in bitter strike and vengeful lock-out. Coarse you were, but never common. Yes, we have all done something to change the childermess to a Childermass of security, health, and a bonnie-looking life. You, Promethean Jim Larkin, with the voice born of the bugle and the drum, Barney Conway and Paddy Walsh of the docks, Paddy Mooney of the horses, Shawn Shelly of the workshop, O'Casey of the pick and shovel; you, W. B. Yeats of the lovely lyrics, Augusta Gregory of the little, the larger, laughing plays and the wisdom of guidance, Shaw of the drama and the prophecies, and Joyce of the sad heart and the divine comic mind, touselling and destroying our mean conceits and our meaner vanities. We all ate of the great sacrament of life together.

> Yes, we had some bread and wine,
> We were the Rovers;
> Yes, we had some bread and wine,
> For we were the gallant Soldiers.

> What car'd we for the red-coat men?
> We were the Rovers;
> What car'd we for the blue-coat men?
> For we were the gallant Soldiers.

>   Nothing, comrades.

CAMBRIDGE

A LONG taxi-drive carried Sean to Liverpool Street Station to catch a train going to Cambridge Town; the town of the three ships passing under a castellated bridge, flanked on either side by a fleur de lys and a rose — the rose of sharon and the lily of the valley. From the station at Cambridge, another taxi would whip him off to the University. A Society of St. Catharine's College had pressed him into coming to give a lecture to the Society's members and their friends. Dear God, now he was on his way there! He was no lecturer; the word itself frightened him. Lecture: connected with the reading of scripture in a church; a formal discussion on some special subject. He couldn't be formal; he hadn't the gift. He had no special subject on which to descant, unless he were to descant on his own deformity of ignorance in all things. All subjects relating in any way to life's thousand activities were special to him; but he knew damn all about any of them. Some society or another in almost every university in England had, at one time or another, asked him to lecture, but he had refused all requests, save one he gave in the London School of Economics and one at Harvard. Even this request from the Cambridge Society's invitation he had first refused; and swearing he would ne'er consent, consented. Oh, dear God, he was on his way there now; on his way to Cambridge to deliver a lecture; to deliver the goods; sitting in a third-class carriage, buzzing along to the College on the Cam; away to Grantabrigge, the old Saxon name of the town. Swing low, sweet chariot, carrying me away from home.

It was odd, he thought, the idea flooding so many minds that the writer of a novel, of a play, of a book of verse, must have a wide knowledge of all things, human and divine. The nearer he got to the town, the more uncomfortable he felt; like as one might feel who kept lurching like a drunken man, conscious of instability, in a church procession, headed by a bishop. Steady, lad! It seemed to him that the Lord had departed out of Shyloh. Even if a writer (as apart from a scholar) did know a lot about some things, it was another matter to expose his knowledge to assembled listeners in an interesting way. That was a gift, often transcending the knowledge itself, for most people came to lectures, if not to be taught, at least to be interested. Chin up, man. Come, let's thump the world with talk.

—Cambridge next stop, thank God; said a voice from the opposite end of the carriage.

He didn't want to be reminded of it. It was all very near now. He'd have to don a mask, like Yeats, the minute the train stopped. Hello, lads! Glad to meet you, and honoured to be within the University. A smile on the kisser, too, and a look of confidence, as if he took lecturing in his stride. Years ago he had stood in halls, on platforms, often made of planks across beer-barrels, at times in the midst of strife, surrounded by armed police, speaking for Ireland or for Labour, without hushing a second for a word, full of his own importance; speaking, maybe, a million words, often with eloquence, as often, maybe, without thought. Idle words? At the judgement day man is to give an account of every idle word he spake. Of every idle word man shall speak, he shall give account thereof in the day of judgement; so Christ said, according to St. Matthew. Every idle word; one by one, not in bunches, but in ones. A terrible thought! It will be a long session for everyman; an all-night sitting in a wilderness of words. What a frightful thing if politicians were sentenced to listen throughout eternity to their own speeches; forced to listen in silence to the speeches of others and their own, without permission even to rise on a point of order; or, indeed, if playwrights had to sit watching the performance of their own plays throughout eternity, or the comic broadcasters forced to sit and listen to their own jokes. The most lamentable punishment of all would be the compelling of the clerics to sit down and listen to their own sermons. A tiresome time for all. Idle words, idly thought, idly spoken, idly sent aroving. The engineers of the soul hoist with their own regards. The wings they thought would fly were only vanes to beat the air, shown to be so now in the infirm glory of this positive hour. What must we do, what can we do? Nothing, but like Shaw's Jack Tanner, go on talking.

The title Sean had chosen for his talk had startled the Committee of the Society. They had never heard anything like it before. He was to speak under the heading of *The Holy Ghost Leaves England*. It puzzled them and probed them with embarrassment. There was a taint of religion in the title, and religion is usually embarrassing, outside of a church, to all except to atheists. Even the clergy, protestant and catholic, feel self-conscious when they pronounce the name of God without the sacristy; as can be seen in the apologetic, self-conscious, tiny homilies appearing, week by week, in the *Sunday Times*, written by this anglican cleric, by that roman catholic priest. The name of God sounds safe now only in Latin. It doesn't quite fit in with the humour of the age. The name seems to have become one of the idle words; and the clerics are to blame, for week in, week out, their thoughts do not touch anything living, or even anything dead.

Hello, lads! Here they were — two officials of the Society waiting for him; St. Catharine's College, the reds and the blacks, holding out their hands in welcome. They had written to Sean saying he was to dine with the Dons, but he had stipulated that he should be with the lads, for he wanted to get into touch with them to hear what they had to say, and what they would do when they bid the University goodbye. Sean had dinner with a crowd of them, all sending over glances, probably wondering what such a curious-looking guy had to say to them. After dinner, a Committeeman told Sean that a professor wanted a word with him. More idle words! Sean hadn't a keen desire to meet one laurelled with scholarship. A poor scholar himself, he could learn more from a student than he could from a professor. He was half-afraid of professors. He asked the Committeeman to call for him in less than ten minutes' time, before he was overwhelmed; and then went round the grass quadrangle to the other college where the Professor waited for him. He was ushered into the apartment, a very comfortable one, with cushioned settee and armchairs, and the floor well carpeted. Well-filled bookcases, tidily set against the walls; everything solid, with a sense of dimness and static confidence over all. Very different from the lousy lordliness of a London or a Dublin pub; but its dimness was illumined gaily by some fine pictures painted by a young Welsh artist, a friend of the Professor's and of Sean's. That was a bond tying them for a while together.

They looked at the pictures, and talked of the hope they had in the future of the young artist, while they sipped port from finely cut glasses. The Professor was a young man of about forty, athletic-looking, quick in his movements, and rapid in his talk. He had the air about him of knowing that everything he thought of must be right. There was no cadence of query in anything he said, even when he asked a question; he had already answered it himself. A man whose every thought was a stride.

—Look here, O'Casey, he said, I want to ask your opinion on whether our universities should or should not have the power to send representatives to Parliament. The Leftists are trying to abolish the long-established practice, and I am one of those appointed to defend it; to vindicate the old traditional right of the universities to have separate representation in Parliament, though vindication is needed only for fools. I needn't tell you that, O'Casey; you know it yourself. It isn't permissible to allow violence to be done to such an important practice.

—Black and red facing each other, thought Sean. Aloud, he said: The privilege will be taken away from you.

—Eh? said the Professor, surprised. Nonsense, man! If it happened, knowledge and culture would be isolated from the people. It would be a disaster, and well you know it.

—The privilege will be taken away from you, repeated Sean.

—What, whether it's foolish or wise, right or wrong? You know, O'Casey, that the privilege, as you call it, is one founded on centuries of experience, on severe common-sense, preventing knowledge and culture from falling into neglect or disrepute; for both begin and end with what the universities think and do.

—When you defend university representation, said Sean, you think only of two, your own and Oxford's. The others don't swim into your vision at all. These two, with all others close behind, don't form the beginning or the end of culture or knowledge, sir. You can't imprison any aspect of one or the other of them in a chair. And, to me, culture and knowledge begin with Baa baa, black sheep; with the song, prose, and wisdom of the nursery rhyme.

—You're trying to be funny, O'Casey. A university is an acknowledgement that knowledge and culture are the flower and fruit of our civilisation.

—The universities may be all that, but their representatives aren't. They have been invariably Tories, and defend, not culture or knowledge, but wealth and the power of privilege. The nursery rhyme, the song of the street, the quips and qualities of the circus, the country fair, the dancing of boy with girl in the evening hours, are the main part of our culture, coming before, remaining behind, and surrounding the university, forging the shape of future life while the university is talking about it.

—Stop quibbling, O'Casey. Stick to the point. I am introducing you to the university.

—And I'm introducing you to life, Professor. This is the first time I ever stood within or without your gates; some years ago, in a runabout through Oxford, I stood there for a moment, going in through one gate and out by another. What is it to me that some think you and Oxford should send special representatives to Parliament? What use are you to me there? University men in the Commons are as useful to culture and knowledge as the Bishops are to God in the House of Lords.

—You don't understand, O'Casey, and, I'm afraid, you don't wish to understand. We don't represent knowledge and culture; we are those things; we bring them in among the materialistic thoughts of men, who, if they weren't reminded of them, would forget them altogether. We make their presence felt there.

—Just as the Bishops make the presence of God felt in the House of Lords.

—You're not a bit funny, O'Casey. Cambridge is too big to be impressed by Irish wit. The question I put to you is more important than the turning of a phrase. You have a grudge against us because you never had the good fortune to pass through a university. We, by our membership of the House of Commons, represent thousands of highly educated men and women in art, science, and literature, among a world of men. You represent only yourself and your opinion.

—On the contrary, sir, I represent millions of men and millions of women, less scholarly, indeed, than your thousands; but highly important all the same.

The Professor was shocked into silence for some moments. A hand lifting a glass of port stopped half-way up, and he stared at Sean for several seconds.

—Oh, come now, O'Casey, he said, rather sharply, don't let conceit run away with you! Don't think the few plays you've written entitle you to represent millions!

—Oh, said Sean, laughing, I wasn't thinking of what I'd written. Therein, I represent no-one. It is in myself that I represent millions, in my upbringing, in my work for bread, in my experience, in my outlook on life, in my education. I am one of the great crowd who know you not, and we must know those to whom we give the power to vote in Parliament. We do not know even that you exist. We don't know the names even of those who represent the universities in Parliament. To recognise your right to stay in Parliament, we must have had a hand in putting you there.

—A damned ignorant attitude to take! And you don't condemn it, O'Casey; you even approve of it.

—Yes, I even approve of it.

—Then you've no mind of your own. You are forced to believe as a party line dictates.

—No, not by any party line; by my upbringing, by my experiences; just as your upbringing dictates your particular point of view. You do your best to infuse your students with your own manner and method, and when you say goodbye to a departing student, you put a hood on his shoulders and a parchment in his hand, hoping that your ideas will be hopelessly embedded in his head. You applaud the continuance of the older law and the older prophets that have gone beyond ripeness, and are turning rotten. It has all lasted long enough. A song from God is meant to sound in every ear, and not merely to be an echo in a university. When a mind becomes great, it leaves the university behind it, and joins the company of man. Coloured hoods are very charming, but they fade if the mind of the wearer isn't broader and more colourable than the hood. Literature, art, and science represent themselves. Milton, Shelley, Constable, Darwin, and Rutherford can go about without their cloaks.

A gentle knock, and the young man whom Sean had asked to come to get him away appeared at the door. I stand at the door, and knock.

—Well? asked the Professor, glass of port in hand; What is it? What do you want?

—Mr. O'Casey, sir — the Committee has sent me to fetch him.

—Mr. O'Casey will come to you in a minute, and as the young man hesitated at the door, the Professor said sharply, Be off! Just a small glass of wine, O'Casey, before you go.

A tart reception to the gentle knock. Bad manners on the part of the Professor, thought Sean. Why didn't he ask the young lad in, set him on a seat, and make him take a glass of wine with the two of them? Sean felt ashamed of the Professor's rude and abrupt order to the student to go. Contemptuous of one within the gates, what must the Professor think of lesser ones without? But wasn't Sean himself far worse and far meaner? He let the lad be snubbed, let the lad go without saying a word. Hadn't the guts to say that the lad had come by a prearranged request by Sean himself to get him away from the Don. Stayed silent as if he had known nothing about it. Afraid of the Professor. A mean and lousy act of cowardice. Let the lad go without a word, without a word.

—Well, goodbye, O'Casey. Don't be so sure that the privilege — as you call it — will be taken away. Think the question over.

—Goodbye, sir. You see, the question doesn't call for much thought from us. We hardly know you exist, and we don't care if you do or you don't. We know as much about you as we do about the rarer fowl aswim on the waters of Victoria Park. You have had a long time of it because we didn't know you were there; but times change, and you are no longer safe in the holy quiets of the past.

—Think it all over, O'Casey. You'll find I'm right. You will have to get above your upbringing, if you're going to live easily with educated people. You must grow up. Goodbye.

—Well, Professor, we're united in our liking for Evan Walters' pictures — that's something, anyway. Goodbye.

Led away with a member on either side of him, a prisoner, and others following, Sean was guided safely through a gentle jangle of colleges — Clare, Peterhouse, Magdalene, Pembroke, Christ's, Trinity, Emmanuel; one of his companions pointing to another, somewhat distant, saying, That's Jesus College, famous as the place where Cranmer studied and began his end by reading too much of the bible. While he was musing the fire kindled. Over a bridge crossing the Cam, and right through the Backs, Sean covering the walls with as many glances as he could get in between the chat that went on and on as they strode forward. Old stones, old stones, where Cranmer got ready for what was coming to him. All old stones, still giving out the fading scent of an old religion; the time when men burned their comrades; sent friends atwist with torture down to hell or swift to heaven up, because they didn't think the right things about Jesus. Old stories, old stories from old stones — Bethlehem, Jerusalem, Damascus. Tell me the old, old story of unseen things above. Here still is the smell of an old theology of the middle-ages, consigning most of us to hell, even destining life to eternal fire from the moment of its conception; when a demon might be swallowed with a lettuce-leaf, incautiously eaten; or hidden in a bubble of the froth of beer (Oh, dockers of Dublin, do take care of yourselves!).

Then only the chosen few could be saved and the many called plunged into inextinguishable flames for ever; a dreadful fear buzzing in the ears of man from St. Gregory up to Newman, and echoed, when the buzz had died, into his ear again by General Booth. Here too are the lingering fabrics of the old fables, of Adam and Eve, the winding-sheet of original sin, which C. E. M. Joad found lying about, dollying himself up in it to go strutting along in it as if sheltered with a cloak of indurable delight. The universities, smothered so long by clerical power and discipline and the Latin Language, are only now beginning to breathe. It took Government commission after commission to get rid of this smothering medieval stuff.

But the cassock rustled around yet. The ghosts of the leaves of centuries were thick under their passing feet. Behind these old stones, God had become old and conventional. Midnight oil was burned here, but rarely daylight. The sun seemed seldom to shine on the books; the wind rarely stirred their leaves. It was all so picturesque and all so dead. How many scholars had gone in behind these old walls, head first; and had come out, feet first, without becoming known to a single worker from one end of England to the other. Professor Coulton's *Four Score Years* brings us close to St. John's and St. Catharine's Colleges, mentions many names of dead and gone Fellows, Professors, Tutors, and Clerics, not one of them able to suggest an echo in the heart of any common man. They are to the plain people as if they had ne'er been born. Unknown to those who lived through the same years with them, in the same land, maybe, in the very same town. Imprisoned for life behind these old stones, away from their own people. Even Coulton himself, a great medievalist, a very fine writer, an extremely brave and honest man — who knows of him? It is a pity that the core of culture and of scholarship should be so safely hidden from the sight of the common man.

There was a blue sky overhead and a cold wind blowing, nipping the ears and forcing hands into pockets of trousers or coat. Sean saw a few bunches of daffodil spears thrusting themselves up through the frosted ground, but no yellow bell yet shook in the wind to give a challenge to the swallow to come before a June sun warmed the withering walls. Through the Backs, over the Bridge of Sighs, a copy of an Italian one, if Sean remembered right. Like the Greek portals in front of English bank, hospital, and poor-house, it pustulated that even an English college had lost touch with English character, song, and building. Out by a gate, through the town to the Fitzwilliam Museum, still between Committee members, more following behind, now increased by some young women friends. A place too full of treasures to see in an hour when contemplation is split to pieces by the aggressive chat of many friends. The one thing he remembered well was a picture by Rembrandt of a young man wearing a plumed hat — probably a portrait of the painter himself.

Cambridge isn't a very distinguished-looking town, in spite of its gay arms of three ships sailing under a castellated bridge, with a fair fleur de lys blooming on one side and a sweet rose on the other. It seems to abide by the fame of its colleges. Here come the colleges! They make up for everything the town may lack. One would think that a town housing a university would be, if not stately, at least dignified. Cambridge is neither. It shows little sign that within it is one of the founts of creative literature, science, and scholarship. It sidles and lurches round the colleges, looking like a shabby fellow waiting for a job from a rich relative. Any free expression of life is muffled up and half smothered by a thick overcoat of colleges.

Professor Coulton, recounting his life, tells a lot about the colleges, but ne'er a thing about the town. A student there for years, then a Professor too, for years. A Fellow of two colleges, he never mentions the town. Am I nothing at all to ye, Professors, who pass me by? He never mentions the Church of the Holy Sepulchre or the Fitzwilliam Museum. When one says He's a Cambridge man, the University is meant, and not the town or county. Sean put several questions to the students about the town, but they weren't interested. They knew their way about it, and that seemed to be about all. Why doesn't the University get into closer touch with the town? Why don't they invite lads and lasses, joining in themselves, to shake their feet in joy, swinging about to the tune of *Haste to the Wedding* or *Greensleeves*, on the green of a quadrangle, the older Dons looking on, and wishing to God that they, too, were in the bloom and bluntness of youth? Had Oxford or Cambridge even any student songs? Sean had never heard of any, and these students walking beside him said they were too busy to sing. Ne'er a Villon here. There were even chapels within the colleges wherein God served the students. The god of the University couldn't well mix with the god of the town. The god of the colleges wore cap and gown and had to keep to the rules. A boat seemed to be their love. The score was made by one college-boat catching up another, and bumping it. He had heard of dear Sydney Morgan, wearing a suitably coloured tie, running along the towpath during a contest, and shouting Go on, Clare!

To secret himself away from the cold, Sean wore an overcoat and his thick red muffler, walking briskly through the streets sadly lighted by an ailing and a fainting sun, noticing that the students wore no overcoats, though gay scarves circled their necks. It was plain that they were far from warmth, and that most of them wore clothes that weren't good enough to keep away the nip of the air or the bite of the wind. The streets were busy with undergraduates wearing nothing warm but their gaily coloured scarves. Were they a hardy lot? Is the undergraduate a hefty fellow, readily resisting cold winds and frosty airs? Quite a lot of them didn't look it. Was it a universal university vanity to go about without an overcoat, however sharply the wind blew or the frost nipped the ear? A foolish vanity, lads, a foolish vanity.

Down to the Common Room where he was to give his talk — a big, rectangular apartment with a grand blazing fire at its upper end. A common room in every way, presenting to Sean — bar the fine fire — an appearance of drab discomfort. No carpet on the floor, the boards themselves looking as if they needed a scouring. No cosy armchairs or settees, no pictures on the walls; no sign of a musical instrument, even of a tin whistle; no attractive lights to make reading profitable and pleasant; no brightness at all, save for the big fire flaming away at the big room's end. A full house, crowded to the doors, instead of the quiet assembly of members promised by the Society. The Chairman introduced the speaker, and announced the title of the talk so softly and cautiously that even Sean, standing beside him, didn't hear the fullness of *The Holy Ghost Leaves England*. Odd how hesitant we are about mentioning any title of the threefold deity we say we worship. With all their Cardinals, Bishops, priests, and parsons, churches and chapels, we are shamefacedly reluctant to mention the names of God the Father, God the Son, or God the Holy Ghost. We will readily speak about Buddha, Mahommed, Krishna, or any other deity or prophet; but strongly dislike to mention our own. In any casual conversation, in almost any secular discussion, not concerned as to whether the Christian belief be true or no, any mention of a member of the Trinity is received with embarrassment, and listened to in a strained hush hush. It was Nietzsche who said that God was dead, and the Christians, in spite of their hymns, churches, catholic heralds, universes, churchmans, and methodist monthlies, seem to be damned glad he is. He no longer gets in their way of making a dishonest living.

One Don came to the meeting. He was a Mr. Henn, a young

attractive man, and, seemingly, very shy. Sean was beginning to learn that souls shaded by cap and gown differed from one another as much as those hidden under costly cloak or simply patterned bib and tucker. Sean enjoyed himself very much, talking, talking, for his audience were young, eager, and ready to laugh at any funny thing he said. Living lads all of them. He felt he was among friends, far younger than he was, of course, but by their lively participation in his informal talk they made him feel as young as themselves, and just as hearty. But all his words were idle; words, idle words; not a damn bit of use to anybody or to himself.

After questions had been asked and answered, in a way, he was invited to a student's room to meet personally some of those who had listened to him; and off he went, guided by two students, and followed by a crowd of student companions. They went up and up a long stone staircase, the ascension protected by an iron handrail, making Sean imagine he was in a Dublin dwelling-house built for the deserving poor. Up, up, they climbed, till debouching to the right from a lobby, they came to the room, as bleak as the Common Room, except that this one had a comfortable armchair in its centre. They led him to the chair and sat him down in it, as if they had enthroned him as the bishop of debate: more idle words. A Dublin kid grown into a figure set down in the midst of the Cambridge Colleges. The room was lighted by one bulb dangling from the ceiling's centre. There were no flowers anywhere (too early in the season, maybe), but a few pictures imposed a bit of beauty on the dull wall, though the light was too dim for Sean to see what they were like. He tried to get the students to talk about themselves and their colleges, but they shelved all his questions, insisting on talking of the drama, a bit of religion, and a lot about Socialism. Sean cast many seeds of thought, hasty and unimportant, into the stuffy air to die there. Perhaps they're echoing round the colleges yet; in the wind o' nights — that sound's the sound of O'Casey's voice, mumblin' in the empty air. Don't listen.

Then suddenly the light went out, and for some moments blotted out completely the dynasty on the armchair and those who sat cramped on the ground around him; then tiny beams from half a dozen hand torches came into play, and relieved the room from its grimmer gloom. It seemed that the college lights went out at a certain hour, warning the students that the time for bed had come. No warning, no bugle-call or drum-tap; just a darkness saying, off to bed now!

—They go out together? What, all over the college? asked Sean, astonished. Yes, all over the college, as our light went out just now. And how do the later students manage in the dark? As best they can. But why do the students submit? It is the rule. We must obey the rules, or go. But this sort of thing treats you all like helpless children. Oh no; it's just the rule.

Sean said no more about the vanished light. It went out according to rule, and the students took it as a matter of course. They didn't seem inclined to question the rule. Sean thought he detected here the sly psychical corrosion of fear. The students were very much afraid of the Masters, and their dogs, the rules. Few here, thought Sean, would be leaders of men, worthy leaders; or leaders in thought; few here would come out to mix with comrades. Many would leave to commit to life the rules they themselves had obeyed as students; trying to force life to remain where it stood. Just to stand; not even to stand and give challenge. As you are. Try no step forward: it might be against the rules. Suffer no new idea to spring from a human head: it might be against the rules; the sacred rules. God Himself was the great Ruler. Was He, too, immersed in the sanctity of rules? He punishes his unruly children; punishes the children for their father's sin when the father has gone underground. So the clergy say. They have carried out the will o' God — on others. Put them in jail; burn them at the stake; exterminate them all rather than one poor rule should perish. It was the breaking of a rule of obedience, Christian teaching tells us, that brought all death, all woe, into the world. It planted deep in man's soul the deadly fungus of original sin. This idea, long an article of faith, has become a fashion, the cold-spur of despair, the *arrah-na-vogue* of death. Professor John Gassner of the United States Columbia College says, 'Contemporary reconstructed "liberals" who exert a literary influence have recently discovered "original sin"'. What the hell is it at all? In a booklet called *Christian Doctrine*, published by Vassalli and Sons, Bath, England, a few years ago, blessed by the signs of *Nihil Obstat* and *Imprimatur* of Westminster, we are told that 'Original sin is that guilt and stain of sin which we inherit from Adam who was the head and origin of all mankind'. The Gaelic catechism strengthens this with the phrase 'in which we were conceived, and born *children of wrath*' — italics theirs. The Gaelic term used for 'wrath' gives the idea of intense heat, of seething, boiling; of fiery rage. And going further into explanations, C. E. M. Joad tells us that original sin explains everything. It hardly explained anything to Dr. McDonald,

Theologian of Maynooth. Joad's new panacea; not one that cures everything evil, but one that damns everything good.

In spite of the church's statement that disobedience was the source of original sin, most ordinary catholics hold that original sin was created by Adam acting the goat with Eve, a belief that gives the priests the delight of having it both ways; for having the desires of sex within themselves, at times voraciously, they can, at the same time, lash out ignorantly and venomously at anyone else showing the slightest sign of it in conduct, book, or play; and this belief hands to the clerics the gift of giving the laity permission to indulge in it, after a few mumbled words have been spoken in a church; a gift that pours a handsome shower of fees into the wide-open pockets of the clerics. Oh, Adam, Adam, why couldn't you keep it down! Hold your hand out, naughty boy! Was it any wonder, now, that Joyce said of Adam,

> He ought to blush for himself, the ould, hay-headed philodophr,
> For to go and shove himself that way on top of her:
> Begob, he's the crux of the catalogue
> Of our antediluvial zoo.

The inner walls of Cambridge colleges must be smoky with the many marks and smudges of centuries of philosophy taught and argued about, day in and day out, written down in thesis after thesis, book after book; their inner airs must be heavy with the incense of centuries of theology taught here, set down in thesis after thesis, book after book; theology pastoral, pastoral-comical, historical-pastoral, tragical-historical; before Cranmer and after him; yet here were a group of students from the various colleges who were doubtful as to what was the wisdom of life, of what life was; having left off even wondering where God could be; students gathered in a room full of themselves and of darkness, seeking explanations still, asking questions of life, and finding answers only in their own experience of it.

What had been called the Truth had often run in and out of the colleges here, ambled through the corridors, crossed the lawns, fed in the refectories, slept in the rooms; Truth carrying a cross in her hand one day, a bible in her hand the next, abandoning both for the *Origin of Species*, which many tried to tear from the hands that held it tight, and hold it tight still. Truth of one kind fluttered in the minds of Latimer and Cranmer, of another kind in the mind of Gardiner, shaking many shoulders to rouse them into reading *The*

Explication and Assertion of the True Catholic Fayth. Yet no mind in any of the bodies here crouching in the darkness thought of either Truth, but sought one of their own making. That's it, by God! Every man must fashion by thought and experience the truth that suits him, the truth he needs.

Universities, said someone, are places where pebbles are polished and diamonds are dimmed. Each lad here sought a proficiency of knowledge that would give him a licence to dangle what he thought he knew before younger minds in minor colleges and schools, and so earn a living. Surrounded by Socrates, Chaucer, and Shakespeare, and all, they were, all the time, fixed to the bread-line. The book of verse, the girl, even the flask of wine, would have to wait till they could easily handle a loaf. Find a job, find a job, was written under every line of Shakespeare, of Chaucer, under every line of poetry or prose the studiers read; under every line they read now as it had been under every line written by Shakespeare and Chaucer, and all the other writers of the time; though Chaucer was saved a lot of worry by burrowing a job out of the Civil Service. All great questions about immortality, the nature of the soul, human destiny, and of God were hedged in by the necessity of satisfying animal life; the significance of human life was tangled up in the desire for a job. God's curse had driven all into a forced-labour camp. Each had to earn bread by sweat of face, or get others to do it for him. After having made life harder by way of a curse, it seems that the Christian God has made its end harder still. Sean wondered how many, if any, of these lads bothered about the *Quicunque Vult* of the Athanasian Creed? Miss Dorothy Sayers emphasises its swashing blow in her *The Mind of the Maker.* 'The proper question to put to any creed', she says, 'is not, Is it pleasant, but Is it true?' 'It isn't', she says, 'that God refuses to save unbelievers; it is the more alarming fact that unless a man believe it faithfully, he *cannot* be saved.' In other words, if he doesn't lap it clearly and faithfully into his nature, he's a gonner. Down, down to hell, say Miss Sayers and St. Athanasius, and say we sent thee thither. Well does Emerson quote the churchman: 'This was Jehovah come down out of heaven. I will kill you, if you say he was a man.' Outside of the catholic church, of the faith, there is no redemption. But, oddly enough, the roman catholic church of America the other day silenced a Jesuit priest for teaching this doctrine. The ones episcopal told him to hold his tongue; he refused, so episcopal authority shoved poor Father Feeney out and slammed the door behind him. So, it seems, they shove out those who won't or can't accept the Athanasian Creed, and, when they've recovered their breath, hustle out those who can and do. Well, here in this room, by the light of the tiny hand torches, a lot was said about Socialism, and nothing whatever about dogma, protestant or roman catholic. Even the echoes of dogma no longer tinkled in their eager ears that had long ago opened to the hearing of other things. Not only here, in this room, in this college, but under the palm and the fig-tree, in the snow-carpeted lands of the north, among the vines, and under the oak and the elm, the ears of man had opened to the hearing of other things.

It was an odd sight with the sitting figures bending towards Sean, those crouching on the floor tucking up their legs to make more room for those crouching beside them; the electric torches throwing out tiny beams of light, now showing a young face tense with thought, a pale hand clenched or resting easily on the back of a chair or a comrade's shoulder; a leg thrust forward along the floor, threading its way among those gathered up, hands clasping the knees to keep them steady; a young mouth opening and closing, busy with the spoken formation of a thought; voices agreeing and disagreeing floating out of darkness; Sean speaking towards that light now, this light then; all in the centre of a curious quietness, for all the colleges were still, and nothing active but the silent grandeur of the night. What did their talking try to do? Tried to untangle a chain or two of all that cling and clang around the heart's desire. He had taught nothing; he had learned something of the ways of a Don; more about the ways of a student; saw within their air of brittle confidence, under the gay colours of their scarves, that they knew as much about the morrow as he knew himself. One by one the torches gave out in the midst of the low voices, till but one remained to give a single glow, like a firefly that had strayed into the room, and had come to rest on the arm of a chair. On the discussion went till some chime or another told them it was two o'clock in the morning, and time to go, for the one torch left would soon give out, and the world would be left to darkness and to them. They rose up unwillingly, for the morrow of life would put wide distances between them and him for ever.

Talking still, they wandered forth from the room, all shaking hands with Sean, each going his separate way, save two, who, linking him on either side, led him down the stone stairs, out of the college, around a quadrangle, over to St. John's College, where a room had been set aside for him so that he could find refreshment in sleep after the labour of his lecture and his talk. They bid good-bye to him at the door, after switching on the light for him, a single, naked bulb hanging from the ceiling's centre again. He was so full of what he had seen and heard that he forgot to ask how was it that while all the lights were out elsewhere, one shone in the room lent to him. Never having asked, he never knew.

There he was, standing alone, in the middle of a February morning, in the middle of a room in St. John's College. Jasus, what a room! A slum room, without a slum room's brightness, defiantly facing him in one of England's primate colleges! The floor was bare and dirty-looking; there was no fireplace, not even a mark where a fireplace might have been. One window, unclad even with the symbol of a rag, looked out on to the night. To the right of the door, a dangling piece of wooden frame-work carried a cord from which hung a patterned curtain, the flower-pattern soiled with the marks of dusty years: this was meant to be the wardrobe, for, behind the curtain, some hooks were driven into the wooden frame. A small cane-bottomed chair sat itself by the staring window. Opposite the door stretched the bed, an ordinary iron-framed one, painted black, but with the paint peeling off in places, showing the rust beneath; over it lay a bedspread, thin and abject, of a dirty yellowish-grey colour, ornamented with a blue-grey pattern; under this two thin blankets, and under these again, clean sheets, once white, but now taking on the colour of fading unbleached linen. There was an air of bruised poverty in the place, more abject than some of the rooms he had entered before, and sadder because of its emptiness. He himself had sat for hours that had mounted into years, studying the beginnings of knowledge, in a room as poor and as bleak as this one; but behind its bitter bleakness had stretched the cosy pattern of a room nearby, where a fire burned, its flames framing his mother mending an old shirt or darning an old sock. If one were a Christian, what would he pray for here? For a quiet death on the pale, dejected bed, for if this room was the usual habitat in a student's life, the best thing for a student to do would be to die. Youth is here, but not youth with a red rose in his breast. Most of the students he had met were too anxious about their future; too strained in an effort to make both ends meet; men of the world hurried by, intent on their business; the world wasn't with them enough.

He peered tensely out of the window, but couldn't see a thing; not a twinkle of a light or a star anywhere; must be misty: just a dark void, and he in the midst of the silence. Earth with her thousand voices is silent now. He shivered; it was damnably cold, too, though he still wore his cap, muffler, and thick blue topcoat. He opened the door, his hand resting on its jamb, and peered out: a black void here, too, without any rapture in it. The light in the room was too dim to go beyond the doorway. He had no torch, but he struck a match, and before it died out, he caught a glimpse of a corridor that led God knew where. He took a step beyond the door, his hand touched the switch, knocking it down and extinguishing the light as he found himself plunging headlong forward to prevent himself from falling smash on his face. Fortunately his outstretched hands struck a wall and not his head, and he stood by it, panting, till he got a calm breath back again. O'Casey wild and loose in St. John's College, Cambridge, in the dead of the morning. Like a thief in the night come to rifle, rob, and plunder. He wondered how far he had shot forward, and hoped there weren't many doors, for then he mightn't know which one was his. Good thing he hadn't crashed against some dignified Don's door. Where the hell was his door? There was a draught blowing through the corridor like a low wind in Jamaica. There were but three matches left in the box. It wouldn't be fun to have to spend the night in the corridor waiting for the Blue of the Night to meet the Gold of the Day; an old song among old stones. How would it go, if he sang it loudly here? Would it be against the rules? And Sean, leaning against the wall, bubbled with laughter. A sound of revelry by night. 'Tis now the witching hour of the morning. He wondered if Wordsworth's ghost had a beat here at times? His old college. Too far away from where he lies now. Did the shadow of him, who thought the bow and arrow more effective than cannon, flit about anywhere here now? Roger Ascham, great at least, as one of the first to coax English language out of its dusty corner, and send it forth to say its own say and speak its own grand message.

He carefully struck a match, and swiftly looked around. Ah, there was the door of his room wide open in welcome. Won't you come home, bill bailey, won't you come home! He will, and cautiously stepping to the door, he wound his arm round the jamb, and switched on the light. Peering down, he saw that there were three narrow triangular steps leading up to the level of the room's floor, so narrow that one would need to step down them sideways. Led in by his friends, he hadn't noticed them before, and so, unaware of them when he stepped bravely out, he had plunged headlong into the corridor. He would open the door softly again. Had he not had a few matches on him, God knows where he might have wandered. Oh, where is my wandering boy tonight! While the matches were giving light, a swift glance around had shown him that there were no pictures in the hall here; not even a poster from the Underground: all bare and drab. No connection with any other firm. The old ecclesiastical idea of seclusion: the students the elect of God instead of the elect of the people. An idea dead that won't lie down. No drums under the windows either; no band ever played on any of the squares.

He closed the door and looked at his watch; on the border-line of three o'clock. Time for bed, for the skip would be knocking at his door at seven o'clock in the morning. The low wind from Jamaica was whistling in under the door; God, he was cold, so the sooner he got under the bedclothes, the better. He hung his coat up on one of the nails behind the faded chintz curtain, put his ordinary coat on top of it, with his muffler hanging over both. He hurried off his jersey, boots, and trousers, and pulled his pyjamas on, tucking his shirt into the top of the trousers, for it was too damned cold to take that off; turned the light out, groped his way across the room, and climbed into bed, shivering. A friendly lot of lads, these students, many of them in such poor circumstances that university life must be something of a torment to them. Poverty was beginning to go a long way up as it went a long way down. He was shivering now with great elation. Colder here in bed than out on the bare floor. No heat in either blanket or coverlet. There would be no sleep for him while he kept so cold. He got hastily up, groped about in the dark, shoved on his trousers and socks, and shot into bed again. Cold as death.

Full of eagerness, a lot of these lads, to meet and answer the questions of life. Brave lads. If only the way was straight before them; if even they could think that their way was straight before them. God, it's colder, colder than it was out in the corridor; frost is flitting about the room. Sweeney, roosting on the frosty fork of a naked tree, was no colder than he, here, buckled up in this bed's centre. Shivering shamefully, he lepped out of bed again, he groped a way across the room, thrust himself into his smaller coat, wound the red muffler round his neck, put out the light, groped back across the room, and shot himself into bed again. But the frosty air nipped as strong as ever, and the low wind of Jamaica sent chill currents down his spine and around his shoulders. Twist about how he might, tug as he would at the miserable bedclothes, it was beyond him to coax a single sign of warmth into where he lay. Up he got once

again, groped about till he found the light-switch to turn on the
light — the only blessing he was to find beside him through the
bitter night. He donned his heavy overcoat, put on his boots, fixed
his cap on his head, and set himself down to spend the rest of the
night pacing the room. Up and down, down and up the little room,
muffled to the ears; up and down till the damned doxy dawn came
to his relief; under the silent bulb of light pendant from the ceiling's
centre: *per amica silentio lumine.* Was there ever anyone else like
unto this one, perishing with cold at Cambridge, in the vast middle
of the night! Up and down, down and up, hour after hour, quietly
treading the floor for fear anyone in the college should be wakened,
and wonder who was walking. Cold as death. Somewhere in the
distance, a clock chimed the quarters, but, though he knew the time
too well, Sean had never looked at his watch so often. At last, the
dawn came to the coldest spot in England. First, he saw her finger-
tips shoving up the shutters of the night, delicate fingers, dimly seen
through a curtain of mist, till the whole hand spread over the whole
sky, and the night was over. Through the grey mist he saw the blurred
outlines of the great colleges, grey walls, zig-zag roof-lines, pierced
here and there by tall, austere chimneys, without a trace of smoke
coming from one of them. Below the mist he saw that the ground
was shrouded in the cold whiteness of a whore frost. Slowly the lazy
sun rose higher, and the bright light adangle from the ceiling turned
into a watery, ghastly gleam, making the poor room look as if there
was about to be a sickly end of its life. Even the skip was late, but
he came in the end, bearing a can of hot water, his mouth opening
a little to say Good morning, sir; I hope you had a good night.
Never mentioning the kind of night he had had, Sean took the water
with thanks, leaving a little to use for shaving, and using the rest to
bathe his swollen, aching eyes; for one of the irritations of life was
that he had to bathe his eyes at least twice a day in water but a
degree away from boiling, so that the lids, heavier than that weighing
down over the one eye of Balor, might remain high enough to allow
the eyes to look out on the world. He was in haste, hurrying over a
wash and a shave that he might slide into his heavy clothes again,
and save himself from frostbite.

Then another wait, and more pacing up and down the room, till
the young guide of the night before came again, hoping, too, that
Sean had had a pleasant night, and they sauntered through the
frosty air to the lad's room, where the morning meal had been laid
out for him. Here there was a generous fire, and with the chair

drawn up beside it, the table pushing itself against the chair, Sean found comfort at last. The breakfast was a sound one of two eggs, a dish of porridge, a number of rashers, a heap of toast, a great pot of tea, and a jar of marmalade. At the opposite side of the table the student busied himself with his own breakfast, starting (as Sean thought) with a saucerful of filmy oats, ghosts of the true grain, dampened with milk poured cautiously from a tiny jug. When Sean had finished one of the eggs, with tea and toast, he noticed the student drawing away from the table as if satisfied, and he asked him if he wasn't going to have an egg and some of the porridge.

—Oh, they're for you, sir, the student said. I've had enough. I never eat more; I find I work well having eaten a light breakfast.

—Eat nothing, then, and you'll work better, said Sean explosively. Good God, man, a young lad like you needs a bigger meal than a saucerful of dried dust! That's no way for the College to feed you. If you go on that way, man, it soon won't be worth a bug's while to bite you!

—Oh, said the lad, with embarrassment, if I needed more, I could get it from the buttery.

—Here, said Sean, pushing them across the table, take the porridge, this egg, the rashers, and half the toast, and don't let me go thinking I've wasted good food.

—Sure you don't want them, sir? asked the student, shyly.

—Quite sure. I never eat bacon, and one egg's enough for one of my age. Muck into them, now, like a lad of mettle. Sean put it off jauntily, realising it was poverty that kept the lad on a diet of dried dust.

The lad mucked into them all right, enjoying the first fair breakfast, probably, he had had for a long time; talking away of his study of English Literature from Chaucer to Shakespeare, so that he might win a Degree in Arts that would flit him out to teach children who had never read a line, and never would, probably, of either poet, and like it, in their life's short journey. It was likely that there were hundreds living here like this young chap, some of them even under harder conditions; for this room had, at least, a fire — though, maybe, it had been lit only to entertain a guest. A number of the rooms Sean had entered had been like his own, fireless and freezing. The poor scholars! Reading Chaucer, reading Shakespeare for a living! Land of warp and worry! Mooching curiously around, he had had a hunt for a bathroom. He found them preciously gathered together in a small group away from the buildings, serving several colleges; and not long there either. An after-thought. Indeed, Dr. Coulton in his *Four Score Years* tells us that in 1922 the Master of St. John's College, speaking about a long-lived Professor, told how he had lived to see the introduction of railways, electric telegraphs, motors, and aeroplanes, adding 'And we hope he will live to see baths in St. John's College'. Anyhow, why worry, said someone, we're never in the college longer than eight weeks. The medieval ecclesiastical affiliation with dirt still lingering on lively in the colleges of Cambridge. Old walls, old walls, and old ways, too.

On the wall facing Sean an elegant, slim oar stretched itself along proudly, held up by brackets. Asking why it was there, Sean was told by the student that his boat had won a competition on the Cam, and that each student of the crew had been presented with the oar he had used; and the glow on the student's face showed he was glad that Sean had noticed the trophy, with the date of the race and the name of the competitor emblazoned on its slender blade. He gets more joy out of his oar than he does out of Chaucer or Shakespeare, thought Sean; and rightly so, for this is something he has done himself. This would be a memento to him all his life. If he married he would show it to his children: rowing on the Cam on such a day against a rival crew, we won, and this is one of the oars that pulled us home. A natural and a noble vanity. All the vanity in Vanity Fair isn't vain. Bunyan was wrong.

The taxi to bring him to the station would be here in a minute or two. Already a group was gathering to bid him goodbye. He had told some of them that he intended to write about the condition of the colleges, but they had begged him to wait a year or two; till they had taken their degrees or diplomas, and had gone for good; for they were fearful that what he might say should do them harm. He went back to his room to collect his grip, where he found the skip tidying the bed that had proved to be such a wretched refuge during the night.

—The college doesn't seem to be busy this term, he murmured to the skip.

—Not busy, sir? We're crammed out, we are; couldn't put up another soul.

—But how is this room empty, then?

—This one, sir? Oh, this was full, but the fellow 'as were 'ere, 'e got took with pneumonia, an' 'ad to be taken 'ome.

Penumonia! In his mind's eye, Sean could see the poor figure on the bed, feeling first the heat of the blood and the tenseness in the side; unsettling, but to be borne till they passed away, and the body righted itself. My people have paid the fees. Only a few days. Vain hope.

> Send speedy help, we pray,
> To him who ailing lies,
> That from his couch he may
> With thankful heart arise.

Soon be better, soon be better, have to be, for the pain became a red pain pinching deep into the lung, pinching deeper, so that he cried out, though no cry came, for it was stifled within the gasping cough that tried to cast the biting lung out of the frightened body, itself now developing a heat of its own, a dry and crackling heat, contestant in its venom with the crackling heat of the lung. Knight of the burning pestilence. Twist on the old, ironic bed, and let your rasping coughs break through whatever chimes may sound softly from the college buildings. In the mean, lonely room, within the meaner bed, away from home, in the midst of scholarly culture, a young lad was gasping out part of his life on a college pallet, silence praying for help, and poverty bathing his brow.

—How is he now? asked Sean of the skip.

—'Ow's 'oo, sir?

—Young lad who had the pneumonia?

—Oh, 'im? 'Ee's dead, sir. 'Eard 'ee just died. 'Is mother come, an' fetched 'im 'ome. 'Adn't the stamina, sir. Lot are like 'im 'ere still. Poor fellas, y'know, sir; always on the scrape. Not the class, really, for the colleges. Thank you, sir! he added, as Sean slipped half a crown into his hand.

The rules! He had just obeyed a college rule himself! Condemning them scornfully among the lads, here in the silent, miserable room, he had confirmed one. An unwritten one, but a rule just the same. Curious conscious and unconscious emotions of inconsistency in the heart of a man.

—Well, goodbye, sir, and the skip had gone, leaving Sean with himself and the lonely room. A boy's lungs had hardened here, sending flaming coughs quivering from a parched mouth. Send some Lazarus that he may dip the tip of a finger in water, and lay it on my burning tongue, for I am tormented in this flame. I am fighting it out, fighting to avoid the cold clutch of the tomb; fighting to get back to Shakespeare, to Chaucer, and to Sidney; here, in this lean room, amid the faded chintz, the naked window, the bare floor, the meagre chair, the drab walls, the unholy bed; while outside stretches out the scholarly land of hope and glory. No more foraging for fees. I did my best, mother, but life was too much for life with me. Open the door, mother, and let me go from this lonely room. Come quick.

Here she is, lad; your mother. Woman, behold thy son. She is come to take you off from this dumb room, and to enfold you with her own cuddling talk. She is come to take away her dying boy to present him with the happiness of a far less lonely death, and a lonelier room at the end.

He went out, and climbed into the waiting taxi, waved a hand to the group of lads waving goodbye to him, and set off on his journey home.

DEEP IN DEVON

THERE is an immense amount of activity, of anxiety, of care, and of thought, in the bringing up of children. It is a harder job than that of any prime minister, of any archbishop, of any general on a horse, or any admiral on a quarterdeck. A mother is busy the livelong day and the deadlong night. She has been left alone too long at the wearing job, and now the man must join in with a sensible helping hand. In spite of all the scientific and mechanical equipment surrounding us, and the colleges and schools, we know next to nothing about the strangest equipment of all — the child, the greatest, the loveliest, and the most delicate equipment we have for the development of life's future. We know more about the child than we did even twenty-five years ago, yet there are still millions of ageing minds who think that the best way to fit a child for happiness and resolution in life is to stuff his delicate mind with a creed, Christian or Communist. For Christ's sake, let the child laugh, let the child play, let the child sing, let the child learn, let the child alone.

A deep talk about schools. Prospectuses fluttering in from various places, all very fine and large and damned expensive. Two boys to be educated now, and another child on the way. Eileen, asking all the questions and answering them herself, wanted a school where the boys would be welcomed as day-pupils, for G.B.S. had advised against boarding the children, saying that a mother's affectionate regard and care should remain breast to breast with children till they had reached an age that allowed them to go forward gay and strong without them. Eileen sought a school where a child's nature would be neither checked nor ridiculed by customs stale; one where no fantasia of pietistic chanting would deafen a child's mind away from its own thoughts; where a child would see trees, herbs, and animals living a natural life, and not as they appeared woven into a nursery-rug, or emblazoned on a nursery-plate or pie-dish.

—Dartington Hall is the place for your boys, said Shaw.

—It's going to cost a lot, murmured Sean, anxiously.

—No more than the others, said Shaw, shutting up Sean. Give the children the good things and the fine things, and, when they grow up, they'll refuse to do without them; and that is what we need, he added emphatically, the refusal to do without the finer things of life.

Eileen thought the world of Shaw, and loved his magnificent, laughing austerity; so it was decided that the two lads should go to Dartington Hall School. Another upheaval for Sean! A change from the city's busy life and colour to the wider and quieter ways of the green country. He feared the country, for it robbed him of much, his eyes there losing a lot of the little power they had. In a city the view was a short one, and his eyes hadn't to travel far to see things; all was at his elbow. The great sky was always a narrow strip, hugged by the city's skyline. In the country the way was wide open, and all around was a great carousel of sky, forcing him to keep his cap well down over his eyes so as to cut most of the sky away, and keep a workable focus in front of him. In a city, on a sunny day, one side of a street was usually shaded, so he could stride along in comfort; in the country, the sun spread everywhere, so he would have to march, head bent, and slowly. In a city, at night, the street-lamps and lighted shop windows were a wide lantern to his feet, so that he could go anywhere safely; but all through the winter, in the country, he would be blind at night, and every step he took from the house then would have to be arranged by some guiding hand. Night-time would take away his independence; and he hated any hand trying to guide him in the way he should go.

Down they went to Devon for the children's sake, carrying all their wealth of worldly goods with them, settling in the busy little town of Totnes, and, once more, going through the arduous orgy of fitting into a new home — a big, clumsy house, full of pretension only, the only one they could get; a one that even a miracle couldn't make comfortable. Totnes is set out so that its main street slinks slowly up a slender hill in the valley of the Dart, Devon's beautiful

Anna Livia Plurabelle. Half-way up the hill of the main street stood
the church, its spire rising over all, and higher up on a spur of the
hill, on the church's flank, stood the circular stone keep of a Saxon
castle. The castle and the church — the two *sine qua nons* of the
long ago. The guardians of God's Truth in the town are plentiful,
for we have in this town the anglican church of the priory and St.
Mary, the roman catholic one of St. George and St. Mary, the
wesleyan church, the baptist church, the congregational church, the
gospel hall, with sundry amateur evangelists, a couple of salvation-
ists, and visits from jehovah's witnesses knocking at our doors to
hand in tracts, sell books, and give a quick word or two about the
surest way to get to God. A little way off, if we happen to stray, in a
beautiful part of the Dart's flow, we knock up against the Benedictine monastery of Buckfastleigh, a simpering silhouette now of
what it was in the Middle Ages when the Abbey owned many fine
fat smiles of the shire. It has its languishing pipe-dream that England
again will be managed by monasteries and pickled in priorities.
Help, help! Help to build up Fountains Abbey! Help to build up
Prinknash Abbey! Names entered in the Golden Book of Remembrance for a guinea a time. Buy away, buy away, fond hearts and true,
and open up heaven for England, their England. A guinea for God.
Guineas are good for us. Send them twinkling in; invest in mona-
hysterical consoles, Jerusalem the golden with milk and money blest.

Here, in Devon, they were anchored on the real red earth, rich
earth, and very fruitful. Here, maybe, Adam was made, for in a
bible Sean had had when a kid, he remembered a marginal note
telling the world that Adam meant red earth; so here, maybe, Adam
was needed into life. Adam filled a vacuum. All he had to do was
to keep his feet, and all would have been well, and all would have
gone on living. God, what a grand world it would have been!
The brontosaurus would have been a pet, and pterodactyls would
have been flying in and out of our windows, chirruping just like
robins! But the man had to fall down. The woman done it, sir —
pushed me down; caught me off me guard. Couldn't keep his feet
for all our sakes; fell, and ruined the whole caboosh.

Here, now, in a house in Devon, he was looking over the page-
proofs of his first biographical book; for, while writing plays and
thinking about the theatre, his mind had become flushed with the
idea of setting down some of the things that had happened to himself; the thoughts that had darkened or lightened the roads along
which he had travelled; the things that had woven his life into

strange patterns; with the words of a song weaving a way through a
ragged coat, or a shroud, maybe, that had missed him and covered
another. His own beginning would be the first word, a little logos
born into the world to speak, sigh, laugh, dance, work, and sing
his way about for a day, for tomorrow he would die. First weave in
a sable tapestry would be the colourful form of her whose name was
Susan, ragged dame of dames, so quietly, so desperately courageous.
Life couldn't get rid of her till she died. She went on going forward
to the end, ignoring every jar, every misfortune, looking ahead as if
she saw a great hope in the distance. A dame of dames, a patient,
laughing stoic. Always forward, with her gleaming black eyes, her
set mouth, forever smitten with a smile; ragged and broken-booted,
still looking forward as if she saw freedom and everlasting truth
beside her. A dauntless feminine brennan on the moor of life.
Thirteen children, and only five surviving. Next door to a Niobe.
Apollo shooting: bring me my bow of burnished gold; and he shot
eight of them. Whizz! Thinned out now; safe; go ahead. Eight little
O'Caseys planted safe in God's acre. *Confiteor meum.* She never
mentioned but three of them — Susan and the two Johns. Maybe
she had forgotten the others. Maybe she thought there wouldn't
have been room in the world for so many; or room in her own deep
heart for so many. She had certainly fought death away from him.
Here he was, deep in Devon, surrounded by his wife and two
children (soon to be three), and the savage grace of a day that is
dead cannot come back to him. Only in sleep might he dream it
back; never again, except in sleep.

Here in his little garden, as the year branched into the month of
August, two rows of runner-beans were gaily climbing up their
tapering bean-poles — called string-beans in America, and scarlet
runners in Ireland. The twining stems have topped the poles, and
hundreds of vivid scarlet flowers hang pensively among their handsome greenery, like rubies resting from their fuller glow. They bring
to his mind the scarlet runner, planted by his mother, that grew up
around the framework of the tenement window. Somewhere, from
someone, she had got a bean, had shown it to him, remarking on its
odd colouring of blackish purple, mottled with pink blotches. She
had coaxed him into getting enough fresh clay from an old dump-
field to fill a small box, and had carefully sown the bean in its
centre, gently tickling it into exhilaration with some rotting dung
gathered by her from the street outside. She had watched the first
leafing of the scarlet runner with delight, feeling sure that a bright

jewel would one day hang from it. When she saw the twisting stem, she knew it was a climber, so she wove threads in and out along the window's side to help it up. Then came the crimson flower, just like the flower of a sweet pea, and all red, and she rejoiced with a quiet joy, her hand touching it gently; and, at times, Sean saw her pouring over the clay the sup of milk she needed for her own tea, flushed with the idea that since the milk nourished her, it would nourish the plant as well; and it seemed she was right, for when the plant was in its prime, the scarlet runner was hanging out its gently vivid, red flowers all around the side of the window's edge. In the later autumn the flowers shrivelled and fell off, the leafage grew dry and wrinkled, and long pods dangled down where the crimson flowers before had fashioned their own beauty. Waiting till the pods seemed to be ripe, she took a number of beans from the pods, and sowed them in the cold clay; but no leaf appeared when the summer came again, nor did any thrust itself up from the clay in the summer of the following year, though she watched it day by day, evening by evening, for the sign of a rising leaf. Her fuchsia, her musk, her geranium, came up steadily year after year, never failing her; but the scarlet runner never came again. Neither he nor she had known that the pods could be eaten, had ever tasted one. Though they had been put before him at dinner while staying at Coole Park with Lady Gregory, he had never connected the succulent green strips with the scarlet runner that had draped with red and green glory the framework around the tenement's miserable window-frame; and it wasn't till they had grown some themselves while they lived in Buckinghamshire, and he saw the blossoms, that he realised he was looking at the red flower which had delighted his mother, that had withered away in the autumn, and had never come again.

Now he was handling *I Knock at the Door*, his first biographical book, which would give her life for an hour again; but some other book soon would shut away the story of her days. The lover of the scarlet runner would be gone for ever; gone after her fuchsia, her musk, her geranium, and her scarlet flower. Fuchsias are still here, hedges of them; geraniums bloom again in countless gardens; musk grows in many places; and his own wee garden here, deep in Devon, is alight with the scarlet stitching of the runner-bean. But not hers. They are gone as she is gone. Thoughts in the memories of the living alone ruffle the dead into living again: the muffled drums of the dead beating a faint roll of remembrance; so faint that the memory ceases to hear it before it ends.

A surprisingly large number of educated Irish have a curious idea of what England is like, of what England is. As in an article called 'Joxer in Devon', appearing in number thirteen of the quarterly, *Irish Writing*, written by Denis Johnston, author of *The Moon in the Yellow River*, *A Bride for the Unicorn*, and other plays, who was a bright young thing for a time in Dublin, and who had the oh-inspiring experience of being educated in Dublin, Edinburgh, Cambridge, and Harvard. He musta missed Cardiff. Selected for one of a number of broadcasts on Living Writers, Denis Johnston came to Totnes to see and to build up what he would say about this living author and his work. He said some curious things. Attention! Sit at ease! Sensitive of talking about himself, Sean chatted of many Dublin things, including the Gate Theatre, of which Denis Johnston had been a Director. Ah, the Gate Theatre? He seemed to be tired of the Gate, for he talked of it in a tired way, as if it were to him but the acrid dust of fireworks that had gone up the night before to make a dark sky falsely gorgeous, to spray the dark sky with fictitious gauds. Each production was as it were a trooping of the colours. They tired one in and tired one out. Most things were done in a tiring, caparisoned rush. MacLiamhoir was getting tiresome, too, in that he still wanted to do the parts of young and handsome laddies, though years had rubbed his bloom away, and a fattening chin had hidden the dear reflection of redolent youth that had stood before the back curtain of age when life was younger. Ah, me, we all diminish when the musk departs from the rose.

The visitor's eye-glance wandered round, and stopped to gaze at two pictures in the hallway, one a Giorgione, the other a Gauguin. He asked whose they were, who had painted them. A shock for Sean! He had thought that the visitor and his circle knew all there was to be known about painting; and as the picture, 'The Sleeping Venus', was one of Big George of Castelfranco's best-known paintings, it came as a swift surprise that the visitor neither knew the picture nor the name of the man who had painted it. The glance then moved to Gauguin's picture: from Gauguin to Giorgione, and back again to Gauguin. Where was that one done? Who did that? Gauguin? Oh, yes, of course — Gauguin. He had got it at last. A new discovery. No glance at the other pictures hanging on the same or the opposite wall — Cézanne's 'Boy in the Red Waistcoat', nor at the lovely golden browns and gentle greens of Simone Martini's 'Angel of the Annunciation', nor at the lovely water-colour by a young Welsh artist, 'Hydrangeas', before which Augustus John himself had stood, looking long at it before he murmured 'That is beautiful'; no glance at the striking portrait of Sean himself by John, or the other John, 'Head of a Gitana', an inch or two from the visitor's nose, a picture exquisite in its delicacy of colouring, its calmness of pose, its quiet lyricism singing of the charm of a beautiful girl. He was interested in art only for what a few pictures might give him to say about his host. This picture by Giorgione, that by Gauguin, fitted him out for the statement in his broadcast of O'Casey's comical attachment to painting, and the epiphany of the man within it. 'O'Casey', he said in his broadcast, 'declared himself by living with these two pictures in the same room.' Denis Johnston must have felt really ill by having to sit for hours in a room where Giorgione and Gauguin almost shook hands with each other. Sat there, pale and white and cold as snow.

Though silent about his own particular selection, the visitor probably thought that it was Gauguin who should go.

It's Gauguin who should go; well, he's the one should know.
It's without grace, it's out of place —
It's Gauguin who should go.

Brightness and boldness frighten the souls of the precious ponderers. The bright scarlet, the purple, the blue-black, the lemon-yellow, and the grand green, afflict the suave-swooning minds of the aesthetic toffs. The fervent way in which Gauguin shows the life of a primitive people in ceremonial form, in impudent line, in vivid colour, irritates the lordly ones as if sand had got into their souls. How beautiful they are, these lordly ones; how beautiful! The swan is their one bird. All other birds are crows to them.

Well, Denis Johnston came to Totnes to gather manna of atmosphere for his talk, and, after staying in it as long as it would take a swift bird to fly over the town, this is what he says about it:

The little Devon town of Totnes is about as English as they come. In decorous bus queues the gloomy housewives stand with baskets on their arms. Odd spectacle of Ireland's only living dramatist with an international repute buried in one of the more arty-crafty corners of England. O'Casey looks a little out of place in these surroundings, and the housewives are inclined to stare after him as he walks by in his cap and his jersey, with a Red Army badge displayed in his buttonhole. The better-informed ones know that it is just another inoffensive literary gent, and they pass the word along — that's Sean O'Casey.

Now Devon is almost all a Keltic County, founded by a Keltic tribe, which gave its name to the county, a tribe that came over long before the gallant Gaels came sailing over the sea to Eirinn, which can be confirmed if Denis Johnston reads O'Rahilly's *Early Irish History and Mythology*. Another branch of this tribe gave its name to Cornwall. In other ways, Devon tells us the story of her Keltic origin. It is still tinted with the tantalising thoughts of fairy lore. The pishgies or pixies of Devon are brothers to the Gaelic shidhe. They do the same curious things — stealing babes from cradles and leaving changelings in their place; misleading travellers in the dark; galloping wildly about on the moorland ponies, a minor manner of the Irish pooka. At times they do good things, threshing a farmer's corn for him; but they must be watched, and food, fresh and tasty, must be left for them on the farmhouse floor. A Devon dairy-farmer, well known to Sean, told him how he had been spellbound one night to the floor of his cattle-shed; how he was surrounded by the pressure of influences hateful and mischievous. He couldn't see but he saw them; couldn't feel, but he felt them; couldn't hear, but he heard them. The flame of his lantern had flickered, gone out, and he stood, stiff and motionless, mid the hot smell from his cattle, his body shivering in the steady trickle of a chilling sweat, his mind trying to move him to the door, his body refusing to stir, so power-less that he couldn't even stretch forth a hand to touch the homely, reassuring body of a cow for comfort, the spiteful influence of some evil thing passing and repassing through him as he stood terrified, body and spirit shaken by the evil influence befouling the byre.

Another farmer told Sean that he had been beset in a contrary way. He had worked in a field all day, and was leaving it in the darkening dusk, but couldn't find the gate that led from the field to the road. He searched where he knew it to be, but it wasn't there; he searched where it might be, but it wasn't there either; he quickened his steps to the quicker beat of his heart, and trotted round the wide field, but saw no sign of a gate, anywhere; anywhere; and the dark-ness deepened so that he ran round and round the field, probing the hedge here, probing the hedge there; but his fingers touched thorns, the needle-like points of holly leaves, and there was silence every-where so that the panting of his breast was loud in his ears, coming slower and slower as his legs grew weary, sagging down towards the earth, till he fell down and lay there, fell down flat and lay there still; lay there till the morning came, and they found him senseless, lying stretched out beside the very gate he had sought for throughout the night, in the darkness, under the stars.

As Ireland isn't anything as Irish as some Gaels make her out to be, so England isn't so English as many Irish think her to be. Half of England, and maybe more, is as Keltic as Ireland herself. Let Denis Johnston listen to the pipe-playing and folk-singing of Northumberland, or to the Cumberland farmers still counting their sheep close to the way the people of Ballyvourney number their scanty flocks. Let him listen any night to 'Dance Them Around' (if folk-custom and folk-song be not too lowly for the beautiful and lordly ones); their band is as Irish as any Ceilidh band in any country town of Ireland. The old songs are neglected and half-forgotten today, and are no longer commonly sung in cottage or farmhouse, just as they are neglected and half-forgotten by Cahersiveen in Kerry and Cushendall in Antrim; though now there is a sleepy interest taken in holding fast to a folk-lore that had almost bidden a picturesque goodbye for ever to the common song a people loves to sing. In listening one night to a gathering in a village hall, near Leamington, in Warwickshire, Sean heard an old woman of seventy-four, the traditional singer of the locality, giving the audience 'Johnny, My Own True Love', just as he had heard his own mother sing it in the days of long ago. It was H. G. Wells who, through *Mr. Britling Sees It Through*, voiced delight in the fact that the bigger part of England's place-names had a Keltic origin; so, what with all this, with Wales by her side and Scotland over her head, adding the Irish and their descendants, England is really more Keltic than the kilt. The old name of London was Caer-Lud, city of Lugh of the Long Hand, and the city's name today is said to mean Fort of the Ships, as she, indeed, is to this day; Lydd in Kent reflects the name of the Irish Lugh, though the English of today regard the myth with indifference, as do the spiritual and imaginative Irish. Bud is the name now. Keltic echoes in myth and story and belief linger on in the countryside throughout Wiltshire, Somersetshire, Dorsetshire, Devon, and Gloucestershire, up as far as, and beyond, Northampton-shire, for

> If ever you at Bosworth would be found,
> Then turn your cloaks, for this is fairy ground.

Over the border, a few short miles away, is Cornwall, packed with the Keltic daylight, with its Derrydown, its Kelly's Round, its Doloe, meaning two lakes. Here are the Hurlers, remains of stone circles, called this name because certain Cornishmen persisted in hurling on Sunday; here are beehive huts, holywells, and all the glamorous clutter left by a receding past. It is recorded that a hundred years ago, West Ireland (Ireland herself) used to play hurley yearly against East Ireland, comprising the counties of Devon and Cornwall. Even the story in T. C. Murray's play, *The Wolf*, had its origin in a Cornish town. Yet another link was that of wrestling, or wrastling, as it was called in Dublin; left hand gripping the shoulder of an opponent, right one gripping his hip. Cornishmen wrestled in their socks, as did the Irish; the Devonmen in their boots, made as hard as craft could make them. The reward for an Irish wrestling champion was a coloured garter worn round the right leg below the knee. Each Sunday, a champion stood out on a green sward in the Phoenix Park, his trouser leg tucked up to show the gaudy garter, and challenged any among those who crowded round him. Sean's own brother, Michael, wore a garter for a year. The Cornish and Devonian prize was either a silver-plated belt or a gold-laced hat, either of which, earlier on, exempted a wearer from being forced into the Navy.

There are some curious remarks hung out to dry in Johnston's article. He says, 'One gathers from some of the sourer pages that O'Casey never felt comfortable in Merrion Square, especially when it was trying to be civil to him'. How nice! Merrion Square, the G.H.Q. of Irish civility. Stirring itself up to be specially civil to him. Sit ye down, an' I'll thrate ye dacent; dhrink up, boy, an' I'll fill your can. Oh, how nice! Well, the fact is that O'Casey never had the chance of feeling comfortable or uncomfortable in the houses of Merrion Square. During his whole life in Dublin, he had been in only one house there — the house of Yeats; and then felt uncomfortable but once, when he talked to the great poet in a terribly over-heated room, while the songs of a hundred golden canaries in a golden cage shattered the harmony of his hearing. Another remark of Mr. Johnston's: 'O'Casey has a profound and deeply-rooted resentment for Yeats, in spite of the poet's efforts to help him'. Really? Well, O'Casey has already written of The Radical Club, formed to try to tumble Yeats off his pedestal, a Club which O'Casey refused to join. But there is more: The Gate Theatre for a long time had a hope that it would scrape the gilt off the Abbey's fame, and, by so doing, take a cubit or two from Yeats's stature. Yeats was too high for the most of them to think of anything but a downfall. The two theatres were rivals in the lights of night; the Gate stood envious of the other's fame.

Another attempt to hurt Yeats, touching Denis Johnston, oddly enough, for he was a Director of the Gate, was that the theatre, by Hilton Edwards, wrote to Sean asking him to give them *The Silver*

Tassie, saying that 'While they thought the play a bad one, it would do good business on account of the row raging because of the Abbey's rejection of the play'. Oh very nice nice oh yes indeed yes very nice indeed. Kill two birds with the one stone — do good business and hurt the Abbey. Though indeed the royalties, even from the Gate, would have been something of a godsend at the time, the request was refused, Sean writing back to say that he was surprised that the Gate Theatre should wish to produce a play they were sure was a bad one. Another incident touching O'Casey's attitude towards Yeats nearer still occurred at the first production of Mr. Johnston's own *Bride for the Unicorn* in the Gate Theatre: Yeats, who was present, rose from his seat during the progress of the play, and walked out of the theatre, part of the audience turning to boo him as he passed them by. Various reasons were given for this action of Yeats, and the poet told Sean himself, afterwards, that he had done so because he thought the production an atrocious one. A few days after the incident Sean got a letter from the lady editor of the Gate Theatre's occasional magazine, an imitation of the Abbey's earlier issues of *Bealtaine*. The letter called upon him, with an air of angry enthusiasm, to denounce as ridiculous the conduct of Yeats. O'Casey's reply must have been disappointing, for it was a loud and blunt refusal to do what was asked of him; so disappointing that the letter of refusal never got no answer; not a line, not a single word.

Mr. Johnston seems disturbed because O'Casey got on with Lady Gregory. He didn't, apparently, and was more uncomfortable with her than O'Casey was in Merrion Square. He didn't catch on; the old tilted head always looked past him. She said no too often. Perhaps she didn't set herself out to be civil to him, even though he was so familiar, oh so familiar, with Merrion Square. The credential wasn't good enough. Oliver Gogarty was another that couldn't cotton on to the old lady for some reason. Even though he was a great friend of Yeats, the old lady's greeting to him was always a hail and farewell; and Gogarty often referred to her as 'that old hake'. Had he called her an old hawk, he would have been nearer the mark, for whenever a difficulty loomed up before her, or before the Abbey Theatre, she went towards it, head thrust out, beak thrust forwards, lips tight, in a quick pounce to set the difficulty aside, or knock it down, and pass over it; the head straight up now, the splendid old face smiling. And in it all, and through it all, she always chose her own wild swans.

The brother of good counsel. He tells O'Casey how he should feel — 'one wonders whether O'Casey hasn't lost the compassion he once had for his fellow-men' — what pictures to hang on the wall, and points out a place where he oughtn't to live. Totnes doesn't suit him, where the housewives stand to stare after him. Well, they don't stand to stare, but stand to talk, for he knows most of them well, and a lot of their children, too. Johnston knows a lot less about the town than he does about a Dainty Tea. Bad and all as Johnston thinks Totnes to be for O'Casey, it has allowed him to write five major plays, three one-act plays, and five volumes of biography. No, Mr. Johnston isn't such a good brother of good counsel after all. The cuckoo's song and the rainbow sometimes come together.

There is nothing sham about Totnes. Next to London, it is the oldest borough in England. All its 'shoppes' are genuine examples of Tudor or Jacobean housing; not in any way so splendid as those found in Conway or Shrewsbury, but as genuine all the same. Neither is there anything 'arty-crafty' about from the bottom to the top of its hill. The housewives who stand in the queues are far from 'gloomy'; they haven't time to be, for they are too busy with the things of life. And there are many Irish incidentals about Totnes: the caretaker of the Drill Hall was a Tipperary woman; the owner of a café was another, but now has one in Stoke Gabriel, a few short miles away; the plasterer who pasted up new ceilings in the O'Casey house, brought down by bomb concussion, came from Roscommon; the parish priest and the O'Casey family doctor are Dublinmen. The one post-woman Totnes had, during the war, came from Tipperary, too. A few miles away, in Brixham, a statue of King Billy stands on the quay, and like Dublin's old figure, has twice been given a contemptuous coat of football-coloured paint. O'Casey is as relevant in Totnes as he would be in Navan or Kells, and more so than in Dublin now; and Johnston's article is pertly and partly proof of it.

Totnes is about the size of Mullingar, but busier, wealthier, and much more lively. Apart from the quiet hurry of market day, gentleness is the first quality to give to it; gentleness in its buildings, and in the coming and going of its people; and in the slow, winding, winding of the River Dart from the moor to the sea. Oh, lord, the natural lie of it is lovely. Except when visitors pour in during the brief summer, the town is so quiet that it looks like a grey-haired lady, with a young face, sitting calm, hands in lap, unmindful of time, in an orchard of ageing trees, drowsy with the scent of ripened apples about to fall, but which never do; hearing echoes of her own voice in the laughing play of children; or in the whispers of that lover and his lass seeking out some corner of the drowsing orchard that is free from any entanglement of time, care, thought, or casual interference.

Though getting some ready money from summer visitors, the town, like so many Irish ones, depends mainly on the farming communities surrounding it. So the eyes of all often scan the sky — not to see the reality of the sensuous enjoyment of its beauty shown by a Constable, a Ruisdael, or a Turner; but to judge the coming weather, for their livelihood depends on it. In a rainy season, they look for a sign of the sun; in times of undue heat, to catch sight of a hidden cloud. Cattle, sheep, poultry, and crops depend largely on what the sky gives; so, when the sun wears his welcome out, or the rain falls too fulsomely on the land, all eyes search the sky for the chance of a coming change.

An old town, stretching out from Lugh of the Long Hand to Winston Churchill and Clement Attlee, a coming together of a strange god and odd men. Years later, it is said, the Romans came clanking along with spear, short sword, and pilum, the time Julius Caesar was mapping out the way the world should go; but it is doubtful if the Romans pierced farther than Exeter, and, held back by the fighting Kelts, ever had a chance to cool their tired and sweating bodies in the waters of the Dart. Fact or fancy, Totnes is a very ancient borough, stuffed with potent parchments signed by kings and princes, giving it a gorgeous right to live. Ancient, too, are its narrow streets, once fitting well the knight's charger, the lady's palfrey, the abbot's mule, and the peasant's cart; now altogether too lean to enclose comfortably the fleet of horning motor-cars and the clattering lorries that shove and push a stammering way through them. Ancient, with its old butterwalk, its guildhall, its Saxon castle, its red-stone church, so commingling with the past that a reminiscent mind might see again an abbot on a mule, padding up the street to a priory, an armoured knight on his war-horse, followed by a squire, the knight carrying on his shield the red rose of Lancaster or the White Hart of the Hollands; or a velvet-skirted damsel or dame on a palfrey trotting through the old archway that was once a town-gate. But no more shall be seen the casqued horseman clattering up the slope to the mouldering castle, a blood-red cross on his surcoat, the head of a poor paynim at his saddle-bow, slain before the walls of Jerusalem the golden; the knight chaunting a merry strain in a merry-hearted mood:

Where I did slay of Saracens
And Haythin pagans many a man;
And slewe the Souldan's cousin deere,
Who had the name doughty Couldran.

The pageantry of banner, banneret, and trumpet, appears suddenly
on occasions in a new way, as when band and banner heralded
Victory Day, and at night, from the Market, began a torchlight
procession of excited relief and thanks, a gathering of the Devon
clans, and a truly moving picture as the procession wended a
flaming way down the hill of the town to the level of a green field.
In this array of light the O'Caseys' little girl of six carried a torch,
innocently honouring the gallant dead who had died that she might
live and sleep unharmed, and grow confidently into a fuller knowledge of life, with all her other thousand sisters and brothers of
Devon's red soil and tor and moorland; the gallant dead who had
put our feet into the way of peace again.

In Devon, many of the women and men never seem to grow old;
they keep going till they skip off for ever. They skip through the
hours till the very last hour of all; though in the hour of middle-age,
they skip more cautiously. The West Country people are human,
talkative, and tolerant; seeming slow to city people, but they work
harder and quicker than any city artisan or labourer. Many work
far too hard and far too long; for, like country people in Ireland,
they are too anxious to lay up for themselves treasure, not in heaven,
but, more safely, in the banks; reminding one of Joyce's sleepy
remark in *Finnegans Wake*:

Anno Domini Nostri Sancti Jesu Christi.
Nine hundred and ninety-nine million pounds sterling in the
blue-black bowels of the Bank of Ulster.

Standing on the top of the hill that carries Totnes so lightly on
its back and shoulders, a lot of what is fine can be seen in the county
of Devon. Overhead, often, a rich blue sky, touched with leisurely
clouds reluctant to leave the silky splendour of their blue bed, though
in winter that same sky can glower grey or glitter with the threat
of a piercing frost. Occasionally, higher than the white clouds, the
dark shadow of a buzzard sails across the sky on wings that never
seem to fly, satisfied with his own rare company. Hidden to the
east lies Torquay, stretching herself languorously, letting herself be
fondled by a soothing sea; a dwelling-place where many who are
old and well-off live, some sick and resentful, trying to imagine they

hear in the sad notes of the Last Post the stirring call of a new Reveille. Away to the west is Plymouth, a fair part of it bloodily scooped away by war; but definite still and as alive as ever; where Drake set foot on his rocking ship to sail out to shatter the bombastic shadow and substance of Spain's Armada, and so disperse the glowing dream of John of Austria, after the Duke himself withdrew from the coloured shadow-play of life. Newly ploughed fields of red earth, spreading out in a view as wide as the eye can cover, aglow with their differing hues, from reddish-purple, reddish-brown, to what seems to be a vivid crimson, separated here and there by squares and diagonals of a green as rich and velvety as the red, a sight to be wondered at and loved. Oh, the Devon people have a beautiful carpet under their feet. Through the crimson, maroon, golden-brown, and green goes the River Dart, binding the colours together with a ribbon of silvery loveliness, awakening in the sight-seer the desire to wait, to linger, and to look on the common clay, and feel how wonderful common things may be.

Though few of the farmers, shopkeepers, or labourers bother about literature or art, rarely thinking of them, or even dreaming about them, Devon is never without a sign that the body and its needs are not all. The other day a farmer visited Sean; he was in a lather of sweat, for he had just helped a brother to gather in the hay from a ten-acre field while the sun shone hot; and, while he talked of the hay and its value, he also talked of his lovely rows of purple, yellow, white, and scarlet sweet peas that were worth nothing beyond the beauty of their bloom and fragrance of their perfume. Though every garden be set aside to grow the things the body needs, there is always a spot there dedicated to a creamy rose or a crimson one. There they are by the fence, beside the door, the creamy and the scarlet roses, showing that Devon, however mindful of the needs of the body, never forgets the beauty of the rose of sharon and the lilies of the valley.

THE DREE DAMES

It was a glorious afternoon of a day tinting a dying June with joy. He sat alone in what was called the sitting-room. The family had gone to swim and jump about in the kindly, sparkling waves of Torbay. He sat in the bulge of the bow-window, an elbow resting on a fumed-oak table that he had laid for tea while he waited for the kettle to boil. He sat sideways, one eye turned towards the garden, the other taking in the rest of the room containing, as Eileen so often said, all the family's respectable pieces, all hers; pieces she had brought from her flat to the new home they had sorted out after their marriage. Not much in it, indeed, but her hand and eye had made it graceful and pleasant to sit in. A deep, bright-brown carpet warmed the floor, stretching itself out with a strain, but failing to come within two feet of the surrounding walls. They hadn't had enough money to allow a carpet to touch the walls; but Eileen had herself darkened the intervening space with a rich walnut stain, and its dark, defiant glistening made the carpet feel richer than it was. A square-backed, square-sided couch and armchair, clad in deep-brown velvet corduroy, faced the hearth, which was brightened by a pale-brown rug, ornamented with geometrical patterns in darker brown, white, and black; all wearing the honest badge of age and use. On a round table, the top of one piece, silken-surfaced and rimmed with walnut, supported by diagonal panels filled with books, lay a wide, shallow bowl of deep yellow, gaily rimmed with coloured patterns resembling the spiral ornamentation of the older Kelts, a wedding-present from Doctor Cummins to Eileen; and on a rose-wood china-cabinet stood the head and shoulders of a young and slender woman, deep in meditation, or breathless with adoration, done in grey-blue porcelain; a mantle covering the bending head and falling down over the shoulders so that the gentle face was half hidden in a niche of drapery: a graceful piece of work so serene, so wrapped in thought that catholic visitors always took the figure to be a symbol of the Blessed Virgin. The Lady of whom an old-time praiser has said that only once has she wrought a miracle of stern justice rather than an act of mercy, when she sent Saint Mercurius to pierce Julian the Apostate with his lance. Pig sticking. But there were other instances of stern justice recorded then, and more in modern times, such as that meted out to three Communard soldiers, who, in a burst of derision, according to a widely read catholic journal, *The Messenger*, fired at a wooden statue of hers, one shooting it through the head, another through the belly, and a third through the heart. That same night, that very same silent night, when all was hushed, a holy priest passing by in the holy night underneath the gaslight glitter of the moon, hurrying home after a quick one, like Chesterton, found them, the three of them, stretched out dead to the living world. And when he came close, through the holy night, and looked closer, he saw, by the light of the loitering moon, that one had a bullet-hole in his head, another, one in his belly, and the third, a bullet-hole through his breast. A sudden flash of lightning from Erewhon made the holy man shiver as it went through him, in at his feet and out by his head, explaining all that had happened as it whirled by, and causing the holy man to murmur piously as he returned to the Everlasting Man for another quick one, Good hunting, oh mighty peers of light effulgent; damned good hunting!

On a higher level, flanking the quiet comeliness of the blue-grey figure, its porcelain shining like watered silk subdued by time, stood a deep-green glass vase filled with the gay loveliness of Cornish anemones. Facing the bow-window stood a Bechstein piano, Eileen's pet property, for touching things musical, Sean hadn't brought into the home as much as a mouth-organ: all Eileen's, for even the table at which he worked had been Eileen's before they were married. On the walls were a Segonzac print, a tiny figure of a man walking along a path through an avenue of towering trees; Van Gogh's 'White Roses' over the fireplace; a lovely water-colour of blue hydrangeas by a young Welsh artist; a tenderly beautiful picture of a Gitana by John; and the same artist's portrait of Sean, the mouth tight closed in a quiver, the face tense, and the eyes seeming to shrink away back from what they may have seen; the dim blues and grey-greens of the picture festivalled with a splash of orange from a handkerchief flowing from the breast pocket of the coat. A kingly present from a kingly man.

So here Sean was sitting in the midst of good things, of grace and quiet charm brought to him by the imagination and sensible selection of his wife; here he sat in close touch with art, literature, and music encased in simple serenity of colour and line and form — as every human being ought to be in hours of leisure; for the young beginning life; for the old ending it. Though security for the future was no nearer to him, yet it would come, too, within the conquest of the people desiring and demanding it, till good things and serene security impregnated and sanctified the life of every human family.

He waited for the tea to brew strong. He sat down to conjure his thoughts into changing images and sprinkle a few glinting spangles on experiences; but he couldn't do it. His mind was vexed and wonderful with the thoughts of a poet, Hugh MacDiarmid, set down in *To Circumjack Cencrastus* and his *A Drunk Man Looks at the Thistle*, books of new thought, daring, and lyrical with fine songs.

Lord God, this fellow is a poet, singing a song even when pain seizes him, or the woe of the world murmurs in his heart. Evidently a scholar, too, knowing Latin and languages, with philosophies from Christ's to that of Nietzsche housed comfortably in his head. He wrote in the Scottish manner, adding riches to the rich music of the Lallans. His verse tore along like a flood through a gorge, bubble, foam, and spray flying from the deep rushing stream. Or like a torch flaming many-coloured, red, purple, jet-black, and through each *a white light like a silence.*

The tea wasn't too good. He'd leave it a while longer to draw better. He hadn't much faith in cosies to give tea a bite. This one was plain brown with a stylised scarlet rose on one side of it so that it looked like a Franciscan friar saying an Ave Maria silently, with the impudent red of a rosette of Revolution impaled in the breast of his homely habit.

> *To think nae thocht that's e'er been thocht afore*
> *And nane, that's no' worth mair than a' that ha'e.*

MacDiarmid, you sling a tough task in the poet's way! However hard and long we think; however bold we be; however fine we write, it's hard to say more than a bare amen to all that's said afore. But you have tried, and, to me, have done it often and done it well; have scrawled many a phrase for Scotland *On the palimpsest o' th' Infinite.* Many a fine phrase. Well in the midst of men's life, of their endeavours, you have shown well that

> *Better's a'e gowden lyric*
> *Than Insurance, Bankin' an' Law.*
> *Better's a'e gowden lyric*
> *Than the Castle's soarin' wa';*
> *Better's a'e gowden lyric*
> *Than onything else ava!*

Than onything else ava. I'm at your side, a mhic o. A gowden lyric's near a thing eternal. Golden lads and girls all must, like chimney-sweepers, come to dust. Ay, indeed; and all the little things we cherish; all the ecstasies and tempests of the soul; all the high hammering out in our minds of wisdom's way; all the pearly prosody of love; in each man's soul, in each man's mind, in each man's way, must go; must die, and come to dust; even the maker himself slinks into dust; some woefu' day. All but the gowden lyric.

Then there's the Tamashanterian joy, wild, relentless, and gay, of his *A Drunk Man Looks at the Thistle,* a many-hued pavilion of verse. Here the gurly thistle is made to grow till it opens out into the gigantic chrysanthemum of Strindberg's play; its jaggy stems and splendid plume are made to grow bigger still and higher yet into a Scottish pine like unto an Yggdrassilian-tree with its roots firm to the good earth's centre, and its higher branches tripping up the angels running about in heaven. And down, down we go in pride and purple postulation, dragging our feet, our souls full with fidgets of shame as we hear him sing out the bitter lonely lament for the failure of the General Strike:

> *I saw a rose come loupin' oot*
> *Frae a camsteerie plant . . .*
> *A rose loupt oot and grew, until*
> *It was ten times the size*
> *O' ony rose the thistle afore*
> *Had heistit to the skies.*

It rose high, then came down 'like the stick from a spent rocket'. It fell here; it rises higher elsewhere. What an odd contrast, starry-wide, lies between T. S. Eliot and this Hugh MacDiarmid! Both are scholars, both are gowden poets; and there the likeness ends. One so cool, the other so passionate. The one, apparently, seeing little of God's countenance in man's mind; the other seeing in man's mind the one way to get to God. T. S. Eliot coasting through a mean or meaner street, indifferently cynical, amenable only to thoughts outside a figure in a doorway, or a face at a window: a poet apropos; the other a part in sympathy even of the vennel's pokiness; unafraid (feeling them even in his own) of the tired limbs and hardened hands of the struggling people:

> *Whaur a' the white-weshed cottons lie;*
> *The Inn's sign blinters in the mochiness,*
> *And lood and shrill the bairnies cry.*

And for a' Eliot's fine philosophy, MacDiarmid's philosophy goes deeper; is braver, and questions man and questions God; challenging the licht said to licht every soul venturing into life; challenging darkness, too.

> *'Let there be Licht', said God, and there was*
> *A little; but He lacked the poo'er*
> *To licht up mair than pairt of space at aince.*
> *And there is lots o' darkness that's the same*
> *As gin He'd never spoken.*

There is resentment in MacDiarmid's Gloria, Eliot's is always disconsolate and desolate; but in the poetry of the Scot, even through its sadness, the shepherd's piping of terli terlow is always clearly sounding.

Sean could easily see MacDiarmid in an evening suit, one or two of the concise creases annulled, maybe, by carelessness; but still trim in it, and handsome, too; and he could see him, as well, in hodden grey, at home with those who have none else; but never T. S. Eliot in the hodden grey. Pity at times the poet does not wear the hodden grey and hob-nailed boot. When this poet traverses *Streets that follow like a tedious argument*, and *Watched the smoke that rises from the pipes of lonely men in shirt sleeves, leaning out of windows*, he never stirs his sympathetic, supercilious mouth to call out even once, What cheer,' me buddies. Yet these may have been some of those who built the home he lives in; carted the coal that gives the heat to warm him; brought to his door the food that keeps him living. And these same images of God, shirt-sleeved and smoking, may, for all we know, be thinking of Shakespeare's native woodnotes wild; or of a daughter freshly married; or of a son lost in a war; or may be solving the mathematical problem of a football pool; if it be the last, though we shrink from the lowly mathematical mind, let us not wander away from his usefulness to life. But few would refuse to be moved by the graceful choice of words by the poet, and the stabbing effect of his images. Would he could show favour to those grimy ones whose minds come no closer than the garment's hem!

Sean had no learning, no knowledge, no instinctive gift, to warrant him to place his hands on men, and say, This man to be a deaconis, this a presbytyr, this one to be an episcopus of poetry. What he set down were but his feelings moulded into words; there they were, and there they'd stay. For the one, whom he had met, as gurly, at times, as the thistle he sang of, he had a strong love; for the other, the elegant rose, whom he had never met, he had a sincere affection; for both, reverence.

In his play, *The Rock*, T. S. Eliot conjures up a church entirely built with hands, though set, quite snug, epergnel in an anglican heaven. Apart from his own chosen words and sparkling phrases, the church he builds is one of wicker-work and moth-eaten canvas. In sentiment and exhortation, the play is a religious dumpling. If ever there was a play about what is called 'religion', to prove that 'religion is the dope of the workers', this is the one; and not Eliot, but his helpers are largely to blame. It is odd that apart from shadowy bishops and an abbot chattering in Latin, there is but one clerical character in the play, a bishop who 'comes in briskly' like Blomfield Bonnington of Shaw's play; and smatters the readers with the dullest dialogue ever donated in poem, play, or novel to any cleric. Yet an odd admission is made by this blowsy bishop who thought of heaven in terms of stone slab, brick, and mortar. The spiritual tenor of the play is the necessity to preserve medieval manners against modern morals; yet, when the workmen complain about the severity of the work before them, he reminds them that 'Men have mechanical devices today that we never dreamed of'! Devices, mind you! Bishop Chasuble watches the bulldozer advancing the kingdom of God. Then Bishop Blomfield Bonnington adds the Crusaders as an example of what 'a few men of principle and conviction can accomplish'! Accomplish! When do would do. Men of principle and conviction! When Christian Venice was more anxious for the destruction of her Christian trade rival, Constantinople, than she was for the liberation of the Holy Places from the Infidels! What good did the Crusade do bar learn the holy Christians a little of the art of cleanliness from the Arabian Knights?

But worse goes before and far worse is to follow. In the preface to the play, Mr. Eliot says 'The Rev. Vincent Howsom has so completely rewritten, amplified and condensed the dialogue between himself (Bert) and his mates that he deserves the title of joint author'. A rascally and conceited interjection. The characters of Ethelbert, Alfred, and Edwin, the workers, are so ridiculously done; are such fakes of pretence and pious posing that one can but throw back the head and give a long and loud guffaw. How sweet to, and familiar with, the workers is this fellow, Howsom! To the workers, of course, who are sweet to him. Here, let me do it, Sean can hear him saying to Eliot; I'll show you what the workers do, what they say, and how they say it. And How! Some dialogue! He even brings on an 'Agitator', and shows us how *he* goes on. Did poet or dialogian never meet and eat with an 'Agitator'? Did either never say 'hello' to Keir Hardie who brought coal dust on his boots to the Commons' carpet; Tom Mann, Bob Smillie, Jim Larkin, Bill McKie, who organised the workers of Ford's Detroit, or Jim Connolly? Pity, pity, they never did. Though Eliot hasn't been chosen, maybe not even called, he would have led the workers in the play nearer God with a song anyway, and would have added dignity to the way the song was sung. Yet how could he sing such a song, when, seemingly, he senses death even in the birth of Bethlehem?

The whole play's about building, yet Sean would nearly swear that neither of them could tell the difference between a bricklayer's trowel and a mason's or a pavior's float; between a Flemish and an English bond; between even a header and a stretcher; or between a straight-edge and a template. He'd swear that neither of them ever saw slaked lime and sand banked together to make the common mortar, or putty run to make that for the finer plastering. He'd say that neither of them ever slung a shovelful of clay from a foundation trench; shouldered a pole for a standard or a ledger, tied a rope to fix one to the other, or to a putlock fixed into the wall; he'd say that neither of them ever even sledged a stone to bring it within the compass of a mason's hammer. All these things wouldn't matter so much if the two creators of the play about building a church didn't set about to patronise the workers; to tell them what to say, how to act, and show them their duty to God, the higher clergy (the fisherman presenting a salmon to an Abbot — instead of snatching one from him), and the upper classes. The building of a church to the mason, bricklayer, carpenter, and labourer doesn't mean a chance to glorify God, but merely a chance to make a living; and the most of them today would rather be building a cinema. Under the way we live, all a building means to the builders is a job. Instead of singing a psalm, Sean could hear Ethelbert and his mates chorusing out

> Th' next who cam' in was a mason,
> A lad as strong as Jason;
> A lad as strong as Jason,
> To join our jolly crew.
> He rattled his trowel against th' wall,
> An' pray'd that churches an' chapels 'ud fall,
> For then there'd be work enough for all;
> When Bunker's Ale was new, me boys,
> When Bunker's Ale was new!

Bread and cheese was the goal of the workers in medieval times, as Geoffrey Coulton points out in his *Five Centuries of Religion*, and grub is the goal of the workers today; and no gem-stained thoughts about the Middle Ages can alter this fact. The right to work is the narrow gate through which alone the workers can enter the kingdom of earth. And who can claim a share in God who does not take the part of man? To Sean's mind, Hugh MacDiarmid makes far more of the Thistle as a symbol for God and man than T. S. Eliot does of the Rose of Sharon. MacDiarmid can rasp and tear the shams of life; but Eliot seems to rasp at life itself, looking at men as living only in so far as they have not yet been buried. Yet with all his well-fifed madrigals of death and desolution, Eliot longs after life. A glow from a warm heart takes the edge from the chilly, searching mind. He desires the people's redemption as we the commoners do: he through the Son of God; we through the sons of men. Let Lisbon-born Anthony of Padua thrill in his trance of self-adoration, kneeling in ecstasy. He has his reward, but not from men. They will hear and hearken and leap at the calling shout of a Garibaldi.

Sean struggled away from his contemplations, praying a kindly curse o' God on Hugh MacDiarmid and T. S. Eliot for forcing him to dwell on their work rather than on his own. To help an escape, he turned his head to look out of the window: there was the limited lawn, more hospitable to plantain, daisy, and dandelion than to grass. It was odd how dandelions adapted themselves to the frequent mowing that cut them down in their infancy; or to the throng of struggling, weedy life beneath the hedges. On the lawn, the dandelions flowered almost level with the ground, or from a tiny stem scarce an inch and a half high; while in the rowdy life beneath the hedges, they pushed and probed their way up through surly bramble, crowding nettle, tough coils of grasses, and buxom docks till on stems a foot and half long, and more, they breathed air, found the sun, and flowered. Up and up and on and on, climbing more steadily than poor MacDonald. In a corner of the hedge, an elder-bush spread about its frothy platter of waxy flowers. A sturdy plant, for hack it how you will, it grows again. One says this tree gave the wood to make the cross for Christ; another that Judas had his last look at the world from it when he dangled there to death. Strange uses for a single plant. In Ireland, Judas would have hanged himself from a sour apple-tree. God's creation: without Him was there nothing made that was made? The elder-tree and its elderberry wine. The dandelion? Medicinal properties. The thistle? Oh, here he was letting the damned thistle into his mind again! He'd stifle thought, and take his tea in peace and gorgeous quietude. He turned away from the window to begin it.

Jasus! Three middle-aged women were standing in the middle of the room, staring at him. Two of them he knew — a middle-aged lass, Donah Warrington, a writer herself, plump and grey-headed; and Mrs. Jen Jayes, a daring-say-nothing, sane secretary, a tall, gangly figure, with the best curve of the body as fluent as an arrow's head. Her head was fenced within a 'kerchief, worn peasant-wise; a face framed for frowning, though it could beam devotedly on anyone well in with the manor set on the hill. The stranger was tall, too, and gaunt; bonily built, the bony structure of the body showing itself more bonily off whenever the sweet lady moved a muscle. She wore no hat or 'kerchief, and the greying hair fell down to the shoulders in slender hanks, hanging untidily. Her face was pale, nay, very pale, and moist eyes peered out from behind wide horn-rimmed lenses. The face, strained into resolution, glared brazenly forward, straight at Sean. The middle-aged lass was dressed in a homely way; the woman sane-secretary as neatly as one would expect a secretary to be; and the figure from God knows where hid some of her gauntiness beneath a thick tweed dress; a sombre bodice filled itself with ripples as it flowed over the bonifying body (no disrespect here: Sean was a damned sight bonier himself); and a brown scarf knotted sideways round her neck gave the wearer half a bohemian, half a hiker look.

—This is Creda Stern, Sean, said Jen Jayes, beaming with grace, and indicating the gaunt lady. She has had a shocking time, and is trying to find a little rest with us up in Dartington. She insisted on coming down to see you before she left us. She insists that you should know the truth.

Sean murmured a howdydo, shook the bony, unpromising hand, while he wondered who was Creda Stern, and why the hell she forced a visit; and what truth she bore as a present for him. He fetched additional delf, poured out the tea, and handed round bread, butter, and jam. He hated these unexpected visits. He wished to retain the privilege of deciding who should come to see him and who should not. This annunciation of an earthly angel wasn't to his liking at all. Playing the hypocrite, he smiled and said it was a lovely day. He talked a little of Dartington and Devon, got a few smiling answers, though the visiting angel said never a word, contenting herself by glaring brazenly, straight at Sean.

—Creda has something important, very important, to say to you, Sean, said Jen Jayes, suddenly. She has the truth for you.

—Creda wants to tell you about her terrible experience, said Donah Warrington.

—Creda has suffered a cruel loss, said Jen. She feels you should know all about it.

—Irreparable, added Donah; and only because she stood for socialism and freedom of thought. Only when she herself told me could I believe it. It's a revelation.

—Creda has had to bear the loss of her husband; taken from her suddenly, without a charge; gone in a moment; taken away for ever, said Jen Jayes. Terrible!

—And where, and by whom! Creda startled Sean by springing up from her chair, and bending towards him, the bony figure glaring down at him sitting at the other side of the table. She was shouting now. Your Soviet Union! By the Ogpu! What do you think of that? I'm a Socialist, and I know; I was there. I know! The truth!

—Creda knows, murmured Jen Jayes.

—Creda saw it happen, murmured Donah Warrington.

—I was there, went Creda on, breathlessly; I and my husband held important positions in the Commitern on the Commissariats of Foreign Trade and Light Industries. I believed in them then. I don't now. She bent over closer to him, squalling, It was all a false dream!

—We all believed, murmured Jen Jayes; but it was all a false dream — Creda knows.

—My husband was taken away without word or sign. He vanished. That's the way it is there: millions in concentration camps. Grey faces everywhere afraid to look left or right, or even behind to anticipate a blow. All hungry, all in tatters — that's the way it is there. She banged the table with a violent fist. A false dream! Now, what do you think of your Soviet Union?

—Take it quietly, lady, advised Sean.

—Oh, do you hear him asking me to take it quietly! she appealed to the others. She turned again to Sean. I'm told you are all for the Soviet Union; that you still dream it is a Socialist country. Do you believe it now? Can you believe it now? Can you? Answer, man!

—Hardly, now, Creda, came a murmur from Donah Warrington. He couldn't now. He knows the truth at last.

—Lady, said Sean, softly, I have been a comrade to the Soviet Union for twenty-three years, and all she stands for in the way of Socialism, and I don't intend to break that bond for a few hasty remarks made by one who obviously hates the very bones of the Soviet people. And the more you shout, lady, the less I hear.

—He couldn't have been listening to me! Creda squealed to the other two. She stood straight up, then bent down again over him. You must listen to me, you must listen to me! I know the truth! Her voice tuned into the semblance of a howl. You can see, can't you, that my husband isn't here? Where is he then?

—That's the question, Sean, purred the voice of Jen Jayes: where's Creda's husband?

—I don't know the hell where he is! said Sean, sharply. He may be anywhere.

—I can't understand you, man! shouted Creda. No-one knows where he is. All that's known is that he was taken by the Ogpu. Can't you understand that? The Ogpu knows. One day he was with me; the next, and nothing was with me but silence. What do you think of your Soviet Union now?

—Well, apparently, silence didn't stay long with you either, said Sean. I've no evidence that he was taken by the Ogpu, he said, beyond your word. That isn't enough for me. Even if he were taken, there's no counter-evidence to show why; for even the Ogpu don't arrest people for the pure fun of the thing. And, if he behaved there as you are behaving here, I don't wonder he was removed as a potential dictator.

—Do you hear what he says? Creda's voice was near a snarl now. He calls one a dictator who fought for freedom all her life, and is doing it now. What singular, inhuman minds the Irish seem to have! She drew back, still bending, her hands resting on the table. Aren't you able to see the truth when it's put straight and clear in front of you? The voice now flew into a fuller snarl. I tell you, Irishman, the Nazis are far superior, and more to be preferred, than your savage comrades in Moscow! Do you hear me?

—I've heard you, lady, said Sean, quietly. You've just told me that the Socialism of the Soviet Union is not only the hope of the workers, but, also, the hope of the world.

Creda was astounded. She stood spellbound and silent for a few moments. Then she moved a little away from the table to hiss out in bitter and steady tones — I confess I can't understand the Irish mind; it is a twisted mind, and utterly irresponsible.

—Aha, said Sean, quickly, there you show your elemental nature. He indicated Donah Warrington. The mind of Mrs. Warrington is as Irish as mine, but to you it is a fine, straight, and honest mind, because that mind agrees with yours. Mine is a horrible mind because it doesn't.

Jasus, Creda was real angry now! She didn't like being caught. No-one does. In her angry face, hatred for Sean was mingled with hatred for the Soviet Union. She started towards the door, and the two other dames rose slowly, and made to follow her. Creda pulled her 'kerchief roughly around her neck till the knot lay in the right place under her chin. She clenched her bony hands, and turned towards him again, half-way to the door. The truth was going away.

—If I stayed here any longer, she said, I'd stifle; I'd stifle. Someone told me you were an intelligent man. She let out a squealing laugh. Intelligent! The fellow's a fool! It is such as you that are the cause of Socialism's failure in the Soviet Union; such as you are responsible for fear, for slavery, and the concentration camps. But your Soviet Union will go rotten. At the first assault on it, it will fall asunder like the rotten thing it is! Oh, I'd stifle if I stayed here longer! She went out, followed by the other two, and Sean, from the window, watched the dree fearsome, fearless dames go down the garden path where the hollyhocks nodded to them, and red, cream, and mauve dahlias whispered a word for beauty to them, but the dree dames passed on sourly, giving no sign by any pause that they felt colour and line and form touching the hems of their garments.

—Strange shadows, thought Sean, sometimes slide in to mar the serenity of a sunny day! What an arrogant mind, what a blustering manner, that woman had! The truth is mine. Some seem to think that truth comes banging at everybody's door. A mind that flushes into a rage whenever another ventures to disagree with it. Out for free thought, yet dragging compulsion into every word she uttered! Only what I say, only in what I believe, is the Truth. An individual authoritarian. Only her truth contained divinity. The way some hurl the truth about: down a man with it! Odd how she believed that she could just rush in and take his own little kingdom of thought by storm. She hadn't given a tittle of evidence to show that what she said had happened was a fact. If the way she had behaved before him was her common manner and method in social life, even in argumentative intercourse, he couldn't wonder that her husband had disappeared. Sean wished he could have disappeared himself: away, away from this rowdy truth. Better the peaceful passion of a lie.

It was comic, in a way, to think how many thought they carried Truth fast in the hollow of their hands. Ready to sell it, too, for a shout. Shout my shout, and you shout the truth. Truth becomes a town-crier. What is Truth? asked jesting Pilate; what is Truth? asked serious Sean; and either was as near to the other in knowing. Truth was rarely a visitor: one had to trudge a long way to find her; and, even when you got to where she was said to be, she was often not at home. She had gone on a voyage of discovery to find herself. Law and Order were out looking for her so that she might be put back safely in her comfortable cage. She could be honoured there; she could even be worshipped there; but there she would have to stay, for it wasn't safe to let her roam at large. It was far better that Truth should be cornered and kept safe from spreading falsehood about in the receptive minds of men. In her cage, she can look happily out on the world of men with safety to herself and satisfaction to them. Here, she is dressed up to the nines and introduced to the best people. At liberty, she has a nasty habit of stripping and going about nude, disturbing peaceable persons, and making them feel self-conscious. It is by no means a pleasant thing to meet this naked lady roamin' in the gloamin' where lay scribes and clerical pharisees are having a respectable and a quiet rest.

Some said that Truth could always be produced out of prayer. Prayer, before and after, could make everything done and said, right and proper and fair and good. Aha, now we have it: truth comes flying into the word said and into the action done. Like the judge of the high court, mentioned in the roman catholic *Universe*, who used to spend hours in prayer before giving a judgement, and always wore a crucifix under his robes. It's very simple, isn't it? The power of prayer. No chance of any mistake. It would solve everything. Imagine all the judges down on their knees a full hour before giving a judgement! Oh, the sight entrancing! Better still, imagine all the doctors down on their knees for an hour before prescribing; the proletariat down on their knees for an hour before dawn to fit themselves for a fair day's work; the employers down on their knees, at the same time, for an hour to fit themselves for giving a fair day's pay. A beautiful arrangement with a slow accompaniment on harps from high above, with sounds of cymbals softened. There's only one foul snag in it — it wouldn't work! The judges would go on giving judgement within the limits of the law, however unjust and un-righteous that law happened to be; the doctors would go on killing and curing in their old-fashioned way; the employers would go on believing they were giving too much; and the workers would go on believing they were getting too little.

What is Truth? Man in his individual nature was still asking the question, and man in the mass was answering it. Facts, though true, were not Truth; they were but minor facets of it. Parts, but not the whole. The great achievements of the Soviet Union; touching material possessions, deprived of all by one war, and most by another, having to start afresh twice with little more than a few flint hammers and a gapped sickle or two. The inexhaustible energy, the irresistible enthusiasm of their Socialistic efforts, were facts to Sean; grand facts, setting the people's feet firmly on the way to the whole truth, calling all men to a more secure destiny in which all heads shall be anointed with oil, and all cups shall be filled.

He looked at the garden's corner where the elder-tree grew; the tree that gave the wood to make a cross for Christ. *Genus Sambucus*, meaning, we are told, a musical instrument. How odd! Wood that can make a musical instrument can make a cross, too. Fifing was going on round the cross today, with prelates conducting — one two three, one two three; one two three four. Happy thing that the tree was so widespread, for much wood had been needed for the martyrdom of man. Every exploitation by one man, or by a bunch of men, of other men was a crucifixion. It was still being done; to the sound of fife and drum when good dividends were declared. A man exploiting himself for the good, for the charm, for the safety of others was a noble thing; a man exploiting man for the grin of gain was an evil thing. But the people are ending the evil. In spite of cowardice and selfishness hidden away under chasuble, cassock, and geneva gown; in spite of a swarm of encyclicals wormy with counsels saying sweet is bitter and bitter is sweet; the people are ending the evil. In the uprising of the peoples, the Spirit of God is once more moving over the face of the waters. No cross on which to hang a man shall ever be made again from the trunk of the elder-tree, or from any other wood. Neither shall a fire ever again be kindled against any man owning up to what fury calls a false religion. Adelphos, the brother; we are all from the same mother.

REBEL ORWELL

IN the midst of bombfalls, blackouts, and all the thrust and over-throw of war, the biographical books appeared, the third one making a pert bow to the public some time before the curtain fell on the tableau of the Nazi collapse, and war-weapons began to be piled before and around the heaps of ruins giving Europe and many parts of England a new skyline that rasped the serenity of the sun and mocked the gentle rain that fell from heaven. The book was titled *Drums Under the Windows*, and all the bum critics of Ireland filled the Irish air with hums, hems, and Hail Marys. Hugh Walpole once wrote that 'O'Casey is an uncomfortable writer', and the Irish critics gave the amen of He is So. So with fingers fidgeting with their beads some of them tried to do it grandly, bowler hat on head, kid glove on hand, elegant cane under an oxsther. Said one flushing critic: 'Honest indignation is one thing, and egotistical protestation another'. Another. Two things in fact. 'Egotistical protestation' is good. A swing of the cane and a touch to the bowler hat. Proceed, sir — we're all listening. 'This reader, approaching without any conscious prejudice, finds the mixture at times irritating, and, in the upshot, unremedial.' Mixture is bad; but still nice, and worthy of bowler hat and elegant cane. Upshot and downfall unremedial. That's sad. But the critic — there is nothing to show his identity — uses fine language, like a persilified white petticoat, dignified, and flavoured with lace. But he spoils it, spoils it, by rudely adding, 'What is the point of punning, or rather "narking" about with the name of a cardinal whom Mr. O'Casey thinks contemptible? Like abuse heard over the garden wall, one's natural impulse is to close the window so as to shut out the sound of it.' No, no; this is not so genteelly written as that which went before, the critic's frightened now. Shut the window! Keep out the sound and the sense! Shut the window! Bang! Gas attack. Let the cry be heard only by the empty street; let the cry be heard only by the passing wind. Shut the window!

A grave and reverend critic, through an article in the *Evening Mail*, a Dublin evening paper, came into Sean's presence, in a most masterly and magisterial manner, to say, 'If you, Mr. O'Casey, could only grasp the fact that vulgarity does not always connote strength, and that for narrative style James Joyce is an insidious and also enervating model, you might, some day, give us a great book which we would read with some advantage to our social education and less of the repulsive-reflex which you excite in us by your rather unnecessary reconstruction of unimportant experiences'. How's that for a rattling fine sentence! The Master speaking seriously to the man. Bow the head. Quite a gent of diction. If O'Casey only would listen!

But these were but comic squeaks compared with the agonised yell George Orwell let out of him when he sat down to read the book, and then stood up to review it. Lots have been written about the honesty, the integrity, the fearlessness, of Orwell. But he had an odd glamour: the farther away he was, the more one liked him; or so Koestler says, adding, 'Thus the greater the distance from intimacy and the wider the radius of the circle, the more warming became the radiations of this lonely man's great power of love'. Keep off! The same writer says of him again, 'He was incapable of self-love or self-pity. His ruthlessness towards himself was the key to his personality.' Bannered balderdash, for no man can be without feeling for himself till he be dead. Self-preservation was a first law of nature to Orwell as well as to all the sorts of men. And Orwell had quite a lot of feeling for himself; so much, that, dying, he wanted the living world to die with him. When he saw, when he felt, that the world wouldn't die with him, he turned the world's people into beasts; Orwell's book of beasts. Since that didn't satisfy his yearning ego, he prophetically destroyed world and people in Nineteen hundred and eighty-four: Doomsday Book. The decay in himself was, in his imagination, transmuted into the life of the whole world. Well, if that isn't self-pity, wrapped sourly up in yearned revenge, then nothing is. It seemed to comfort his ailing nature to believe that he was leaving a perishing world; a world that would soon ignobly and terribly die. He was a lordeen of Shalott who saw life in a mirror, not the lovely and coloured life the Lady saw, but the misshapen figures and manners born in his own ailing mind. He was wild that the world of men and women noticed him not, but went on fighting. They plunged forward into resolute hope, while he embedded himself deep in self-pitying despair; for Koestler himself tells us that 'Orwell's despair had a concrete, organised structure, as it were, and was projected from the individual to the social plane'. He yearned to drag all life down with himself into his own stony despair. Life dissolved, not even into amber, but into grey stone. Tried hard, too, to do it through the books he wrote; and he went wild to hear, in a muffled way, the sounds of life at work, and life's loud laughter a long way from it all. Koestler enthrones this poor wailer among the rebels, saying, 'His life was a consistent series of rebellions against the condition of society in general and his own predicament'. Rebel indeed! Rather a yielding blob that buried itself away from the problems of living that all life has to face and overcome. No fight in him; always a running away and a yielding. What did he rebel against? One can understand rebellion against his own predicament; but here even there was no resilient opposition to it; but rather a hugging of it and a hastening to places where it was bound to grow worse. As regards his rebellion against the condition of society, did he do a hand's turn to improve it? Rather, in desire and malignant prophecy, he tried to make it worse. The mass of the people never knew him while he lived; had never heard of him when his life had ended. He has been dumped beside Jonathan Swift, but Swift hasn't turned his head to look at him; for Swift was an intense star in Ireland's sky, while poor Orwell's pin-point of light hadn't even the power to point a way to where the greater star was blazing; Swift was known to all Dublin, and almost all of Dublin followed his body to the grave.

Koestler tells us that George Orwell was 'a dish-washer, a tramp, and a sergeant in the Burma police'. He was a dishwasher and a tramp and all! A pseudo-secular worker-priest. Probably never sang the bum-song in his life; the dishwashing tiring him in less than a week. One doesn't find experiences by seeking for them: they come naturally, according to the time, the place, and the conditions, or they don't come at all. He was a sergeant in the Burma police all right, for the sergeant's shout echoes strongly in a lot of his work; and, particularly, in the persistent egotism that all should think as he thought, or suffer for it. He was no rebel in his books, for in his ripest time there was a great mass of readers flourishing well within the context of despair, so that his thoughts floated far, and were gathered into a warm reception-room. Here, and in many other places, there was a concourse of kafka-koestlerian souls waiting to carry his books about on velvet cushions; so that, instead of making souls uncomfortable, he filled them up with gratification; all drooping in a sunny darkness of despair, ready, to all appearances, to pop into the rotten mouth of death. They were saying to the newly-born, Abandon hope ye who enter here; they were murdering life's little children in their beds.

Orwell's *Animal Farm*, hailed so heartily as a great original work, isn't so original in form or substance as the hearty hailers thought it to be. A similar tale appears the time the English language was beginning to be timidly lisped in a welter of French and Latin. It appears in a poem called *Vox Clamantis*, written by Gower when he was frightened near to death by the rising of the peasants led by Wat Tyler and John Ball. Gower tells of the crowd changed into beasts, asses fierce as lions, who will bear no more burdens, oxen who refuse to draw the plough, dogs who bark at huntsmen; all led by a Jay, representing Tyler, who harangues them, probing the air with shouts of Down with the honourables, Down with the Law! The Jay is killed, but the whole of life is left in disorder; there is a scene of whole-hearted corruption, though there is a beat in the poem of a hope higher than Orwell's despair; for Gower ends by saying that the voice of the people is often the voice of God. In Orwell's book, the voice of God is gone; no sound of the people's voice; only the yell from Orwell. Gower is the poet who is the measure of Orwell, and not Swift. Someone has said that Gower is of value only as a measure against the greatness of Chaucer; and, in the same way, Orwell is of value only as a measure against the greatness of Swift.

Loud cheers are given, wonderful claims are made for his honesty: 'The most honest writer alive; his uncompromising intellectual honesty was such that it made him appear almost inhuman at times; his integrity was never touched'. Never? Let this amazing integrity speak for itself, in one instance, anyway, throughout his review of *Drums Under the Windows*, in *The Observer*. He opens with, 'W. B. Yeats once said that a dog does not praise his fleas, but this is somewhat contradicted by the special status enjoyed in this country by Irish Nationalist writers'. Does he mean that Irish writers are fleas in the hairs of the British bulldog? Is that honesty, is that integrity? It is a curious connection to give to a poem written by Yeats, and dedicated to 'a poet, who would have me praise certain bad (Irish) poets, imitators of his and mine'. Is Orwell, at an opposite pole to Yeats, angry with Irish writers because they don't imitate him? His manner, his mood? Is the use of the plural but camouflage for an attack on the singular O'Casey, who would have none of his mood, none of his manner? Status! What status have Irish writers had in England? Shaw? But Shaw was no Nationalist. Yeats then? But Yeats told Sean himself that he was over forty before he handled a five-pound note; and it was Sweden that gave him the Nobel Prize. James Joyce? Read this great writer's Preface to the American edition of *Ulysses*, and learn of the wonderful status Joyce had here. O'Casey? Ah, he, him, first and foremost. Well, we'll see.

Orwell goes on, 'Considering the story of Anglo-Irish relations, it isn't surprising that there should be Irishmen whose life-work is abusing England; what does call for remark is that they should be able to look for support to the English people, and in some cases should even, like Mr. O'Casey himself, prefer to live in the country which is the object of their hatred'. Get outa me country! A curious cry from such a lover of freedom and all humanity to yell. A jingo snarl — and from Orwell; from the person who was stridently, or pretended to be, out for universal freedom of thought, the fellow who, it is said, fought against uniformity in life; now balling out a curse on the head of a writer because he happened to be Irish. Hadn't the savvy (had it all right, but had set it aside to suit his malicious purpose) to realise that O'Casey could no more help being an Irishman than Moses could help being a Jew.

Orwell knew that the support given to O'Casey by the English people wasn't amazing; knew it well. Let's get this clear; put forth a few hot facts in this cold war. Two-thirds, and more, of the support he got came from the United States; half of the other third from his own country, the rest from Britain, including an odd hand from the Scot and the Cymru. He lived in England, but so far from living on her, he paid more in tax to her revenue than he received from the south coast to the banks of the Tweed. An uncle had fought and was wounded at Balaclava, a brother had fought in the Boer War, another in the first World War, a nephew in a submarine, a son of his had served in the Royal Artillery, and another was serving in the Artillery now. Wasn't this the record of as good a giver as what was given by this yelling Orwell? Yelling out against 'abusing England', while he himself was abusing and cursing the whole of life.

'England was the object of O'Casey's hatred.' To say simply that this remark is a lie is but to give it a good name; it is more, inasmuch as it throbs with malice, too. Certainly, he had no liking for the England that was Orwell and his abune companions. But he had steeped himself in the culture and civilisation of the broad, the vital, the everlasting England, not through means provided by solicitous English Governments, but by desperate, never-ceasing efforts of his own; half a life's work which shows, not a hatred, but a great and a consuming love for England's culture. He knew England's history better than that of his own country, and that was saying a little; knew it, probably, better than Orwell himself, for in his work Orwell seemed to be strangely distant from it; ignoring the great English souls of the past, ignoring those of his own time, content to gratify his own tangled thoughts by shouting out rot and rust to England's future.

This defender of England, lover of all her values, showed in his review that he was ignorant of one of the best-known pieces in the whole of English literature. His voice rises to a special scream when he describes Cathleen ni Houlihan marching along singing what he thought to be an Irish 'Nationalist' song:

Singing of men that in battle array,
Ready in heart and ready in hand,
March with banner and bugle and fife
To the death, for their native land.

Get outa me country! We won't let you sing these ballads, breathless with hatred of England, here! But this ballad breathed love for England, for it was written, not by an Irish Nationalist, but by Tennyson. It is sung by Maud in the poem of the same name, known to most, but unknown to England's great defender, Orwell. One would imagine that an educated Englishman like Orwell would have known it almost off by heart; but Orwell had never heard the Voice by the cedar tree, in the meadow, under the Hall. Yet the wreathed garlands on Tennyson's grave had hardly had time to wither when Orwell came into the world of England.

This logos of lamentation complains that the book is so written 'as to make it difficult to pin down the facts of chronology'. Facts of chronology is damn good. But there are quite a lot of facts of chronology that haven't been even pinned up yet. As a chronological fact, on what day of the year was Christ born? Mohammed? And what was the year, the month, and the day, on which Buddha first sat down under the Bo tree? He goes on, 'Sean did this and Sean did that, giving an unbearable effect of narcissism; the book is written in a sort of basic Joyce, sometimes effective in a humorous aside, but it is hopeless for narrative purposes'. Basic Joyce! Bad or good; right or wrong, O'Casey's always himself. Of course Sean did this and did that, because he was alive, and will go on doing this, doing that till something called death stops him. Everybody's doing it, doing it, doing it. The low note about cogging from Joyce is particularly ironical, seeing that in his first venture, sent to Sean for an opinion, Orwell himself tried to imitate Joyce, not here and there only, but in whole scenes as near to the genius of Joyce as Sean's few verses are near to the poetical genius of Shakespeare or Shelley. Orwell goes on, 'Literary judgement is perverted by political sympathies, and Mr. O'Casey with others like him are able to remain almost immune from criticism. It seems time to revise our attitude, for there is no real reason why Cromwell's massacres should cause us to mistake a bad or indifferent book for a good one.' Well, that's a good one! Here's a lad indeed with honour set in one eye and death i' the other! Cromwell's massacre of Irish citizens is to be changed to a massacre of Irish writers by angry English reviewers. All nationalities are to be equal within the British Commonwealth, but some nationalities are to be more unequal than others.

—I wondher why the fellow showed such venom in a review, murmured Donal o' Murachoo, as he and Sean trudged through piercing points of sleet, a bitter red wind from the east numbing their backs; I wondher why?

—I imagine I know, responded Sean. Ten years ago, Gollancz, the publishers, sent me a book in proof-form, called *A Clergyman's Daughter*, written by Mr. Orwell. In a letter they said they hoped I'd find time to read it, adding that though the Firm didn't think the book maintained an even keel, they were sure the scene in Trafalgar Square was one of the most imaginative pieces of writing they had ever read — equal to Joyce at his best. They asked me if I had time to read it, and liked it, to write them a line they could quote, with, of course, permission to use my name.

—Aha, the name, the name! ejaculated Donal. Not a whisper of complaint from him then about an Irish Nationalist writer's status. Oh, no, not when he was hot-foot after a puff of praise behind him. The higher the status, the more he was pleased.

—The name was all he was after, Donal, though the name had no authority, either in training or experience, as a reviewer. Christ! This sleet's cutting the skin off my face! Let's take shelter somewhere.

—That was his single-think; the double-think came afterwards, said Donal. Did you send the magic line that Orwell wanted?

—No, then, I didn't, Donal.

—Then what did you do, love, and what did you say? crooned Donal.

—I had my own integrity to guard. I returned the proof-copy, saying I couldn't agree with the publisher's pinnacied praise of it. I said that the scene in Trafalgar Square wasn't even imitation Joyce, and curried the remarks with another advising the publishers to suggest to the author to try to keep 'and so and so's and so forths, with etc. etc. etcs.' well out of any future book he might write. Orwell had as much chance of reaching the stature of Joyce as a tit has of reaching that of an eagle.

—Good advice, son; but why didn't you reply to his review of *Drums Under the Windows*?

—That I did, Donal, but the one reward I got was a civil note from the Literary Editor of *The Observer* saying he had sent on the comments to Mr. Orwell. He answered never a word, Donal. Like Dr. Gogarty and Mr. Louis McNeice, Orwell shot silence at O'Casey, because either the comments were too ridiculous to be noticed, or too difficult to answer.

—Let Boyos like Orwell say what they like, said Donal, giving a higher hitch to his coat-collar, there will always be a spot of green in an Irishman's eye. O'Casey's song and dance have as much right on the stage of life as Orwell's bastard ballet of lamentation. He stopped to look up at a sign that a lamp above flooded with light, showing clearly a golden Crown and a crimson Rose. What about here? he queried; looks trim, looks cosy, and the two of us near perished.

Shoving a glass-panelled door from him, Donal led the way into the lounge, into a glow, made brighter and cosier by the sound of the slashing sleet and bitter wind without. There was a fine sheen from many bottles, black and brown, green and golden; a gripping glitter from polished tankards, never used now, looking like sturdy old men watching with scornful wonder the more delicate ways of present-day drinking; a softer shine came from many glasses, and all were wrapped up in an enveloping warmth, from which crept the soft caress of a heady smell, vaporising itself from the fumes of whiskey and of beer.

Donal got two whiskeys, hot, and he and Sean sat down on a leather-cushioned bench facing the bar; sipping their drinks with quiet delight, letting the soft, lazy comfort of the Rose and Crown seep through secular body and secular soul. Over at the far corner of the bar two men were seated on high stools, drinking iced beer, each with an eye on the crowd, though remaining intent on themselves.

—Wonder who are those two set-aside birds perched on the high stools at the far corner of the bar? Bedammit, he went on, answering himself, the lean one's Orwell; but who's the other with the cocky stance and stony stare, like an ageing owl, once wise, now witless?

—That one's a gossop-writer in an evening paper, one who, in his mind-nurtured column, said the British Prime Minister had allowed the British Council to send the Dublin Gate Theatre all over the Balkans as an advertisement for Britain, acting the plays of O'Casey, who laughs as loud at the British as he laughs at the Irish; though a little inquiry would have shown the blown-up duffer that the Gate Theatre never did an O'Casey play; so neither the Prime Minister nor the British Council had been guilty of misbehaviour in encouraging O'Casey 'to laugh at the British'. So, Donal, me man, it's out of the British book and off the British stage with the Irish O'Casey.

—God spoke first, said Donal. Looka, Sean, looka — towards the door! Is me eyesight going queer? Tell me if you see as well or as queer as meself.

Sean looked, and saw a bright young lady tripping into the lounge. She was dollied up regardless, in a suit of steel-blue faille, gold-threaded, shimmering; with large stand-away pockets and narrow velvet belt. Over all, she wore a coat of smooth *velour de fouine*, lined with brilliantly blue silk, having a winged collar and voluminous sleeves. Handsome she looked, and handsome she knew she was, and, oh, the sight entrancing!

—It's Cathleen ni Houlihan! ejaculated Donal, fear in his eyes, and pride in his voice. As handsome a heifer as ever, though not quite as slender as she used to be. Look at her varnished nails, her clouded eyelashes — they don't fit in with her past manner of modesty. Among the English she shouldn't shape herself like that — nylons too! Doesn't look a bit like as if she came out of a cloud of disasther and woe!

—You don't expect her to come here dressed as she's shown on an Abbey Theatre poster, do you?

—Her get-up doesn't seem suitable, Sean, considering the way so many poets wrote about her; it does Ireland disservice. She looks too loud and gay to worry respect out of the English. Aw, she's seen us! She's making straight for us!

Over she came with a twittering run, a musical motion rippling her legs and hips, her fresh face flushed and smiling, her hands outstretched.

—I seen yous, the pair of yous, the minute I waltzed in; and glad I am that I won't be a bird alone here. I was lost alone in the hotel I'm in, and so I run down in a taxi to have a quick one here to warm me up a bit. Welcome to the Rose an' Crown, me rattlin' boys from Paddy's land. Well, how are yous? Why the silence? Aren't yous goin' to ask me to sit down?

—Sit down, do, please, Cathleen, daughter of Houlihan, said Donal, made almost mute by the new look of his mystical love.

—Thanks, kindly, she murmured, sitting down facing them, stroking her skirt into attractive alignment with the contour of her shapely legs. Whisper, lads — don't call me Cathleen. I'm over here incognito, and known now as Lady Shan Van Vogue. Got a bit tired of being a tall, white candle before the Holy Rood. A real lady, mind you, and she slapped Donal on the shoulder. Isn't either of yous goin' to ask me if I have a mouth on me? Mother o' God, it's a cold welcome I'm gettin'.

—Your coming took us by surprise, said Donal, rising slowly; would you like your lemonade warmed?

—For God's sake, man, I need something with a keener kick in it than lemonade — cold or hot!

—Shush! Careful! warned Donal. Not so loud. Those two boyos on the high stools have their ears cocked, and are watching you.

—Let them watch! said Cathleen, with a lovely toss of her head; they'll see something they'd like to have at home.

—Deh, deh, Donal clicked his tongue. Cathleen, please, remember where you are.

—Aw, for God's sake, man! I'm where I haven't to watch every step I take, or do reverence to ould rusty partialities. Looka, agra, she said to Sean, get me a tidy gin with a slim splash of lime in it, and let another nip of comfort go with it by yous tellin' me how're things with the pair o' yous.

—I'm not sure it was wise of you to come here to the Rose and Crown, said Donal.

—You don't say? said Cathleen, caustically, Ara, man, I had to come or go outa me mind, off me head — go demented, I mean. She gracefully sipped at the warm gin Sean had brought her. I come over here for a harmless flutter, for a little of what I fancy. The homeland's nuts on rushing towards the first house in heaven. A twicenightly business now, and quite a few doin' well on it, thank God.

—Cautious, Cathleen, cautious, murmured Donal.

—Ah, you! retorted Cathleen. Every county's vying with the one next to it as to how many volleys of prayers they let fly into heaven; a continual *feu de miserére* of missions, retreats, an' novenas. All our poets, dramatists, an' storytellers, are lyin' day an' night, flat on their bellies, just because a leadin' poet, Patrick Kavanagh, has declared that if only the poets an' writers fling themselves prostrate before God, an' admit their dire disthress, they may be admitted into a new dispunsensation; for, said he, all the great poets, says he, were, an' are, those who lie prostrate before God. Before God, it's terrible over there, over there, I'm tellin' yous, gentlemen.

—Still, I think you should have stayed at home to keep the old flag flying, said Donal.

—Oh, you do? Well, I don't. You go over, an' keep the old flag flyin', if you're that eager. You go over an' care for the poets lyin' prostrate. An' are they comfortable? They are not! An' do they want to lie prostrate? They do not! An' are they spoutin' great poetry? They are not! It's just that they daren't get up. The nation's watchin' them from window an' door. Bendin' over one of them, with a sweet Tipperary lass be my side, before I left to come here, I heard him mutter that the longer he lay the worse he got; an' when I poked him in the back with me snow-white wand, symbol of purity, tellin' him to get up, an' talk to the pretty lass beside me, an' be a man; he only dug himself deeper, moanin', Oh, if it wasn't for the wife an' kids!

—I don't know that you're going to be any better here, murmured Donal.

—Don't you? I do. I'm betther already. Here a girl can show the curve of a calf, of a bosom, even of a bottom, without fearin' to have to face fury.

—Dtch, dtch, Donal clicked his tongue. You're sadly changed, Cathleen. In front of the English too! We should behave, while still showing we're Irish and proud of it.

—Aw, that boast's a batthered one now, Donal. There's small use of bein' proud of what none of us can help.

—Looka! said Donal suddenly; looka, something's happening to the boyos on the stools! They're vaporising into the whiskey-fumed air! Whisht, Orwell's saying something!

—Hear me, my people, said the voice from the top of the vapoury column into which the figure was changing; why should the Irish have a status in our comfort-mongering Rose and Crown? Pack them back to their bracken-clad fields, their stony roads, their tousled houses.

—Drive the Irish from our stages throughout the ages, tare and ages, whispered the weakening voice of Gossup from the vapoury wisps he was fast becoming.

—From our literature, too; away, away, whispered the voice of Orwell; out of its pages throughout the ages, tare and ages; let no Irish thought taint our English civilisation! Away!

—For God's sake! ejaculated Donal, the mien of the secular scholar rising up in him. There's no such thing as English civilisation — it's a mingling through the ages of many others — Syrian, Jewish, Hellenistic, Roman, with the Scot, the Cymru, and the Gael brightening it all up a bit. The very rosary beads we twist through our fingers had their origin in Syria, and the column keeping Nelson in the air has a Syrian root. If we all haven't drunk from the well at the world's end, we've all had a sip from the well at the world's beginning!

—Out of the books, off of the stage, went the dying whisper out of the vapour dying down to silence as the two souls dissolved into the warmth of the whiskey-fumed air, and left nothing but a slightly darker air hovering over where the two souls had been sitting. The dour departed.

—Never mind them, buddies, called out a voice from the lounge's centre; me own father's mother was an Irishman.

—Same here, called another voice from the far end; sure, me own mother's father was an Irishwoman. Sing us an Irish song, and forget them. A chorus of easy-going English voices murmured approval, and gentle knockings of the tables gave encouragement to the call for a song. Sing us one of your Irish songs, one of your heart's desire; sing us one that you used to sing around the cabin fire.

—Go on, Donal, me son, pleaded Sean; sing from our hearts out.

—Do, Donal, pleaded Cathleen, laying a white, coaxing hand on Donal's knee; sing, an' show we're Irish without shame to ourselves, or danger to anyone else.

So Donald leaned back in his seat, and sang:

All round me hat I wear a band of green ribbon O,
Careless of what any lofty mind may say;
If anyone should ask me why, I'll tell them Eire wove it
All round me hat, an' there it's destin'd for to stay.

All that she is or was is woven in that ribbon O,
Her chieftains lyin' low in cloister'd Clonmacnoise today;
Th' bugle-call of Finn that shook the mountain high, the valley low,
Cuchullian's chariot-rush that took th' foemen's breath away.

All that her saints have done, her sinners' gay mortality,
Th' time they stood undaunted up, th' time they slipp'd an' fell;
Th' beauty of the oldher books an' all th' songs her poets sung,
Are woven in this ribbon green, an' woven fair an' well.

All th' Ulsther chiefs defendin' Eire from the Norman Law;
Tone tossin' on the sea, an' damnin' all its din;
Emmet takin' Ireland's hope down with him to a grave unknown,
When people had no peace without or gleam of hope within.

Th' rout of priests who ordhered Irish souls away to hell,
Who saw a Chieftain sent from God in Charles Stewart Parnell;
Larkin's apostolic voice that rang the workers out of sleep,
An' made undaunted fighters from a flock of baain' sheep.

An' them comin' lather when daffodils danc'd in th' sun,
When many were th' whispers that poor Ireland's days were done;
When Pearse an' all his comrades beat a roll upon an Irish drum,
A roll that's beatin' still to bring a rally yet to come.

So all round me hat, I wear a band of green ribbon O,
Zone of our faults, our fights, our love an' laughter gay;
All that Eire is or was is woven in that ribbon O,
An' there it stops till life is dead an' time has ebb'd away.

HEAVILY HANGS THE BROAD SUNFLOWER

THE first book of biography came before the eyes of those whose ears were listening to the stuttering, muttering rumble of war. Everyone was becoming tense; the nation was beginning to rise up on its toes. A great part of the world was about to do a ballet battle-dance in ruin: a slow movement to muted violins, tuneless; the con-ductor's baton a beat behind the rhythm; the music dwindling low at times to a querulous lullaby, always asking, never answering; till of a sudden the crescendo came, deafening the very sounds the music gave itself, shrieking a fierce overture for the tens of thousands of British men, women, and children, who, in a day or two, would be flung from the uproar into the odd stillness of a land of shadows. Neither England nor France had had the foresight to make an ally of the Soviet Union before, and they couldn't screw their courage to the sticking-place to make an ally of her now. England's Prime Minister, Chamberlain, had so many children that he didn't know what to do, and he had no Ma to advise him. He crept out at night to the building of the Soviet Embassy, and looked up at the lighted windows, murmuring, Shilli go in or shalli stay out? He had courage only to look through a window to see the time by the shadow of the Kremlin clock, watching the hands creeping towards the time when churchyards yawn; thought the clock was fast, and hurried back to Downing Street, where the cautious clock was comfortably slow.

See him standing up at the Lord Mayor's Banquet to speak, in the midst of the smell of food, the odour of wines, the rustle of silks, the glitter of jewellery. Hear him speak the word: We stand where we stood, we stand where we are, where we stood before, we stand still, and we refuse to sit down. Hear, hear. We shall stand fast, stand steady, stand forth. All listening? Yes, all listening. Gog and Magog agog with interest. What is the wild wave saying? No one there, no one anywhere, knew anything about the shape of things to come. No one knew that the daft god of the Nazis would soon be flinging down fire and brimstone on England's pleasant land, or that the smoke of the city would soon go up as the smoke of a furnace, nor did the daft god know that the very fire he created would one day make a cinder of himself. Gog and Magog are with us: no one can harm us. A confident fellow is speaking. I warn Herr Hitler! A great clap-clapping of hands. A very confident fellow. I warn Herr Hitler that we shall stand by Czecho-Slovakia; I warn Herr Hitler that if he attacks Poland, England will read the riot act; throw all she has on the side of right and justice, and the British Army will march, tramp, tramp, tramp; and show the world that Europe is still a Continent fit for zeros to live in; if Germany attacks Poland, England will immediately go to her aid! How? March across the Continent? Through Germany to get to Poland? A short cut. Too dangerous for ships to sail through the Skagerrak, so fill up small boats with men, and let them pull to the port of Gdynia. With a long, long pull, and a strong, strong pull, gaily, lads, make them go! If neither way be possible, then tunnel a way to Warsaw! The Lord Mayor felt he'd like to conk Hitler with the mace; but it might have been better had he conked Chamberlain. Britannia had changed her trident for an umbrella. Let us under outa the rain. Attention! Umbrella down. It ain't gonna rain no more. Poor man! He gave England all that was in him to give; but national tension tightened the life out of him; and events beyond were far beyond the stretch of his terminal mind.

No one wanted war in England, and poor Chamberlain had a distressing time fitting in the possibility of war with the mood of the people. The effort hastened his end. There was none of the excitement among the people which had emblazoned the passions of the previous one. People were guessing what it might be like, and they didn't relish what they saw in their mind's eye. Thousands and thousands of disabled veterans of the last war were dragging themselves about still; the Cenotaph stood to remind them of the million of young Englishmen who had gone from life a few years before, and the young men of the day had no wish to follow them down to earth. Crêped thoughts still lingered in English souls today. All were sullenly silent, and all waited. Look, it's bending a little — the broad sunflower. Ah, the first of wintry fear on the sunflower's stem. Germany and Italy alone of Europe were ready to go out to cheer on every public pathway and bid the nations bid themselves goodbye. Hitler had his banner hanging from every German window, had turned every road into a route-marching avenue, every square in every town into a parade-ground. Mussolini had the ledges of every window of Rome worn away leaning out to tell the people that Hitler was the new *lux mundi* and he the *lux mundi secunda*, godsent, godborn, goose-gospelled.

The one bright thing in England's pleasant land was the British Blackshirts, headed by Oswald Mosley, a chromium-plated tapper-tit, trotting through the London streets, trumpeting *De Profundis Britannicum*, like toy soldiers embowed with what looked like life for a brief spell, self-ridicule investing them with its honour as they chalked their symbol, the Flash within the Circle, on the road wherever two streets crossed. The string in the egg; the egg and I. Mosley thought he was leading a crewsade, but he but led a wandering to and fro. He had one thing in common with Hitler — no sense of humour. Mussolini was funny in himself, Hitler was sinister, Mosley ridiculous. Some big-business men applauded him and supported his movement for a time because they thought he would prove to be the Deliverer of the Goods; a deliverer who would flatten the organised workers into a thin tail that would wag delightedly for whatever might be kindly given to the dog. We Want Mosley, chanted the Blackshirts, but no one else took up the cry, and the winds of life blew even its echoes away before many had time to hear it. Once, in the Albert Hall, Mosley, after a funfare, came forward in a tremendous pool of electric light to tell the English people how to live, how to die, and how to do their shopping. Stood out in the fierce white light that beats upon the drone. Stood there talking. Bands playing and audience chanting Mosley's the Only Boy in the World, and England's his Only Girl. England's Pick-me-up. The Duce Anglicanem. The living Song of the Shirt. Shirts were in demand everywhere. Men on the make were everywhere seeking fresh gods and postures new, and the symbol was a shirt. Even Ireland started to wear them; but to give her her due, those who bought them soon sold them to be used as football jerseys. It was a Shift that caused the great commotion in Ireland; a Shirt everywhere else: Song of a Shift in Eirinn, song of a Shirt in Sasana. Mosley led the stuffed shirts in England. He caused quite a sensation of fear among some of our Communists, who didn't know a bumbell from a Jo Anderson, me Jo John. The Blackshirts couldn't get going. They were heard in silence, and, after a meeting, seemed to slink away, rather than to depart; fold their taunts like the Scarabs, and silently steal away. They never seemed to be at ease in their shirts; not in any way at ease like a Scot in his kilt; not even like a would-be saint wearing a hairy one. Mosley, seemingly, hadn't it in him to go far. His vision seemed to be limited to what he saw in the looking-glass. Malice through the looking-glass. Not a tap came from Drake's Drum, though some Communists thought they heard it thundering. Hitler's and Mussolini's sad success had added cubits to Mosley's stature. Yet the apathy shown to his cause by the English people and the ring of clenched fists around him kept him in a corner. It was maddening.

Far away in Berchtesgaden, the umbrella and the axe sat together in the best room there, sipping tea and talking. Chamberlain listening, nodding his head, and occasionally asking Hitler what time o' day it was; Hitler outstaring him, the madman's glare already lighting up the bulging eyes; Ribbentrop beside him, smiling covert encouragement over to the British Prime Minister: Now, Mister Prime Minister, you can really see what a really charming laddie he is; the English Ambassador, Nevile Henderson, hanging his head in embarrassment, knowing well that the Prime Minister Chamberlain's talk was convincing Hitler that England's shoulders could no longer carry a coat of mail.

—Well, we've had an interesting and a profitable talk, said Chamberlain, rising to go. He gently touched the swastikaed arm of the Furor: Don't forget, son, that you have promised me to be a good boy. Now, you won't go too far?

—I promise, said the Furor, the lidless eyes staring and fascinating the Prime Minister; all I want are the Sudeten hills and the villages at their feet: when they are mine, I shall be satisfied.

—Fair enough! said Chamberlain, ignoring a warning nod from the head of his Ambassador, whose keener mind possibly foresaw that Britain's life stood breathless in the middle of her autumn, to be followed by a frost that would never soften. Heavily hangs the broad sunflower over its grave i' th' earth so chilly.

All through the ferment, the ebb, and the flow Sean worked at the second volume of his biographical book, calling it *Pictures in the Hallway*, and a play which he called *Purple Dust*, the play coming into the world before the book. Soon in many places, there would be no pictures in the hallway, no hallways in which to hang any, no homes even for hallways. Soon umbrella-carrying Britannia's set and serious face would be ripped open, the slashed cheeks would be blood-dripping, with no time to stitch the gashes close. Let the blood drip and splash pitiful patterns on the pavement; no time to sew up the wound; no time: it will mean disfigurement, but life is at the last, long hazard now.

George Jean Nathan, the famous American critic, had welcomed the play, and had promised to do all he could to bring about a production in New York; and Sean was content to wait for one. Then a curious thing happened: he got an unsigned letter from a London Theatre Club asking an option on the play. A woman's name printed on the top of the letter indicated her to be the Secretary, and he wrote to her, politely saying that he was expecting an

American production, and couldn't give permission. After some delay, a letter, signed by the producer, came along to say that the play had been in rehearsal for some time, and would O'Casey kindly give formal permission to the production by the theatre. No, O'Casey couldn't, and wrote to say so, adding that he didn't like the procedure of a group putting a play into rehearsal before getting permission from the author. Then a third letter from the producer told a strange tale: not only had the play been fully rehearsed without first even hinting to Sean that they were thinking of doing it, but Mr. James Agate had been invited to see the play and give his views on it in the coming issue of the *Sunday Times*. Agate came, watched the rehearsal through, and, on the following Sunday, denounced the play as a worthless one; more, that it was an attack on England when England was helpless and unable to reply! Lil'Allegro to the watch-tower came, and tranceposed himself into the custodian of the British Commonwealth. He wroped himself in the Union Jack and over England's head his arm he flung against O'Casey. God, he was fierce! The world could hear him snorting!

> Hold thou my casque, and furl my pennon up
> Close to the staff. I will not show my crest,
> Nor standard, till the common foe shall challenge them.

Was it dislike of the author and the play, or love of England that made the Ego strike? This critic had great influence, and Sean did himself harm by not sending him a monthly bouquet of flowers. Sparse as the response to the play in a book or on the stage might be, the response was likely to die altogether now that a war was about to begin. Yet, to bring a play through to a full rehearsal, without telling the author anything about it, till a prominent critic had come to see it and to write about it in his next review; and to expect that the author would not object to all that, was, indeed, a very strange thing to think, and a stranger thing to do.

Mr. Chamberlain came home waving the talismanic umbrella. Is it peace, Jehu? It is peace! Herr Hitler has met an old man in the half-way house, and has promised to be good; has promised to go over the hills only. He will go for the Reds, thought many, maybe Chamberlain, too. We need have no fear. He will level Moscow. He won't harm us. He as much as told Mr. Chamberlain so. He calls the Russians sub-humans, and, maybe, he's right. I, for one, could never cotton to them. They are too vital for words. They think far too much about life, and all that life can do, as George Borrow saw and said during the black and frosty drip of the Crimean War. They should be stopped, and Hitler may be the man to do it. Pray God he may think quick about it. The Brown Shirts will soon be over the border! What border? Whose border? The Soviet Union's border. Do you tell me that? That I do. Huraah!

No hurry; no necessity to hurry with that job, said Hitler: that can wait. It will be no more when it comes than a jolly garden party where a few shots are fired. I'll tame the fiercer first. Show France and England who's who there, here, and everywhere. The Russian venture won't be more than a rather long hunt; the chase will be half-blinded by banners, ears will buzz with gay bugle-blowing, and, of course, a few will be hurt to take monotony out of the march. Heil Hitler! Sieg Heil! would soon be shouted in the Kremlin. It will be fascinating to spend a fortnight there, looking around, and bring a few souvenirs back to Berlin. The Bolsheviks must be in a sweat — that is if there be any of them intelligent enough to realise that their days are numbered by me. Our Nazi Army will go through the Red one like a hot knife through butter; even the English generals, admirals, and prime politicians know that well. The Red Army is but a moving heap of shreds and patches. My army will pave the way to Moscow with rusting Russian faces. Moscow will become a shooting-lodge for the Junkers and the generals. It will be an amiable and a thrusting day when the Nazi tanks thunder through the Red Square, and the Volga becomes the eastern Rhine. And Hitler combed his hair.

But the infatuated bastard didn't do that; he did this: on a fine September morning, he sent his thanks thundering over Poland's border straight for Warsaw. What the hell was the fellow doing? You've disappointed us all; you've taken the wrong turning, you fool! So Chamberlain took off his gloves and, uniting with France, declared war on Nazi Germany, but his bold words went up and up and over, only to be lost amid the smoke and fire of blasted Poland. Not even a war correspondent could be sent to help the Poles. France's time was coming soon, and England's too, for sparks from Poland's fires would shortly set brave London burning.

The Nazis got a shock when they came to the river Bug, for there, on the opposite bank, stood battalions of Red Army men watching them; cannons pointed, if you please, across the river towards the Wehrmacht men.

—Christ is risen! shouted the Nazis over to the Reds, knowing that this was a Russian exclamation common on Christmas or

Easter Day — they couldn't remember which.

—He is risen, indeed! shouted back the Reds; and you're to come no farther — we'll take care of what's behind us.

The Furor wasn't pleased; indeed, the Furor was furious. This wasn't the act of a pal. Here were Stalin's Reds lined up on the bank of the Bug, with artillery and tanks facing his invincible Wehrmacht, and telling them, impudently, to stay where they were; to come no farther. Stalin must have a bad mind. After all, Hitler's word was Hitler's word. Aha, Stalin, my boy, you wait! Oh, when he did thump down on these Reds, his fist would thump them like the hammer of Thor! Better and wiser if they took what was coming to them lying down. Whom the gods would destroy, they first make mad. He'd leave this line of least resistance to the last; but when he got going, he'd leave nothing of these Bolsheviks but bundles of rags and bones blowing aimlessly about their own snowy steppes.

Bang! Jasus, what was that! Was it a car rattling o'er the stony street, or was it the cannon's opening roar? No, no; sit down; it's all right. Just Eire banging her big front door shut on *I Knock at the Door*. Hear the holy Confraternities shouting from behind it:

—Get away, old man; get away from here! The very mention of the book leaves a fume behind. Oh, do get off the doorstep. Go where you can't be seen or heard. The bad drop's in you. Vatican's raidar renders news that St. Patrick's rending his whiskers, threatening to rip the shamrocks off his stole, if you is let inside the house. It's not silk you have in your wallet, nor apples for ladies to eat of. You, Joyce, Shaw, and George Moore, are the remaining echoes of the Lamentation of Aughrim. You're shut out!

Sean guessed that his books must prove very embarrassing to any intelligent mind reviewing for the Irish papers. However a reviewer may jib or fidget, he must always express opinions with a big X in front of his eyes. Once, Sean got a letter from M. J. McManus, then Literary Editor of De Valera's daily, *The Irish Press*. He wouldn't have written at all, Sean thought, if he hadn't had a reason, for a tailpiece to the letter said that a book of his own would shortly be published. This is a bit of what he says (he is dead now, so this enunciation can't make him lose his job): 'I enclose a review of your book which you may not have seen, and which, I think, is the first to appear in an Irish newspaper. I liked the book immensely, and only regretted that owing to circumstances which prevail in this country — and of which I am sure you are not unaware, — I could not give my appreciation an altogether free vein. The Literary Editor of a paper which has a large sprinkling of clerical shareholders cannot always say what he wants to!'

Bang! went the door against *Purple Dust*, too, against *The Star Turns Red*; sent to go as exiles, along with the outcast *Within the Gates*, *The Silver Tassie*, and *I Knock at the Door*; followed by lesser bangs of library doors shutting to keep the books out in the street. Ireland was hardly any longer worthy of her name. McManus dismisses her with the contemptible title of 'this country'; a country where so many were never afraid to die is now a country where so many are afraid to live. The clerical shareholders are listening. The writers of Ireland must get instinctively to know just what not to say. One may argue with Micky Muldoon, but not when Mickey becomes the Reverend Michael Muldoon, or, worse still, the Right Reverend Michael Monsignor Muldoon; unless one is brave enough to suffer loss. The slogan of Ireland's writers and thinkers now, according to Mr. Sean O'Faolain, is 'If It Wasn't For The Wife And Kids'. Ireland's a decaying ark anchored in western waters, windows bolted, doors shut tight, afraid of the falling rain of the world's thought. All to give God a quiet life, and keep Irish souls safe, so that the heads in Ireland are dwindling down to knobs.

Out of hearing of the guns, stretching away from the threat of them, Ireland busied herself shutting everything up. She had shut out all mention and meddle with the U.S.S.R., shut out Joyce, O'Casey, and allowed Shaw only to look over the garden wall; and now she set about shutting out the war: but, in the end, she had shut out little. Shaw was jauntily climbing over the wall, Joyce and O'Casey had a foot in, preventing the tight shutting of the door, and her sons and daughters were pouring out over to England through the upper exit of protestant Ulster; pouring out in such numbers and in such excitement that Ireland won far more honours in the war, in proportion to her twenty-six-county population, than any other member of the British Commonwealth; and Stalin's name, if not loved, was better known all over Ireland than any of her best bishops, protestant or catholic, sitting snug on a carved ecclesiastical bench.

Lower and lower, in England, the broad sunflower was bending; lower and lower the hollyhock and the tiger-lily. Hitler, abroad in the night, had suddenly laid violent hands on Denmark and Norway; the Furor was among the fiords, so large detachments of British had been landed to link up with the Norwegian fighters, and drive the Nazis away; detachments of men, Mr. Churchill said, who not only had never experienced such shape of country or condition of weather in winter, but had never even imagined them. Their experience of snow had been of a few flying snowballs thrown in fun, quick, before the snow had melted, or of some makeshift snowman in some back-yard; and whose highest hill was Primrose Hill in the north-west, or Lavender Hill in the south-west of London. Now they were up to their waists in snow, piled about towering mountains, whose paths they couldn't see, whose ways they didn't know; men who had never laid eyes on a pair of skis, even in a shop window. Even had they known how to use them, there were none here to use. Nor artillery either. How could they have got guns here; and what good would they be, were they here, for there was nothing to fire at, except the mountains. The guns were down at the jetty, bereft of ammunition, standing idle, up to their arses in snow. Mountains towering over the beset soldiers, frightening them with their nightmare gleaming, enclosing them silently round about, so that they knew not where to go; men murmuring at one another, Don't lie down in it; keep moving; keep moving for God's sake; I can't, for if we move we may tumble down into snow, deep as a sea. Brave men, they had turned from pushing the Nazis out into pulling themselves, pulling, pulling themselves out of the snow. Falling snow, falling, falling to deepen itself under us. No vision now farther than what we feel. Touch him, touch me, keep together; nothing around us now for miles but tangles of falling snow, weaving a winding sheet for us. Don't say that; for you, and not for me. The quiet, still fall of it over us, all around, everywhere. The snow shall be their winding-sheet. Cold here is the snow of all the years, and falling still. Look, the shadows in the snow are blue like the Virgin's cloak. Where is Our Lady of the Snows that she cannot stop its fall on poor and patient men?

And those at home in England waited for news, news of victory that came this way and then went that way and was lost. Then rumours came creeping to them of deepening snow still falling, and of men stumbling about in it; men chittering with cold, faces pricked to bleeding by the sting of the icy flakes; men with frost-bitten feet; men whose hearts were aching, hearts were hopeless, seeking a way back through the piled-up snow beneath them and the snow falling on the fallen snow, jacketing them with its clinging coldness. To the people waiting, news came later, mentioning casually, through the news of exciting movement, that many sons of anxious mothers, husbands of anxious wives, lovers of waiting sweethearts, had disappeared under the deepening snow forever. The silent weeping behind closed doors was beginning in English homes; many rachels were weeping for their children, because they were not. Soon they would hardly have the time to weep, or the heart either.

Then, suddenly, like a thief in the day, the good catholic, Hitler, struck deep in the month dedicated to the Blessed Virgin:

> Oh! by Gabriel's Ave,
> Utter'd long ago,
> Eva's name reversing,
> 'Stablish peace below.

Passing through the silvery gateway of summer, Hitler's hosts swept into Holland, and ere the clock could strike ten strokes, Rotterdam was less than half itself, the poor half still left was trembling, and looking as if about to fall. In less than a week's time the Nazis held Holland, and were sweeping with a laugh over Belgium, tossing town after town behind them in the manner of light-hearted gifts to Nazi Germany, till the King of the Belgians, sprinkled with the flowery dust of May, slid from his horse, tired, to seek a rest in the lap of Hitler; and British tank and armoured car, decorated on either side with battalions of dubious infantry, plodded over the magic imagined imaginot line to drive the Nazis out of Belgium, and prevent them from crossing into France; the time-burrowing Frenchmen polished the buttons of their half-buried guns, voiceless now, and forever to remain so; while the Nazi panzers shot over the line, merrily, merrily all the way, darting in and out through British and French divisions, till, giddy with turning and twisting, the British and the French made for the sea, leaving all they had behind them, an amaze of guns, tanks, and equipment, and leaving to others the task of digging up the red poppies of Flanders to make fresh room for the additional dead.

> Ho! Stand to your glasses steady!
> 'Tis all we have left to prize.
> A cup to the dead already —
> Hurrah for the next that dies!

The twilight war was over; the real tension had begun, and the first wrinkle of war-care began to seam England's face. As Sean listened in fancy to the booming of the guns in Belgium and France and heard, between the booms, the steely rush-along of the panzers (wondering how near these would come to them in time), he had to get on with the labour of living, and run after the best way to bring a new life into the world, for Eileen was far gone towards the birth of her third baby — one of the thousands of babes born in the black-out; hidden away from the lights of the world. Within the glare of guns firing, within the tale of ten cities crumbling into dusty rubble, heaping themselves over buried men and women; within the chorused cry of scorched humanity, left bare of all but bare life, bewildered women bore children about within them, and were busy laying restless hands on calico and wool to knit and stitch together things protective for the infant entrants to a shattered world. Even in this, sewing up some of the coming wounds of war.

Hitler's roar of Fiat Tenebray had set all England snatching light away from life, in lane, road, street, and byway. Nowhere must a rayeen of light be seen once the sun yawned out a dismal cheerio to the declining day. Even the flame from a farthing candle demanded a curtain on a window. Angrily-moving hands and cursing lips each evening pushed frames of cloth or thick black paper against the windows, tight up, tighter, tighter, ere a candle could be lit. Black cloth and black paper got hard to get, and increased their price, and many a family in many a room, for many a night, had to sit in darkness, while the shadow of death crept nearer, before they could make a screen to hide themselves from the stars. Many an ankle was twisted, many a wrist strained, many a spine ricked, putting up the black-out curtains for the night. In the O'Casey house, the windows in four of the rooms were bow-shaped, big bullies, stretching from floor to ceiling, and weary was the way of life before these could be screened to the satisfaction of the peering, prodding eyes of some special constable. There were more than twenty windows in the rambling house, each to be darkened every evening, uncovered every morning, an irritation so penetrating that seven of them were permanently blackened out, leaving half of the house in perpetual twilight — the twilight of the cods. No light could hang in the hall, for that would have meant a curtain within behind the door to prevent light showing when the door was opened; so for six long years, Sean had to feel his way up and down the stairs, through the hall; a good practice, for England was becoming the kingdom of the blind. Outside, save when the moon shone, the deep darkness separated town and district from their own existence. Every city, town, and village had darkened itself out of visible existence. All over England tens of millions of hands blacked out their homes every evening at the same moment of time. An example, most noble, of expendable and expandable energy. Up arms, and at 'em! Oh! the bleak bother of the black-out, the funereal piecing away of the windows, with Peace a disheartened fugitive, hiding somewhere in the outer darkness — no-one knew where!

Sometimes, at night, Sean wandered a little way down the road, while Eileen was having her baby in Torbay Hospital, whose walls were now bolstered up with sand-bags, the latest unornamented cushions feverish hands were making everywhere, idly thinking to coax the hurt out of a bomb exploding: hands trying to shove a hurricane aside. So, sometimes, when all the darkness was there, Sean, armed with a walking-stick, went out by the garden gate, and tapped a way along the path beside the Plymouth road, looking forward, looking back, but seeing nothing. There were houses all round, but they remained invisible and silent; hushed and waiting. There were people here, there, but they were not seen, and rarely heard in the darkness that pressed against the breast, the back, and down on the head oppressively; so silent that even the cocks seemed to have forgotten to crow. Occasionally, a figure, silhouetted by the hushed footfall, would go by silently on the other side of the road, or, more occasionally still, one would steal by on the path beside him, mentioning his passing presence by a hushed Good night, as if a word, too, as well as a gleam of light, might soar upwards, and tell a hovering enemy something. Once or twice a bus passed, no longer so swift, but rather searching a way along from Plymouth to Torquay, or Torquay to Plymouth, a pin-point of light from a headlamp giving a sluggish safety to the way onwards; its lights shrouded, the window-panes purple-blue, so that, in the dusk or the darkness, it moved like a thick shadow along the silent road, stealthily steering through the night to its journey's end; as if it were the ghost of a brighter bus stealing one more visit from the route it had so often travelled through before. When meetings were held in the town, and those who had attended set out for home, they went silently, walking carefully as if their footsteps might, if let down loud, give an enemy an idea that a town was near; no gossiping along the way, but a steady, cautious wending of the way back; an unhurried quickness in the movement homewards; a quiet opening of a gate, a pause, the quiet opening and quieter shutting of a door, then silence, complete and brooding, came again, leaving the night to darkness and to him. No gun had yet been heard, no hostile aeroplane had yet purred shrilly overhead; but everything and everyone were waiting to see and hear them soon. Heavily hangs the hollyhock, heavily hangs the tiger-lily.

Fear was here already; hunger was coming too. Ship after ship bearing corn and oil to England was going down, slowly or suddenly, in this sea's side, in that sea's centre, and England was threatened with a lean and hungry look. Feed us, heavenly Father, feed us! Feed us with a shepherd's care! Produce more food! Rip up the garden, the public park, the playing-field, and lawn, and sow! Dig up the pleasant places, abolishing colour and perfume. Dig, dig, dig for victory. A potato a day'll keep Hitler away.

There may be gas, poison-gas, too! Gas that blinds, gas that chokes, gas that turns a lung to a rotting cinder! Oh, what a tide of woes! Make millions of gas-masks and make millions of money. It's an ill wind! Call them respirators, and it will sound nicer. Get them from your Warden. Attention! Gas-mask drill! One, two, three — Thumbs under the band; chin thrust firmly into the sack; over the head — so! One, two, three! Practise wearing them. Make them comfortable by getting used to them. Put the baby into the bag-respirator, and see that whosoever pumps air into the bag doesn't stop for a second, or the babe may suffocate. Don't forget to remember. Put the baby in daily, and get it used to the horror. Blow the kid up. Carry your gas-mask everywhere with you — to theatre, to shop, to church, to bed with you, even on first night of honeymoon. Flimsy things of rubber and tin, with a pad of cotton, but guaranteed to keep you alive, gasping for an hour or two during a gas-attack. So now you know. Carry it always. Churchill does, so he does, carries it about with him everywhere, slung around his shoulder like a tiny, brand-new accordion. A Service one, better nor yours, but, still, a gas-mask. A goggle-eyed and snouted nation. Handsome days.

Gas-masks weren't enough. Thousands harried about, and busied themselves turning out cubby-holes, larders, and little rooms, to turn them into protective chambers against gas, storing in them a tin or two of food, a box of biscuits, a can of water, a bottle of rum, and a bible. They pasted strips of paper by the sides of windows and along the sides of doors, covering every crack they could see in window, door, and wall; over cracks in the ceiling, too, and cracks in the floor. They must paste. I paste, I paste! When the alarm goes, don't get excited — excitement hinders breathing — don't rush. Put on your gas-mask quietly and firmly, walk with dignity into your gas-chamber, without any fuss; close the door, seal it up, and sit down to wait patiently till the decontaminating officer knocks to say hello. Sing a hymn to yourself, if you feel the least bit nervous.

Oh God, our help in ages past,
Our hope for years to come,
Be thou our guide while troubles last —

Oh, God, I'm stifling! There's no air! I stifle! Keep calm, you fool! Stifle, if you want to stifle! What if you do itself? Hundreds of thousands are in a' worse plight than you are, woman!

The Nazis held Europe, now — save where lines of red flags from the Black Sea to the ice-floes of the Arctic held them back from owning it all; and over on the beaches of France were thousands of planes with wings swept back, ready for flight, and thousands of panzers, too, the snouts of their guns stretching out, stretching over, stretching out towards England. Invasion!

Heavily hangs the broad sunflower,
Over its grave i' the earth so chilly;
Heavily hangs the hollyhock,
Heavily hangs the tiger-lily.

ORPHANS OF THE STORM

(Not a drum was heard, though something like a funeral note was sounding.)

No drum, no drum, the orphans come; thousands of them, phalanx after phalanx of them, row after row of them; down to Totnes on the River Dart, down to the apple-trees in bloom, rosy umbrellas to shade them from the sun, sweet-smelling, and promising fine fruit. They were coming to a blossomy welcome, the time the gnarled branches were hidden under sprays of fragrant silken beauty. But the winter would come, and the trees would have to fight the frost and the chill irony of the wintry winds, making them wince and wonder. The pines seemed to enjoy the push of the fiercer winds, tossing their branches gaily, this way and that; the oak stood spread out, facing them, indifferent to where the winds came from, or how fierce they blew; the elm stood straight, like a guardsman, un-yielding, as if it murmured, If I fall, I fall; the beech swayed gently to and fro, not indifferent, but as if resigned till the time came for the winds to go; the apple-tree alone seemed to resent the change, to complain, and to sigh for the time of its blossoming again.

But now the winter's away, so come, kids, to the gathering of clusters of the rosy-red buds, soon to open wide to the sun and the searching bees. God's will is wending with ye. He maketh me to lie down in green pastures. Don't be afraid — the bosom of the West Country's a warm one. Come along, boys and girls of London, and hide among the apple-blossoms from the bombs. But the small faces, staring from the carriage windows as the train drew into the station, had no elation in them; no shine of hope. They were unexcited faces, silent, looking quietly out on what was passing, seeming to sense that this was no excursion for them; that this visit wouldn't be a race around and home again, but one that would keep them away from all they knew for a long, long time. The little sweeneys in the apple-trees. Coming to purgatory to escape from hell. A hades without the asphodel. Down to the populous solitude of bees and birds. Away, away from the bright lights, the throngs, the homely thunder of the buses, the shows crowding around one; away from all the glitter, fume, and dirt of London; away, away; to a land that would tilt them into a quietness more than half-way to the quietness of death.

Silently they came, for no fife shrilled a tune, no drum beat out the step; along in column of companies, teachers beside them to see them safely deposited; no sound save the simple patter of their feet along the hardened road, many carrying millboard suitcases, some bearing parcels who couldn't afford more, armed with a day's ration of biscuit, tin of condensed milk, bar of chocolate, and an apple. Gas-mask slung round each slender shoulder. The musk had gone from the rose. Gas-masks among the apple-trees. A new fruit growing on the human body. A growth, a tumour, a welt. Hang up your gas-mask on a weeping willow-tree. On they marched so slowly, ticketed by name of parent and name of school so that they shouldn't be lost who were half-lost already. Don't diddle and fiddle with your gas-mask so, Neddie. It's government property, and may creep between you and death one day. One day, I crept between death and Ned o' the hill. The Devon children stared at these new lives marching from the wrath to come. Some of the Devon women were weeping quietly as they watched the buds of London humanity go by, while the apple-trees, doing their best, nodded their budding fruitfulness to these young strangers, seeming to say in the confidence of their gentle movements through sun and breeze that the juice of the apple was as good any day as the juice of the pampered grape.

Every kindly home in Devon was searching among racks, in presses, and in boxes, to find something to give them; or preparing a refuge for these little spare parts of life receding from the busy banks of the Thames to sit down on the quiet banks of the Dart, and, maybe, weep there; for many there were who would never see their home again; many whose fathers and mothers would soon be lying still under cairns of brick and stone; many, oh, so many. Help the kids! And badly many of them needed help, for they were miserably clad, and had been miserably fed over many years. The three who came the O'Casey way — Doris, aged ten, Zoë, aged six, and Bobbie, aged four, were in a woeful state. What they had on had declined into rags that fairly stank; they were stunted and thin. In some way, they had evaded examination, and so it was found that their hair was a garden of lice and bonnie bunches of nits, so providing Eileen with the shock of her life. She had never seen the like, though Sean had seen it, and felt it too; for the grey repulsive louse with its dirty lustre of clustering nits is the dull tiara the crowded tenement puts on the heads of the children. They had never sniffed the savour of cleanliness, so they did everything they had to do wherever they happened to be at the time, leaving whatever they had done behind them for others to plant their feet in it, and cry out curses on their lice-ridden heads.

These kids had been nourished when England's wealth stood undisturbed: they weren't the result of plague, pestilence, famine, or war; they were the result of poverty forced upon them by a rotten life foisted on man by rotten masters, Baldwin's Best. And master missionaries, hundreds of them, protestant and roman catholic, were out in afric's sunny fountains and on greenland's icy mountains, trying to force worse conditions into the life of little Asians and Africans; conditions that had made the life of their own little ones as unlike life as life could be.

Speaking in a lecture entitled *Missions Under Judgement*, given in Dublin University in February 1952, the Rev. D. M. Paton, M.A., is reported in *The Irish Times* as saying, 'The Christians and the churches they support are as reactionary as part of the whole Western Imperialistic conception; and the actual policy of the Missions tends to preclude, and not to foster, a dynamically self-supporting church in China. I blame the whole church structure in China for maintaining an atmosphere of western civilization, a policy that made the Mission, both socially and religiously, a failure.' Look you, young African and Asian people, you won't get to see even the hinderparts of God, if you don't learn to strut through this life in the best western manner. Father Geraghty, a roman catholic missionary, writing in the February No., 1952, of *The Far East*, a missionary journal, reports, 'I have just concluded a tour of our territory in part of Northern Korea, and found destruction everywhere. Chunchon, the provincial, and three other towns have been levelled to the ground.' Probably, thousands of men, women, and children levelled with them. But not a whisper of denunciation from this kindly father of God; not a breath of blame for the rough and savage work done by shaggy hands, by the shag-haired villainy of war. The priests, Father Geraghty said, were just waiting round for peace to come. They're still waiting. Waiting for a chance to teach the Koreans the love of Christ in the midst of the ruins of their little homes and the ruins of their dead; with the incense of napalm bombs rising round the throne of God. Time for a Tea Deum.

Is it any wonder that things are as they are with our children at home here, and abroad among those termed heathen, when we peep into the kind of schools and colleges set apart for them who are chosen to lead life at home, and who go over the seas to bring the dusky-skinned ones and golden-skinned ones to the knowledge of what is termed truth, and into the wonderful way of Western Culture? Send out the manna and the manacles. Three articles, published in the magazine of a famous roman catholic college for training men for the priesthood, tell us something about the way of seminarian life with these biretta barons. The ex-seminarians who wrote the articles knew they would be overlooked by Collegian Censors, so they larded their criticisms with professions of love for their Alma Matter, who had been more than something of a bitch to them. Says One, 'I grieve against you because you didn't teach me manners. This I learned in a thousand ways — when I sat for interviews, and didn't *know* how to behave; didn't know how to speak properly, didn't know what to do with my hands.' Not even manners! Says Two, 'The newcomer found the first term as hard as did Tom Brown the first year of his schooldays. The newcomer was the perpetual butt of the bully, the cynic, the wisecracker. His duties were multitudinous, ranging from fetching handballs that had crossed the ball-alleys to polishing the seniors' boots.' The fag! Fag in a fog of duties. Again, 'Class was a big problem, with a liberal use of the cane to encourage the flagging mind. We may smile now, but our hearts came as near to bursting as ever they will that morning the gates opened to release us for our first Christmas holidays!' Out into the holy night, silent night at last. We may smile now; smile, smile, smile. Open the gates, and let us through. Says Three — from an ex-student of a famous English roman catholic college — 'New arrivals are the occasion of the ceremony of *bushing*, conducted by the older students. This is a form of baptism in a gorse bush — an experience one either enjoys or does not enjoy, according whether one was an older student or a newcomer.' And the holy, civilised fathers, so close to culture and Christ, keep their eyes shut. Says Four, 'Seminaries have always had a bad name: A jumble of memories of things cold, things unpleasant, things miserable — cold, wet days spent walking up and down, up and down a corridor or a shed, cold, badly-prepared quality meals, cold (poor) dormitories, cold classrooms. When thrust out into life, many of the neglected matters are set right or short-circuited. The rest of the Seminary's mistakes are thrust on a world which already has enough of its own. The students' immaturity in face of their new-found freedom at university or in a job is responsible for "berserk bend" and failed examinations which are so often the seminary student's initiation rite into adult life. Mediocrity characterises our educational system at every level.' Cold comfort to prepare for leadership. Says Five, after giving similar details, 'If I have exaggerated, I ask forgiveness, and I repeat that I love you. Having gone so far I am tempted to say one more hard thing, that if I had a son, I doubt I should send him to you.' We hear you. Food, clothing, shelter, the trinity of need worshipped by all life; in the secular seminary, in the ecclesiastical seminary as well as in the mind of the atheist and in all the homes of the working-class. What on earth do the saints think of all this? But these same souls, ripe for glory, have been nourished on bread and cheese and meat, washed down, probably, with a tot of wine. Oh, no, no! Oh, yes, yes, yes! The *Confessions* of St. Augustine, the *Meditations* of St. Alphonso de' Liguori, the poems of St. John o' the Cross, all had their roots in bread and meat and cheese. Who provided for these chaps? Did they do for themselves? Did they buy their food, carry it home, cook it, before they golloped it down? Did they wash up the dirty dishes, carry the coal from cellar to fireplace, and kindle the fire that warmed them? Of a winter's morning, with their fingers nipped with frost, did they empty the ashes before they set a fire to make their coffee, toast their bread, to strengthen them for another day's worship? Were all these things, and more, done for them so that they might have a good time in writing a poem, inditing a confession, making a meditation? It is said that it takes ten men to keep one soldier in the field; how many, more or less, does it take to keep a saint on his knees? If they didn't do any of these things, having things done for them, then what the hell did they know about life? Leave it all to the drudge, the lay brother!

Hidgiology doesn't say much about these common things. Puts them behind a sacred curtain, leaving hoy polloy to believe that the holy ones live on sweet airs from heaven; or, at the worst, on watercress, spring onions, and water from a well. Ketch them doing it, doing it. Even St. Bernard found he had to eat well, for we are told 'He had lived on common food for a long time, but even this great man, in his later years, garnished his table with tenderly done capons, fine muttons, and fair wines, to balance his belly back to order. Almost all the other monks had begun living on the best long before, waxing furiously fat in eating, idleness, and sloth; as the great Abelard tells us, saying, "Every lean fellow, when he reacheth the stew-pond of the cloister, soon waxeth as fat and well-liking, that seeing him again after a brief period, thou shalt scarcely know him for what he was!"' But these things lie hidden behind a rood screen. Men like to feel like gods, but the body's needs stand obstinate in the way. The never-resting body has a lot to do to keep the soul alive — the poor, despised lay brother of the spiritual man.

The educational way of life, where the dear little shamrock grows wild, is little worse, but no better, than that where the ladylike rose is bedded out to bloom away its beauty. The protestant secondary schools, the grammar schools, are equal, or almost so, with the roman catholic seminaries in their rush-hours after results, their over-crowding, their poverty in amenities, their coldness, physical and spiritual, and the mediocre mutter of their education: consolidated decadence over and under and in them all. The pupils are orphans in the storm of dusty questions, dusty answers, dogma, traditional definitions, with most heads empty of any thoughts of their own.

Then there's the curious servility and rigid idea of obedience in conduct, question, answer, that attaches pupil to teacher, the dangerous lack of friendship between the two. In every one of these schools, church and state, there is a never-ending buzz of Sirs among the desks: yessir, nosir, I willsir, I won'tsir. The teacher has to handle far too many to be able to be friendly with any of them. He has to rule, not with a kindly hand on a shoulder, but with a box and a shout. He has to carry the buzz of yessir and nosir with him even to the playing-fields and running-track. No teaching-dick calls a pupil Harry, and no pupil would dare call a teaching-mister Dick. The young are fed with information as cattle are fed with hay and mangels.

Here, the children of the crowded cities, of the little houses, the human sparrows of London, come in a sad parade, to the loneliness of beech, ash, elm, and oak, to shelter among the apple-trees from the bomb, from the bite and the blight of its blasting; down to Devon bearing the banners of their enormous tribe, their lack of harmonious insight, their narrow visions, their lassitude towards creativeness, and, some of them, their lice; not yet knowing how to ask, not yet knowing how to seek, not yet knowing how to knock at the door of life; each with his tin of condensed milk, his apple, his biscuit, and his gas-mask.

For a time, Devon forgot about its bulls, cattle, and sheep, to think out how best to show affection to these dear little souls, only a few of which came in nice clean faces and nice clean stoles; so deferential, so demure, that the sound of birdsong seemed an intrusion; but when this big wave of young life broke up and splashed itself abroad, the Devon folk were bewildered at the destructive fluttering of uprooted infancy. They told to all who would listen that Us be near driven mad with them evacuees, all muckin' up house an' home till us be near an end. I says to schoolmaster, I says, Us'll be left naked if they don't quieten quick; but 'ee shook 'ead, an' says, Frank, says 'ee, there's a wor on; an' I says to 'ee, says I, Ay, says I, an' us is in they middle of it now.

But many changed after a year's stay, recognising order and the special aspects of the country; helping where they'd hindered; planting where before they had rooted things out of life. A friend who, in his youth, had been a champion sheep-shearer, with his wife, took two lads into his cottage. The garden, pride of the couple, became a waste; a great armchair, bought for comfort during leisure hours, had its lovely chintz cover ripped off, its stuffing pulled out; yet in less than a year's time, the garden looked as good as ever, the chair, renewed, was never harmed again. The lads had changed, and when the time came for them to return home, the old couple bade them farewell on the station platform amid many tears and kisses from the lads to the old couple, from the old couple to the young lads.

Eileen was shocked by the difference in the interest shown to the poorer children and that shown to those who came from well-off schools. It was made positive and particular; the richer ones never even saw the others. They were safely hidden behind their own apple-trees. Never saw a kid rougher than themselves. If they did, it was from a distance, and in the company of a smart teacher or a cautious nun. One rich convent school settled itself snugly in

Sharpham, a lovely place a few miles up the River Dart from Totnes, surrounded by lawns and deep woods that were garlanded with heronries, so that the lives of the children were pushed away from all untowardness in a lovely and dignified seclusion, for they were somebodies, so they were. These indeed were they who had dear little souls, nice clean faces, and nice white stoles. The parish priest often visited them, and as often came back with a beaming face.

—Such lovely children — delightful! he would say; so well-mannered, such a credit to the nuns. All so charmingly dressed, with nice clean faces and nice white stoles. It is always a pleasure to visit Sharpham House.

These little ladies were not for burning. Precious jewels, precious jewels, Christ's robe adorning, rich gems for his crown. If only one could see clearer than through a glass darkly, it would surely be seen that the Guardian Angels watching over these little ladies, in nice clean faces and nice clean stoles, were better dressed, shone more brightly, looked far more respectable, than the Guardian Angels set to hover over the common kids. All England's; the tattered and the tidy; the one in the nice clean face, the one with the snotty nose and the finger poking at the lice in the hair; all England's, though, as Disraeli saw, one would think that they belonged to different nations.

A few of the young exiles were different — almost too quiet to be mortal. They ate sparingly and in silence, as if it was all bitter bread. They grew thin, pushing aside the affectionate anxiety of a foster-mother; going silent to school, coming sullenly back again to wait for night and loneliness so that they might weep in peace; weeping beside the waters of Devon for the lost bright lights, for the stimulating thunder of the passing red buses, for the crowded streets, for a home they had loved; and, later, maybe, for a kind mother now sinking deeper into the ground, the bond between them broken forever. Oh, we who pass these things by, even go through them as hurrying helpers, and then forget them — we, too, are destitute, and sit in the deep valley of the shadow of death.

RED LAUGH OF WAR

THE shout of war had become more than an echo; it was close to every ear now, a bellow. Hitler's heil was hurrying for honour everywhere. Soon the battle would close in, thick and bloody. The waste land wondered at its own scurrying to defend itself. Everyone was out preparing; all were one. Corporal Nym lived by Pistol, telling winds and walls what he would not do if the Nazis came his way; and Pistol lived by Nym. Pickwick side by side with a Weller learned to hold a hose; and Prufrock was fitting on a steel helmet, reconciling himself to a sharp and stinging death in the midst of what he called his duty. The threat of death was bringing the waste land to life again. Oh, Mr. Prufrock, what shall I do? Our home's become my husband's grave, and my babes are buried, too. The Englishman, so clever in his foolishness, was fighting for his life, and the Irishman, so foolish in his cleverness, was fighting with him. It was more than touch and go now; it was all touch and little go, for England was nearly naked. Not much else save the symbolic trident remained in her hand. A few lonely-looking tanks, a few guns, and a few ageing aeroplanes were all she had to call her own. Oh, Mr. Prufrock, what shall we do? God has turn'd away, and left the most of it to you. We have a few guns, a few tanks, a few old aeroplanes, and we have the spirit of a brave people. All of what she once had had been left scattered along the way to the coast of Dunkirk. All her treasures of destruction had been abandoned to the Nazis. Prufrock and his friends could be armed only with a pike and the courage to use it. He had a splitting headache from the pressure of the steel helmet on his head; his legs ached in every joint from the dint of drill; his hands were torn by barbed wire learning how to make a prickly barricade. The ageing Churchill stood by the wireless to promise the British people a succession of gala years of toil, sweat, and tears; Prufrock beside him, murmuring Get us the tools, sir, and we'll do the job. Prufrock, you have busy days before you. He took off his collar and tie, put a muffler round his thin neck, raw with the sun, the wind, and the rain; he covered his thinning hair, thin legs, thin arms with steel helmet and battledress. More clearly than ever before, he saw the Eternal Footman holding his coat, heard him snicker, and was not afraid. Things were too active, too terrible, to let fear get in the way. Home they brought her warrior dead. Who is it? Some bloke named Prufrock.

Lonely men, leaning out of windows, in their shirt sleeves, were lonely no longer; things were too terrible, too active, for them to be lonely. In carpeted rooms, with pictured walls, and cushions on the settee, women no longer came and went, talking of Michael Angelo. They were buzzy fixing helmets on curls, natural or permed, cutting them down a lot to let the helmet cover the nape of the neck; flitting out of their rooms to join the Waacs, the Wrens, or to fix Red Cross armlets on a sleeve of their coats. Men and women were measuring out life now, not with coffee spoons, but with rifle, tommy-gun, sling, splint, and bandage. A bitter change, but not all evil. Common life had to go on, but with a very different rhythm. Things were changed, changed utterly. Church worship in any sense of thought towards a Prince of Peace or a Father of Love was demolished in the fire and detonation of the struggle. All political diversions ran from the stage as the curtain rose upon war. Fee fum family reunion. A whole people massed communistically for such a war as had never been known before; no peace, no sign of peace, till one side or the other lay dead. The chastisement of Hitler was upon us all. Invasion! Well, fight! Than to be subjects of Hitler's herrenfolk, better to be

A pair of ragged claws,
Scuttling across the floors of silent seas.

The gentle town of Totnes, cuddling itself in its quietness, jumped out of its gentleness, and jumped into action. All classes strained themselves into activity, ready to fight in the streets, in the fields, on the hills, against the Nazis. Invasion! They meant it, too, nearly killing themselves with preparation. Fellows of well over fifty ran and jumped about, climbed walls, and flung themselves down to the field on the opposite side, unmindful of a broken leg or a cracked skull; old codgers did bayonet drill and turned somersaults till one's eyes grew blurred and one's head grew dizzy looking at them. Sprained arms and ankles, pulled muscles, and black eyes sprouted out everywhere. In every corner, one heard the crack crack of rifles going and the explosions of hand-grenades, till it seemed that England was blowing herself to pieces. Busy people were getting ready for their own burial. For a long time, the Home Guards were very excited, and did everything at a bound. A driver of a car, or a passenger in one, had to be wary, and keep an open ear for the cry of Halt! A heedless driver, or a scornful one, would hear a bullet whistling past an ear, or, maybe, feel one tearing through his back. All were on the watch, for no-one knew how soon, or where, the Nazis might show themselves in the London thoroughfares or in the Devon lanes. That they would come, and soon, was certain. Hitler had set the whole world the job of wasting energy, time, and thought.

Eileen was never so busy in her life. Minding the latest infant, she forced time to let her gain a first-class certificate in the science of first-aid; she practised how to deal with an incendiary bomb, creeping, done out in dungarees, on her belly into a hut filled with old furniture, set ablaze with magnesium. Within smoke and fume, and heat of the blaze, she worked the hose of a stirrup-pump — first the spray to gradually coax the flaming venom from the home-made bomb, the spray from the nozzle was turned to the jet till the flames died, and curling smoke round the charred furniture showed that danger was over. Then, each day, she hurried up to Dartington to help with the midday meal for the refugee children, watching warily and brightly over her own flock in her spare time; for she and he often spent anxious times till their two lads were safely home from school, having passed through the sullen black-out of the bitter wintry evening. So many women had been called to the colours that housewives with children had now more work than three of them would be expected to do normally. Then there were the lectures given to teach us all how to deal with injury from poison gas, that turned the flesh into a green cindery rot; how to deal with burns from an incendiary bomb, or from fire caused by one; how to deal with shock, with splintered bones, with severed arteries: Everyone was learning anew and in a fresh way that God was Love.

All road sign-posts were swiftly taken down, all names of places blotted out from railway stations, so that all England quick became a land without a name. The district was segmented by geometrical design into sections, sub-sections, and semi-sub-sections, each having its own letter and number as well as its warden, sub-warden, and semi-sub-warden, with messengers, callers, and couriers added to them, topped by a head-warden over all. There were those who wore khaki-coloured helmets, those who wore black ones, those who wore white ones; first-aid wardens, ambulance wardens, rescue-squad wardens, and churchwardens — the land bristled with wardens. No-one was left out, grandsires and old women forming part of England's guard. The men pulled up their socks, the women their skirts. Cut your here up to your ere, your kirtle to the knee. Barriers were put up to check tanks at various parts of the roads, and one stood on the road directly in front of the O'Casey garden gate — thick portly pillars of concrete so placed that passing cars had to wriggle in and out through them. But convoys of heavy guns and tanks couldn't go through, so the portly ones had to come down, to be replaced by V-shaped angle irons, set into sockets of concrete, which were left on the sides of the road, ready to be thrust into the concrete sockets as soon as the rumble of the Nazi tanks shook the English roads, and tightened the hearts of the Devon people;

the military experts seemingly unaware that the invading tanks had but to sidestep the barriers to make their way through the gardens fronting the houses, and go on their way, gay with the prospect of goring out England's vitals, belching fire and smoke, as if the dragon, killed by George, had come to life, had bred a host of his kind, and had gathered them together to destroy altogether the cocky consequence of the tarnishing legend.

One day, suddenly, the local park, the town, and the district flooded up with American troops, white, chocolate, and black. Men from almost all the States were represented by those who sat, who sang, and slept in the tents that formed line after line in the grounds; men from the borders of the Great Lakes, men from the West, from New York, and from Texas, too. All in for fight. Sean often sauntered round the camp, for there were few restrictions, and the Americans were comradely, and ready to talk. Even the lonelier sentries meandering around the fringe of the camp were glad to halt for a few moments to say Hallo, guy. How different these sentries from those around Buckingham Palace or those who had once kept watch over Dublin's Bank of Ireland! The American sentry had his rifle right enough, so many rounds of ammunition, and his greyish-green helmet was pressed down on his head, but there the military formality ended. No sane person would think of entering into conversation with a sentry around Buckingham Palace; it would be low treason. He has ceased to be a human being for the time being, and must comport himself as if he were a changed man. Puppet passes; major movements by strings.

The American sentry carried his rifle sloping across his arm, the barrel resting in the socket of an elbow. He sauntered round, stopping, maybe, to look at the scratch baseball match his comrades were playing; or gazed after a girl that happened to pass by, calling to a comrade within earshot that that was a good-looking dame. One of them Sean spoke to was from Kansas City, a lorry-driver in a store there, he told Sean. He wasn't a big fellow; rather one of the smaller men of the detachment; thin, too, but wiry and firm in his stand. His face was thin, made to look thinner by the enveloping steel helmet. His nose stretched down, thin and long, coming down more than half-way over his upper lip. The biggest mark in his face were the big, brown, wide-open eyes that gently and quietly stared out from the long thin face; eyes that saw little outside what they had already seen at home. The big, brown, wide-open eyes always carried about in them an image of Kansas City. Back in Kansas, he would forget the faint impressions, not only of Totnes, but of England. The Yeomen of the Guard in their scarlet and gold, the Horse Guards Blue, on their nobly-formed horses, found no nest in his thoughts: Kansas men, Kansas women, and Kansas town were all the world to him. He was satisfied with the streets of his city, its life, and the roads of Kansas and Missouri.

—Don't get this place, he said to Sean. Wha's its name?

—Totnes, the oldest town in England, bar London, and it's near the coast of a county called Devon.

—Ay, Devon, he echoed tonelessly. A long way from my home town, he added, after a pause; a long way; yessir.

—You'd like to be back in Kansas City? Sean queried.

—I sure would! he said quickly, a gleam of interest coming into the big, brown, wide-open eyes. Kansas suits me, suits me fine. Yessir, I'd like to be back in Kansas. Guess I will, one day.

—Devon's a very lovely county, said Sean, hoping to interest him into asking questions.

—It sure is, buddy, he responded, again tonelessly. Kansas suits me better. I'm Kansas born an' Kansas bred, an' I jus' can't get goin' anywhere else; I really can't.

—Well, I hope Kansas City will like Totnes Town, murmured Sean.

—It sure will, murmured the sentry; it sure does. It's a small hang-out, though, ain't it, buddy? Guess it could be dumped down in Kansas City's smallest street, and not be in the way. You could carry all that's goin' round here under one arm. But the people are swell; gotta give them their due; swell, yessir.

—Where do you go from here? asked Sean.

—Dunno, buddy. That's only our second hop. Wonder what the next hop's gonna be like? The eyes went dead again, hiding any sign of an image of Kansas. Well, so long; be seeing you. Gotta get goin' the round; and he turned away to continue his sauntering parade, slow and mechanical, round the camp, seeking silence and solitude to bring the image of Kansas into the big, brown, wide-open eyes again; and a red laugh of war stung the ear of Sean.

Each was homeless near a thousand homes. Oh, to be home again, home again, home again, under the apple-boughs down by the mill. Throughout the camp there was an air of gay, almost reckless, bewilderment, mild, but bitter, as if the G.I.'s silently thought it unwise to be here. The innocents abroad. Far away from Jelly Roll and from Lead Belly, from their racing simple songs, their wisecracks. Where is now the merry party I remember long ago! Laughing round the Christmas fire, laden by its ruddy glow. Or in summer's balmy evenings, in the fields among the hay? They have all dispersed and wandered far away, far away. Some have gone from us forever; longer here they could not stay — Oh, change it, buddy; don't make gloom gloomier. Who was it, what bastard laughed in that harsh, red way?

One or two of the tents had a ukelele-player, who could be heard strumming out lively notes, with, maybe, some comrade singing some jazz-song or hot ditty: singing sorrow and fear away. Away, away! A hard thing to do, buddies. It didn't sound merry. If one came from Chicago, another from Texas, they were all, all lonely and all far from home; from things familiar, from a sweetheart's kiss, from a mother's fussy care, from a wife's companionship, from all things settled. They had been hunted from the serene monotony of peace to the savage, purposeless monotony of war. Privacy was gone, and all lived an alice-in-blunderland life, with death, maybe, round the corner of the next hop. Some of these men, many of them, perhaps, may be phantoms already, gay as so many of them pretend to be. The Spirit of Pity no longer hovers over, no longer probes, the heart of war; the Spirit of Irony only gets where war is waged.

The Stars and Stripes flying from a tall pole at the camp's entrance made the place American territory, but it refused to make the place a home. The kindly and talkative Devon folk made things as easy and as natural as they could for the soldiers, but the Americans, white and black, carried but an image of home in all their eyes. The life in camp was dirty, dull, and boring. Besides, the guns were being stuffed now with something more than wadding and powder. There was more of death than of pageantry in their booming. None here sought death at the cannon's mouth. The next camp might be a camp of a dead brigade, and far away from Brooklyn. Gay as they might be, they all knew that they faced towards the front where the graveyards were. Many comrades were already under ground in the Philippines and other isles of the Pacific, never again to return to Dixie Land, to the cornfields of Kansas, or hear the patter of their own feet on the pavements of Broadway. It was all dreadful; yet here in the recreation grounds of the little town of Totnes, hundreds more were waiting to join the dead. However they might hang out the colours of motley, however they might play their ukeleles, however they might shout their wisecracking comments on an improvised baseball game, the camp had around it a deep black border.

The panzers were racing over Russia! Totnes was busy presenting things, making toys, holding concerts and dances to provide funds for Mrs. Churchill's Russian Red Cross Fund. In the window of the Anglo-Soviet Headquarters stood three huge photographs, four feet tall and three feet wide, of Churchill to the right, Stalin to the left, with Franklin D. Roosevelt in the centre. The Soviet Flag was seen for the first time in Totnes, and hundreds wore a little Red Star in the breasts of blouses or in the lapels of their coats; for the fight of the Red Army had modified the fear, and had removed the very present danger of invasion; while through all the hurrying activities moved the American soldiers, attending concert and dance, their convoys of great guns and tanks rumbling along the street of the town, often to the gentle accompaniment of a tinkle tinkle from a ukelele playing somewhere from a tent in the camp.

The panzers were racing over Russia! We're owre the border, and awa'! Russia first; England next, and within a year the Wehrmacht will be doing the Lambeth Walk along Piccadilly and the Mile End Road. Race on, my brave warriors, invincible and hitlarious! Let the united drums of a united herrenfolk beat a united roll when Hitler enters Moscow! Henceforth, the world would form its life to the beat of Hitler's heart. Race on, my men! This is the way that Hitler rides, a gallop, a gallop, a gallop! Another day or two will see the Russians parking their cannon, garaging their tanks, and the Red Army dropping their rifles to lift their hands, and cry for peace. But the cannons went on blazing, the Russian tanks split the German tanks in two; and at Stalingrad, Germany's woe began. Oh, weep for the German dead; the young and sprightly ones lie still forever! Red laughter of war echoing over the graves. And Hitler heard it; yes, Hitler heard it. It would soon be louder.

The work for England and for the Soviet Union went forward in the little town of Totnes. The rose and crown looked fine beside the hammer and the sickle. Sean helped as well as he could, addressing envelopes and delivering circulars, for one thing. He tapped at the door of a Totnes bungalow to deliver a circular notifying a meeting. The door half opened, and he saw half of a middle-aged woman standing there, crying silently, crying deeply. Mechanically, Sean extended the letter; she made no movement to take it; she didn't look at it; just looked aimlessly before her, crying silently.

—Notice of a meeting, he mumbled, trying to think how he could get away quietly.

—I don't want it, she said, tonelessly; don't want anything now. Just got a telegram telling me son's killed; killed, an' us doesn't know how or where. No grave of his own even, for us heard they are buryin' 'em in bundles now, an' us doesn't know where; doesn't know where. Crying silently and deeply, she slowly and silently shut the door.

She hadn't had the comfort of hearing her son's last moan, hadn't had the joy of committing his body to the grave. She had been denied the mystery of sorrow in stroking her loved one's body for the last time, like Gilderoy's sweetheart, who, at least, had had that gaunt privilege:

> Wi' tears, that trickled for his death,
> I washt his comely clay;
> An' siker in a grave sae deep
> I laid the dear-lued boy.

Not even that; not even that much elation for the mother.

It was everywhere: it followed Hitler about; it sounded soft, ironic, murderous, in the ears of the Nazis racing across Russia; it trickled through the fancies of the Americans digging trenches by the side of their camp, offset by deep pits for ack-ack guns; it circled round the British depriving England of a name, the hurried medical inspection of youth, the drill-donned gas-masks, the call for identity cards, heard in the sound of the siren's wail, gurgled through the curses misspent fixing black-outs over the windows, its derision blurred blasphemously the gasps of a deep-wounded, dying lad, and here a gust of it had swept through a humble Devon bungalow, soft, ironic, murderous — the red laugh of war.

IN CELLAR COOL

DAUB the name of Dunkirk in black and gold on our banners. Forget the place, and forever remember the time. An ugly smudge, gold-circled, in the people's fight for freedom. Hitler comes with tanks descending upon us. Backward to the beaches! The sea must save us. Between the devil and the deep blue sea. The Nazi Army is but a mile behind. Hitler's chosen people are on top. Forward to the beaches! Left right, left right, left right, left right. We are very tired, oh, kings and captains. Forward to the beaches! Tramp, tramp, tramp, the boys are marching. Hundreds of thousands of British troops and tens of thousands of Frenchmen are marching to the beaches, and the tramp of their marching feet becomes the pulse of England's heart: the pulse of Irish hearts in England, too. From every road, north, south, and east, press on to the beaches. Pile your rifles by the hedgerows, for they are useless now, useless now. They can kill no longer. Rank your tanks, your guns, across the wider roads to check the panzers, for guns and tanks are useless now, useless now. Let the spirit drag the legs, let the legs drag the bodies along: we must get to the beaches. Can you hear the sea? Not yet, not yet. Left right, left right.

What was that flame ahead of us on the road. God damn it, the Nazi guns are firing on us! Right incline; don't look to the left; never mind them; pass them by; close your ears to the squealing. Let the wounded attend to the wounded; let the dead bury the dead. Start a song, lads; someone start a song. We thank with brief thanksgiving whatever gods may be that no life lives forever, that dead men rise up never, that even the weariest river winds somewhere safe to sea. God, that's a meek, mournful ditty. That won't help, help us along, Long river of wearied men mus' just keep rolling along. A long journey through long days without end, seeing the day rise and the night fall. Don't stagger; keep straight, keep right on left right to the end of the road. Jesus! the Stukas are over us and the flames are pillaring the way forward and the ground is twisting under us. Looka, the trees are on fire, and the grass so green is brown and black and burning. Right incline! Eyes right! Close all ears to the squealing: let the wounded attend to the wounded, the dead bury the dead. What sounds are those? The scream of the sea-gulls, the cry of the curlews. The beaches are before us! Pass the word behind to halt. Halt? Why are we halting? What are them in front doing; what are they thinking of? Why the hell are we halting? For Christ's sake, push on! The Stukas will be here again in a moment. Bad enough to feel sick when a bomb falls and we on the move; how'll we feel when a bomb falls on us standing still! Forward to the beaches! Halt; the beach has as many men as a beach can hold. Oh, when will my head rest on the pillow at home while the vacant midnight passes? The boats and ships are loaded and gone; we must wait for another embarking before we move again. Halt! Stand at ease!

How far are the beaches now? Two miles; five miles; ten miles. How long till we get there, get there? We're too tired to stay still. If we rest, we rust, and joints will bend no more. We are all crooked men already. The burdens are heavy; burden of sweat under arms, between the thighs, running down breast and back; burden of aching limbs, and the tightening pain in the head. Why do the damned seagull and curlew come in so far, deceiving us, deceiving us into thinking the beaches are but a few steps more? Many steps more; many, many: oh, the beaches, the beaches! Burden of fear in the heart. England's armed pride, armed no longer, bent and broken, stumbling along to the beaches, the road swaying under them, the Stukas over them, the cheers of the conquering Wehrmacht behind them; and the wayside full of the wayside flowers, wild flowers, gaily yellow, brilliantly blue, flaming red, safe in the sunlight, and silently shaming us; over the blossoms the birds everywhere, no tightness in the head, no ache under the wing; birds everywhere, yellow-backed, red-breasted, blue-tailed; busy nesting, shaming us in their song. Oh, the foxes have holes and the birds of the air have nests. We're all very tired. Who's that murmuring ahead? What's he muttering? Our Father which art in heaven, hallowed, hallowed, hall. No use, buddy; waste of time, waste of breath. The Stukas are between your words and the place where they've got to go if an answer is to come. May be a dead man before the words can dodge the Stukas, and go on to the top. The aches of hell are all on this one road. The head is drooping, drooping, drooping down. Must be sleep. Forgot about sleep; had to keep moving. Drive the thought of sleep from the seeking mind. What's that gentle humming? Such gentle humming never came from distant Stukas. Bees! Odd things in the air. Bees flying about like the birds and the Stukas. If only the Stukas would go, and leave the birds, the bees, and the men alone. The road has become a corridor towards sleep; more — towards life. Why don't we go on? What the hell are we waiting for? Keep the head up. I hate sleep, I hate it! We're moving again! You in front — for Christ's sake, lift your feet! On to the beaches, the beaches. Through the sunshine, with the birds and the bees, move the men. Oh, when shall my head rest on a pillow at home while the vacant midnight passes!

Dunkirk was one of England's darkest victories. Having nothing left, she gained all back in time. Near four hundred thousand men, sound in wind and limb, were sailed, steamed, ferried and dragged over the waves from Dunkirk to Dover. It was as if the whole army had swum the Channel. My old Kentucky home, good morning! England, who had traduced herself with gloom, now took hold of hope, and confidence had become a great golden chip on her shoulder.

But very few had much time to rest their heads on a pillow at home, for all were now ordered into the fury of regrouping and re-training to be ready for the coming fight in the coming invasion. Some even saw the parked barges of joking Germans racing over the sea to Dover and Dungeness; even over the sea to Skye.

A halt of a few seconds came after the exodus from Dunkirk, a heated halt. All in England were waiting for something to happen, something worse than the worst they expected. Send us the tools, America. They're a long time acoming. Hardly a gun in the house. We can't fight with umbrellas. Send them soon; send them quick; send them now. The bombers will come splitting palace and slum, and what shall we English do then, poor things! They were waiting with long-handled shovels to be used to scoop up incendiary bombs, nice and calmly, and carry them, blazing, out to garden, yard, or street; waiting with stirrup-pumps to put out any fire started by any incendiary bomb that had evaded the prod of the shovel; waiting with their heaps of sand lying outside of front or back doors to be sprinkled over a big flame caused by a bunch of bombs, too many to be carried out by the scoop of a shovel; the Home Guard waiting for the enemy with long-handled pikes to thrust and thrust, parry and thrust, advance and thrust, till their shirts were red, and the Nazis fled like a cowardly caravan. Full of fear and anxiety, but their hearts were strong; the British were at their best; their hearts sang; sang

> That song, whose breath
> Might lead to death,
> But never to retreating.

But all got ready to crouch. They knew not yet how they would have to go through the earthquake, the great wind, and the fire. There had been straight talks and roundabout arguments as to where lay the best place to crouch should an air-raid come. A safe, strong hiding-hole. No use to go into a church, for sanctuary had lost its meaning: altar rails or altar horns were no damned good now. Even the bird sanctuaries might suffer. Some said the coal-cellar, some said under the stairs, a few poor minds said under a table. Hoosh the cat from under the table. One thing was laid down as a law — always be behind a wall and always keep away from the windows, for they had become mad, magic casements, opening out on to a terrible death. Some built Hans Anderson shelters at the ends of their little gardens, damp, unhealthy holes, more dangerous than the bombs themselves. Under the kitchen in the O'Casey house was a cellar about as big as a double and a single bed, laid side by side. The floor was of earth, moist and maggoty, giving out a musty smell. This they tried to strengthen by a few uprights and struts; covered the floor with straw and the straw with canvas; added a few kitchen chairs, cushions; set up a shelf on the wall for a jug of water, biscuits and some sweets for the children, with a pack of cards for a possible game. This cellar was reached from the outside by a number of steep, slippery steps of firebrick, requiring great caution and some gift of balancing when descending them; but to get to these it would be necessary to circle half the house. Experience told them that in the haste of an air-raid, it would be quite easy to break a neck. It wouldn't do; Sean had a lame leg for a week after trying a quick descent. So a trap-door was cut out of the kitchen floor, and a roughly-made step-ladder brought them down from the kitchen into the mouldy and miserable place that wouldn't make a decent tomb. There, then, was this handsome zone of security waiting for them when the tense moments of a bomb-raid came flooding over them. Safety right beneath their feet. Now thank we all our God with hearts and hands and voices!

Everything was ready: the long-handled shovel rested beside the heap of sand outside the front door; the scullery window had been gummed over so as to prevent it splintering in a blast, though, of course, a blast not only took away the windows, but the doors and walls as well. The box of first-aid equipment was ready to hand; a large clothes-basket in which to carry down the baby girl, and with Eileen's knowledge of how to deal with almost anything except death, they waited, as all others waited, for the terror to come. The heavens were hung with black.

Then, one night (one night of love), at eleven o'clock, pip emma, the three children in bed, Eileen getting ready to go into hers, and Sean working away at the biographical book, *Drums Under The Windows* and the play, *Red Roses For Me*, the Siren sounded — a series of rising, descending, wavering wails, sending a shiver through all who heard it. The bomber is acomin' in. Get going! Hurry, hurry! Get the children up; carry the baby down; hurry, man, hurry, woman! Where's the first-aid box? Where in th' name o' God's the first-aid box! Oh, do hurry, or the bombs may be down on us before we get to the cellar. The blankets, the blankets — don't forget the blankets! And down they climbed, down to the mouldy, maggoty cellar, meagre candlelight showing them in a wavering way how to settle down, maybe for the rest of the night; perhaps, forever. Now, overhead, they could hear the whirring burr burr of the aeroplane-engines; over the roofs of Totnes, over this very house; no one speaking; all listening, bar the babe in the basket; all knowing that a direct hit would make a united bloody blot of them all. Sean's stomach was so tense that it seemed the skin holding it could stretch no farther. They seemed to be lower now — the engines were louder. His nerves vibrated busily, making the heart give a quicker beat. Eileen looked quite calm, showing no signs of tenseness; cool customer. Both had to look unconcerned so as not to agitate the children, though the elder boy seemed to be as calm as his mother. Sean and the younger lad of six years were the only two who shook. Sean died several times that night, though no bombs fell; not on Totnes, but they were falling thick and fast a little distance away. The minutes filling into hours were dotted with the sharp, snarling rumble of exploding bombs, and the sudden tremors the explosions gave to the house made them all crouch closer, tightening the nerves to throw the tremor off. It was a queer thought that the ragged, runabout guttersnipe of Dublin's dirtier streets should be crouching in the cellar under the kitchen of a Totnes house. Yet no change, for the cellar was a slum, with filth below them and terror overhead. A big change among the changes of many-coloured life, and far from a pleasant one. The many-coloured dome had turned dark, and above it chaos and old night had begun to reign again. Millions were crouching as they were crouching here. The monstrous ego squatting in Berlin or Berchtesgaden was making millions do what they were never born to do; an ego with a senseless, smiting arm stretching from Berlin to the Volga, up to the Arctic snows, and down to this little town of Totnes. All were being bitten, and no brazen serpent, now, to heal the bites: nothing but the making of an aeroplane to equal Hitler's and a bigger gun to smash the gun that he was firing. Where were the bombs falling? It mightn't be long till they were falling here, so what was the use of worrying out a guess? But still they worried, and still they guessed, while the baby slept and the two boys sitting on the floor nodded forward in tendentious sleep; nodded till they stretched themselves out, and were covered with the blankets and the overcoats worn by Eileen and himself.

All were miserable and cold now; even the children were moving uneasily under the blankets; as if the clothes had taken into them the coldness of the damp from the floor under them and the walls around. He could stick it no longer. There was little safety here, anyhow. If a bomb gave even a glancing blow to the house, it would go stumbling down on top of them, and all would go down to dusty death by suffocation. Sean had liefer die under a tree, behind a hedge, or walking fast or slow along a road. He looked at his watch — near half-past two, with the burring drone of the aeroplanes still sounding overhead. He couldn't stick the numbness of body and bone any longer. A cup of tea! Would it be wise to leave the cellar? Wise or unwise, he'd go. What better way to die than to be brewing tea when death came? He went up, made a pot of tea in the scullery, and brought it down to the perishing family. Jasus, wasn't it sweet! Whisht! Heavy steps coming down the steps outside; a desperate scraping as the boots slipped down most of the way; a catching of breath, and a hurried curse; then a knock at the cellar-door.

—Who's that?

—Me. 'Arry, and in came a Home Guard, in steel helmet, full uniform, and rifle in hand.

—Near broke neck on steps, he panted. On watch for paratroopers; expecs 'em drop anywhere. He rubbed his neck; near broke she acomin' down. Know where th' bastards is bombin'? Plymouth! They're pastin' Plymouth. Swarmin' over she, an' only a few ack-ackers defendin'. He sipped from a cup of tea. Th' bastards! Sean noticed the hand holding the cup trembling. Jus' relieved fr'm guardin' bridge. Poundin' Plymouth, poundin' she to bits!

The Siren sounded the All Clear at last; the Home Guard hurried off to rejoin his comrades; the blankets and children were lugged up out of the cellar, and were guided to their beds, Sean and Eileen elated that no bombs had fallen, and that sleep was before them for the rest of the night. No sooner had they begun to remove their clothes than the Siren sounded the Alarm again, and the whole weary, wasteful performance had to be borne once more. Down, down in the cellar cool again; down in it till half-past six before the All Clear sounded, rising from it once more, weary and worn and sad. To hell with it! Sean had learned the sound of the Nazi planes, and he and Eileen decided that for the future Sean wouldn't rouse them till he heard the Nazi planes circling directly overhead, and sensed any danger of an attack, let the siren sound how it might. They decided, too, that they would stay in a room, and seek the cellar no more.

Sean did most of his work at night when all were in bed, and the house was soundless. One night, typing away at a biographical chapter, he thought dimly that he heard the snarling burrr of Nazi planes, but was too busy to care; and, anyway, if there was any danger, the siren would send its wail to him. He was sitting at a big table, in a ground-floor room, facing towards the Plymouth road. Suddenly a shattering explosion shoved him and the chair a good way away from the table, the typewriter lepped up a foot from its pad, glass of a window crashed out on to the floor, the hall-door shook violently, and the whole house shuddered. The family came rushing down, covered with anything their hands first found, and all gathered in the hall, for planes were dropping bombs very near. Some had fallen a little way up the Plymouth road, in a field bordering the roadway, making a huge crater, and sending a row of houses opposite into a panic, so that the windows twisted, the ceilings fell, the doors buckled, and a little child was near blinded by the dust of a ceiling falling all over her. Had the bombs dropped thirty yards farther east, they would have fallen on the road, directly in front of the houses, and then there wouldn't have been many left alive within their walls. Again, and once again, shattering explosions, tossing the door about, shaking the house, and sending the hall where they crouched rocking so that it seemed ready to change its shape like a crushed-in cardboard box. Night after night it went on, till it seemed concussion was the natural form of the earth's emotion.

Night after night, Plymouth was pounded, till one thought it must have swallowed itself up in its own flame and its own erupting dust. At night, even after the Alarm had gone, and planes were circling viciously about in the sky, the people living on the Plymouth road would stand outside staring at the tremendous glare of fire filling the south-western sky, just a few miles away, showing plain where Plymouth was burning; burning amid the sharp rumbling of exploding bombs; a sky that seemed to say that hell was no longer beneath us, but seemed to have ascended and to reign where heaven used to be. Evening full of the aeroplanes' wings. In the broad bosom of that red, flaming plenitude many a Nazi airman died, many a British mother's son, many a British sweetheart's boy, found death, too, in that red sky-glow made by Plymouth's burning. Light at evening tide.

> Last night as I lay on my pillow, last night as I lay on my bed,
> Last night as I lay on my pillow, I dreamed that my Bonny was dead.

So he is, lass: a dream come true.

In the flame beneath, of which that in the sky was but a shadow, men died with a quick curse, or before a sudden prayer had finished; women stretched themselves over screaming children as the walls came toppling down on them imaging their arms of flesh to be fit props to keep the tumbling stones away from smiting their little ones.

When the Heinkels, the Junkers, the Dorniers, and the diving Stukas had shed all their bombs and departed, smoke-harried men and women sweated and cracked their muscles to reach, here and there, a faint cry heard somewhere at the bottom of a tangled ruin; daring to add some of their own lives to the already dead in an effort to dig out a living soul from a heap of smouldering débris. All kinds went down in the Plymouth bombing; many a sprig of a Tess of the D'Urbervilles, many a pair of blue eyes, many a Farmer Oak, many a Sergeant Troy, a Marty South, a Diggory Venn, Bill Brewer, Jan Stewer, Peter Gurney, Peter Davy, Dan'l Whiddon, Harry Hawk, old Uncle Tom Cobley, an' all; good souls, gay and morose, sensible useful souls — all thrust together in the terrible companionship of violent death.

A friend of Sean's, an ack-ack gunner, home for a few days' rest and a few nights' sleep, half staggered to a chair, on a visit for tea to empty himself of the thoughts he had had while helping to hit a bomber darting through the clouds, and snatch him down to death; his eyes red with staring into flame, so worn out that his crimson-topped forage-cap remained on his head throughout his visit.

—Looks like Plymouth's gone, he said, looks like they 'as done it to she. Yes, Sean, mister, looks like she's gone. He seemed to be sinking into deeper exhaustion through rest in the deep chair. Yes, mister Sean, he went on, now too tired to try to open the slitted eyes, Plymouth's woeful place; don't 'ee never go near she again, for 'tis death's front parlour now. Day after day, week after week, us was at guns afirin' up, afirin' up, afirin' up, till all us wanted from Nazis was chance of a little sleep, sleep. The few guns us 'ad was tired, too, afirin' up an' up. No rest for guns, no rest for 'em afirin' of 'em up. No, mister; keep on your toes, an' keep afirin' up was hourly order. Seen whole skyline agoin' down; houses, docks, churches, chapels, shops, just athrowin' theyselves down flat on knees, on faces, alyin' flat in flame, with us afirin' up, afirin' up, afirin' up! Ten blows for one, us'll give the bastards yet; ten blows for one!

The gunner seemed to drowse, his face haggard, his skin bitten into visible pores by the sharp smuts flying about and around the smoking city; his hands restless, the fingers moving about among the buttons of his tunic, up to his cap, along his chin, and down to the tunic again; his eyes closed, though the darkness made the flames he had passed through much more visible still. Sean gently took from the gunner's mouth the cigarette threatening to burn his lips, and put a fresh one in its place, the soldier never once trying to open an eye; still, save for the hands giving flickering touches to his tunic buttons, down, up, down again, darting unsteadily from the top tunic button to the tiny ones on his crimson-topped cap, down again along the row of tunic buttons, up again to touch the chin, and down again to the buttons on the tunic, his nerves showing in tiny crinkling waves under his skin, stretching, and then crinkling again. A rough-cast face disturbed, clear-cut honesty its one testimony to grace: his whole soul now a crunching cry for vengeance.

—Th' shelters was useless, Sean, came in a murmur from the depths of the chair, and the tired hazy eyes flickered open to a half-slit; a fool's fart would have knocked they down. Blasted to bits all tumblin' down with they fallin' buildin's. An' fortunes was made out of they, Sean; fortunes. Doesn't bear thinkin' on. He stretched himself, made half an effort to rise, and lay back again. When us started firin' up first, us tried to hum The Old Hundredth, but us couldn't get further 'n the first line — you know, Sean, All people that on earth do dwell. No go. All people was afightin' each other. Kill, kill, or be killed! He wrenched himself from the chair, the hands still flickering over and along the buttons. When the old mind gets tired, Sean, mister, I says to she, I says, There's a war on, mate, an' don't 'ee forget it. Us must get home for a rest. A rest is all us's needin'; a long, long rest. Thanks for tea, mister Sean, an' for the happy talk; does one good, does she. But the tired body slid back into the chair again, the weary eyes closed once more, the flickering hands went more slowly from button to button, and the tired soldier dozed.

Here was a chap who should have been guiding a plough, or driving a tractor, now spending years of his life, in sun, rain, frost, and snow, at the arse of a big gun, firing up to the firmament; loading shells instead of loading hay; trying by the probing light from a magnified candle to nick an enemy in the higher air, and send him tumbling down. Asleep now, and harmless, even pathetic; but dreaming it, dreaming harm, surely; encouraging himself to hold on till the time came to give ten blows for one. Here, a father seeks a son, there a son seeks a father; there a mother scrounges in the ruins for a child, here a child is wailing for a mother; a husband burrows for a wife, a wife watches others burrowing for her husband. All were hunting for the dead. Give a glance, and go, mate. No time to look; there's a war on. Ten blows for one. Vengeance is mine, saith the gunner.

Stick it, grim gunner: the time is coming when for every home demolished in Plymouth, ten will sink into rubble in Hamburg and Berlin. They may blast our streets away, but we will blast away their cities; level them so that not one stone will be left to balance itself on another; the people who once trod entranced through cities, sure and proud, will seek refuge in their ruins, like conies seeking shelter in the rocks. Nothing left for them but holes and corners; scream it out, gunner — holes and corners! Smother the terrible testimony in the drum-beat of bombs exploding!

Sleep on, grim gunner, and take your peace; and dream your great dream. The time cometh and is at hand, when your gun shall be idle and silent, cloaked against the weather; when you may sit calm on a bench in the inn, drinking your beer, and chuckle, gunner, when you hear the German kid scream and the kid's mother scream, and the kid's father yell in agony, for the cities and the towns where they have their habitation shall fall upon them, splintering their bones and squashing their ripe flesh till it is flesh no longer; and you shall laugh, grim gunner, for there shall not be a corner in city or town, be it never so small, that shall not be inflamed with the terrible blaze from a bursting bomb. Then you will have time and breath to sing All people that on earth do dwell, remembering God's mercy is forever sure.

The tired eyes twitched half open, and the gunner's soul urged the gunner's body out of the chair's comfort. He stood up, a little crookedly, blinking at Sean, the fingers still playing wistfully with the buttons.

—Must go, he said. Want rest, long sleep; yes. Don't 'ee worry, no, don't 'ee worry, Sean, mister; we'll bust they bastards soon. Carry on.

He moved crookedly to the door, and went out, Sean going with him to the garden gate to watch him walk towards town and home; watch him walk unsteadily, with occasional jerky pauses. He faced round, suddenly, shook a fist in the air, and shouted, Don't 'ee worry; us'll get they bastards soon! Then he turned, and went on shakily, as if uncertain where he was going; as if he were walking in a half-sleep, as, almost certainly, he was.

Life kept on going into new years, and Christmas was celebrated more scantily than in former times. The decorations on the Christmas tree were shoddy, and had abandoned their scintillating brilliancy; peace on earth to men of good will had swindled into a mocking injury of the inquisitive Oh, yeah, brother! The bells of Christmas had croaked themselves into silence. Harder times than those of Dickens were upon all like a pall without a break. Spiritual ack-ack guns throughout days of national penitence kept afirin' up, afirin' up, petitions for help, but heaven seemed to be far and away out of range. Aforetime, kids had seen apparitions in Lourdes, kids had seen apparitions in Fatima, kids had seen apparitions even in little Knock; but, now, the time seemed to have dimmed their eyes. Most probably, they were shivering with cold and fear in some Nazi concentration camp, or were hiding in an Anderson shelter, or crouching under a Morrison table, biding away from the bombs. No apparition appeared in Westminster over the anglican abbey, or over the roman catholic cathedral; none was seen anywhere; none. Even the Angels of Mons, it seemed, had dwindled into old-age pensioners. The skies were too dangerous now for angels to be knocking about. The baby girl, Shivaun, who had been carried down to the cellar in a clothes-basket, now was a sturdy kid, running round and prattling away; even attending a nursery school: but still the bombs were falling, and the black-out as keen and wearisome as ever.

On a bright, brisk morning, after the children had gone to school, Eileen and he were busy washing up the breakfast things, when, half-way through the work, they heard the rasping roar, continuous and angry, of an aeroplane, somewhere above them; a roar that filled the scullery so that they couldn't hear each other speak.

—Ah! shouted Sean into Eileen's ear, one of our aeroplanes in trouble!

He rushed to the window, flung it open, and stretched out to get a clearer view of the sky. Yes, there were one — two — three, flying by, skimming the O'Casey roof and the roofs beyond, flames spitting out of every fuselage. Then came a long, shattering explosion, shaking their nerves, and rocking the house under their feet and over their heads; an explosion that seemed to grow louder as it rumbled fiercely along.

—God, the house's falling! shouted Eileen.

—Come along to the front of the house! he shouted back, the explosions turning the shout to a whisper; and the two of them ran from the back of the house to the front room facing the road; but this room was rocking more violently than the other.

—Out of the house, into the open! he shouted, catching her hand and hauling her to the window, but push and push as they would it wouldn't open to them. Then, suddenly, they saw that the hasp was on the window, and ten men couldn't have pushed it up. Holding each other's hands, they stood in the centre of the room to laugh splendidly at the frantic and ridiculous efforts they had made to open a bolted window by main strength; the snarling rumble of the explosions forgotten in a hilarious sense of humour; laughter that sounded through the explosions shaking out a window, sending down the greater part of two ceilings, and loosening the trembling house in all its joints.

They unhooked the hasp, flung up the window, and ran out to shelter beside a loaded lorry standing alone, without a driver, in the centre of the Plymouth road, the air all round full of a biting acid smell of fumes mixed with burning wood and scorching brick. Half the railway-station was in ruins, the bridge had been damaged, walls flung down, Totnes main street was a river of glass, and all the roofs around were battered, broken, and slit with machine-gun bullets. A number of persons were wounded, and an Air-Force officer, just released on leave, and waiting at the station for a train to take him home, was killed; wending a way home, he went too far; stepped over time into eternity. No wound showed on him, not even a scratch, but his lungs within had been burst asunder by the blast, as two strong hands coming together would burst a toy balloon. When the raid was over, soldiers returned to the lorry, and told Sean and Eileen that they couldn't have selected a more dangerous place to shelter, for the lorry was loaded with explosives. Another fine laugh for them, sitting by the fire that night, the black-out up, the danger past for the present.

Through it all — the bombing, the black-out, the drills, the departure of loved ones into a paramount and pungent danger; the arrival of telegrams to some family telling it briefly that a loved one had vanished; the lengthening of the Roll of Honour, and the swelling lists in the local papers of simple rhymes, like

> Time passes, shadows fall;
> Love and remembrance outlast all;

for nothing dies but something mourns: through them all, life went on, harder now in its everyday problems, so that, with ration cards and allocated points, with a heavy scarcity to select from, the housewife was ever in a maze of figures that toppled to a tangle as soon as they were settled to a tidy-looking sum. Many an old woman, an old man, or a young girl, go along silently, now; no longer eager to stay for a gossip; wordless where they used to babble; two have lost a son, one a lover. But still life hurries on, too busy to halt for a moment of mourning. Too much mourning to mourn at all. The winter-time is the hardest, when the black-out lasts too long, and makes the gayest heart moody. Winter's bosom-pals, the cold rains, fierce winds, nipping frosts, and sullen snows have been with us far too long; and so all welcome the snowdrop slowly and sturdily pushing its white way up through the cold earth and the rain-sodden grasses, its stem of gentle green bearing its tiny white flag of promise that though winter be still here, spring's not far behind. There they are in a drenched meadow by the Dart, or on the moor, demure and thoughtless, but confident under the grey, grumbling skies of aged and agued winter; tiny and fragile angels of the annunciation sent by spring to tell all that life will soon be new-born under sunnier skies, and sit in the lap of an ampler earth.

The snowdrops send a stir through the hearts of many living in the little houses stretching themselves along the hedgy roads, nestling under the shoulders of the hill, or hiding away in the deeper dip of a valley. The people murmur among themselves, saying, Soon they snowdrops will be adottin' they woods, an' maybe clusterin'; an' us'll go gether them. They wonder if the broad fields will nurse more of them than they did last year. Women too old for uniforms, or privileged by family burdens; girls too young for uniforms, and many children, will search out their oldest clothes and strongest boots to be found in press or box, to equip themselves against muddy or snowy road and sodden woods; and among the country-folk will be a sprinkle of those who have been blown thither by the red, flaming winds that turned their little city homes into desolate confusion. They will fetch out old baskets, and trim them anew, so that the blossoms may be carried back without bruise or blemish. Some will sigh for a pair of wellington boots, for the grass will be high, and will be plump with the rain that has fallen so fast and so often, making foot, ankle, and knee numb with the sappy wet, and will saturate the pendent skirts of the blossom-hunters, making the skirts cling madly to the cold, perishing legs of the enthusiastic thieves. They will bear the flowers home, not to decorate a mantel-piece with a graceful tribute to the Virgin or to that angel who drove Eve from the Garden out into the snow, and who, breathing on the snowflakes as they fell, left snowdrops in full blossom behind: they pull them out, pluck them up out of the snow to market them. They trim their stalks respectably, wrap them thoughtlessly in moistened paper, pack them decently into suitable cardboard coffins, and hurry them to the steaming train; for the well-off of London cry out for them, and they carry a good price back to those who had plucked them from their cool beds in the hidden places of the snowy woods. They droop quick in the hot breast of a London dame, and wilt as fast when they are forced to form for a minute a pool of quiet glory on the polished corner of a pompous table. Throw them in the dust: many more fresh and fair ones left where these ones fading first were snatched from the snow.

It must be that upon each tiny snowy blossom there lies now a tiny crimson stain, for where they grow, the ground often shuddered, wondering why, and they have trembled many and many a time with the sigh of many a dying Englishman, the near-by sigh of a dying Englishwoman, and the dying English child sighing a bewildered farewell to all that killed her. Their tender and reclining loveliness fits no way into the warm and cosy bosom of even the prettiest woman; nor do they sit satisfied in the blue bowl on the polished corner of a grandee's table. They are not for the world-wise, the wasteful-minded, or the whirling dancer. This little plant with its green leaves touched with white, its white flower touched with green; these three pale sepals holding the tiny, green-speckled white cup, enclosing the tinier yellow pistil, like a midget queen, beneath her canopy, cloaked in saffron. These pale pages of their lustrous sisters, the daffodils, may rest in peace only in the bosom of the very young when the very young are dead; to lie quiet on the young breast, replacing the red rose of life snatched from the mouth of those who died too soon. Breathless and afraid these blossoms feel, where red wine-spots stain the purity of linen, where silver glistens, where words are many and the voice is loud. Rather let them rest in peace upon the breast of the young who haven't had their day.

Through all life's twinings, its affection and animosity, the war went on; the men went off to die or came back mangled; the bombs still fell; the black-out was still as tense as ever: the tale of a wasted life was still being told. Sean and Eileen had bought a Morrison table with its thick steel top, and this had been set up in a little room off the hallway, ten feet from the front door. Under this table, Eileen, the girl of three, and the boy of six lay flat, while Sean and the elder boy of thirteen sat in the hallway, just outside the door of the room where the rest of the family lay under the steel table, whenever bombs were falling in the nearer neighbourhood. The table was said to be able to bear up brightly against the shock of a tumbling house, however big, and to preserve a cavity where those under it could possibly last out life in semi-suffocation till a Rescue-squad had time to dig them out of their huge burial mound, and give them better air to breathe. A wan hope under a wan protection; but it gave more confidence than any useless prayer or any old-fashioned hymn. There they were, Eileen and the two younger children flat on their bellies under the steel table, the little girl laughing at the experience, the younger lad merry, too, but sobering when the house shook; the older lad, quiet and unmoved, sitting on a chest beside Sean, glum, though trying, too, to look unconcerned, but cocking his ears to distinguish the nationality of the aeroplane engines throbbing, snarling, throbbing overhead; his work laid out on a table in another room, abandoned when the raid came, waiting for him to come back to writhe towards a competent interest in it again, when the raid ceased, and the All Clear sounded; his heart in his mouth whenever a bomb fell near, and the explosion made the windows jump, and the hall-door, a few feet away, bulge in and out, with a rattling snarl as rapid. as a frantic roll beaten by a frantic pair of hands on a tightly-laced drum. Oh, in war, there is neither song nor sermon. Oh! let the winter go, let the spring hasten, let the summer come, let the autumn linger, and let this damned war die away out of life; let Hitler and his chums die with it; and all who may ever want war again, die too; so that we may have time to look at, ponder over, and enjoy, our desolation.

SHAW'S CORNER

A LETTER came when stars were paling, came from Charlotte Shaw; a letter that was kind and homely; a letter that was law; written in that style of handwriting so oddly like that of her great pard; the confident manner of its phrasing sending out the idea that the invitation was a minor command to come when you're called; inviting Eileen and him to lunch in Whitehall Court. Indeed, an invitation connecting itself with a visit to G.B.S. was a command that few would like to disobey or ignore. A visit to him always made Eileen's heart and his own beat a little faster. Mrs. Shaw liked Sean, but seemed to like him in a bitter way; a shrill kind of attachment. She looked upon him as a somewhat refractory fellow, and was too anxious about him. She had resented his silent refusal to accept the offer of her husband's mediation in the contest with the Abbey

Theatre over the rejection of his *The Silver Tassie*. She seemed to think that Sean's choice to fight it on his lone was something of a snub to her great husband. She was eager to direct him in the way he should go, through literature, through art, through drama, through life. She had an earnest admiration and deep respect for some things that Sean wouldn't stop to look at twice; and she vehemently resented his demolishing regard for George Russell's works, for she placed Russell firmly before Yeats, taking him to her bosom as Ireland's most brilliant, spiritual, and powerful avastar. Avast! Her cheeks glowed whenever she muttered the magic symbol of A. E., as if this diphthong had within it the whole kind kingdom of heaven. To Sean, he was Ireland's brazen Buddha. One sentence criticising anything said or done by Russell would tense the curiously soft face into a flint-look, cold anger sparking from its flushed compression. Numerous times, she had commanded Sean to honour and obey the genius of A. E., but Sean had smiled and registered a refusal in solid silence.

Another writer she had tried to force into his esteem and affection was the scholarly Miss Helen Waddell, a fellow-adorer of George Russell. Mrs. Shaw sent him Miss Waddell's *The Wandering Scholars* and *Medieval Latin Lyrics*, calmly commanding him to give direct attention and whole-hearted admiration to the works. They were the works. But Sean side-stepped away from Mrs. Shaw's peppermint-explosions of You Must read and re-read them till you Understand them, and so gradually get to realise how fine they are, and get to Love Them. Come with me and be my love. But Sean hadn't the time. Or the scholarship. Anon, sweet wag; anon, anon!

Later on, she tried to make the philosophy of Gerald Heard a pulse-beat in his mind, but he slipped away from Heard without even hearing him speak. Mrs. Shaw used every call to lunch to mention something he should do or not do, or name a book he should read which would wave him along some one-way road of spiritual life and mental wisdom; her great husband gazing at her all the time, silently, with a patient, quizzical face. He had such an affection for her, and she was so necessary to him in his going out and his coming in, that he rarely tried to cross her; or, maybe he thought it best to let the advice given be left or taken, according to the nature of him or her to whom it had been offered.

Once at a lunch, with Charlotte at one end of the table, Shaw at the other, Eileen at one side, Sean facing her at the other, the group looking like a four-leaved shamrock, Mrs. Shaw, grim-faced, waiting for the lunch to be served, and the maid to go, Shaw chatting about the sharp spring air that tingled the cheek and nipped the ear. Sean had long noticed that Charlotte ate heavily, a great pile on her plate, thickly covered with whatever sauce went with the main dish; that she leant forward determinedly to swallow whenever she filled a forkful, using a sluggish energy to bring it to her mouth and get it down quickly, quietly rebuking him because he ate sparingly, never allowing a heap on his plate; for, however hungry he might be, a piled plate shoved away any desire to eat. Mrs. Shaw felt the cold keenly, and she sat over her plate, hunched up, a shawl round her shoulders, and an electric fire beside her chair — symptoms, probably, of the dread disease that, later on, shoved her into the grave. Shaw sat erect in his high-backed chair, eating his baked eggs and vegetables, and drinking his milk with graceful ease; chatting away, evoking a burst of laughter from Sean, a rippling one from Eileen at some witty comment given about some former incident, startling Mrs. Shaw away from her attention to her plate, and delighting the great man himself, who leant farther back on his stately chair to give a musical laugh himself. While Sean was eating his share of apple-tart, Mrs. Shaw suddenly asked him what he was doing now.

—Nothing at all, at the moment, he said; for he had no wish to undergo a catechism of what it was about, how it was growing, and when it would end; he added: Nothing at the moment; I'm afraid I am an idle man just now.

—Too busy quarrelling, she said, rather viciously. I hear you have quarrelled with Agate now. You will have to learn a better way of conducting yourself. You will get nowhere by these senseless disputes.

—Not even into heaven? queried Sean, not knowing what to say to this sudden assault, and trying to put it aside with a hasty laugh.

—It's no light matter, she said. Quarrelling with people this way, you will have enemies everywhere. Why do you do it?

This was unexpected, and damnably embarrassing to him. Eileen, more embarrassed even than Sean, lifted her head, smiling uncomfortably; bent her head, lifted it again, hoping that Sean wouldn't burst out in resentment at Mrs. Shaw's rebukes. He had, apparently, been led into a trap: brought to a private, personal lunch so that Mrs. Shaw could go at him to her heart's content. She didn't seem to realise that she was doing now what she was condemning him for, with the advantage of being the hostess, and so making it hard for Sean to reply. Silent for a moment, he then said, If a critic judges a writer by what a writer may say to him or even about him; if he denies merit in a work because of dislike for the author, then he's not a critic, but a dastard.

—There you go again! she said, angrily. You must learn to be more agreeable to critics. You mustn't go on disturbing important people in this reckless way; you must be made to check this reckless urge towards opposition. You must control him, she added, turning suddenly on Eileen; you must advise him, and modify what he is inclined to say; while Shaw sat straight up in his chair, listening; silent.

—Sean is too honest, ventured Eileen. He says things in a very blunt way. It seems unpleasant, I know, but I think he is right.

—He isn't right! said Mrs. Shaw, emphatically. He's too peevish, too peevish altogether. You shouldn't encourage him. She turned swiftly towards Sean again. Why do you do it?

—Why do I do it? echoed Sean, trying to think out what he ought to say to such an attack by such a woman. Somehow or other, I am made to do it. Your own husband did it, and does it still, Mrs. Shaw.

—There you go again! she said, and the too soft face crinkled with vexation. You quarrelled with Yeats, you quarrelled with A. E., as great a man as Yeats, and, in some respects, a greater one — no, you don't think so, I know, she said quickly, sensing Sean's rejection of her claim; and now you've quarrelled with James Agate.

—I didn't quarrel with Yeats, said Sean, quietly; I differed from him on a question of drama; so, too, with Agate: I withstood him to his face because I thought he was to be blamed — if he doesn't like it, he can lump it.

—You see, you stay obstinate! No-one will have a good word for you if you go on in this irritating way. Why do you do it?

—I have to, said Sean; I can no else. Something within me speaks before I am aware of it, and the harm is done. Sean was trying to be good-humoured. Maybe it's the prompting of what some venture to call the holy ghost.

—What do you exactly mean by the holy ghost? The voice was sharper than before, and the soft face was flushed and even quivering a little with anger. You must learn to define your words before you use them. Just what do you mean?

—He means, said Shaw, in a calm, even voice, never moving the white, clinging hands from the back railings of the high chair; he simply means, Charlotte, that he has got something and I've got something that you haven't got.

Sean had been several times to lunch with them when they had
lived in Adelphi Terrace; and he had wandered round the district,
remembering how many great men had lodged and dodged about the
streets: Garrick, Pepys, Turner, and even Peter the Great. Dust of
time was everywhere, and mustiness clung to hall, stairway, and
room. Streets crowding after each other's heels everywhere; houses
pressed so close together that few found space to breathe in. How
we cling to old and dying things! To things Doric, Corinthian, and
Ionic, as if these were to be the everlasting architectural for all ages;
as if no new thought of building could infuse human imagination
with forms as fine, and far more suitable. And for family worship
no finer forms of furniture than those of Sheraton, Chippendale, and
Hepplewhite; lost now with the fop, the dandy, the curtsey, the low
bow, and the jewelled snuff-box. All gone; gathered up and taken
away by the groping hand of time. The hardier things about them
stayed, table, chair, and ceiling; snuff-box, necklace, and sword;
stuffed into a museum, and set out in ritual tier and row; the men and
women themselves no more than the scintillating dust of England.

Sean entered by the wide-open doorway, climbed the stairs,
fumbled a long time with the chevaux-de-frise, spears against un-
invited probers. He got it open at last, passed through, and was
guided by a maid into the presence of the great man and his wife.
A vast experience to the shy and inexperienced Sean; but the genial
twinkle in the sage's questioning eyes, and the soft, motherly
welcome of Charlotte dissolved the nervousness, and Sean's nature
fused pleasantly with the Shaw household. At a lot of these lunches,
curious customers gathered to meet the Shaws. Only on a few
occasions did Sean see sweet feminine face and form and hear
elegant or sturdy talk from visitors. Looking like human goofies
(Sean himself among them; for once Shaw had asked John Dulanty,
Eire's Ambassador, How lovely Eileen Carey had come to marry
such an ugly fellow as Sean. Although it was little known, and few
thought it, Shaw, like every intelligent Irishman, had a keen eye for
a good-looking woman.) 'Mostly, Mrs. Shaw's cronies', a handsome
young visitor once whispered to Sean. How singular, Sean thought,
Eileen and a handsome young Russian named Duiska looked, caged
among so many gnarled and uncouth guests, gabbing away importantly to Mrs. Shaw and her white-bearded sage. Shaw alone put
brightness and daring into the current remarks, though they forced
him to give opinions of persons and things, long ago dead, and never
before the eyes of the present generation. The faded puppets of long-

dead dramas, Balfour, Bonar Law, Bannerman, were marched about and handled, by this one, by that, as they munched and munched meat and swallowed wine round the round table.

At one of the lunches there were a man and his wife who were crooked as cods in a pot. Both were lame, and each carried a stick to help them over a stile, one veering to the right, the other to the left, as they toddled along. The man's voice sounded like the sound of a saw going through a rusty nail embedded in wood the saw was cutting, and whatever humanity was left in a sourpuss was evicted by a black patch over one eye. His wife sang the praises of some osteopath, who, she said, had straightened her into what she was now, Mrs. Shaw nodding in agreement, and mentioning that her own bones had been put into a smart conception of what they were originally meant to be by another osteopath. The husband assailed Shaw with some old history of something that had sucked from political life and usefulness a man named Sir Charles Dilke in the days of Gladstone, forcing Shaw to prod his mind back to a reconception of, and to comment upon, an event that had died, and lay like a log, deep buried under the loam of time. Shaw was plagued with persons insisting on hearing his opinions past and gone, who came with pick and spade to disinter the near-forgotten dead, and make them look lively again: the encumbrance of the remembrance of things past.

At a lunch given by Lady Lavery (whose face appeared on the first issue of Ireland's national pound note), wife of the painter, Shaw entertained everyone present with racy accounts of incident after incident, while Lady Londonderry, Mrs. James MacNeill, wife of Ireland's High Commissioner, and others, enjoyed themselves; the magnificent head of Augustus John, moving slowly on his broad shoulders, gazing at the company, the brilliant, piercing eyes seeing all in anything worth seeing, noticing nothing where there was nothing to notice. Afterwards, when most had gone, and Mrs. Shaw with Mrs. MacNeill was upstairs looking at a recent painting, by Sir John, of a prelate — Archbishop Mannix if he remembers right, he who had led the hostility to Dr. O'Hickey, in Maynooth, the time Mannix was President of the College — Shaw walked firmly up and down the dining-room, pausing for a moment to say to Sean, Great strain on one this necessity to keep talking during the time of a luncheon.

—Why the hell do you do it? asked Sean. Is it vanity, his mind asked, silently; is it just trying to shine? Shine out, fair sun! We're all doing it, doing it, doing it.

—They all expect it of me, Shaw said; and one can't sit in silence, staring at the others.

—Why not? queried Sean. If the others can stick it, you can; and, if they can't stick it, they'll talk themselves, and save you some of the strain. Augustus John talks only when he feels like it. Unless talk comes spontaneously to me, I'm dumb. I don't make conversation at lunch a question of conscience.

—That's sound advice, said Shaw, halting in his patrol, slanting back his remarkable head, and letting out a musical laugh. Shaw stops talking — what would the world say!

Sean wondered if Shaw really took all this in so as to sit more silent sitting at a foreign table, reserving his queer, salient talk for the time he would be at his ease sitting at his own. Under those bristling eyebrows, behind those brilliant Irish eyes, over that thick-ended nose, under that frosty pow, thinning thickly now, the alert, witty, and peerless mind peered out at the present, peered into the future; almost faultless, utterly unafraid. Oh, Shaw, there is not your equal now! When shall we see your like again!

Chesterton prancing about, commodore of the cosmos, wrote a book setting forth Shaw as a connoisseur of mistaken opinions and belief. In a debate, Shaw was always merciful to Chesterton. Miss Ward tells us that 'each would sacrifice his life rather than hurt the other'. Bosom pals. Not like Cuchullain and Ferdiadh, who loved each other as few did; yet in the fight of the ford, each strove to wound the other; and though they halted in the evening to bind up each other's wounds, they kept hard at it till one of them was killed. Shaw was merciful to Chesterton as anyone might be to someone angling obliquely for a possible conversion; and Chesterton was fulsome with Shaw in a childish effort to show how close the roman catholic church came to Shaw's idea of religious and social life. Keep the door ajar. Indeed, Miss Ward is clearly puzzled as to what to say about their differences because she doesn't want to make them too pronounced. She, too, was helping to keep the door ajar. She says 'Chesterton was, however, in agreement with the ordinary citizen and in disagreement with Shaw as to much of Shaw's essential teaching. And here we touch a matter so involved that even today it is hard to disentangle it completely.' Hedging! Today? Yesterday, today, and for ever, Miss Ward.

Shaw was a member of an expanding universe, Chesterton of a narrowing one. Chesterton grew in childishness as Shaw grew in grace. Bawling out that he was the one man who understood Shaw,

Chesterton showed, in his first few comments on the dramatist, that he didn't understand a thing about Shaw's idea of *John Bull's Other Island*. Shaw didn't bother, for you couldn't tell a thing to Chesterton. He was incapable of assimilating anything outside of himself. Shaw sought out chances to face things, Chesterton rushed after every chance to avoid them (Dreyfus!). It is funny to think of him trying to reflect Tolstoy, Blake, and Browning from the mirror of his shifty mind. It's a wonder he didn't try to write about Joyce; but Joyce beat him, for he was too great a catholic for Chesterton's mind to manage. Hide him from me, heaven!

Fear, ever behind Shaw, was ever in front of Chesterton. According to his sister-in-law, he feared sickness, or even to speak of it; hated to think of, discuss, or debate death, except in its relation to fanciful murder done by faraway denizens in his lurid detective fiction. Like the title of one of them, he himself was the sign of the broken sword. Chesterton, to maintain his cosmos of cosmic comprehension, of God, of man, and of all things, from everlasting man to tremendous trifles, had to proclaim that, to him, Shaw was an open book, and that he, and he alone, had the hand to close it. But in his jump into cosmic comprehension from what he thought to be the kernel of the church, he became but another old woman who lived in a shoe. We are told in the life of this tremendous trifle that Chesterton showed 'deeper thought' in his play, *Magic*, than Shaw did in his, because, evidently, he 'believed in the love of God and man [as if Shaw didn't!], he believed in the devil and that love conquers diabolical evil'. See the conquering zero comes. He dismisses every writer greater than himself with a gentle, recessional wave of the hand from a cloud of the love of God — Ruskin, the Brontë sisters, Tennyson, Tolstoy, and, of course, George Moore (but not a word about Joyce); takes them down as one would china figures from a shelf, gives each a chestertonian spit and a catholic polish, and puts it back again; all of them, in Chesterton's mind, abashed that they had not kept right on to the end of the road to Rome. But the newer roman catholic writers, Mauriac, Waugh, Grahame Greene, seem to doubt the power of love in conquering diabolical evil. Their thoughts seem to go too damned deep for words. With them it seems there's no love left anywhere to conquer anything.

Seeing how popular he was, how he splashed his concepts about in paper, magazine, and book, his rush to get his words recorded, so mad and so breathless that it took a litter of publishers to print his books; seeing all this, it is odd that so few (if any, bar his wife) followed him into becoming a *persona gratis romanorum*. One would imagine he'd have marched in at the head of a crowd. He doesn't seem to have caused even an *honoris causa* conversion. He fiddled for Shaw, as did many others. The roman catholic church would have got a tremendous kick out of Shaw's conversion to the faith — their faith. Many of them thought that Shaw had already got flashes of the truth as it was in Father O'Flynn, and they hoped on to the last. Flickers of faith. Would Shaw become a Catholic Movie? Once, a letter from Mrs. Shaw to Sean, asking him to lunch, told him a Father Leonard would be there, the letter's tone implying that the priest was a familiar figure to the Shaws; but Father Leonard didn't come, and Sean never knew what kind of a bloke he was, except that he was an Ess Jay; never heard his name again. Probably a number kept praying for Shaw's conversion. All together — pray for the wanderer, pray for him! What a catch he'd be! If he would only come knocking at the door. Knock, knock, knock. Whisht, is that him? Oh, if he only would venture under the portals of St. Peter! At times, he seemed so near, then, in a laughing moment, he was farther away than ever. Miss Maisie Ward tells us that when visiting Shaw and Wells, the two 'able and indeed brilliant men betrayed not only an amazing degree of ignorance concerning the tenets of Catholicism but also a bland conviction that they knew them well'. If Miss Ward had talked to the parish priests, she might well have found that they were more ignorant of the tenets of catholicism than were these two able and brilliant men. Dr. Mc-Donald, forty years Professor of Theology in Maynooth roman catholic college, tells us how on a ship heading for Belfast, he met a young doctor, a Scot, who was astonished at the small amount one had to accept in dogma in order to become a catholic. The Scot asked time to consider what McDonald had told him, and, in the morning, he asked the Professor, in all honour, to tell him that if he explained the faith to the priests of Ulster as Dr. McDonald had explained it to him, would the priests recognise it as the faith that each and all avowed. 'As an honest man', adds Dr. McDonald, 'I was forced to admit that they would not.' Miss Ward sighingly complains about the laughing way in which Belloc and Chesterton tried to answer Shaw's and Wells' denials of the doctrine of The Fall. 'Perhaps', she says, 'they did not realise where the beginning must be made in instructing otherwise instructed men on the subject of Catholicism.' They didn't know the beginning, and, seemingly, they didn't know the ending either. They did not know because they were not told! Miss Ward adds, rather pathetically, 'Has any Catholic ever explained the philosophic meaning of Transubstantiation to Shaw?' Answer her, answer her! Not a damned one, apparently, Miss Ward. Since Dr. McDonald, forty years Professor of Theology in Maynooth College, found the going hard, rejecting a lot of common and high-brow catholic teaching, including Belloc's and Chesterton's Fall, is it any wonder that Wells and Shaw found the coming harder?

How men like Belloc and Chesterton could think that such sensible, secular minds could seek shelter under the roman dome of dogma is difficult to understand. But Shaw's gentle way of turning aside roman catholic supplications for submission left him open to the patter of pietistic hope. He might do it. He might, he might do it!

Multitudes of minds have been explaining the meaning of the philosophy of transubstantiation, the semi-catholic philosophy of consubstantiation, and the philosophies written round the other church tenets, for the last thousand years, or more; yet they stand still, waiting, unexplained, even to the roman catholics themselves. Indeed, the whirling controversy goes down even to the origin of man himself, all along, down along, out along way. Looks like Chesterton, Belloc, and Miss Ward spent a good deal of their lives stretched out comfortably on the plush-covered, cushioned roman couch of traditional thought; and didn't notice many things; or were dozing deeply when they happened. Not so St. George Jackson Mivart, who died when Sean was already twenty years old. Mivart was made a Dr. of Philosophy by the pope of 1876, four years before Sean was born; and M.D. by the University of Louvain, in which he was given the Chair of Philosophy of Natural History; then in a blaze of blackened roman candles, he was excommunicated by the roman catholic church four years before his death. Among others, here are a few things said about this brave man by Dr. McDonald, Professor of Theology in Maynooth roman catholic college: 'Here, in Mivart's *Primer of Philosophy* — given to me, mockingly, by Dr. Walsh, afterwards Archbishop of Dublin — was what was being said every day, quite near us; not by lunatics or demons, but by men of great scientific attainments, who deemed it a duty to say what they said. The book stimulated me in a way I never felt before. It was the beginning of a new life — the life which I have led ever since, and which I am likely to lead while I live at all. Few things pained me more than that Mivart, to whom I owed so much in the

way of religious and scientific instruction, should, at the close of his
life, have had such a struggle and have suffered such eclipse; that he
did, throughout, what he deemed his duty, I cannot for a moment
doubt; neither, however, do I doubt, that he was wrong objectively,
in attributing to the Church, as definitive, what she never taught
definitively; but that such a man should be plunged into such misery
by non-definitive teaching — a fate which I myself barely escaped,
if by God's grace, I do escape it — shows how good men, by ultra-
conservatism, may be doing the devil's work when they are most
zealous for God and religion.'

The church that had no room for a Mivart could hardly have the
strength to squeeze out a place for such as Shaw, such as Wells; no
room in the bin. No room, really, even for Dr. McDonald, who
fashioned out his own faith (as he tells us) far away from the mouth-
ings of infallible fools. It is odd that neither Chesterton nor Belloc
ever mentioned McDonald's name. Chesterton was forty-six when
McDonald died; he was in Ireland after the World War, plunging
into the roman catholic world there, but, apparently, never heard a
whisper (or, if he did, kept his mouth shut) about one of Maynooth's
most remarkable priests. It is odder still that Dr. McDonald never
mentions this prancing champion of catholicism on his white horse,
or when, in lighter moments, he was doing his comic catholic can-
can, though Chesterton was famous in roman catholic Ireland, and
his sayings were being quoted by priest, poet, and peasant. But then,
we are told that 'his awe and reverence for a priest were enormous',
and that he would listen, 'head bowed and hat off', to anything a
priest might say, however fatuous'. Add that this was a man who
didn't like to speak of sickness, didn't like the mention of death, put
Walt Whitman out of his house, and refused to let Ibsen in, as well
as declaiming against giving a vote to a woman — hardly a competent guide, either in secular or religious philosophy, to such a man as
Wells or such a one as Shaw. How Belloc and Chesterton could for
a moment imagine that such sensible secular minds would jump for
shelter or crawl for shelter under the roman dome of dogma is
difficult to understand. Still you never could tell what thought
might change the thoughts of the devil's disciples. Shaw's gentle way
of turning roman catholic supplications aside left him open to the
patter of pietistic hope. He might submit. He might do it, he might
do it. He jarred at times, though: like the unintentional way he hurt
a hopeful mother superior, who, when he had gone, exclaimed What
a horrid, blasphemous fella! When I asked him would he join up

with us, he replied, Yes, I'd like to; but think what a terrible thing it
would be if the world had two popes! Setting up an equality with the
Holy Father. The villain! Still he might, might do it.

> The dame made a curtsey,
> The dog made a bow;
> The dame said, 'Your servant',
> The dog said, Bow-wow.

The odd thing was that the probing minds of Mivart, McDonald,
Wells, and Shaw were, in fact, coming closer to God, while, it
seemed, the minds shrinking away from question and quiz, turning
their backs on pillar of fire and cloud, were covering their eyes with
their hands, rather than see or sense the back parts of God as he
passed by on his way to others. Those thinking to hold up the church
were knocking her down, those apparently knocking her down were
holding her up: perhaps, now and then, heaven likes a joke.

Shaw's *pied-à-terre* in London was a roomy and comfortable one,
and for all that it must have heard, many times, many great arguments about it and about, the whole impression it gave out was one
of commonplace serenity; a cushioned recess for the mighty mind.
Here was nothing vulgar, nothing modern either, in furniture,
picture, or stone, except the painting of Shaw himself by Augustus
John, hung so high that the eyes of Shaw or of his wife never met it
during their sitting down or standing up in the room. The head had
to be thrown back on the shoulders to see it, and Shaw never, far as
Sean knew, pointed it out to a visitor. Let it hang there quietly out
o' the way. Eileen's eye caught sight of it the moment she entered
the room, and halting to stare, she cried out, happily, A John!

It was amusing to see the half-startled way Shaw turned up his
head to squint at the picture, turning his head down again, to wait
patiently till Eileen and Sean had ended their look at it. Perhaps it
was too lyrical, too far away from the cloudy emphasis of a photograph, too sensuous, though the sensuousness was a gentle mingling
of lovely silvery greys and gentle blues, giving it a look of gay loneliness; and from these lyrical greys and gentle blues peeped impudently the wise and humorous face of the dramatist and the fighter.
A suggestion from Eileen that it should be placed where the eye
could see it comfortably evoked no comment from Shaw and but
the short statement from Charlotte that G.B.S. didn't like it well
enough to change it from where it was. Ricketts was about the
furthest that Shaw got towards the enjoyment of the painter's art.
He preferred the ghastly picture of himself done by John Collier to

the lyrical impression of himself done by John. It would seem that he had gunned the art of painting away from him by a multitude of shots from his camera. What a great loss this lack in the Shaws was to Ireland! With their wealth how many fine pictures they could have gathered to be presented, some time, to Eire's National Gallery, or to the Municipal Collection housed in Parnell Square. His friends didn't help him any, for few, if any, cared a damn about Raphael or Renoir. Few of those pictured beside him had shown any desire to mingle their souls with the old painters or the new; indeed, some of them — like the Webbs — were as deaf as the mole is blind to all art and all literature. They spent their working-hours and leisure sorting men and things out in tier and row. They never sought out a second for a song and a dance. What would the Webbs have thought had they seen Joyce suddenly indulging in his mad, amazing, wild-man dance on a bridge of the Seine? Shaw would have wondered, and laughed; the Webbs would have hurried away, for it wouldn't have been either possible or seemly to have tucked away such an item into a pyramid of statistics. Dublin workers, had there been any there to see it, would have remained hushed for a few moments, and then they'd have hilariously joined in — hoosh the cat from under the table! Joyce, for all his devotion to his art, terrible in its austerity, was a lad born with a song on one side of him, a dance on the other — two gay guardian angels every human ought to have. And what is the universe but a dance of orbs? Brooks Atkinson in his *Once Around the Sun* tells us that the Dog Star's Procyon is rushing towards us at the rate of two and a half miles a second; and many other stars are rushing away; this way, that way, in the expanding universe: so if we go wild at times, as Joyce did, we are errant in magnificent company. Life will be on a high plane when life becomes a song and a dance and a serious thing.

Music. A harpsichord. Shaw's crest and arms. A lovely one, encased in polished yellow wood, standing in a prominent part of the room. Shaw's heart was here. He was blessed with a deep love for, and a deep understanding of, the melody, intricate, rippling and majestic, that flowed from, and thundered out of, the magic weaving of sounds by Beethoven, Brahms, Wagner, and Mozart. These were his God be praised. These glories balanced safely his lack of feeling for the glories of painting in the past and the present outspread of its experimental valour. Shaw had deeply what Sean lacked altogether. Not altogether, maybe, for he could, at least, love the melodic bars in opera, oratorio, and symphony. But Shaw had the knowledge of music in brilliant abundance, and this, maybe, gave him his serenity, as it, maybe, did to Joyce, too. The lullaby to irritation and anger in David's harp still sang through the music of the day. It wasn't, of course, that Shaw was always serene. He very often felt the flame of indignation alight within him; he felt anger at stupid things said and cruel things done; and he felt the sick heart when fools assailed him. He could calmly set down hard things without a quiver in a bristling eyebrow when writing of revolutions; but he was always damnably reasonable: 'Even in the first flush of the Soviet Revolution, the Soviet was more tolerant than we were when our hour came to revolt. We frankly robbed the church of all it possessed, and gave the plunder to the landlords (a lot of them catholic, by the way). Long after that, we deliberately cut off our archbishop's head. Certainly, the Soviet made it quite clear to the Russian archbishop that if he didn't make up his mind to accept the fact of the Revolution, and give to the Soviet the allegiance he had formerly given to the Tsar, he would be shot. But when he very sensibly and properly made up his mind accordingly, he was released, and is now, presumably, pontificating much more freely than the Archbishop of Canterbury.'

Music helped to keep Shaw calm, and made a fine dramatist of him, for music sings in most of his plays. Oh, lackaday, that Sean had so little of its solace! One had to be a constant practiser, or a constant listener, to know or feel anything right about the form and style of beautiful sounds which we call music. How is the ordinary man to enter into an intelligently emotional enjoyment of music? Sean could think of but one way: listening. Listen to the band, for that was what an assembly of eminent musicians really was, though given the lordly, and deserved, name of an Orchestra. Now that their three children were constant listeners to Beethoven, Mozart, Bach, and the rest, flowing from the wireless, the gramophone, and, more simply, from the stately piano they had in their best room, he was often sprayed with beautiful sounds. But it was but a lovely baptism. Too late, now; too late. He would never be able to go further than the porch of the temple; never see the lights gleaming on the altar; never hear the full hymn sung.

Had Mrs. Shaw lived longer, Shaw would have lived longer, too. She cushioned away a lot of the hardness of life for him. She was his woeman of the guard. She travelled a lot, following the sun for warmth, and he went with her; for boat-decks, cabins, and foreign lands with her were better than Ayot St. Lawrence without her.

Constant comfort and companionship departed from him with Charlotte. He tried to take it cheerily, but he was just an old boy whistling in the dark. In a letter to Sean, he said he was all right, but damnably lonely. A lone one at last. The state of a lone star; and to remain damnably lonely till he departed too. Though they had their differences. Once, sitting pleasantly by the fire, just four of them, Shaw, Charlotte, Eileen and Sean, chatting generally about the drama, Mrs. Shaw suddenly asked Sean which did he think was G.B.S.'s best play; Sean replying, immediately, that it was *Heartbreak House*. Shaw's face lit up instantly, and he took his elbow from the mantelshelf to give fuller attention to what Sean had said; but a cloudy look settled on the face of Charlotte.

—Do you? said Shaw, delightedly. That's odd. Few do, though I think myself that it is my best play. Charlotte doesn't like it.

—Nonsense, said Mrs. Shaw to Sean: *St. Joan* is the best play G.B.S. has written.

—No, no, said Sean, innocently and fervently. *St. Joan* is his most popular play, maybe. It is a lovely play, but a compiled one. *Heartbreak House* is deeper, far more original, and nearer to life. It is as a fine symphony with flaws in it is to a perfectly modelled folk-air. There is no heart-break in *St. Joan*; she burns too triumphantly. G.B.S. knew this, and so he added the Epilogue.

—It cannot compare with *St. Joan*, said Mrs. Shaw — a note of finality in her voice. I don't like *Heartbreak House*.

Shaw saw that there was disorder in poverty, and he liked order, said to be 'heaven's first law'; he saw that there was disease in poverty, and he liked health; he saw that there was death in poverty, and he loved life. He was the first saint to declare that God no longer liked to look upon the face of the poor, so different from the Jesuit, Vaughan, who, well-fed. well-clothed himself, said that the poor were God's own aristocracy. What voice has shouted Dope? Banish poverty from our midst and from our ken, and with it her foul breed of deformed men, deformed women, deformed children. Force the Christians to seek divine election through their own efforts and development, and suffer them no longer to feel they are jolly good fellows by doling out to others what they never miss themselves. Take the wine away from them, and let them drink a little water for their stomach's sake. To the Lyons with the Christian rich! Shaw is the workers' War-cry!

There is sense for everyone in Shaw's Corner who hates the ulcerous misery of poverty. He was one of those who never hesitated to say into the ears of the man isolated by wealth, and in the ears of the multitude, that what are called man's petty and insignificant needs are related to the stars. 'Men honoured Christ', he said, 'so long as he remained a charming picture in a golden frame, or hung helpless on a varnished cross; but men begin to yell with alarm when the picture leaves the frame, or when the figure comes down from the cross to become a moving, terrible force in the world.' The picture is out of the frame now, the figure is off the cross, and Christ now marches in the surge forward of the masse-men. Blok saw him march through Leningrad at the head of the Red Guards, and he has appeared in China amid cheers; today, too, his shadow falls on Africa: Lo, I am with you always — March! Left, left, left!

Some critics say Shaw was no poet (indeed, Sean remembers arguing against this precious aversion of men and women to others, having greater gifts than their own, in Dublin, thirty years ago, with Sarah Purser, a notable lass of the city of that day); that he was one almost incapable of emotion. Hens cackling, cocks crowing, at the eagle's whistle. There is poetry in a lot of his plays, emotion in some of them, and laughter and thought in all of them. A fine synopsis of active and poetic life — tears, laughter, thought, and song. He will live in the life following his own for his jewelled courage, his grand plays, his penetrating wisdom, his social sense, his delightful, effective criticism of the theatre of his day, his fight for Ibsen, Wagner, Brahms, his uncanny knowledge of children, his battles for womanhood, and for his brilliant leadership in the thought of man.

A great man, but not great enough for the closed shop of saintship in the Christian church. Indeed, a name to be mentioned with great caution; and so the churchmen slip down to the hell of mediocrity. No, no; not Shaw. What a scandal it would have aroused had Shaw been allowed to climb into a pulpit! Bernard Shaw in the pulpit of Westmonaster Cathedral. Monastrous! Do stop him from playing such fantastic tricks before high heaven as make the angels laugh. Church in danger! The gates of hello are prevailing against her! Even the figures in the stained-glass windows are climbing out to go. Mention a more suitable name. Here's the Prefect of the Sacred Congregation of Rites, and there's the Reverend President of the Anglican Convocation; so, mention a more suitable name — we're listening. Johnny Appleseed, sirs. Who's he, and what did he do? Done millions of miracles, sirs; scattered appleseeds wherever he went. Appleseeds? You don't know your catechism, son. Don't you know what the apple has done to man? *Mala mali malo malu, melo contulit omnia mundo.* Oh, sirs, I am sorry. It seems to me as sweet as honey. Oh, Plautus! Oh, preserve us! Well, mention another — we're patient. We're eager to have as many saints as *per se* possible. Hiawatha's a name, sirs, I mention with glee, for the way to make honey he taught to the bee; to Red Men, he gave agriculture, and more — he cur'd them whene'er they felt sick or felt sore. A pagan chief he must have been, and we've no room for pagans here; we drink no wine, but sit and sip the sober excellence of beer. No dionysiac thought or laughter can enter here, now or hereafter. So get you gone, you brazen smarty, and lecture to life's cocktail party!

If not saints, then bishops! What a grand bunch they'd be on the bench — Shaw, Joyce, and Yeats! Stop them! Rerum novarum oram pro noram. Maanooth is in an upsoar. Oh, catholic herald, come blow your horn, before a wild oak comes from the little acorn. St. Patrick's coming down on a winged horse. Was there ever such a one as the Bull from Shaw; was there ever such a one as the Pastoral from Yeats; was there ever such another as the Encyclical from Joyce! They'll ruin and maruin us. Oh, soggart, aroon, is it dhreamin' I am as I'm standin' up stiff in a medley of fear, for the heads are all harps and the harps are all heads in the things that I see an' the things that I hear. We're betrayed! Who's that running about like a kingaroo? Belloc. What's he shouting, what's he shouting? They Do Not Know Because They Are Not Told. They don't; we do, don't we — oh, boy! What are the three boyo bishops doing now? Blessing the people. Blessing them — what with? Shaw's blessing them with his plays and Yeats is blessing them with his poems, and Joyce is blessing them with the comic laughter of a brooding mind. They'll destroy us. If they're let go on, they'll quench the *ignis fatuous* of the faith! They're doing God down, harming heaven; taking all the smoothness out of it, and the velvet away from under our walking. The Universe is going mad. Such things to happen in Catholic Times! And we thinking they were stretched out among the Defunctorum, with the tablet of non este fideles over them. Under the silentio luna. What's Father O'Flynn doing that he isn't here to help? Let him come to the fore now, and bring his wonderful way with him, for it's well wanted. They're the devil's disciples. Undermining truth. What's that bounder, Yeats, saying? Would that the Church were Anything but Merely Voice. Oh, they do not know because they are not told. They've been told often, but they won't listen; they refuse to hear the voice of truth — the gang of hearetics!

What's Yeats saying now? That he's fallen from himself because he hasn't seen for a long time the Prince of Chang in his dreams. What Chang, which Chang, whose Chang? Is this Chang in the cullender of saints? No, no; he isn't. I guessed he wasn't. It's these free libraries is doing all this detriment. Shut the doors, Richard! Where's the Catholic Herald? He's on the rumparts of infidelium proclaiming a dies irae erin on all shinners. It's too late now. Oh, Leonore oh oh ora pro woebis. What's Shaw saying, saying? Saying that no church shall ever have a creed. Wants to take our one remainder, leaving us without a screed. We're in a bad way, Mick. What's the other boyo bishop, Joyce, doing? Taking down verbatim a discussion between the Mooksee and the Gripes. What's them? Are they civil or religious disorders, or what are they? No one knows? There'll be nothing here now but the wind and the rain, and chilly water under every tired foot halting for a rest. Even the older dogs know the road no longer. These three boyos are whispering their strange thoughts into every Irish ear, and every Irish ear is cocked to hear them. This land will soon be nothing but a weed in a garden of noses — no — poses. Oh, what am I saying! Soon be nothing but a nose in a garden of weeds. Oh, I'm going mad! Impetuous heart, be still, be still.

—Conthrol yourself, Mick, and let some sound of sense get into what you're saying. More things grow in Ireland than the three-leaved shamrocks. Say what you like and pray how you may, there'll always be a gay song deadening the sound of a *de profundis*. It would be a big, bright blessing in disguise if even a few of our bishops had some of the imagination of Yeats, a tittle of the wit and deeper sense of Shaw, and a little of the royal ribaldry of Joyce to test our thinking.

—I won't listen. Are you letting yourself emerge into their meaning, too?

—And if I am? It's near time we got something fit for a man or a woman to read; something having a jolt in it as well as a jingle. Your heaven seems to be responsible for a helluva lot of rotten literature.

—Don't say that; you mustn't say that, man! What we read is safe reading, and that is our only need. We must have virtue at all costs; and no inquiries, no questions. D'ye hear me talking? No inquiries, none at all, I'm saying!

No, no, it wouldn't do. Unsettling saint; never do for us. Let St. Peter go back to his sedia astoria in Rome, and Patrick to his stone stand on Tara's Hill or Croagh Patrick. The names mentioned aren't a quarter good enough to be thought of by the roman catholic church, or even good enough to win a thought from an anglican pulpit. They are man's saints; our saints, registered in the wide church of humanity; if not for social service, then for heroic virtue in the integrity of their art: the people's choice.

Yeats got a large medal from a Swedish artist, and was so dazzled with the design that he decided to form an Irish Academy of Letters. A circular, signed by some prominent Irish writers, was sent out, appealing to others to become founder Academicians or associate members. The circular came to Sean signed personally by Bernard Shaw. Shaw was asking a favour from Sean; the first favour ever asked, and Sean saw himself threatened with the hardest refusal he had ever had to face. Shaw had fought by his side in the Abbey Theatre controversy over *The Silver Tassie*, and now Sean had to refuse the one favour the great man asked of him. He didn't know what to say, though he knew what he would do — refuse to join. Indeed, he had sent a laughing, critical article about the scheme to *The American Spectator*, and its editor, George Jean Nathan, had replied, saying it would appear in the next number. Sean didn't like institutions powered to decide what was good literature and what was not good: they had made too many mistakes before. They were inclined to look kindly on those who flattered their own work. He spent a long, long time thinking out a loving letter in whose core was a firm and final refusal. The letter of refusal was sent to the sage, but no answer came back. It was but an incident in a busy life. No malice touched Shaw's nature; he was the most forgiving man Sean had ever met. Nothing mean ever peeped out of his thought or his manner; the noblest Irishman of all Irishmen. Sean and he met many times again, but neither of them ever once mentioned the Irish Academy of Letters.

Later on, when the O'Casey family shifted down to Devon to be near the school Eileen had chosen, on Shaw's emphatic recommendation, for the children, they rented a house that was the only one vacant for miles around that could shelter them in a partially suitable way; a pretentious place, originally built by some lower middle-class snob who feinted towards being an ape of his betters. The landlord didn't like the look of Sean, or mistrusted anyone trying to make a living by writing (small blame to him for that), and demurred about agreeing to the tenancy, demanding credentials as to the prospective tenant's character and good repute. As to his character, Sean told him he would ask no one to trust it, for he couldn't trust it himself. Though he knew many who would readily give him a bad name, he knew no one who would give him a good one. This made the landlord more dubious, but he brightened up when he was promised a guarantor who'd pay the rent, if Sean didn't. The landlord agreed to allow the tenancy if the name Sean gave proved to be satisfactory. Not wishing to bother G.B.S., Sean wrote to Mrs. Shaw, and asked her to do him this favour. Almost immediately, a letter came back asking them to lunch in Whitehall Court to talk about the matter. After lunch, before a fine fire, Mrs. Shaw started questioning; asking how much a year the house would be, including rates, if Sean was working at anything; if a play, had it any prospect of production; while G.B.S. leaned over the back of the chintz-covered sofa, listening to all that was said by Mrs. Shaw sitting on the sofa's centre. Sean was put through a means test, his face flushing, his nerves urging him to walk out of the room, out of the house, his necessity riveting him to where he stood listening.

—Oh, give it to him! suddenly ejaculated Shaw from the cloud of questioning. He has told you all you need to know. Mrs. Shaw stopped dead, and immediately changed into a gracious readiness to do all she was asked to do.

But all for nothing. When Sean handed out the news that Mrs. Shaw would stand as guarantor, the landlord let a snort out of him, jumped from his chair, ran to the farther end of the room, and almost shouted, It's no good; I'll not take any woman's guarantee! I won't let you into the house on any woman's name. I'll let no woman meddle in my affairs!

Oh, Jesus! First Mrs. Shaw's hesitation and distrust; now this old-fashioned fool's rejection of a name Sean had gone to so much trouble to get! So Sean had to write to Mrs. Shaw telling her that her signature would not do. G.B.S. then took over the guarantee, first indulging in a spicy correspondence with the landlord's solicitors, and a subsequent letter told Sean that the business had been carried through:

4 WHITEHALL COURT, LONDON, S.W.1.
17th October, 1938.

MY DEAR SEAN,

Your landlord, being a dentist, has developed an extraction complex. He proposed a lease in which I was not only to guarantee all your covenants, but indemnify him for all the consequences. I said I did not know his character, but knew enough of yours to know that the consequences might include anything from murder to a European war; so I re-drafted the agreement. The lawyers, knowing that their man was only too lucky to get a gilt-edged (as they thought) security, and that his demands were absurd, made no resistance. I mention it as you had better watch your step, not to say his, with the gentleman. Anyhow I had a bit of fun with him. I seem to have picked up completely. The anaemia was not really pernicious. I am glad to learn that the two miniature O'Casey's are happy among the young criminals at Dartington and that their mother is now one of the Beauties of Devon. Charlotte sends all sorts of affectionate messages.

G. B. S.

The fun Shaw had had cost Sean guineas he could ill afford, for the lawyers charged for all the letters. But the great-hearted G.B.S., Sean thought, imagined he'd have to pay, not only the costs, but the rent as well, and so he thought he might as well have a good laugh out of the loss. Sean thanks heaven, feasting, that G.B.S. never had to pay a red cent of costs or of rent. The Agreement is with T. Cannon Brookes of Cannon Brookes and Odgers, London, who cried out that he wouldn't part with it for anything. T. Cannon Brookes is a direct descendant of Napper Tandy (the one who Met with poor old Ireland, and shook her be the Hand, according to the famous ballad of *The Wearin' o' the Green*. Napper Tandy afterwards became a general of France's Grande Armée, and lies buried in Bordeaux), with the Napper Tandy nose which he has handed on to his tall son, and whose little son is sprouting the same nose too.

Then came the long, sad shock of Charlotte's illness; the gradual distortion of the stout body, the sinking away from association with the companion she had loved and guarded so long. The great and sensitive man had to watch the life of his wife declining day by day; the flag of companionship slipping down the staff. She is very much deformed, he wrote to Eileen. Though the day ends the same way for us all, there is infinite variety in the place, time, and manner of its ending. There was a great deal of goodness dying side by side with Charlotte Shaw; and the greatest good was the care she gave to the people's champion. Still she was there while the shadow of herself lingered in the home; there beside him. But shrink from it as he might, he had to let her go at last. She is dead, G.B.S.; ay, indeed, she is dead right enough. Shaw's Corner suddenly expanded into a wide and desolate world. One was taken and the other left. Put a brave face on it, man. I will, I will; but icy death that has taken Charlotte has touched me, too, as he passed. My wife is dead. She was called Charlotte; a good woman, a very good woman; and, now, she's gone. Alone, at last. Oh, Charlotte, where art thou, and why art thou silent, thou pulse of my heart? The place is full of shadow, even when the cuckoo calls. The summer is icumen in, but it will always be,winter, now. Life is like a withered tree; what is all the world to me; life and light were all in thee. I am very busy trying to answer the thousands of letters of sympathy coming from the four quarters of the earth. It will take months; I am very busy. Ah, my heart is sair, I darena' tell, my heart is sair for somebody. Busy, yes, busy. A fistful of dust about the garden blows. I said to the rose, the brief day goes. Silence everywhere. The housekeeper talks, the maid talks, the visitors talk; but there is silence everywhere. Silence in my own heart. I wander lonely as a cloud, a lone, lorn critter. The brief day goes. She was old; she had her day; the day soon goes. The evening star is gone, the shine has faded from the morning star.

> I'm here alone, I'm there alone;
> All that was here is here, yet all is gone;
> The star that glittered, the sun that shone.
>
> Visitors come and go,
> To laugh, murmur, and crow;
>   All has been said and done.
>   Death faces a friendly foe;
>   Tho' there's still things I'd like to know.
>
>   I'm withered to creaking bone,
>   And I potter round here alone.
>
>   A few more years shall roll,
>   A few more seasons fade;
>   This mind of mine, if it shall last
>   Behind death's lone façade,
>   Shall question many things mismade:
>   Shall question unafraid.
>   Oh, Charlotte, well-beloved, I hear you
>   calling me.

Eileen and Sean sent several letters to him to assure him that he was far from being forgotten, but no reply came to the letters, and both were troubled. Sean wondered if they had been kept from him (afterwards, Shaw seemed to confirm this, for when, on a visit to Ayot Saint Lawrence, Eileen told him she had written some time ago, the old man said she must be mistaken, for he got no letter). Then Sean thought Shaw might be too tired or too busy to be bothered with him. Later on, a letter from George Jean Nathan, the American drama-critic, told him that he had written to G.B.S., enclosing one of his books, but had got no acknowledgement. They all puzzled over the reason why Shaw could be so silent. Later, Sean forwarded to Shaw a letter from a Dublin friend, Peadar O'Donnell, editor of *The Bell*, pleading for a preface to a book written by an ex-soldier of the Irish Republican Army. This brought an affectionate reply from G.B.S., saying he had written to Peadar pointing out why he couldn't write the Preface, adding that Peadar couldn't have had a better introduction than one from Sean. Then came word from George Jean Nathan, saying Shaw had acknowledged the book, and had written 'Attaboy! Write a thousand of them. I like your stuff, and rank you as Intelligent Playgoer Number One!' So all smiled again, George Jean in New York, the O'Caseys in Devon, for all was well with the glorious sage of Ayot Saint Lawrence.

After they had sent him, at his request, a portrait of the family, Eileen on his invitation went, with John Dulanty, Eire's Ambassador, to have tea with him, caged now in his own home, where they had a fine time, John Dulanty brimming over with stories, Shaw commenting on them with many a musical laugh, Eileen adding her own merry laugh and good humour to the party. But the day soon goes. Some time later came the news of the accident; he had fallen while pruning a plum- or a pear-tree, and had broken a thigh. And he was ninety-four; there was small hope now, said Eileen, he is so old. No, no, said Sean, though, in his heart, he feared that Shaw, at last, was on the way to the land o' the leal. Carry him off to the hospital, where, it was said, the great man was quite chirrupy. It is odd to think of so many unable to see that this manner was assumed by Shaw to veil his shyness, to conceal his hatred of having to be helped by others; and strangers, too. To be helpless and dependent on others was a taste of horror for Shaw. Meagrely patched up, Shaw returns to his home, and soon after, hearing that she is in London, Shaw asks Eileen to come to see him. She goes, and that night her voice from London comes down to Devon over the telephone to say, Sean, Shaw is dying! Can you hear? G.B.S. is dying.

—Nonsense! went the voice of Sean from Devon up to London. You're imagining things. He's no more dying than I am.

—If you saw him, Sean, you'd know he was dying.

—He'll rally out of it. He'd rally out of anything.

—Not out of this, Sean; not out of this. When he looks at you, death looks at you, too.

Some days after, Eileen heard from John Dulanty that Shaw would like to see her again, but she put it off, having to give a lot of time to two of her children who are with her in London. But the thought that she should go down again to Ayot Saint Lawrence keeps coming into her mind. She should go, she shouldn't go, she couldn't go. She would ask John Dulanty as to whether she should or should not go; for she feared to disturb Shaw, or receive a snub from those who had charge of him. She journeyed down to the Ambassador's office, but he was out. That settled it: she would not go. The secretary asked her to come the following day, and Eileen, murmuring that she would, decided that she wouldn't. Anyway, it was hardly likely that Shaw really wanted to see her. He had always liked her greatly, wondered sometimes why she had married such a one as Sean, at times gently teasing her about it. He liked her intelligence, not only of her mind, but also of her heart; so natural, vivid with friends; so real and generous with children. She understood as many didn't the odd, sparkling mind in the weakening body of Shaw; the mind still gay and as unpredictable as ever under the shawl of age. But she wouldn't go to John Dulanty's office to-morrow, and so would never see the bold G.B.S. again. But in some strange way, the thought that she should go never left her mind, and, on the morrow, she went down to the Ambassador's office, and met him as he was going out for the biggest part of the day. He came forward, saying Ah! I want you! He told her Shaw would very much like to see her, adding that, if she hadn't come, he would have written to her. Like Sean himself, John didn't believe that Shaw was dying, saying so to Eileen, and adding that when he was in Ayot Saint Lawrence a week or so ago, the old man was in fine fettle; but Eileen still fears that she is right, and that Greatheart, Captain Valiant, is dying; that the last moments of this battler, this lover of laughter, are saying farewell to the world and us all.

The Ambassador tells her to ring up to see if a visit would be all right at the moment. The housekeeper answers Eileen, goes away to ask Shaw, and comes back to say that Eileen is to come at once, for Mr. Shaw would very much like to see her. So Eileen goes down to stay for a few minutes, but remains for a long, long time with the departing Titan. He is slowly leaving the ken of the world, chatting in whispers so low that Eileen has to bend down close to the gentle face to hear what he says, sinking into a doze occasionally that was the shadow of coming unconsciousness.

He was lying in a sloping position in a bed against a wall, in a ground-floor room; lying there, waxen-faced, calm and patient; his eyes, bright as ever, shaded by the bushy brows, common sense alert in them, humour still aglow in them: living to the last. Another bed, narrower, lay alongside a wide window, looking out into the garden, sanctified now with the dust of his Charlotte; the flowers and walks he loved hidden away from him for ever. Looking round while he dozed, Eileen saw on the wall a big photograph of the upright Stalin, full face, handsome and jovial, and, near by, one of Gandhi — both fine fighters, like Shaw himself, fighters in different ways; equals in ideal and outlook, fundamentally three in one: the world's peoples have spoken by and through the three of them. Eileen panted a little, very quietly, so as not to disturb the dozing Shaw, for the room was very hot, vainly assailing the coldness of death creeping over the life of the losing leader. The young woman and the old man; the one in life's centre, the other about to slide away from its oldest circle. The keen eyes slowly opened again, and she bent low to catch his whispering chat.

—I'm going, at last, Eileen; and I'm glad of it.

—Nonsense, G.B.S. You'll rally out of it, and live for us all a long time yet.

—No, no, Eileen; no longer. I want to die. What good would it be going from this bed here to that bed there; and all the time to be handled by those I don't know; by strangers? No, it is time for me to go; and he slid into a stilly doze.

—Are you there, Eileen? Are you still there? he whispered, coming back to the world again for a few moments.

—Yes, I'm still here, Eileen whispered back. Tell me if I bore you, or if you wish me to go away.

—No, no, he said, in a hasty whisper; stay till I sink into a deeper sleep.

—A sleep will do you good, she said; you'll be better then — not rightly knowing what to say.

—No, I'll never be better, he whispered back. Then the bright eyes closed again, and the long, lean figure lay still, the handsome hands, transparent now, lying quiet on the quilt. Eileen waited till the eyes opened again, the wan but still powerful face turned towards her, and a gentle smile creased the whitening lips; I have no desire to live longer. Could you stroke my forehead for a little while? — it seems to soothe the pain; and she stroked the high forehead gently, feeling that Shaw imagined himself back in his childhood, with his mother watching over him.

—It is very pleasant to feel the touch of a soft Irish hand, and to hear the sound of a soft Irish voice. He was going from the world with his comrade-fighters, Gandhi and Stalin, watching from the wall. A quizzical smile flickered over his face. It will be interesting, anyhow, Eileen, to meet the Almighty.

—I'm sure, G.B.S., that He and you will get on well together.

—I'll have a helluva lot of questions to ask Him, and the old humorous look lighted the wasted face again.

—Wait for Sean, she whispered; wait till he joins you, for he is a bit of a fighter.

—I'm a fighter, too, and the whisper became emphatic; but here my fighting is finished. It's up to Sean, now.

—Sean is too old, said Eileen quickly; he's seventy, now.

—Well, then, it's up to one, or both, of the boys, if their lives aren't wasted in another war.

Quietly and softly, he stole away into a sleep, and quietly and softly Eileen tiptoed out of the room, leaving him looking as if he were already dead. Outside, she talked for some time to the nurse. Then, suddenly, the bell, fastened to Shaw's shoulder, rang to bring attention. When the young nurse went in, he asked her if Eileen had gone, and was told she had not, but was about to go. He said he'd like to say goodbye to her. She went back, sat down by the bedside, and with a lovely smile that flashed back into his face the younger Shaw to view again, he said, Goodbye, Eileen, goodbye; give my love to all the O'Caseys. She lingered there over the goodbye till the great, tired soul sank into sleep again, a deeper sleep than before; then she stole from the room, and left Shaw's Corner, and left the great householder in sleep, that he might be free to go forth to meet death, to give death welcome, and see death bow before his greatness.

He died two days later. These were his last words: That youth might not be wasted in another war. Kind man, brave man, wise soul, indomitable spirit of the indomitable Irishry.

Many tries have been made to press down the world-stature of Shaw. Critics have derided his plays; politicians have jeered at his socialism; defenders of institutional religion cocked noses at his philosophy. Little chitterers reaching up puny hands to pluck at his knees and tumble him down. Life can't change. Oh, unchangeable, sinful, sinner human nature! Original sin has got us all by the short hairs! With Grahame Greene life is a precious, perpetual, snot-sodden whinge. With Shaw, a poke from a living, forward-thrusting hand — pip pip! Theirs a pat from a hand damp with death.

Every character in every play is a puppet, in so far as every character does, or says, what the author thinks it should say or do.

There is no part in any play, bad, good, or great, which is independent of its creator. The author says to his character, do this, and he doeth it; come, and he cometh. Of course Shaw often uses the characters in his plays to voice what he thinks about man and his methods; but no more so than dramatists who are no more in skill and creation than, physically, a tom thumb is to a giant. They all weave their own opinions into what the characters in their plays say. Some critics say there is no poetry in Shaw's plays (how often have the Dublin bravos signed this in the air with a sawing hand!); and no emotion. There is poetry in the very description of the Syrian sky at the opening of *Caesar and Cleopatra*, in the way the Bucina calls, in the two great figures dwarfed between the paws of the Sphinx, in the rush of the Roman Legion into the Palace, halting to cry Hail, Caesar, when they see him sitting alone with the Queen of Egypt; poetry, and emotion, too. There is poetry and fine emotion in the scene on the banks of the Loire in the play of *Saint Joan*, and in the Saint's sorrow when she sees that while the world venerates her at a safe distance, the same world wants her no nearer; here is ironical emotion, shot with sadness stretching out to the day that is with us, for, with Christians now, it is not, Get thee behind me, Satan, but Get thee behind me, God. There are poetry and emotion in *The Devil's Disciple*, a heart-sob, indeed, at the end of the first scene when Essie, the natural child, finds a friend, and cries to show her joy, to get the devil's disciple's blessing in Oh, yes, you may cry that way, Essie. Indeed, the whole play is shot through with emotion, and he who doesn't feel it is neither critic nor man. There is poetry and emotion in *Candida*; poetry of a minor key in the way the doctors regard the thoughtlessness of the artist, Dubedat, rising into a major key at the death of the artist when the play is ending; it flashes through every scene of *Heartbreak House*; and stands dignified and alone in the character of Keegan in *John Bull's Other Island*; the poetry and emotion gleams out in the revelation that God is close to Feemy Evans, the fallen woman of the camp, though the respectable humbugs wouldn't let her finger-tip touch the bible. The English critics are afraid to feel: Eton and Harrow seem to have groomed them against the destitute dignity of tears. They are cross-grained against any visible sign of emotion. The Irish aren't. George Jean Nathan in his preface to *Five Great Modern Irish Plays* says, 'Perhaps the outstanding mark of Irish dramatists by and large is their shameless emotional candor. They write what they honestly feel, however possibly embarrassing. The Irish alone as a playwrighting nation appear to appreciate the human heart for what in all its strange and various moods it is, and the Irish alone with a profligate beauty and a lyric artlessness permit it to tell its true and often aching story.' Emotional expression in Shaw's plays is seldom shameless; but it is often plain and outspoken, reaching those who haven't locked humanity out of their hearts.

His comments upon the theatre of his day stand dauntless still, though almost all the plays he saw and spoke about are dead, and vaulted now where no man's mind can reach them. The Notorious Mrs. Ebbsmith, sore disturbed, stormed for a day or two, then sighed, and gave her queen-seat to Lady Wayneflete. Michael's Lost Angel stretching out arms to keep away intruders, was hustled out and off by the wild sanity of the Devil's Disciple; and all the mouthing crew of cant and humbug hurried off to hide from purging laugh and biting wit of Shavian play and Shavian preface. He was the greatest British playwright of his age; none equalled him then, none equal him now. None of those who learned from him have yet thrown a wider chest than his own. Dead though he be, none can yet venture to sing the *Nunc Dimittis* of Bernard Shaw, either as prophet or playwright.

What time has been wasted during man's destiny in the struggle to decide what man's next world will be like! The keener the effort to find out, the less he knew about the present one he lived in. The one lovely world he knew, lived in, that gave him all he had, was, according to preacher and prelate, the one to be least in his thoughts. He was recommended, ordered, from the day of his birth to bid goodbye to it. Oh, we have had enough of the abuse of this fair earth! It is no sad truth that this should be our home. Were it but to give us simple shelter, simple clothing, simple food, adding the lily and the rose, the apple and the pear, it would be a fit home for mortal or immortal men.

That was one of the great and courageous virtues of Shaw — he made the most of life. The earth was his home, and he loved it. He was at home among the mortals. His epiphany was the showing forth of man to man. Man must be his own saviour; man must be his own god. Man must learn, not by prayer, but by experience. Advice from God was within ourselves, and nowhere else. Social sense and social development was the fulfilment of the law and the prophets. A happy people made happy by themselves. There is no other name given among men by which we can be saved, but by the mighty name of Man. It was wise and good of Shaw to give himself no grave.

SUNSET

VICTORY DAY was born in a bluster of bells. Confined within the cell of silence during the years of the war, they rang out now as if every ringer were a Quasimodo swinging from the ropes. All of them; everywhere: bells of St. John Lateran, of St. Jim Clatterin, of St. Simon Slatterin, of St. Finian Flatterin, of St. Nicholas Natterin: bells of St. Mary's, bells of St. Clement's, and bells of Old Bailey; bells of St. Martin's and the big bells of Bow. Hellsbells brazen bounding about, with Saints George, Andrew, David, and Patrick, bowing acknowledgements. Sean stood, half deafened, in the midst of the din from the bragging bronze, a din that would have caused Dickens to clap his hands over his hearing; a din that would have prompted Keats to write about bells tolling as he did of those that rang in his day:

> The church bells tolled, a melancholy sound,
> Calling the people to some other prayers,
> Some other gloominess, more dreadful cares.

The bells were trying to be merry now — harder, faster, pull, pull, pull! Ding dong dell, Europe's in the well. Who knocked her in? Hitler's scurvy sin. Who'll pull her out? Ah, therein lies the doubt; no one knows a thing about the rightful way to pull her out, said a brawny boy scout, musing by a scout redoubt. Ring out, wild bells, to the wild skies. Belling the ruins. Weeds are growing where stately buildings stood. Sit down solitary amid silent ruins, and weep a people inurned and their greatness changed into an empty name. Ring out, wild bells, to the wild sky! God is clapping his hands! Christians, awake, salute the happy mourn! Ring out the hot war, ring in the cold war! Hitler, the world's blunder, is a withering handful of ashes sourly sinking within a world of ruins; the great cod-god gone. Mussolini is hanging, head down, naked, from a hasty gibbet, his glory gone, his bawling jellied in his battered brain; the end of the huddling half-god.

It was indeed right to peal the bells, to try to feel gay, to dance a measure in honour of the silence which came when the cannon's mouth was shut; to cheer for the joy of peace that was the sweet voice, the luminous cloud. For a moment, forget the wounded, the maimed, and leave the dead to bury their dead, while the people snatch a fearful thrill from a moment of peace: and so the people of Totnes rejoiced, the Mayor in his red robe, the Town Clerk in his black gown and white wig, the Town Sergeant in his embroidered coat and his new cocked hat, and all the people with them; the little children, the young, the middle-aged, the old, in their best attire, trailed down the hilly main street under the setting sun, under the evening star, trailed down carrying torches, Sean's wife and his little girl among them, singing a song to the hour that had brought them victory and peace; and in the midst of the torches' light, the music of a band, the riotous peal of the bells, his old age stands, serene and bright, and lovely as a Lapland night. No, no; not quite, for the look of the land without and the feeling of the heart within mock the loveliness of a Lapland night, laugh at the serenity of old age.

Wherever we may stand in England, there are ruins around us, and the breath of old age is thickened and harried with aggressive smoke; smoke coming between us and the light from the torches; envious smoke, blurring even the sound of the song. The smoke from ten thousand ruins is rising, sullying the silver solace of the evening star; the flames are flickering round the blackened stones still. Poor me, poor me! The dead lie down beneath the ruins, the dead that are blackened and burning still. Has anybody here seen my Jesus? Has anybody seen my Lord? Poor me, poor me! Did He see the smoke, did He feel the fire? A sky of smoke and a floor of fire. The roadways gone, no pathway left. Did He hear from the blast the sigh of the burst one? Did He hear the scream of a mother maddened for a child that was but is not now? Has He seen a woman's fingers scraping timber and stone away from the ruin of her man? Or a man's sad finding but flame and a fuming and a line of dead where his home had been? Oh, I see too much, know too much. Many dead here, many there; many maimed and many marred. Oh, Jesus, trouble's going to bury me down! Where is my young son? My younger daughter? Where is my young husband? My young wife? Bring me the black cloak for my body, the black hat for my head. Poor me, poor me! Give me many tears to waste away this ache. Oh, has anybody here seen my Jesus? Has anybody seen my Lord?

When the gatherings had dispersed after the Victory Toasts had been drunk with wine or beer, and the people had gone back to the chair and table, England sat down to count the cost, and couldn't do it — the quicker the rush to the horizon of recovery, the faster it scurried away. All she had left was her pride and a hot cross bun. Her last glittering foreign investments had been snatched from her hands. The once wealthy England was now like Mrs. Squeers measuring out tea, sugar, meat, cheese, eggs, and coal, so that most might get a little lick to preserve the longing. Gloomy honours appeared on her flag — Mend and Make Do, Eat Less, Wear Less, Do Without; their one uplifting thought — others are worse than we. The British People, fearsomely heroic throughout the uproar and bustling bloodiness of war, now had to be heroic through lean years, years that dragged them close to the snarling snout of want. Let the people sing, said one fellow; put out more flags, said another; but the people were in little mood for warbling, and bunting was needed for patching shirt and shift so that the poor body might present a respectable façade to the gaping world. The broad straight road had disappeared, and England now walked unsteadily over a crazy pavement. Tomorrow had vanished, for the day that was had in itself more than enough to think of, so help us God. The women defiled themselves into a queue stretching from one end of England to the other. Through the summer hot and sweating, through the winter's damp and desolation, the women were inching, inching along in a never-ending queue. It often took a woman months to grab hold of a coat, a pair of knickers, a pair of shoes for a child. A-hunting we will go, a-hunting we will go! The sharing out of points and rations became a geometrical problem. The nation was living on its spare parts. After the querulous quietude of the queue, there was the rush home to wash, to sew, to cook, to get the children to school; more than ever now, the indomitable housewife became the pushed-about pathfinder of life. If women were not what women are, the world would perish overnight.

Some Irish sent up a titter, thinking that England would soon be as the old Bards had foretold — trudging through frost without a shoe on her foot. It was no laughing matter for the English, and, soon, the Irish found that it was no tittering matter for them. England down meant Ireland up no longer. A poor England on her flank was as big a menace as a wealthy England had been. England was no longer such a responsive market. Coal was Ireland's big need, but England could spare but a paper-bagful. Constirnation! No miracle, no novena could bring to Ireland the coal she needed. No coracles appeared carrying miraculous draughts of fuel. Depend on yourselves. Shinn Fane. Burn everything except English coal. Turf turf turf! Oh, Eire, turf is the only wear and smile in thy cry. The dear's cry — turf on me left hand, turf on me right one; turf before me, turf behind me. De Valera and his cubinette were in a state of ecstatic coalition. It's turf that gives me heart all its joyous elation. Fianna Fail was dancing the baile baile. There's nothing we cannot do without it.

I met with Napper Tandy, an' he took me be the hand,
This turf'll be the one an' sure salvation of the land;
Three things we've got'll keep us great, an' speed us on our way —
Our turf, our Irish Sweep, and shawls of gallant galway gray.

In the hundreds of rotten, leaky, Irish schools, the happy children were learning all about the evolution of the idea of a sod. The old bog road's thick with cheering crowds on their way, trot trot trot to bother the bog; a slawn on every shoulder, all singing the new national anthem — *The Bog Down in the Valley O*. Turf is what'll enlighten our darkness. Listen, before yous begin digging: did yous hear that they're going to build the new catholic cathedral outa turf? D'ye tell me that? Ay, roof and all. Ay, and they're going to make all the new bishops' croziers outa bog-oak so's to keep things in harmony. I'm telling you turf's a thing'll never peater out. Let England keep her coal — it's a turf stage. Let turf electrify the land. The whole land under turf-ray treatment. Electric teashocks everywhere. Staggering thought! Electric hares and prayers; electric spires and lyres in the new land of shrines, sepulchres, and shams. Electrical vibrations in the Lenten pastorals short-circuiting sin and shocking souls into ample nodes of *senora pro nobis na hEireann*.

The sun is half-way under the horizon's rim, a sad decline when it symbolises the lost loveliness of life's full day. Pale gold and paler green but thinly garland the sober livery of the evening's end. The day is dying drowsily in a lovely bed. The night is near. Swift to its close ebbs out life's little day. Life's day ebbs swiftly, but life's day is not a little one: it is big with grandeur and may be bright with glory. Oh, twilight, stay with us another hour and keep the last and loving light of day from fading!

A rumble of low, blaguardly thunder from the right. Rowdelum Randy, the insinity divinity tinkers are at it again: a first production of *The Silver Tassie* causes definite desolate protests in Vienna, and a first production in Berlin almost provokes a riot, though the comedy was shouted, the cry against war whispered, and the crippled Harry prevented from crushing the Silver Tassie in the last act; all to avoid offending roman catholic churchmen, in fear of committing a breach of the cold war. Rowdelum Randy: a Dublin friend, working in Birmingham, going homeward once more on a holiday, brings a copy of *Drums Under the Windows* with him, lends it to his brother, who reads it in the quiet of the night, and leaves it beside his bed when he goes to work in the morning early; the mother enters to make the bed, picks up the book, reads a little of it, thunder shakes the house; she rushes to the fire, burns the book, and rushes to get the priest to bless the building. He blesses it, and the dangerous vibrations from O'Casey's book are bent back; push, push, lads; bent back to poor old Pagan England again. Wipe the sweat from your face, lads; wipe your face; the sweat away. With all this rumbling of thin thunder, comes a soft limelight love from many letters bloated out with Dublin Catholic Truth Society's tracts, like *Tolerance Thumbs Up Too Much of a Good Thing*, by the Reverend Daniel Lord, S.J.; the booklit lanterned with a *nihil obstat* and an archiepiscopal *imprimi potest*, with the news that the booklit is reprinted by the kind permission of The Queen's Work, St. Louis, U.S.A.; tailed by a warning that 'this edition must not be sold in the United States or Canada'; and a coda reminding all that 'this booklet is to make God known and loved', and that 'you cannot serve him better than by passing it on to a friend', or 'if you cannot find a friend, leave it to Providence (thumbs down!), and deposit it in a theatre, a bus, or a park seat'. Deposit is good. Deposit account. Make him known. Give him plenty of publicity. The heavens that declare his glory, and the firmament that showeth his handwork aren't enough by a long chalk: we must floodlight his glory with booklits.

Some British reviewers seem to have a coy way of avoiding any touch with an author commenting on what they may have written about his work. Those who aren't rich enough to have an ivory tower, shrink into a shell. When *I Knock at the Door* came out, Oliver St. John Gogarty shrank away from its candour, and, writing in the *Sunday Times*, said he was gravely shocked at what he called 'the unlocking of the heart'; and instanced the habit and example of the Chinese of reticence and silent fortitude. This, too, when the red flare of revolution had appeared in the Chinese valleys and the Chinese hills! But Oliver St. John Gogarty hadn't heard a word about it. The time of Chinese reticence was over. A letter telling him all about it was sent to the paper, which, refraining from publishing it, forwarded it to the reviewer, but Oliver never replied: practising personally his own gospel of reticence. The willow pattern plate must not be broken. Silence. Silence never betrays you.

Sean was mystically confronted by another ghostly silence on the part of the celebrated poet, Mr. Louis MacNeice, when he made some comments on a review of his book, *Rose and Crown*. In

the review, Mr. MacNeice said, 'O'Casey assumes that everything
Roman or Latin is alien to England. Odd for an admirer of Milton.
In refusing to hear anything good of the Middle Ages, O'Casey is
equally perverse. As a playwright he might have remembered that
there were once Miracle Plays and that some of these were very
gay.'

Gay? Oh, God! Old and gay! These Miracle Plays are moulded
from episodes in the Scriptures, few of which were gay; none of
them very gay; The Fall, Expulsion of Adam and Eve from the
Garden of Eden, Killing of Abel by Cain, Israelites in Bondage.
And Mr. MacNeice calls these gay! Even the events culled from the
later Testament, and made into plays, aren't what would be called
gay. Such as Massacre of Innocents, Flight into Egypt, Temptation
of Christ, The Betrayal, Remorse of Judas. To call such entertainments gay would seem to say that Mr. MacNeice has turned humour
all tapsalteerie O. Most of them are clumsy and terribly dull —
including the worshipped preciousness of *Everyman*. Even these,
though, were frowned on by the church! 'It is forbidden him by
decree to make or witness miracle plays, because miracle plays, once
begun, become gatherings and sights of sin.' Even this poor, dull
gaiety was condemned by the church of the Middle Ages. Thou
mayest kill, an thou will, but 'thou shalt neither dance nor laugh.
But the ghostly frown was no extinguisher of the peasant dance
round the maypole, or of the lover's desire for his lass, or the lass's
desire for the desire of her lover; for these were life, and the church
could not kill life.

Perhaps Mr. MacNeice confused Miracle Plays with Morality
Plays coming to us afterwards. It was only when life started to pull
itself out of the Middle Ages that we come to more human thought
peppered into the Morality Plays, a very different genre from the
Miracle Plays. Even these couldn't be called 'very gay', containing,
as they did, more of satire than of merriment. By far the best of
them is Lyndsay's *Ane Satyre of the Thrie Estaitis*. Here we find
little laughter in the Pauper's story of how, when his old feyther died,
the landlord took his grey mare, the vicar his best cow; the same
vicar took his second-best cow, and got the Clerk to take away the
Pauper's clothes, after his wife had died of grief, leaving him only
with a groat, which, we are told, he intends to give to a lawyer as a
fee to win, through the law, justice from the church; to which, when
he hears it, Diligence replies, 'Thou art the daftest fuill that ever I
saw; do you expect to get remedy from the clergy by means of the

law?' Diligence knew more about the gay customs of the Middle Ages than does Mr. MacNeice.

Sean admired Milton, not because of his Latin, but because of his English, despite the fact that Milton was Latin Secretary to Cromwell. In the Preface to the First Edition, the editor, Humphrey Moseley, says, 'It is not any private respect of gain, Gentle Reader, for the slightest pamphlet is now adayes more vendible than the works of learnedest men; but it is the love I have to our own Language that hath made me diligent to collect, and set forth peeces both in Prose and Vers as may renew the wonted honour and esteem of our English tongue'. Aha, the English tongue! Who cares now about Milton's Latin Elegiarum? His Latin illusions are but the tiny Latin buttons on an English suit of serge. Milton was as English as Hobson, the University's carrier in the poet's day. He was an English oak that sent out a few sparse sprays of the gadding vine. Born in Bread Street, buried in Cripplegate, Milton was a great Republican, and, to Sean, an Englishman to his heart's true core.

Sean in his ignorance couldn't understand the orgiastic idea that there was something inherently divine, poetical, and tremendous in the Latin language; that among the battling languages around, it was an Emanuelian manifesto of human speech. Strong an idea today as ever it was. We are told that all the monarchical titles on Elizabeth the Second's Great Seal of England are shrouded within the wonder of aloofly-warbling Latin words. The language of bible and prayer-book, of Shakespeare himself, wasn't classy enough for the great, grandiloquent Seal of England. No, sor. At one time it was everywhere and everything, separating the people from all life outside of their hovels of clay and wattles made, their spare-ribbed pig, their shabby cow, and their woeful patch of arable stone. It was the earth, the zodiac, sky, sun, moon, and stars; hail, dew, thunder, and lightning; it was the signpost to heaven for all. God spake it, and the devil, too. It is still plastered over many things: on banners, coats-of-arms, army slogans, of navy, of air-force; sign-posts to an earlier grave. It forms divine mottoes for diocese, city, and church bell. Bold-faced, it bears a preface on a raw book of Dublin street ballads. 'Looka, lad', said Molière once to Sean, 'a laudation in Latin is of marvellous efficacy at the beginning of a book.' It puzzled people for centuries, and plundered them of knowledge. Sean had heard it mumbled beside a coffin, and had seen wistful and weary kids intoning *Tantum Ergo* and *Salutaris Hostia*, little members of a Latin hymn-class in a Dublin school, a music-master leading them on, the parish priest present to prod them on, an irritated gob on him because of the children's hesitation over unfamiliar and foreign words.

Latin, they say, is the soul of all literature, and Virgil the soul of poetry. Soul of Rome! Shakespeare but a player on pipes of reed compared with the outspreading symphony of poetry composed by the honey-spouting Virgil. Are these appellants for Latin right? he wondered. A big claim, with very few to verify it. Of the thousands of millions of people crowning this earth with human life, how many are there who could lie back on divan, sit straight in a chair, and enjoy the poetry of Virgil? Very few. And of these fewer still who could translate him in such a way as to show him shining to those who read him in English. Are there even a few who could do this? Ne'er a one, ne'er a one. Who could give in English sense and English music the rolling O of Virgil, imitating lamentation for the falling stones of Troy? Or all the S's combining to give the hiss to the snakes destroying Laocoön and his sons? Ne'er a one — not even James Joyce. And why Virgil alone? There's reason to believe that heaps of poems by other Romans perished because they hadn't the influence of grander persons to help in preserving them. When an emperor stands by you, the world does, too. Folk-lore and the songs of the people died with these other Romans. Many, or some, of those might have had with us, had they been more fortunate, as great a name as Virgil. He wasn't the only one who sang fair and sang to the music of man's soul.

Ford Madox Ford says of Horace's *Dulce ridentem Lalagen amabo, dulce loquentem* that they are 'the most beautiful words ever written about fortunate love'. He adds that they cannot be translated, and then says they mean 'I shall love the sweetly-smiling Lalage'! He goes on, 'There is no word for loquentem; it means "conversing", or more in French "devising"; it certainly doesn't mean "chattering" or "prattling"'. No? Then what the hell does it mean? Indeed, Ford Madox Ford says of Propertius's poem of his Cynthia sinking to death in the Ionian Sea that 'no translation can give the poetic feeling or equivalent of the extraordinary beauty of the Latinity of this poem. Faced with the incomparable, ringing, marble, bas-relief of the Latin, you will be overcome by paralysis. [Poetriomelitis.] The English with its harsh sounds and soft, gluey effects of meaning as compared with the clean Latin, can hardly ever be marble or ringing.' The same writer says somewhere else that he has always held that the most exquisite poetry in the world was contained in the following four lines of Tibullus:

Te spectem, suprema mihi cum venerit hora,
et teneam moriens deficiente manu
flebis et arsuro positum me, Delia, lecto
tristibus et lacrimis oscula mixta dabis.

Well, there's a marble slab for you to make what you can of. Indeed, the whole of Latin literature is but a cemetery of marble slabs jutting up here and there to show the passer-by what he may be missing. Footman, pass on! Latin has slunk into the silence of the grave. Canned into cold storage, with no-one able to rede the labels on the tins. One wonders if the Latin be so high and the English so low; if the Latin language be really so grand and glorious as Ford Madox Ford, here, and T. S. Eliot, there, make it out to be. Certes, in translation, it is more like plywood than like marble. It has no ringing sound in it, not even the sound of Gregory's swashing blow. Shakespeare himself (probably, like Sean himself, because he didn't know it) usually uses Latin to raise a laugh. Sad sight, sad sound, sad sense. But if it be such a mighty language, why did it die? Why did ye die, why did ye die; Conn the Shaughraun, why did ye die! Time was when the English Parliament's marble halls constantly heard round ringing Latin phrases, when members bullied each other with quotations from Virgil, Propertius, Lucretius, Horace, and Ovid; long, long ago; oh, long ago. Now, they quote themselves. Why couldn't they keep the Latin poets on their laps? It couldn't have been Communism that ordered their liquidation. Latinity was a warm thing in the schools and colleges the governing-class attended; gave them their Latin cue; and sent them forth with a loquacity half as old as time. Perhaps it died because, when we grow up, the world is too much with us. The fact is, life leaves us far too soon. It keeps us busy. We haven't the chance, even if we had the wish, to spend a lonely life reclining by Windermere's Lake or on the banks of Loch Lomond, sipping fiery or mellow Scotch, or lowering wild Falernian wine, chanting Virgil. We have to watch our muttons.

The one claim that Latin poetry is all it is said to be seems to be the claim that a translation can never touch the beauty, the regularity, or the dignity of the original. No-one can contradict the claim, since, if we could, we should have to know the Latin familiarly and well; which few of us do. Is this lady latinum as fair as they say? Come now, press your hand to your head, and think — SPQR or USAR or USSR? Latin civilisation has downed us into a literary demurity. Ovid, Horace, and Virgil peep over the cotswolds and the quantocks with the rising of every sun, and we are tired of them since they have to speak to us by signs. Latin has put English into a toga, and English looks damnably affected in the garb. When a car was invented holding more than a couple, it was called an omnibus, so frightening the people that they short-circuited it into bus, which is bad enough, and not near so good as folkwagon; so agon-bite of inwit is more piercing than qualm of conscience. Anyway, reduced to a translation, Latin pales off into a ghost. None of them Sean ever read equals a poem by Yeats or a sonnet by Shakespeare. What's this now? Just caught a glimpse of it: *Everyman's Encyclopaedia*, in its article on Latin, says 'Latin is not naturally suited to the writing of poetry. The Romans were not themselves an imaginative race, and the long, sonorous Latin words do not fall easily into lyrical metres. In the hands of Horace and Virgil it received its finest form as a poetic instrument.' Now, what bounder said that? Some gutter-snipe! Not an Eton or a Harrow laddo, certainly, or even a Grammar-School scholar. Oxford giving a Doctor of Civil Law degree, *sonorus causa*, to the United States Secretary of State, told him, in rich Latin, that he was a jolly good fellow, a gay honour few would have known about, if it hadn't been put into English the following day by the British Press. A few must have smiled and nodded their heads, and nodded at one another when they heard the Latin rolling along like ole man river, as Roman Senators did when Cicero spoke Greek.

Still the Latin hasn't the gift of turning itself into a charming English changeling, and the purple stipple given to it by them who know it must be taken for granted. But the English translations of Latin hymns and poems in Miss Waddell's book are as flat as pancakes, without salt, sugar, or spice. It is very odd that an awed honour is still given to anything which comes hopping lamely out of the Latin. Sean was one with Whitman's regard for this persistent reverence for something, chiefly because that something was unfamiliar to the general man. Whitman didn't like it, and the old man sang out for American preference, his wide-brimmed hat covering Manhattan, his beard flowing out in the winds of the world:

> Come, Muse, migrate from Greece and Ionia,
> Cross out please those immensely overpaid accounts,
> That matter of Troy and Achilles' wrath, and Aeneas',
>   Odysseus' wanderings,
> Placard 'removed' and 'to let' on the rocks of your snowy Parnassus.

And uncles Remus and Romulus, too, me lad, for we have had a fine fill of them all, and some of us want to turn to sturdier native fruits and wine of the mind and spirit, for our nature's inclined to be cloyed with

That soft bastard Latin,
That melts like kisses from a female mouth.

Bona roba of literature. It was always pathetic for Sean to see Grammar-School lads shoving Latin verbs and nouns into their memories, things which they didn't enjoy and could never understand, for, when they broke loose from school at last, Lucan for them was lost, Seneca dead as a doornail. Thousands of them leave school yearly, but one never sees a Virgil or a Horace in an ageing grammar-school hand; nor, for the matter of that (to move to the lords of Latin) do we see a Juvenal or a Catullus in the hand of priest, monsignor, or bishop; no, not even an abbreviated copy of the Aquinas's *Summa* in the original Latin; more often, probably, a detective tale in a back pocket of their pants. Sean remembered telling a priest of a friend, known to both of them, that he had gone into the priesthood, and received the comment, 'Aw, he mastered the Latin grammar'. Well, the Latin is more than a grammar, a lot more, if it's a language at all. The most of these have just enough to read the Canon of the Mass and browse over the breviary: a quick browse often. Lord, they have taught them Latin is sure waste.

Latinlore twisted the neck of art for years so that she couldn't whisper that there was anything else in the world. For instance, the statue of King Billy in Dublin looked more like an illegitimate Caesar than it did an English or a Dutch king, and pictures painted by Poynter and Alma ta ta Tadema showed Rome at its worst, giving her a decline and fall that Gibbon never meant her to have. Johnson spoke to Frenchmen in Latin (though the Frenchmen couldn't understand him) because he wouldn't speak to a mere Frenchman in a foreign jargon. Some of the literary men of the time bescreeched him to write Goldsmith's epitaph in English, but the learned one refused 'to disgrace the walls of Westminster Abbey with an English inscription'. Said Emerson, 'the barbarians who broke up the Roman Empire didn't come a moment too soon'; and it is near time present-day barbarians broke up the literary empire she left behind her; for, as Stobart says, 'The great Latin writers are truly and really classical, apparently, because they did not write as they spoke or thought'. So, apparently, the Latin left to us is a purpled Latin never spoken by the bulk of the people, by

those watching the circus, those ploughing the fields, those tramping
the roads — legionary, centurion, or even captain; the little left is
the Latin of those who were afraid to write as they spoke or as they
thought.

And translations, however good, won't do, even for the Latin
wearing a toga with its purple stripe. Says Stobart again, 'Latin, of
all languages, least permits of translation. You have only to translate Cicero to despise him.' Good God — Cicero; no! And thousands
of our schoolboys blue in the face trying to do it. But a louder voice
than Stobart's — that of Ford Madox Ford — says 'I carried six
lines of a poem by Propertius in my head for fifty years before I
ventured to translate them, and then, comparing them with the
original, found they didn't fit, and violated the dignity of the
original'. For fifty years. Fifty years agrowing! No use of knocking
at the door of original classics; there's an ironical curtain between
them and us; their pictures don't suit our hallways; their drums no
longer sound under our windows. None or few of the translations,
read by Sean, seemed to come up to those made from the Gaelic.
Even the satirical poem or two in Miss Waddell's collection can't
compare with the satires of MacConglinne, for instance; and even
Adeste Fideles or *Tantum Ergo* are thin things compared with the
passionate faith and courage expressed and recited in *The Deer's
Cry*, better known or unknown as *St. Patrick's Breastplate*; or St.
Ita's lovely little lullaby to herself with the Infant, Jesus, on her
breast,

> Jesu, thou angelic blossom,
> No ill-minded monk art thou.

Or Crede's lament for Dinertach, whom she loved, when he was
brought in wounded before her from the battle of Aidne,

> There are arrows that murder sleep
> At every hour in the bitter-cold night.

In a review of *Rose and Crown*, Louis MacNeice, the well-known
poet, said 'O'Casey assumes that everything Roman or Latin is
alien to England. Odd for an admirer of Milton.' Not a bit odd.
O'Casey would like very much to know Latin himself, but, before it,
he would put any living language of Europe as far more important.
Latin isn't any more alien to England than it is to France, Germany,
Hungary, or Russia. As a dead thing it is alien to all things living.
It is a bright thing for scholars. For instance, if Coulton hadn't
been such a one, he could never have written his books on the
Middle Ages, and Sean could never have enjoyed them. But even

University Fellows don't commonly talk Latin among themselves. They used to; they no longer do so. Neither do the priests; not even the cardinal priests. At one time, Latin was the expressed power of the Church and the State, hiding everything from the common people, giving the things of the Church and the State a grandiloquent air of divinity. It had a divine rite of its own. But the English language was its enemy; it fought the Latin ceaselessly, gaining strength every time it touched its own good earth. Even the Anglo-Saxon Latinists — Clerks Adhelm, Alcuin, and Bede — couldn't stop the English manner and spirit from jumping about in their dignified Latin prose and poems; time and change finally confining it to a few words on the arms of the lords, ladies, and bourgeois gentlemen, and the brassy cap-badges of the ` serving soldiers. Even many members of the roman catholic faith have declared their wish that there should be less of Latin and more of what they call 'the vernacular' in their church services. After all, The Lord be with you is as good a fellow as *Domine vobiscome*.

Fitter for the purple-flushed ones in college, school, and home to love the languages on their own doorstep, tongue of Scot, Cymru, and Gael, than to hell-bend over ones as dead as any dead thing can be. The English language, after many hoary centuries, is vivid, valorous, strenuous still, and glowing for them, to them, who use it, respect and love it; and, hard as it may sometimes be, it can often melt like kisses from a woman's mouth, and a lovely mouth too. So the English first and foremost, though, but for the Latin, we shouldn't have known about Hercules, who with his club killed Cerberus, that three-headed canis, and calmly strangled serpents with his mighty manus.

As the comments on Oliver St. John Gogarty's review of *I Knock at the Door* in the *Sunday Times* remained unanswered, so the comments on Mr. MacNeice's review of *Rose and Crown* in the *Observer* remain unanswered to this day, this day. The rust was silence. Perhaps they feared there was a red ray in the comments; or, more likely, they thought the comments to be silly, and, out of charity, decided to do the commentator no further harm. Maybe it was the pity that gave before charity began. We shall not quench the smoking flax. Clever and delightful poets, both of them; but one didn't know much about China, and the other didn't seem to know much about Miracle and Morality Plays. Still there was a kinship between him and Louis MacNeice in their outlook on drama. Mr. MacNeice writes in the *Radio Times* in 1952, 'I have attempted in *One*

Eye Wild something similar to what I did in two earlier programmes. Both of these were experimental and tried to combine two techniques, those of realism and symbolism.' Attaboy!

Sean was now near to the door again, about to go out of life's house by the same door as in he went. It was a wider door now than when he first knocked at it. A few more drinks. As he drank, change in all he saw. He felt hustled. It wasn't that change was here: that is no new, no startling thing. Changes were busy before the first man was able to give his first indicative grunt. Changes moved through all the changes, through the Plantagenets, the Tudors, the Georges, through the slow, plushy years of the Victorian satisfaction, yawning up its gratitude to God for trying to keep things as they were; saved from self-satisfaction by its group of great men and women, and many fine things done in their time. It wasn't the changes that hustled him; it was that so many changes have come so fast; so fast that he and all the old come halting on behind. Science has presented life with more life than present life can comprehend or hold. Worlds in bunches away beyond the Milky Way, and worlds alone in space; with new worlds unfolding themselves beneath the microscope and within the atom; new worlds still hidden from the myopic eye of the microscope and the equally myopic eye of the telescope nosing among the stars. New worlds of vitamins, cells, viruses, moulds, chromosomes, isotopes, superseding spermaceti for an inward bruise; new worlds for all, with a new world of democracy thrown in, garlanded with glory and with danger too. Aristotle is becoming a ghost.

The sun is more than half-way beneath the horizon's rim, and its pale gold and pale green garlands are paler now, paler, and turning grey. The day is dying, dying drowsily in a lovely bed. Swift to its close ebbs out life's lambent day. Oh, twilight, stay with us another hour and keep the last and loving light of day from fading!

OUTSIDE AN IRISH WINDOW

THROUGH it all, how fared my sweetheart when a boy; The little Dark Rose; Ireland to you, sir? Nicely, thank you all. In the midst of the heavily-hanging hollyhock, the broad sunflower, and the tiger-lily, the shamrock had dimpled its way through life, untouched, except by the morning dew. The people went down Sackville Street as if nothing was happening next door; though tens and tens of thousands of Ireland's sons and daughters flocked to seafights and landfights, so that in every place where tiny crosses stand, Irish names are found. Ireland had her own problems, her own life to live, her own death to die. Busy saving her soul. She was growing holier day by day, according to statistics, 50 per cent this year above the norm; not good enough, but encouraging. All Ireland's temporal activities had been placed under saintly protection — Textiles under St. Clotherius, Building under Saints Bricin and Cementino, Brewing and Distilling under St. Scinful, Agriculture under St. Spudadoremus, Metal Work under St. Ironicomus, Pottery under St. Teepotolo, Fishing under St. Codoleus, Book-making under St. Banaway, the whole of them presided over by the Prayerman, St. Preservius, a most holy man of great spiritual preprotensity, who was a young man in the reign of Brian Boru, and who passed to his rest through a purelytic seizure the day he tried to read the first few lines of Joyce's damnable *Ulysses*.

Ireland had developed tone, too: gentlemen had their morning coats and tall hats, judges their red robes, senior counsels flung black silk gowns over their shoulders and planted fine white wigs on their law-loaded heads; and formal etiquette was made obligatory in all formal gatherings, causing acute distress to those put down into a low category, though they all belonged to the old and honoured clan of the great Dull Cash; and the President trotted about in the manner of the old English Viceroys, surrounded by his gold-braided Blue Hussars (at present in pawn to save something that might help to balance the Budget), lifting the taller to anyone bidding him the top of the morning; cloppety clop clop through the streets of Dublin, aidescamp on either side of him to keep the wind away.

> Aidecamp, aidecamp, look after me ease,
> Protect me from touch of the commoner's pleas,
> Please, and their fleas;
> Aidecamp, aidecamp, protect me, do, please,
> From the savage mavrones and the wicked machrees,
> And from Sweeney, there, swinging, mad, out in the threes!

This is Sackville Street, sir, and that's Mr. Costello speaking outside of the Bank of Ireland, and he telling the world that Ireland's greatest need today is dollars — can you see clear, stranger? And hear clear, too? Right: the curtains are drawn, but they're thin, and the window's wide. First get the dollars, stranger, and all the rest will be added — ahem, amen. There, in front of Parnell's statue,

stands Dev, and I hope you hear him saying that Ireland's the foremost spiritual state in all the world. So we are. The very ships that
leave our harbours now have strings of coloured lights a-swing from
mast to mast, exactly like rosaries, stranger, so that, when they're
lit up o' nights, the deckhands and stokers can say the rosary in tune
with the hum of the engines. We're not like England, with her mouth
open against fasting, and the same mouth shut against prayer. Turf
and theology, stranger, were our two main props throughout the
quiet years of the war. That youngish woman, crying on the back
doorstep? Oh, that's the Widda Malone whose two kids, a boy of
five and a girl of six, were whipped away from her, one being put
in an Industrial School, and the girl in a Convent School, because
the Widda couldn't keep them properly on her pension of sixteen
shillings a week. There was a tinkle of a murmur about it, some
interfering gets saying that if the Widda had got what it would cost
the convent and the school to keep the kids, she'd have been able to
keep them in clover. Taking the children from their natural guardian,
the gets said, because the woman pleaded for the kids to be left with
her, and the kids yelled to be let stay with their mother. Wasn't
Christian, the gets said. The kids'll soon be made to like where they
are, stranger, for a cane's a fine convincer.

That fine, out-stepping fellow on the other side? A bishop,
stranger, who'll stand no nonsense. When a City Council and its
architect chose a site for a new school, a site he didn't like and
thought unsuitable, he soon and short told them to build it on a site
of his choosing; and when the Council decided to keep to their own
selection, he soon and short told them they were behaving in the
Continental manner of disrespect for their priests; a gentle warning
that sent them running to vote as one man, bar the architect, for the
holy bishop's choice. The bishop's ring rang the bell.

That imposing-looking laddo, over in the corner, leaning on the
edge of the mantelpiece, in the tweeds, in danger of taking fire any
minute from the maroon waistcoat he's wearing? Sh! you'll waken
Mr. Doyle. Wait till this lad coming up the street's passed us, for
one's got to be careful these days. Oh, it's only Dan. Sh! The sayin',
'You'll waken Mr. Doyle', 's a way we have of warning. Morra,
Dan.

—Morra, Mick.

The laddo in the tweeds, stranger, is Ireland's literary copper
cockoo. No-one knows how he landed among the poets and writers.
He just suddenly appeared. He perches in a clock-case office in the

Irish Times, one of Ireland's National Dailies. Every Saturday as the clock strikes the hour of a dark rosaleen dawn, the portcullis shoots up, and me bould cockoo steps out to give his private views about writers, poetry, and prose, without conception, without respect of persons. Once, he says, 'Looka', he says, 'Looka that Padraic Fallon fella writing that deplorable series called his "Journal", in *The Bell*, where what he doesn't say, and the manner in which he doesn't say it, is the most interesting part of his thesis. It is not altogether fanciful to regard his extraordinary capacity to talk a great deal while committing himself to the bare minimum of communication. All our writers dislike taking up a position without first ensuring that all possible avenues of escape are open.' The grim, copper cockoo paused to let this sink into the listening souls. Have you got that much cockooed? Right. On we go again: 'The Irish writer, that boneless wonder, is an expert at wriggling. He will not be committed; he will not be taken quite seriously, because he does not really take himself seriously. He adopts not a position but a pose. Thus Mr. Fallon's rollicking, rambunctiousness; Mr. Clarke's arch pranks among pierrots and ancient Irish monks; Mr. Iremonger's grim detachment; Mr. O'Farachain's metrical acrobatics are all sleight of hand. The escape tunnels are all safely secured. Even Mr. Patrick Kavanagh, when he comes to writing prose, is the deftest side-stepper of them all.' Have you that much cockooed down, stranger?

—He's got it down all right, Mick.

—Right. On we go again: 'In Ireland the critical faculty — critical in its denigratory sense — is hyper-developed. In a society firmly based on the principle that "what goes up must come down", everyone waits maliciously with beady eyes cocked for the collapse of the next victim. The almost audible sharpening of knives, the gleeful anticipatory chuckle of those ranks of Tuscany who make a lifetime's occupation of forbearing to cheer, would make the strongest think twice about exposing himself in the arena. The only future would seem to be a literature of Artful Dodgers.' Mavrone for Ireland and for Irish Writing! There y'are, stranger — a sad state of affairs.

—I dunno, Mick. What do we want writers for anyhow? They only create confusion.

Oh, St. Anthony Guide, St. Anthony Guide, is O'Casey to go back to this? To become, maybe, a Member of the Acodemy of Blethers. A high extinction. A good death, Bona Mors. Dignified defunctorum. Immortelles all. No flowers by request. Lay them to rest where the shamrock's growing. Little field of renumbrance. Each little tablet over each little head. And you'll remember me. We will try; till we go ourselves. Looka that one writing in the corner, stranger; from here you can see what is being written. 'Stay where you are, O'Casey, in England, where, if there isn't wisdom, there is sense, and some decency of manners.' And the other writing in the far corner — read: 'All the new plays would have been better had they remained senseless on the typed-out paper. Dublin has changed so much! Pseudo-intellectuals, social climbers, racketeering politicians and businessmen, all squabbling and scrambling for power and position.'

—Isn't that a right one, Mick! The ignorant get, even if he is known well among literary gents and ladies, to defie his country!

—That noise, stranger? Echoes, only echoes, The land's full of them. Isn't it, Dan?

—It is that. Mostly wailing echoes after the emigrants. Won't you come home, won't you come home? Come back again; come back some time. The heart-cry of the Gael! Heard so often that the very echoes of the land have learned them. Hasn't she, Mick?

—She has that, Dan. The one you're hearing now, stranger — come over nearer, bend your ear down, for we speak of such things seldom. The one you're hearing now like quiet thunder, is the echo of the hurried patter of boots over the pavements. It came out of — listen, for this tale's a whisper. A week ago, the International Affairs Association (what the hell it's doing here, I don't know) heard the editor of the roman catholic paper, *The Standard*, giving a lecture on 'The Pattern of Persecution in Yugo-Slavia', with the papal nuncio, Monsignor Mickey O'Hara, sitting nice and easy in a front row. At the end, Dr. Owen Skeffington proposed that the meeting be flung open for a discussion (always a dangerous game), and the meeting voted in favour of the idea. Up sprang a country gentleman, named Hubert Butler, who, low and behold, began to talk of the part Cardinal Stepinac took with Pavelič, the Fascist leader, in forcing them of the orthodox church over into the roman ditto. Yep, yep! stir your stumps for your spiritual good, till you're all mangled and ironed out into good, hearty roman catholics. Go on, yep! to your sure salvation! At the nonce, up bounced the noncio, and out he flounced, beset with such indignation that he forgot to bang the door after him. Close the meeting quick; oh, quick; no more talk; no, none! What you're hearing, now, stranger, is an echo; the echo of what happened immediately after. The echo of the thudding of boots worn by them racing along to the nuncio's dwelling to apologise for what had happened; and to beg his big blessing. It's been echoing here, there, ever since — hasn't it, Dan?

—It has that; and, if you listen cautious, stranger, you'll hear within it a curious strain of music which an anthropologist said is the tune known as *The Man Who Struck O'Hara*. Bar a few fluttering letters in the Press, no-one spoke. Better let it lie. The thing was like a harp in the air — everyone listened, but no-one heard. No poet or peasant spoke. Thersites said nothing; Miles na Gobaleen said nothing; Quidnunc said nothing. Neither priest nor parson spoke. Didn't notice a thing. The whole of Ireland was undergoing a retreat. Silence.

Later, it was discovered by someone that Dr. Skeffington was to be principal speaker at a meeting organised by the Students' Union. Some members of the Vocational Committee who had control of the Union, had a chat, without calling any formal meeting, and decided, mum con, that Dr. Skeffington's name gave a dark decoration to the Student's programme, and that it would have to exit (excuse me, stranger, using Latin, but it comes natural). So, on orders from the Vocational Committee's members, the name of the clever and well-known Doctor got the sign of the cross-off from the programme. Didn't it, Mick?

—It did, Dan. At the night of the meeting, the Vocational Committee and their butties took over the Hall, let their friends in, keeping out even the distinguished persons invited by the Students, locked the doors, and guided the meeting in the way it should go. Didn't we, Dan?

—Ay, did we, Mick, without a whisper from the Students, afraid of the catholic cleric's ecclesiastical punchios; and the lecture on 'Can the Individual Survive?' would have gone fine, only for the get on the platform who condemned the banning of Skeffington, using honeyed words that made the meeting agree with a vote that the banning was wrong.

—Sh! You'll waken Mr. Doyle, Dan. We don't want that shame known, stranger. You see, if Skeffington and his pal, Butler, were left to open their gobs to bewilder us, there would be no freedom of thought left in the country from one end of it to the other. If the blithers aren't prepared to voicify wholesome opinions, then they must be made to keep their mouths shut. We're working towards a population of holy, practising imprimaturs, stranger. Hear that bugle call in the distance? The *Dies Irae*, Reveille of the Maria Duce, a most commendable body, filling a long-felt stunt. We must insist on proper reverence to our bishops and our nuncio. Why, looka here, just imagine, our Ministers, Ministers, mind you, scorning the jestice of ceremonial dress, attended the Eucharistic Congress in soft hats, soft hats, mind you, while at the secular Ottawa Conference they were there in all the sweet attire of morning clothes and silk hats, an indecent dereliction, making Oliver Gogarty, the poet, write the lines,

> Who wore soft hats for Christ the King,
> And toppers for King George.

you see, stranger, if things were let go, where would we be? Just think of the happy picture of Christ reviewing a Guard of Honour of Ireland's best in morning clothes and toppers!

What's what, stranger? That blaze in the distance? Oh, that — that's the blaze of burning books. Little Mary Cassidy, a county librarian, has warmed the whole country by the burning, off her own bat, of 443 books, 'because they were unfit for publication'. Sniff! This one smells bad, too! To the stake with it! Bought and burned. A woman of much importance. The bishop's book-keeper. What a lovely job. What a lot of thrills one might enjoy reading so many books that have to be burned. Reading sub nosa. We're putting a proper shape on things. Every foreign artist coming over here has to show his points, especially Americans; some have had to either sing 'I Am a Little Catholic', or put on the uniform of a catholic boy scout, and do a saunter down O'Connell Street, to show all and sundry how he defers to the devotion of the land. I'm saying, stranger, that it won't be long till we're a land of saints again. A land of perpetual prayer, a perpetual spiritual Tostal — Ireland at home to God! We've made a great beginning, and soon every levee at our President's Residence'll be nothing less than a levee of saints. Eh, Dan?

—A laudable entherprise, up to a point, Mick, up to a point; but it's soldiers we want now, an' not saints, seeing that we're in the throes of talkative preparations. All our generals and colonels, coupled an' crossed with military experts, are arguing here, there, how best to act if tens of thousands of Russian parathroopers came dropping down from the Irish skies on to Tara's Sacred Hill, or on to the Mountains of Mourne that sweep down to the sea. You haven't to think twice to see the pickle we'd be in then. That's our present problem; though some don't seem to realise it. D'ye know what that ignorant eejut, Muldoon, the Solid Man, said when he was told that the Russians could come down from the Irish skies in swarms?

—No, then, I don't, Dan.

—The venomous eejut said it would be betther and fitther for us to guard against the swarms of green flies and swarms of black flies that dhrop from the Irish skies and destroy the crops!

—Did he, now? Such persons should be arborised into places where they couldn't be heard talking, Mick. Go on, Dan, me son; go on approvin' of us.

—You see, Mick, we're too small to fight the Russians on our own. It isn't that we haven't the courage.

—You're right there, Dan. He's right there, stranger. We have the courage, right enough. Let me like a soldier fall, wha'? You're right, Dan; we're twice too small; we'd have to have help.

—No use either, Mick, of looking to allies too far off from us, like France or Italy — they'd take years to come.

—So they would, Dan, so they would.

—You see, Mick, Ireland's so important, that, in a war, Russia would need to take her over in an hour; an hour, Mick. Does that ring a bell?

—Yis; a whole peal of them. But then, wha'?

—Well, man, we'd have to get help at once, at once.

—Then what about England, Dan?

—England! Why, man alive, she'd be fighting for her life, and couldn't let us have even a policeman from point-duty!

—Well, then, wha'?

—America's our only man, Mick. Organised battle on our part wouldn't be worth a damn; a guerilla war no good either.

—So what, Dan?

—What we need, Mick, is swarms and swarms of jeeps.

—Jeeps, be jeepers!

—Yes, jeeps, Mick; each with a driver, a spare driver, a commander, and a wireless operator. Every able-bodied man in Ireland in a jeep here, a jeep there, with a sten-gun, a hammer and pliers, head-phone, and a jeepsie walkie-talkie — that's the one solution, Mick.

—And a trailer to every jeep, Dan — you forgot that.

—Aw, man, use your brains; think a little! How the hell could a jeep jump a hedge with a trailer attached?

—But, Dan, what would the ordinary cars and pedestrians do

and the roads buzzin' with jeeps? You haven't thought of that; I don't like the idea at all. Man alive, there wouldn't be a man, woman, child, or chicken left alive in the country. No; count me out.

—Aw, think again, Mick. Your thoughts aren't exact enough yet to gather it all in: Looka, if they were all done for aself, wouldn't death on our own roads be better than exportation be the Bolsheviks to an unknown destination? Take that in, Mick.

—I am taking it in; you're not the only one who can take things in. What exportation are you walkie-talkiein' about?

—Looka, Mick, the expert put it plain before us all; the military expert, mind you. A nation like Russia that holds fifteen millions and more in concentration camps, and has eliminated twenty millions more and more be vast and frequent purges, man, wouldn't cast a thought about eliminating thousands of Irishmen, women, and children, the expert said, or wait to think twice about exporting the rest of us. It would be only child's play, he said, to the Russians.

—A thrue saying, Dan; thrue for me, thrue for you, thrue for all. Pity all this wasn't said to the eejut laddo with his swarm of green flies an' swarm of black flies.

—It was said, Mick.

—It was, was it? I bet that bet him! An' what did the Solid eejut say to all them homers?

—And where, said he, would the Bolsheviks find the ships and the trains to cart our people to exportation, four millions of us? he says: Siberia's a long way off, if you ask me, he says.

—Huh huh; that was a sensible question, Dan, and a sensible remark for the eejut to make, anyhow.

—How was it a sensible remark, and how was it a sensible question, Mick? Where's your brains, man? The Bolsheviks wouldn't be dreaming of Siberia, man, and the Isle of Man only a few feet away from our own green border.

—Aha, Dan, I bet that had him bet. He hadn't had the imagination to think of the Isle of Man — the eejut!

—Divil a bit it bet him, Mick.

—No, Dan?

—No, Mick; sorra a tremor it took out of him. He just let an eejeeotic laugh outa him, saying, Counting the millions of relatives of them in concentration camps, with the millions of prisoners themselves, an' the millions more of relatives of them who've been purged, he says, making in all hundreds of thousands more of bitther enemies to the Russian Government, then the nation that can stand to that, and then send millions of more paratroopers flutthering down through the skies on to Erin's lovely shore, is invincible, says he, an' we're wasting our time thinking out a way to fight them.

—An' did he say that, now? Wasting our time! Isn't that shockinly reaving! What about our well-known love of country? Why didn't you counther him with that, Mick?

—I did, so I did.

—An' how did the eejut react to it?

—Looka, says he, prodding me in the chest with his forefinger; looka, he says, if the Bolshevik land is the kinda country you're saying it is, then the Russians that'll dhrop from our Irish skies on to our emerald sod will be, says he, some poor divils seekin' asylum.

—Seekin' asylum, is it? What, a lunatic asylum it is he must be meanin'.

—No, no, man; an ordinary asylum, an ordinary asylum.

—What ordinary asylum? There's no ordinary asylum. When a body says We've taken a certain party to the asylum, we mean a lunatic asylum, don't we?

—Yes, yes, but——

—There's no but about it, Dan. An asylum's an asylum — there's no but about it.

—Yes, there is.

—There isn't, I'm telling you!

—I'm telling you there's different asylums; for instance, a deaf-and-dumb asylum.

—Maybe, but the parathroopers dhropping from our skies won't be deaf an' dumb, will they?

—I know they won't. For Jasus' sake, don't thry to be as big an eejut as the other fella!

—Who's an eejut?

—You're talking like an eejut now.

—You're talking like an eejut yourself! A fully fledged one! Wantin' to flood the counthry with jeeps! While you're at it, will you kindly tell us who's goin' to provide the hundred thousand jeeps to go gallopin' around and lay us all out, dead as mackerel, on the roads of Eireann; every man-jack of us and every woman-lizzie of us that hasn't the good fortune to be sittin' safe in some of them! An' if we put into every one of them, as your expert advises, a dhriver, a spare dhriver, a commander, an' a wireless-operator with his walkie-talkie, addin' all them stretched out flat an' dead on the

roads, will you tell us who's going to look afther the common things
that have to be daily done to keep the counthry goin'? Aha, you're
silent now! That's bet you! An' listen, another thing: While America
might be dhroppin' the jeeps, what's to prevent the Bolshies at the
same time from dhroppin' their parathroopers an' filling the jeeps
as they touch down, to let them go scamperin' all over the roads,
takin' over the Turf Board, the Tourist Association, the Hospitals
Sweep, the Court of Chancery, the Catholic Young Men's Society,
the Protestant pulpits, the Abbey Theatre, and the President's
Residence, forcin' the unfortunate members of Maria Duce to do
point-duty at street corners an' cross roads; an' ending, maybe, with
the plantin' of a Red Flag in the hand of St. Patrick's Statue standin'
helpless on a windy hill in the centre of the lonely Plains of Meath!
That's what your jazzin' jeeps would do — provide the Bolshies with
a rapid an' logical means of locomotion throughout the whole of our
unfortunate counthry! Isn't that so, stranger — God, he's gone!
The sensible man wouldn't stay to hear the ravin' of an eejut com-
mendin' jeeps. Well, I'm goin' too!

—Goodbye, Mick. Think it all over; take your time. Say what you
like, but cantherin' jeeps on all our roads alone could purse the land
into safety.

Woman and war — two terrible dangers. Wherever she goes,
rings on her fingers, bells on her toes, she trails behind her devotion
that should go to God, destruction that should never come near
Man. What's that, what's that! Lightning flashing before her,
thunder rolling behind, and a voice from the midst of them. What
voice, whose voice? McNamee's voice, bishop of Ardagh and Clonmacnois's episcopal Pistol thundering out the Rule that No Dance
must last beyond twelve o' the clock, no Bar to be in any Dance Hall,
no revelry in Lent in Clonmacnois today, or in Ardagh either.

A hand's stretch away, in Sligo,

> Among hydrangeas and the falling ear-rings
> Of fuchsias red as blood,

Catholic energy and art painted a picture of real life, when a girl
went to work for an unmarried farmer, aged fifty-six, with the
blessing of her parents, but against the will of the clerics and their
henchmen; an occasion of sin — the priest objects; so, one morning
early, when the hoar frost was out, the first postman of the morning
found the girl in her shift chained and padlocked to a telegraph pole,
too frozen to moan, or give signal of life; while the farmer stretched
himself out in his kitchen, bruised and bloodied as red as the

fuchsia's ear-rings, from a beating given in the cause of honour and virtue, though no untowardness had passed between him and-the girl; but the danger had been there, so the clerics stayed dumb, and the police folded their arms till the district became calm, and a hush hush came down among the hydrangeas and the falling ear-rings of fuchsias red as blood. Where Yeats lies buried, far away now from fuchsia and hydrangea, and from the over-blown bleat of the clerics; but still in County Sligo, in Drumcliff; still there, but quiet, and resting.

Barrum, barrum, barrum; Yeats's drum tapping as in his play, *The Resurrection*. A rattle in the wood where a Titan strode. Barrum, barrum, barrum.

> The herald's cry, the soldier's tread,
> Exhaust his glory and his might:
> Whatever flames upon the night
> Man's own resinous heart has fed.

Is there a heart among us now with enough resin in it to provoke a flame that would roast a spud? Tiny holy candles flickering around Ireland, fainting wills-o'-the-wisp; woeful; but ne'er a torch; ne'er a one blazing anywhere.

> Heads bent, we go; go stumbling on
> Where others ran:
> A pray'r for me, a pray'r for you,
> And pray'rs for Jack the journeyman.

What's that? An eagle's whistle! And another, a number of them! Jasus, there are eagles flying among the grey tits and the flat snipe! Brennan's still on the moor. There are brave men and women in Ireland still; and will be, will be, always, for ever.

AND EVENING STAR

THE sun has gone, dragging her gold and green garlands down, too; gone from the sky, leaving him to live in the glimmer of midnight, to share the last few moments of life with the tender loneliness of the evening star. Soon it will be time to kiss the world goodbye. An old man now, who, in the nature of things, might be called out of the house any minute. Little left now but a minute to take a drink at the door — deoch an doruis; a drink at the door to life as it had been with him, and another to whatever life remained before him. Down it goes! Slainte!

The whole earth's a place of never-ending arrivals and departures; Glad to see you is but the echo of goodbye, Sally, goodbye, Sue. Still the interlude, strange interlude, was a fine and exciting one. He had lived and fought through twenty years of the nineteenth century and through more than half of the twentieth, and ginger, i'faith, is hot in the mouth still. Good going. The evening star was the one lantern to his feet now; the morning star would never again be bright for him to see. It was sad, but within him sadness faded quick, and the evening star was beautiful. It was a long look-back to the time when he remembered wearing the black-and-red plaid petticoat — a little rob roy; and he sitting on the doorstep of a Lower Dorset Street house, watching the antics of the older and braver kids let loose on the more dangerous roadside; in his ears the sound of lorry, dray, and side-car, with their iron-rimmed wheels, clattering over the stony setts of the street; in his nose the itching smell of dusty horsedung. A long look-back to the time, kneeling, cold, on a chair, looking out of the window to watch the rain pelting down on the pavement, each impact of its falling watery lances forming tiny, swirling circles that his mother said were pennies. He had been rich while the rain had been falling. Not the Father, the Son, or the Holy Ghost; not the sun, the moon, or the stars were this kid's, or that kid's, gods; but the penny. The kid who went to the catholic catechism, or the kid who went to the protestant sunday-school, worshipped the penny. As it had been then, so it was now — though no longer a kid in a red-and-black plaid petticoat, but an old man: he still stood at the door waiting for pennies. Most artists do. They stand at the door, on the pavement, hat or cap in hand, hoping some god may prompt some passer-by to sling a penny into the patient, waiting cap.

Odd why so many thought authors with any name must be very rich fellows. He himself got appeals to help a charity by fishing up some forgotten trinket from some long-neglected drawer. Dip a hand down, said one request, and you will probably pull out a pair of gold cuff-links, a gold cigarette-case, or a gold watch, long hidden away from memory. Pull away, and up she rises! Lucky dip! The old figure developed from the kid in the red-and-black plaid petticoat never could, and never would be able to thrust down a careless hand and pull up a gold watch from a neglected drawer. A civilisation in which millions are hard put to find shirt or shift, harder set to find a house to live in, that condones a condition permitting a fortune-flushed hand to pull a forgotten gold watch from a dusty drawer, is a civilisation needing the curse of God and the hammer of man to its changing.

When Sean was twenty, the first tweed cap, worn by Keir Hardie, came suddenly into the House of Commons. Gents empanelled in glass-encased offices, looking over ledgers at God, didn't bother even to look up. The one tweed cap among the crowd of glossy toppers caused a disturbance, but only one of loud laughter. Bah! Pooh! Who is this so weak and helpless; who is this in yonder stall? A miner; went down into the pit when he was ten; never got a spot of schooling. Must be very embarrassing to Black Rod and Sergeant-at-Arms. It is, and to the Constable at the gate, too; doesn't quite know if he should permit a tweed cap to come in. It is trying. Comes from some god-forsaken place in Wales, I'm told. How'd he manage to get here? Freak election. Helped by that red-headed fella who writes plays and things — Shaw's the name, I think. Ephemera-mental. Eh, you, tweed cap — whom do you represent? Me, sir? Yes, you, sir. Oh, I represent only the miners, railway-workers, men at the plough, men behind the counter — all earning a living by hand or brain; in short, sir, the people of England, Wales, Scot-land, and Ireland; and in a way, the world.

Curious how religions, ancient and modern, harp on the futility of life. How they fill it with pain, uncertainty, and woe. Brief life is here our portion; life is but a walking shadow; life is but an empty dream. Even Buddha, gentle as a dewdrop upon a lotus blossom, sitting without a stir under the Bo tree, calls men away from this life. They find it damned hard to go, for no man is so old as to believe he cannot live one more year. Even if life be all that Buddha made it out to be,

> *Ache of the birth, ache of the helpless days,*
> *Ache of hot youth and ache of manhood's prime;*
> *Ache of the chill, grey years and choking death,*
> *These fill your piteous time.*

Kneel down, and say your prayers, and be off — there's nothing to keep you here. Yet man finds it hard go to, and so he does. 'The pleasure of life', yells out a rebellious Elizabethan, 'what is it but the good hours of an ague?' Truth in this, too, but is it all the truth? Not to him. There are many, many beautiful things in life, but life is too short to see and enjoy more than a few of them. Now that is sad if you like. There are honest men here, and women still as fair as the evening air clad in the beauty of a thousand stars. Must we close our eyes for ever on the holly-tree in berry, or the rowan-tree in berry and in bloom? It is the many beauties of the earth that make life hard to bear, knowing that life must end, and all the beauties of the world say farewell to us. Oh for permission to be old and gay; thousands of years, thousands of years, if all were told.

There was struggle still under the quietness of the evening star, and he, longing to sit down in a deck-chair to enter into what Yeats called 'the red flare of dreams', found he had to keep busy defending his corner in life. Nothing to be frightened of, for some poet has said that 'all things declare that struggle hath deeper peace than sleep can bring'.

A young Irishman, named Patrick Galvin, who, he says himself, has written thirty poems, a few short stories, and has produced a magazine of his own, has leapt into view on the London-Irish scene, whipped off his coat, and has offered (no holds barred) O'Casey out to fight; prefacing the contest with an open letter to the *Tribune*, then sent on to the *Irish Democrat*, a copy of which flew down to Devon. 'I've seen your three one-act plays', the letter says, 'and they have, to my astonishment, confirmed in me once for all the suspicion, previously held at bay, that you are not a Socialist.' Oh, what a fall is here, my countrymen! 'Am I right in deducing that the whole theme and setting of *The Hall of Healing* derive from a fifty-year-old memory?' Quite right, lad, and I told you so myself, which you could have seen had you taken the trouble to read the *Irish Times* of December 28, 1951. There your deduction is given an *Imprimi potest*. In a letter to the editor, O'Casey says, 'Dear Sir, Little did I think when I wrote *The Hall of Healing* that the conditions of fifty years ago in the dispensaries of the poor would be the same today'. At that time, the Mother and Child Bill was being contested in the Dail, with the hierarchy in the close background; and things said in the Dail, and letters and an article published in the Press, showed that the old dispensary conditions still held bad. The notorious Red Ticket, that exacerbated some of O'Casey's days, was still the method of communication between patient and doctor, and, for all he knows, flourishes still. On August 5, 1953, a day right under Patrick Galvin's nose, Radio Eireann announced that a new Dispensary was about to be built, at a cost of something over a thousand pounds, in Killashandra, Co. Cavan, to replace a shack that had existed there as a dispensary for near on a hundred years. And what kind of a Dispensary, these days, can be built for the price mentioned? Are they building there a small cabin of clay and wattles made? How much would it cost if it was being built for the care of the soul and the vanity of clerics? Maybe the clergy have got the Young Men's Catholic Association, or the members of Muintir na Tire, to work for next to nix. The old O'Casey goes through the world with one eye open, but Patrick Galvin seems to meander along with both eyes shut.

But let the lad go on: 'Even as caricatures I find your characters false. As a fellow-countryman of yours I cannot but ask you to consider whether it is not a dis-service to Ireland, to the working-class, and to the cause of progress, that they should be offered to the public ostensibly in the name of Socialism.' He goes on still: 'I have long admired your work. The conclusions forced on me by *The Hall of Healing* have been an unpleasant shock to me [Christ, I am sorry! S. O'C.]. I shall now have to re-read you from start to finish to see whether what I assess in this play as an attitude of profound contempt for the poor — as I have heard others say, and have denied — has been latent in your work from the beginning. Not only are your *Hall of Healing* characters frauds: The style seems to me a fraud too. . . . What are the rest of us to make of it (English as well as Irish, to say nothing of the rest of the world), save a new and peculiarly un-acceptable stage-Irishism? Have the progressive Irish fought so long against the Stage Irishman, so convenient to their [*sic*] exploiters, only to have him handed back to them on a "socialist" plate by you who are held to be progressive too?'

Mea culpa! Please, sir, not on a 'socialist' plate, sir, no; rather on a majollican plate I hand out my plays, a plate decorated, not with galvinian socialist mottoes, but with colour and gay decoration. A few more tinderclaps: ' Had you not better in your own interests and ours, stick to the lines of sheer music-hall farce, of which *The End of the Beginning* is a dazzling example, or develop and delve deeper into the strain of Yeatsian fantasy with which you have a modicum of a success in *Time To Go*? Unless you would care to return to Ireland and find out what goes on? Your *Hall of Healing* I frankly consider an insult. To use a Dublin expression, "you were just coming the bliddy hound". The whole play was pure codology from start to finish.'

Now, sir, just a minute: The play, *End of the Beginning*, is almost all founded on a folk-tale well known over a great part of Europe. All O'Casey's children have read it under the name of *Gone is Gone*. If Patrick Galvin had searched a little in his own beloved country, which he is so eager to guard from all touches derogatory to her excellent name, he would have found the story glowing in Sugrue's (An Seabhach) *An Baile seo 'Gainn*, decked out in good Gaelic too; but these patriotic persons seem to enshrine all their patriotism in their shouting. Like the Gaelic magazine, *Iris*, which reached him in Devon, and to which he at once subscribed, because it seemed to be courageous and animated, to find that, after a few more months, it had died, because only, as he was told, eighty copies of the magazine were sold, and a heavy loss was suffered by the promoters. An Gaelic abu! *Time to Go*, oddly enough, is founded on another Irish folk-tale, but Mr. Galvin can have the pleasure of seeking its whereabouts for himself.

One more criticism from the young poet, and then his trumpet coda: 'The old woman who "doesn't want much", and is managing on five shillings a week (This, God save us and guard us, is presented as the present day!).' Well, O'Casey's own mother often worked for a week for less than five shillings a week; and he and she lived for weeks on her old-age pension of ten shillings a week, which, if I can add two to two, comes to five shillings a head. Now, the galvin-gallant coda: 'I know the Irish *lumpen-proletariat* and the Irish Working Class. I know them as well as you do and much more recently. There is far more in them than you seem to imagine. I myself am a demonstration of how a man can emerge from the fecklessness and shiftlessness of the lumpen-proletariat into genuine working-class consciousness and knowledge, and I am far from believing myself to be a phoenix. [If not a phoenix, then a V.I.P.?] The hopelessness you portray in *Hall of Healing* is out of date. Do you honestly believe it yourself? Come off it! If you and me were in some old pub for half an hour over a bottle of stout I'd either talk the indifference out of you or we'd kill each other.'

A fierce young fellow, but he'll have to go to that 'some old pub', and drink the bottle of stout alone. Rightly or wrongly, Sean ranks these letters with the ones he gets carrying little holy pictures, rosary beads, catholic truth society tracts, notes of pathetic appeals to be converted to Truth, and notes of indignant denunciation. As for Sean, were it in his power, he'd make all the young Irish poets happy, and all great.

The younger ones coming into life could never be the same as the older ones going out. He saw as he stood by the door how different this generation was from the one which had enfolded him. If the old don't recognise this, the young ones will harass them. Go down, thou bald-head! To serve one's own generation is almost as much as one can do; and no humiliation is hidden in any inability to dominate a new one. In his own three children, he felt and saw the tremendous change that had come over life since the days of the black-and-red plaid petticoat; and he himself, thank heaven, had done a few things to bring about the change — bar in Ireland, where they lingered fifty years behind the rest. The young were busy in the house of life that the old were leaving; throwing out some of the musty stuff, bringing in the fresh and the new; changing the very shape of the house itself (though there were many young ones coming into life who were mouldier than the older ones going out of it); placing new pictures on the walls; knocking out walls separating one family from another; polishing everything with a newer glow; opening the windows wider.

Oh, the world was a busy place now! The one lonely tweed cap had become a great multitude such as no man could number; multitudes of all lands, of every colour, of every race. The tractor and combine, great land-gods, had appeared in the fields; the skylon and nylon had appeared in the street. The one part of civilisation that hadn't changed, daren't change, was institutional religion. This was the sulky laggard in man's forward march; a dangerous and a malicious laggard; a mistress of sabbathage.

When he thought of all the common routine of life that had to be gone through — to eat, to drink, to sleep, to clothe ourselves, to take time for play, lest we perish of care, to suffer and fight common and uncommon ills, then the achievements of man, in spite of all these, are tremendous indeed. Away then with the whine of being miserable sinners, with the whine of we've no abiding city here, with the whine of pray for the wanderer, pray for me! We've important things to do. Fag an bealach! How many tons of coal have we delved from the mines today? How many railway waggons have we loaded? How many yards of textiles have we woven? How many schools, hospitals, houses, cinemas, and theatres have we built? How many railway-engines, carriages, and trucks have we put on the lines? How many ships sent to sea? Fag an bealach! Work is the Reveille and the Last Post of life now, providing for man, making leisure safe, enjoyable, and longer, profiting body, soul, and spirit, having a song in itself, even when the sun sets on old age, and the evening star shines a warning of the end.

There were personal activity and personal disappointments as well as those disturbing a community. There was the perennial difficulty of getting a play produced, and, worse still, the poverty of producer and of production that inhibited any performance given. Apart from the Irish Players in their heyday, and the production of *The Silver Tassie*, all were bad, a few worse than others, and one worst of all. 'To see a bad play given a fine production', says George Jean Nathan somewhere, 'is a bad thing, but to see a good, aspiring play badly done, is to witness a betrayal of the drama.' And there are quite a few traitors to the drama among managers, producers, actors, and among the playwrights, too. Of course, the theatre, by and large, is nothing higher than a money-making game. The drama's altar isn't on the stage: it is candlesticked and flowered in the box-office. There is the gold, though there be no frankincense or myrrh; and the gospel for the day always The Play will Run for a Year. The Dove of Inspiration, of the desire for inspiration, has flown away from it; and on its roof, now, the commonplace crow caws candidly.

Whenever he ventured to think of what was the worst production of a play of his, his heart's blood pressed into his head, and all the world became red. Even critics, often tolerant of things done badly, declared it to be a butchery of a play. And one had to bear it quietly, though the heart was stung. Never before had Sean seen such an assured and massive incompetency in a producer assigned to an English theatre or such managerial support given to incompetence. He was the cockiest clacking cod Sean had ever encountered, adazzle with iridescent ignorance of the drama; a fellow who should never have been allowed even to pull a curtain up from the stage of a tuppenny gaff, yet the manager clapped him on the back continually. The play, admittedly, was a difficult one, probably a clumsy one, possibly, even, a bad one; but the shocking production failed, in every possible way, to show whether it was one, or all, of these; failed to give the slightest guidance to an experimental playwright. The fellow's gone now, making his exit by way of a gas-oven, giving in a kitchen a better production than he ever gave on a stage.

In a recent letter, George Jean Nathan refers to 'the rapidly-dying theatre'. A sad saying from such a man. Is the theatre, so long sounding the Reveille, to be heard now tuning into the Last Post? Maybe. During the production of his last play, Sean heard the Last Post clearly; but has given the fool's answer since by writing three one-act plays, and two of three acts each. George may be right: looks like the House of Satan's sinking into the turfy mud of mediocrity, with only the box-office remaining safe on the top of the bog.

Ah, some young body singing in the house of life! Sighs and songs never leave it. Beside the sigh, there is always the song. A young heart full of golden nonsense singing the challenge of love to any power in the path of a maid's way with a man.

A sour-soul'd cleric, passing near,
Saw lovers by a rowan-tree;
He curs'd its branches, berries, bloom,
Through time and through eternity.
Now evil things are waiting where
Fond lovers once found joy,
And dread of love now crowns th' thoughts
Of frighten'd girl, of frighten'd boy.

The rowan-tree's black as black can be
On Killnageera's lonely hill.
And where love's whispers once were warm,
Now blows a wind both cold and shrill.
Oh, would I had a lover brave
To mock away its power,
I'd lie there firm within his arms,
And fill with love one glorious hour!

Then branches bare would leaf again,
The twisted ones grow straight and true;
And lovers locked within its ken
Would nothing fear and nothing rue;
Its bloom would form a bridal veil
Till summer days were sped,
Then autumn berries, red, would fall
Like rubies on each nestling head.

The singing heart. The young may-mooning. Oh, foolish lover and foolish lover's lass, know ye not that love is corrupt with the corustcation of original sin? A sense of beauty at the sudden sight of some image; image of cloud, flower, fern, or woman, lingers less than a moment. Silence the sigh, for man has made many an ever-lasting thing out of a moment of time. The lover and his lass are for ever acting on the stage of life, and Marlowe's glimpse of fair Helen's beauty didn't die with him in a tavern brawl. The primrose's gentle yellow blossom dies; every season a last rose of summer sheds its petals on the cynical earth; but the rose is always with us, and the primrose blooms again.

He looked over Jordin, looked over, and what did he see, what did he see? An atom bomb coming, an atom bomb coming to carry him home, carry him home, carry him home. No angels planing over the clouds now, no sign of a cross in the sky. Oh, Helena, Helena, have a heart, and help us! Real things are hurtling around there now — the whole firmament is full of flying saucers. There's saucers aflying in the air. Prospero, Prospero! They'll leave not a wrack behind! Don't look up, brother; keep your eyes on the ground, sister — earth's new orb is dangling dangerously over us all; botchlandt über alles. Dangle it, darling, dangle the flaming gem over our heads; over the heads of the Queen and her ministers of state, and all that are put in authority over us; over the head of the cleric fumbling for God at the altar; over the heads of the lover and his lass lying nervously under the hawthorn-tree; over the mother suckling her child; over the old stepping warily towards their end. Zip! There goes a city! Send them up to heaven hot. All the saints wondering. What is this that they have done unto you?

> You haven't an arm and you haven't a leg,
> You're an eyeless, noseless, chicken-less egg,
> You'll have to be put in a bowl to beg.

The flame from the angel's sword in the Garden of Eden has been catalysted into the atom bomb; God's thunderbolt became blunted, so man's dunderbolt has become the steel star of destruction. War minions are going about giggling. We can't let it be wasted; we must use the damned thing. We can't let all our work go for nothing; and the word Inevitable is cradled within everything they say. We have the atom bomb. Twinkle, twinkle, mighty bomb, bring us safe to kingdom come; when you come with clouds ascending, doing harm that needs no mending; from the palace, hall, and slum bring us safe to kingdom come. Never worry, what the wind is, what the whether — God can stick the bits together. We have the atom bomb — get that into your head. We're ready for anything now. Warships sail with decks half-cleared for action; no general wears a nosegay to soften the arrogant air of his crimson tabs; the guns are polished, primed, and pointed: we're ready for anything. Zip! any minute now. Oh, Walt Whitman, saintly sinner, sing for us!

> Walt Whitman, one of the world's good wishes
> Is the one that wishes you here today,
> To sing Shake Hands to the world's peoples;
> To listen, cock-eared, in a way of wonder,
> To all that others have got to say;
> Then with your own embracing message,
> Lead all correctly, or lead astray,
> For either is goodness with God, and gay,

Like song of a thrush or screech from a jay;
They'll mingle miles on, from each other learning
That life's delightful at work or play.
So enter in spirit the sharp contentions
Of brothers belling each other at bay,
And soften the snout of the menacing cannon
With the scent and bloom of a lilac spray.

England isn't in a good way, there's no denying it. At times, they seem to stand without breath or motion, flattening out their kidneys, as Wyndham Lewis says, with great draughts of thin beer. They haven't yet been able to come out of the dive they took in the last great war. Each English person is said to owe as much as it would take him to earn throughout a lifetime. The English do not welcome the possibility of another war. They can't absorb another one. They snap out of any talk that mentions a word of war. The more they are driven to the thought of war, or preparations for war, the more they are magnetised by the thought of peace. Most of them seem to be in the condition that if another war came upon them, they'd stand still and wait for death. Anyway, it wouldn't take long to come to them. Looks like the generals, who seem to be kept alive by the thought of war, will have to wage a little one of their own. And, indeed, most folk would be glad if none came alive out of it.

The generals don't like the look of things. They are uneasy about this ineptitude for war, cold or hot. General Montgomery's plea for a Supreme Commander to direct the Cold War met with a cold response. 'Exactly how that could be done, I haven't thought out', he said; 'it's not my job, really. I'm the Hot War chappie — if it comes. It is because we don't win the Cold War that they hand it over to Hot Wars. When the politicians get completely mucked up about the Cold War, they hand it over to Us.' Over to you, chappie. As if he were talking of hot and cold springs; as if careless of the bitterness, the ruin, the hurried burial of the messed-up dead, and the cry of woe that lies in the accursed core of the conceited and applauded villainy of war. There is no more room for any more ribbons on the generals' tunics. The young aren't prepared to die to hang a tawdry glory out on a general's breast.

The generals don't like this. They love guns as kids love candies. They call upon people to get ready for war as if they were calling upon them to get ready for a walk. 'The sight gladdens my old eyes', a general is alleged to have said, when he saw a heap of Korean dead; forgetting that where there are Korean dead, there will be

American dead, British dead, and, maybe, Irish dead too. The Korean dead don't lie lonely. The price we pay for a heap of Korean dead is a heap of our own dead; put out an eye, and lose one ourselves; a loss for a loss; I'm dead, you're dead, he's dead, we're all dead. Every day, every hour, there are many who will never knock at the door again. The military mind is indeed a menace. Old-fashioned futurity that sees only men fighting and dying in smoke and fire; hears nothing more civilised than a cannonade; scents nothing but the stink of battle-wounds and blood. Only today, as this is being written, a memorial was unveiled to men who died in the First World War. Memorialising only half done when the tide of the Second World War swept over the work. Looks like, if generals had their way, the tide of a Third World War would sweep over all before men had a real chance to see what the last war looked like. So we hang together as best we may, going through a life that has become a corridor of war memorials, built in honour of the young who gave their lives gallantly for his nib's sake; with obeliskan officers standing at every corner shouting: Prepare to fight; prepare to die; prepare to meet your enemy! Aw, go to hell, and leave our little world alone; our little lives rounded with a little sleep; our little streets, our little homes; we want them all, we love them all — we'll die in our beds, you tabb'd and uniformed sons of bitches!

Imagine it — an expert's vision of jeeps dashing about the Irish roads while he sat here under the sunset and the evening star. Such talk, such things, such talk, in Ireland, while the echoes of Yeats's voice and Lady Gregory's lingered there still, floating over the Irish Sea to glide into his own ear as he sat listening here. The new divinity — the jeep. For all her holy dedications, there are odd gods in Ireland today. Poor prospects and poorer men. Full of green tits and flat snipe. Nothing now but hallowed hollow men. A prayer for me, a prayer for you, and a prayer for Jack the Journeyman. Not a word now about the Lane Pictures. One of Lady Gregory's last letters written to him — probably the last — says:

DEAR SEAN,

I had a few days in London, arriving Sunday, leaving Thursday, and had hoped to be able to go to see you and make acquaintance with your wife and son. But I had a good deal of business to go through, and I hurried home because of my grandson having returned from Cambridge; and his mother not having returned from the Continent. I was very disappointed, a real disappointment. I am so seldom over here, and only went because I had promised to attend the National University St. Patrick's

Day Dinner some time ago. I had hoped to be able to say a few words about the Lane Pictures then, and that the New Gallery had begun, but a strike had put this off, and I thought silence best, until, at least, the foundations had been laid. Perhaps you will be coming to Ireland again? I hope so, and that you will let me know. Yours as ever.

A. GREGORY

Dead now, and buried, too. And the pictures buried with her. The lowliest theft ever done by an English Government on Ireland, in face, too, of protests from eminent Irishmen, Scots, Welsh, and eminent sons of England herself. Hugh Lane, who went down in the *Lusitania*, neglected to get witnesses to his will, and, though thousands of wills made by British soldiers, unwitnessed, were made legal, Lane's wasn't, and the Government of England's decision became God's dictum pictorum Laneiensis. The goddamn, rotten, lousy thieves! But then the green tits, the flat snipe, and the white-collared crows of Ireland don't care a damn about them. There are only souls wafting about Ireland; souls empty save for the Pap in the Paper Pastorals published during Lent and Christmas time. Yet Renoir's 'Umbrellas' give a glory to God that all the Pastorals ever written could never do. Souls sinking down to the earth. Souls sprawling over a sweep-ticket. Four kinds — hearts, clubs, diamonds, and spades. Hush! Voice from above: bing crosby singing over the wireless. Oh, mighty soul, transcentdentaliser of man! A cultured, cheering group are forming, right now, a Society to give Bing a month's free holiday in Ireland, with an illuminated address from Maria Duce, to be presented by Mick McGilligan's daughter, Maryanne; right now; yessir. Shut up — let's listen! Now.

Bing on the one end of the tape, Eton on the other. Odd things, odd things bury themselves in life. There are numbers of a certain class, good, often intelligent, Christians, who think the kingdom of heaven less important than the Kingdom of Eton's way-in, way-out. They lay an infant on Eton's doorstep before it has learned to suck; before it has been baptised. One sent into the world from Eton is more important than one sent in by God. Yessir. It was never very important to God, he could easily get on without it; it is no longer of much importance to man. The lad in the topper, eton suit, with the nice cane, is no longer the guaranteed lord of the future. They must now sing for their supper and fight for their place with man. The red carpet no longer trails straight from the school-porch to the front door of government posts. Imitation etonia sed imitation Christi has become a cod.

Come on out of these arched and cloistered academes of uniformity in accent, in dress, thought, manners, and superficial conduct, lads, and join the crowd. There are a lot of grand gossoons among you, but you hide yourselves in the fear of being different from what your father was. Let the old boy be a warning to you to change your tune. You are just feeding yourselves on mould. Harrow and Eton no longer impress — they are becoming comical. Forget your tony school for a minute, and take a decko at yourself in the glass, dollied up in your ancient dress, topper and all, and tell yourself what you think of yourself. Your uniform isn't even slightly picturesque like that of Christ's Hospital. You aren't dressed in it; you are encased in it, like sacred statues encased in cellophane. Tear off these mummifying wrappings, for sense's sake, and let your energy and imagination loose for the good of all. Come off the fading red carpet on to the rough road of life, where all your brothers and sisters, without the law of a dead tradition, go. Lads of the shiny toppers and the wide-leaved straw hats, come off it, for life has no longer any time, any longing, to look upon you as life's pretty pampernils. Hurry up, if one day you don't want to be stuffed into a glass case for a wonder and a show.

Old, oh, so old! Yet he couldn't see the logic of the calendar or give ear to the ticking of the clock. He knew that the bit of life-tapestry he was weaving would come to an end before long. Soon the loom he was at would go clack clack clacking no more; nevermore. He had to go to make room for the young; recognise as Tennyson did that

> Old men must die, or the world would grow mouldy,
> Would only breed the past again.

Well, the clack of his loom had always gone with the louder clack of life. The loom worked slower now, but there was no rust on it. It was a little tired, a little worn, for it had never rested, and never would. The young are knocking at the door. The old must decrease, the young increase. He hoped his children would throw a wider chest than his own. Down below, the elder lad hammered a frame together for a picture he was painting, the younger lad, laying aside biology for a spell, was blasting out music from a fine second-hand trombone, the young girl was merrily tapping out a Mozartian minuet from the piano — all indifferent — all careless of the tumult of mind afflicting the old codger up above, labouring over finding words for his wonderful work. Heartless youth; didn't give a damn how they distracted him. Thinking of themselves only. And who else should they be thinking of, in God's name?

> When the rain raineth and the goose winketh,
> Little wots the gosling what the goose thinketh.

And why the hell should it? It is only the young who possess the world.

Past achievements, failures, experiences, were echoes in his ear now; all echoes under the sunset and the evening star; echoes of places where he had lived and moved and had his being; echoes all echoing around everywhere, in the strength of the day, in the still deep of the night.

> Echo, I will not talk with thee,
> For thou art a dead thing.

He couldn't linger long among a crowd of echoes, however charming they might be; there were too many things to think of, too many things to do: things to think about, things to do in the home, in the wider community of the nation, in the widest community of the world. The world now was like a jig-saw puzzle; though some had fitted the pieces well and securely together, others, in conference, committee, assembly, and what not had jumbled the pieces so confusedly that few knew even where to look for the most of them. The nations of Europe have fallen into a screaming coma. A lot of them are yelling out for help. America's feet are worn away running from one to the other. Oh, there's another one down! Prop him up, buddies! But before this guy is properly propped, two more are down on their backs; and soon there's a queue lying, dead to the world, waiting to be lifted to their feet again. The coma conquers them. Neither dollars nor machinery are worth a damn if the people haven't the will to do. A nation, though immersed in wealth and cluttered with machinery, but without a will, would surely, if slowly, die.

Ireland's idea of safety with her roads adance with jeeps was neither a will nor a way. He had just read in an Irish journal that a roman catholic dignitary, preaching in an Irish town, had condemned Communists, their friends, and their friends' friends, adding, as a sorrowful affix, that for the whole year there had been but one marriage in the town. Ha ha ha! Looks like Ireland was becoming like heaven itself, where they neither marry nor are given in marriage. Ha ha ha! Last May, the Blessed Virgin's month, before the bloom was on the rye, a letter came to Eileen from a woman living in a

Dublin cottage slum, with eight children to keep. The last baby had come six years after the seventh, and had left the mother prostrate for months. Ever after she was to feel the effects of the strain. She wrote:

'My dear Mrs. O'Casey, Thank you for your letter. We all had flu. Una got it Bad and I have her in Bed with Pluresy at the Moment. She is not quite as bad as she was she is a bad fighter and lets everything in on her lets hope she wont be long till she is well again. You know I am a Bad letter writer cant think of what to say when I sit down to write. Ill say goodbye for now Ill get this off to you and get the kids to bed love to Shivaun Sincerely Chris.'

A bad fighter, letting everything in on her! A bad character for a slum-child. Written, probably, in the irritation of a great weariness, or written out of a vague reason for the child's lack of toughness; for the woman, Chris, was a fine mother and a very kind one; but she had too many kids to keep and care for, and, now, with all things dearer, it wouldn't be long till thousands of other kids would cease to be fighters, and would let everything in on them. Anyway, it was far more urgent for the defence of the country to have jeeps prancing along the roads than to fill the bellies of the nation's children with the food they urgently needed. Let the kids go — we need jeeps; we do, be jeepers!

Same here, same in England. All was needed for the arms, and little needed for the man. Even in the wealthy and imperative United States, many a still, small voice cried out in solitary places. Writes an American mother to him:

'Not knowing a mother, I was brought up by a grim, hard-working father, who, bending over a noisy sewing-machine, six days a week (doing that still today at sixty-six). We were never hungry, but there were many things daily to remind us that it happened to the best of working-class families; that our furniture as well as next family's could be put out into the street; that Santa Claus wasn't abroad at Christmas time, or sitting in the grocer's shop; that the landlord was a force to be reckoned with almost on the lofty level of the Government and the Lord above. Today, they gave my little girl a bit of metal on a chain to wear around her neck. It's called a Dog-Tag [der Tag!]. United States soldiers wear it in Korea and wherever they are. That's if Russia bombs us we'll be able to identify the pint-sized remains. The stamped letters with the child's and father's names are supposed to be especially durable. Flame-tested, I guess. Neither I nor my child will ever wear one.'

There is no need to wear them, O little girl and grown-up woman. Soviet bombs will never fall on New York City, unless New York bombs fall on Moscow first. There would be no gain to either city if each destroyed the other, for both would be gone, and the world would miss them. There is no danger, no danger, for though man be foolish, men are not fools. Each great city will go on living; living in its own vigorous, beautiful way.

He was writing now in the Fall of the Year, while the leaves of the trees were taking a last flutter through the air, whispering a goodbye to life as they fell. Sere and yellow, they were useless now to the tree; they had done their work, and the newer buds beneath were busy pushing them off; pushing them away from life, never to return again. Sere and yellow leaf, fall fluttering, and fade from all you knew, carrying to earth with you some tender fragment of the summmer's dream. So are many now, so was he — waiting for that gentle but insistent push that would detach his clinging desire, and send him, like the tumbling autumn leaf, sinking from life's busy tree to the dull flavour of death in the kingly dust where all men mingle in a sleep unending.

Outside, in the tiny garden, the few flowers have faded, or have been shoved from life by the sharp frost of the night before. The tall hollyhocks have toppled, leaving a few lingering rose-like forms on one dismantled stalk nuzzling itself into the chilly clay. Only the michaelmas daisies are topped with fading stars of crimson and mauve, and in the sullen hedge, hacked into rough-arrayed order, a few golden-brown blossoms still peer out from the prickly barberry-bush. A spreading bloom of a purple dahlia and the crimson disk of a single one have slunk heavily to the ground, oozy with a brownish slime that almost hides the memory of their bygone brilliancy. A short time ago, he had watched two big, handsome bees, delicately furred and red-banded, in the yellow centre of the crimson dahlia-disk, one bee in its core, the other on its fringe. Honey-drunk and half-dead they seemed to be. After a long time, the furry fellow on the fringe sleepily began to press himself deeper into the yellow core of the crimson disk, his twitching legs moving about to get a firmer grip, touching the other fellow's legs in the centre, who, with the tiniest show of irritation, shoved them twitchingly aside, just as a woman in the honey-hush of sleep might sleepily shove away from her body the wandering legs of a husband. Dead the blossoms, half-dead the bees, and the leaves all round fluttering down. A beautiful sadness everywhere. But in a few days the crimson disk will be there again, the purple-spreading dahlia will flaunt its pomp in the world's face, and the bees will buzz and hum and buzz again, as if the sun shone always and the frost was all over for ever. Even the winter has her many beauties, even for the old who shiver; the crisper air; the cold mists of morning, the fretted framework of the trees against the sky, the diamantling frost biting a harsh beauty into the earth's soft bosom; the stillness of the earth herself under it all, waiting for the spring. Ah, yes; to the old, spring and its budding bring a welcome as well as to the young. Sweet spring, full of sweet days and roses.

Even here, even now, when the sun had set and the evening star was chastely touching the bosom of the night, there were things to say, things to do. A drink first! What would he drink to — the past, the present, the future? To all of them! He would drink to the life that embraced the three of them! Here, with whitened hair, desires failing, strength ebbing out of him, with the sun gone down, and with only the serenity and the calm warning of the evening star left to him, he drank to Life, to all it had been, to what it was, to what it would be. Hurrah!

THE END